METHODS AND MATERIALS FOR
SECONDARY
SCHOOL
PHYSICAL
EDUCATION

METHODS AND MATERIALS FOR

SECONDARY SCHOOL PHYSICAL EDUCATION

CHARLES A. BUCHER, A.B., M.A., Ed.D.

Professor and Director, School of Health, Physical Education,
Recreation and Dance, University of Nevada, Las Vegas,
Las Vegas, Nevada; Consultant to the President's Council
on Physical Fitness and Sports

CONSTANCE R. KOENIG, B.A., M.S., Ed.D.

Associate Professor of Physical Education,
State University of New York College at Brockport,
Brockport, New York

SIXTH EDITION

with **124** illustrations

The C. V. Mosby Company

ST. LOUIS · TORONTO · LONDON   1983

MOSBY

A TRADITION OF PUBLISHING EXCELLENCE

Editor: Nancy Roberson
Assistant editor: Michelle Turenne
Manuscript editor: Sylvia Kluth
Book design: Nancy Steinmeyer
Cover design: Diane Beasley
Production: Kathleen L. Teal, Mary Stueck

595819

Cover photo by A. Hubrich from H. Armstrong Roberts, Inc.

SIXTH EDITION

Copyright © 1983 by The C.V. Mosby Company

Previous editions copyrighted 1961, 1965, 1970, 1974, 1978

Printed in the United States of America

The C.V. Mosby Company
11830 Westline Industrial Drive, St. Louis, Missouri 63141

Library of Congress Cataloging in Publication Data

Bucher, Charles Augustus, 1912-
    Methods and materials for secondary school
physical education

    Includes bibliographies and index.
    1. Physical education and training—Teacher
training. 2. Physical education and training—
Study and teaching (Secondary) I. Koenig,
Constance R. II. Title.
GV363.B73   1983   613.7′07′12   82-2243
ISBN 0-8016-0874-0   AACR2

GW/VH/VH 9 8 7 6 5 4 3 2 1   02/B/286

Preface

The sixth edition of *Methods and Materials for Secondary School Physical Education* has gone through a major revision. There are four new chapters: Chapter 5, "A Sports Program for the Secondary School," Chapter 6, "Legal Liability and Physical Education," Chapter 8, "A Philosophy of Physical Education to Guide the Teacher," and Chapter 12, "Teaching for Mastery." In addition, there have been major revisions in most of the other chapters in order to keep this text abreast of the latest developments in the fields of general and physical education. Particular attention has been given to such recent innovations as *Basic Stuff Series I and II;* health-related physical fitness; mastery learning; cognitive, affective, and psychomotor learning; and the legal implications of Title IX and P.L. 94-142.

This text is not a general methods and materials text that covers all educational levels. Instead, the focus of attention is on the secondary school since the unique needs of adolescent boys and girls require such treatment. As a result, this text uses the adolescent student as a focal point in discussing the many factors that require coverage to effectively teach physical education to secondary school boys and girls.

Thanks to Carmen Smith for typing the manuscript.

Charles A. Bucher
Constance R. Koenig

Contents

PART ONE

The community, school, and student

1

The community and the secondary school

Instructional objectives and competencies to be achieved

After reading this chapter the student should be able to

1. Describe some of the factors in the community that influence general and physical education programs in the schools
2. Understand the community's attitude toward the functions of the school
3. Discuss how the community affects the physical education program
4. Discuss and diagram the various types of administrative structures for the community and the school
5. Describe the place of physical education in the administrative structure of the school
6. Indicate the titles and roles of key administrative personnel in a school district
7. Describe how, through community involvement, physical educators can enhance their school's physical education programs

Our modern society is dynamic, flexible, demanding, and self-centered. The space age is freeing men and women from the confines of the atmosphere, permitting them to reach into outer space, even the moon, and to probe the depths of the seas. This era is having an increasingly profound influence on society. The skilled worker has had to become a highly trained technician, and the professional has had to become a specialist. Widespread use of computers, which are the children of the space age, has increased the pace of life. More people need more education to understand and control the machines that are the core of modern life. Each highly complicated electronic vehicle that is launched into space or dropped into the sea is the result of increased technology and of the refinement of the machines of science, industry, and education.

Our world becomes more complicated year after year. Not only are there many problems that affect us domestically, such as the need for more education, increasing specialization among vocations, problems of the inner city and of the environment, and a faster living pace, but there are also growing international problems.

Only a little over 20 years ago, our world was a relatively uncomplicated place in which to live, become educated, and earn a living. During brief periods of world peace, domestic and international unrest was not in the forefront of the news. Students in high schools, colleges, and universities were willing to adapt themselves to required courses and curricula in order to have a job and a steady income. Today's youth, however, realize that schools and universities must change as the world changes and are calling for improvements in curriculum, faculty, and administration. Student activism has indicated that young people will no longer endure outdated pedagogy. We have "new" secondary school students, and we are gradually giving them "new" secondary schools geared to the needs of tomorrow.

Today's secondary school students live in a computer card world. They have never known international peace or domestic stability; instead they are intimately familiar with a constantly fluctuating society, community change and upheaval, electronic marvels, and educational evolution. It is not technology per se that has brought about the changes in secondary schools but the effect technology and new developments have had on all the factors that combine to influence and control secondary education. Society at large, the changing structure of communities, students and parents, educators, administrators, and the schools themselves are all intimate parts of educa-

Fig. 1-1. The secondary school is an important part of the community.

Courtesy Strix Pix.

tional evolution. Today's society is, for most people, an open one. People have become highly mobile, and more money is spent on more and more consumer goods and services.

This last decade has been marked by increased suburbanization. Many persons have chosen to leave the cities to seek out the supposedly quieter, more stable, and relatively more peaceful life of the suburbs. Many former urbanites prefer to commute to work many hours rather than live in crowded, industrialized cities. Many cities are now largely the domain of lower socioeconomic groups who cannot leave because the suburbs cannot house or employ them or because they find that society has effectively closed the door on

upward mobility. The cities represent one of the nation's major problem areas. Transportation, crime, pollution, the high cost of welfare services, and inadequate housing are only a few of the critical ways in which cities are suffering.

Society is also becoming more internationally minded. New communications media have helped to bring the world into every home. News is relayed from country to country at the time it happens, shrinking the size of the world and increasing the possibility of international understanding. The youth of today are especially concerned and actively demonstrating this view through involvement in secondary schools, United Nations clubs, and international relations clubs.

Fig. 1-2. Cities represent one of the nation's major problem areas. City of Seattle, Wash. with the Kingdome in the foreground.

Many older youths have turned to other humanitarian activities such as antinuclear projects. Young people opposed to war actively demonstrate against it.

Our wealthy, knowledgeable, mobile, and highly automated society is still fighting the ills of poverty, discrimination, and unemployment. Social problems, especially those of minority groups, have directly affected large segments of the population. Many of our citizens in this affluent society live in poverty, lack money for adequate medical care, attend schools that do not meet their educational needs, and rarely venture outside their own neighborhoods. Additionally, lack of adequate education and training prohibits these individuals from obtaining employment. Political unrest and general dissatisfaction with government bureaucracy have been characterized by scandals and the misuse of public office.

Society is concerned with its environment. The pol-lution of the air and water, the destruction of our natural resources, overpopulation, and the increase of wastes have caused great concern among a large segment of the population. Environmentalists are deeply concerned that outdoor recreational resources are being threatened and that potentially hazardous living conditions for future generations are being created.

The energy crisis has resulted in skyrocketing prices for oil and gasoline as well as a shortage of these commodities. As a result, many activities requiring travel have had to be curtailed, with most people making adjustments in the consumption of energy.

The feminist movement has resulted in women playing a much more important role in all aspects of societal endeavors. It has helped to open up new job opportunities, has provided equal pay with men in many positions, and has made it possible for girls and women to participate in new experiences, such as sports that formerly were solely the province of the male.

The community

The vast changes taking place in society are leaving their imprint to a greater or lesser degree on each school and community in the United States. Although some communities, because of their location, conservatism, or other factors, are changing more slowly than others, most are different from what they were only a few years ago.

The nation's economy is responsible for austere school budgets with cutbacks in physical education, including athletic programs. Research conducted by the National Education Association has disclosed that many of the nation's largest school districts are operating under crisis conditions because of financial problems. In addition, students are questioning whether some educational requirements, including physical education, are necessary. As a result, some physical education programs are becoming voluntary rather than required.

The demand for an end to discrimination against minority groups has led to community discussions regarding such matters as bussing, hiring of black teachers, and equal salaries and opportunities for women as well as men teachers. Population mobility has raised questions about what kind of educational program is needed for a nation on wheels. The alarming dropout rate in our schools, with large numbers of young people who have neither the skills nor the self-reliance needed for gainful and satisfying employment, has elicited a recommendation to assign top priority to career education. More community and parental concern for education has led to a demand for greater accountability on the part of educators. Computers have made school class scheduling and record keeping easier. In the big cities of the nation there has been a move to decentralize large cumbersome school districts in favor of small community districts, which it is hoped will result in better administration of and more lay involvement in the running of the schools.

Both schools and physical education programs reflect, as in many ways all education does, the communities in which they exist. The community is that subdivision of people, homes, and businesses that make up a school district. It may coincide with the geographical limits of a city, town, or village, such as San Diego, California, or Denver, Colorado; or it may include two or more political subdivisions, such as the Bedford School District, which includes the towns of Bedford, New Castle, North Castle, and Pound Ridge, New York.

In any event, the local community plays an important part in the philosophy and formulation of the school's physical education program. Therefore, a knowledge of the community and the secondary school are important to the physical educator so that he or she may better prepare for the experiences to be encountered.

What is the structural organization of the community? What factors play a part in the financing of the schools? In regard to the schools, who is responsible to the citizens of the community? What influencing factors should be considered in establishing a philosophy of education? How is the physical education program affected by the community?

In this chapter these and other problems as they relate to the community and the schools and specifically to physical education will be discussed so that physical educators may be better able to understand and work with their particular situations.

COMMUNITY FACTORS INFLUENCING EDUCATION

Many factors have a bearing on the school system and its programs. Although these factors could be termed external, in that they are related to influences outside the school and the teacher-pupil relationship, their importance cannot be overemphasized. Therefore, school programs must be planned around the needs and interests of the community and the students. It further must be remembered that the school is only one community agency that contributes to the education of children. Therefore, the physical education program must be related not only to the individual but to the family and the community as well.

Economic conditions. One of the problems facing every community today is how to obtain enough money to close the gap between the amount and quality of education that is needed and the financial support that is available. Some of the factors that determine the cost of education listed by the National Education Association are the problem of securing an adequate number of teachers at salaries high enough to attract and hold them; the need for counseling and guidance; the need for adequate facilities and equipment; the need for enough classrooms to implement a modern program; and the need to lift poverty-stricken districts to a respectable level of support.

The community that is able and willing to meet these needs will have a sound educational system. In relation to physical education, this means well-planned physical plants—both indoors and out—and enough qualified personnel to administer a sound, safe, and varied class program, an inclusive intramural program, a full interscholastic program, and a practical adapted program.

In poorer areas many students have after-school jobs and, furthermore, because of crowded conditions, cannot study at home. In this situation, nearly all educational experiences must take place in the school if they are to take place at all. Special dress or equipment requirements must be kept to a minimum because of the financial status of the majority of families. In addition, the physical facilities and equipment available will depend to some extent on what the community can afford to pay.

In densely populated areas the schools may be crowded. Class size must be a component of program design if the maximum benefit within the limits of facilities and number of students is to be achieved. Obviously, many more curricular options are available in schools that can afford manageable class sizes. At the same time, lower salaries, larger classes, less equipment and supplies, fewer personnel, and limited intramural and interscholastic programs often result in inferior programs.

Fiscal problems have no easy solution, but the implications for physical education, as for all education, are monumental. The economy of a community may have particular impact on the physical education program. In an economically weak situation, the classes are apt to be overcrowded, with far too many students for an effective teaching-learning situation. There may be inadequate locker and shower facilities, as well as inadequate teaching stations both indoors and out. Equipment may be worn or in short supply, and new equipment may be difficult to obtain. In a situation where students are employed after school, it may be difficult to operate an intramural program. Lack of staff may dictate that physical education personnel assume a variety of nonteaching duties, such as lunch hour supervision and study hall and bus duty. In a community where the schools enjoy strong economic support, the reverse will be true.

Religious groups. Fifty to one hundred years ago, religious groups had a great and direct influence on the administration of a community's affairs, including school programs. In recent years the increased separation of church and state may have diminished the influence of religious groups.

The church school is another consideration. Many children spend part or all of their school life without attending a public school. With conditions as crowded as they are in many public schools, this helps alleviate further overcrowding. Support for public education, however, is understandably less from this group.

A few religious groups frown on certain activities that a school may endorse such as social dancing, Saturday or Sunday athletic contests, and family life courses. Where a particular church has considerable influence, it may mean a complete breakdown of parts of the school program that may be needed and wanted by many students.

To meet these problems, physical educators must base programs on educationally sound principles and be certain that the school administration is supporting the program. If a question arises, they should be prepared to explain the program with supporting evidence to representatives of the community's churches and to listen carefully for valid criticisms and suggestions for improvement.

Politics. In communities where school boards are appointed, merit and qualifications for the job may be taken into consideration. However, in other instances, appointments may be made on the basis of political patronage. Where board members are elected, the entire voting community has a voice in who runs the schools. However, this sytem may also have drawbacks. Although interested candidates who can do a good job run and sometimes win election, aspiring politicians often run for the school board and then use the position as a stepping-stone in their careers. The process of education is frequently only a minor consideration to such politically motivated individuals. Further, in a community that favors one political party over another, the candidates of that party, rather than the best person for the job, may be elected.

Not only the school board but local politicians as well may have a voice in running the schools of a community. The local press and radio also reflect local political views toward the schools through editorial comment. It is the school board, however, that hires and fires teachers, approves budgets, and decides on new construction. Thus the teacher is ultimately responsible to the school board, which as a group is responsible to the community.

Strong support of a school board by the community will be reflected in the physical education program, ensuring a better chance that qualified staff will be hired, will teach satisfactorily in a healthful environment, and be retained for further service. Budget requests and appropriations are most likely to be honored where the school board receives community support and in turn supports its teachers and their programs. Where the school board is ineffective and inefficient because it is politically maneuvered, all of education suffers.

Climate. Another consideration is the geographical location of the community. Planning must take the following aspects into consideration:

1. *Amount of time it will be possible to be out-of-doors.* It would be unreasonable to spend large amounts of money equipping and maintaining an oversized gymnasium in southern California or Florida where much more time will be spent out-of-doors than indoors. Conversely, in the northern states, more time will normally be spent inside because of the weather.

2. *Activities that will be of interest to local residents.* The inclusion of and emphasis on skiing and ice skating in the program in northern states would certainly be understandable, whereas more emphasis on tennis would be reasonable in Arizona and Texas. This does not exclude ice skating from the program in the South or the Southwest, although facilities would have to be available. The emphasis on winter sports in the South, however, would not approximate

that in the northern section of the country. It is necessary to determine the activities and interests of the community as they relate to the climate in order to make efficient use of funds.

Sociological and cultural backgrounds. The composition of the community has a bearing upon the physical education program. The races or nationalities, wealth or lack of it, educational backgrounds, and ages of the residents are just a few of the sociological and cultural factors that should be considered when planning a program.

The program in a low socioeconomic area should include many opportunities for active participation as an outlet for aggressive tendencies that may be more prevalent in such an area. In requiring proper gymnasium attire, it is important to recognize that some pupils may not have the money to purchase sneakers or gym suits. However, it may be possible to stockpile uniforms as pupils outgrow them; yet it is necessary to be tactful when making them available to pupils. It is also important that showers be taken because some of the pupils may not have other opportunities to take baths at home.

If the child resides in the inner city, play space is usually limited to the streets and neighborhood playgrounds. Thus it is up to the school to provide a well-rounded program of motor experiences for such students. If the parents of a child are poverty-stricken, there will be little money for recreational activities. If different ethnic groups are represented in the student body, new sports and activities might be included in the program to enhance students' pride and respect for their own heritage. It makes much more sense, for example, to keep activities relevant to students' backgrounds than try to teach deck tennis to inner-city children.

In other communities, residents may be college graduates and fairly well-to-do. The physical education program should make use of the educational interests of these fathers and mothers to encourage support for programs, facilities, special equipment, and supplies. The program may include individual activities such as golf, tennis, and archery, since the students will probably be able to make use of these skills out of school.

The great problem of meeting the needs of children

Fig. 1-3. The sociological composition of the community influences the physical education program.

Courtesy University School of Nashville, Nashville, Tenn.

from varied backgrounds presents a challenge to the teacher in working not only with pupils but with their parents. It is therefore important to know the parents of children in the community. Such knowledge could come from an analysis of the following items concerning the parents: (1) interest in the parent-teacher association, (2) participation in various organizations that are important in the community (groups such as the League of Women Voters, garden clubs, and Junior League may indicate a higher educational background and socioeconomic status), (3) participation in hobbies and leisure activities (golf and tennis clubs and riding stables may indicate a higher socioeconomic area), (4) interest in school sports activities, which may indicate interest and potential support if properly channeled by the physical educator, and (5) the desire to conform (the danger lies in the possibility of conforming to mediocrity).

Differences in taste, attitude, and race or nationality are minimized in the gymnasium and on the athletic field. Breaking down false beliefs, recognizing abil-

ity, and giving a feeling of belonging can be accomplished in the field of sports. Physical educators can help combat the harmful social and cultural variances within the community by means of a good program.

Attitudes toward education. Is the community willing and able to support the schools? How has it voted in recent referendums relating to school expansion or expenditures? Does it regularly cut the school's operating budget? If so, it is possible that the community is either unable or unwilling to meet desirable educational expenses.

A beginning physical education teacher should be conscious of the handicaps of equipment and supplies that are old or in short supply, classes that are overcrowded, or facilities that are inadequate. The amount of relief that can be expected is largely dependent on the attitude of the members of the community.

Another aspect worth noting is the degree of acceptance of educational trends approved and used in other communities or sections of the country. For instance, are antiquated strength tests, an excessive amount of formal work such as calisthenics, or heavy apparatus being used? Is the term "physical training" still used? The answers to these questions indicate attitudes of the community toward schools that may have a part in the eventual success of the physical education program.

Consideration must be given to parents' ideas for their children's education in the design of any school program. All social groups have goals for their children, and these determine what programs the community will support and sanction. There is a need for clear lines of communication between curriculum planners and the community.

Pressure groups. A pressure group can be defined as an organization or group of people working to achieve a common goal. There are groups or organizations in every community that attempt to pressure others to elect a certain candidate, repair a street, reduce a tax, or perhaps change the physical education program. Examples of pressure groups are a dads' club desiring to sponsor a football league, a church group wanting to eliminate social dancing in the school, and a citizens' group trying to rally support for a school referendum.

Pressure groups are not necessarily negative. In fact, quite often the opposite is true, and sometimes one pressure group is formed to combat the goals of another group. It is also true that many organizations believe they are helping physical education programs when in reality they are doing a great disservice to the students. For example, a fraternal organization that gives expensive prizes or awards or sponsors a football league at the elementary school level usually does so out of a desire to be of service to the community and the school. Only by fostering an understanding of the possibly harmful effects of overemphasizing competition can the physical educator effectively oppose such influences.

When physical education teachers are members of the community, there are often opportunities to discuss ideas on an informal basis. Such discussions provide an excellent chance to encourage, dissuade, or rechannel the energies of a group of interested community members. Speaking at meetings, interpreting a good program, and sending home happy, understanding students are probably the best ways to resist undesirable group pressures.

THE COMMUNITY'S ATTITUDE TOWARD THE FUNCTIONS OF THE SCHOOL

Both the community's and the professional educator's attitudes toward the functions of the schools have been well publicized. A recent Gallup Poll indicated that many Americans feel that the most important qualities for students to develop in school are, in order of priority: learning to think, developing facility at human relations, becoming willing to accept responsibility, and acquiring high moral standards, eagerness to learn, and the desire to excel. At the same time, the public believes that the qualities most neglected by schools are high moral standards, thinking for oneself, eagerness to learn, willingness to accept responsibility, desire to excel, and adeptness at human relations. According to the survey's respondents, only 13% of the schools in this country deserve an "A" rating, 29% a "B," 28% a "C," 10% a "D," and 6% a failing grade.

According to another survey, the following tasks must be accomplished to improve our schools:
- Basic skills need to be taught more effectively.
- Better discipline should be provided.
- Individual needs of students must be met.
- Better parent-school relations should be established.
- More time should be spent on moral development.
- Career education should be emphasized.

Many communities also feel that there should be more emphasis on the "basics," sometimes referred to as "The Back-to-Basics Movement in Education." A Gallup Poll regarding the public's attitude toward the schools shows a strong emphasis on educating the nation's children and youth in basic learning skills. The public wants its young people to achieve high standards in subjects such as reading, writing, and arithmetic. The quality of education in the basic intellectual disciplines, it says, has deteriorated and must be improved. According to Brodinsky,* the back-to-basics proponents want the following reforms:

1. Spending the major part of school time in the elementary grades on reading, writing, and arithmetic

*Brodinsky, B.: Back-to-basics: the movement and its meaning, Phi Delta Kappan **58:**522, 1977.

2. Devoting most of the time in secondary schools to English, science, mathematics, and history
3. Changing teaching methodology to emphasize teacher-directed activities, frequent testing, and homework
4. Stressing discipline, required courses, and few (if any) electives
5. Basing promotion from grade to grade on skill mastery and demonstrated achievement as indicated by passing marks on tests
6. Eliminating such ''frills'' as sex education, volleyball, weaving, and flute practice
7. Eliminating such social services as driver education, guidance, and physical education
8. Placing more emphasis on patriotism

What has created the back-to-basics movement? Some of the reasons are associated with the public's current stress on accountability, the conservative trend taking place in society and in education, the disintegration of the family, the poor writing and reading ability of students throughout the nation, and the troubled economy, which has resulted in less money for education and the feeling that a program stressing only the basics will be more economical.

The back-to-basics movement has made considerable progress in recent years, as evidenced by the following facts:

- A greater emphasis placed on basic subjects in the curriculum by four-fifths of the nation's school boards
- The popularity of the competency-based learning approach
- The great number of existing competency-based teacher education programs
- The Council for Basic Education's statement that many, many school systems throughout the United States have adopted its fundamental or traditional concepts, including such states as Florida, which has passed legislation requiring pupil performance rather than social promotion as a basis of promotion
- The prediction of several educators that in the near future almost all states will require minimal competency testing for promotion and graduation
- The reduction of personnel and the deemphasis of physical education in some schools and colleges

Fig. 1-4. Basketball is a popular sport in the secondary school.

Courtesy Barbara Ann Chiles, Aledo, Ill.

The back-to-basics movement in education has many implications for physical education. Since some of the advocates of this movement look on physical education as a frill and as a social service that cannot be justified in today's educational programs, it may mean survival or nonsurvival for some programs as they are known today. The best strategy, it seems, for physical educators to follow in counteracting the back-to-basics movement is to show how physical education is one of the "basics" and why it should be so viewed in today's educational curriculum. To do this, physical education leaders must set forth clearly and articulately how and why it is part of the general program of every educational institution. *Basic Stuff Series I and II* (see Chapter 4) is part of this attempt to justify the role of physical education.

THE COMMUNITY'S ATTITUDE TOWARD THE COST OF EDUCATION

The community's attitude toward the cost of education is becoming increasingly clear in these uncertain economic times. Education budgets are being scrutinized very carefully and, in many cases, austerity budgets adopted. Needed capital improvements are frequently delayed or abandoned altogether, while essential personnel are not being hired.

The budget crunch caused by the taxpayer revolt in California and the passage of Proposition 13, and more recently, the passage of Proposition 2½ in Massachusetts could forecast what may happen in other states and communities. Proposition 2½, passed by 60% of the electorate, states that local property taxes will be limited to no more than 2½% of assessed valuation, compared to the 6% to 8% that had been previously assessed in many communities. As a result, educators see this legislation as a threat to the schools. Some persons feel schools may not be able to stay open, and some believe that physical education and athletic programs will be the ones most seriously hurt. There has already been a reduction in some school systems in the number of participating athletic teams, particularly of the subvarsity type. Some school districts are turning elsewhere for funds to finance their programs, including persuading businesses to provide matching funds, appealing to alumni for financial help, and encouraging local citizens to make tax-free

donations. As one person said, "2½ didn't say 'eliminate programs' but rather 'change the way you pay for them.'"

A survey of 1,000 Directors of Physical Education and Athletics in the State of New York showed that 62% have had to cut programs, reducing funds for supplies, transportation, and specific sports. Many of the Directors indicated that in order to survive, they were financing at least part of their program through such means as booster clubs, participation fees, lotteries, student work projects, and other promotional activities.

COMMUNITY STRUCTURE

Through a knowledge of the composition of the community and its governing bodies, physical educators will be better able to understand the problems facing the community. Further, any suggestions for improvement of curriculum, school plans, facilities, number of personnel, or school philosophy will be more meaningful when they are based upon local community conditions. It is necessary, therefore, to investigate and obtain information about the community, evaluate these facts in the light of professional knowledge, and plan a course of action.

Size. Is the community a compact industrial area, such as Scranton, Pennsylvania, or does it sprawl over the countryside, as does Berkeley, California? The answer to this question has much significance for both school and physical education program. In a compact area, for instance, there is little or no transportation problem. Afterschool activities, such as intramurals and varsity team practice, are not greatly affected because public transportation is available to take students home. In a sprawling community, lack of public transportation can be a deterrent to many activities. Solutions to these transportation problems may include convincing school authorities to provide extra transportation, enlisting the aid of the local parent-teacher association, and coordinating efforts with other departments, such as music or dramatics, thereby involving enough students to warrant extra transportation.

Another problem of community size involves future growth, particularly in light of the exodus to the suburbs. Has the community reached its peak growth, or

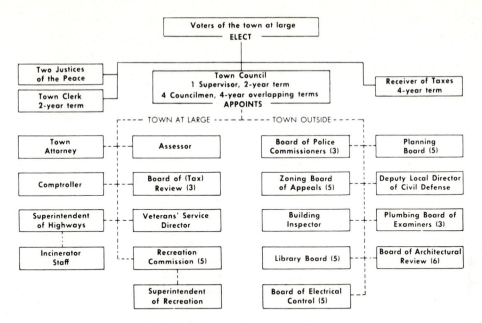

Fig. 1-5. Structure of a town government.

is it still expanding? Do facilities amply provide for the current number of students? What are the plans for new facilities? Do these plans properly provide for physical education space, equipment, and teaching stations?

Type. Is the community predominantly residential, such as Darien, Connecticut, or Berkley, Michigan? Educators in such communities may assume that the parents will take time to inquire about and participate in educational planning. Active and interested parents who put their energies to work in helping administrators and teachers are of great help. Involved parents can help the physical education program by supporting its activities; helping to obtain new facilities, equipment, and supplies; and gaining an understanding of the program. In an industrial community or in a culturally disadvantaged one, residents may be less inclined—perhaps because of time—to concern themselves with education. In Flint, Michigan, however, a public interest in education brought more people into the schools at night than during the day.

Flint has developed the school-community idea to the point where each school has an evening center,

and most have gymnasiums that are at least 100 by 100 feet in area, as well as other community rooms. In addition to the evening recreation centers, there are child health programs, in-service training for teachers, an outdoor camp, Big Sister organization, adult education programs, tots and teens groups, a stepping-stone program, and other programs.

This program was begun in 1935 by the Mott Foundation in cooperation with the Flint Board of Education. Its purposes are threefold: (1) to make possible the maximum utilization of school buildings and school facilities as well as other community resources—personnel, material, and organizations, (2) to act as a pilot project in testing and demonstrating to the local board of education and other communities the possibilities of what may be accomplished, and (3) to stimulate, by demonstrating what can be done, constructive influences not only in this community but eventually in other parts of the state, the nation, and the world.

The values of the Flint program are obvious. Important also are the attitudes of the taxpayers when they are able to see and use the buildings for which they pay. Flint was blessed with the Mott Foundation, but most communities can achieve community-centered schools for very little extra cost.

Unlike Flint, many industrial or business villages, towns, or cities do not have a positive attitude toward education. There may be little room for playing fields and recreational areas. There may be a large number of older residents who no longer have school-age children. The attitude of the public is of great importance because many residents may feel little sympathy for public school problems, particularly since most solutions to these problems involve an increase in taxes.

In addition to the older residents, there are those parents who send their children to private or parochial schools and who have no desire to pay twice for education. They must pay their taxes, which are used for public education, but they have a vested interest in minimizing these payments.

Although there are always many parents interested in the schools and their problems, the support of a majority of the population is necessary. This requires public interpretation. In Flint this positive attitude has been achieved through a community-centered program. In Norfolk, Virginia, an interest has been manifested in education through a program of health and activity instruction and intramurals. This program developed because of close cooperation in the fields of health and physical education, which led to an integrated core of instruction.

If community support is not present, it is the responsibility of the school and of every individual in the school to foster it through careful planning.

Governing body. Three main types of governing bodies determine the form of local government: the mayor-council, the commission, and the city manager.

The *mayor-council plan* places primary control of administrative matters in the hands of an elected mayor. The council, elected by the citizens, handles local legislation. There are variations in the organization of this plan. Some communities have a dominant mayor, others divide the responsibilities of the mayor and the council relatively equally, and still others have a weak mayor, with the bulk of duties handled by or through the council. The mayor-council plan is still the most prevalent. The majority of small cities use it in one

form or another, as do such large cities as New York, Boston, San Francisco, and Detroit.

The *commission plan* has had its period of growth and is now generally regarded as being in eclipse. The city of Galveston made this plan popular just after the turn of the century. There were five commissioners elected by the people. One was designated as mayor, but only for the purpose of presiding at the meetings. He had no veto power and shared administration proportionately with the other commissioners. This type of plan is still used by some municipalities, but its popularity is on the wane.

The *city manager plan* is growing more rapidly than any other type of city government. In this plan, a career person trained in public administration is appointed by the council and made responsible for the conduct of municipal administration. There are variations in this plan, such as the council keeping certain appointment rights. Most plans leave only two duties in the hands of the council: (1) the right to pass necessary ordinances and resolutions and (2) the right to select the city manager.

The growth of the city manager plan has numerous implications for education. The concentration of powers in a professional person (the manager is supposed to be nonpartisan and is generally chosen from an approved list) usually brings about wider use of modern administrative procedures, which generally are credited with unusually effective standards of modern administration.

The implications of the governmental structure—whether it is city, village, town, or other type—for the school and the physical education program are numerous. Knowing it well will provide an understanding of the following:

1. *The chain of responsibility*—that is, who the local district leaders are and what they have to do with appropriated monies
2. *The use of modern governmental structure*—that is, the degree to which the community is operating under an archaic form of patronage or an efficient modern structure that attempts to cut unnecessary costs and meet today's challenges
3. *The pressure points in the community structure*—that is, how public sentiment for needed school expenditures can best be made known and impressed on local officials

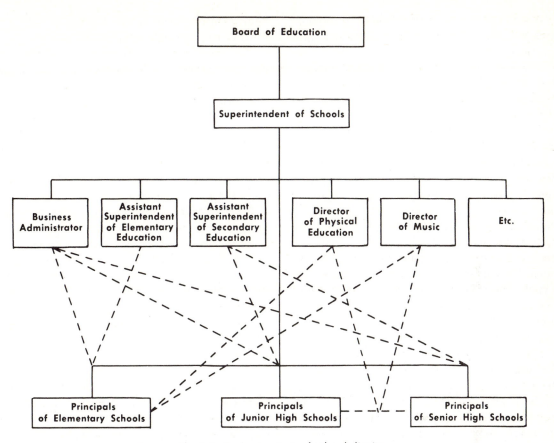

Fig. 1-6. Basic structure of school district.

It is the responsibility of a teacher to know as much as possible about the local government.

Board of education. The board of education, or school board or committee, as it is known in some areas, is the administrative unit whose responsibility it is to develop policies for the educational program in the local schools. Some communities have a single commissioner of education, but most cities and districts retain the board plan. This is true in spite of the widespread movement to single-headed departmental control in such areas as police, fire, and health—perhaps because of the reasonable success of the board plan and the caliber of most board members, who are usually able to remain aloof from local politics. Whatever the reasons, the board plan appears to be here to stay, and most educators seem to prefer this type of administration.

A board of education may be financially independent, allowing it to fix its own tax rate within limits set by the state and to spend the money as it sees fit. In many cities of more than 25,000 people, as well as in some smaller communities, the boards are financially independent. When a board is fiscally dependent, it recommends the amount it needs to cover the cost of its budget, but the municipal administration decides on the amount the board will receive. If the full amount is not given, the board must reduce, eliminate, or adjust budget items to fit the allotted amount.

It is important for the physical educator to keep the board aware of problems facing the teacher and to recommend some realistic solutions. Further, it is necessary to channel this information through the principal, director or supervisor, or superintendent.

Composition. Boards of education for school districts evolve from acts of state legislatures. In most cities, boards are elected by the voters. There are places, however, where the mayor appoints members. Regardless of how they obtain their positions, their terms vary from one year to about four years. The usual term is three to four years. Terms are frequently overlapped to ensure continuity in membership.

Size. Boards of education are gradually diminishing in size, from the 30- and 40-member boards of yesteryear to the five- and nine-member boards seen most commonly today. The number of board members ranges from three, who represent a small local district, to 15 in some large cities. The smaller boards of today seem to produce better results by working more efficiently and with greater harmony. As a rule, most members serve without compensation, although very nominal salaries are given in certain areas.

The National School Boards Association indicated a few years ago certain characteristics of school boards in 42 cities throughout the nation having more than 300,000 population. Most of these school boards have seven, five, or nine members, in that order. Three cities have boards with fifteen members. The composition of school board members (3% of whom are women and 13% of whom are blacks) is broken down as follows: businessmen, 103; lawyers, 66; housewives, 51; physicians, 22; ministers, 11; and college professors, 8.

Most of the 137,000 members of the nation's approximately 25,000 school boards are elected. Among the large cities, only Philadelphia, Pittsburgh, and Washington, D.C., choose boards through a committee of court judges. In Boston, Detroit, Los Angeles, and St. Louis, school boards are elected.

Duties. The board of education's responsibilities may be summed up as follows:

1. *Establishes policies and legislates*
   a. Curriculum—including physical education curriculum (in accordance with certain state regulations)
   b. School calendar—including time and days when interscholastic contests may or may not be played
   c. School entrance age—set by the state in some areas

2. *Provides means for carrying out policies*
   a. Prepares budget—including salary scale, arrangements for time off or extra pay for coaching, and policy regarding coaching duties
   b. Hires superintendent and other personnel (on recommendation of the superintendent)
   c. Votes tax levies, if fiscally independent, or recommends adequate levies to those who have the fiscal responsibility
   d. Plans and executes building and maintenance program (within limits mentioned above)—including new physical education plants and facilities

3. *Sees that policies are efficiently carried out*
   a. Visits schools
   b. Receives oral and written reports on progress

The board also represents the public in the preparation of its policies and budgets, interpreting to the public the needs of the school in terms of plant, facilities, and working conditions. Although there are some specific duties and responsibilities of boards of education and of superintendents, there is no exact line where the duties of the board end and those of the superintendent begin. This must be worked out together toward a common goal. The superintendent of schools, however, is the professional education leader, and members of the board of education are lay personnel. This, of course, has implications for the responsibilities of each.

There is a growing awareness among professional and lay leaders alike of the need for reform of school board operations. Such reforms have been advocated by so important a group as the New York Committee on Educational Leadership and are receiving support in some of the more progressive sections of the country. These improvements include (1) the transfer of all administrative functions that encumber school board operations to the superintendent of schools, (2) better procedures for screening school board members so that the "office seeks the man rather than the man seeking the office," (3) elimination of required annual public votes on school budgets and substitution of budget hearings, and (4) improved procedures for selecting superintendents of schools.

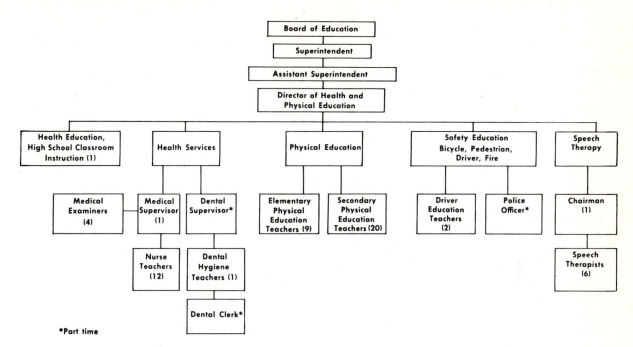

Fig. 1-7. Administrative structure of school district with director of health and physical education.

STATE AND NATIONAL INFLUENCE

Since education is a state function, the state legislature is responsible for it. Although most states follow similar administrative structures, they differ in details. In every state there is usually a commissioner or superintendent of education as well as a board of education.

State departments of education emphasize cooperative planning. They do not serve merely as law enforcement agencies. Although most states have the power to change school districts, they prefer to leave as much choice as possible to the local districts; however, they will bring pressure to bear where necessary. They are always ready to provide consultant services to help in the solution of local problems.

Recently, at the request of an eastern city, the state department of education conducted a school survey in that city. The recommendations included in the survey covered many aspects of education. The imminent threat of the withdrawal of state aid was one of the factors that hastened the city's compliance with many of the basic recommendations made as a result of the survey. In the field of physical education, improvements came in the addition of teachers, an increase in allocation for supplies, and the expediting of plans for reconditioning and enlarging existing physical plants.

A knowledge of the minimum state standards will enable the beginning teacher to determine whether the school has provided the educational essentials. If the recommended standards have not been met, an attempt to make improvements should be made. Since one responsibility of state departments of education is to improve physical education programs, consultants are usually available to local schools and districts for (1) evaluation of program content, (2) assistance in curriculum revision, (3) guidance in problem situations, and (4) assistance in public relations. State department representatives will usually work to find ways of improving curricula, standards, and facilities.

Since the Constitution of the United States does not carry any provision for federal education, the state has assumed the responsibility. Yet the state has limited its own action primarily to guidance and the specification of minimum requirements, leaving a major part of the obligation of education in the hands of the local district and thus placing more responsibility on the physical educator to constantly interpret his or her program.

The school within the community

The school, as the hub of the educational program, should reflect societal changes that are meaningful and important to the students who attend these institutions since they have the responsibility of educating tomorrow's citizens. Furthermore, the school should work directly with the community, parents, and students in a manner consistent with the changes taking place. For physical educators and school administrators to do this intelligently, the structure and role of the secondary school must be clearly understood.

The beginning physical educator, particularly, in order to perform his or her role in the most effective way possible, should know and understand the way the school system is structured in the community, how the secondary school fits into this structure, the personnel who play key roles in the educational process, the facilities utilized, and the programs being offered. Although the goals of education are similar, means will differ from one school system to another. The lack of such knowledge and understanding can result in personnel problems, disregard for proper channels of communication, and failure to utilize important program resources or gain acceptance for innovative ideas.

STRUCTURE

School district. A school district is that subdivision responsible to the state for the administration of public education. Districts vary greatly in size and function. They may be formed on township and city lines, according to elementary or secondary levels, or they may use other divisions. The trend is away from having many, overlapping, ineffectual districts and toward the use of larger, more effective districts. The National Education Association reports that from 1948 to 1958 the number of school districts in the United

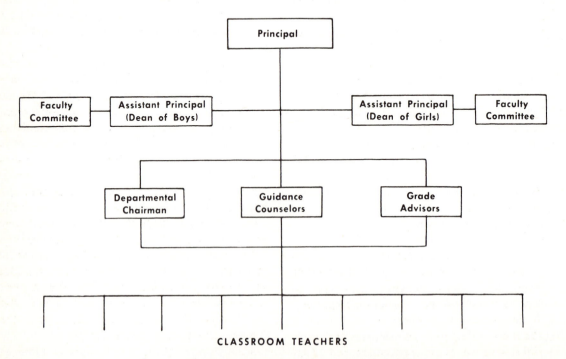

Fig. 1-8. Administrative structure of one secondary school.

States dropped from nearly 102,000 to 48,043. In recent years the number of school districts has been reduced still further; at the present time there are approximately 30,000.

Local school districts operate under authority granted by the state. The school district, which is administered by a board of education, is therefore legally responsible to all the people of the state, not only to those of the school district. The fact that a great amount of local freedom is allowed does not alter legal responsibility. (The school board's duties are explained earlier in this chapter.) Agents of the board, such as superintendents and principals, are the administrators who concern themselves directly with school problems.

The implications of district organization bode well for physical education. As districts become larger, their ability to support and maintain proper physical education plants, personnel, equipment, and supplies should increase—hence, the probability of a more comprehensive program.

School system. The size of the system dictates the number and type of duties of its school administrators. In a small system the superintendent performs many separate functions. In a larger system he or she is concerned primarily with coordination and public relations, while the many details are handled by assistant or deputy superintendents, department heads, subject supervisors, and principals.

The pattern of school organization at the elementary and secondary levels is in a period of transition, as reflected in various plans.

1. In the traditional high school, or 8-4, system, the four-year high school is preceded by the eight-year elementary school.
2. In the combined junior and senior high school, or 6-6 or 7-5, plan, the junior and senior high schools are combined under one principal.
3. In the three-year junior high school, or 6-3-3, system, the junior high school is grouped separately under one principal. Although the junior high school usually includes grades seven to nine, there are exceptions to this organization.
4. In the four-year high school, or 6-2-4, system, the four-year high school is similar to the traditional high school in organization, and the junior high school consists of two grades.

5. The middle school plan, for example, the 4-4-4 plan, retains the old high school idea but groups the upper elementary grades, grades five to eight, in one unit.

There are many arguments that can be set forth for each plan of school organization. The physical, psychological, and sociological aspects of the school setting and of child growth and development, the need for effective communication between schools, the range of subjects, the facilities provided, and the preparation of teachers are all pertinent to the selection of administrative organization. One survey of 366 unified school systems with pupil enrollment of 12,000 or more, conducted by the Educational Research Service, showed that 71% of these school systems were organized on the 6-3-3 plan, 10% on the 8-4 organization, and 6% on a 6-2-4 pattern. Other patterns included 7-5, 6-6, 5-3-4, and 7-2-3.

Elementary school. In most elementary schools the pupil is with one teacher most of each school day. The only change comes when a specialist handles the class for a period one or more times each week. These specialists may include the physical educator, music teacher, science teacher, art instructor, and an occasional resource person. In very small rural schools one teacher may instruct grades one through six in the same classroom.

In some elementary schools all physical education is handled by the classroom teacher. In other situations a physical education teacher may meet with the elementary class weekly or biweekly and prepare a program for the classroom teacher to use during the intervening days. In other elementary schools the physical education specialist sees the children two or three times weekly.

Middle school. One pattern of organization being considered by many school systems is the middle school concept. Most simply stated, a middle school is for boys and girls between the elementary and high school years—grades six, seven, and eight, and sometimes five. Communities that have adopted the middle school pattern are Bridgewater, Massachusetts; Bedford Public Schools in Mount Kisco, New York; Sarasota County, Florida; Saginaw, Michigan; Easton, Connecticut; and Independence, Ohio.

Some of the advantages of the middle school include the opportunity for more departmentalization, better stimulation of students, special teachers and special programs, and better student grouping.

Some of the disadvantages of the middle school include the lack of evidence to support its value, the social adjustment problems occurring when ninth graders are placed with twelfth graders, the possibility that youngsters in the middle school will be pushed too hard academically and socially, and the necessity of altering administrative techniques and procedures.

Secondary school. The junior high school is usually composed of grades seven, eight, and nine, and the senior high school is composed of grades ten, eleven, and twelve.

It is difficult to present a picture of a typical secondary school because of the variety in the size of the schools. They range from small rural schools with fewer than 100 pupils to large city schools that house student bodies numbering in the thousands. There are, however, certain basic factors that are true regardless of size or location:

1. Secondary education is usually coeducational.
2. Guidance is offered in most schools by specially trained personnel.

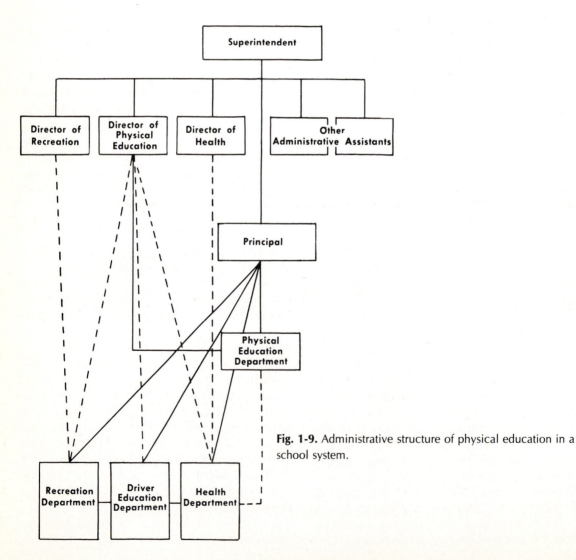

Fig. 1-9. Administrative structure of physical education in a school system.

3. Extracurricular activities are an important part of the program.
4. Secondary schools are prepared to offer terminal education as well as college preparation.
5. Individual courses of study are prepared for the students.
6. Teachers are specialists in subject areas.

The present tendency toward centralization and consolidation is a result of the limitations of the small high school:

1. *Meager curriculum offerings*—inability to hire teachers for small groups of gifted children
2. *Inadequate equipment and facilities* (such as library, gymnasium, shops, and laboratories)—because of lack of funds for these expensive areas
3. *Inferior opportunities for social development*—small number of children of comparable age and interests
4. *Inferior staff*—lower pay scale and living conditions as a result of lack of available funds

The larger high schools are generally able to offer a much more varied curriculum. Many educators have pointed to the necessity of challenging our gifted pupils and bringing along the slower ones. In the large high school the opportunity to meet these and other objectives is more readily available. Among recommendations for improving American secondary schools are

1. More student involvement
2. Minischools
3. Use of paraprofessionals
4. Use of community resources
5. Teacher accountability
6. Flexible scheduling
7. Differentiated staffing
8. Individualization of programs
9. Self-paced instruction
10. Grouping according to ability

The opportunity to meet children's needs is greater in a larger school—one with a graduating class of at least 100 pupils. In a large school there are usually a

Fig. 1-10. Physical education class at Mount Pleasant Senior High School, Wilmington, Del.

sufficient number of gifted pupils to fill a special class. The more experienced and better teachers are attracted to the larger school by better salaries and working conditions. The curriculum is more varied because full-time teachers are hired to teach languages, sciences, and other needed courses, as well as to work remedially with slow readers. Guidance personnel are also more readily available.

Specialists almost always handle the physical education program on the secondary level. In some junior high schools the arrangements are similar to the elementary school procedure, but more and more schools are using physical educators to handle the entire program, as they do in senior high schools.

PERSONNEL

Responsibility for the operation of the local schools rests with the board of education. The board hires a professional educator to administer the school system. This practice, about 150 years old, started when the educational process outgrew management by existing town officials. Now, as then, administrators attempt to solve the ever-present problems of public education.

Superintendent. The chief school official hired to supervise a school system is the superintendent. In a small community he or she may double as the principal of a high school and may be referred to as the district supervising principal. In larger communities he or she has an office staff and possibly an assistant to handle myriad responsibilities. In large cities or towns numerous assistants, deputies, or associates assist in various duties. Included in the superintendent's charge are these responsibilities:

1. *School organization*—establishing the school structure for the system
2. *Curriculum development*—establishing groups to conduct curricular revisions in all areas
3. *Personnel recommendations*—recommending to the board those individuals needed to fill vacancies
4. *Administration of all the school plans and facilities*—supervising maintenance, construction, and repair of all plants and facilities
5. *Budgetary recommendations*—submitting budget recommendations to the board of education

6. *School-community relations*—fostering good public relations through public appearances, meetings, and so forth
7. *Advice*—advising the board regarding policy changes, procedures, and practices, presenting educationally sound, workable suggestions
8. *Publicity*—keeping the board informed, giving reports on educational trends and notice of special school activities

To assist in these responsibilities and make recommendations to the superintendent, there may be any or all of the following individuals as part of the administrative organization in the school system: assistants for secondary education and/or elementary education; business administrators; school health assistants; personnel assistants; public relations assistants; curriculum assistants; and directors of special areas such as art, music, library, industrial arts, physical education, and buildings and maintenance.

Principal. In each school within any system, the principal is the chief administrator. His or her duties vary, depending on the size of the school. In a small building the principal may teach some classes in addition to assuming supervisory and administrative responsibilities. In larger schools he or she is not only relieved of teaching duties but also has some administrative assistants. They may include an assistant principal, guidance personnel, department heads, deans of girls and boys, and a custodial head.

The principal's responsibilities are similar to the superintendent's. They consist of executing the educational policy as outlined by the superintendent, directing the instructional program, promoting harmony and a democratic feeling within the faculty, encouraging and directing good school-community relationships, and supervising the maintenance of the physical plant.

It is usually difficult for a principal to know all the pupils in a large high school, but as a rule the pupil-administrator relationship will be much better when the principal is able to know pupils personally. Many administrators drop in at a rehearsal, team practice, or sports event not only to observe the teacher but also to let the students know that they are interested in their activities.

The principal also works closely with parents. He

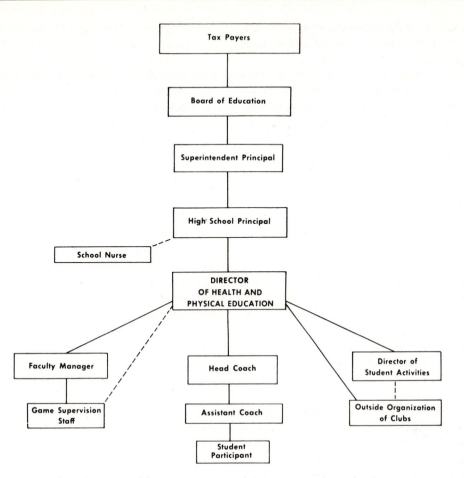

Fig. 1-11. Athletic organization chart in a secondary school.

or she plays an important role in the local parent-teacher association and in community affairs. The principal meets with parents to discuss student problems regarding college, grades, or discipline or acts as the intermediary to bring parents and teachers together to discuss these problems. The work is time-consuming and tedious.

One of the responsibilities of a principal is to establish a democratic administration. This means that faculty members participate in the formulation of policies. Of course, it is the principal's decision to use or to discard any suggestions, but the successful and wise administrator listens to faculty suggestions—whether in open meetings, through committees, or in personal conferences. Faculty committees are usually appointed by the principal to work with specific problems, such as grading, graduation, discipline, and the honor society. The committees present to the faculty and the principal recommendations to be used in the formulation of school policies. A knowledge of the formation and the functioning of these committees can be invaluable to the new teacher. It is also important to know the function and frequency of staff meetings and the channels through which problems, questions, and innovative ideas may be presented. Knowing how to approach the supervisor can play an important part in the satisfactory adjustment of the beginning teacher.

Department heads. Depending on the size of a

school system, there may be heads of special subject matter areas. These heads assist the superintendent by coordinating the work of the teachers and programs in their special fields.

Similarly, in larger high schools there are department heads to assist the principal. These people usually teach a number of classes, but their assignment also includes supervision, organization, and guidance. In smaller schools a department representative is often appointed by the principal to act as a liaison between the administration and the department when it is inconvenient to meet with the faculty as a whole.

In the field of physical education it is the usual practice in the larger school systems to have a director or supervisor who coordinates the work and supervises all the physical education teachers. In the smaller systems the superintendent or an assistant in charge of secondary or elementary education may supervise the physical education teachers.

Teachers. Teachers are hired by the board of education on recommendations from the superintendent, who usually consults with a principal or department head.

In small schools a teacher may teach two different subjects and possibly on two educational levels. This situation is not generally prevalent in larger schools. Physical education teachers on the secondary level usually teach physical education full time.

It is becoming more common to use specialists in health to handle all health instruction; however, in many systems the physical education teacher still doubles as the health teacher and possibly as the driver education teacher as well. Specific problems and details that the new physical education teacher must face are discussed in Chapter 9.

Custodians. Responsibility for the maintenance of the building rests with the principal. It is customary for a principal to delegate this responsibility to a head custodian. The importance of this aid to creating a good teaching atmosphere becomes evident when the temperature is too high or seats are in disrepair and conditions are not satisfactory for effective learning. A means of communication between the teachers and custodians is usually established so that these environmental factors can be quickly controlled and kept at optimum standards.

The school's custodians are often the physical educator's best friends and allies. Where they are treated with respect, the gymnasium and locker and shower rooms usually are kept in spotless condition. Frequently, the custodians are also responsible for maintaining the playing fields and for marking lines. If the physical educator takes cognizance of these individuals, his or her work can be made much easier. Where good relationships exist, the custodians will go out of their way to help repair a piece of equipment, to build a special item, or to mow the field an extra time. Poor teacher-custodian relations can have disastrous effects on the entire physical education program.

Specialists. The size of a system usually determines how many specialists will be part of the professional staff and just what their duties will be.

Medical staff. A large system may include a full-time physician in charge of the nurses and part-time physicians who assist in the yearly examinations, follow-up of remediable defects, and examination of athletic team participants. The medical staff in a smaller system may consist of a nurse who is assisted for a few hours weekly by a local physician.

Some schools authorize the nurse as the only person who can excuse a student from a physical education class for the day. This individual can assist the physical education department by observing and referring students who need advanced medical or dental treatment. The nurse also has knowledge of those students in need of a modified program and can act as a liaison between the physical education department and the family physician. The school nurse is an invaluable resource person for the physical education team.

Supervisory personnel. This area may range from numerous assistants in a large system to a superintendent or supervising principal who is the primary supervisor in a small school.

Curriculum specialists. Responsibility for the curriculum may be placed in the hands of committees of classroom teachers, or it may be delegated to curriculum specialists.

Guidance specialists. Professional workers in guidance may include psychologists as well as other guidance personnel. Some students manifest various behavioral and emotional problems. The school guidance counselors have dossiers on each student and can

Fig. 1-12. Physical education class at Mount Pleasant Senior High School, Wilmington, Del.

guide the physical educator in the most effective way of handling a particular problem. The guidance people are usually backed by school psychologists and social case workers, who may have or who can obtain further helpful information. The physical educator should seek the assistance of these people. A mishandled problem can create further problems, especially where a chronically disruptive pupil is concerned.

Because of their unique position in the school, the guidance counselors are often in a good position to observe and evaluate physical education programs. They frequently hear the student's point of view in counseling interviews and can relate nonconfidential comments to the physical educator.

Business administrator. The details of business administration may be assigned to an individual or to a staff responsible for the maintenance and repair of all plants as well as the distribution of all supplies, texts, or equipment.

Cafeteria personnel. Supervision may be handled on an individual basis in each school, or it may be handled through a head dietitian responsible directly to the superintendent.

FACILITIES

An excellent educational program does not necessarily require an ideal plant, nor does an ideal plant guarantee a good program; however, they complement each other. School construction is a major problem in the United States. Since the physical education plant is one of the most expensive items in the school, this problem is of particular interest to the physical educator. Multiple use of the physical education areas, such as the gymnasium, playing fields, and pool, undoubtedly engenders more support from the voting public for school construction. This implies the use of the facilities during evenings, weekends, holidays, and summers, in addition to school hours. Some communities that make extensive use of their school plants are Oakland, California; Spokane, Washington; and Norwich, Connecticut. Public reaction to educational expenditures is generally more favorable in such communities. This is undoubtedly true because many of the residents themselves are involved in the use of the school building, have a better understanding of where their money goes, and are therefore more inclined to support educational referendums.

Multiple use of facilities is not a panacea for education but has implications for the physical education teacher. Extensive use of facilities and proper interpretation to the public may help alleviate some of the problems relating to plant and facilities.

CURRICULA

Today's secondary schools vary greatly in the type of courses offered and in size and organization. If the trend toward centralization and consolidation of districts continues, it will help most schools to offer comprehensive programs and greatly raise the level of education.

There are three basic curricula offered on the secondary level. Some schools offer all three, which provide a sound, comprehensive program, while others offer only one or two.

General. The general curriculum is usually a terminal education program. It meets state requirements for graduation and covers basic courses in English, history, science, mathematics, physical education, art, and music.

College preparatory. This program includes the same courses as above at an advanced level plus added units in any or all of the following subjects required for college entrance or used for advanced standing: foreign languages, sciences, mathematics, music, and art.

Vocational or career education. The vocational curriculum includes basic courses in English, history, practical mathematics, and physical education, as well as specialized courses in such vocational areas as bookkeeping, typing, welding, auto mechanics, food trades, and designing.

In most schools grades seven and eight follow the required courses; grade nine allows for some exploration; and the tenth, eleventh, and twelfth grades allow students to follow their chosen course of study. This pattern is usually selected through the joint effort of the pupil, parents, and guidance personnel.

In some small schools the choice may be limited; therefore, students may be forced into patterns they would not select if given a choice. In some larger cities special schools meet the needs for special courses. In many cities there are schools that concentrate in a particular area, such as science, music and art, machine and metal trades, aviation, and food trades.

The type of course a student follows in high school has no bearing on the amount of physical education required. It is generally accepted that this instruction is necessary for all students.

Physical education in the school

For beginning teachers to better meet their responsibilities, it is necessary to understand the place of the physical education department in the school and the responsibilities of the personnel in the department.

STRUCTURE

The position of physical educators sometimes is more complicated than that of other teachers. As teachers, they are under the direct supervision of the principal of the school. In many systems, however, a director or supervisor of physical education represents the superintendent of school in this special area. Yet this supervisor usually does not have direct control over department members. Although responsible for the coordination of all physical education in the system, the director functions as an advisor to the principal and superintendent. The relationship of physical education instructors, their director, and the principal is a delicate one and should be understood by new teachers so that they may avoid obvious pitfalls. Beginning teachers should find out the disposition of responsibilities in the system.

PERSONNEL

In the field of physical education, the responsibilities of personnel will depend on the size of the system. In a small school one person may handle all the physical education duties from kindergarten through the twelfth grade. In other communities the responsibilities may be divided among director, chairman, and teachers.

Director or supervisor. There is a trend that recognizes the necessity for one person to oversee and coordinate all physical education in a school system. In at least one state a physical educator may become certified as a Director of Health, Physical Education, and Recreation. This person's responsibilities are to help establish policy; see that it is carried out; organize and administer girls' and boys' physical education programs at all levels; check facilities; coordinate programs; supervise teachers; help prepare the budget; organize all athletic programs, including scheduling, arranging for officials, transportation, equipment, and insurance; and assume responsibility for all equipment and supplies. In some communities these responsibilities are divided between the coach at the high school and an assistant or deputy superintendent.

The responsibilities of a director who has been charged with administering the fields of physical education, health, and recreation are varied.

General duties of the director

1. Implement standards established by the state department of education and the local board of education
2. Interview candidates for positions in special areas and make recommendations for these positions
3. Work closely with the assistant superintendent in charge of business affairs, the assistant superintendent in charge of instruction, and specialized and classroom teachers
4. Coordinate areas of health, physical education, and recreation
5. Supervise all inside and outside facilities and equipment and supplies related to special areas (this responsibility includes maintenance, safety, and replacement operations)
6. Maintain liaison with community groups; for example, hold educational meetings with doctors and dentists to interpret and improve the school health program, schedule school facilities for community groups, and serve on various community committees for youth needs
7. Prepare periodic reports regarding areas of activity
8. Coordinate school civil defense activities in some school systems
9. Serve on the school health council

Physical education duties of the director

1. Supervise total physical education program (class, adapted, intramurals, extramurals, and varsity interscholastic athletics)

2. Administer schedules, practice and game facilities, insurance, and equipment
3. Maintain liaison with county, district, and state professional groups
4. Upgrade program in general

Chairperson. The chairperson of a department is usually appointed by the principal or superintendent of schools. In some schools there is no formal department head; an individual is appointed by the principal to act as representative of the department. In most instances this person is the immediate supervisor of the physical education teachers. Part of his or her responsibilities may be to assist in the evaluation of a new teacher's performance. The person involved with this administration may teach a full program and receive extra compensation for duties rendered, may be relieved of some or all teaching responsibilities to allow time for administrative duties, or may merely be the department representative and have no supervisory responsibilities. In some cases this same individual may also be the athletic director, which means planning all interscholastic athletics.

Teachers. Teachers of physical education handle physical education classes, assist in curriculum evaluation, make suggestions for the improvement of the program, handle intramural and interscholastic programs, and assume other obligations to the school that fall to the lot of every teacher.

In a small secondary school the physical education program may be conducted by only one teacher for the girls and one for the boys. In such a situation each teacher must assume total responsibility for all areas of the program, including teaching, care of equipment, budget making, and directing intramural and extramural programs, as well as assuming any other responsibilities that may accrue from undertaking all phases of the job.

In a large secondary school there are frequently several male and several female physical educators. One of these teachers may serve as department chairperson and in turn be responsible to a supervisor of physical education who serves the entire school system. In this hierarchy each teacher is usually asked to assume responsibility for a particular area, such as equipment maintenance or the ordering of library ma-

Fig. 1-13. The physical educator should play an effective role in community. Physical educator at Hampton Institute, Hampton, Va., demonstrates tennis grip to student.

terials and audiovisual aids. This arrangement fragments the operation of the overall program but frees each teacher to devote more time to teaching. Similarly, department chairpersons and supervisors can devote more time to serving as resource people and to general supervision of the program.

Two of the main challenges facing a new physical education teacher are to be accepted as part of the total school and as an important part of the physical education department.

1. *Part of the total school picture.* One way in which a physical educator may gain the respect of colleagues is to share the so-called boring, routine jobs that are so much a part of the school day. These may involve distribution of supplies, detention assignments, lunchroom duty, or graduation practice. It is well worth the effort to shoulder a share of daily responsibilities.

As a member of a school faculty, the physical educator should show an interest in school activities and projects of all kinds. There is always something to be done, such as helping with the annual concert, the dramatic presentation, or the magazine drive, as well as participating in parent-teacher association meetings, staff meetings, and even faculty social functions. The physical educator should know the teachers in the school so that they will have the opportunity to gain a new respect for and understanding of the physical education department. This could very well lead to a more honest evaluation of the physical education program and to new supporters for its rightful place in the school curriculum.

2. *Member of the physical education department.* As is true for any new faculty member, the physical educator must demonstate capability, flexibility, and sincerity to his or her peers. This requires doing the

job as efficiently as possible and respecting the experience and seniority of colleagues.

INTERSCHOLASTIC ATHLETICS

The interscholastic athletic part of the physical education program may involve controversy. It is unfortunately true that there are some coaches who go to extremes in the handling of their teams. These coaches drive their teams unmercifully, attempt to pressure teachers to keep players eligible, believe they have to win at any cost, and devote too much of their time and energy to their teams—to the detriment of their physical education classes.

It is important that the interscholastic sports program take its proper place in the total program. Among its worthwhile aspects are its great value in challenging the athletically gifted child, kindling and keeping aflame the spirit of a student body, and uniting the members of a school and giving them a proud feeling of belonging. Interscholastic sports are, however, only one part of a physical education program.

INTERPRETING PHYSICAL EDUCATION*

Too often the physical educator or coach is considered separate from the education staff: the faculty educates students; physical educators exercise them.

The challenge of this attitude must be met by physical educators. They must have a sound philosophy of education and an understanding of the place of physical education in the development and growth of the child. They must also be exemplary in the performance of duties. Finally, the interpretation of physical education must be directed not only to faculty members but to the community as a whole.

Physical educators have many means of interpreting the program. Speaking at meetings of the Parent-Teacher Organization (and at clubs such as Rotary, Elks, Masons, and Kiwanis) is an accepted and effective method of presentation. Physical education demonstrations, sports nights, and athletic contests can also generate good publicity.

The best selling point, however, is the student in the physical education class. If pupils understand why they spend hours on the playground or in the gym-

---

*See Chapter 7.

nasium, their reactions and comments at home are the best means of interpreting the program to parents. To accomplish this, however, students must receive more than a chance to play ball. There must be an understanding of the accumulated values of a well-rounded program. Students, then, can be the physical educator's best salespersons. If they are educated well, the opportunity to do an even better job can be anticipated because of increased school and community support.

KEYS TO SUCCESS IN PHYSICAL EDUCATION

Certain characteristics are essential for a sound general and physical education program in the secondary school.

Administrative philosophy and policies. The administrator of a secondary school may or may not view the physical education program with favor. Where the administration values physical education, it will be easier to have homogeneous classes, and physical education will not be the last class to be scheduled. Where the administration is cooperative, the physical education program will be placed on a par with academic courses. The administration often sets the policies in regard to uniforms, excuses, and the grading system. The teacher must abide by these policies. The administration also assigns extra duties to teachers. Where physical education is given its rightful place in the curriculum, the physical education teacher has a minimum of extra duties during the school day. Lack of homeroom duties means time to ready the equipment for the day. Lack of study halls and lunch duty frees the physical education teacher for teaching, and lack of afternoon bus duty allows time for the management of a good intramural program. In any case the physical education program must be conducted within the existing administrative framework.

Faculty relationships. Teachers should work together not only to coordinate subject matter but to support and coordinate those special events that are so much a part of school life. The efforts of all teachers should be harmonized to culminate successfully in a music festival, school dance, general organization membership drive, athletic event, or other school-sponsored project.

The physical educator must strive to maintain cooperative relationships with the rest of the faculty. Social conversation with other faculty members allows for an interchange of ideas. Understanding is developed and concepts are formed about other areas of the curriculum. It is also in this area that the physical educator can articulate the relationship of the program to the rest of the school. The physical educator should always remain professionally ethical and refuse to discuss confidential information about students or to participate in a discussion that is concerned with gossip about students, other teachers, or the administration.

Teacher-parent relationships. When teacher-parent relationships are good, parents believe that they can approach their child's teacher to discuss any prob-lem, and the teacher believes that he or she can call on parents for assistance when necessary. A relationship of mutual respect provides the basis for a frank discussion between parent and teacher of problems and possible solutions.

To know the parents helps the teacher to understand the child. By joining the parent-teacher association and attending its meetings and social events, the teacher is able to meet the parents in a relaxed and informal atmosphere. It is here that the teacher can explain programs and answer parents' questions. The physical education program in a secondary school thrives on good public relations, which starts with the parents of the community.

Teacher-student relationships. When teacher-student relationships are good, mutual respect exists be-

Fig. 1-14. As a result of competency-based certification, teachers of physical education must demonstrate qualifications for teaching various physical skills. Physical education instructor demonstrating her competency in teaching tennis as part of Hampton Institute's training program, Hampton, Va.

tween pupils and teachers. The teacher who is aware of the need and the methods for earning this respect is able to establish rapport with pupils, which greatly contributes to the success of his or her program.

Besides teaching students, the physical educator must know and guide them and try to inspire them. In some schools student respect for teachers is totally lacking, and good discipline is difficult to maintain. Safety alone requires that physical education classes be well disciplined. A new teacher must be especially cognizant of the fact that students will test him or her. They want to know how the teacher will react to disrespect, horseplay in class, and bad conduct in general. Where the school administration has set strong behavior policies, the teacher will receive backing in maintaining these standards. Where behavior policies are weak, the teacher must set high standards and be consistent in applying them.

A martinet never develops close rapport with students. The good disciplinarian who respects and knows students as individuals will be able to do so, tempering discipline with understanding and respect for the student.

Good teacher-student relationships also develop in, and are carried over to, areas outside the classroom. The teacher who attends football games and concerts and helps to chaperone dances and social affairs has the opportunity to develop a working and companionable relationship with students. Students will respond in kind to respect, understanding, and interest.

The community school movement

The community school movement, although concerned with teaching children, emphasizes the role of the school in helping to meet the needs of the community. This concept is based on the premise that residents of a village, town, or city will work together to improve their community if opportunities are provided for them to make greater use of their schools. The community school, therefore, offers its facilities and resources, thereby helping residents of the community in joining to resolve their common problems. The community school view recognizes that the community needs the schools, and the schools cannot accomplish their purpose without the help and support of the community. The school further gains by using the community as a laboratory for enhancing learning possibilities.*

Physical education and community involvement

The community considerably influences the development of the physical education program. In those schools and institutions where the community provides funds for programs and wants to be involved, there are particular implications for program development.

Smith† recently indicated the extent of community involvement in Darien, Connecticut, public schools, demonstrating how various groups there were involved in a curriculum study project. A Task Force on Physical Education, appointed by the Board of Education, consisted of 13 members active in the community and business life of Darien. The Task Force established objectives and strategies to achieve them. Its design provided for a survey of 600 students in the school system, the schools' coaches and staff members, 1,000 Darien residents selected from tax rolls, and 40 organizations with a direct or indirect interest in athletics and recreation. Furthermore, the Task Force established criteria for program evaluation.

The project resulted in rewriting curriculum guides for each level of instruction (K to 6, 7 to 9, and 10 to 12), setting up student advisory boards and student intramural councils, creating a physical education inventory system, establishing a faculty manager position in the secondary school, instituting a full-day inservice workshop for physical education teachers, holding regular meetings with community agencies, and developing a coaches' handbook.

"Physical education is alive, well, and growing in Oklahoma City," according to Willet,‡ who points out what can be accomplished through a team effort of administrators, teachers, parents, and community.

---

*The Flint, Michigan, program discussed earlier in this chapter is an example of the community school concept.

†Smith, N.W.: Community involvement—through a curriculum study project, Journal of Physical Education, Recreation, and Dance **52:**16-17, June 1981.

‡Willet, L.: Physical education—alive, well, and growing, Journal of Physical Education, Recreation and Dance **52:**18, June 1981.

Physical education programs there, despite tight budgets and staff reductions, have gained outstanding support, both financial and moral, in the last four years. For example, there were no elementary school physical education specialists in the Oklahoma City school system in 1972. However, in the 1979-1980 school year, 31 new physical education specialists for elementary schools were hired. Three more were added in 1980-1981. In addition, 80 minutes of physical education instruction were provided each week by specialists, a maximum class size of 35 students was established, and the administration advocated the development and implementation of a system-wide physical education curriculum. Financial support was also provided to purchase hundreds of balls, ropes, mats, and other equipment, and monthly inservice sessions were held for new instructors.

In order to reach the public, special events, with extensive media coverage, were planned. One of these events was a Physical Education Exposition, planned and implemented by the physical education staff to demonstrate skills and activities learned in the program. Another event involved 5,000 fifth grade students in a Fitness Festival.

Physical education teachers accepted the responsibility for developing positive public relations with faculty, administration, students, and community members. The public in Oklahoma City responded with enthusiasm, giving physical education excellent support and devising many money-making schemes for projects such as the installation of creative playgrounds.

Clay,* in his article on the Norfolk, Virginia, physical education, health, and safety program, indicates how community awareness and involvement have resulted in an outstanding physical education program. He contends that what is most important for gaining community support is the instructional aspect of the physical education program. He also discusses methods that have been used successfully over the years to interpret the program to the public.

School-parent communication. Effective school-parent communication utilizes several techniques.

First, a *Handbook for Pupils and Parents* is given to each student in the school system at the beginning of each year. The *Handbook*, which discusses the nature and scope of the program, is taken home by the students, who brief their parents. Second, a Student-Parent Interest Survey is conducted by the physical education and research departments. This survey is designed to determine the interests and leisure-time needs of both parents and students and to ascertain whether the physical education program is meeting these needs and interests.

Government and agency cooperation. An impressive number of agencies and businesses in Norfolk cooperate with the physical education department. The Norfolk Chamber of Commerce has developed an ''Adopt-a-School'' Program whereby a business or corporation supports a nearby school or one in which it is particularly interested, helping in numerous ways to contribute to its physical education program—for example, by building facilities. As a result of this project, the Chesapeake and Potomac Telephone Company adopted Granby High School and constructed the Granby Community Track, officially dedicated on June 5, 1980. This $100,000 facility was built through volunteer effort without cost to the public.

The United Virginia Bank adopted Maury High in the spring of 1980. Although it had a new gymnasium, swimming pool, and tennis courts, it lacked a track. As a result of the Bank's efforts, friends and alumni of the school raised $15,000 with construction companies contributing the rest.

Many other agencies and community organizations contribute to Norfolk's physical education program: the Norfolk Parks and Recreation Department helps by providing six instructors annually to teach pupils swimming; the Norfolk Police Department and Tidewater Rape Crisis Center conduct a crime resistance program; the Norfolk Public Works Department installed walkways and ramps at an outdoor education facility; and the Norfolk Mayor's Youth Commission provided the physical education department with two outdoor swimming pools.

Community sponsors. Several community organizations in Norfolk sponsor activities for the school program. For example, the Northside Norfolk Rotary Club sponsors an Annual Leisure Time Track and

---

*Clay, W.B.: First class and getting better, Journal of Physical Education and Recreation **52**:19-21, June 1981.

CHECKLIST OF SELECTED ITEMS FOR EVALUATING THE SECONDARY SCHOOL'S PHYSICAL EDUCATION PROGRAM'S RELEVANCY TO THE COMMUNITY

	Yes	No
1. The physical education program utilizes such community resources as parks, swimming pools and bowling alleys, as well as people with expertise in various physical education activities and such methodology as visual aids and curriculum development, in providing a rich experience for the students.	☐	☐
2. Physical education takes into account the economic background of the community in planning activities (for example, weekend skiing trips may be too expensive).	☐	☐
3. Physical education takes into account the physical needs of the residents of the community (physical fitness, nutritional needs, and skill levels).	☐	☐
4. The physical education program takes into account the climate and other natural features of the community, making greatest use of the out-of-doors, providing seasonal activities, and the like.	☐	☐
5. Physical education works cooperatively with closely allied community agencies such as Boys' Clubs, PAL, YMCA, YWCA, CYO, YMHA, and YWHA.	☐	☐
6. The physical education program, in its offering of games, dances, and sports, provides for the interests and needs of people in the community with different ethnic backgrounds.	☐	☐
7. Physical education interprets articulately the value of its offering to the children and other residents of the community.	☐	☐
8. Physical education works closely with the community's communication media to properly interpret the program, including the role of educational athletics in the school.	☐	☐
9. Physical education interprets the athletic program to the townspeople and encourages proper behavior of spectators at sports contests to reflect favorably on the school.	☐	☐
10. Physical education interprets to school authorities the need for community utilization of its facilities in order to further its objectives for the adult population.	☐	☐
11. Physical education takes into consideration the attitude of the residents toward education and the level of aspiration for their children.	☐	☐
12. Physical education takes into consideration such community problems as drugs, violence, and school dropouts in its curriculum planning.	☐	☐
13. The physical education program takes into consideration the religious beliefs of the community in planning and carrying out its offering.	☐	☐
14. Physical education provides a viable program, where feasible, during school vacation periods.	☐	☐
15. Physical education provides advice and counsel for community physical fitness and athletic programs.	☐	☐
16. Physical education does not yield to community pressures to utilize questionable professional procedures to develop outstanding athletic teams.	☐	☐

Field Demonstration; the Khedive Shrine Temple sponsors Sportscope, the annual physical education demonstration; the Cosmopolitan Club of Norfolk and 36 cooperating organizations sponsor a Health Education Fair; the Tidewater Heart Association and the Norfolk Paramedics train health and physical education teachers to teach cardiopulmonary resuscitation to all eighth, ninth, tenth, and eleventh grade students; the Tidewater, Virginia, Lung Association and other organizations provide instruction in smoking and alcohol; and more than 75 agencies provide instructional materials, financial aid, or other assistance to the physical education, health, and safety department.

The Norfolk physical education program is an excellent example of how community involvement can enhance offerings and service to the community and provide for the interests and needs not only of students but of the adult population as well.

Self-assessment tests

These tests are designed to assist in determining if material and competencies presented in this chapter have been mastered.

1. Describe the community in which you live and give specific illustrations as to how it has affected the school's physical education program.
2. Prepare a plan that you would follow as a physical educator to ensure an effective working relationship between the community and your school's physical education program.
3. Draw a governmental organizational chart of your community that shows existing offices and positions.
4. Prepare an administrative organizational chart of your school district. Include in this chart a detailed breakdown of the various administrative units in the high school and how physical education fits into this administrative structure.
5. You are presented with the proposal that the administrative structure of your school be changed. Discuss how schools differ and what administrative plan you feel would be most helpful to implement a viable physical education program.
6. List the key administrative positions in a school district. Opposite each position list the duties performed by the person holding that position.

Points to remember

1. There are different types of communities in which teachers work; the nature of each type of community has many implications for physical education.

2. Many community factors, including economic conditions, religious groups, climate, sociological and cultural backgrounds, attitude toward education, and pressure groups, affect education and physical education.
3. There is an urgent need for cooperation between physical education, health, and recreation.
4. The structure of a school district has implications for physical education.
5. There are many types and characteristics of secondary schools.
6. The place of the physical education department in the total school picture is important to the program's adequate functioning.

Problems to think through

1. What are the advantages to the physical education department in a community where the board of education is fiscally independent? Fiscally dependent?
2. What would you, as the physical educator, do in a community where there is a movement to organize a highly competitive sports league for junior high school students?
3. What are the implications for physical education in the drive to consolidate or centralize small school districts?
4. What are some of the considerations that face a new teacher?
5. How may a coach avoid alienating members of the school faculty?
6. What are the advantages of a secondary school that has a graduating class of 100 pupils?
7. Of what value would a director, chairperson, or supervisor of physical education be to a school system?

Case study for analysis

All teachers are responsible to their principal. Many physical education teachers are also supervised by a department chairperson and/or a director or supervisor of physical education who represents the superintendent of schools. Analyze the chain of responsibility of all physical education teachers in a school system containing one senior high school, one junior high school, and four elementary schools. Consider possible friction points among the supervisory personnel. How can physical education teachers avoid difficulty in their relationship with their supervisors?

Exercises for review

1. Describe the composition of the board of education in your community and the powers and qualifications of the members.
2. What are the pressure groups in your community that may affect the physical education program?

3. List five facets of a program of physical education that are successfully performed in communities near your own.
4. What are the responsibilities of the superintendent of schools regarding physical education?
5. To whom may the new physical education teacher turn for help and guidance? Indicate specific areas in which the new teacher needs assistance and the individuals who may be of greatest value.
6. Prepare a speech that you could use to interpret physical education to a parent-teacher association, men's club, or sports night dinner.

Selected readings

American College of Sports Medicine: Encyclopedia of sport sciences and medicine, New York, 1971, Macmillan Publishing Co., Inc.

Bannon, J.J.: Leisure resources—its comprehensive planning, Englewood Cliffs, N.J., 1976, Prentice-Hall, Inc.

Billings, T.A.: About people who never grew up . . . by one of them, Phi Delta Kappan **57**:18, April 1976.

Broer, M.R.: Efficiency of human movement, Philadelphia, 1973, W.B. Saunders Co.

Bucher, C.A.: Administration of health and physical education programs, including athletics, ed. 8, St. Louis, 1983, The C.V. Mosby Co.

Bucher, C.A.: Foundations of physical education, ed. 9, St. Louis, 1983, The C.V. Mosby Co.

Bucher, C.A.: Physical educatiion for life, New York, 1969, McGraw-Hill Book Co.

Calam, J., and Patenaude, J.: The schools ain't what they used to be—and probably never were, Saturday Review, April 29, 1972, p. 52.

Cassidy, R.: Societal determinants of human movement; the next thirty years, Quest **16**:48, 1971.

Fusco, G.C.: Improving your school-community relations program, Englewood Cliffs, N.J., 1967, Prentice-Hall, Inc.

Hecht, G.J.: What must be done to meet the needs of all American children? Parents **47**:10, 1972.

Hitchcock, C.: An analysis of the responses of directors to a survey on the effect of budget cuts and austerity budgets on athletic programs, New York State Association for Health, Physical Education and Recreation Journal **30**:3, 22 June 1978.

Kalakian, L., and Goldman, M.: Introduction to physical education—a humanistic perspective, Boston, 1976, Allyn & Bacon, Inc.

Kindred, L.W., et al.: The school and community relations, Englewood Cliffs, N.J., 1976, Prentice-Hall, Inc.

Levine, D.U., and Moore, C.C.: Magnet schools in a big-city desegregation plan, Phi Delta Kappan **57**:507, April 1976.

Lewis, F.C.: Self-abuse as a teaching device, Phi Delta Kappan **57**:533, April 1976.

Patton, C.V., and Patton, G.: A year-round open school viewed from within, Phi Delta Kappan **57**:522, April 1976.

Penman, K.A.: Planning physical education and athletic facilities in schools, N.Y., 1977, John Wiley & Sons, Inc.

Rainman, E.S., et al.: The educational community—building the climate for collaboration, Pittsburgh, 1976, Allegheny Intermediate Unit.

Resnik, H.S.: The open classroom, Today's Education **60**:16, 1971.

Schurr, E.: Movement experiences for children, Englewood Cliffs, N.J., 1980, Prentice-Hall, Inc.

What happens when the money runs out? Athletic Purchasing and Facilities **5**:44-48, July 1981.

The secondary school student

Instructional objectives and competencies to be achieved

After reading this chapter the student should be able to

1. Identify the characteristics and needs of secondary school students
2. Understand why teenagers act as they do in searching for identity
3. Appreciate the developmental tasks that boys and girls face in their teens
4. Describe the physical, emotional, social, and intellectual changes that take place in the adolescent person and their implications for teaching physical education
5. Identify the differences between boys and girls in regard to height, weight, skeletal changes, and primary and secondary sex changes, and the implications of these changes for teaching motor skills in the physical education program
6. Indicate the characteristics of boys and girls in relation to their social development and how an understanding of these characteristics may help the physical educator to better meet the needs of secondary school students
7. Identify the characteristics that determine when a young person reaches maturity

Today's secondary school students are going through turbulent times and, as a result, need as much help and guidance as the school can provide. At the same time, it should be pointed out that the extent to which young people are helped will probably correlate with the degree to which educators understand the physical, emotional, social, and intellectual growth that takes place during adolescence.

As indicated by the statistics concerning the school dropout rate, many problems are troubling today's adolescents: use of alcohol, tobacco, and harmful drugs; involvement in acts of violence; and the high rate of teenage suicide. According to a 1981 report prepared by the United States Department of Labor, more and more young people are dropping out of high school before graduation. Across the nation, approximately 11 out of every 100 youths 14 to 21 years of age have dropped out of school. In the state of California, for example, which has more dropouts than twice the national average, the rate ranges from 13% among 14-year-olds to 30% among 17-year-olds. Reasons for dropping out include dislike of school, economic problems, and pregnancy.

The National Institute on Alcohol Abuse and Alcoholism indicates that 3.3 million teenagers, or about 19% of the adolescent population, are problem drinkers or are using alcohol for destructive purposes. Furthermore, alcoholism develops two to five times faster in a young person than in an adult. The Institute also points out that alcohol is especially dangerous for adolescents because it may prevent them from accomplishing important developmental tasks essential to a happy and productive life. In addition to preventing normal development, alcohol abuse hinders the acquisition of appropriate skills to cope with stress and handle adult responsibilities.

The University of Michigan's Institute for Social Research conducted a survey of high school seniors in 1980 and found that 65% had used some illegal drug during their lifetime, 39% using a substance other than marijuana. Although the Institute's latest study reflects a drop in daily cigarette smoking by high school seniors—21% as compared to 29% in 1977—obviously many teenagers continue to smoke.

Violence is prevalent among young people, particularly ''gang'' violence, which has been spreading at an unprecedented rate since the early 1970s, according to a 1980 report of the Harvard Law School's Center

Fig. 2-1. The secondary school student.

Courtesy University School of
Nashville, Nashville, Tenn.

for Criminal Justice. In Los Angeles alone, 351 people died in 1980 in gang-related incidents. New York City, Chicago, and Philadelphia annually report many gang-related deaths. During the 1970s violent crime rate per 100,000 population increased in the United States from 363.5 to 535.5, a rise of about 48%. In 1970 the number of violent crimes reported to police was 738,820; the number jumped to 1,178,540 in 1979, up about 59%. Murders increased 34% during the decade. The day after President Reagan was shot, the Federal Bureau of Investigation released the information that 13% more violent crimes were committed in 1980 than in 1979. Reasons listed for crime among youth include unemployment, school dropout, discontent with nuclear projects and environmental destruction, desire for thrill, and selfish pursuit of monetary or other gains.

It is interesting to note that while the overall death rate for the American people dropped 20% between 1960 and 1978, it grew by 11% for young people aged 15 to 24 years. According to many experts, alcohol, drugs, and violence are the leading cause for this rise in deaths among young people. Suicide is now the third leading cause of death among teenagers and, in the 15 to 24 age group, the third leading cause of death among males and the fourth among females.

On a brighter note, Doctors Daniel Offer, Eric Ostrov, and Kenneth Howard, in their controversial new book (controversial primarily because their survey utilized the questionnaire method), *The Adolescent, A Psychological Self-Portrait* (1981, Basic Books), report their analysis of 1,300 normal youngsters. Among their findings are that 85% of the adolescents tested reported being happy most of the time, that 7 out of 10 said they liked the changes that were taking place in their bodies, that they were satisfied with their parents and their parents with them, and that, although they experience anxiety, it does not result in all-pervasive and unceasing tenseness.

Fig. 2-2. Violence in sports.

From Coakley, J.J.: Sport in society, ed. 2, St. Louis, 1982, The C.V. Mosby Co.

The need for physical educators to know and understand adolescents

Physical educators in today's secondary schools face student populations quite different from those they found several years ago. Teenagers and their environments have undergone extensive changes that must be understood because of their implications for teaching. National attention is being focused on the struggle of adolescents for existence, and it is this increased interest in teenagers that has brought about further changes in their environment. Students in several communities, for example, have evaluated their own secondary school curricula and suggested changes.

Today's students are being studied while they study and are being influenced while trying to exert influence. The student has achieved a unique importance in the structure of education, and it is this individual that the teacher must try to understand. The forces and pressures being exerted upon adolescents while they undergo an important phase of personal growth and development combine to make adolescence a difficult period of adjustment. The teacher must try to assist them in every way possible.

TEACHER EXPECTATIONS IN A SECONDARY SCHOOL POPULATION

In a school of 500 students a teacher should be prepared to find 500 different individuals, each one advancing through various stages of the adolescent process, and each one at a different level of development. While many of the students may be college-bound, others require education that fit them immediately for life.

Secondary school students have a variety of cultural backgrounds and bring with them a vast assortment of needs, fears, hopes, abilities, and problems. Those individuals who require special attention—the mentally retarded, the culturally disadvantaged, and the

Fig. 2-3. Physical educators need to know and understand adolescents.

Courtesy Panama Central School, Panama, N.Y.

physically handicapped—must be identified so that programs may be tailored to meet their needs. At the present time the federal government is spending large sums of money on special education programs for these individuals. Yet less than one half of the eight million handicapped persons are receiving the special programs they require. Many of these students are still enrolled in public secondary schools, and physical educators have a responsibility for providing them with an equal opportunity to develop their physical capacities. This may be done through the adapted program of physical education or through assignments within the regular class program. The individualization of teaching can best accomplish these goals.*

WHAT IS THE ROLE OF THE SCHOOL?

The school must identify and recognize the nature of each student. It must strive to help all secondary school students to find themselves, for this is the cen-

tral problem of adolescence. The development of self-esteem and the identification of the self are vital concerns of every teenager. Too often in the school environment, factors such as class distinctions, differing values, and unrealistic standards threaten rather than reassure students. Too often schools demand conformity instead of independence of thought and action. If the purpose of the school is to develop worthy citizens, it must start by helping them feel worthy and competent within themselves.

The physical education program provides excellent opportunities for the development of these needed competencies. The feeling of importance derived from team, group, or squad membership, the feeling of freedom of expression in movement, and the pride in accomplishment when points are scored for a team are all competencies that are natural outcomes of physical education activities. More important, however, is the recognition of the self as defined by a body concept, which can be developed through participation in a well-balanced program. Research indicates a close relationship between an integrated self-concept and the confidence needed to face life. Those who feel

*Chapter 17 discusses the different types of atypical students and the contribution that physical education can make to them.

satisfied with their body's ability to move, express, attract, feel, and react are more apt to feel satisfied with their total adjustment to life. On the other hand, unhappy students are frequently displeased with their body image. Physical educators have a vital responsibility for the development of healthy attitudes toward the body and should therefore provide positive experiences through well-planned and well-executed programs.

Understanding the complex changes of adolescence is a large task for students and for teachers. The implications for teaching are many because of the relationship between student development and achievement in education. Therefore, it has always been helpful for the beginning physical education teacher to understand in detail the physical, social, emotional, and intellectual changes that take place in the adolescent. But the upheaval in American culture has complicated the maturational process. As a result, the many changes taking place in American culture in recent years have left an imprint on our young people—our students. As a result, unless teachers of physical education know and understand their students—their characteristics and needs, their goals and aspirations, their developmental tasks, the factors that affect the development of their personalities, and a multitude of other forces and facts that play upon them—they can never have a truly successful physical education program. Consequently, in light of the fact that we have a new breed of students in our secondary schools and that boys and girls are our chief concern, considerable space is devoted to this most important consideration.

WHAT IS ADOLESCENCE?

Adolescence may be defined as the period in life between childhood and adulthood. Generally, *preadolescence,* or childhood, spans the ages from 11 to 13 for girls and 13 to 15 in boys, *early adolescence* from 13 to 15 for girls and 15 to 17 for boys, *middle adolescence* from 15 to 18 years for girls and 17 to 19 for boys, and *late adolescence* from 18 to 21 years for girls and 19 to 21 for boys.

Kurt Lewin, the psychologist, says that the adolescent is in "no-man's land." He or she is neither a child nor adult and is caught in the middle of over-

lapping forces and expectations. As a result, the physical educator who works with adolescents needs to understand what happens during the transitional period between childhood and adulthood in terms of developmental tasks, the influence of peer groups, the implications of sexual maturation, and the desire to achieve identity. The physical educator should also strive to help adolescents achieve status and independence, develop a satisfying philosophy of life, and to attain goals.

Robert Havighurst* lists ten tasks, presented here in adapted form, that need the adolescent's attention during the period of adolescence:

1. Achieving mature relations with peer group of both sexes
2. Achieving a male or female social role
3. Accepting one's body and using it effectively
4. Achieving emotional independence of adults and parents
5. Acquiring assurance that economic independence will be a reality
6. Selecting and making the necessary preparations for an occupation
7. Making preparations for marriage and a happy family life
8. Developing intellectual skills
9. Achieving social skills that result in responsible behavior
10. Developing an ethical value system

During childhood, students live in an environment created for them by others. Adolescence, on the other hand, is really the halfway point in their life cycle—a bridge between childhood and adulthood. It is a period of "growing up" when they prepare to go out on their own. It is, in the words of one authority, "the period during which a young person learns who he or she is and what he or she really feels." It is the time during which a student becomes a person in his or her own right. Another important fact for physical educators is that it is the time when the foundations of a physically active life are formed and when the student develops positive or negative attitudes toward physical education.

---

*Havighurst, R.J.: Human development and education, New York, 1953, Longmans, Green and Co.

Fig. 2-4. High school physical education coeducational activity.

Courtesy Bill Henderson, Toms River, N.J.

Adolescence is therefore the span of years when the student can take care of "unfinished business" left over from earlier developmental stages. This does not mean the student fights old battles or nurses old hurts. But if he or she has not built a strong and satisfying self-image, the teen years offer the opportunity to try out new ideas and work out more satisfying behavior patterns.

The teens can be divided into three phases that differ from one another and that young people experience at different times. *Puberty* (controlled by endocrine changes) is marked by rapid development of the reproductive system accompanied by the "gang spirit." It is followed by the *transition period* during which interest shifts from same-sex to opposite-sex friend-

ships. *Late adolescence* is characterized by idealism and by romantic attachments to members of the opposite sex. In addition to the overall developmental tasks of adolescence, each of these phases has something special to contribute to the growth of personality.

WHO AM I? THE QUESTION OF IDENTITY

How does a human being with new properties and new functions fit in with the self-image developed in childhood? A teenager often asks the question, "Who am I?" because the self of teens is not the self of childhood or later adulthood. Young people may be drawn in two directions and may not always be sure whether, in a given situation, to act like a child or an adult. They cannot leave childhood permanently behind until their identity (incorporating the physical, mental, emotional, and social changes that have taken place) has been securely established.

During the teens young people try on a number of personalities in the same way they try on hair styles and clothes to find those that best suit them. In establishing a true identity, a host of mannerisms and attitudes may follow one another. This accounts for the rapid changes in many teenagers' friendships, interests, and plans. The midteens especially may be a period of moods that swing like a pendulum from high to low.

During the teens students may have feelings of dissatisfaction and may need a boost to their self-image. For this reason they are most sensitive to criticism. They may feel out of step as they replace one personality with another. They want to know who they really are because their self is in a state of flux.

SEARCH FOR SELF

The search for self that takes place in the teens may assume such outward forms as choosing a new name or spelling the old one differently. This device reflects a wish to announce the "new me" independent of the infant named by parents. Parents may find it hard to remember that the Patsy of yesterday is the Patricia of today, or that "Sonny" or "Junior" is now to be called by his proper name. Teenagers often experiment with handwriting and try to project their new personalities by adding flourishes or adopting a different slant in their penmanship. On the more serious side, they may also join in rallies and movements to attack social injustices—often to the consternation of adults. All of these attitudes and mannerisms (and there are likely to be many more) contribute to the formation of a life-style typical of themselves and no one else.

The ideal self. By the time students reach the teens, they have a pretty good idea of the kind of person they want to be. In terms of personality, this is their *ideal self*. It is based on many models and various experiences. The ideal self allows them to match their actions against a standard. Their ideal self helps direct the resources of their personality toward unifying the various selves established in earlier stages of development. Thus their self-image in the teens has two sides—a "real" (natural) self and an "ideal" (moral) self.

They are constantly working to balance their self-image—their real self—with their ideal self. Unless they do this, they may be in a state of conflict or tension. When their real self harmonizes with their ideal self, they feel comfortable and at ease. They are happy with themselves. When there is a gap between what they are and what they would like or expect themselves to be, feelings of guilt and inferiority crop up.

To the degree that they accept or reject their sense of self, their life will be pleasant and satisfying or disquieting and tense. Physical education offers many opportunities to help students accept themselves and bring into more harmonious balance their self-image with their real self.

DEVELOPMENTAL TASKS

Young people abound in energy during their teens. They are ready and eager to test themselves in new situations and will work to overcome obstacles and difficulties. Developmental tasks are usually undertaken in a spirit of adventure. Most teenagers like a challenge and welcome responsibility. Those who felt insecure as children, however, or whose wills were given too little chance to develop at the appropriate time may shrink from new challenges.

Because the teens pose many special problems, the developmental tasks of this period deserve separate consideration. Some tasks persist throughout the teens, and some predominate during one or another developmental phase. A mature personality brings the physical, mental, emotional, and social achievements and failures of all developmental stages together into an individual identity. When this has been done, all the resources of the personality can be directed toward self-actualizing activities.

Reality principle. Children and adults characteristically act to secure their needs in different ways. Children usually act according to the pleasure principle. That is, they follow the path of least resistance to meet their needs. The pleasure principle spurs them to act on impulse. To act on the pleasure principle is sure to cause problems because it ignores the fact that actions have results.

Mature people can put off gratifying their needs

until the appropriate time. This basis of action is called the reality principle. To act according to the reality principle requires a person to consider the effect of what he or she is going to do before doing it. Children lack the experience to link cause and effect. It is a developmental task of the teens to change the base of action from the pleasure principle to the reality principle.

Reality checking. Teenagers can draw on a wealth of past experience to meet the challenges of daily life. All present impressions must be checked for accuracy against past experience. This process, called reality testing, measures current observations, ideas, attitudes, and reactions against other things one feels, knows, or has experienced.

Reality testing is one of the important mental functions to be developed in the teens. A person cannot respond to the environment appropriately unless he or she first tests reality. Reality testing must be employed to gauge strengths and limitations accurately. A realistic personal assessment leaves one free to use, shape, and develop abilities. Reality testing helps to base what one thinks and does in every area of life on a dependable foundation. It helps to distinguish fact from fantasy, reason from emotion, and evidence from wishful thinking. Thus it is the basis of sound decision-making.

Toleration of stress. Change, conflict, and tension are to be expected in life. After the period of protected childhood, teenagers may suffer considerable tension when first exposed to the "hard facts of life." Mature people can endure physical hardship and discomfort. They can also withstand repeated and intense disappointment, failure, and other real stresses. They can

Fig. 2-5. At end of adolescence, student will be a young adult. Student in physical education class, Regina High School, Cincinnati, Ohio.

tolerate failure or the possibility of failure as well as success. To tolerate stress does not mean to give in or avoid it. It means to continue in spite of it—to overcome, rather than to be overcome. Each experience in the teens should contribute to tolerance of stress and thus prepare for the more complex problems to be encountered in adult life. Physical education offers many opportunities to endure physical, social, mental, and emotional stress. It can provide a laboratory for meeting problems head on, whether it involves losing hard-fought athletic contests, failure to achieve a high rating in a physical fitness test, or one of the many other situations that constantly occur in this program.

Physical growth and self-image during adolescence

The adolescent grows and develops in four different ways: physically, emotionally, socially, and intellectually. The physical educator should be conversant with each of these four areas. Physical changes in the teens have a dramatic effect on personality development, but there are also many carry-overs from childhood. Illness or injury, the level of nutrition, and the amount of sunshine and exercise received during childhood will have physical aftereffects in the teens. Irregularities in hormone secretions can cause startling physical and personality changes. Endocrine imbalance affects height, weight, growth, and development. In the teens, normal changes in the endocrine system herald the onset of puberty.

The teens, a time of rapid growth, are sometimes an awkward age. Just as second teeth looked so large to students when they were in the first grade, arms and legs seem to grow at different rates while youngsters are in high school. In the teens their noses and chins may also seem out of proportion for a while.

It is sometimes hard for young people to accept the fact that wide differences in rate of growth, muscular development, and coordination can be expected at their age. Teenagers differ from children and also from adults. They differ physically, biologically, and intellectually among themselves. Some differences are controlled by genes, and others are the product of environment. Still, human beings put the "finishing touches" on their own personalities. Many of the things that make them different from other people are the results of their own ideas and efforts.

PERSONALITY AND APPEARANCE

Physical appearance influences personality because, after all, it is the first thing people notice about individuals. Physical differences may or may not be "handicaps," depending on their effect on self-image. Extreme good looks or startling beauty can be liabilities if they interfere with personality development. Many people develop fine, strong personalities in spite of disabling physical handicaps. Helen Keller triumphed over the triple handicap of blindness, deafness, and mutism to make meaningful contributions to the world. Some people, because of a weak self-image, magnify a small defect so that it cripples development.

Physical characteristics affect the self-image of boys and girls differently. Tallness, for example, has a favorable effect on a boy's self-image, whereas a girl may be unhappy if she seems taller than the boys and girls around her. A person whose skin is marred by acne feels different about himself or herself than does one whose complexion is clear.

Basic feelings of acceptance or rejection toward oneself are often expressed in personal hygiene and grooming. Neglect or excessive care may reflect feelings of inferiority. A desire to falsify appearance may reveal an individual's negative self-image. Extreme tastes, either in dress or grooming, may cover up feelings of rejection. A girl with a poor opinion of her looks may use too much makeup. A boy who does not feel he is accepted as a young man may grow a beard or moustache. On the other hand, indifference to detail in dress and grooming sometimes reflects a self-image so secure that no outward "show" is needed to support it. As a person's physical appearance alters and he or she gains experience, the self-image changes and personality grows.

Physical development

The secondary school student passes through four stages of development, which are generally labeled preadolescence, early adolescence, middle adolescence, and late adolescence. It should be understood that each individual develops according to his or her own growth pattern, but in general the stages may be identified at certain age levels. Because of the complexity of physical development in the adolescent and the differences between boys and girls, it is necessary to consider each phase of their growth separately. Height and weight, skeletal changes, and primary and secondary sex changes will be discussed, with the differences in boys and girls explained at each level of development. The implications for physical education will also be included in the discussion.

HEIGHT AND WEIGHT

Probably the most obvious physical changes during adolescence occur in height and weight. These changes result from increased hormone production, which in turn causes the sudden growth spurt of the preadolescent and early adolescent period.

Girls 11 to 13 years old become taller than boys of the same ages but then show slower increases in height until late adolescence. A rapid increase in weight also takes place at this time or following the growth in height. Girls are frequently heavier than boys at ages 12 to 14 years, but with the onset of menstruation a leveling off period occurs.

The sudden growth spurt in boys does not come until approximately two years after that of the girls, and it continues to a greater extent until around 20 years of age. Boys show an even greater increase in weight and also continue this gain for a longer period than do girls.

These changes have definite implications for the physical education program. First, boys and girls have a real concern for their physical development. Participation and total involvement in physical education activities provide an opportunity for them to forget their own self-concerns and to lose themselves in the enjoyment of the game.

Second, in regard to regular class activities in which height is an important factor, as in volleyball or basketball, it may be advisable to distribute the tallest boys and girls among the squads for the best playing results. Also, the coeducational program at the junior high level, where differences in sizes are most obvious, must be carefully organized to minimize any

undue embarrassment experienced by both boys and girls. Dancing activities may be difficult to conduct because the boys are shorter than the girls, whereas relays, games of low organization, badminton, volleyball, and similar activities may have great success. However, it should be noted that in communities where social dancing is established and promoted for this age level, this activity will probably meet with success.

One of the most important factors that the physical education teacher should consider is the personal self-consciousness and embarrassment suffered by teenagers in regard to their physical development. This is particularly true in physical education classes, where emphasis is placed on physical skills and bodily coordination. Students who are concerned with overweight or underweight conditions frequently seek excuses from class participation, showers, or exercise because of their discomfort, fatigue, and ineptitude. The teacher of physical education has a real opportunity for guidance in such cases by offering suggestions on healthful nutrition and proper exercise. A sincere interest and understanding of individual problems can direct the student's self-interest toward a solution of problems and motivate him or her to put forth increased effort.

SKELETAL CHANGES

Some of the adolescent increases in height and weight may be attributed to changes in the skeletal structures, which cause differences in body proportions at this time.

The bones of the growing youth change in length and breadth as well as in density (mass). Studies of x-ray films show that a definite relationship may be found between skeletal age and age of puberty. In other words, a child's bony growth continues at approximately the same rate and time as other facets of development and is complete when the sexual function is mature.

These skeletal changes cause differences in body proportions common in adolescence, such as disproportionate growth of the long bones and muscles of arms and legs. Facial contours change, and as the nose lengthens, the hairline changes and the second molars appear.

Several implications for physical education are involved here. With these constant changes occurring in their skeletal framework, adolescents need considerable exercise to maintain good tone in their large muscles. The teacher must use caution, however, during strenuous activities and guard against fatigue and strain in this age group. Adolescents also need a broad understanding of the changes taking place to offset disappointment and discontent when skills suddenly seem less adequate.

In relation to the competitive aspects of the intramural and interscholastic programs, especially among early adolescents, skeletal growth, muscle strain, and fatigue should be considered. Physical educators must, of course, follow state regulations in regard to competition.

PRIMARY AND SECONDARY SEX CHANGES

Besides the sudden spurt in height and weight, the next most obvious adolescent change is in sex characteristics. There are two levels of changes to be considered here: the primary sex changes, which involve the reproductive organs, and the secondary sex characteristics, which include those traits generally attributed to masculine and feminine appearances. Growth of facial hair on boys and breast development in girls are examples of secondary sex characteristics.

The primary sex change in girls is the development of the organs of reproduction (ovaries and fallopian tubes), which signal their maturation with the onset of the menstrual cycle. This signpost of adult function is of major importance to growing girls and usually occurs between the ages of 12 and 14 years, although, in a few cases, it may be earlier or later.

The implications of this cycle in teaching physical education are many. In the first place it is essential that a healthy attitude toward menstruation be fostered by requiring all students to dress for classes and to participate in some, if not all, the activities. Girls should not be allowed to pamper themselves on these occasions but should learn to lead a regular, normally active life. There are, of course, exceptional cases—girls who are under a doctor's care and who may need additional rest at this time.

Instruction in proper hygiene and cleanliness, as well as in helpful exercise to relieve tensions, is an-

other area in which the physical education teacher can be of great service to adolescent girls. Special provisions for showering may have to be made, however, to spare them real embarrassment. In schools with individual stall showers and dressing areas, there is no problem, but in other instances, girls having their menstrual period may need to shower earlier or substitute a sponge bath for a shower at the end of class.

The reproductive organs of boys (penis and testes) do not mature until approximately two years later than girls' reproductive organs, at approximately 14 to 16 years of age. Because growth of the male organs is external in nature, overdevelopment or underdevelopment is often a cause for much self-concern. Teachers should show care and understanding, fostering on the part of all students an attitude of acceptance of individual variations. Locker room antics and teasing about this personal characteristic can develop an unhealthy dislike for physical education and should not be permitted.

The main female secondary sex characteristic that develops in adolescence are the mammary glands. Other minor changes include growth of pubic and axillary hair, settling of the voice, and broadening of the hips. These changes begin the slow process of development at around 10 years of age and continue long after the menarche.

In boys secondary sex characteristics are similar to those of girls: pubic and axillary hair, plus facial hair, as well as a deepening of the voice, broadening of the shoulders, and development of a waistline. These changes generally appear around the age of 12 years and continue into late adolescence.

The teacher of physical education should recognize the great importance these changes have in the minds of the students and the deep concern they feel about their growth and development. The teacher should help the students understand the process of growth itself and should guide their thinking toward an appreciation of individual differences.

The teacher should also assist students in overcoming some of the problems that usually accompany sex changes. Acne, caused by the increase in glandular activity, and body odors, for example, may both be discussed by the physical education teacher, and hints may be given for improving these conditions. Group

Fig. 2-6. Secondary school student playing tennis as part of the program at University School of Nashville, Nashville, Tenn.

instruction on personal cleanliness and hygiene and individual, personal consultations in extreme cases are services that the teacher can perform for adolescents.

OTHER SYSTEMIC CHANGES

Other physiologic systems also undergo further development. The circulatory system, which includes the heart and blood vessels, continues to grow steadily during adolescence. This growth may be identified by a normal increase in blood pressure. However, the pulse rate seems to decrease in adolescence, although girls maintain a higher rate than boys.

Respiratory system changes are also evident in adolescence, as reflected by measurements of vital capacity. Large increases are registered in both boys and girls from ages 10 to 14 years, with a subsequent slowing down in girls' capacities, while boys' capacities continue to increase.

The digestive organs continue to grow during this time, necessitating more and more daily nourishment

and thereby making greater demands on the adolescent body.

The nervous system is more fully developed before adolescence than are the other systems, but there is thought to be an increase in the complexity of brain connections, with a subsequent increase in the types of thought processes. These developments continue until late adolescence.

Systemic changes should be considered as part of the total adolescent developmental picture, each having some bearing on the teaching program. In regard to respiratory and circulatory changes, adolescent students should be watched carefully for signs of fatigue and exhaustion. Their appetites are usually large because of changes in digestion but, because improper food habits are generally prevalent, they need guidance in this area. The further development of the nervous sytem, with increases in the types of thought processes, has implications for the knowledge and appreciation adolescent students can now acquire. The teaching program may therefore be geared to more advanced aspects of strategy, rules, and philosophical ideas.

BASIC MOTOR SKILLS

Consideration of basic motor skills and their development during adolescence is a very important concern of the physical education teacher. The following observations seem to hold true in many cases:

1. *Accuracy.* Girls are usually better than boys in this skill throughout adolescent development.
2. *Agility.* Girls are more agile than boys until around 13 years of age, at which time boys surpass the girls in this respect.
3. *Control.* Girls perform with more control than boys in early adolescence. The boys become superior after the age of 14.
4. *Strength.* Boys are generally superior to girls in strength, but a greater degree of differentiation is seen with their maturity.

Basic motor skills are an essential part of the program in physical education. Therefore, changes in adolescent performance of these skills have definite implications for teaching. For girls, emphasis should be placed on continuing improvement in balance, agility, control, and strength. Boys need to work, particularly in the early years, on accuracy, agility, and control, whereas in later years stress should be placed on their ability to achieve accuracy.

The differences in basic motor skill performances should be kept in mind when various aspects of the program are planned. With coeducational groups, for instance, activities requiring strength would not be chosen because of boys' superiority. When expectations of athletic performances are estimated, these same skill differences and changes should be considered. The teacher should realize that a change in students' interest and satisfactions takes place as their motor skills change and develop. In motivating students, therefore, different techniques will be necessary at each age level.

HEALTH ASPECTS

Although adolescence is sometimes described as one of the healthiest periods of life, a study of illnesses and problems of secondary school students is quite revealing to teachers. Figures gathered from 19 clinics across the United States indicate that the most frequent diagnoses of adolescent patients show these health problems to be most prevalent: obesity, acne, allergy, seizures, and orthopedic problems.

The physical education program should consider what contributions it might make through its curriculum to alleviate the number one problem, obesity. At the same time, physical education teachers should realize that injuries, along with upper respiratory infections, are frequent problems for their students and must consider ways to ensure student safety and freedom from exposure to disease.

A comparatively new problem in high schools in the larger urban areas across the country involves student pregnancy. In many instances it is the girl's physical education teacher who first recognizes the symptoms, and therefore she should be aware of the type of help currently available in the schools for such students.

Although the health and vitality of adolescents are usually good, every teacher should be aware of other aspects of student life that may cause difficulties. The physical education teacher should take advantage of every opportunity to offer guidance in health matters. The need for proper diet, rest, and exercise is easily related to athletic performance, and discussions of these factors can be very valuable. Guidance in proper body mechanics and posture, which is also a responsibility of the physical education teacher, is very important to adolescent health. Every program of physical education should contain a unit or series of classes devoted to postural studies for the identification of defects and improvement of postural conditions.

FITNESS ASPECTS

It is of utmost importance that physical fitness be an objective of the physical education program in junior and senior high schools. Students undergoing the constant process of change need to pay particular attention to achieving and maintaining a high level of fitness. It is at this stage in their development that a true appreciation of activity and fitness for its own sake is formulated. Physical education teachers have a great responsibility in this area because physical fitness is an important element of their program.

The physical development of the adolescent is a very complex process. Its relevance to the physical education program makes it essential that teachers understand thoroughly the various aspects of growth and development in order to meet the needs of adolescents and help them understand better the process that is taking place.

Emotional development

The emotional development of adolescents is just as complex as their physical development, but it is not as easily defined or measured because there is no exact pattern of development to follow. To discuss this phase of adolescence, it will be necessary to picture briefly the basic human emotions and the adolescent adjustments and responses that are distinguishable from those of childhood and adulthood.

BASIC HUMAN EMOTIONS

It must first be realized that the adolescent, like human beings of any age, experiences the three basic emotions—fear, anger, and joy—and their variations. It is in responses to stimuli and specific situations that the growing adolescent differs from other age groups.

ADOLESCENT RESPONSES

Adolescent responses tend to be extreme in nature. Members of this age group are either highly excited or greatly depressed, and rapid changes of mood are typical. For this reason adolescence is sometimes described as a period of heightened emotionality.

Adolescents develop emotionally at the same time that physical, social, and intellectual maturation is taking place. Signs of extreme emotional responsiveness may be seen as early as the preadolescent stage, and the developmental process continues slowly, with completion in late adolescence. Boys mature approximately two years later than girls in this respect as well as in other phases of development.

The heightened emotional responses of adolescents can best be understood in terms of the changing needs that cause them and that in themselves form a pattern of emotional development. A study of these adolescent needs, therefore, is necessary to interpret their relationship to physical education.

ADOLESCENT NEEDS

The emotions of adolescents are aroused in response to the adjustment needs peculiar to their stage of development. They must adjust to a changing physical state, to a heterosexual interest, and to an environment free from parental control. Other adolescent needs that must be satisfied are shared by all human beings. They include security, achievement, affection, adventure, and well-being. Adolescents, however, in satisfying these needs, find methods that are limited to their particular age group and that undergo changes as different stages of development are reached. It is this transition in satisfaction-producing factors that provides a clue to adolescent emotional development and that should be studied individually in respect to each student's needs.

Affection. The early adolescent seeks many friendships with individuals of the same sex, whereas in middle adolescence friendships with the opposite sex begin. These friendships become even stronger in late adolescence, while friends of the same sex continue to hold interest. Also in late adolescence relationships with adults are more friendly as authority relaxes, and eventually friendships with the same sex dwindle in number as they deepen in intensity.

Problems in regard to affection usually arise either from fears centered around the making or losing of friends or from conflicts with them. Still others may stem from a desire for continued affection from parents, which is in conflict with a simultaneous need for independence from them.

All teachers need to understand the basic problems faced by teenagers in reference to their need for affection. Physical education teachers should provide many socializing situations in which friendships may be fostered and further the process of adjustment to the opposite sex through coeducational activities.

Achievement. In early adolescence achievement is realized through success in many and varied interests and hobbies. In middle and late adolescence, as interests center upon fewer, more important areas, achievement is sensed through accomplishments in these areas. These later interests usually stem from the adult role that the adolescent determines is most suitable, and success is felt as this ideal approaches reality.

Fig. 2-7. Adolescents have a need to achieve success in their physical education activities. A high school student at Tates Creek High School, Lexington, Ky.

Problems of adolescents generally stem from lack of achievement in the areas of interest at each age level. For example, receiving poor grades in school becomes a problem when an interest in a college education is aroused.

Teachers of physical education should realize that many students find satisfaction in superior performance and achievement in their field. For those students who have difficulty performing in physical education, the teacher should try to provide a program varied enough so that in some particular activity or sport a sense of accomplishment may be derived.

Adventure. In early adolescence the variety of interests in many different areas affords satisfaction of the need for adventure. Striking out on one's own with the new freedom that this age permits provides much excitement in middle adolescence, and this same satisfaction is present in late adolescence. The major problem occurs when gratification of this need for adventure is gained from improper experiences, as seen in the juvenile crimes of today.

In physical education this need for excitement and adventure may easily be met through the challenge and thrills of sports and competition. The program should therefore be set up on a broad scale to provide satisfaction through afterschool activities for as many students as possible.

Security. The early adolescent seeks security in his or her social world through the gang or crowd. The middle adolescent finds similar pleasure in smaller groups or cliques, and the late adolescent begins to be satisfied with more adult relationships, having found inner security.

The main cause of insecurity in adolescents is inner turmoil. Because of the uncertainties life holds and the doubts of success, adolescents do not dare to rely on themselves. Instead, they seek security in whatever else they can find: the gang, the club, the world of books or music, or some other facet of life.

The physical education teacher has a very real responsibility to foster feelings of security in each student in all activities. Students should feel at ease in the gymnasium, and this goal may be accomplished by giving concrete instructions and establishing definite procedures and regulations so that students will know exactly what is expected of them. This, together with consistency in handling routine procedures, discipline problems, and other everyday occurrences, ensures feelings of security in physical education.

Sense of well-being. A sense of well-being is brought about by adjusting the picture of the self through various mechanisms. Adolescents employ the same methods as all human personalities: rationalization, blame, compensation, and use of excuses, to name a few.

Superiority in physical pursuits provides one outlet for adjusting the self-picture of individuals who have difficulty in academic work. Students who can achieve in some area of physical education naturally augment their sense of well-being or sense of worth. Elementary classroom teachers have said that the key to all learning is making children feel good about themselves in regard to whatever they are trying to do. Surely this same principle applies to students of all ages.

Physical education teachers should be aware of the abnormal extremes to which human personalities may go when overrationalizing or overcompensating. When teachers recognize these extreme cases, they should make the proper referrals to the school psychologist for study. In this way the teacher does a service to students who need help in regaining their sense of well-being.

Adjustment to physical change. The adjustment to the changing physical self has been discussed previously in this chapter. From the emotional standpoint it should be emphasized again that this is a source of great concern to all adolescents.

Adjustment to heterosexual interest. This discussion will be expanded in the section on social development, but the close relationship of heterosexual interest to emotional responses should be pointed out here. Many adolescent fears and worries center around this particular phase of development, necessitating a real contribution on the part of the physical education program through coeducational activities to relieve tensions.

Freedom from parental control. In adolescence there is a particular need to gain freedom from parental control, yet the conflicts in the treatment of adolescents by adults cause many problems.

At home adolescents begin to assume adultlike responsibilities in relation to household chores, baby-sitting, holding parttime jobs, and receiving an increased allowance. At the same time, however, they still are restricted in many matters, such as using the family car, dating, and observing curfews. These discrepancies in treatment frequently seem senseless to the adolescent and are difficult to reconcile.

At school this dichotomy—treating adolescents partially as adults and partially as children—continues. Rules and regulations are established about smoking, dances, and conduct, while at the same time the students are allowed to run the school government, athletic organizations, and other school activities.

To help adolescents feel secure without depending on parental or other adult controls, the physical education teacher should try to offer many opportunities for the development of self-responsibility, self-discipline, and self-reliance. This may be done through assignment of leadership positions and through class planning of rules and regulations of conduct. Students who are allowed to participate in formulating their standards of behavior better understand the necessity for rules and, consequently, follow them more willingly.

An understanding of the many adolescent worries and needs helps the physical education teacher make provisions in the program to overcome these emotional difficulties. It is also important that additional problems be avoided in the school situation, and the teacher who understands possible areas of concern, such as security, is better able to provide a healthy teaching situation. Students who are emotionally upset learn little, and they need help in controlling emotional responses. It is the responsibility of teachers to assist them in achieving this goal.

MANHOOD AND WOMANHOOD

Boys and girls are transformed into men and women in the teens. The activity of hormones on the reproductive system at the onset of the teens emphasizes sexual differences. The fact that men and women possess different reproductive structures and functions shapes their psychological and emotional development. Until the adolescent period, personality development is largely the same for boys and girls. From

the teens on they follow different paths to achieve a mature identity.

Physical and psychological functions are generally established before they can be fully used. This is also true of the reproductive function. During the teens the reproductive urge joins hunger, thirst, and safety as among the most powerful human drives. Reproduction, however, involves not only the individual but a partner and society as well. The sex drive requires special understanding so that it can be controlled and directed not only in terms of personal needs but in line with social values.

Physical differences. At one time women were believed to be "the weaker sex." Research has shown, however, that more boy than girl babies die at birth. In general, life expectancy is longer for women than for men. Furthermore, girls mature (from about the age of 6 through the teens) a year or two ahead of boys. This is the reason girls are often taller than their male peers. Earlier emotional maturation also explains their readiness for social events sooner than most boys.

Emotional differences. The nature, strength, and timing of sexual feelings are different for boys and girls. The difference in their emotional and psychological involvement in the matter of sex is partly explained by their differing biological roles. A woman's reproductive system prepares her for childbearing and nurturing. Thus her total personality may become involved in feelings of love. Traditionally, society considered marriage to be the fulfillment, biologically and otherwise, of a girl's personality. A girl's feelings (possibly because girls mature earlier than boys) may center on marriage long before boys of her age are emotionally or economically ready for it. Traditionally, boys accepted the fact that economic independence was required to care for a wife and family, and a great deal of his energy was directed away from the home and to his work. In the United States today, however, many question these traditional attitudes. There is an increasing tendency for the man and woman to share economic responsibilities and for both to find satisfaction in their careers. Although some portions of society hold to the traditional views, many alternatives are now available to those who do not.

Social development

Social development can be thought of in terms of the adolescent's relationships with friends of his or her own sex, with friends of the opposite sex, and with adults. In each area, different stages of growth are found, appearing later in boys than in girls, and to a different degree. The developmental process itself is based on the adolescent's desire to break away from parents and to assume selfhood in the social world.

RELATIONSHIPS WITH SAME SEX

In early adolescence the individual finds a place in the social world by becoming part of a large group, which usually consists of age-mates of the same sex. This occurs with girls in junior high school and somewhat later, perhaps in the ninth or tenth grade, with boys. Groupings usually evolve among youngsters from the same school, classes, neighborhoods, and social backgrounds. They provide standards of behavior, such as manner of dress and speech, as well as opportunities to learn how to act with people in various situations.

In middle adolescence the dictates of the peer groups continue to be strong. However, the crowds break down into smaller, more cohesive cliques that promote snobbishness and prejudices not usually found in the larger groupings. With girls these close friendships maintain an extreme importance that continues into the college years, while boys seldom rely as completely on friendships.

One of the crowd. At every stage of the life cycle, teenagers want to feel that they belong. A child's feeling of belonging centers on the family. In the early teens group membership, characterized by the "gang spirit," takes the place of family dependence.

During the early teens the opinion of peers is more highly valued than that of adults. Teenagers may ignore family or teacher approval and turn instead to the crowd for support and reassurance. Their approval reinforces individual self-confidence. Teenagers often excuse their actions by saying "everybody's doing it."

In the early teens boys and girls are still largely separate from one another in interest and activities. Friendships are formed among members of the same sex. Being one of the crowd gives boys and girls the feeling that there is safety in numbers. Boys seem more attracted to moving in a gang than do girls, perhaps because in the teens their aggressiveness (an emotional by-product of increased endocrine activity) takes more active forms. Boys, moreover, are intensely loyal to the group, whereas girls tend to be more personal when loyalty is involved. Girls who do move in gangs often join a group of boys.

Clubs and gangs. Many clubs are organized to promote common interests among teenagers. Shared enthusiasm for drama, folk music, stamps, cars, chess, or science holds some groups together. Club membership strengthens personality by making the individual less self-centered.

Gangs often form because of a mutual gripe or grievance. Even though a gang may not always seek socially approved goals, membership in it can increase a person's ability to share with others and to minimize self-centeredness. So far as the individual member's personality development is concerned, this is helpful. Sometimes gang members feel powerless as individuals and consequently use group force to gain their ends. This not only injures society but damages the individual's personal development. Just when young people should be building a secure self-image, they become overly dependent on others.

Group membership serves a positive purpose if it contributes to independence. If conformity to group standards replaces dependence on the family, however, one form of dependence has been replaced by another. When instead of depending on the family a person depends on the group, there is no net gain in independence.

The person who relies too heavily on the group for approval may have a weak self-image and be overly dependent on others for clues to his or her true worth. It may be that the individual's personality is too weak to stand without group support. If it lasts beyond adolescence, group membership without other independent interests may be a sign of immaturity.

Difference and conformity. To break with the past a person must be different from the way he or she was in childhood. Although teenagers want to be different from children, they do not want to be too different from their peers. Teenagers feel a strong urge to adopt group standards as a mark of being "in." If a young person has not developed a strong sense of self-worth, being different in any way can be a source of misery and humiliation.

But group approval usually requires conformity in dress, behavior, speech, mannerisms, possessions, and attitudes. Fads in attire (dress, hair styles) and behavior (posture, speech) become badges of membership in the "in" group. As people develop strong individual personalities, they gradually discard such conformity in favor of making their own choices.

Following the leader. The group—be it a club or a gang—usually takes its identity from one person who initiates action and inspires loyalty. But who is the leader? He or she is a person who has a secure (not necessarily mature) self-image.

The leader's "power" is usually based on qualities that group members would like to possess. They identify with the leader's weaknesses and strengths and may imitate oddities of dress, speech, and behavior. Such loyalty provides followers with a chance to develop weak areas of their personalities. But the leader may have the problem of being too sure of being "grown up," may feel there is too much to risk in giving up any detrimental traits, and so may fail to mature further. As a result, this individual lacks the insight to understand that the loyalty and admiration on which he or she depends is bound to pass.

Search for popularity. In the teens, group acceptance is usually measured in popularity. Being well liked can be an important goal to a teenager. To be accepted by a club, a sorority, an athletic team, or a fraternity is often considered proof of popularity. Some teenagers will sacrifice anything in the quest for acceptance and approval. This is especially true if they felt rejected in childhood. Popularity should not serve as a crutch for a faltering self-image. It can never substitute for the inner security that comes with a strong self-image.

There are two important implications for physical education stemming from this phase of adolescent social development. One concerns leadership and the other clique formations. Because the development of *leadership* qualities is a fundamental phase of physical education, the program should provide many opportunities for promoting and guiding good leaders. The

formation of leaders' clubs in junior and senior high school provides a structured situation wherein leadership qualities may be developed and practiced by many interested members. Learning to select good leaders may also be considered an outcome of physical education, and this factor should have carry-over value into out-of-school group activities.

Another phase of the physical education program that should transfer to social relationships is understanding the injurious effects of cliques. The socializing phase of physical education activities, such as teamwork, should focus on the equalities of all individuals and promote consideration for and cooperation with people of all races and religions. The harmful effects of ostracizing a few people—so frequently found in small clique formations—should be discussed during class organization, with the hope that desirable extracurricular practices will be followed.

RELATIONSHIPS WITH OPPOSITE SEX

In early adolescence, between the ages of 10 and 12 years, boys and girls generally exhibit an antagonistic attitude toward one another.

In middle adolescence, girls of 13 and 14, who are now developing physically, begin to take an active interest in boys, parties, and mixed social functions. Boys, however, seem less interested in girls. Between 14 and 16 years of age boys return this interest in the opposite sex, and social activities consume a great deal of an adolescent's time and energies. It is usually at this point that pairs begin to develop. By the age of 16 or 17, adolescent adjustments to members of the opposite sex are nearly complete.

In the early teens groups of boys and groups of girls are likely to socialize with one another. One reason that a hangout—drugstore, pizza parlor, street corner, record shop, or youth center—may be popular is that it provides neutral ground for male and female groups to enter separately and without prearrangement. The fact that girls mature sooner than boys changes this relationship. As time goes by, boys and girls no longer look at each other with the indifference of childhood. For a while new feelings may make them uncertain of how to behave. By the end of the teens, however, they should be at ease in one another's company.

First love. Strong interest in members of the opposite sex is characteristic of late adolescence. Writer Atra Baer described it as the time when ''Johnny Jones now writes in chalk, his love for Mary on the walk.'' Before the individual becomes seriously interested in one person, he or she has usually been interested in the opposite sex as a group. The attraction is a general one. A boy has usually been ''in love'' with a number of girls at the same time. A girl has sought and enjoyed the attention of more than one boy.

It is in late adolescence that most people have their first real experience of love. In first love, adoration and blindness to the other's faults and shortcomings is typical. Romantic love implies feeling without action and worship from afar. It focuses only on perfection and ignores flaws.

The experience of young love can ripen into mature love, and some ''childhood sweethearts'' have made successful marriages. Those who have strong self-images and who have completed their developmental tasks are most likely to make lasting marriages early in life. A happy marriage brings together all the feelings of friendship, companionship, romance, and family life that the individual has previously known. This kind of love is a part of emotional maturity where all earlier experiences are brought together. It is not achieved when a person is trying to ''make up'' for a lack of love in childhood.

''Real'' love. Love (unlike fear, anger, or sex) is not an instinct but a group of emotional tendencies. It includes tenderness, friendship, admiration, devotion, pride, respect, aggressiveness, submission, protection, loyalty, and adoration. Each of these has previously been felt separately in the course of personality development. In the mature personality, an attachment is formed on the basis of an integration of these emotions. Thus love is not a feeling only but a relationship involving the whole personality. The part each emotion plays in a relationship varies with circumstances and the individual. Friendship, for example, looms large in a marriage between childhood sweethearts, who are more likely to be aware of each other's faults and shortcomings and so marry with a realistic view of one another.

Physical attraction also plays an important part in real love. Physical fitness and a strong physical image are assets for young people. Beauty has biological value. When strong and fit individuals marry and raise families, their children will usually inherit the desire for strength and fitness, too. Natural beauty has survival value for the human race. To a large extent beauty goes with health, and healthy parents can better care for and protect their offspring. Survival of offspring after birth also requires tenderness, protectiveness, and patience. These qualities reflect emotional maturity. Establishing a stable home for the development of new personalities involves the cooperation of mature people. Without it, children are exposed to insecure family relations. In such a setting warped personalities are likely to develop.

Boys and girls together. More and more the social standards in the United States and in other countries accept women as equal partners in life with men. Since Title IX was passed and since business, the professions, and politics have opened their doors to women, the two sexes must learn to appreciate each other as co-workers and companions. Fortunately, one of the tasks of teenage development is for boys and girls to learn to think of each other as human beings.

Boys and girls who know each other as friends, who talk openly on a variety of subjects, and who participate together in physical education activities are learning to accept one another as persons. They have a chance to see the ways in which they are alike. They can also observe the social, psychological, and emotional ways in which they complement one another. Not every relationship that boys and girls or men and women share is romantically inclined. When romance develops out of friendship, however, it is much more likely to strengthen self-concepts than does romance based only on physical attraction. Solid friendships with boys and girls bolster self-esteem and self-confidence and improve the individual's self-image. The midteens are the time when boys and girls have the widest opportunity to develop friendships with the opposite sex.

Friendship encourages the spirit of sharing. It is a developmental task of the teens to learn to share not only material possessions but thoughts, feelings, and ideals. By the end of the transition period a boy and a girl may communicate secrets and problems in the same way they once did with a best friend of the same sex.

Fig. 2-8. Secondary school student engaging in weightlifting exercise.

In this period of mutual interests personal qualities such as politeness and consideration are strengthened. Interest in personal grooming gains importance. It is a time when many matters are shared in preparation for the collaboration required in marriage. Friendships with members of the opposite sex enable teenagers to test personal relationships in anticipation of making a permanent choice in marriage.

The development of an interest in the opposite sex as well as such legal requirements as Title IX have two important implications in the physical education program: the planning of coeducational activities and the individual class program.

Coeducational activities for the early adolescent in junior high school should provide an opportunity for relaxed socialization without undue embarrassment. At this level boys and girls are at various stages of development, ranging from no interest to too much interest in the opposite sex. Activities should therefore be those already familiar to the students, such as badminton, volleyball, tennis, or recreational games. Knowing the activity helps the adolescent overcome the fear of socializing. Simple mass dancing activities may be successful when well organized and taught, particularly in communities that promote social activities in junior high school.

The senior high school coeducational program should include learning experiences that will be useful when students complete their education. Bowling, golf, and other individual sports may be introduced at this level if facilities permit.

The individual program of physical education must take into consideration this changing heterosexual drive. Younger girls love to play all kinds of games, but with physical development comes an increased desire for attractiveness, grace, poise, and balance. This aspect of their interests can and should be served in the teaching program, with dance and fitness activities stressing these goals.

The difference in sexual roles, although changing in today's culture, has always been reflected in an unfortunate split in social values and a "double standard." That is, society sometimes approves one form of behavior for boys and men and another for girls and women. Boys have more freedom and are less subject to social criticism than are girls. The "boys will be boys" attitude is an example of this. When social conventions are disregarded, girls suffer the burden of social disapproval more than boys do, although to a far lesser extent than they once did.

RELATIONSHIPS WITH ADULTS

Preadolescents usually accept adult authority, whereas early adolescents begin to resent it and try to assert themselves above such authority, except in cases of hero worship. In middle and late adolescence the students become more receptive to adult helpfulness and seek advice from those who represent fields in which they are strongly interested. Then at the end of adolescence, adults are met on a more friendly basis, and socially mature individuals find that they can enjoy casual friendship with everyone.

Conflict between generations. Because they are adventurous and willing to take responsibility, teenagers want to make choices on their own. They resent interference in choice of clothes, hairstyle, friends, books, and recreation. Each generation has a different point of view concerning appropriate behavior. Teen-

agers who insist on having their own way may be considered rebellious and disobedient. Their conflicts with adults usually center around friends, a car, money, use of time, and telephone privileges.

Sometimes the gap between the generations makes communication difficult. A teenager may feel for a time that adults just "don't understand." Parents, too, may shake their heads over the fact that they just do not seem to "get across" to their children. They will express concerns as to "what the new generation is coming to."

Relations to authority. One's personality needs guidelines throughout life. During the teens parental discipline, firm but reasonable, is still helpful. This form of guidance, which respects a young person's individuality, reinforces feelings of trust and security.

Parents who have shared in their children's early efforts to adapt and socialize will not need to worry about control and discipline in the teens. All their training in discipline will have taken place long before. By midteens, self-discipline should be well established. Teenagers who do not get along well with parents, however, will usually resist authority from other sources. They may protest the supervision of teachers, the regulations of the police, as well as the advice of parents.

It is sometimes hard for parents, teachers, and children to give young people enough discipline to assure trust and enough freedom to support individuality. Sometimes teenagers are more vocal concerning their rights than concerning their responsibilities. It is a developmental task of the teens to demonstrate self-discipline before asking for greater freedom.

Another developmental task of adolescence is breaking childhood ties and forming new ones. To grow up one must reshape links with the past, a past that includes family and friends. These ties may be based on affection, authority, respect, responsibility, closeness, or possessiveness. Teenagers come to see that those who were loved in childhood are neither all-powerful nor all-perfect. At first this recognition may cause shock, pain, and disillusion. When they realize that "nobody is perfect," they can accept other people's flaws and imperfections without loss of respect and affection. They should also be able to face their own.

Fig. 2-9. Secondary school students have a variety of cultural backgrounds and bring with them a vast assortment of needs, fears, abilities, hopes, and problems. Secondary school students in the training program at Hampton Institute, Hampton, Va.

In addition to making new friends, adolescents have the developmental task of forging adult ties with family: interest in, acceptance of, and concern for its members. To see parents as human beings with their weaknesses and strengths and their favorable and unfavorable personality traits and to feel strongly about them in spite of these is a big step in the process of growing up.

In adolescence teenagers live in their own society with many of its own standards and values. This state lasts for about as long as they look back across the teen bridge to childhood. It becomes less important in the midteens as they look forward to taking their place in adult society.

Emotional transition. At about the age of 13 or 14 in girls and about 15 in boys, a phase of self-absorption sets in. This is a period in which the teenager appears to be given over to self-examination and often to long periods of wanting to be left alone. A new point of self-discovery is often preceded by a period of depression. This may reflect a fear of not meeting adult expectations. Parents and teachers are likely to be surprised by this sudden change because it is in marked contrast to earlier gang activity and "bosom buddy" loyalties. This period usually precedes a person's first real interest in a member of the opposite sex.

During this time young people feel a strong need to be close to the parent of the opposite sex. Boys at this age will be more gallant and protective toward their mothers. Girls become especially affectionate and considerate of their fathers. When, through force of circumstance, parents are neither physically nor emotionally close to a child, these feelings may spill over to teachers, relatives, or older friends. This form of intimacy helps young people understand the needs, interests, and personalities of people unlike themselves. Much of the sensitivity and understanding teenagers later bring to marriage is learned in this phase of life. A successful relationship with parents in this stage increases self-confidence and strengthens personality.

It is possible at this time to become overly attached to a parent. This usually reveals insecurity held over from earlier developmental stages. It suggests that the individual was not prepared by his parents or parent substitutes for true psychological independence. If the parent has also felt emotionally deprived, he or she may rely too much psychologically on youngsters in this stage and may have difficulty letting go when the time comes. An overly intense attachment between children and their parents may hinder rather than promote personality development.

This change in the adolescent-adult relationship has two important implications for physical education. One concerns class management and the other the problem of hero worship. Because the younger adolescent tends to be resentful of adult authority, the physical educator should encourage class members to manage themselves as much as possible. Through guided group planning the adolescent can set proper standards of behavior and therefore has no reason to rebel. Students are then motivating themselves and providing self-direction—thus fulfilling educational as well as developmental goals.

In regard to the second factor, hero worship, it should be pointed out that in physical education, in which an informal teacher-pupil relationship is likely to be established, hero worship and infatuations easily develop. This can become a serious problem for the student involved, for such strong feelings often become very time and thought consuming, to the detriment of the individual. If such an attachment develops, the wise teacher remains objective and tries to be friendly and helpful and, at the same time, remote in other relationships with the student. Fortunately, these infatuations are usually shortlived, and when they are properly handled no personal misunderstandings or ill feelings result.

The social growth of the adolescent is of great importance both to him or her and to the school. The physical educator should assist in as many ways as possible in the development in all three aspects: relationships with friends of the same sex, with those of the opposite sex, and with adults.

Boys and girls are less concerned about material security and more concerned with basic human values. They resent the differences between what adults say and what they do. They want to participate more in deciding their own future. They are articulate and inclined to express themselves regarding the major issues of the day.

Some specific social characteristics of today's students that have deep implications for the teacher of physical education are:

- *Today's secondary school students want to be involved.* Boys and girls desire a say in respect to the decisions that affect them. They want to participate in the curriculum they will follow, the rules and regulations that control their actions, and the matters that will affect their future. They wish to have a voice in policy decisions, be on school committees, and evaluate courses and teachers.
- *Today's secondary school students are not inhibited.* They voice what they believe, which often is different from what adults believe. They want to know why they have to do certain things and why certain procedures and practices are followed.
- *Today's secondary school students have a new image of themselves.* Students recognize that they are human beings who have rights in this society and a say in what happens to them, what happens to their families, and what happens to their country. They are no longer content to let adults and others make decisions for them. They utilize their economic, political, and social power. They stress the value of the individual in society and the need for each person to have equal opportunities.
- *Today's secondary school students may be antiestablishment.* They may be skeptical of adults, of the school administration, of government, and of older people in general. They have seen the materialism, discrimination, pollution of the environment, war mongering, and other evils associated with past generations and want to bring about a change.

- *Today's secondary school students have goals different from adults'.* Students' goals differ particularly in respect to such matters as money, security, challenge, and position. According to a recent survey, young people indicated that their three greatest sources of satisfaction listed in priority order are family, leisure, and occupation.
- *Today's secondary school students are educationally oriented in different ways.* Instead of memorization of dates; they want to know the reasons for the movements and events behind the dates; instead of merely knowing about historical events, they desire to understand the underlying forces that resulted in these significant events.
- *Today's secondary school students are not part of the crowd.* Each student wants to be considered for his or her own self and talents. Girls, for example, want to have the same rights as boys. Students do not want to be treated in an impersonal manner and exposed to an impersonal curriculum. They do not want to be required to perform the same school tasks that other students, whose abilities, needs, and interests differ from their own, are required to perform. Students feel they must be dealt with as they are and not as they are expected to be.

What the secondary school student wants is illustrated by the demands of students as listed in a study conducted by a student task force in North Carolina. The survey involved students from representative high schools in the state. Their major demands include the following:

- Administrators should maintain a constant dialogue with students.
- Legitimate requests of students should be dealt with promptly and fairly.
- Student dissent should be sanctioned if it is legitimate and does not disrupt the educational process.
- Seminar sessions should be held regularly with students for discussion of current school problems.
- Students should be permitted to form committees with powers to investigate and propose solutions to problems of unrest.
- Students should be urged to respect the school as their institution of learning.

- The local high school should be given responsibility for all rules and regulations.
- Clear communication lines should be established between administration, faculty, and students.
- Student government should be given as much responsibility as possible.
- The principal should write a column in school newspaper as an avenue of communication.

As a result of these demands, new and innovative methods and educational programs in North Carolina were established, students were given a voice in planning their own course of study, and they were appointed to committees and given a chance to revamp the grading system.

Intellectual development

The teens are a period of mental growth. A teenager's interests extend in many directions and are stimulated by new experience. The fact that students are no longer confined to the narrow limits of their immediate environment opens new horizons. Heightened learning and planning ability and improvement in the capacity for self-expression help teenagers to develop minds of their own.

The ability to conceptualize and to grasp abstract ideas increases rapidly in these years. During this time young people can approach the upper limits of their intellectual potential. With these new powers the teenager undertakes the most complex tasks of the life cycle—establishing a system of values, forming lasting personal relationships, choosing a career, and developing a pilosophy of life.

The adolescent does not go through a great intellectual growth spurt or change as in other phases of development. At this time there seems to be an expansion of powers, however, as well as an increase in capacities. The continuing growth toward intellectual maturity is extremely varied in individuals, with a high degree of this development being reached at any time between the ages of 16 and 25 years. Boys and girls are alike in this respect, and the wide range of ages points out the individualized nature of intellectual growth.

Adolescent intellectual advancement may be discussed in reference to four general areas: memory, concentration, imagination, and reasoning power. The power of memory, which is so strong in childhood, seems to decrease in adolescence. Actually, however, it is the adolescent's lack of interest in making use of this capacity to memorize that causes this decline.

The powers of adolescents to concentrate increase, particularly in areas of work in which they are greatly interested. The adolescent's ability to use imagination also increases at this time. Of greatest importance in relation to schoolwork is the distinct increase in adolescent powers of reasoning and judging. It is this phase of intellectual development that distinguishes growth away from childish ideas, permitting the student to generalize from past experiences to integrate moral values and knowledge into a philosophy of life.

The importance of this intellectual development of adolescents to the physical education program lies in its relationship to teaching methods and the influences exerted by the teacher. The teacher must be sure to consider the variation of intellectual abilities when presenting instructions and explanations. As students progress through high school, the material presented in physical education class should require more and more reasoning power and judgment. Thought questions should be included in tests rather than simple true-false or multiple-choice types. Strategy and game concepts should become a part of the teaching program, for adolescents are now able to understand more fully this phase of physical education activities.

The teacher should also make use of teaching methods that promote creative thinking on the part of adolescent students. Units on modern dance obviously foster creative thinking in girls, but sports units for both boys and girls may be constructed to take advantage of improved adolescent powers of imagination and analytical thinking. Students should have an opportunity to work out team plays in basketball, for example, or to develop their own exercise patterns, drill formations, or football plays. The teacher can use the problem-solving technique to accomplish this, asking the students to think out some specific solution to a given game situation.

The other important aspect of adolescent intellectual development that affects the physical education teacher lies in the student-teacher relationship. Because adolescence is the period in which adult attitudes, moral values, and a philosophy of life become formalized, the teacher of physical education should

exemplify those ideals that are most suitable to mature living. For example, the physical education teacher should try to promote positive attitudes toward health and physical fitness: a desire to maintain good health, a desire to continue physical pursuits for enjoyment, and an appreciation for the benefits of physical exercise. As an influence on adolescent moral values, on their concepts of right and wrong, and on their prejudices, which are now taking final shape, the physical education teacher should have clearly defined values that are consistently applied and worthy of imitation by the students. The ideals of respect for all individuals, no matter how different they may be, should be promoted in physical education, together with the real meaning of sportsmanship.

ESTABLISHING GOALS

Young people have earned the right to make their own decisions when they assume responsibility for them in terms of the reality principle. Each decision that is made and attitude adopted influences future growth. Thus it is always important to select positive aims and goals.

Goals established in the light of the reality principle are usually positive and therefore unifying. Negative goals undermine stability. In a general way we can call positive goals "right" and negative goals "wrong" to the degree that they promote personality harmony. Each person must select goals that harmonize his or her personality by assessing abilities and admitting shortcomings.

WHAT DO THEY BELIEVE?

The question "Who am I?" can hardly be separated from the question, "What do I believe?" For this reason it is important as the teen years pass for young people to formulate a philosophy of life. Their philosophy of life is an overall system of ideas that determines what they believe and how they will behave. To maintain their psychological balance, they must follow a consistent code of conduct. This does not mean merely establishing predictable behavior, because even conditioned behavior is predictable. Human beings who function like clockwork have lost an important element in the enjoyment of life.

People's values differ according to their education, environment, and personal needs. Some people act on

CHECKLIST OF SELECTED ITEMS FOR EVALUATING THE PHYSICAL EDUCATION PROGRAM'S RELEVANCY TO THE STUDENT IN THE SECONDARY SCHOOL

	Yes	No
1. Activities are provided that will enable each student to feel successful and worthwhile.	☐	☐
2. Students are helped to relate to one another, to members of the opposite sex, and to adults.	☐	☐
3. Students are provided an opportunity to have a say in the development of the physical education curriculum and consequently will be more highly motivated to participate in a program that is meaningful and interesting to them.	☐	☐
4. Students are helped to understand the reason for the activity in which they are participating.	☐	☐
5. Students are grouped in classes according to their abilities.	☐	☐
6. Teachers know all students and help in solving their problems.	☐	☐
7. The community is involved in the physical education program; for example, father-son and mother-daughter activities.	☐	☐
8. Instruction is provided in new sports, such as scuba diving, in which students have an interest.	☐	☐
9. Students have a voice in policy-making decisions, are represented on important committees, and participate in the evaluation of courses and teachers.	☐	☐
10. The physical education program is kept abreast of the changing times in society and the changing nature of students, with student needs being met in a realistic, meaningful manner. (Today, some students find their programs repetitious, time consuming, of little value to the unskilled, and so on.)	☐	☐
11. The program gives equal opportunities to girls and boys.	☐	☐
12. Opportunities are provided students for leadership roles.	☐	☐
13. Students are represented at faculty meetings.	☐	☐
14. The physical education program meets the needs of minority groups.	☐	☐
15. Communication channels are available whereby students can submit their grievances to the administration.	☐	☐
16. Intellectual as well as physical capacities of students are challenged.	☐	☐
17. The curriculum provides for a sequential advancement from basic skills to more advanced skills.	☐	☐
18. Individualistic hair styles and dress codes are permitted where they do not affect the health, safety, and performance of students.	☐	☐
19. Physically handicapped, mentally retarded, emotionally disturbed, and culturally disadvantaged students are provided for in the physical education program.	☐	☐
20. Sufficient variety and progression exist in activities to satisfy individual differences.	☐	☐
21. The intramural, varsity athletic, and other extracurricular activities meet the needs of students.	☐	☐
22. The program is designed to develop the optimum potential of each student.	☐	☐
23. The objectives of the physical education program are clearly understood by students.	☐	☐
24. Students have the opportunity to participate in activities that stress individuality and acceptance.	☐	☐
25. Students have the opportunity to participate in activities that will be of value to them not only now but also in the future.	☐	☐

"common sense" in daily life. Others embrace a religious teaching. Some people operate in line with material considerations; others formulate a philosophy based on intellectual or spiritual values. No set of rules imposed by others can cover every detail of one's life. As one gains experience, a pattern gradually emerges that shows the kind of behavior that balances different areas of one's personality and brings peace of mind. These ground rules form part of the young person's way of life.

A sound philosophy is one that is consistent in terms of inner personality and appropriate in terms of outer reality. It promotes good adjustment and brings personality into harmony with the environment. A weak philosophy upsets the steady state. Without a philosophy of life or at least a personal guide for action, it is difficult to make day-by-day choices in terms of long-range goals.

Religious doubts and philosophical questioning are increasing concerns of the adolescent. Physical education teachers never know when their actions, thoughts, or beliefs may be idealized or when guidance and advice may be sought. They must therefore be ready to serve and to answer students to the best of their abilities and must recognize that many values are best learned from example.

Achieving maturity

When all parts of the personality are in harmony, the young person has achieved *self-direction*, that is, is able to use personal resources to reach self-made goals. Establishing self-governing behavior is an important developmental task of the teens and is made possible by the successful completion of earlier tasks.

To provide steady support for the total personality, the appropriate rules, regulations, and values of society must become part of each young person's attitude. When this process is accomplished one's life is guided from within and is not subject to the "whims of fate." It has become *inner directed*. This capacity develops throughout the teens as conscience, aims, goals, and values are built into the personality.

When developmental tasks are completed, the young person's personality has become aware of itself (self-conscious) and critical of itself (self-critical). To

be self-conscious or self-aware means that one part of an individual's personality recognizes the other. Most importantly, it is in command of itself under the direction of the will (self-controlled).

The mature conscience. In a classic example of cinema art, Walt Disney told the story of Pinocchio. Every time the puppet did something wrong, his conscience in the form of an insect, Jiminy Cricket, was there to "bug" him. In a dramatic way, this characterized the role of conscience in personality. A mature person recognizes conscience not as an outside force directing action like a policeman directs traffic but as a necessary and functional part of his or her inner life. Conscience plays the part of an outside critic, but it is still a real part of each person.

Conscience monitors the relations between the real self and the ideal self. A person's real self is the self of needs and drives. The ideal self develops with experience and education. Children handle their instinctual demands in such a way as not to break rules set by their parents or other people who may punish them. However, although fear is a natural and necessary emotion, one cannot seek the "right" thing to do out of fear without damaging one's personality. A pattern of behavior based solely on fear makes demands incompatible with psychological well-being and mental health. Acting on fear, a person may appear well behaved, but his or her adjustment will only be on the surface.

The gratification of instinct is always primarily pleasurable, but emotions, depending on their nature, may be pleasurable or painful. A mature personality has established some form of harmony among its impulses. This cannot be accomplished without the expenditure of considerable energy. A mature conscience helps a young person to behave so that he or she not only does the right thing but feels the value of such socially constructive emotions as honesty, kindness, generosity, loyalty, and perseverance.

MATURITY

When all the elements of an individual's personality—body, public personality, inner self—combine, we say that personality is integrated or mature. Personality has become a reliable unit that one can take for granted and depend on. It maintains a steady state in which physical and psychological needs are faced and met. One can feel that this stage has been reached when he or she can say, I am the kind of person who (1) has come to accept myself, physically and mentally, (2) has accepted the selves of others, (3) is accepted by others, (4) has learned to master and adjust to my environment, and (5) acts on the basis of my own values and experience.

Maturity, however, is not the end stage of growth. It is rather, the secure foundation on which continuing growth and self-realization take place.

A final developmental task of adolescence is the foundation of a sense of commitment. That is, the entire personality, unified toward satisfying goals, is directed toward self-completing activities. It is concerned not only with what is best for itself but what is best for others and for society as a whole.

Self-assessment tests

These tests are designed to assist students in determining if material and competencies presented in this chapter have been mastered.

1. Prepare a table and list the principal characteristics and needs of a boy and a girl in each of the grades 7 to 12.
2. Think of some teenaged boy or girl that you know. List some of the mannerisms, interests, plans, and attitudes he or she expresses that reflect a searching for identity.
3. Prepare a list of developmental tasks that boys and girls face in the secondary school.
4. Complete the following chart regarding changes that take place during adolescent growth and the implications these changes have for teaching physical education:

Changes that take place during adolescence	Implications for teaching physical education
Physical changes	
a. _____	_____
b. _____	_____
c. _____	_____
Emotional changes	
a. _____	_____
b. _____	_____
c. _____	_____
Social changes	
a. _____	_____
b. _____	_____
c. _____	_____

Intellectual changes	
a. _____	_____
b. _____	_____
c. _____	_____

5. You are in charge of a ninth-grade coeducational physical education class in volleyball. How would you provide for differences in height and weight and other physical differences in boys and girls in the class?
6. Title IX requires coeducational physical education classes. Indicate the social characteristics of high school boys and girls and how you would provide for these social characteristics in the high school physical education program.
7. Define the term maturity. Describe in specific terms how you would know when a boy or girl reaches maturity.

Points to remember

1. Some of the characteristics of secondary school students have changed over the past several years.
2. The needs of secondary school students, in light of these changed characteristics, should be attended.
3. The question of identity is a primary concern for teenagers.
4. Developmental tasks include growth in physical, emotional, social, and intellectual areas.
5. The process of adolescent physical development and the stages undergone are different in boys and girls, and each individual follows his or her own particular growth pattern.
6. The emotional responses of adolescents are different from those of adults because of their varying needs.
7. Social development in adolescence is recognizable by the changes in relationships with friends and adults.
8. Intellectual growth is experienced during adolescence and plays an important part in mature living.
9. The process of growth and development in adolescents has many implications for the physical education program.

Problems to think through

1. How can we capitalize on the varying interests exhibited in junior high school students?
2. How can we promote and further good social relationships in junior high school students when heterosexual interests develop?
3. Why do some teenagers belong to ''gangs''?
4. How can physical education help teenagers to achieve a sense of identity?
5. Why is there a generation gap between some students and adults?

Case study for analysis

You are assigned to a high school in your community. It is your responsibility to develop a physical education program that meets the needs and characteristics of one of the grades in this high school. Analyze the student body and develop a physical education program from this analysis.

Exercises for review

1. List several reasons why it is very important for teachers of physical education to know and understand their students.
2. Why is adolescence called a bridge between childhood and adulthood?
3. What constitutes a wholesome relationship between the student and authority?
4. What are some signs of peer group influence and how can this affect physical education?
5. To what extent should teenagers make their own decisions?
6. What steps should be followed in helping a student whose emotional adjustment is questionable in a school where a nurse is not in daily attendance?
7. How would procedures regarding monthly periods be outlined to a class of seventh grade girls?
8. In what way could proper class and locker room management benefit the ostracized high school boy?
9. What adolescent individuals in the modern world of sports should be singled out as examples of athletic achievement?
10. What advice should be given the adolescent youth, ordinarily proficient in physical activities, who falls below par?

Selected readings

Arnheim, D.D., Auxter, D., and Crowe, W.C.: Principles and methods of adapted physical education and recreation, ed. 3, St. Louis, 1977, The C.V. Mosby Co.

Arnheim, D.D., and Pestolesi, R.A.: Elementary physical education: a developmental approach, ed. 2, St. Louis, 1978, The C.V. Mosby Co.

Berg, K.: Maintaining enthusiasm in teaching, Journal of Physical Education and Recreation 46:22, 1975.

Blair, G.M., and Jones, R.S.: Psychology of adolescence for teachers, New York, 1964, The Macmillan Co.

Bronson, D.B.: Thinking and teaching, The Educational Forum 39:347, 1975.

Bucher, C.A.: What's happening in education today? Journal of Health, Physical Education, and Recreation 45:30, 1974.

Caldwell, S.: Toward a humanistic physical education, Journal of Health, Physical Education, and Recreation 43:31, 1972.

Dacey, J.S.: Adolescents today, Santa Monica, Calif., 1979, Goodyear Publishing Co., Inc.

Friedenberg, E.Z.: The vanishing adolescent, Boston, 1959, Beacon Press.

Friedenberg, E.Z.: Coming of age in America, New York, 1965, Random House, Inc.

Grinder, R.: Adolescence, New York, 1973, John Wiley & Sons, Inc.

High school kids "turned off" by education, White Plains Reporter Dispatch, Oct. 20, 1971, p. 10.

Murphy, G.: What can youth tell us about their potentialities? Bulletin of the National Association of Secondary School Principals 50:10-24, 1966.

Oliva, P.F.: The secondary school today, New York, 1967, World Publishing Co.

Riley, M.: Games and humanism, Journal of Physical Education and Recreation 46:46, 1975.

Snyder, E.E., and Spreitzer, E.A.: Family influence and involvement in sport, Research Quarterly 44:249, 1973.

Stallings, L.M.: Motor skills: development and learning, Dubuque, Iowa, 1973, Wm. C. Brown Co., Publishers.

Taggart, R.J.: Accountability and the American dream, The Educational Forum 39:33, 1974.

United States Department of Health, Education and Welfare: Dialogue on adolescence, Washington, D.C., 1967, U.S. Government Printing Office.

Vodola, T.M.: Individualized physical education program for the handicapped child, Englewood Cliffs, N.J., 1973, Prentice-Hall, Inc.

Williams, W.G.: Does the educational past have a future? Kappa Delta Pi Record 11:103, 1975.

Youth's faith . . . (editorial), New York Times, May 8, 1970, p. 20.

PART TWO

Goals and program considerations

3

Developing goals—what should physical education be doing for the student?

Instructional objectives and competencies to be achieved

After reading this chapter the student should be able to

1. Describe the nature and importance of developing goals in physical education
2. Identify the bases and procedure for determining the specific goals that physical education should strive to achieve
3. Outline and discuss the objectives of general education
4. Name and present a rationale for the major objectives of physical education
5. Present data to support a priority of objectives of physical education
6. Show how methods and materials for teaching physical education are important to the realization of its objectives

What are the goals toward which physical educators should strive in the secondary school? Will the selected objectives, when achieved, contribute to the physical, mental, emotional, and social well-being of the student? What are the main contributions that physical education can make to the new breed of student who is attending the junior and senior high schools of this country?

Thus far we have considered the secondary school in the context of a changing community and school environment. We then looked at the student. In developing this next logical step—articulating the goals and objectives of physical education—it is well to keep in mind four basic guidelines.

• *Goals must be clearly identified and should be understood by the student.* Surveys indicate that the purposes for which physical education programs exist are not always clear in the minds of students or are thought to have little value. This should not be the case. When students take physical education, they should clearly understand at the outset the purpose of the program and the benefits and values to expect as participants. In addition, the goals should have been so carefully thought through and selected that the student will recognize their immediate and future importance.

• *Goals should have scientific worth.* The physical educator should select achievable goals that are backed by scientific investigation. Unfortunately, some teachers make wild claims for physical education that they can neither prove scientifically nor achieve.

• *Goals should be relevant to society, education, and the student.* The aims of physical education should reflect the changing society, education, and student discussed earlier. Physical educators will be remiss if they fail to evaluate and select their goals with these changes in mind.

• *Goals should relate to the cognitive, affective, and psychomotor domains.* Objectives of physical education should reflect directly or indirectly three domains, namely, the *cognitive,* with its emphasis on knowledge and the development of intellectual abilities and skills; the *affective,* which relates to attitudes, values, interests, and appreciations; and the *psychomotor,* which refers to motor and manipulative skills. Furthermore, the interdependence of the three domains in relation to student learning should be recognized. For example, students do not think or behave without feeling; they respond as total beings. Annarino's operational taxonomy reflects this human characteristic.

Operational taxonomy for physical education objectives*

PHYSICAL DOMAIN (ORGANIC DEVELOPMENT)

Proper functioning of the body systems so that the individual may adequately meet the demands placed upon him by his environment

A. **Strength:** The maximum amount of force exerted by a muscle or muscle group
 1. Static (isometric): The maximum force exerted without any change in muscle length
 2. Dynamic (isotonic): The maximum force exerted by shortening or lengthening the muscles
 3. Explosive (isotonic): The release of maximal force in the shortest period of time
B. **Endurance:** The capacity to persist in strenuous activity for periods of some duration
 1. Muscle: the ability of a muscle or muscle group to sustain effort for a prolonged period of time
  a. Static: the ability of a muscle or muscle group to sustain effort in a fixed position
  b. Dynamic: the ability of a muscle or muscle group to repeat effort in a movement
 2. Cardiovascular: the ability to persist in strenuous activity dependent upon the combined efficiency of the blood vessels, heart, and lungs
C. **Flexibility:** The range of motion in joints
 1. Extent: the ability to extend joint motion as far as possible in various directions
 2. Dynamic: the ability to repeat flexing and extending movements

PSYCHOMOTOR DOMAIN (NEUROMUSCULAR DEVELOPMENT)

The harmonious integration of the nervous and muscular systems to produce desired movements

A. **Perceptual motor-abilities:** those abilities needed for recognition, interpretation, and response to stimuli for performing some type of task
 1. Balance: the ability to maintain body position or equilibrium
  a. Static: maintaining a specific stationary body position
  b. Dynamic: maintaining equilibrium while performing a movement

---

*Annarino, A.A.: Operational taxonomy for physical education objectives, Journal of Physical Education and Recreation **49:**54-55, Jan. 1978.

2. Kinesthesis: the awareness of the position and movement of one's body or parts in space
  a. Body image: a self-concept of one's body and its relationship between one's self, others, space, and the world around
  b. Body awareness: recognition and control of the body and its parts
  c. Laterality: distinguishing the difference between left and right sides of the body and of left and right within one's own body
  d. Directionality: distinguishing between and among left, right, up, down, front, back, and distances in space
  e. Dominance: consistency in the use of a preferred side in performing a task
 3. Visual discrimination: the ability to receive, recognize, and differentiate between and among objects in space through visual cues
  a. Visual acuity: to differentiate and understand various sights
  b. Visual tracking: to follow objects with coordinated eye movements
  c. Visual memory: to recall and reproduce movement from past visual experiences
  d. Figure-ground relationships: to distinguish and select an object from its surrounding background
  e. Perceptual constancy: to recognize familiar objects presented in a different size or manner
 4. Auditory discrimination: the ability to receive, recognize, and differentiate between and among sounds
  a. Auditory acuity: to receive and distinguish varying pitch and intensity of sounds
  b. Auditory tracking: to locate sounds and follow their movements
  c. Auditory memory: to recognize sounds from past experiences
 5. Visual-motor coordination: the ability to integrate visual cues and specific body parts to produce a desired movement
  a. Eye-hand coordination: the relationship of the eyes with the hands to gain control, accuracy, and steadiness
  b. Eye-foot coordination: to integrate the eyes and foot to judge accurately the speed and direction of an object for kicking movement
 6. Tactile sensitivity: the ability to receive and use cutaneous cues for enhancing motor performance
B. **Fundamental movement skills:** manipulative skills involving the body or an object
 1. Body manipulative skills: those movements restrict-

71

Developing goals—what should physical education be doing for the student?

ed to moving one's self by locomotion from space to space; nonlocomotor movements of moving one's self or body part within a space

a. Basic locomotor skills moving the body from one place to another
   (1) Walking
   (2) Running
   (3) Leaping
   (4) Jumping
   (5) Hopping

b. Basic nonlocomotor skills moving a part or body part within a place
   (1) Bending
   (2) Stretching
   (3) Twisting
   (4) Turning
   (5) Hanging
   (6) Posture

c. Locomotor combinations: combining two or more locomotor skills
   (1) Skipping
   (2) Galloping
   (3) Sliding
   (4) Starting
   (5) Stopping
   (6) Changing directions
   (7) Falling
   (8) Landing
   (9) Rolling

d. Nonlocomotor combinations: combining two or more nonlocomotor skills
   (1) Swaying
   (2) Swinging
   (3) Lifting

2. Objective manipulative skills: the use of the various body manipulative movements in propulsive and receptive skills

a. Propulsive skills: giving impetus to an external object
   (1) Throwing
      (a) Underarm
      (b) Sidearm
      (c) Overarm
   (2) Pushing
   (3) Pulling
   (4) Striking
   (5) Lifting

b. Receptive skills: receiving of external objects
   (1) Catching
   (2) Trapping

3. Sport skills: the more complex skills which apply specifically to performance in a sport, game, or dance
   a. Individual skills
   b. Dual skills
   c. Team skills

COGNITIVE DOMAIN (INTELLECTUAL DEVELOPMENT)

A. **Knowledge**
   1. Game rules
   2. Safety measures
   3. Game etiquette
   4. Terminology
   5. Body functions

B. **Intellectual skills and abilities**
   1. The use of strategies
   2. The use of judgment related to distance, time, form, space, speed, and direction in the use of activity implements, balls, and self
   3. Solve developmental problems through movement
   4. Understand the relationship of physical activity to body function and structure
   5. Knowledge of the immediate effects of activity
   6. Knowledge of long-range effects of activity

AFFECTIVE DOMAIN (SOCIAL-PERSONAL-EMOTIONAL DEVELOPMENT)

A. **A healthy response to physical activity**
   1. The development of positive reactions through either success or failure in activity
   2. An appreciation of the aesthetic experiences derived from correlated activities
   3. Recognizing the potential of activity as an outlet for tension release and use of leisure time
   4. The ability to have "fun" in activity
   5. Appreciate outstanding physical performance as a spectator

B. **Self-actualization**
   1. An awareness of what the body is capable of doing at a specific time
   2. The knowledge of what one is and the ability to accept this knowledge of one's capacity and potential
   3. Willingness to set a level of aspiration that is within reach and be motivated to seek this level

C. **Self-esteem:** Self-perception refers to all of an individual's basic beliefs about self based on past experience; self-esteem refers to the individual's personal evaluation of these beliefs.
   1. The individual develops perceptions of physical performance in a specific activity or of general physical ability.

Student–parent confusion

Many students and parents are confused about the real worth of games and sports as part of the school program. Over the years we have had the opportunity to discuss physical education with many people. Some of their comments reflect this confusion: "It's exercise done to command." "A matter of arms and legs and good intentions." "Something that entertains the students—a necessary evil." "Physical fitness and physical education are the same." "A good device to keep the kids off the street." "Just an extracurricular activity—a frill, a fad." "It certainly isn't part of the educational program—merely an appendage." "Too much time should not be devoted to it—above all, don't take time away from science and mathematics."

If physical education and play do not mean more than these comments indicate, they should be abolished from the school program. After all, there are more than 100,000 leaders getting paid several million dollars annually in this specialized field today. Approximately 60 million school children are being exposed to their programs. Gymnasiums, swimming pools, playgrounds, and recreational facilities are being constructed at a cost of billions of dollars to taxpayers. An up-to-date gymnasium costs more than $400,000 and a 75-foot swimming pool more than $150,000. Even the basketball that the kids bounce up and down the floor costs $30. The average gymnasium is one of the most costly parts of the school building and takes up space equivalent to 10 to 14 classrooms. Why pay all these teachers, construct these expensive facilities, and take up valuable space unless they have beneficial results—unless they are an important phase of education?

Students and parents are demanding the answers to such questions. They have become vitally interested in education. For parents, this interest has mushroomed until today there are over 15 million members of parent-teacher associations throughout the country. They want to make sure their children have the benefits of worthwhile educational experiences. They vote for funds only for programs they consider sound.

As these parents scan the educational programs of their communities, they should become increasingly aware that boys and girls do not learn, grow, and develop only during those hours spent at their desks in reading, writing, and working with paper and pencil. There are other times that may be even more important: time spent in taking a trip to the zoo, going to camp, attending a dance, and, *yes,* playing on the field, in the gymnasium, or in the swimming pool.

Knowledge of objectives— an important consideration

On the shoulders of the teacher of physical education rests the responsibility for interpreting to students, their parents, and the public in general the objectives of their specialized field. This responsibility cannot be met unless the teacher understands clearly the goals of education, students, and physical education and how they fit into the total educational picture. Trying to work without such vital information would be analogous to a carpenter's trying to build a house without blueprints to guide him. Furthermore, all these goals must be compatible with the educational development of each boy and girl in the secondary school and must contribute to it.

Each student of physical education and each teacher in the schools should know the goals they are trying to reach. These aims represent the worth of this specialized field, they show the contribution that can be made to young and old alike, and they provide a guide for action in our day-to-day programs.

Recent developments with implications for physical education

Some recent developments in the United States that have implications for the objectives of physical education and what it should be doing for the secondary school student are: health related physical fitness, *Basic Stuff Series I and II,* and self-help preventive medicine.

HEALTH-RELATED PHYSICAL FITNESS

Physical fitness is a very desirable quality. However, there are many definitions and several components of physical fitness. The question that should be asked is, "Fitness for what?" Should the focus be on physical fitness that contributes to general health or

73

Developing goals—what should physical education be doing for the student?

physical fitness that assures outstanding performance in some particular sport? Both forms of physical fitness are comprised of identical qualities; these include cardiovascular function, strength, body composition, and flexibility. However, physical fitness for performance requires greater development. AAHPERD, through its Task Force on Youth Fitness, advocates that for the general population the greatest need is for health-related physical fitness.

Cardiovascular function, one of the fitness components, is regarded by experts as the most important of the four in terms of health. Diseases associated with the circulatory system are among the principal causes of death throughout the world, and vigorous physical activity seems to improve cardiovascular function and, consequently, to reduce the incidence of these diseases.

Body composition, the second of the physical fitness components, relates to the makeup of the body in terms of muscle, bone, fat, and other elements. The percentage of body fat is particularly significant since an excess amount requires the individual to exert more energy for movement, and it may reflect a high fat-saturated diet. Furthermore, it is believed that obesity contributes to degenerative diseases such as high blood pressure and atherosclerosis. It can also result in psychological maladjustments and may shorten life. A balance between caloric intake and caloric expenditure is necessary to maintain proper body fat content, and exercise is one effective method of control.

Strength, the third component in physical fitness, is the capacity of a muscle or muscle group to exert force against resistance. It is needed in all kinds of work and physical activity. Strong muscles better protect body joints and are less prone to sprains, strains, and other muscle difficulties. Furthermore, strength helps in maintaining proper posture, provides for greater endurance and power, and helps combat fatigue. Strength also is a very important element for succcess in sports, which is why most athletes pay particular attention to developing various muscle groups.

Flexibility, the fourth component in physical fitness, is that quality that permits freedom of movement. It is a measure of the range of motion allowed by a body joint or joints. Flexibility is very important

for performance in most active sports. It is also important for good posture and for carrying on many of life's activities. In addition, it can help prevent muscle strain, orthopedic problems, and headaches.

BASIC STUFF SERIES I AND II

Basic Stuff Series I and II, developed by physical education leaders, presents a conceptual approach, offering valuable information that focuses on the "why" of physical education for elementary and secondary school students. It covers such areas as exercise physiology and relates them to three basic age groups: early childhood, childhood, and adolescence. The series, when implemented, will help to gain academic respect for physical education.*

THE HOLISTIC HEALTH, SELF-HELP MEDICINE, AND WELLNESS MOVEMENTS

Holistic health and medicine is based on the premise that an individual's health is the result of many forces: physical, mental, social, environmental, genetic, economic, political, and spiritual. Therefore, simultaneous attention should be given to all these forces. As a result of this view, many doctors are attempting to deal with the various aspects of the patient's life that might be relevant to his or her health.

Self-help medicine stresses that individuals should assume a greater responsibility for their health by paying more attention to aspects of life-style that affect health, such as smoking, alcohol consumption, physical activity, and diet, in order to prevent, as far as possible, various maladies and diseases.

The *wellness movement* emphasizes the need to provide measures that will prevent disease rather than treat illness. In other words, if individuals can prevent disease they will not have to worry about treating various types of illness. Wellness assumes that many deterrents to good health can be prevented if people eliminate the controllable risk factors in their life-style that cause sickness.

The secondary school student should be aware of these movements and be prepared to achieve the goals they espouse. This means the development not only

---

*Basic Stuff is discussed in detail later in this chapter.

Fig. 3-1. Gymnastics helps to develop strength—a component of health-related physical fitness.

Courtesy President's Council on Physical Fitness and Sports.

of physical skills but, equally important, the mastery of knowledge that will provide the self-direction needed to promote good health.

MASTERY LEARNING

Mastery learning is based on the assumption that nearly all students can learn if they are given sufficient time and the material is presented in a way that they can understand. The procedure followed in those places where it has proved successful is presentation of material to an entire group of students. Then an evaluation is conducted, and those students who have not mastered the material are given a second chance. The material is presented again but in a different way and in a manner that is better understood by those students who did not master the material the first time. Mastery learning operates under the assumption that there are no failures; everyone succeeds. This process

has the same implications for physical education that it does for other subjects.*

OLYMPIC CURRICULUM

The education committee of the United States Olympic Committee has prepared booklets designed to incorporate the ideals associated with the Olympic Games into the curriculum of several subjects, including physical education, in the elementary, junior high, and senior high schools of the nation. Physical educators will want to review these booklets and determine if this material has value for their programs.

HUMANISTIC EDUCATION

Change is necessary to humanize the school so that students feel a sense of identity and belonging and are

---

*Mastery learning is discussed at greater length in Chapter 12.

75

Developing goals—what should physical education be doing for the student?

actively involved in the decision-making processes that affect them. Certainly educators should be concerned with humanization and involvement processes.

NEW GAMES

New Games represents an innovative approach being utilized by some physical educators. It is based on such concepts as "Any game can be a new game," "Anyone can play," "Creating a new game is part of the fun," "We play for the fun of it," "It is the process of finding a game we all want to play that is important," and "We learn about play by playing." The New Games organization holds training sessions for individuals interested in this movement.

Development of goals for the physical education program

Physical educators in the secondary school should use a logical, step-by-step approach for arriving at the goals they wish to accomplish in their programs. The following steps are suggested as a specific way in which goals may be determined. Each step is presented in the form of a question, and the questions proceed from general to specific considerations.

WHAT IS THE PURPOSE OF EDUCATION?

Physical educators should be aware of the purposes for which formal institutions of learning exist. This changing nation has basic objectives for educational programs that are well grounded in democratic ideals. Some of these objectives, discussed later in this chapter, were formulated by the Educational Policies Commission.

Physical educators should next determine how their field can best help to accomplish the basic goals of education. Furthermore, they should recognize the place of physical education in the total sphere of general education—that it makes a contribution to the physical, mental, emotional, and social development of the student.

WHAT IS THE SCHOOL'S PHILOSOPHY OF EDUCATION?

Physical education goals should be compatible with the philosophy of education in the school where the

physical educator works. Therefore, the physical educator should be familiar with the goals of education of the secondary school and relate them to the physical education program. A careful study of the school's goals should be made, and confusion about the school's philosophy should be clarified through discussions with the administration. Most schools have developed goals in written form. Schools without such documentation should be urged to formalize their goals. One school, for example, states its aim—"to promote healthful living by developing physical fitness, emotional stability, and appreciation of the ideals of good sportsmanship. . . . In our entire program we consciously support good physical and mental health habits, which are specifically taught in physical education [and] family living. . . . Through sports and other extracurricular activities we encourage participation in and enjoyment of rewarding recreational activities."

WHAT ARE THE NEEDS AND INTERESTS OF THE STUDENTS?

The physical education program exists for the students, and thus their needs and interests are a vital consideration. These needs and interests may be determined in a number of ways and by using a variety of resources, including school records, observation of students, talks with parents, inventory of students' interests and suggestions, examination of the literature and professional research that specifically relates to this subject, and consultation with specialists in the school program, such as the school physician, the nurse, and the guidance counselor. Any program that is developed should be compatible with the needs and interests of the students in a specific school. The procedure of studying students carefully should be a continuous one so that the goals are flexible and meet the changing needs of the students.

WHAT IS THE FIELD OF PHYSICAL EDUCATION TRYING TO ACCOMPLISH?

The goals of physical education should be compatible with the professional aims of leaders in the field who espouse the views of professional organizations such as the American Alliance for Health, Physical Education, Recreation and Dance. Professionals in physical education continue to be active in such endeavors as establishing standards for programs at every educational level, developing tests in such areas as physical fitness, and publishing materials such as *Basic Stuff Series I and II*. These activities represent the thinking of many leaders in the field and should be taken into consideration in setting goals for physical education programs.

WHAT ARE THE INFLUENCING FACTORS RELATING TO SUCH ITEMS AS FACILITIES, STATE REGULATIONS, AND STAFF?

A basic premise for the development of physical education goals is that they must be established within the framework of factors essential for their accomplishment. For example, it would not be a worthwhile goal to insist that each student know how to swim if there is no swimming pool or water available for such instruction; or, if a state regulation does not permit the use of a trampoline, it would be foolish to list such an activity as a goal. Individualized instruction in many activities is not possible without adequate staff. In addition, there are other influencing factors, such as climate, local school regulations, available equipment, and administrative philosophy, that must receive the attention of the physical educator in the development of goals.

WHAT DOES THE NATURE OF THE COMMUNITY INDICATE ABOUT THE TYPE OF PROGRAM THAT IS NEEDED?

The community itself—its social, economic, political, and physical makeup—should play an important role in the development of goals. For example, Americans are becoming aware that the type of education needed in the inner city and in poverty areas of this country is different from that of suburbia. The program must be geared to the boys and girls who dwell in these neighborhoods. The fact that they are physically, emotionally, socially, and educationally disadvantaged has implications for education. That many of the students are antiintellectual must also be taken into consideration. Ethnic concerns are another pertinent element.

The physical education program has particular value and can make a valuable contribution to many boys and girls if it is related particularly to the conditions that exist in their communities and to the type of educational program needed to meet their needs and interests. A consideration of the community is also important in that its support and cooperation are needed if an excellent physical education program is to be developed.

WHAT IS THE PHYSICAL EDUCATOR'S PERSONAL PHILOSOPHY OF GENERAL AND PHYSICAL EDUCATION?

After all the previous steps have been taken into careful consideration, physical educators should give thought to their own personal philosophy of general and physical education. Their training, experience, and thought have resulted in a realization of what is valuable, what is educational, and what type of program will make the greatest contribution to young people. When the first six steps, plus the development of a personal philosophy, are synthesized, they should provide a valid formula that, when implemented, will result in an outstanding program.

Objectives of general education

Teachers of physical education must first be concerned with general educational goals since physical education is a part of general education. It is important to understand the purposes of education—why schools, teachers, and curricula exist. Physical education is one part of the educational program, as is geography, science, mathematics, foreign languages, or art. Each field of specialization should keep its sights on the purposes of general education if it is to justify its rightful place in the schools. If each area of specialization in secondary education established its own objectives irrespective of the overall goals of education, chaos would result and programs would probably conflict and become distorted, depriving the students of a well-balanced educational experience. Therefore, each area of learning must realize that it is a part of the whole and that the whole is greater than the sum of its parts.

The educational objectives that are most widely supported today are those developed by two educators, Bloom and Krathwohl. Their taxonomic system divides objectives into three domains: (1) *cognitive*, (2)

Fig. 3-2. Soccer as part of the physical education program at Brockport Central School, Brockport, N.Y.

affective, and (3) *psychomotor.* The three are interdependent, continuous, and responsive to individual needs and the developmental tasks of the learner.

For purposes of this discussion the goals of general education set forth several years ago by the Educational Policies Commission, and which incorporate the cognitive, affective, and psychomotor domains, may be used. This influential policy-forming group pointed out that there are four major categories of educational objectives: (1) self-realization, (2) human relationship, (3) economic efficiency, and (4) civic responsibility. As one studies these objectives it can be seen that they relate to the cognitive, affective, and psychomotor domains discussed on pp. 76-77.

The objectives of self-realization are concerned with helping the individual to become all that he or she is capable of becoming. For example, education

should help each student to speak, read, and write effectively, to acquire fundamental knowledge and habits concerned with healthful living, and to develop ability to use leisure time in a wholesome manner.

The objectives of human relations are concerned with assisting the individual to fully understand and relate to human beings and to work cooperatively with them. Thus education should help to develop such qualities as an appreciation of the home, friendships, courtesy, the value of human welfare, and the ability to work harmoniously with others.

The objectives of economic efficiency relate to the individual as a producer and a worker as well as a buyer and a consumer. Therefore, these objectives stress, on the one hand, such things as the importance of good workmanship, selecting one's vocation carefully, occupational adjustment, appreciation, and efficiency and, on the other hand, such matters as consumer judgment, buying, and protection.

The objectives of civic responsibility pertain to the function of the individual in a law-abiding society. These goals apply to such traits as citizens' responsibility to other citizens, to country, and to the world; responsibility for being tolerant, scientific, critical, sympathetic, and cooperative as a member of a free society; and responsibility for developing an unswerving loyalty to the democratic way of life.

The four categories of objectives oulined by the Educational Policies Commission point to the overall purposes of education. The goals of physical education, therefore, must be compatible with and reinforce these objectives. The education that takes place at the gymnasium, playground, dance studio, swimming pool, and other play facilities can contribute much to the accomplishment of these worthy objectives.

Goals for secondary school students*

Teachers of physical education, in addition to understanding and appreciating the goals of general education, must also be familiar with the goals that are unique to boys and girls who are pursuing their sec-

---

*See also Chapter 2 for a further discussion of goals for secondary school students.

…cation. General educational goals …ation objectives must be interpreted …n terms of what students need at each …opment and at each educational level th… …h they pass. At the secondary level teachers sho… be aware of the developmental goals and tasks that boys and girls are accomplishing and continually try to utilize the physical education program as a means of helping students accomplish these worthy goals. Some of the developmental goals of secondary school students include:

1. *Understanding of self.* Students should understand themselves physically, mentally, emotionally, and socially—how each aspect of self is reflected in personality and how to strive for integration of the various aspects of self so as to function harmoniously as a whole.

2. *Feeling of security.* Young people become secure by acquiring skills that protect them against danger and help them earn a living and meet physical needs. They should develop inner security that encourages them to love, possess self-confidence, and have a feeling of belonging.

3. *Realistic attitude.* Young people should discover their abilities and interests, grow in understanding of self, and know their needs and capabilities. They must learn to be realistic in self-appraisal, to accept themselves, and to deal with situations and problems honestly and objectively.

4. *Self-sufficiency.* Young people become increasingly self-sufficient when they develop skills and interests that provide freedom from dependency on family and group. Then they are increasingly able to make decisions, do original thinking, and work out personal plans.

5. *Flexibility.* Young people profit from the thinking and experiences of others and are tolerant and understanding of their feelings.

6. *Social-mindedness.* Young people should establish satisfying relationships with boys and girls and with parents and adults, should serve as participating citizens in school and community, should learn about the social environment, should gain experience in group living, should learn to respect the rights of others, and should conform to the standard of acceptable behavior.

7. *Balance.* Young people should develop a variety of interests that may include sports, drama, music, and history rather than focus on one activity such as basketball or reading.

8. *Sense of personal worth.* Young people should have self-respect, self-esteem, and a sense of pride, achievement, mastery, usefulness, and success.

9. *Emotional stability.* Young people should exercise self-control and adjust to changes in a mature manner.

10. *Intellectual improvement.* Young people should develop basic mental skills, acquire knowledge, learn about the natural and physical environment, develop better understanding of the scientific approach to learning, grow in ability to listen, read, think, speak, and write, and become motivated by learning.

11. *Value consciousness.* Young people should appreciate the difference between what is right and wrong and the importance of striving for excellence, scholarly behavior, and proper ethical conduct.

If the boy or girl in secondary school can achieve these developmental tasks before completing this phase of education, he or she will have gone a long way toward becoming an educated and well-adjusted person and thus will have laid the foundations for productive, happy, and healthful living. Physical education can play an important role in helping each young person to be successful in accomplishing these goals.

What the physical education program should do for each student

The physical education program should

1. *Develop physical powers*

Body awareness	Coordination	Balance
Strength	Flexibility	Accuracy
Endurance	Speed	Posture
Muscular power	Agility	

2. *Develop skill in many activities*
   Movement fundamentals
   Fundamental activities (running, jumping, skipping)
   Individual sports (tennis, golf)
   Team sports (basketball, baseball, track and field)
   Gymnastics (tumbling and apparatus)
   Aquatics (swimming and diving)
   Rhythmic activities (dance)

79

Developing goals—what should physical education be doing for the student?

3. *Facilitate understanding of movement and physical activity*

Movement principles (role of gravity, force)

Contribution of physical activity to physical health (weight control, muscle tonus, relief of nervous tension, relaxation, absence of fatigue)

Contributions of physical activity to mental health—for example, a desirable body image (research indicates the attitudes and feelings of a person toward the body affect personality development); outlet for aggressions; release from tensions

Contributions of physical activity to academic achievement (research indicates there is a correlation between motor development and academic achievement: development of motor skills promotes physical fitness and better self-concept)

4. *Provide a meaningful social experience that encourages:*

Success in play activities

Recognition and a feeling of belonging

Knowledge to play by the rules

Development of such social traits as honesty, sportsmanship, and reliability, which contribute to the development of a socially desirable personality

Development of respect for other members of the class

Development of respect for leadership

Contribution to proper group adjustments

Major objectives of physical education

The general objectives of physical education are usually stated in broad terms without distinction between boys or girls. The physical education profession has selected, through its leading authorities, the general objectives of physical, cognitive, and motor development and affective and social adjustment.

PHYSICAL DEVELOPMENT AND THE FOUNDATIONS FOR EFFECTIVE MOVEMENT

Physical development refers to the building of organic power through development of the various systems of the body. It is concerned with a state of vigorous health and physical fitness. Physical power is built into the individual partially through participation in a program of physical activities adapted to the needs of the individual. Such participation, if engaged in wisely, results in the ability to sustain adaptive effort, to recover, and to resist fatigue. The value of this objective is that an individual will be more active, have better performance, and be healthier if the organic systems of the body are functioning properly. Physical activity helps these organs to function properly. Through vigorous muscular activity, the heart provides better nourishment for the body, and the person is able to perform work for a longer period of time with less expenditure of energy. Such a condition is necessary for a vigorous and abundant life. Throughout the entire day, a person is continually in need of vitality, strength, endurance, and stamina—both to perform routine tasks and to meet emergencies. A well-planned physical education program can help equip the student with these essential items. Thus *health related physical fitness*, stressing cardiovascular function, body composition, strength, and flexibility, should represent an objective for each secondary school boy and girl.

The physical foundations on which effective movement takes place are body awareness, strength, endurance, muscular power, coordination, flexibility, speed, agility, balance, and accuracy. Through mastery of such elements, students find personal meaning, significance, and the development of a healthy and positive self-concept.

MOTOR DEVELOPMENT AND MOVEMENT SKILLS

Neuromuscular skills are concerned with proficiency in the performance of physical activities. They include the coordination, rhythm, accuracy, and poise that lead to excellence in various games, sports, and physical skills. Motor development is concerned with cutting down wasted motion, with performing physical acts in a proficient, graceful, and esthetic manner, and with utilizing as little energy as possible in the process. This has implications for one's work, play, and any other activity requiring physical movement. This objective is sometimes referred to as ''motor'' development, a name that is derived from the relationship between a nerve or nerve fiber that connects the central nervous system, or a ganglion, and a muscle. As a consequence of the impulse thus transmitted,

Fig. 3-3. Physical education should develop skill in such activities as dance.

movement results. The impulse the nerve delivers is known as the motor impulse.

Motor, or neuromuscular, development is essential to physical education. With increased cortical control of the body there is less wasted motion; consequently, coordination and skill are increased. Greater skill and proficiency and fewer errors mean more enjoyment of the activity and a greater desire to engage in it since it is natural to like to do those things in which one excels. Consequently, it is very important to the physical education profession, to the individual, and to society in general to develop in the individual many and varied skills, increasing the probability of a fit population that is motivated to participate regularly in physical activities.

Physical education should help students develop movement skills. This means that boys and girls will learn to move confidently, meet and solve new movement demands that are encountered from day to day, and interact efficiently with other students through movement. It means that students will move in a skillful manner in the various activities that are a part of the physical education program as well as in situations they encounter during their out-of-school activities. It means that students will develop efficient use of locomotor, nonlocomotor, and manipulative skills. It

81

Developing goals—what should physical education be doing for the student?

means they will develop a sense of rhythm, time and spatial relationships, and visual-tactile coordination.

COGNITIVE DEVELOPMENT

Cognitive development implies the need to understand and appreciate the structure of movement and the ability to solve movement problems. It refers to an understanding of such movement principles as the role of gravity and force in the execution of physical movements. It includes an understanding of facts concerning the relation of physical activity to weight control, relief of nervous tension, mental health, relaxation, absence of fatigue, and muscle tonus. It includes an understanding of the many concepts incorporated in the publications, *Basic Stuff Series I and II*.

Cognitive development involves knowledge and judgment. It is concerned with an accumulation of knowledge essential to enriched living and the ability to think and interpret situations encountered in day-to-day living. This acquisition of knowledge occurs when the person gains information concerning the body, the importance of exercise, the need for a well-balanced diet, and the values of good health attitudes and habits.

Cognitive development also includes knowledge of sanitation, disease prevention, community and school agencies that provide health services, rules and regulations in regard to various games and allied activities, techniques and strategies involved in organized play, human relations, and many other items useful in living a full life. The ability to think and to interpret situations is developed through many experiences in games and sports. These experiences foster alertness and the ability to diagnose a situation under tense conditions, make a decision quickly and wisely under highly emotional conditions, and interpret human actions. A body of knowledge is stored away so that it can be called on at some future time to help make discriminatory judgments, discern right from wrong, and distinguish the logical from the illogical.

AFFECTIVE DEVELOPMENT

Affective development is concerned with helping the student adopt or establish acceptable interests, appreciations, attitudes, and values relating to physical education and physical activity. This objective relates to the worth or value students attach to physical activity in their own or other persons' life-styles, as well as to such matters as personal behavior in game and sport situations. This can range from a desire to improve group skills to assuming responsibilities for the effective functioning of a group such as a squad or team. Through participation in an excellent physical education program, each student can learn desirable ways of associating with others, the need for cooperation, and the importance of being dependable, courteous, and honest.

Affective development is also concerned with the development of an attitude that fosters good health habits and helps develop a personal regimen that contributes to physical fitness. Thus the student appreciates the contribution that physical activity can make to his or her physical, mental, social, and emotional welfare.

SOCIAL DEVELOPMENT

Social development entails adjustment to self and to others and development of desirable standards of conduct essential to good citizenship. It represents one of the main contributions of physical education to modern society. Through physical activities the individual, under qualified leadership, can be aided in making adjustments. Physical education carries its own drive. Most children and youth do not have to be motivated to engage in many of the activities that are offered. They want to participate of their own free choice because of an inner drive that propels them into action. Under such conditions rules and a framework for conduct can be established to which the individual will conform. Good human relations are developed when there is respect for ability, individual desires are subordinated to the will of the group, aid is given to the less skilled and weaker players, and the realization exists that cooperation is essential to the success of society. Physical education further aids in developing a feeling of belonging, regard for the rules of sportsmanship and fair play, courtesy, sympathy, truthfulness, fairness, honesty, and respect for authority. All are essential to good human relations— one of the most important keys to a peaceful and democratic world.

Of social value is a healthy self-concept. Since boys and girls may be accepted or rejected by their classmates because of their physical characteristics and performance, it is important for students to develop physically, not only for self-awareness but to enhance their social image. The physical educator can help achieve this goal by creating a climate conducive to the development in all students of a positive self-image.

Instructional and performance objectives

Once major objectives for the total physical education curriculum have been identified, it is important that they be accomplished through established instructional objectives for teaching units within the program. As grade level courses are formulated, sequential instructional units should be designed, incorporating appropriate objectives drawn from the goals of the total curriculum. Using unit instructional objectives as a foundation, physical education teachers next organize their daily lesson plans, including specific performance (behavioral) objectives that are in fact the outcomes of that day's learning process. This final step brings the program into the classroom and represents the critical translation of goals into real learning. Chapter 11 includes details for writing instructional and performance objectives.

Priority of objectives in physical education

Leaders of physical education are beginning to ask such questions as: Is one objective of physical education more important than the others? Where should the emphasis in physical education programs be placed? Physical educators cannot do everything; what comes first? Does physical education have a master purpose? Is there a hierarchy of objectives?

Historically, we have seen that physical education in its early days was primarily concerned with organic development. However, at the turn of the century with the introduction of the "new physical education," other objectives more closely identified with general education, such as social development, were included.

Today there are varying viewpoints in regard to the question of priority of objectives.

A survey of selected leaders in the field of physical education who were asked for their views about a hierarchy of objectives, produced some interesting information. Most professionals contacted felt that organic development and motor development are the objectives that deserve highest priority because they are most uniquely related to physical education, they are essential for fitness throughout life, they provide the impetus for the program, and they represent the objectives that can more readily be achieved. After organic and neuromuscular development, these leaders indicated that the objective most widely accepted as important is cognitive, mental, or interpretive development. The reasons listed for the importance of this objective included the significance of developing a favorable attitude toward physical education if any objective is to be achieved at all. In addition, education is primarily involved with developing a thinking, rational human being in all matters, whether it be physical development or other aspects of living. Social development ranked lowest in the survey because all areas of education deal with social development—that it is not the unique responsibility of one field such as physical education.

The survey of national leaders in physical education reflected another important consideration. Many professional leaders, stressing the national curriculum reform movement taking place today with its increased emphasis on educational priorities, believe that physical educators should rethink their positions in regard to their place in the educational system. They should reexamine how they can, through rigorous effort, make their greatest contribution in today's changing world.

Rosentswieg* conducted a study in which 100 college physical educators in Texas ranked 10 objectives of physical education. These instructors ranked organic and neuromuscular objectives highest; however, men and women disagreed about the primary objective of physical education. The statistical results of the study are illustrated in Tables 3-1 and 3-2.

---

*Rosentswieg, J.: A ranking of the objectives of physical education, Research Quarterly **40**:783, 1969.

83

Developing goals—what should physical education be doing for the student?

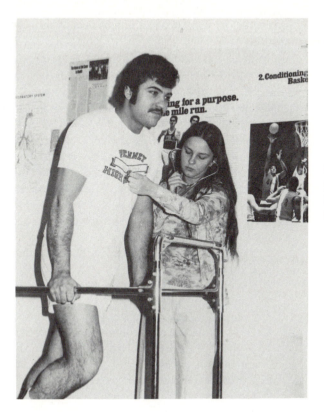

Fig. 3-4. Students participating in exercise physiology program as part of the physical education program at Penny High School, East Hartford, Conn. Girl is listening to boy's heart rate.

Table 3-1. Comparison ranking of objectives of physical education*

Objective	Ranking
Organic vigor	1
Neuromuscular skills	2
Leisure-time activities	3
Self-realization	4
Emotional stability	5
Democratic values	6
Mental development	7
Social competency	8
Spiritual and moral strength	9
Cultural appreciation	10

*From Rosentswieg, J.: A ranking of the objectives of physical education, Research Quarterly **40:**783, 1969.

Table 3-2. Ranking of objectives by sex*

Objective	Ranking	
	Males	Females
Organic vigor	1	2
Neuromuscular skills	2	1
Leisure-time activities	3	3
Self-realization	4	4
Emotional stability	5	5
Social competency	6	8
Democratic values	7	7
Mental development	8	6
Spiritual and moral strength	9	9
Cultural appreciation	10	10

*From Rosentswieg, J.: A ranking of the objectives of physical education, Research Quarterly **40:**783, 1969.

Achieving health goals through physical education

Since physical education has a direct relationship to the health of secondary school boys and girls, the ultimate objective of any health education program is to maintain and improve the health of the youngsters in the schools. This refers to all aspects of health: physical, mental, emotional, and social. The school has the responsibility to see that all students achieve and maintain optimum health, not only from a legal point of view but from the standpoint that the educational experience will be much more meaningful if optimum health exists. A well child learns more easily.

Physical educators will find many teachable moments that contribute to achievement of health goals. The opportunity is provided to impart scientifically accurate information that will contribute to better health habits on the part of students when they ask: "Why will it be necessary to take showers?" "Must we bring clean towels?" "Why must uniforms be clean?" Physical educators trained in the biological sciences can provide accurate information on various topics that directly bear on the health of students.

Physical educators can see that the health services of the school and community are understood and utilized by the students in the physical education program, whether they involve emergency care, health appraisal, communicable disease control, or other health measures.

Physical educators should provide an environment that promotes health, growth, and learning. For example, they should cooperate with the custodian in providing safe and sanitary facilities that meet acceptable health standards; in providing proper ventilation, heating, and lighting in the settings for physical education activities; in seeing that all equipment is in a safe and clean condition; and in providing a proper social and emotional atmosphere for the management of the program. They should conduct regular inspections of facilities and equipment, institute rules that will promote safety in various activities, establish procedures to be followed in the event of illness or injury to participants, and provide proper insurance protection.

Physical educators should be cognizant of the health of students in their program, be continually alert to their health practices, encourage them to improve, and take an interest in each student's total physical, emotional, social, and mental health.

Physical educators can help in the attainment of several specific objectives that the health program is attempting to accomplish in the schools. These are (1) to provide boys and girls with *health knowledge* that is reliable and based on scientific facts, (2) to help young people develop desirable *health attitudes,* and (3) to stimulate students to develop desirable *health practices.* Some specific areas in which the physical educator at the secondary level may help in the achievement of these worthy objectives are:

1. Safety education as applied to physical education activities
2. Accident prevention as applied to physical education activities
3. Dangers of self-medication
4. Dressing for warmth, comfort, and protection
5. Sanitary practices involved in physical education participation
6. Available community health services
7. Organic systems of the human body
8. Good body mechanics
9. Physical limitation and fatigue
10. Effect of depressants upon the human body
11. Effect of stimulants upon the human body
12. Structures of the human body
13. Safeguarding eyes and vision
14. Physical defects and how to correct or live with them
15. Communicable and noncommunicable diseases and minor health disorders—how to prevent and control
16. Nutrition and weight control
17. Good grooming
18. Importance of an adequate and a balanced use of free time for relaxation and recreation
19. Relationship between exercise and good health
20. Need for physical activity to develop and strengthen the body
21. First aid procedures
22. Amount of sleep and rest a student needs

85

Developing goals—what should physical education be doing for the student?

Fig. 3-5. Instructor in physical education at Hampton Institute in Hampton, Va., helps students to achieve health goals.

23. Necessity and importance of the medical examination
24. Physical fitness and health
25. First aid
26. Drugs and physical health and athletic performance

Some of the health attitudes that the physical educator can help to develop include an interest in the following:

1. Attaining and maintaining good health
2. Obtaining accurate scientific information concerning health
3. Forming proper nutrition and eating habits
4. Preventing accidents
5. Recognizing the roles of physical activity, sleep, rest, and relaxation in physical fitness
6. Separating health facts from fallacy
7. Understanding one's physical limitations

8. Correcting any remediable body defects
9. Developing good health habits
10. Evaluating one's health habits and making needed changes
11. Understanding how one's body can function to utmost capacity
12. Using the body in an efficient and graceful manner in sports activities and daily life
13. Mastering and enjoying a wide range of physical activities
14. Providing for play and large-muscle activities, as well as daily relaxation, in order to realize optimum achievement in physical and mental well-being
15. Knowing how various organic systems of the body work together
16. Acknowledging health responsibility as a member of a school, community, and family

17. Accepting reasonable responsibility in keeping the school, home, and community environment neat and clean
18. Participating in social and play activities with others
19. Being a good sportsman and taking failures and successes in stride
20. Learning to accept physical handicaps of self and others
21. Recognizing the effects of drugs, alcohol, narcotics, and tobacco on performance in physical activities

Some of the goals with which every physical educator teaching at the secondary school level should be especially concerned are to:

1. Prevent the spread of infection and insist that each member of an athletic team or physical education class have an individual towel and drinking cup and personal articles of clothing
2. Prevent the spread of infection (such as colds, influenza, mumps, and measles) and not permit students with an infection to exercise or engage in a strenuous workout
3. Give proper first-aid treatment promptly to floor or mat burns or other abrasions and wounds suffered in physical activity
4. Have a physician present at all interscholastic contests in which the injury hazard is great
5. Refuse a player reentry to a game following a severe injury, particularly when unconsciousness or injury to the head or spine has occurred
6. Work closely with the medical adviser and health department in all matters that are medical in nature, such as treating infected wounds, and honor all excuses from physicians
7. Maintain a sanitary environment in the locker and shower rooms, gymnasium, swimming pools, and other facilities of the physical education department
8. Insist on clean clothing and towels for all types of physical education activities
9. Discuss with physicians, the medical society, nurses, and other qualified persons the school policy that should govern health-related excuses from physical education

10. Encourage students with colds and other illnesses to remain home
11. Make the health and welfare of students the primary considerations in planning all physical education and athletic programs
12. See that students have adequate medical examinations if they participate in any of the various phases of the physical education program
13. Conduct an athletic program in which contests are adapted to the physical capacities and other needs of the student
14. Plan the playing seasons for athletics so they will be of reasonable duration, eliminating postseason contests and making sure players are well conditioned before competing
15. Encourage all boys and girls to receive proper sleep, rest, and nutrition and develop other desirable health practices essential to physical performance and sound health
16. Eliminate boxing as part of the physical education program
17. Be qualified in first aid
18. Allow time in planning classes to permit change of clothing and showering
19. Provide an opportunity for each student to participate in physical education class and the intramural sports program
20. Give appropriate guidance to community groups sponsoring organized competitive athletics
21. Offer a wide variety of activities based on students' interests and needs
22. Group students for participation on the basis of their abilities and needs.

Principles to keep in mind in furthering health objectives

1. Only those physical activities compatible with the pupils' health status should be included in the program. This means that such factors as students' strength, organic or functional disorders, muscular development, physical disabilities, and coordination, as ascertained through medical examinations, are taken into consideration.

87

Developing goals—what should physical education be doing for the student?

2. All students should participate in the physical education program.

3. Class size should be sufficiently small to permit effective instruction and activity. A general guide is to enroll not more than 40 pupils in a class.

4. Every possible precautionary measure should be taken to provide for safety and to prevent accidents.

5. The intramural, extramural, and interscholastic athletic programs should be laboratory periods for the class instructional program and should be conducted in the light of the welfare and health interests of those who participate.

6. Every school should have a well-defined plan that provides for the proper medical and health considerations of each pupil. This means that there should be well-thought-through policies governing procedures for such matters as prevention of disease, emergency care in event of accidents, environmental sanitation, and medical examinations.

7. The physical education program should establish and enforce sound hygienic standards.

8. The physical education teacher should be sure that each student understands the effects of certain food, drugs, smoking, and the use of alcoholic beverages on physical performance.

9. Teachers of physical education should have an understanding and an appreciation of the school health program and a desire to further the health of their pupils.

Leadership—the key to accomplishment of professional objectives

Good leadership is essential if the goals of physical education are to be realized. Without qualified leaders, programs with the most elaborate facilities and materials will fail. These leaders must have certain general and specific qualifications if they are to do an acceptable job, which includes

1. *Sound judgment, logical thinking, common sense, and the ability to discriminate right from wrong*

2. *Functional use of written and oral English* since the use of English is essential in effectively presenting programs to the public. In addition, because physical education leaders are emulated by the thousands of youths who engage in their programs, they must set a good example by using correct English.

3. *Acceptable health.* Leaders should be free from any physical or mental defects that would prevent successful leadership. Leaders should be in a state of buoyant and robust health so that they may carry out their duties regularly and effectively. They should be able to teach by doing and to participate in the activities they recommend to others. Good health is essential if this function is to be performed effectively. Most important, however, the physical education leader should be an example for the profession that stresses the importance of a healthy body.

4. *Pleasant personality.* Such traits as enthusiasm, friendliness, cheerfulness, industry, cooperation, dependability, self-control, integrity, and likableness are essential to working with people in a manner that will ensure the success of the programs concerned.

5. *Interest in and understanding of human beings.* Leaders should be familiar with the needs of the atypical as well as the normal individual. They should be conscious of the interests and capacities of those with whom they will work. Leaders should enjoy working with people. They should get along well with others, be interested in people, be able to obtain their respect, and be able to adapt to various social settings. Such qualities as patience, loyalty, tactfulness, sympathetic attitude, sincerity, friendliness, tolerance, reliability, and a good temperament are some of the essential attributes to develop if this qualification is to be met.

6. A *sincere interest in the profession.* Leaders should be willing to contribute generously their time and effort to the advancement of the profession. Individuals must believe in what they are doing and conscientiously strive to promote their work so that more people may share its benefits.

7. *Skill in many of the activities that constitute the program.* Skill is essential in appreciating and demonstrating good performance, instilling confidence, knowing the work that constitutes the profession, and adequately interpreting the program to the public.

8. *Technical training.* Specialized training is essential for the field of physical education. An understanding of the fundamental sciences and of scientific principles in the areas of philosophy, administration, and methods and materials, in addition to many other areas of knowledge, is necessary to the development of physical educators.

Physical education work has appeal to many, but not all are qualified to become leaders in this field. Only those who meet the essential qualifications should be considered, for in their hands, methods and materials may be used effectively and wisely.

Physical education leaders often remark that inadequate facilities are preventing them from doing a good job, that it is impossible to have a good program without essential indoor and outdoor equipment, and that the program is not recognized because of these deficiencies. Acres of beautiful green grass, spacious gymnasiums, and special equipment for sports and other physical education activities are very helpful. Other things being equal, they result in programs that better meet the needs and interests of the public than do programs that have poor resources. However, teachers must strive to do an effective job with what is available. Programs must be built on the status quo while effort is expended to obtain more and better facilities. Many needs can be satisfied by improvising and by obtaining auxiliary playing fields and space to tide the program over an emergency period. Doing an effective job with what is available is one of the best ways to stimulate good public relations to the point where additional facilities will be provided. The public must recognize the need for the program and how it is helping to build a better community. When the community is able to see how the program can be further aided by additional facilities, the response will be greater. If the leader exhibits apathy, indifference, and lassitude because ample resources are not provided, the response will be negative.

There is an increasing need for better qualified leaders in physical education. There must be a stringent selective policy for all preprofessional students, and standards must be established that allow only qualified individuals to become members of the profession. Only in this way will it be possible to adequately meet the needs and interests of the public, obtain their respect and enthusiasm for this work, and realize the potentialities of this great profession.

The fact that many undergraduate students and leaders in physical education do not have sufficient knowledge of the many activities that comprise their programs presents a problem. Better professional preparation in our colleges and inservice education in the schools will help in solving the problem.

Another problem encountered by many professional leaders is that of large instructional groups. Under these conditions the ratio of leaders to participants is usually very low—a few leaders responsible for many students. To do a sound instructional job under such conditions, the instructor must not overlook several important factors. There must be advance planning that takes into consideration all the equipment, visual aids, and other materials that will be needed. There must be good organization of the class, of materials, and of other essential items. Good teaching methods and proper techniques must be utilized. Safety precautions must be stressed. These items deserve attention even in smaller classes but require special attention in large groups.

Importance of methods and materials in realizing physical education objectives

Where do methods and materials fit into the total picture of leadership and teaching of physical education? The goals of physical education are worthy ones and should be accomplished in the most economical, thorough, and beneficial way possible. Since the activities that comprise physical education are the media through which the objectives are to be achieved, the activities should be taught using the best possible methods of organization and presentation. The methods and materials used should represent the experience and training of those who have worked with these activities for many years and who, through their training and experience, know the method that is most effective under various situations. The use of such methods and materials will result in the best teaching and learning situations, with consequent interest, acquisition of knowledge and skill, and proper attitudes on the part of the learner-participant.

The methods and materials selected by teachers for

89

Developing goals—what should physical education be doing for the student?

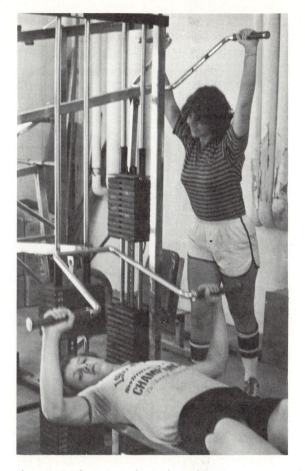

Fig. 3-6. Students in a physical conditioning program at Panama Central School, Panama, N.Y.

physical education classes should reflect the *most recent* information from research in teaching methods and subject area. Teachers who year after year teach the same activities using the same teaching methods rob the student of the benefits of the latest research and developments in educational fields.

New materials. Professional associations, state education departments, and publishers of educational texts are continually developing new materials that are important for teachers in physical education (see Chapters 15 through 18). *Basic Stuff Series I and II*, for example, should have significant impact on programs across the country. This collection of booklets developed by the National Association for Sport and

Physical Education—an association of the American Alliance for Health, Physical Education, Recreation and Dance—presents concepts and principles drawn from various disciplines. In the spring of 1981, AAHPERD sponsored a workshop to train leaders from every state and district association to carry information about this series back to their organizations for distribution. It is hoped that the knowledge and ideas developed in these booklets will be passed on to teachers in school districts across the country for implementation into school curricula.

Series I of the *Basic Stuff* texts consists of six booklets written by scholars from the major disciplines in physical education: "Exercise Physiology," "Kinesiology," "Motor Learning," "Psycho-Social Aspects," "Humanities," and "Motor Development." Using the latest information and research findings, the authors present concepts and principles that underline the objectives of activities, sports, exercise, and dance in programs for kindergarten through grade 12. The three booklets in *Basic Stuff Series II*, entitled "Early Childhood," "Childhood," and "Adolescence," written by practitioners in the field, include ideas for presenting the concepts found in Series I in ways appropriate to each of the three educational levels.

The authors present information from each of the six disciplines in a question-and-answer format, organized around six major purposes related to student participation: health (feeling good), appearance (looking good), achievement (doing better), social (getting along), esthetic (turning on), and coping with the environment (surviving). By helping youngsters to learn *about* performance and to understand the *whys* of what they are doing, educators should create the physically educated student who possesses skills, knowledge, and attitudes that last a lifetime.

New methods. Educational researchers continue to seek answers to questions about the art and science of teaching. What characteristics distinguish the outstanding teacher from the one who does an adequate but less than outstanding job? What methods of teaching produce lasting rather than tentative learning? Recent investigations into teacher effectiveness and mastery learning are beginning to provide some answers. These topics are discussed in later chapters (see Chapters 11 and 12).

Why people differ on how objectives should be achieved

Although history shows there is agreement among educators in regard to the importance of physical education at the secondary school level, some persons differ about the way physical education programs should be conducted. The many reasons for such differences of opinion include such considerations as a person's own schooling and background, parental conditioning, and philosophy of life and education in general. A person who has experienced a physical education program that did not concern itself with his or her needs may feel that physical education has little worth. In addition, some persons have given considerable thought to what is important in education. They may be realists and believe that the value of physical education comes only from a scientifically formulated curriculum—that is, activities selected on the basis of scientific evidence as to their worth, supported by principles of anatomy, physiology, kinesiology, and biomechanics. Others may be pragmatists and feel that physical education is of value only when the curriculum is based on the needs and interests of the learner and when such learning is accomplished through the problem-solving method. Still others may be naturalists who believe that physical activities develop more than strength and fitness—that is, through physical activity students learn to become contributing members of a group, develop high moral standards, and learn to express themselves better. Some individuals may subscribe to existential belief that there should be freedom of choice in physical education programs, with a variety of activities that emphasize the development of creativity.

The philosophy that seems to cut across the thinking of a majority of persons today, especially educators, is one that stresses the individual student, recognizing that young people have different needs. Individualized learning, they stress, is important for all students, including the normal, retarded, and otherwise handicapped. Furthermore, they feel that education is concerned with more than only academic excellence—that it is also concerned with such values as social effectiveness and a student's health and well-being.

Self-assessment tests

These tests are designed to assist students in determining if material and competencies presented in this chapter have been mastered.

1. Given: two departments of physical education in two different secondary schools. One department has clearly outlined goals it wishes to achieve. The other department has not given any thought to such goals. What do you project about the nature and scope of each department's program of physical education?
2. Develop a modus operandi for determining the goals a physical education program should achieve.
3. Without consulting the text, state in your own words the objectives of general education.
4. You have been asked by the Parent-Teacher Organization to give a speech on the major objectives for the physical education program in a secondary school. Prepare an outline of this speech indicating each objective and your rationale for selecting it as a goal.
5. List what you consider to be the order of importance of each of the objectives of physical education. Present documentation to support your thinking.
6. For each of the objectives of physical education, indicate how methods and materials are important to the accomplishment of that objective.

Points to remember

1. An understanding of the goals of physical education.
2. Importance of knowing the objectives of physical education.
3. Scientific principles upon which physical education programs need to be based.
4. The role of the leader in accomplishing the objectives of physical education.
5. Importance of methods and materials in achieving the objectives of physical education.

Problems to think through

1. Why is a teacher who does not know the objectives of his or her profession somewhat like a ship without a rudder?
2. Why should the goals of physical education give support to and help accomplish general education goals?

Case study for analysis

Select a secondary school and study its program of physical education to determine how well this system is accomplishing the four major goals of our profession.

91

Developing goals—what should physical education be doing for the student?

Exercises for review

1. Read four professional books in the field of physical education, and list and discuss the goals of physical education as described by the authors.
2. Categorize the specific values of physical education under each of the four major objectives.
3. What knowledge should a student possess in regard to physical education?
4. Describe a physically educated student.
5. Why is leadership so important in the achievement of educational objectives?

Selected readings

American Alliance for Health, Physical Education and Recreation: Knowledge and understanding in physical education, Washington, D.C., 1969, AAHPER.

Annarino, A.A.: The five traditional objectives of physical education, Journal of Health, Physical Education and Recreation **41**:24, 1970.

Ariel, G.: Physical education: 2001, Quest **21**:49, 1974.

Bloom, B.S., editor: Taxonomy of educational objectives. Handbook I. Cognitive domain, New York, 1956, David McKay Co., Inc.

Bloom, B.J., et al.: Handbook on formative and summative evaluation of student learning, New York, 1971, McGraw-Hill Book Co.

Bucher, C.A., and Thaxton, N.: Physical education and sport: change and challenge, St. Louis, 1981, The C.V. Mosby Co.

Bucher, C.A., and Thaxton, N.: Physical education for children: movement foundations and experiences, New York, 1979, Macmillan, Inc.

Bucher, C.A.: Administration of physical education and athletic programs, ed. 8, St. Louis, 1983, The C.V. Mosby Co.

Bucher, C.A.: Foundations of physical education, ed. 9, St. Louis, 1983, The C.V. Mosby Co.

Cratty, B.J.: Teaching motor skills, Englewood Cliffs, N.J., 1973, Prentice-Hall, Inc.

Dillon, S.V., and Franks, D.D.: Open learning environment: self identity and coping ability, The Educational Forum **39**:155, 1975.

Gronlund, N.E.: Stating behavioral objectives for classroom instruction, New York, 1970, Macmillan, Inc.

Harrow, A.J.: A taxonomy of the psychomotor domain, New York, 1972, David McKay Co., Inc.

Jewett, A.L., et al.: Educational change through a taxonomy for writing physical education objectives, Quest **15**:32, 1971.

Martens, R.: Social psychology and physical activity, New York, 1975, Harper & Row, Publishers, Inc.

Maslow, A.: Psychological data and values theory. In Abraham Maslow, A., editor: New knowledge in human values, Chicago, 1971, Henry Tegnery Co.

Park, R.J.: Alternatives and other ways: how might physical activity be more relevant to human needs in the future? Quest **21**:30, 1974.

Robb, M.D.: The dynamics of motor skill acquisition, Englewood Cliffs, N.J., 1972, Prentice-Hall, Inc.

Rosentswieg, J.: A ranking of the objectives of physical education, Research Quarterly **40**:783, 1969.

Tanner, D.: Using behavioral objectives in the classroom, New York, 1972, Macmillan, Inc.

4

A relevant physical education program

Instructional objectives and competencies to be achieved

After reading this chapter the student should be able to

1. Describe the component parts of the total school physical education program
2. Indicate the role of the basic instructional physical education program as it relates to the other component parts of the total program
3. Define what is meant by the adapted program and the contributions it makes to the secondary school student
4. Discuss why curriculum reform is essential to the future of physical education as a profession
5. Apply the procedure for developing a curriculum in physical education to a specific situation
6. Demonstrate how physical education activities should be selected for any given group of secondary school students
7. Plan a yearly, unit, and daily program in physical education
8. Utilize a systems approach to the development of a physical education curriculum
9. Propose a plan for bringing about desirable changes in a school's physical education program and outline the procedure to be followed if changes are necessary

Physical education is an integral part of the total educational process and has as its aim the development of physically, mentally, emotionally, and socially fit citizens through the medium of physical activities that have been selected with a view to realizing these outcomes. This definition of physical education is recommended for this important field of endeavor.

• *Physical education should be an integral part of the total system of education.* Its value is determined by its contributions to the objectives of education in general. It is one part of the total educational process and therefore must contribute to the achievement of the objectives of general education.

• *Physical education should promote the optimum physical, mental, emotional, moral, and social development of each student as a contributing member of a free and democratic society.* It is concerned not only with training the physical self but with the mental, social, and emotional aspects of human development. Its worth is associated with such qualities as health, organic efficiency, character, and personality. It helps each pupil in the process of normal growth and natural development.

• *A study of needs and interests of students is essential in determining the type of program content and methods for a physical education program.* The program does not exist apart from the student. The program must be made to fit the needs and interests of students, not the students made to fit the program.

Components of the secondary school physical education program have been listed by many authors and under a variety of terms. The four components of the school physical education program used here are (1) the basic instructional class program, (2) the adapted program, (3) the intramural and extramural programs, and (4) the interschool program.

The basic instructional class program

Where sound basic instructional class programs of physical education exists, they have been developed on the basis of the physical, social, mental, and emotional needs of the students. A broad and varied program of activities, both outdoor and indoor, progressively arranged and adapted to the capacities and abilities of each student, is offered.

Following are some important considerations for the basic instructional class program of physical education at the secondary level for boys and girls.

INSTRUCTIONAL NATURE

• *The physical education class is a place to teach the skills, strategy, appreciation, understanding, knowledge, rules, regulations, and other material and information that are part of the program.* It is not a place for free play, intramurals, and varsity competition. It is a place for instruction. Every minute of the class period should be devoted to teaching boys and girls the skills and subject matter of physical education.

• *Instruction should be basic and interesting.* Skills should be broken down into simple components and taught so that each individual may understand clearly what he or she is expected to accomplish and at the same time how it should be done. Utilization of demonstrations, loop films, models, slide films, posters, and other visual aids and materials can help to make the instruction more meaningful and interesting.

• *Instruction should be progressive.* There should be a definite progression from simple to complex skills. Just as a student progresses in mathematics from simple arithmetic to algebra, geometry, and calculus, so in physical education the pupil should progress from basic skills and materials to more complex and involved skills and strategies.

• *Instruction should involve definite standards.* Students should be expected to reach individualized standards of achievement in the class program. A reasonable amount of skill—whether it is in swimming, tennis, or another activity—should be mastered, depending upon individual differences. Laxity and indifference to achievement should not be tolerated any more in physical education than in any other subject area in the curriculum. When boys and girls graduate from high school, they should have met definite standards that indicate that they are *physically educated.*

• *Instruction should involve more than physical activity.* All physical education classes do not have to be held in the gymnasium where physical activity predominates. A reasonable proportion of class time, perhaps as much as 10% to 20%, can be devoted to discussions, lectures, independent study, working on learning packages, and meaningful classroom activity. Outstanding coaches often have chalk talks for their players, in which they study rules and regulations, strategies, execution of skills, and other materials that

are essential to playing the game effectively. This same principle can be applied to the physical education class period. There is a subject matter content that the student should know and understand. Physical activity should not be conducted in a vacuum; if it is, it has no meaning and will not be applied when the youngster leaves the class and school. As the student understands more fully the importance of sports and activities in life, what happens to the body during exercise, the history of the various activities in which he or she engages, and the role of physical activity in the culture of the world, the class takes on new meaning and physical education takes on new respect and prestige.

• *A textbook should be used.* Just as other subjects in the secondary school program utilize textbooks in their courses, so can physical education profitably use a textbook. Assignments can be made, discussions held, and tests given—all of which will provide the student with a much more meaningful learning experience. Physical education should not be a "snap" course. It has content, and knowledge and appreciation are to be gained from this subject just as they are, for example, in American history. One high school physical education textbook for student use is Bucher's *Physical Education for Life.**

• *Records should be kept.* Adequate records by the instructor provide tangible evidence of the degree to which objectives are being met by the students. This means that data on physical fitness, skill achievement, knowledge of rules and other information, and social conduct—such as sportsmanship—should be a part of the record.

• *There should be homework.* It is just as reasonable to assign homework in physical education as in general science. There is a great deal of subject matter to be learned and many skills to be mastered. If teachers would require their students to work on various activity skills and knowledge outside of class, there would be more time in class for meaningful teaching.

• *Each student should have a health examination before participating in the physical education program.* An annual health examination should be regarded as a minimum essential to determining the

---

*See Selected Readings.

Fig. 4-1. Students engaging in judo exercise as part of physical education program.
Courtesy New York University.

amount and nature of physical activity that best meets each student's needs.

• *The teaching load of physical educators should be determined not only by the number of instructional class periods assigned but also by the total number of activities handled by the teacher both in class and outside of class.* To do efficient work a teacher should have a normal work load—not an overload. Professional experts have established that class instruction should not exceed five hours or the equivalent of five class periods per day.

STUDENT REQUIREMENTS

Physical education fills a need of every child, just as do English, social studies, and other school experiences. Physical education became part of the school offering as a required subject to satisfy such a need and therefore should be continued on the same basis.

All students should take physical education. No one should be excused. If a boy or girl can come to school, he or she should be required to attend physical education class. At the same time, this presupposes that a program adapted to the needs of *all* pupils is provided.

If physical education is not required, many students will not have the opportunity to participate in this program because of the pressures of required courses. In addition, the student looks upon those subjects that are required as being the most important and the most necessary for success. If physical education is not on the required list, it becomes a subject of second-rate importance in the minds of some students.

Various subjects in the curriculum would not be offered unless they were required. This is probably true of physical education. Until state legislatures passed laws requiring it, this subject was ignored by many school administrators. If physical education were taught on an elective basis, it could be crowded out of the school curriculum in many communities. Either the subject would not be offered at all, or it would have to be eliminated because of low enrollment.

Even under a required program, physical education is not fulfilling its potentialities for meeting the physical, social, and mental needs of students in most

Fig. 4-2. Girls' archery, Hughes Junior High School, Los Angeles Unified School District, Los Angeles, Calif.

schools. If an elective program were instituted, deficiencies and shortages would increase, thus further handicapping the attempt to meet the welfare and needs of the student.

Physical educators should try very hard to convince administrators, school boards, and the public in general of the place of their special subject in the curriculum of the secondary school. Only as this is done will the subject occupy an important place in the school and become a respected required offering.

DAILY PERIOD

On the secondary level there should be a daily period for physical education or, through flexible scheduling, a system that provides adequate time for a meaningful physical education program. Although this does not exist in many schools at the present time, it should be a goal toward which all leaders work. The great amount of subject matter, skills, and activities to be covered and the need for regular partici-

pation in physical activities are two good reasons that a daily period is so essential.

CREDIT

Physical education, like other major subject matter offerings, should carry credit. It is included in the curriculum because it contributes to educational outcomes; thus credit is justified by the contribution physical education makes to the achievement of goals toward which all educators work.

VARIETY OF ACTIVITIES

Some physical education activities that should be covered in the secondary school are:
- *Team games:* baseball, softball, basketball, touch football, volleyball, soccer, and field hockey
- *Dual and individual sports:* track, badminton, table tennis, deck tennis, handball, horseshoes, tennis, archery, golf, and shuffleboard
- *Rhythms and dancing:* movement fundamentals,

social dancing, folk dancing, rhythms, square dancing, and modern dancing
- *Aquatic activities:* swimming, diving, lifesaving, scuba diving, water games
- *Outdoor winter sports:* skating, snow games, ice hockey, skiing, and tobogganing
- *Gymnastics:* tumbling, pyramid building, apparatus, rope climbing, and acrobatics
- *Other activities:* self-testing activities, relays, corrective exercises, camping, and outdoor education

To best meet the needs of the secondary school student, the types of activities should be many and varied. The junior high and early senior high school programs should be mainly exploratory in nature, offering a wide variety of activities, with team games modified in nature and presented in the form of lead-up activities. Toward the end of the senior high school years, there should be an opportunity to select and specialize in certain activities that will have a carry-over value after formal education ceases. Furthermore, many of the team games and other activities should be offered in a more intensive manner and in larger blocks of time as the student approaches the senior year. This allows for greater specialization in selected activities.

As a general rule, boys and girls at the secondary level, including both junior and senior high, can profit greatly from rhythmic activities such as folk and social dancing; team sports such as soccer, field hockey, softball, baseball, touch football, volleyball, and speedball; individual activities such as track and field, tennis, paddle tennis, badminton, hiking, handball, bowling, archery, and fly casting; many forms of gymnastics, such as tumbling, stunts, and apparatus activities; and various forms of games and relays. These activities will comprise the major portion of the program at the secondary level. Of course, the activities should be adapted to boys and to girls for either separate or coeducational play.

The adapted program

The adapted program refers to that phase of physical education that meets the needs of the individual who—because of some physical, mental, or cultural inadequacy, functional defect with potential for improvement through exercise, or other deficiency— temporarily or permanently may have difficulty participating in certain physical education activities. The adapted program can correct faulty body mechanics, develop physical fitness, and provide a meaningful program of physical education for students who may otherwise not be able to benefit from such an experience. The word ''adapted'' refers to the same special program known by terms such as ''corrective,'' ''handicapped,'' ''individual,'' ''modified,'' ''remedial,'' ''atypical,'' and ''restricted.''

Health examinations such as medical or physical fitness tests often indicate that some of the pupils are not able to participate in regular physical activity programs. The principle of individual differences that applies to education as a whole should also apply to physical education. Physical education leaders believe that as long as a student can come to school, he or she should be required to participate in physical education classes. Adherence to this tenet means that programs must be adapted to individual needs. Many boys and girls who are recuperating from long illnesses or operations or are suffering from other abnormal conditions require special consideration in their program of activities.

It cannot be assumed that all individuals in physical education classes are normal. Unfortunately, many programs are administered on this basis. One estimate indicates that one out of every eight students in our schools is handicapped to the extent that special provision should be made in the educational program.

Special provisions under an adapted type of program also need to be made for such high school students as the mentally retarded, the physically handicapped, the poorly coordinated, and the culturally disadvantaged. Culturally disadvantaged students, for example, often have had only limited physical education experience, either because their families have moved frequently or because they may have attended inner-city schools without adequate facilities and staff for a sound physical education program. In some cases they have had no prior training at all and have not developed the fitness needed to cope with a regular physical education program.

In summary, students having such atypical physical conditions as the following may profit from an adapted

Fig. 4-3. Wheelchair—up and down ramps.

Courtesy Julian Stein, American Alliance for Health, Physical Education, Recreation, and Dance (1900 Association Dr., Reston, Va. 22091), and Rehabilitation Education Center, University of Illinois, Champaign-Urbana, Ill.

program: (1) faulty body mechanics, (2) nutritional disturbances (overweight or underweight), (3) heart and lung disturbances, (4) postoperative or convalescent problems, (5) such disorders as hernias, weak and flat feet, and menstrual problems, (6) emotional disturbances, (7) poor physical fitness, (8) crippling conditions (such as infantile paralysis), (9) cultural disadvantages, (10) mental retardation, (11) disruptive tendencies, (12) poor coordination, and (13) gifted or creative minds.

An adapted physical education program can help these students develop the skills, fitness, and ability they need to find enjoyment and success in sports, games, and recreational activities.

FUNDAMENTAL CONSIDERATIONS FOR A SOUND ADAPTED PHYSICAL EDUCATION PROGRAM

1. A thorough medical examination is a prerequisite to assignment to the adapted program.

2. Through conferences the teacher can gain from the student much information concerning his or her interests, needs, limitations, and abilities.

3. The program of activities should be adapted to the individual and his or her atypical condition. Special developmental exercises, aquatics, and recreational sports can play an important part in most adapted programs.

4. There should be a periodic evaluation of student progress.

5. Complete records of each student should be kept. Such information as the nature of the handicapping condition, the recommendation of physician, special activities, interviews, progress, and other pertinent data should be recorded.

6. Excellent teacher-student-nurse-physician-administrator rapport is essential to an effective program.

7. The teacher of adapted physical education should work very closely with medical and guidance personnel.

8. Teachers of adapted physical education should have a sincere interest in handicapped students and should recognize the real challenge in helping them.*

---

*See also Chapter 17.

Intramural and extramural athletics programs

Although the intramural and extramural athletics programs are discussed in Chapter 5, they are listed here since they are components of the total physical education program.

The interscholastic program

Although the interscholastic program is discussed in Chapter 5, it is listed here since it is a component of the total physical education program.

Methods of improving physical education programs

An analysis of present-day physical education programs shows that they can be improved through:

1. Outlining clearly defined goals to be achieved by students at each grade level

2. Developing meaningful programs that are developmental in nature and that are characterized by progression from kindergarten through grade 12. Programs should also utilize performance and behavioral standards to assess accomplishment.

3. Individualizing programs for each student (normal, physically handicapped, mentally retarded, poorly coordinated, culturally disadvantaged)

4. Utilizing effective teaching techniques such as team teaching, independent study, student involvement, alternate programs, and applying the techniques that promote motor learning

5. Having sound instructional materials for each activity in the program. Materials on activities graded according to skill ability; audiovisual materials such as records and film; materials on the human body such as charts on organic systems, posture, safety, and first aid; and physical education textbooks that can be used by the students should be included.

6. Evaluating each student's progress toward established goals—for example, utilization of valid and scientific tests of physical fitness or skill and a sound grading system

7. Having a comprehensive record system of factors such as each student's skill achievement, physical fitness, posture, physical defects, and medical examinations, which follows the student from kindergarten to grade 12 as scholastic records do

8. Providing for a consulting service and inservice education of faculty. Teachers and administrators should have ready access to experts in all phases of physical education, including curriculum development, testing, teaching techniques, and instructional materials. There should also be provision for periodic inservice workshops for teachers of physical education and coaches.

Developing the curriculum

A well-developed physical education curriculum is more than just a course of study or a program of activities. It is a statement of the philosophy behind the physical education program. It is a set of principles guiding the staff in all phases of classroom and extraclass instruction. It is a series of objectives and goals to be achieved by those who learn. It is the program, progressive in nature from year to year and season to season, providing the best opportunity for education to the majority of students as often as possible. It is the measuring rod beside which the achievements and accomplishments of students and staff alike may be evaluated. The curriculum is all these things—a culmination of the united efforts of the many people who serve to develop it.

The purpose of a curriculum is to provide the best type of physical education program possible for students in a particular school situation. It is the responsibility of a curriculum committee not only to determine the type of program but to construct an appropriate progression of activities.

CURRICULUM COMMITTEE

The curriculum committee is usually established by the school administrator or superintendent of schools and directed to develop or revise the course of study. The head of the physical educaiton department may serve as chairperson, or the committee may select its own leader. Other members may include the physical education staff, a representative from the administration such as a school principal, individuals from the health and recreation departments of the school or community, and selected classroom teachers from the elementary grades.

The size of the committee can vary and depends largely on the size of the school and community to be served. The group may be further enlarged by visiting specialists or consultants in curriculum design who are called in to advise and guide the workshop meetings. In some school systems, developing a new curriculum may be labeled inservice education and members serving on committees may receive credits toward salary increases for their participation. When university personnel are used as consultants for curriculum workshops, committee members may be able to receive graduate credits. Serving on the curriculum committee should be a very rewarding and enriching experience for new and experienced teachers. Although completion of the study may require a full school year and after-school meetings, if a worthwhile program of physical education is the result, the entire school system and the community benefit.

STEPS IN CURRICULUM DEVELOPMENT

Collection of data. Many facts and details should first be gathered by the committee to serve as a background or foundation on which to build the new curriculum. Several factors influence a course of study, and they should be identified, analyzed, and understood. To prepare for constructing a curriculum, therefore, subcommittees should be established to investigate the following areas:

• *The current program of physical education.* The present curriculum should be evaluated in terms of student achievements and progress. Specific weaknesses and strengths of the program should be identified and areas for expansion studied. Are the proper activities being scheduled for students? Are students meeting or exceeding minimum physical fitness standards? Are more teachers or teaching stations needed at any level? These and similar questions need answering.

• *The needs of the students.* A curriculum is successful only to the extent that the students benefit from it. They learn, they achieve, they develop, and they are better prepared to face the future as a result of experiences in physical education. Therefore, it is essential that the basic needs of the students be identi-

fied. Two areas require investigation in this respect. Current research findings related to adolescent growth and development should be studied, and a survey of student interests and attitudes should be taken. The results of these two studies of the needs of students should yield helpful information and background material.

The school's community. A curriculum should fulfill the specific needs of the school's particular community. It is essential to survey the community in terms of its prospective growth and change, school population expansion, and recreational needs. Similarly, it is important to survey community feelings in regard to the physical education program itself. Would the community approve construction of athletic facilities for increased interscholastic programs, for example? Is there a desire to use school facilities for adult recreation programs? Is there an increasing need for other recreational activities? All these areas should be fully investigated before beginning the actual development of a curriculum.

The surrounding communities. The physical education curricula of schools in neighboring communities should be surveyed as well as those of distant schools similar in size, geographic location, and climate. Much can be learned from the successes of others, and valuable ideas may be gained in this way. For example, if a course in scuba diving has been successful in other schools, the curriculum committee may want to consider such an activity in its own school program.

The current trends in society and education. A study should be made of recent trends in society and in the field of education in general as well as in physical education. The latest techniques and methods of teaching, such as team teaching, learning packages, self-paced instruction, and programmed learning, should be considered. Research findings in relation to the learning process, grouping, and group dynamics should be studied. The identification of learning theories and concepts regarding motor learning that are compatible with today's physical education programs should be given careful consideration. Information on improved equipment, new resource materials, new films, and new books and games should be collected. It is particularly in this area that real stimulation and

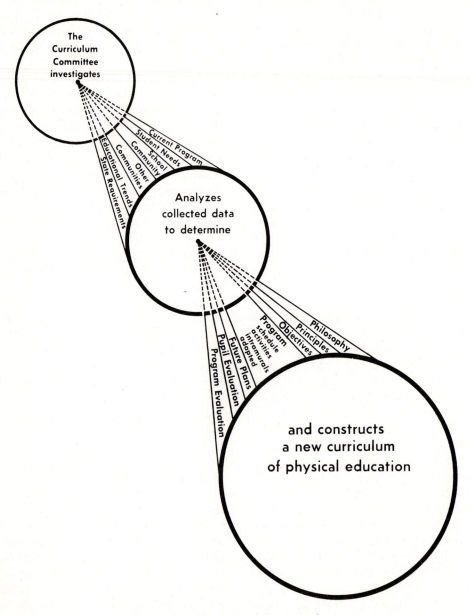

Fig. 4-4. Development of the curriculum.

impetus may be found for changing a program. At the same time provisions may be made for program experimentation and research.

The state requirements. An investigation of state regulations and requirements should also be made to ensure acceptance of a new or revised curriculum. At the same time, in order to prepare for any future requirements, it should be determined whether any changes in state standards are anticipated or are in progress.

When the subcommittees have completed studies in each of these six areas and have gathered as many facts and materials as possible, the committee as a whole should then be ready for the next step in curriculum construction.

Analysis of materials. The materials thus collected should be considered by the entire committee and serve as a basis for rebuilding the curriculum. Recommendations of the subcommittees should be heard, and the committee as a whole should then determine the direction for the program and outline necessary changes for the present and future.

Constructing the curriculum. When the data have been thoroughly analyzed and the committee has agreed on the fundamental directions of the new curriculum, smaller working groups may again be appointed for the purpose of constructing the curriculum. Using their findings as a basis on which to work, these new committees might prepare the following:

1. A statement of philosophy of the physical education department compatible with the school's philosophy of general education

2. A set of principles for teaching, incorporating new methods, materials, and techniques at specific grade and ability levels

3. A set of goals and objectives for students at each grade level with provision for individual differences

4. An outline of class activities identifying levels at which new materials should be introduced to ensure progression within the program

5. A schedule of classes, including suggested size of classes, time allotment, class sessions per week, and teacher assignments

6. An intramural and extramural program outlining activities to be included and standards for participation

7. An adapted program including methods of appraisal and referral and suggested time and types of activities for class sessions for each type of atypical condition

8. A prospectus for the years ahead suggesting additions needed in facilities and equipment and increases needed in the teaching staff and budget to accommodate innovations and expansion in the activities program and the school population

9. A synthesis of evaluation techniques covering individual record cards for students at different levels and methods of reporting and assessing achievement of objectives

10. A technique for the yearly evaluation of the total curriculum and staff, with suggested methods for curriculum revision if necessary

It should be noted here that a curriculum does not dictate to a teacher exactly what must be taught during a particular class hour. Rather it serves as an overall guide for the establishment of the program within a school. It provides consistency, progression, and structure for the total physical education program without binding or stifling the individual and collective creativity of the staff.

Adoption of the curriculum. After the curriculum has been developed, the committee as a whole should reconvene to amend and to adopt it; then it should be sent to the administration for approval and action. Subsequently, the physical education curriculum should be revised as frequently as the need dictates.

Anticipated changes in physical education programs

Traditionally, physical education curricula have been developed in a haphazard manner. Activities have often been scheduled during the fall, winter, spring, and summer seasons of the year without any logical, scientific, or systematic basis. Sometimes teachers of physical education have scheduled those activities in which they are most interested and proficient without regard to what is best for the student. Sometimes there has been insufficient consideration of objectives and how the curriculum relates to the achievement of these objectives.

In recent years many physical educators have tried to develop a more logical means of determining the activities and programs that should be included in a curriculum. In some cases, formulas have been created that help to determine the activities that should be scheduled. In other cases, step-by-step procedures have been developed that provide a rationale for matching goals with activities. Such methods of scientific curriculum development are very encouraging.

The physical education program in secondary schools will experience many changes in the years to come. Students will play an increasingly active role in determining the type of program that will best meet their needs and interests. This will be reflected in such innovations as more electives, from which students can select those activities in which they wish to specialize. In addition, there will be independent study,

Fig. 4-5. Rock climbing.

Courtesy Jerry Taylor and State University College of Arts and Science, Pottsdam, N.Y.

which will allow a student to spend an entire semester working on some sport or other project. Furthermore, students will be permitted to take tests that, if passed, will provide exemption from part or all the physical education requirement. Performance and behavioral objectives will also be widely used.

The physical education program will become more instructional in nature. Physical education will emphasize involvement in community programs and greater utilization of community resources in the organization and implementation of the curriculum.

The years ahead will see the extensive utilization of computers and measuring instruments to accurately group students in physical education classes according to abilities, traits, skills, physical fitness, and previous experience. Textbooks will be used in physical education classes as routinely as in other subject matter fields. Emphasis on movement will pervade the program throughout the school life of the student. The adapted program will also receive much more attention. In general, physical education programs will be aimed at developing physically educated students, with a trend away from teacher-centered learning toward student-motivated learnings. The conceptualized approach will focus on identifying the most important concepts to be transmitted to the student: those that define the domain of physical education and its significant contributions to human beings.

A well-developed curriculum is a prerequisite for teaching and learning and the key to successful daily programming. It requires much time and thought to construct an extensive course of study that encompasses the present and future needs of an ever-changing student body and community. However, it must be done if students are to pursue a relevant curriculum in physical education.

Redesigning the curriculum— what one state is doing*

Physical educators were invited from various sections of New York State to a workshop entitled "Rede-

---

*The University of the State of New York, The State Education Department: Final report on the workshop on the concept of "redesign" for New York State physical educators held at Stamford, New York, Oct. 11-13, 1970.

sign of Physical Education.'' A preliminary feature centered on two questions asked of workshop participants, the answers to which are particularly relevant to this chapter. One question was: ''If I had the power to change my physical education program, the first problem that I would work on would be—.'' Some of the selected answers indicate new directions for physical education:

- Individualize learner goals.
- Relate physical education to the rest of the curriculum.
- Step up electives.
- Improve staff and student communications.
- Reevaluate the relevancy of objectives.
- Reinforce basic classroom learning through physical education.

- Eliminate repetitious content.
- Provide relevant course choices for each student.
- Meet needs of students.
- Reinforce the curriculum in behavioral objectives.
- Provide a more relevant curriculum.
- Develop a program that is interesting to all students as well as enjoyable.
- Revitalize staff.
- Recognize individual abilities and offer challenges to each.
- Provide flexibility in program.
- Redesign entire curriculum.

The second question asked of physical educators who attended this conference is especially pertinent to the development of a relevant curriculum: ''What

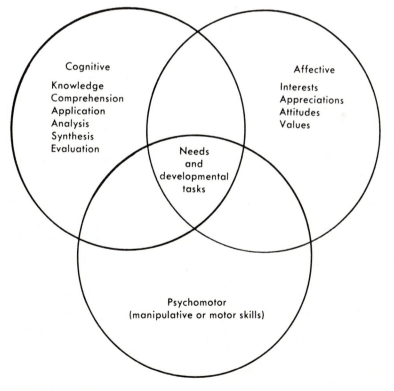

Fig. 4-6. Attention to behavioral objectives strengthens the curriculum. Cognitive, affective, and psychomotor domains are interdependent, affecting the learner's system of needs and developmental tasks.

will be the characteristics of physical education in the 1980s?'' Some selected answers were:

- Recreation oriented
- Elective in nature
- Less structured physical education classes
- Greater use of resources in community
- Stress on individuality
- Growth of girls' interscholastics
- Pupil planning
- More coeducational activities
- Individualized curriculum
- Increased voluntary participation
- New concepts in facilities
- Interdisciplinary curriculum
- Use of audiovisual television aids
- Teacher-student/teacher-teacher/student-student planning
- Involvement of community and student in planning curriculum
- Emphasis on behavioral change in students

Selection of activities

Activities such as team sports, individual and dual sports, rhythms, calisthenics, self-testing, and leisure-time and movement education activities should receive special attention. To provide students with a program consisting merely of popular team sports is neither adequate nor beneficial. Therefore, the following principles are offered as a partial guide for determining the activities to be included in a balanced program of physical education.

SELECTED PHYSIOLOGIC PRINCIPLES FOR DETERMINING ACTIVITIES

1. The physical education program should provide ample opportunities for a wide range of movements involving the large muscles.

2. The facts related to human growth and development are important considerations in curriculum construction.

3. The differences in physical capacities and abilities among students should be provided for in the program.

4. The physical fitness needs of students must be met by the physical education program.

Physiological characteristics are a major consider-

ation in the selection of activities. It is necessary to understand the physical characteristics of boys and girls at all levels of growth and to consider them in selecting activities. The program must be rewarding for students at all levels of ability.

SELECTED PSYCHOLOGICAL PRINCIPLES FOR DETERMINING ACTIVITIES

1. The physical education program should consist mostly of natural play activities.

2. Activities should be selected in the light of the psychological age characteristics of the student. For instance, the program should provide more coeducational activities for adolescents because this type of program meets the needs and interests of this age group.

3. Activities that are valuable in providing an emotional outlet for the student are needed.

4. The selection of activities should provide for progression. In the junior high school the fundamentals of tumbling and apparatus work, along with simple stunts, may be taught. In the senior high school the student should progress to more advanced work and more challenging combinations.

5. The selection and placement of activities should allow for sufficient time for the basic fundamentals of the skills to be learned.

6. Activities should be taught so that each student develops a more desirable self-concept and experiences a feeling of success.

7. Activities should be selected that best meet the seasonal interests and other concerns and abilities of the students.

8. Psychologically, activities should provide a healthy outlet for boys and girls; they should be challenging, yet within the student's physical and mental capabilities. There must be an opportunity to continually improve and develop knowledge and skills— that is, there must be a progression that will keep interest high and develop abilities to a point where an activity can be enjoyed for the pleasure of doing it correctly.

SELECTED SOCIOLOGICAL PRINCIPLES FOR DETERMINING ACTIVITIES

1. The curriculum should be rich in activities adaptable to use in leisure time. For example, such

activities as golf, tennis, and swimming should be included in the program, if possible.

2. Activities should be selected for their possible contribution to youths' training for citizenship in a democracy. The opportunity to participate in a team sport, select a captain, and be a member of a cohesive unit should be available with proper teacher guidance.

3. The curriculum should be suited to the ideals of the community as well as to its needs. It may be of value, for instance, to include square dancing, swimming, or bowling to meet the interests and needs of a community.

4. The activities that are particularly rich in opportunities for individual pursuit, such as gymnastics, are especially desirable.

5. Activities that reflect nationwide interests should be provided in the program. It is important to understand and have a working knowledge of popular American pastimes, such as baseball and basketball, because of the values inherent in these team sports and because of their national recognition and acceptance.

6. The curriculum should provide opportunities for students to develop leadership qualities.

Planning the total program

The goals of physical education can be achieved only through the execution of a well-made plan. The teacher in the physical education program has the responsibility to design the unit and daily learning tasks in terms of overall objectives. This can be done only through careful and thoughtful planning of every physical education experience so that it may be a purposeful one for each student and a step toward the attainment of the goals. See Tables 4-1, 4-2, and 4-3 for suggested curriculum design for dance, gymnastic activities, and games and sports.

PLANNING THE YEARLY PROGRAM

The program of study for a single year is based on the total curriculum, with specific objectives and activities selected according to the age and grade level of students. The program for the year should be exact and yet flexible enough to accomodate the changing needs and abilities of the students. Steps in planning for the year include both selection of objectives and activities and evaluation.

Fig. 4-7. A volleyball class at Panama Central School, Panama, N.Y.

Table 4-1. Curriculum design for dance activities*

Developmental objectives		
Cognitive	*Affective*	*Physical and psychomotor*
Interpret various social customs and racial characteristics through dance Express individual personalities spontaneously Understand various types of dance Understand the value of social contacts through dance Realize the value of dancing as a lifetime activity Use dance as a creative experience	Enjoy group participation Feel "at home" in activities of a rhythmical nature Realize that dancing is socially important Appreciate the importance of social etiquette at dances Enjoy participating in or attending dance programs	Promote growth toward accurate rhythm Develop skill in dancing with a group (square dance) Develop good poise, balance, and body control through dance Understand dance activities aid in development of pattern or rhythm in many games

*From Annarino, A.A., Cowell, C.C., and Hazelton, H.W.: Curriculum theory and design in physical education, ed. 2, St. Louis, 1980, The C.V. Mosby

Table 4-2. Curriculum design for gymnastic activities*

Developmental objectives		
Cognitive	*Affective*	*Physical and psychomotor*
Understand personal limitations and how to adjust to them Discover personal strengths and weaknesses Know the importance of skill, strength, speed, and endurance in relation to physical performance Show originality and creativeness in activities	Develop pride in growing ability and achievement Develop courage and self-confidence Develop some concepts and attitudes concerning standards of performance Appreciate the attitude of prevention (safety)	Improve body control and flexibility Develop strength Improve cardiovascular endurance Develop poise, grace, balance, and kinesthesis

*From Annarino, A.A., Cowell, C.C., and Hazelton, H.W.: Curriculum theory and design in physical education, ed. 2, St. Louis, 1980, The C.V. Mosby

Suggested units	Suggested activities	Evaluation criteria
Adventures in rhythm	Music used as accompaniment for tumbling and athletic fundamentals	Do boys and girls mix freely at dances?
	Cheerleading	Can they make a combination of steps fit together to give variety to their dancing?
	Free exercise	Do they move smoothly and rhythmically in a square dance?
United Nations festival	Folk dances of countries belonging to United Nations	Can they call a simple square dance?
Tap and clog dances	Tap routines	Do they show some degree of interest and skill in dancing?
	Composition of a tap dance	
	Arkansas Traveler	Do the pupils enjoy dancing?
Square dancing	Dive for the Oyster	Do the pupils show originality in creating movement rhythmical patterns?
	Take a Little Peek	
Social dancing	Ballroom dancing	
	Contemporary dancing	
Modern dance		
Jazz		
Ballet		

Co.

Suggested units	Suggested activities	Evaluation criteria
Stunts and tumbling	Review:	Is muscular development evident?
	Forward roll	Can pupils appraise their own performance and progress?
	Backward roll	Do the pupils enjoy self-competition?
	Somersaults	Has coordination been improved?
	Pyramids	Do pupils assist and spot one another?
	Cartwheels	What is the number of stunts performed from selected and graduated checklists for the development of routines?
	Headstands	
	Handspring	
	Advanced:	
	Combinations	
	Routines	
	Free exercise	
Apparatus	Balance beams	
	Uneven and even parallel bars	
	Mini-trampoline	
	Vaulting box	
	Rings	
	Horizontal bar	
	Horse	
	Ropes	
	Hoops	
	Balls	

Co.

Table 4-3. Developmental objectives: Cognitive, affective, and physical and psychomotor

Developmental objectives		
Cognitive	*Affective*	*Physical and psychomotor*
Demonstrate knowledge of advanced sports	Learn to sacrifice students' own personal "whims" or desires for the purpose of group or team success	Develop skills in the fundamentals of all sports activities
Know how to officiate in several sports	Learn to appraise and evaluate their own abilities	Develop desirable physiques
Know how to critically evaluate general team play	Learn to participate in large groups	Are especially efficient in at least one team and one individual or dual sport
Understand the rules, strategy, and techniques of various team and individual games and sports	Learn to control emotions in situations (games) highly charged with tension	Develop well-coordinated bodies
Understand the necessity for good equipment and its care	Learn to abide by rules and accept the official's decision as final	Develop the ability to pace themselves in competitive games
Understand the contribution of sports activities to the development of mind, body, and personality	Participate in wholesome leisure time activities	Gain poise and overcome awkwardness and self-consciousness
Understand responsibilities to others	Enjoy the fun of using and testing their growing abilities and strengths in team situations	
Understand and respect the possibilities and limitations of the human body	Respect the skill and ability of others (opponents) with the realization that they furnish opportunities to test personal skill, endurance and self-control	
Learn to think and act "on the spot" in game situations		

*From Annarino, A.A., Cowell, C.C., and Hazelton, H.W.: Curriculum theory and design in physical education, ed. 2, St. Louis, 1980, The C.V. Mosby

Objectives. In planning the yearly program, teachers should select specific objectives from those outlined in the overall curriculum, with selection based on the particular age group and developmental status of the class. A secondary objective of the goal of physical fitness, for example, may be the development of accuracy. A subordinate objective based on this factor may be the improvement of accuracy in the layup shot for basketball. Similarly, the methods of teaching activities should be selected specifically to meet these objectives. Yet plans must be adaptable, since some students may already be proficient in the skills.

Activities. The activities to be included in a particular year of study are usually outlined in the curriculum. However, the teacher should determine the amount of time to be devoted to each activity, according to the needs and desires of the group. In schools that promote student planning, the teacher may base some decisions on the results of discussions with students. For example, one class of ninth-grade girls may wish to study field hockey exclusively in the fall, while another group may want to combine field hockey with tennis. However, the teacher must ultimately decide the program for the year, after considering such factors as the seasons of the locality, the facilities and equipment available, and the size and needs of the group.

Evaluation. Methods of evaluating the year's work should be planned in advance. Student achievement and program content should be surveyed in terms of the established objectives. Procedures for evaluation are outlined in a separate chapter, but the teacher should realize that planning is an essential part of the yearly plan.

(Grades 11 and 12—games and sports)*

Suggested units	Suggested activities	Evaluation criteria
Team sports	Football-type games	Have the students had written tests on rules and strategy?
	Touch football	Have they been given standard achievement tests?
	Soccer	What are their attitudes toward their activity, selves, officials, team-
	Speedball	mates?
	Field ball	Has a sportsmanship behavior checklist been made?
	Field hockey	Have they been evaluated for promotional team work and cooperation?
	Basketball-type games	To what extent are activities used for recreation?
	Basketball	
	Volleyball	
	Softball	
Individual and dual	Archery	
recreational	Badminton	
sports	Golf	
	Tennis	
	Handball	
	Fencing	
	Deck tennis	
	Table tennis	
	Horseshoes	
	Racquetball	
	Bait and fly casting	
	Track and field	
	Snowskiing	

Co.

PLANNING THE UNIT OF TEACHING

A unit of teaching refers to the period of time during which a particular sport or activity is studied. The program for the year has several units of teaching, some scheduled for six weeks, eight weeks, and other amounts of time. The use of units in teaching physical education is of great importance to the quality of the learning experience. Unit teaching provides direction and structure to each class meeting, and the students recognize each session as being a distinct part of a whole. The physical educator, guided by the unit goals, offers progressive instruction for their attainment, and the students should be aware of the purposes of activities within the unit. In planning the unit, the teacher must consider the specific objectives and activities to be included in the unit. Because this phase of planning is the basis for daily instruction and the learning experience itself, its importance must not be underestimated.

Objectives. Specific objectives established for the year form the basis of the subobjectives in the unit plan. These subobjectives should relate to all four goals of physical education (see Chapter 5), for they are the steppingstones to achievement of overall goals. For instance, an objective may be broken down in terms of (1) *goal*—physical skill, (2) *objective*—to develop throwing power, (3) *specific objective (yearly plan)*—to improve pitching accuracy, and (4) *subobjective (unit plan)*—to pitch fast balls over the plate. Subobjectives would be established for each of the four goals in this manner, with the age level and developmental needs of the students the determining factor in estimating accomplishment.

Activities. The choice of activities to be included

Fig. 4-8. Intramural basketball at Regina High School, Cincinnati, Ohio.

in each unit of study should be made on the basis of the established subobjectives. Certain principles should be kept in mind while planning the activities in order to make the unit a complete series of learning experiences.

1. Provide a variety of learning experiences (relays, games of low organization), techniques (drills, skull sessions), and materials (audiovisual aids, outside reading).

2. Provide activities that are appropriate to the needs, age level, and developmental achievements of the group.

3. Provide activities that are progressive in nature.

4. Provide flexibility in planning so that unforeseen

interruptions and delays during the course of the unit do not hinder achievement of unit objectives.

5. Provide a definite form for the unit by introducing new skills and activities on a weekly basis or with each class session (depending upon the frequency of classes) so that students recognize progress within the unit.

6. Provide activities that promote the greatest amount of participation for the greatest number of students by utilizing all facilities and equipment available.

7. Provide for appropriate ending activities in the unit: methods of evaluation based on predetermined, specific objectives as well as some type of special, climactic activity such as a tournament, demonstration, performance, or similar presentation toward which the work has been building throughout the unit.

Table 4-4 is a sample unit taken from the yearly plan with its activities and subobjectives.

An alternative to the unit plan, called the day's order, is sometimes used. In this approach activities vary from day to day. However, within a semester of teaching, the same amount of time would be devoted to each activity as in the unit plan. When scheduling problems prevail, this plan facilitates use of gymnasium space by more than one class, for one group could be working on basketball while the other class concentrates on trampoline or apparatus work on the sidelines.

PLANNING THE DAILY LESSON

The final step necessary in the planning phase of teaching is the lesson plan itself. This has as its basis the unit plan of objectives and activities but is a complete analysis of the step-by-step procedures to be followed during each class session. This plan is probably the most important one because it represents the real contact with the students and what they should be learning. It therefore needs to be very carefully thought-out from beginning to end, with many principles followed in selecting procedures and definite objectives established for attainment.

Objectives. Each lesson must have its own set of definite objectives. Unless the teacher knows exactly what should be accomplished during the class period, the students also will not know the daily objectives.

Table 4-4. Sample basketball unit (six weeks)

	Physical fitness	Physical skills	Knowledge and appreciation	Social development
Week 1	Endurance Speed	Passes Dribbling	History Safety Rules: ball and line violations Assign notebook	New squads Discussion: leadership Elect captains
Week 2	Endurance Speed Agility	Review passes and dribbling New: reverse turn and pivot	Rules: footwork and fouls	Group responsibility in drill practice
Week 3	Endurance Speed Accuracy Agility	Review pivot New shots: layup, chest, and one hand	Offensive techniques	Safety-shooting practice
Week 4	Endurance Speed Agility Accuracy Balance	Review shooting New: foul-shooting	Defensive techniques Planned plays	Teamwork Group planning
Week 5	Endurance Speed Agility Accuracy Balance	Review shooting Tournament	Etiquette in tournament Strategy Review rules	Continue group planning and teamwork
Week 6		Evaluation of skills	Written test Notebook due	Evaluation of social cooperation Needs and plans for next unit

Procedures. An outline of procedures should be written down for each class meeting. The various methods of teaching and the progression from one type of activity to another should be carefully worked out. The following principles for the daily lesson plan should be helpful in planning procedures for a single class period:

1. Provide maximum participation for all class members. When choosing a method of teaching, the physical educator should consider the size of the class, the facilities and equipment, and the time allotment and select those procedures that allow the greatest amount of practice for the most students.

2. Provide maximum instruction and supervision. The physical educator should select formations and drills that allow instruction for small groups and supervision for the entire class.

3. Provide for safety of students. Group formations and game situations should be set up so that students are protected from danger. This includes hazards from

stationary equipment and from adjacent practicing groups.

4. Provide for the health of the students. Methods of instruction should be selected in accordance with the capacity of students for overexposure, fatigue, and extreme heat or cold.

5. Promote student interest and enthusiasm. The physical educator should strive, by varying the teaching patterns (games, drills, relays) and increasing the complexity of the work, to heighten student responses.

6. Provide for the growth and development of the students. The choice of methods should be dependent on the skill levels and accomplishments of the participants, and performances either far above or below the estimated limits of their abilities should be avoided.

7. Promote learning by proceeding from what is already known by the group to what is unknown. The students will thus be able to understand the relationship of new learning to what they have already learned.

Fig. 4-9. Wrestling at Brockport Central Schools, Brockport, N.Y.

8. Provide for self-evaluation by students and for evaluation by the group and the physical educator of daily accomplishments. In this way improvements and progress are recognized and advancement toward specific goals is kept in mind.

9. Promote carry-over values and transfer of learning into daily life situations. Students who learn cooperation and good sportsmanship on the field or in the gymnasium, for example, need help in applying such learning to other experiences. The physical educator should make references to everyday situations to pave the way for application of these traits.

10. Promote creativity on the part of each student. Contributions of new ideas and theories from all the students should be sought by the physical educator. An atmosphere should be established in which all students feel free to express themselves.

One final note in regard to the daily lesson plan concerns flexibility. Although it is essential that this plan cover the full time allotted to the class and be adhered to as closely as possible, the physical educator must be sensitive to the group's response to the procedures. It is apparent that the class tires quickly in a particular drill formation or that one of the procedures is not successful, the physical educator should

go on to a different phase of the lesson. It is always wise to plan more than the time allows so that in such instances valuable time will not be lost for lack of organization or preparation. During the outdoor season, alternate daily lesson plans should be prepared for use indoors on rainy days. In this way no time is wasted because of inclement weather.

A daily lesson plan drawn from the ninth-grade unit on basketball provides an example of one approach.

A systems approach to curriculum development in physical education

The systems approach to curriculum development in physical education includes seven steps:

1. *Identify the overall basic or developmental objectives of physical education* (example: organic development, skill development, cognitive development, social-affective development). These represent the objectives physical educators are attempting to achieve for each boy and girl. For a fuller description of each of these objectives see Chapter 5.

2. *Delineate each of the basic or development objectives listed in the first step into meaningful subobjectives desirable for each boy and girl to accomplish.*

Date: January 10
Class: Ninth grade boys and girls (approximately 30)
Teacher: Mr. EJM
Activity: Basketball (pivoting)

Equipment: AV loop film; six basketballs
Time: 48 minutes
Area: Gymnasium
Group organization: four assigned groups

Behavioral objectives

1. Each student will practice/drill with partner for eight minutes or until he has successfully completed 25 of each of the three types of passes (overhead, underhand, and chest) as previously taught. Passing station is in southwest corner of gym.
2. Each student will improve by one second his or her score for performing the zigzag dribbling course set up in the northeast corner of the gym. Improvement should be shown within eight-minute practice/drill at this station.
3. Each student will view loop film on pivots in northwest corner of gym, actively following directions provided for practice of pivots. Practice and viewing should take place in approximately eight minutes.
4. In the southeast corner of the gym each student will follow given directions on pivoting drill, actively working with a partner to complete passes with pivots. Practice will continue for eight minutes or until successful completion of 25 passes to partner, using pivots off left side and right side.
5. Each student will record his or her own progress at the end of class.
6. Each group leader will be responsible for the conduct of his or her group and will record progress of each group member on progress charts at end of class.

Time	Learning activity	Organization	Teaching behaviors
0-5 min.	Preparation for class Individualized shooting practice at baskets	Free organization for shooting at six baskets	Assist practice Check roll as class enters gym
5-37 min. (approx. 8 min. ea.)	At learning stations; 1. Review passes 2. Review dribble 3. Observe pivot loop film 4. Practice/drill pivoting then	Four groups, one at each station Rotate at 8-min. interval, or individuals rotate on completion of tasks	Assist groups (emphasize safety: keep balls under control, in assigned areas; throw only to a *ready* receiver)
	At baskets for shooting	Individual shooting practice after completing four stations	Work with pivoting
37-39 min.	Evaluation reporting	Report to leader	Collect balls and progress charts
	Question period	Informal around teacher	Question group
39-48 min.	Showering and dressing		Supervision

Questions for evaluation

1. How many of you were able to complete all your passes? To improve this skill?
2. How many of you were able to take one second off your zigzag score?
3. What is the purpose of a pivot? Why should we be able to perform to both sides? Describe balanced position. What violations pertain to pivoting?
4. Did you all record your scores with leaders?

Notes for next time:

Identifying the subobjectives brings into sharper focus what needs to be accomplished and makes much more manageable the achievement of the overall basic or developmental objective. Some examples of subobjectives of each of the overall developmental objectives are:

Organic development objective
Subobjectives:

Cardiorespiratory endurance	Posture
Muscular strength and	Flexibility
endurance	Speed
Coordination	Agility
Balance	Accuracy

Skill development objective
Subobjectives:

Locomotor and nonlocomotor activities
Movement fundamentals
General motor ability
Specific motor ability in game and sport skills

Cognitive development objective
Subobjectives:

Understanding of principles of movement (role of gravity, force)
Knowledge of rules and strategies of games and sports
Contribution of physical activity to health
Contribution of physical activity to academic achievement
Problem solving

Social-affective development objectives
Subobjectives:

Sportsmanship
Valuing
Participation
Group orientation
Attitude toward physical education
Respect for other students and leadership

3. *Identify the characteristics of the students in terms of each subobjective identified in step 2.* A characteristic, for example, of seventh-to ninth-grade students concerning the subobjective of cardiorespiratory endurance (an organic development objective) is that boys and girls at this level tire easily because of the rapid, uneven growth that takes place during this period. On the other hand, tenth- to twelfth-grade level students have either reached or nearly reached phys-

iological maturity and therefore are much better equipped to engage in vigorous activity for an extended period of time.

The characteristics of students at each educational level are analyzed in terms of the subobjectives identified in step 2. Where pertinent, distinctions between boys and girls should be taken into consideration. As a result, it is possible to see the relationship between accomplishing desired goals and the specific characteristics of the students for whom the goals are set.

4. *After identifying the characteristics of students, it is important to determine needs in relation to characteristics.* For example, because seventh- to ninth-grade students lack cardiorespiratory endurance, they need physical education experiences that account for fatiguing factors associated with time, distance, and game pressures. On the other hand, the much greater physiological development of tenth- to twelfth-graders reflects a need for more vigorous activities. Students also need guidance about matters such as amounts of activity, food habits, rest, and sleep.

5. After identifying developmental objectives, subobjectives, characteristics, and needs and seeing how all of these relate to students, *the next step is to identify appropriate activities.* For example, the schedules for students in grades seven to nine should include sports such as soccer or field hockey, in accordance with the specific school's facilities, utilizing modified and well-defined rules, including such factors as shortened periods of play, smaller playing areas, frequent time outs, and unlimited substitutions.

6. In conformance with a recent trend in curriculum development, this systems approach in physical education suggests the *listing of specific performance objectives for students in relation to their characteristics and needs and the activities appropriate to their age, physical condition, and abilities.*

For example, a performance objective for the cardiorespiratory endurance subobjective in a seventh- to ninth-grade group could be: "Given an exercise that measures cardiorespiratory endurance—for example, running a quarter of a mile—the student is able to perform without undue fatigue and with a quick heart rate recovery." A performance objective for a tenth to twelfth-grade group of students might be: "The student runs ½ mile and is able to perform without

Fig. 4-10. Intramural volleyball at Regina High School, Cincinnati, Ohio.

undue fatigue and with a quick recovery of pulse and heart rate.'' Performance objectives provide specific levels of accomplishment that indicate whether the desired objective and goals have been accomplished.

7. *The final step is to identify methods and procedures for instruction that will be most effective in achieving the desired goals.* These methods should provide variety for the students and include the application of sound motor learning theories (for example, mass versus distributed practice) and the understanding and appreciation of certain basic concepts relative to the accomplishment of the objectives (for example, follow-through helps to guarantee accuracy, which is a concept in skill development).

Development of the subobjective of cardiorespiratory endurance for seventh- to ninth-graders, for instance, might include a laboratory experiment with conditioned and nonconditioned animals, an explanation of the role and worth of cardiorespiratory en-

durance in organic development and physical fitness, an explanation in simple language of some research that indicates the physical fitness status of the students' age group, actual participation in activities that develop this quality, and an explanation of performance objectives and practice for their accomplishment.

The seven-step systems approach to curriculum development in physical education provides a logical and scientific step-by-step method for determining which activities will be offered to accomplish objectives compatible with student characteristics and needs; then it establishes performance objectives to assess whether students have met each objective. The utilization of such a systems approach assures a much more meaningful physical education program. It makes possible in our schools programs aimed at helping students become physically educated in the true sense of the word through a well-planned physical education curriculum.

To recapitulate, the systems approach to curriculum development in physical education consists of:

1. Identifying major developmental objectives of physical education

2. Delineating each major developmental objective into meaningful subobjectives

3. Identifying characteristics of students in respect to each subobjective listed in step 2

4. Identifying the needs of students in light of their characteristics listed in step 3

5. Identifying the physical education activities that meet the conditions outlined in steps 1 through 4

6. Listing performance objectives for each physical education activity in terms of conditions in steps 1 through 4

7. Identifying the best methods and procedures for instruction

Role of students in program planning

The teacher of physical education should devote some thought to the role of students in program planning. How much opportunity should they have in planning their own course of study?

The answer to this question lies in the philosophy of the department concerning student creativity and free expression. It may be believed that students should share in many phases of the planning or that they should contribute only to planning within a single unit or part of a unit. Some measure of student contribution should be sought, however, because of the inherent values of increased motivation, understanding, and creativity it affords.

Motivation. When students assist in making plans for class work, they are motivated and stimulated to participate to a greater extent. They believe that they have a share in the goals and thus a genuine desire for their accomplishment.

Understanding. The discussions necessary to bringing out student suggestions require leadership and guidance from the physical educator. Some of the purposes of physical education might be pointed out to the students at this time to widen their understanding of the program as a whole. In this way their suggestions become consistent with their own needs and with the goals of the program.

Creativity. Developing individual creativity, a general educational goal, should be included among the

Fig. 4-11. Coeducational physical education activity.

Courtesy Bill Henderson.

physical education objectives. Allowing students to contribute their own ideas and express their feelings is one way in which a creative atmosphere can be effected. While it may be difficult to promote this kind of rapport, it is indeed worth the attempt.

Problems. There are certain problems connected with student-teacher planning and the incorporation of the students' ideas into the program. In a large school where use of facilities is tightly scheduled and a prescribed regimen of activities must be followed, students would need guidance in taking these factors into consideration.

Another problem that arises in regard to student planning stems from the type of leadership offered by the teacher. There is a real art to promoting good class discussion to bring out the contributions of all students, and the physical educator must devote a great deal of time to planning key questions and ideas and to developing skill in this area.

Individualizing instruction

After incorporating student suggestions into the program, the instructional phases of physical education may be further individualized with the inclusion of variable goals for individual achievement. Inasmuch as each student within a class has attained a certain level of ability in a particular sport, the goal for that student should be improvement of his or her own skill level. Therefore, the student needs freedom to work at his or her own level of interest and rate of speed.

The student should strive to improve according to developmental tasks based on previous record and performance. For example, in a skill such as pitching a softball or a baseball, proficiency levels for some students might indicate further practice to improve accuracy and speed, whereas other advanced students may need to proceed to practicing various styles of pitching (fast ball, slow ball, inside and outside curves). Thus, in a prescribed curriculum, some students would be working on advanced skills earlier than suggested in the written guide. It must be remembered, however, that individual development rarely follows a defined pattern; consequently, freedom to explore and expand must be provided.

When the teacher has completed all phases of plan-

ning—for the curriculum, the year, the unit, and the daily lesson—and has incorporated student ideas where possible, the time has come to carry out the plan.

Concepts in physical education

The process of education is undergoing a revolution in many areas of the curriculum. The sciences, mathematics, and languages especially are utilizing new teaching methodology and new technological devices, drastically revising curricula. Today's secondary school students are familiar with concepts and areas of knowledge that formerly were reserved for college-level courses.

Physical educators are well aware that they also must adapt physical education to the demands of this era. They have found that today's students require and react well to a conceptualized approach to physical education and that this approach to teaching helps to stimulate curriculum reform in their field.

Today's physical educators realize their first task is to educate students about their bodies and the scientific principles that underlie the use of the body and to teach them to use their bodies effectively and efficiently to maintain health and fitness. The conceptualized approach to teaching physical education integrates the mental aspects with the physical.

In using the conceptualized approach, the teacher serves as a guide rather than as a storehouse of information. Students learn, for example, the principles of body leverage, hip rotation, and foot and leg placement in throwing a softball by experimenting. The physical principles involved are best understood when they are ideated by the students themselves. This approach depends on the background of the physical educator and his or her willingness to place much of the burden for learning on the students themselves. It also demands that the physical educator utilize instructional materials, such as *Basic Stuff Series I and II**, geared to secondary school students and that each student be assigned readings and outside work based on the text and related experiences in the physical education classroom.

The conceptualized approach to physical education

---

*See Chapter 4 for a more detailed discussion.

helps students to understand why certain activities are selected for inclusion in the program and why such activities as physical fitness and the lifetime sports receive such great emphasis. In this atmosphere students are drawn closer to the program which helps make physical education activities a respected and pleasurable aspect of the school day.

Projecting physical education into the future

What will physical education be like for the secondary school student of the future? Based on a knowledge of current advances in education and technology, some tentative projections can be made, but even these will be subject to change in the light of new events and discoveries.

The cost of education is constantly rising while physical education facilities have to be financed and built to accommodate students and teaching staffs. New materials, especially plastics, will probably be used extensively for gymnasium floors to reduce the constant need for refinishing thus saving on maintenance costs. Synthetics will be utilized on outdoor surfaces to make them more usable for longer portions of the year. Geodesic domes will house multiple-use gymnasiums and auxiliary physical education rooms, and air-supported structures will provide additional teaching stations.

An increasing emphasis on research in physical education will lead to more scientifically formulated curricula. Much of the benefit from this research will result in better programs for the atypical student. Mainstreaming will be utilized more and more frequently. Students in regular physical education classes will be assigned textbooks and will make use of special audiovisual aids. They will be able to analyze their performances through instant playback devices housed in physical education projection rooms.

Curricula in the secondary school will be broadened and increased, and students will be given a wider choice in the selection of activities. Alternate pro-

Fig. 4-12. Coeducational activity at Brockport Central Schools, Brockport, N.Y.

grams will be introduced. A wide variety of lifetime sports will be offered, along with physical fitness work, dance, and the usual variety of team and dual sports and activities. Portable pools will help to make swimming instruction a possibility for every student. There will be an emphasis on student-centered learning through the conceptualized approach, and the students will take on an increased responsibility for the program.

As physical education continues to assert itself in the secondary school curriculum, it will gain greater respect. This will help to decrease class size, to give classes a more homogeneous balance, to provide an individual program of physical education for every student, and to release the physical educator from the burden of nonteaching duties. Physical educators will become more expert in their own field, will attend more inservice and graduate courses, and will be more knowledgeable about education in general, which will help the profession to gain full community respect and support.

Athletics will become more educational for both boys and girls. The current trend toward varsity-level competition for both sexes as provided for under Title IX will continue and intensify, but these programs will be balanced by expanded intramural programs serving the needs and interests of all the students in the school. Interschool competition will place stronger emphasis on the individual and the effects of competition.

As sophisticated communications and transportation media continue to make the world seem smaller, the international aspects of physical education will emerge. More and more students and physical educators will cooperate in international exchange programs, and Olympic and international sports and events will become vital parts of the secondary school program.

We cannot know or predict all the changes the future will bring. We may find that the philosophy and objectives of physical education will have to be drastically revised from year to year. Continued space exploration may result in significant advances in the understanding of human physiology and psychology that will affect our programs. Government-sponsored research and pilot physical education programs,

changes in professional preparation, and revisions in general education will also have a profound effect on physical education, as will our need to serve handicapped students more meaningfully and our efforts to stabilize domestic and world conditions.

Bringing about change in the physical education curriculum

If physical education is to grow and gain educational respect, the traditional type of physical education must be evaluated carefully and alterations made in light of the changes taking place in society and general education. To bring about change, physical educators must (1) look at the catalysts that bring about curriculum change and (2) examine the ingredients essential to change.

CATALYSTS THAT BRING ABOUT CURRICULUM CHANGE

Changes occur in physical education curricula as they do in other disciplines. There is usually a continuous list of myriad proposals for change. Each proposal should be considered on its own merits and put to the test of whether or not it has value. In addition, numerous factors influence change.

National associations and agencies. The President's Council on Physical Fitness and Sports is an outstanding example of one national governmental agency that brought about significant change in programs of health, physical education, and recreation throughout the United States and the world. Through their speakers, publications, and statements through the media, many changes have taken place in the schools and colleges of this nation. In some communities physical fitness has become the overriding purpose of programs of health education and physical education, sometimes at the expense of the other objectives of these fields and a well-balanced program of activities.

Examples of other national associations and agencies that play a part in curriculum change are the National Education Association; the American Alliance for Health, Physical Education, Recreation, and Dance; the United States Office of Education (for example, Title IX regulations); the Association for Supervision and Curriculum Development; and the American Medical Association.

State associations and agencies. As national organizations influence the curricula of our schools and colleges, so do state organizations. State boards of education or departments of public instruction; state bureaus, departments, or divisions of health and physical education; state education associations; citizens' committees; teachers' associations; and associations for health, physical education, and recreation are a few examples of organizations that influence curricula. Through the publication of syllabi, sponsorship of legislation, enactment of rules and regulations, ex-ercise of supervisory powers, allocation of funds, and initiation of projects, organizations promote certain ideas and programs that initiate changes in schools and colleges.

Research. Research brings about change. As new knowledge is uncovered, more information is acquired about the learning process, new techniques are developed, and other research is conducted. Change eventually ensues if the research is significant, but the change may be slow in coming. It usually takes a long time for the creation of knowledge to penetrate to the grass roots, where it becomes part of an action program.

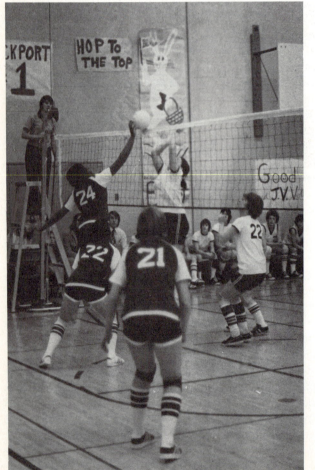

Fig. 4-13. Volleyball action at Brockport Central Schools, Brockport, N.Y.

In the field of physical education, research on motor learning, the relationship of health and physical fitness to academic achievement; movement education; cognitive learning; physiological changes that occur in the body through exercise, smoking, and environmental factors; and the relationship of mental health and physical activity represent a few examples of research that have or will have a bearing on programs throughout the country.

College and university faculties. The leaders in education from the campuses of the nation who serve as consultants, write textbooks, make speeches, and are active in professional associations help to bring about changes in education in general and in the special field of physical education.

Social forces. Such social forces in the American culture as the civil rights movement, automation, mass communication, student activism, black studies, sports promotion, and collective bargaining through unions are a few of the movements sweeping the nation that have implications for curricula in schools and colleges. In addition, social trends involving attitudes toward sex, driving, alcohol, tobacco, drugs, and narcotics affect programs. Times change, customs change, the habits of people change, and with such changes the role of educational institutions and their responsibilities to their society frequently change.

INGREDIENTS ESSENTIAL TO CHANGE

Change is a process that takes time. The steps through which change usually occurs are as follows: (1) Physical educators become aware of a needed innovation—for example, movement education in the elementary school. (2) As more and more people become interested in the innovation, an interest stage develops. Interest in movement education has been generated through experimental programs, workshops, writings, and other means of communicating the idea to educators. (3) There is an evaluation stage, in which physical educators determine the values that the change has for their programs—values that relate directly to the student and the goals of physical education. (4) More extensive experimenting with the idea takes place. (5) The change is adopted. Movement education has gone through these steps in many school systems and consequently adopted. However, many of the schools in the United States have not changed their program to incorporate movement education into their schools. Therefore, more change needs to take place not only in respect to movement education but also in many other areas.

Miller,* in her article, entitled, "A Man to Fill the Gap: The Change Agent," points out that each profession needs to bring about change to lessen the gap between what its associates know and what they practice, which requires change agents. Miller defines the change agent as "a professional who has as his major function the advocacy and introduction of innovations into practice" or a professional person who tries to influence decisions that will bring about the adoption of new ideas. In bringing about change, the change agent, according to Miller, should be aware of seven principles. They are presented here in adapted form as they relate to physical education.

• *The change agent must be well informed as to the needs and characteristics of the client system.* The students and others, such as the physical education staff in a school where individuals desire change, are the client system. It is important for the change agent to base plans on the client system's needs.

• *The change agent must develop a close relationship with the client system.* A mutual trust and respect must exist between the client system and the change agent, for change cannot effectively be brought about without confidence in the change agent.

• *The change agent must realize that change is not a unilateral undertaking but, instead, is a mutually cooperative affair.* The autocratic director of physical education who orders the innovation will never succeed. Change is a cooperative procedure between the change agent and the staff of the school system. As a result, there may be compromise and modifications, but the changes will be more permanent and better accepted by the staff.

• *The change agent should enlist the support of key leaders in the client system.* Key leaders among the students in the school system, as well as other persons, can help to ensure that the change is accepted by the client system and is adopted. Their involvement is essential in getting the entire student body and staff to accept the new development.

---

*Miller, P.L.: A man to fill the gap: the change agent, Journal of Health, Physical Education, and Recreation **40**:34, 1969.

CHECKLIST OF SELECTED ITEMS FOR EVALUATING THE PHYSICAL EDUCATION PROGRAM'S RELEVANCY TO A MODERN SECONDARY SCHOOL

Educational philosophy   Yes   No

1. Educational philosophy of the school encourages innovation.   ☐   ☐
2. Close school-community relationships are encouraged.   ☐   ☐
3. Educational program is relevant to the times.   ☐   ☐
4. Faculty and students are actively involved in the total educational program.   ☐   ☐
5. Education is individualized for each student, including culturally disadvantaged, physically handicapped, and mentally retarded.   ☐   ☐
6. The worth of a physical education program is recognized.   ☐   ☐
7. A clear written statement of educational philosophy exists, with educational objectives enumerated.   ☐   ☐

Administration

1. Administration represents a means to an end (an excellent educational program) rather than an end in itself.   ☐   ☐
2. Administrative structure enhances and facilitates the implementation of the educational program.   ☐   ☐
3. The school, including physical education, has a meaningful and accurate system of record keeping.   ☐   ☐
4. School records are accurate and up-to-date.   ☐   ☐
5. The school is open to the community.   ☐   ☐
6. Faculty and students play an important part in decision making and policy formation.   ☐   ☐
7. The school utilizes community resources.   ☐   ☐
8. Adequate facilities, supplies, and equipment exist.   ☐   ☐
9. Sufficient teaching stations exist to carry on a meaningful physical education program.   ☐   ☐
10. Scheduling is done in an effective manner, including the utilization of flexible scheduling.   ☐   ☐
11. Meetings are held regularly with the faculty to share new ideas and methods and discuss common problems.   ☐   ☐
12. Students have representation at important administrative and faculty meetings.   ☐   ☐
13. School facilities are utilized on a 12-month basis.   ☐   ☐
14. Facilities are designed to meet program needs, permit effective instruction, and ensure pupil safety.   ☐   ☐
15. The community is kept informed concerning educational objectives.   ☐   ☐
16. Equipment and supplies are checked periodically to ensure that adequate amounts are available and in good condition.   ☐   ☐
17. Administration is democratic.   ☐   ☐
18. The school building is utilized to its maximum potential.   ☐   ☐
19. The administration is receptive to innovative teaching techniques.   ☐   ☐
20. Office practice is efficient and represents a valuable service in carrying out educational objectives.   ☐   ☐
21. The administration understands the needs of physical education and its contribution to the achievement of educational goals.   ☐   ☐
22. Channels of communication are readily available to faculty and students.   ☐   ☐
23. The school conforms to Title IX regulations.   ☐   ☐

Students

1. Students participate in curriculum planning.   ☐   ☐
2. Students have the opportunity to evaluate the physical education program.   ☐   ☐
3. Students are assigned to physical education classes on the basis of their physical development, needs, and achievement.   ☐   ☐

Students—cont'd

	Yes	No
4. Students find school and physical education a pleasurable and worthwhile experience.	☐	☐
5. Students participate in a program that meets their individual needs.	☐	☐
6. Students are properly grouped for activities, according to ability and other relevant factors.	☐	☐
7. Students have good rapport with teachers.	☐	☐
8. Students have the opportunity to develop leadership potential.	☐	☐
9. Students are permitted to pursue individual dress and hair styles, providing they do not interfere with the rights of other students or their own health, safety, and performance in school activities.	☐	☐

Teachers

	Yes	No
1. Teaching assignments are made with regard to teacher's interests, strengths, and experience.	☐	☐
2. Opportunities are available to experiment with new teaching methods and materials.	☐	☐
3. The beginning teacher is provided with proper orientation to school and role to be played.	☐	☐
4. Evaluations of teachers are objective, with a view to improving teaching ability and service to students.	☐	☐
5. Accountability is required for outstanding teaching and service to students.	☐	☐
6. Salaries are assigned according to the role teachers play in the educational process.	☐	☐
7. Faculty meetings are attended regularly.	☐	☐
8. Leadership in teacher's specialty is provided for the community.	☐	☐
9. Excellent relationships exist with students.	☐	☐
10. Student leaders and paraprofessionals are utilized to develop the leadership qualities of boys and girls and to allow teachers to devote more time to teaching.	☐	☐
11. Creativity is regarded as an important quality.	☐	☐
12. New developments in special field are well known, understood, and applied.	☐	☐
13. Harmonious working relationships exist with other members of the faculty.	☐	☐
14. Professional activity is recognized as being important.	☐	☐

Physical education program

	Yes	No
1. Innovative ideas are utilized.	☐	☐
2. Students participate in the development and evaluation of the program.	☐	☐
3. Classes are of sufficient length to permit meaningful participation in scheduled activities.	☐	☐
4. The intramural program provides for maximum participation of all students.	☐	☐
5. Transportation is provided for athletic events.	☐	☐
6. A close working relationship exists between the physical education and health programs, including school physician and health services.	☐	☐
7. Provision is made for individual differences.	☐	☐
8. Progression is a characteristic of the program, with a smooth transition from elementary to junior high school and from junior high school to senior high school.	☐	☐
9. Physical education is an integral part of the total educational offering.	☐	☐
10. Program evaluation takes place periodically, resulting in necessary changes.	☐	☐
11. The program is relevant to the times, the student, and the role of education in modern society.	☐	☐
12. The Title IX regulation regarding sex discrimination is adhered to.	☐	☐

• *The change agent needs a well-developed plan and strategy for introducing change.* The plan for bringing about change in an organization cannot be a hit-or-miss affair. Foresight and planning must be used to decide the timetable for moving from one step to the next, for identifying the key leaders who in turn will influence others, and for formally approving the change. In addition, the techniques to be used, the communications media to be solicited, the persons to be seen, the meetings to be held, and the information to be imparted must all be carefully formulated so that nothing is left to chance.

• *The change agent must be willing to change and to keep up with the times.* To be effective in bringing about change in others, the change agent must be a model of change. He or she must reflect an image of self-renewal and self-improvement. Such a person is needed to empathize with others and to be sensitive to the change process.

• *The change agent needs to help others to become change agents.* The change agent's success will be determined in large measure by how well he or she gets other members of a staff or organization to become change agents themselves. They, in turn, will be abreast of the latest research findings in their field, have a recognition of the need for innovation, possess the ability to make wise choices as to what innovations will best help the client system, and be willing to try new ideas and practices.

Self-assessment tests

These tests are designed to assist students in determining if material and competencies presented in this chapter have been mastered:

1. Define the term "physical education."
2. A teacher has been in a school system for 25 years. She indicates that the physical education curriculum she developed a quarter of a century ago is the best physical education program for her school. The program includes field hockey and soccer in the fall, volleyball and basketball in the winter, and softball and tennis in the spring. What is your answer to this teacher?
3. Get permission from a junior or senior high school to observe its physical education program. After your observation, apply what you consider to be a sound procedure for curriculum development, and construct a physical education program for that school.
4. Given a group of seventh-, eighth-, ninth-, tenth-, eleventh-, or twelfth-grade students, indicate what activities you would select to be included in its physical education program. Justify your selection.
5. Prepare a yearly plan for the teaching of physical education for a tenth-grade class. Then, follow through and develop a unit plan for the teaching of swimming. Finally, develop one day's session plan that would be included in the swimming unit.
6. Utilizing the systems approach in the text, prepare a physical education program for a given group of seventh-grade students.
7. Imagine you are a faculty member in a secondary school that urgently needs to have the physical education curriculum updated and revised. The faculty is composed of elderly teachers who wish to preserve the status quo. What procedure would you advocate to bring about desirable change in this program?

Points to remember

1. Curriculum planning is a group process.
2. The physical educator has a major responsibility in the formulation of a physical education program.
3. A curriculum guide for a school system is a set of minimum standards.
4. There must be understanding of student and learning theories to produce a valid curriculum.
5. A curriculum study must fit the school system and the society in which it will operate.
6. Activities must be properly selected.
7. A systems approach may be used in curriculum development.
8. Evaluation is a never-ending process for a curriculum.
9. The daily plan, the unit plan, and the yearly plan are all outgrowths of the overall curriculum.

Problems to think through

1. How detailed should a curriculum guide be in regard to length of time spent on an activity and items to be covered in a listed activity? Why?
2. Should there be room for initiative by the physical educator working from a curriculum guide? Why?
3. Compare two schools where the same activity may be handled differently. What may make it necessary to handle this activity differently?
4. Why is it important to understand the nature of the student in curriculum planning?
5. What administrative details would limit a curriculum?
6. How can a systems approach be used to develop a physical education curriculum?

Case study for analysis

Select a secondary grade level (boys or girls) and prepare, in outline form, a curriculum for one 20-week semester. The school has separate gymnasiums for boys and girls, an outdoor turf area, two teachers for each class of 60 to 80 pupils, sufficient equipment and supplies for the largest class, and three periods of physical education weekly for each student. Analyze specific objectives, time allotment, activities, and fundamentals. Simulate a school situation by working in a committee groups.

Exercises for review

1. What steps should be followed in the preparation of a curriculum?
2. How may a physical education teacher make a contribution to a curriculum study?
3. What principles should be considered in the selection of activities for a program?
4. Who may be a part of a curriculum study group?
5. Plan a six-week unit on badminton for seventh graders.
6. Plan a daily lesson within that unit.

Selected readings

Bannon, J.J.: Leisure resources—its comprehensive planning, Englewood Cliffs, N.J., 1976, Prentice-Hall, Inc.

Brameld, T.: A cross-cutting approach to the curriculum: the moving wheel, Phi Delta Kappan, March, 1970, p. 346.

Bucher, C.A.: Physical education for life, New York, 1969, McGraw-Hill Book Co.

Bucher, C.A.: Dimensions of physical education, St. Louis, 1974, The C.V. Mosby Co.

Bucher, C.A.: Administration of physical education and athletic programs, ed. 8, St. Louis, 1983, The C.V. Mosby Co.

Bucher, C.A.: Foundations of physical education, ed. 9, St. Louis, 1983, The C.V. Mosby Co.

Crosby, M.: Who changes the curriculum and how? Phi Delta Kappan, March, 1970, p. 385.

Curriculum for people, Today's Education 60:42, 1971.

Kidd, F.M., et al.: Guidelines for secondary school physical education, Journal of Health, Physical Education, and Recreation 42:47, 1971.

Metcalf, L.E., and Hunt, M.P.: Relevance and the curriculum, Phi Delta Kappan, March, 1970, p. 358.

National Advisory Council on Education Professions Development: Mainstreaming: helping teachers meet the challenge, Washington, D.C., 1976, The Council.

Shane, J.G., and Shane, H.G.: Cultural change and the curriculum: 1970-2000 A.D., Educational Technology, April, 1970, p. 13.

Silberman, C.E.: Crisis in the classroom—the remaking of American education, New York, 1971, Random House, Inc.

Singer, R.N., et al.: Physical education: foundations, New York, 1976, Holt, Rinehart & Winston.

Toffler, A.: Future shock, New York, 1970, Random House, Inc.

University of the State of New York, The State Education Department: Final report on the workshop on the concept of "redesign" for New York State physical educators held at Stamford, New York, Oct. 11-13, 1970.

U.S. Department of Health, Education, and Welfare, Office for Civil Rights: Final title IX regulation implementing education amendments of 1972—prohibiting sex discrimination in education, Washington, D.C., 1975, HEW.

Van Til, W.: Curriculum: quest for relevance, New York, 1971, Houghton Mifflin Co.

Willgoose, C.E.: The curriculum in physical education, ed. 2, Englewood Cliffs, N.J., 1974, Prentice-Hall, Inc.

5

A sports program for the secondary school

Instructional objectives and competencies to be achieved

After reading this chapter the student should be able to

1. Understand the relationship among the intramural, extramural, and club programs; the interscholastic athletic program; the adapted program; and the basic instructional program
2. Identify the values claimed for sports as well as the harmful impact they may have on secondary school students
3. Discuss the characteristics of youth and their implications for sports programs
4. Prepare a set of guidelines for intramural, extramural, and club sports programs at both the junior high and senior high school levels
5. Prepare a set of guidelines for interscholastic sports programs at both the junior high and senior high school levels
6. Prepare a set of guidelines for sports programs for girls at the secondary school level
7. List the key provisions of Title IX and their implications for sports programs in the secondary school
8. Identify key personnel associated with sports in the secondary school

Sports have popular appeal. This appeal is revealed by the number of individuals involved in sports both as participants and as spectators, the variety of sports, the media coverage of sports programs, and the large sums of money spent on sports. In 1977, it was estimated that approximately 20 million youngsters between 8 and 16 years of age were involved in non-school sports programs.* A 1979 sports participation

*Thomas, J.R., editor: Youth sports guide for coaches and parents, Washington, D.C., 1977, The Manufacturers Life Insurance Company and The National Association for Sport and Physical Education.

survey conducted by the National Federation of State High School Associations revealed that some 5.6 million students participated in high school sports.

The recent increase in the number of sports being engaged in by people of all ages also points out the popular appeal of sports. There has been a significant increase in the number of participants in such sports as paddle ball, racquetball, road running, tennis, golf, bowling, cross-country skiing, and backpacking.

In terms of media coverage, the number of hours devoted to sporting events on television (10 to 12 hours almost every Saturday and Sunday), the number of pages covering sports in the newspapers (more space devoted to sports than all the arts combined), and the number of magazines about sports (for example, *Sports Illustrated, Sport, Inside Sports, Runners World, Body Building, Pro Sports*) all attest to their popularity. In addition to regular television coverage of sports events, many additional hours of network time are focused on special sporting events such as the Super Bowl, All Star Basketball Game, and the Olympic Games.

Millions of dollars are spent each year by manufacturers to advertise their sports products. Correspondingly, millions of dollars are spent by consumers on sports paraphernalia. In addition to the money spent by manufacturers and consumers, vast sums are spent by college and professional organizations for sports programs. The astronomical salaries paid to professional superstars is one illustration, with some professional players earning $1 million or more annually.

Relation of sports programs to other components of physical education in the secondary school

The basic instructional program in physical education is looked on by most physical education leaders as the foundation for adapted, intramural and extramural, and highly organized athletics programs. The instructional program includes the teaching of concepts, skills, and strategies. The intramural, extramural, and club programs provide opportunities for students and participants to utilize these concepts, skills, and strategies in competitive games and contests. This part of the physical education program is often referred to as the laboratory where the individual has an opportunity to experiment and test what has been learned in the instructional program.

Both intramural and extramural activities and in-

Fig. 5-1. Running the hurdles in track.

terscholastic athletics are integral phases of the total physical education program in a school. Each of the component parts has an important contribution to make to the achievement of objectives. Yet it is necessary to maintain a proper balance so that each phase enhances and does not restrict other phases of the total program.

Values claimed for sports at the secondary school level

Physical fitness. Sports contribute to physical fitness. Through the intensive training provided for competition, various components of physical fitness, such as strength, speed, endurance, agility, and coordination, are developed. The participant submits to an arduous training program, essential to excellence in competitive athletics. Many students willingly and voluntarily participate in these vigorous conditioning programs to prove their worth and ability in sports competition, thus enhancing their peer status.

Skill. Sports contribute to the development of physical skills, which leads to a high level of proficiency essential to achievement in the sports arena. The development of skill, furthermore, results in recognition, a feeling of belonging, achievement, and other psychological benefits for the participant. In addition, skill has proved to be a medium of upward social mobility for many minority groups.

Individual development. Self-discipline, self-realization, and a desire to achieve are individual qualities that many sports leaders say can be developed through sports. Individuals acquire a self-image through an assessment of how they believe they appear to others as well as themselves. To realize and assume their roles, participants must be cognizant of the roles of others. Only by differentiating themselves from others, and by perceiving the attitudes of others toward them, may players perceive their own self-image. Furthermore, self-evaluation is based on a continuing perception of the attitudes of others toward themselves. Therefore, an individual's self-concept depends, in part, on having opportunitites to observe others. The highly dynamic and competitive nature of athletics provides many such opportunities for comparison.

Self-control, many sports leaders claim, may also be enhanced through athletics. The ability to withstand or adjust to emotional stress is believed to be a result of the stress adaptation mechanism that is conditioned by exercise. Athletics provide the exercise leading to stress adaptation and, in addition, provide a highly charged atmosphere in which the individual may test and develop his or her ability to exercise self-control.

Self-discipline may also be developed since sports require a great deal of self-sacrifice. The player is called on to subordinate personal desires and wishes to those of the group, to accept the consequences of personal decisions, and to submit to strenous training programs and training rules.

Social development. The playing field provides a laboratory for the individual to compete as well as to cooperate. An individual must first compete with other members of the team for a position, then must cooperate with teammates when they compete with other teams. Under wise and effective leadership, sports leaders maintain, the playing field will provide a place for fairness, adherence to the rules, understanding and respect for others, and the ability to accept decisions and defeat.

Other values. The benefits of sports have been extolled by many research studies and references in the professional literature. For example, they have indicated that sports are a source of fun and enjoyment and an acceptable outlet for excess energy. They provide a common bond for unifying a school and student body, keep students from dropping out of school, provide an opportunity to learn worthwhile skills, develop physical abilities and fitness, and test a broad range of physical, interpersonal, leadership, and intellectual skills. Furthermore, these references suggest that sports build confidence and improve self-concept. In a practical sense, it is pointed out, they provide opportunities for scholarships and success that lie outside the formal academic structure. A study in Philadelphia, for example, showed that of 1,129 college-bound seniors participating in the athletic program, nearly 50% received scholarships.

In regard to sports motivating students to stay in school, a 3-year study in Cleveland, Ohio, showed only two dropouts among 391 athletes in a school within a setting where, at the time the study was

Fig. 5-2. Field hockey in Lexington Public Schools in Lexington, Mass.

undertaken, more than 40% of the general student body dropped out.

Conditions under which athletics become sociologically valuable

All participants as the focus of attention. There must be equal opportunity for all students to participate in the competitive athletics program, with activities that are individually adapted to the student. Athletics can be valuable when all students are given the opportunity to learn, to practice, and to play and when playing facilities and the coach's time are allocated among all students.

Focus on the individual student. Athletics must be molded and shaped for the student—not the student for athletics. Instruction must be fitted to meet the needs of the players; sports should be included that are appropriate for the age, maturity, skill, stage of growth, and physical condition of the participant.

Potential harm caused by sports

Ego-centered athletes. There is a great glorification of the star athlete by both the school and the community. These few select youngsters are frequent-

ly singled out from the team to receive special publicity and attention. There is a concentration on the few superior players instead of the many. An overemphasis on publicity often results. Consequently, these youngsters may develop inflated ideas about themselves. They begin to assume that they are "special" and should receive extra favors because of their reputations.

Winning at all costs. Some coaches have changed college transcripts in order to make players eligible, used educational monies for their own benefit, and physically abused players in their desire for winning teams.

False values. False values may likely be developed because of the emphasis placed on the star athlete or even athletics in general. The team practice session or the actual game may become more important to the youngster than any other out-of-class activity; a boy may begin to acquire the attitude that he is destined to become an "All-American" and therefore must give his full time to this endeavor. And, as the community becomes more interested in the program, the youngster may become more concerned that the spectator be pleased and less concerned about personal needs.

Harmful pressures. When parents and members

of the community develop the kind of interest in interscholastic sports that has as its main objective "winning," pressures that affect the players are likely to result. A boy or girl may feel the need to win to please the public and gain acceptance. Thus constant overstimulation of the student occurs as he or she strives to reach adult goals.

Loss of identity. Athletics can lead to a loss of individual identity. At a symposium* on problems of the black athlete, one of the major issues was the dehumanization of both black and white individuals. Symposium chairman William Ruffer emphasized the point that the athlete is not a college student in the generally accepted definition of the term. College athletes sometimes have a special dining arrangement, live in a separate dormitory, and may take a reduced academic course load. They have a controlled life guided by athletic directors and coaches, who are not always sensitive to their needs. College athletes also lead a socially regulated life. Although many colleges are reforming their athletic policies, some are still pursuing strict authoritarian procedures that prevent athletes from making their own decisions and living their own lives.

Inequitable use of facilities, leadership, and money. Athletics are only one phase of the total physical education program. Yet the amount of facilities, the number of personnel, and the proportion of money to be spent are often distributed to the interscholastic program in an inequitable proportion.

Distortion of the educational program leading to overspecialization. At times so great an emphasis is placed on producing successful athletic teams that the educational program may suffer. The academic achievement of both the participants and the nonparticipants may begin to diminish as student interests are captured by the constant excitement and tension of their team and their heroes. The young competitive player may become one-sided, with athletics becoming much too large and important a part of the individual's thinking and purposes.

Aggression and violence. Two theories of aggression have been proposed that directly involve athlet-

ics. One theory states that aggression is instinctive, and because society is aggressive by nature, athletics serve to channel these tendencies. The other theory asserts that aggression is learned behavior, and athletics aid in teaching aggression. Therefore, one might deduce that athletics contribute to a violent society. Although these two theories appear to be incompatible, they hold a valuable lesson for physical educators. Rather than accepting or rejecting either theory, one must reconsider sports curricula and evaluate the degree of aggressiveness produced by an activity in terms of both value and harmfulness to the participants.

Characteristics of youth that have implications for sports programs*

With an estimated 5.6 million students participating in school sports, a sound program is necessary if these individuals are to receive the positive values that sports can provide. Those persons responsible for organizing and conducting sports programs require helpful information and guidelines.

Physical characteristics. The adolescent growth spurt, with its increase in both height and weight, is the most noticeble sign of puberty. The amount and distribution of fat changes and the proportion of bone and muscle tissue increases. Throughout adolescence, height increases by about 15% and weight increases about 50%.

Despite general characteristics of growth patterns during the different stages of development, there are wide variations from person to person. It has been reported that a group of 12-year-old boys or girls will customarily include individuals whose body cells are not yet at the maturity level of the average 10 year old, while others will have maturational ages equivalent to 15 chronological years. Boys and girls also differ in the rate at which they achieve maturity. In boys, for example, height and weight increase sharply from 12 to 16 years of age, and in girls, height and weight increase sharply from 10 to 16 years of age. At 15 years of age, most girls have reached their final

---

*Ruffer, William A.: Symposium on problems of the black athlete, Journal of Health, Physical Education, and Recreation **42:**17, Feb. 1971.

*See also Chapter 2 on the secondary school student.

stature, while most boys do not complete their growth until 17 years of age. The body density of males is greater than females at birth and becomes greater during adolescence. The male skeleton also becomes larger and denser during adolescence than the female's.

In terms of body proportions during adolescence, one of the most noticeable changes is in the trunk of the body. The trunk widens at the hips in girls and at the shoulders in boys; the waistline drops in both sexes. Growth of the trunk accounts for about 60% of the increase in height from puberty to adulthood. A layer of fat develops in the hips and legs in both boys and girls. This fat soon disappears in boys but remains in girls. The increase in growth of the trunk

area, along with the previously increased length of the arms and legs, gives the young adolescent an awkward, gangly appearance. The early growth of hands and feet adds to the young adolescent's ungainly physique. In fact, the hands, feet, and head are the first body parts to reach their mature size.

The immature skelton is the most vulnerable part of young athletes engaged in competitive sports. The growing ends of the long bones (epiphyses) in the immature skeleton are particularly susceptible to continuous heavy pressure, blows, and sudden wrenching. If such stresses are severe enough, they may derange the normal process of bone growth and result in permanent damage.

Fig. 5-3. Skiing is a popular sport.

Courtesy Department of Intramurals,
Club Sports and Recreation, Colgate
University, Hamilton, N. Y.

The appearance of primary and secondary sex characteristics signals the beginning of puberty. A change in the shape of the hips (to become more round and wide) and the development of breasts are characteristic of girls during puberty. Menstruation also begins during this time. In the United States, the average age for the onset of menstruation (menarche) is 13 years of age, with a range of 10 to 17 years of age. In boys, puberty is signaled by the appearance of semen, pubic hair, a lower voice, and growth of the penis and testes. Boys' skin becomes coarser and thicker during puberty, and the pores change. The fatty glands become active and produce the oily secretion that results in acne during adolescence.

Social and emotional characteristics. The adolescent experiences many social and emotional problems. These disruptions are caused by the many changes taking place in the youth's life; the awkward and gangly appearance, the newly experienced sex drives, exaggerated self-assertiveness, and the strong desire for peer group approval all serve to create social and emotional problems for the adolescent. During this period of development, young people vacillate between alertness and irrationalism. They strive for recognition and form close associations with others, at first with members of the same sex and later with members of both sexes.

The development of the self-concept that started during late childhood is a large part of the concerns of adolescents, who are seeking to discover a place in society. Since their self-concept is determined mainly by the way others view them, they have a strong desire to receive admiration and approval from others. The older adolescent, for instance, takes great pride in personal grooming to gain the needed admiration of peers.

Extreme differences in physical appearance can greatly affect youngsters' emotional and social development. They react to differences in physical appearance in various ways, depending on whether these differences are used positively or negatively. For example, a boy or girl who is much larger than his or her classmates might develop a poor self-image and withdraw because of the size difference. On the other hand, if the increased size differential enables the person to excel at sports or some other activity, it could lead to a positive self-concept because of the admiration and approval athletes get from schoolmates.

Guidelines for sports programs

Sports programs should, of course, provide proper conditioning for participants under adequate medical supervision and competent coaches. The type of sports program that will make the greatest contribution to youth will

- *Base the type and intensity of competition on the growth and developmental level of the participants.* Sports programs for youths of junior high school age should consist of intramurals, extramurals, and modified varsity competition.
- *Emphasize the educational values of sports participation.* The development of the total person should be the overall objective of all sports programs for youth. Both school-sponsored and agency-sponsored programs should stress the development of cognitive and affective outcomes as well as the psychomotor domain. For example, participants should be helped to develop good sportsmanship qualities, leadership and followership qualities, a positive attitude toward sports, a knowledge of rules and strategy, and a high level of skill in a variety of sports activities.

The sports program in schools should be a part of the physical education department, with funds provided by the regular educational budget. If fees are charged for admission to games, they should go into the general fund.

Intramural, extramural, and club athletics programs

Intramural, extramural, and club activities comprise that phase of the school physical education program geared to the abilities and skills of the entire student body, with voluntary participation in games, sports, and other activities. The program offers intramural activities within a single school and such extramural activities as ''play'' and ''sports'' days that bring together participants from several schools. It is a laboratory period for sports and other activities whose fundamentals have been taught in the physical education class. It affords competition for all types of individuals—the strong and the weak, the skilled and the unskilled, the big and the small. It also includes both sexes. It is not characterized by the highly organized features of varsity sports, including their commercialism, numerous spectators, considerable publicity, and stress on winning. It is a phase of the total physical education program that should receive considerable attention.

Whereas intramural, extramural, and club activities are intended for the entire student body, varsity interschool athletics are usually designed for students who have a greater degree of skill. Intramurals are conducted primarily on a school basis whereas extramural and varsity interschool athletics are conducted on an interschool basis.

There is no conflict between these phases of the program if the facilities, time, personnel, money, and other factors are apportioned impartially—according to the degree to which each phase achieves educational objectives rather than stimulating public appeal and interest. One should not be designed as a training ground or feeding system for the other. It should be possible for a student to move from one to the other, but this should be incidental in nature rather than a planned procedure.

If conducted properly, each phase of the program can contribute to the other, and through an overall, well-balanced program, the entire student body will come to respect sports and the great potentials they have for improving physical, mental, social, and emotional growth. When a physical education program is initially developed, it would seem logical to first provide an intramural program for the majority of the students, with the interschool athletics program coming as an outgrowth. The first concern should be for the majority of the students, which is characteristic of the democratic way of life.

Although the intramural, extramural, and club athletics program is designed for every student, in practice it generally attracts the poorly skilled and moderately skilled individuals. The skilled person finds his or her niche in the varsity interschool athletic program. This has its benefits in that it is an equalizer for competition.

JUNIOR HIGH SCHOOL LEVEL

In the junior high school the main concentration in athletics should be on intramural and extramural activities. It is at this particular level that students are taking a special interest in sports, but at the same time their immaturity makes it unwise to allow them to engage in a full-scale interscholastic program. The program at this level should provide for all boys and girls, appeal to the entire student body, be well supervised by a trained physical educator, and be adapted to the needs and interests of the pupils.

The American Alliance for Health, Physical Education, Recreation, and Dance, the Society of State Directors, and many other professional groups have gone on record in favor of a broad intramural and extramural junior high athletics program. They believe that it is in the best interests of youth at this age level.

The junior high school provides a setting for developing students' fundamental skills in many sports and activities. It is a time of great energy and a time when physiological changes and rapid growth are taking place. Youth in junior high schools should have proper outlets to develop in a healthful manner.

Because of the differences in maturational levels among youth, some will need a more competitive sports program. A modified varsity sports program is recommended for these youngsters. The modified sports program should consist of some of the sports provided for students of senior high school age, but the sports should be adjusted to suit the needs, interests, and maturational levels of the participants. Examples of modifications include limiting the number of games to be played, limiting travel distance, regulating the number of players (either increasing or reducing as needed), and decreasing the length of games. The sports program for older adolescents (16 to 18 years of age) should provide opportunities for the highly skilled as well as those youngsters of average skill. To accommodate all persons in this age group, a varsity-level sports program should be provided in addition to the intramural and extramural programs. All of these activities should be extensions of a broad instructional program of physical education.

SENIOR HIGH SCHOOL LEVEL

At the senior high school level the intramural and extramural athletics program should develop its full potential. At this time the interests and needs of boys and girls require such a program. These students want and need to experience the joy and satisfaction that are a part of playing on a team, excelling in an activity with their peers, and developing skill. Every high school should see that a broad and varied program is part of the total physical education plan.

The program of intramural and extramural athletics for boys and girls should receive more emphasis than it now has at the senior high school level. It is basic to sound education. It provides a setting in which skills learned and developed in the instructional program can be put to use in a practical situation, with all the fun that comes from such competition. It should form a basis for the utilization of skills that will be used during leisure time, both in the present and in the future. Since so many teenagers lose interest in physical activity, the intramural and extramural program can help to maintain such an interest.

Corecreational activities should play a prominent part in the program, and many of the activities in the high school program adapt themselves well to both sexes. Play and sports days also offer a setting in which girls and boys can participate and enjoy worthwhile competition together.

SPORTS CLUBS

The concept of a sports club, which specializes in a particular activity, originated in Europe. Club teams are often established, with equipment and other expenses usually paid by the membership. The administration of the club is composed of either voluntary or paid coaches, managers, and officers. Some high schools have also established clubs in various sports.

Sports clubs offer many advantages. They present opportunities for students and others to engage in activities which interest them and which are not provided for in the physical education program; they offer chances for self-administration, self-financing, and self-planning; and they provide occasions for students and faculty to participate together.

Sports clubs also provide an opportunity for social

group experiences and the enjoyment of a particular sports activity. Clubs are based on many different interests, including water ballet, table tennis, boating, ice skating, skiing, soccer, karate, trap and skeet, weightlifting, archery, bowling, boxing, canoeing, cricket, racquetball, judo, lacrosse, dance, mountaineering, parachuting, hang gliding, rifle and pistol, rodeo, rugby, sailing, scuba, fencing, flying, and parachuting.

Most sports clubs in schools make provision for student administration and financing. Financing may be generated by the student body through such sources as student fees, dances, and exhibition games. A relationship with the athletic administration of the institution to facilitate matters of equipment and facility use, eligibility insurance, travel, injuries, and program assistance should be made a part of the club's bylaws, with procedures and policies clarifying this relationship.

In many organizations sports clubs are the responsibility of the intramural administrator or administrator of the physical education program. In this case, the administrator guides the club in relation to such things as constitution and bylaws, membership qualifications, dues and fees, advisors, officers, coaches, scheduling, and financing.

PRINCIPLES UNDERLYING SOUND INTRAMURAL AND EXTRAMURAL PROGRAMS

1. The goals of the intramural and extramural programs must be consistent with those of general education and physical education.
2. The supervision of the intramural and extramural programs should be the responsibility of qualified physical education personnel.
3. The planning and management of the intramural and extramural programs should be based on democratic principles and allow for participation by students as well as faculty.
4. The facilities of the entire physical education department should be available for the intramural and extramural programs to permit a wide variety of activities and maximum participation.
5. The units of competition in intramural and extramural programs should depend on such factors as the size of the school, needs and interests of students,

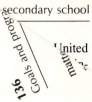

natural formation of groups within the school, and other considerations that will lend flavor to the competition.

6. Tournaments should be conducted to permit maximum participation of students.

7. Eligibility requirements should be designed to enable maximum participation of the student body and to protect the health and welfare of the participants.

8. Achievement can be recognized by some token of recognition, but awards should not become a primary motive for participation.

9. Officials should be well qualified so as to promote better play and maintain safety.

The interscholastic program

Varsity interschool athletics have an important place in senior high school. Whether they should exist at the junior high school level is controversial, but varsity interscholastic competition at the senior high school level can help players achieve a higher standard of mental, moral, social, and physical fitness, provided the overall objectives of physical education are kept in mind.

Varsity interschool athletics represent an integral part of the total physical education program and should grow out of the intramural and extramural athletics program. Athletics, with the appeal they have for youth, should be the heart of physical education.

Fig. 5-4. Girls volleyball at University School of Nashville, Nashville, Tenn.

JUNIOR HIGH SCHOOL LE...

There has been considerab... advisability of varsity athleti... junior high school level. The... by some professional organizati... taken by leaders in the field... that highly organized interschool a... ...ograms are questionable as a part of junior high school programs.

There are two sides to the question of junior high school varsity athletics, and at times they both sound convincing. Opponents have offered facts to indicate that it is risky business to permit boys and girls to play varsity interschool athletics at this level of growth and development. Those who favor these activities have shown that programs have been conducted in a safe and sound manner.

Both sides would agree, it seems, that more research is needed to determine the right policy to follow. Educators would probably be on the safe side to wait until the results of these investigations are available before encouraging varsity participation. Above all, they should follow some sound and basic principles.

1. The main object of athletics should be healthful participation and fun.

2. Every student should have opportunities to participate in a varied program of many physical activities and sports both in physical education classes and in intramural and extramural programs. These phases of the total physical education program should receive priority for the junior high schools.

3. Occasional competitive experiences in selected activities on an informal basis such as sports days and play days can be profitably conducted.

4. A complete medical examination is a prerequisite.

5. Proper leadership consists of persons who know and appreciate the physical and emotional limitations of students, the fundamentals of first aid, the sport itself, and how to condition and train players for the activity. A certified physical educator should handle such activities.

6. Because of the transitional stage in the development of adolescents of junior high school age, specific modifications should be made regarding such

males and females on all levels are much more equal in the 1980s.

PHYSIOLOGICAL CAPABILITIES OF GIRLS

From the scientific point of view, Klafs and Lyon—in their book *The Female Athlete**—list some of the physiological capabilities of girls.

1. Females are competent to participate in strenuous activity under all conditions in which men can participate.

2. Females have not in any way reached their potential in terms of performance.

3. Physiologically, females compare favorably to males; however, they will always function at a 20% to 30% handicap in power and strength because of their size and structure.

4. Current obstetrical and gynecological data refute the idea that severe exercise causes undesirable effects.

5. Endurance performance is no more damaging or overtaxing to the female than to her male counterpart.

6. The female's emotional reactions under stress are no different from those of the male; "emotional" reactions are more likely to be the result of social and cultural mores than psychophysiological factors.

7. Such differences as do exist between the sexes must be kept in mind when selecting physical activities and sports for the female. Activities should be designed or modified when necessary to take advantage of both her body structure and functions.

8. Age is not, nor should it be permitted to be, a barrier to sports activity and competition. The values of such participation are pointed up not only by the beneficial aspects that can accrue but by the fact that participating mothers are most insistent that their daughters should be activity conscious.

Furthermore, these authors stress that through a training and conditioning program, it is possible to achieve such results as increased muscular strength, increased oxygen consumption, higher maximum volume of blood per heartbeat, lowered pulse rate, more economical lung ventilation, ability to perform more work aerobically, quicker recovery after exercise, and more efficient heat dissipation.

THE CHANGE IN ATTITUDE TOWARD FEMALE ATHLETES

There has been a gradual change in the attitude of the general public as well as professionals in physical education regarding participation by girls and women in sports. When college men began to organize athletic competition in the 1800s, participation by girls and women was frowned on. Girls and women were allowed to be spectators, and some were even encouraged to be cheerleaders, but the dictates of society forbade participation by females in competitive sports.

By the beginning of the twentieth century, women began to participate in sports at some colleges. In the eastern colleges, this participation was limited mainly to play days and sports days, with an occasional invitational meet with several schools participating. The situation was different in other parts of the United States. For example, a survey in 1909 revealed that nearly half the colleges in the Midwest and West engaged in intercollegiate competition.*

The attitude of leaders in the field of women's physical education toward sports for girls and women paralleled the attitude of the general society. The platform statement issued in 1923 by the Women's Division of the National Amateur Athletic Federation indicated the thinking at that time. The stress was on participation in an informal manner and not on high-level competition. The group endorsed participation by girls and women in athletics that

Promotes competition that stresses enjoyment of sport and development of good sportsmanship and character rather than those types that emphasize the making and breaking of records and the winning of championships for the enjoyment of spectators or for the athletic reputation or commercial advantage of institutions and organizations.†

---

*Dudley, G., and Kellor, F.A.: Athletic games in the education of women, New York, 1909. Henry Holt and Co. Cited in Van Dalen, D.B., and Bennett, B.: A world history of physical education, Englewood Cliffs, N.J., 1971, Prentice-Hall, Inc., p. 451.

†Sefton, A.A.: The Women's Division—National Amateur Athletic Federation, Stanford, 1941, Stanford University Press. Quoted in Lumpkin. A.: Let's set the record straight, Journal of Physical Education and Recreation **48**:40, March 1977.

---

*Klafs, C.E., and Lyon, M.J.: The female athlete, ed. 2, St. Louis, 1978, The C.V. Mosby Co.

The emphasis was clearly on intramural and informal extramural sports activities for girls and women in 1923. That attitude prevailed until the 1960s. Probably the first tangible sign of a change in philosophy by women leaders of physical education toward the participation by girls and women in varsity athletics was in 1967 with the organization of the Commission on Intercollegiate Athletics for Women (CIAW) by the Division for Girls' and Women's Sports (DGWS). The women acted on their changed attitude in 1969 by sponsoring national championships in both gymnastics and track and field. Athletics for girls on the precollegiate level usually followed the lead of the institutions of higher learning.

In some cases, girls and women participated in highly competitive athletics before it was approved by leaders of women's physical education organizations. In Michigan, for instance, the girls' high school team of Marshall won the state basketball championship in 1905 and was greeted by ''bonfires, 10,000 Roman candles, crowds, noise, Supt. Garwood, ex-major Porter, and all red-corpuscled Marshall.''*

Females in a few black colleges in the South also participated in highly competitive sports during the early 1900s, especially basketball. It was noteworthy, however, that a highly competitive track and field program for girls and women (known as the Tuskegee Relays) was started in 1929 by Tuskegee Institute in Tuskegee, Alabama. Several of the normal schools and colleges in the local area participated in these relays.†

Today women are freely participating in almost all phases of American society on an increased basis, including participation in sports and athletics.

---

*Van Dalen, D.B., and Bennett, B.: A world history of physical education, Englewood Cliffs, N.J., 1971. Prentice-Hall, Inc., p. 451.

†Thaxton, N.A.: A documentary analysis of competitive track and field for women at Tuskegee Institute and Tennessee State University, unpublished doctoral dissertation, Springfield College, 1970. Springfield, Mass., pp. 77-79.

Fig. 5-6. Girls' competitive basketball.
Courtesy Barbara Ann Chiles, Aledo, Ill.

ADMINISTRATIVE GUIDELINES FOR SPORTS FOR GIRLS IN THE SECONDARY SCHOOL

The following guidelines are intended to help those school personnel faced with the task of either starting an athletics program for girls and women or providing coeducational sports. They are consistent with the most current information related to the medical, psychological, sociological, and educational aspects of sports for girls and women. Further, they reflect a philosophy of athletics as an educational experience for the highly skilled as well as the less skilled student. Thus school personnel should:

1. Conduct athletic programs in accordance with regulations endorsed by governing bodies such as the National Federation of State High School Associations, National Association for Girls and Women in Sports, and the Association for Intercollegiate Athletics for Women.

2. As a general rule, provide separate teams for males and females when size, strength, or other special conditions place girls and women at a disadvantage in some sports (football and wrestling, for example). In special cases, allow a highly skilled girl or woman who wishes to participate in a sport offered for males only to try out for that sport

3. Maintain an educational emphasis in the athletics program and plan schedules so that students will not be away from school and classes for long periods of time

4. Modify the rules to equalize competition in managing coeducational teams

5. Provide qualified coaches for all girls and women's sports, including competent men, with the aim of selecting the best qualified person

6. Base the athletic program on the needs, interests, and capacities of the participants

7. Encourage and facilitate research on the effects of athletics on girls and women

8. Although there are wide differences of opinion concerning athletics for girls and women, there is agreement that in any type of athletics program for them—intramural, extramural, or varsity—special consideration must be made for the participants. The program cannot be a duplication of boys' and men's athletics. There is also strong support for the idea of making women responsible for the administration, coaching, officiating, and management of the female athletics program.

Coeducational sports

Coeducational sports should be offered in the schools because of the sociological and cultural benefits that can accrue from such participation. In some cases, however, coeducational sports should be limited to the intramural and recreational levels. In instances when one or two highly skilled females would not otherwise have the opportunity to participate in a particular sport, they should be allowed to participate with males.

A 1977 Gallup Youth Survey Poll revealed that the most popular coeducational sports among teenage boys and girls were tennis, swimming, track, basketball, and baseball.

The main reason for not advocating coeducational participation in many sports on the interscholastic level is the physiological difference between males and females. Since the ratio of strength to weight is greater in males than in females, girls would be at a decided disadvantage in those sports requiring speed and strength, including all contact sports and some noncontact sports such as track and field and volleyball. If coeducational varsity teams were encouraged, males would dominate since girls' reduced capacity in speed, size, and strength limit the number who could make varsity teams.

Sports for handicapped persons

Persons with handicaps can receive the same benefits from a program of competitive sports as nonhandicapped persons do. Arnheim, Auxter, and Crowe* list the following reasons for including adapted sports activities in the physical education program.

1. There are many students assigned to an adapted physical education class who are unable to correct an existing condition, but who also are unable to participate in regular physical education. A program of adapted sports would be ideal for such students [because it would give them some form of physical activity].

---

*Arnheim, D.D., Auxter, D., and Crowe, W.C.: Principles and methods of adapted physical education and recreation, ed. 3, St. Louis, 1977, The C.V. Mosby Co., pp. 170-171.

2. Students in the adapted physical education program need activities that have carry-over value. They may continue exercise programs in the future, but they also need training in carry-over types of sports and games that will be useful to them in later life.

3. Adapted sports activities may have a therapeutic value if they are carefully structured for the student.

4. Adapted sports and games should help the handicapped individual learn to handle his or her body under a variety of circumstances.

5. There are recreational values in games and sports activities for the student who is facing the dual problem of . . . overcoming some type of handicap; some of his [or her] special needs can best be met through recreational kinds of activities.

6. A certain amount of emotional release takes place in play activities and this is important to the student with a disability.

7. The adapted sports program, whether it is given every [other] day or several weeks out of the semester, tends to relieve the boredom of a straight exercise program. No matter how carefully a special exercise program is planned and organized, it is difficult to maintain a high level of interest if the students participate in this kind of activity on a daily basis for one or more semesters.

Federal legislation, specifically P.L. 94-142 and Section 504 of P.L. 93-112, has undoubtedly played a great part in improving the educational opportunities of the handicapped. Yet the Joseph P. Kennedy Jr. Foundation probably has focused more attention on sports for handicapped persons than any other single organization or legislation. The Kennedy Foundation can also be credited with promoting and motivating others to provide significant services to handicapped persons through its many programs and activities. The most visible activity promoted by the Kennedy Foundation is the Special Olympics, organized in 1968 and designed to provide mentally retarded youths, 8 years of age and over, with opportunities to participate in a variety of sports and games on local, state, regional, national, and international levels.

The basic objectives of the Special Olympics are to:

1. Encourage development of comprehensive physical education and recreation programs for the mentally retarded in schools, day care centers, and residential facilities in every community

2. Prepare the retarded for sports competition—partic-

ularly where no opportunities and programs now exist

3. Supplement existing activities and programs in schools, communities, day care centers, and residential facilities

4. Provide training for volunteer coaches to enable them to work with youngsters in physical fitness, recreation, and sports activities*

Thousands of people volunteer to coach mentally retarded youngsters in Special Olympic events such as track and field, swimming, gymnastics, floor hockey, and volleyball. The volunteers include professional atheletes in many sports.

A Special Winter Olympics was started in 1975 for mentally retarded children and young adults. These games are sponsored by New York Special Olympics, Inc., which is affiliated with the International Special Olympics. Nearly 300 retarded and handicapped children and young adults gathered at a Catskill Mountain ski resort in Woodridge, New Jersey, to participate in the Fourth Annual Winter Games. Events included tobogganing, snowshoeing, downhill and cross-country skiing, and figure and speed skating.

Wheelchair sports are another specialized series of athletic events designed for handicapped individuals. Wheelchair sports were initiated in Veterans Administration Hospitals all over the United States as part of the medical treatment for disabled veterans returning home after World War II. The stated purpose of wheelchair sports is to "permit those with permanent physical disabilities to compete vigorously and safely under rules that are kept as close to normal rules as possible."

The first National Wheelchair Games in the United States were held at Adelphi College in 1957. A total of 371 athletes competed at the twenty-third National Wheelchair Games at St. John's University, Queens, New York, in 1979. Wheelchair basketball was the first sport in the Wheelchair Games. Currently, track and field events, archery, dartchery, lawn bowling, table tennis, snooker, weightlifting, and swimming are also included in the Wheelchair Games.

---

*Stein, J.U., and Klappholz, L.A.: Special Olympics instructional manual, Washington, D.C., 1977, AAHPER and the Kennedy Foundation, pp. 1-2.

Fig. 5-7. Mentally retarded persons preparing for soccer in the Special Olympics.

Courtesy The Joseph P. Kennedy Jr. Foundation, Special Olympics, Washington, D.C.

Competitors are grouped at the Wheelchair Games according to various disability classes: quadriplegic, paraplegic, and amputee. The various classes are also broken down into levels, based on degree of disability. For example, Class IA includes incomplete quadriplegics who have involvement of both hands, weakness of triceps, weakness throughout the trunk and lower extremities, and loss of voluntary control. The most severely disabled compete in this class. The next classification (IB) includes those incomplete quadriplegics who have some upper extremity involvement, but less than IA, with other disabilities similar to those of IA.

Sports opportunities are also available for persons in special schools for the handicapped as well as in the regular schools where handicapped students are mainstreamed. In some cases, handicapped students in special schools are permitted to compete against athletes in regular schools. For instance, the Texas University Interscholastic League (UIL) has rules that allow mentally retarded students to participate in all levels of interscholastic athletic competition. Provided they meet certain requirements, special students are allowed to compete in athletic contests when they participate in Texas Education Agency–approved secondary school programs.*

*American Association for Health, Physical Education and Recreation: The best of challenge, vol. II, Washington, D.C. 1974, The Association, p. 21.

Fig. 5-8. Girls' intramural softball at Colgate University, Hamilton, N.Y.

Key personnel in intramural, extramural, and club programs

Some of the key persons involved in a successful intramural and extramural program are the director, students and participants, unit managers, captains, officials, and an advisory council.

The director. Many schools and other organizations have established the position of director of intramurals and extramurals. In some cases, other titles that relate to the same position are used. The director is responsible for establishing programs, getting adequate funding, involving the community, and evaluating the success of the program. Some of the more specific duties of the director include:

- Providing an organizational structure that will best serve the program
- Planning programs
- Organizing tournaments and other forms of competition
- Supervising and maintaining facilities, equipment, and supplies
- Supervising personnel
- Attending and planning intramural council meetings
- Interpreting the program to the membership, administration, and general public
- Coordinating the program with allied areas such as the physical education instructional program, program for the handicapped, and varsity athletics

ing professional meetings

ring student or member opinion as to program needs
- Supervising the program
- Preparing budgets
- Evaluating the worth of the program

Student involvement. Student involvement in all phases of education has been steadily increasing, including participation in the administrative aspects of intramurals and extramurals in high schools. The roles of student leaders may range from serving as officials to being managers and office assistants.

Student director and unit manager. In some school programs the director of intramurals and extramurals appoints an upperclass student who has been involved with the program as student director. This student director may have such responsibilities as procuring officials, working with managers, issuing supplies, and scheduling.

Student unit managers have an important responsibility because they are in charge of a particular sport or activity. They usually work closely with the team captains and manage supplies and equipment, team rosters, and entry sheets, notifying teams of time and date of contests and clarifying eligibility rules.

Officials. Capable officials are vital if the program is to be run successfully. They should have special qualifications, including a knowledge of their activity, the participants, the goals of the program, and the organizations's philosophy of competition.

Intramural and extramural council. An important feature of the overall administration of an intramural or extramural program is the establishment of a council—usually an elected council with representatives from the participants, central administration, intramural staff, health department, and staff. This body is influential in the establishment of policy and practices for a broad athletic program.

The council assists the director and staff and serves in an advisory capacity. In some cases it plays an important role in the decision-making process. Councils usually have representatives from the various participating units who disseminate information to the individual teams. The council also helps in making decisions about program operation as well as serving as a sounding board for ways in which the program may be improved.

Key administrative personnel in interscholastic athletic programs

The key administrative personnel in the interscholastic athletic program include the director of athletics, coach, athletic trainer, and athletic council. Other personnel may be involved in athletic programs, such as assistant or associate athletics directors, athletics business manager, facility director, administrative assistant, equipment manager, and ticket manager.

DIRECTOR OF ATHLETICS

The athletics director implements the athletics policies established by the council, board, or committee. Responsibilities of the athletics director include preparing the budget for the sports program, purchasing equipment and supplies, scheduling athletics contests, arranging for officials, supervising eligibility requirements, making arrangements for transportation, seeing that medical examinations of athletes and proper insurance coverage are adequate, and supervising the program in general. The athletics director should be trained in the general field of physical education as well as in athletics—preferably with a background that includes a major in physical education as well as experience as a player and a coach.

In a school with a large athletics program, the director might work closely with a faculty manager or business manager of athletics. Such a director might be in charge of officials, hire ticket sellers and ticket takers, develop programs, assign security, keep financial records, pay guarantees, and be in charge of security. The director of athletics in some large programs may also have an assistant to help with such responsibilities as scheduling, staff supervision, eligibility, budgets, purchasing, travel, and insurance.

THE COACH

One of the most popular phases of professional physical education work is coaching. Many students who show exceptional skill in an interscholastic sport would like to become members of the profession in order to coach. They feel that, because they have proved themselves outstanding athletes in high school, they will be successful in coaching, which is not necessarily true. There is insufficient evidence to show that exceptional skill in any activity necessarily guarantees success in teaching that activity. Many other factors, such as personality; interest in youth; knowledge of human growth, development, and psychology; intelligence; integrity; leadership; character; and a sympathetic attitude are essential to coaching success.

Coaching should be recognized as teaching, and coaches of sports teams should be hired for their abilities as teachers as well as their expertise as coaches. Because of the nature of the position, a coach may be in a better position to teach concepts that affect daily living than any other member of a school faculty. Youth, with their inherent drive for activity and action and their quest for the excitement and competition found in sports, look up to the coach and, in many cases, feel that he or she is the type of individual to be emulated. The coach should, therefore, recognize his or her influence and see the value of such attributes as character, personality, and integrity. Although a coach must know thoroughly the game he or she is coaching, these other characteristics are equally important.

Coaching is characterized in some organizations by insecurity of position. Whether a coach feels secure depends to a great extent on the administration. Coaching offers an interesting and profitable career to many individuals. Yet these educators should recognize the possibility of finding themselves in a situation where the pressure to produce winning teams may be so great as to cause unhappiness, insecurity, and even the loss of a job.

Four qualifications characterize the outstanding coach. First, this person has an ability to teach the fundamentals and strategies of the sport: he or she *must* be a good teacher. Second, there is a need to understand the player: how a person functions at a particular level of development—with full appreciation of skeletal growth, muscular development, and physical and emotional limitations. Third, he or she understands the game coached. Thorough knowledge of techniques, rules, and similar information is basic. Fourth, the coach should be a model for the players, a person of strong character. Patience, understanding, kindness, honesty, sportsmanship, sense of right and wrong, courage, cheerfulness, affection, humor, energy, and enthusiasm are imperative.

Unfortunately, the only qualification some coaches possess is the fact that they have played the game or

sport in high school, college, or the professional ranks. It is generally recognized that the best preparation is training. In light of this fact, several states are attempting to see that coaches, particularly at the precollege level, have at least some instruction in the field of physical education.

Certification of coaches. AAHPERD's Task Force on Certification of High School Coaches, established to set standards for coaching certification, identified essential areas: (1) medical aspects of athletic coaching, (2) sociological and psychological aspects of coaching, (3) theory and techniques of coaching, (4) kinesiological foundations of coaching, and (5) physiological foundations of coaching. Coaches should be encouraged to seek training even if certification standards have not yet been required by their particular state. The trend toward certification is growing, and thorough training of all coaches is essential to the health and performance of athletes.

Noble and Sigle* conducted a survey of 50 states and Washington, D.C., regarding the certification of coaches. The responses provide the following information.

- In 34 states nonteachers are allowed to coach either on a regular basis or as an emergency device.
- In 20 states there are no minimum requirements other than age.
- In 8 states a teaching certificate is required.
- In 1 state a Red Cross first aid course is required.
- In 1 state attendance is required at a rules clinic in the sport an educator coaches.
- In 1 state coaches are required to have a knowledge of developmental skills of the sport they coach.
- In 5 states (Iowa, Minnesota, Pennsylvania, South Dakota, and Wyoming), paraprofessionals are required to complete a coaching preparation program.
- In 15 states limitations are placed on nonteaching coaches, such as barring them from head coach positions in all or some sports and assigning a teacher to accompany the group on road trips.

---

*Noble, L., and Sigle, G.: Minimum requirements for interscholastic coaches, Journal of Physical Education and Recreation **51:** 32-33, Nov./Dec. 1980.

- In 8 states (Arkansas, Iowa, Minnesota, New York, Oklahoma, Oregon, South Dakota, and Wyoming) additional requirements are necessary, such as completion of certain courses, working experience in physical education, knowledge of first aid, coaching experience, and certification in physical education.

Evaluation of coaches. The Beaverton (Oregon) School District has a form that they use in the evaluation of their coaches.*

THE ATHLETIC TRAINER

The profession of athletic training has taken on greater significance in recent years with the increase in sports programs and the recognition that the health of the athlete is an important consideration. Today's athletic trainers need special preparation to handle duties that include the prevention of injuries, administration of first aid and postinjury treatment, and rehabilitation work. Such preparation, if possible, should include a major in physical education, certification by the National Athletic Trainers Asociation, and/or certification as a registered physical therapist. Furthermore, trainers should have such personal qualifications as emotional stability under stress, ability to act in a rational manner when injuries occur, and a standard of ethics that places the welfare of the participant first.

The financial situation of many schools prohibits the hiring of a full-time athletic trainer. Some schools, however, find it feasible to provide this service by hiring a person who plays a dual role. Such an individual might have another part-time school assignment, such as coach, assistant athletic director, health service supervisor, or teacher (someone in the adapted physical education program or in another subject area); might teach on the college level in an athletic training degree program; or might work as a secretary or nurse.

---

*Pflug, J.: Evaluating high school coaches, Journal of Physical Education and Recreation **51**:76-77, April 1980. (Courtesy American Alliance for Health, Physical Education, Recreation, and Dance, 1900 Association Dr., Reston, Va.)

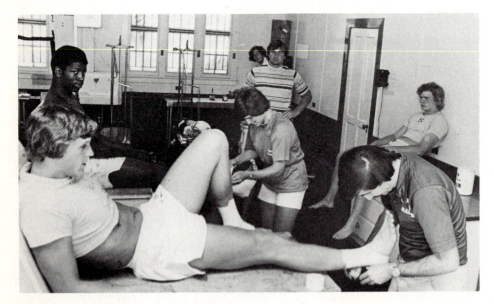

Fig. 5-9. Athletic training has no sex barriers.

Courtesy John Cramer, Cramer Products, Inc., Gardner, Kansas.

Name _____   DEPARTMENT OF ATHLETICS   Evaluator _____
                          School District No. 43
Assignment _____   Beaverton, Oregon   Date _____

COACH'S EVALUATION

COACH'S SELF-EVALUATION (to be completed prior to the start of coaching assignment)

1. Statement of personal goals and/or program goals as they relate to your coaching assignment

_____

_____

2. Statement of self-evaluation on applicable criteria relative to completion of goals statement (to be completed at the conclusion of your coaching assignment)

_____

_____

3. ATHLETIC COORDINATOR'S EVALUATION (to be completed subsequent to the coaching assignment, then reviewed with the coach)

CODE: Scale of 1-5, with 5 highest competency. If blank, not applicable

	Circle one
A. ADMINISTRATION	
1. Care of equipment (issue, inventory, cleaning, etc.)	1 2 3 4 5
2. Organization of staff	1 2 3 4 5
3. Organization of practices	1 2 3 4 5
4. Communication with coaches	1 2 3 4 5
5. Adherence to district and school philosophy and policies (eligibility reports, inventories, budgets, rosters, insurance forms, and follow-up, scores reported)	1 2 3 4 5
6. Public relations	1 2 3 4 5
7. Supervision	1 2 3 4 5
B. SKILLS	
1. Knowledge of fundamentals	1 2 3 4 5
2. Presentation of fundamentals	1 2 3 4 5
3. Conditioning	1 2 3 4 5
4. Game preparation	1 2 3 4 5
5. Prevention and care of injuries (follow-up with parents)	1 2 3 4 5
C. RELATIONSHIPS	
1. Enthusiasm	1 2 3 4 5
a. for working with students	1 2 3 4 5
b. for working with staff (support of other programs)	1 2 3 4 5
c. for working with academic staff	1 2 3 4 5
d. for the sport itself	1 2 3 4 5
2. Discipline	1 2 3 4 5
a. firm but fair	1 2 3 4 5
b. consistent	1 2 3 4 5
3. Communication with players	1 2 3 4 5
a. individual	1 2 3 4 5
b. as a team	1 2 3 4 5

Continued.

Name _____ DEPARTMENT OF ATHLETICS Evaluator _____
School District No. 43

Assignment _____ Beaverton, Oregon Date _____

COACH'S EVALUATION—cont'd

D. PERFORMANCE

   1. Appearance of team on the field or floor   1 2 3 4 5

   2. Execution of the team on the field or floor   1 2 3 4 5

   3. Attitude of the team   1 2 3 4 5

   4. Conduct of coach during game   1 2 3 4 5

E. SELF-IMPROVEMENT

   1. Attends in-district meetings and clinics   1 2 3 4 5

   2. Attends out-of-district clinics   1 2 3 4 5

   3. Keeps updated by reading current literature   1 2 3 4 5

4. Review by Building Athletic Coordinator with Coach (District Athletic Coordinator will review all evaluations before forwarding to principal.)

_____

_____

_____

5. To be placed in working papers of principal and forwarded to the personnel office with yearly teaching evaluation.

Original—Building Principal   Signed by Coach: _____

Canary—District Athletic Coordinator   Signed by Evaluator: _____

Pink—Building Athletic Coordinator

Gold—Coach

Athletic trainers should complete a 4-year college curriculum that emphasizes the biological and physical sciences, psychology, coaching techniques, first aid and safety, nutrition, and other courses in physical education. They should be competent in accident prevention, emergency treatment, and rehabilitation of injured athletes. They should also be able to work closely with administrators, coaches, physicians, the school nurse, students, and parents in a cooperative effort to provide the best possible health care for all athletes under their jurisdiction. In addition, they are also responsible in many college programs for development and supervision of a student athletic training staff.

Specific courses required in professional preparation programs for athletic trainers include anatomy, physiology, physiology of exercise, applied anatomy and kinesiology, psychology, first aid and safety, nutrition, remedial exercise, health, techniques of athletic training, and laboratory practice in the techniques of athletic training.

More women should become involved in athletic training. Women are more likely to be open about personal problems to other women. Yet in may undergraduate physical education programs, women have not received adequate preparation in athletic training. Furthermore, most athletic training in women's competitive sports is performed by men who often cannot handle the physical and emotional trauma suffered by female athletes. Thus, a woman may be reluctant to seek the services of a male athletic trainer. Injuries and other related problems occur as regularly in women's sports as they do in men's, and women should be adequately trained to meet these situations.

THE ATHLETIC COUNCIL

Many schools have some type of athletic council, board, or committee that establishes athletic policies for the institution. It may involve only faculty members, or it may also involve students. Such councils, boards, or committees are responsible for giving the athletic program proper direction in the educational program.

The composition of such committees or councils varies widely from school to school. In some the principal may serve as chairman; in others this position may be held by the director of physical education or other faculty member. The committee may include coaches, members of the board of education, faculty members, students, or members of the community.

Some of the functions of athletic councils at the high school level include making policy, approving awards, advising the athletic department on problems that arise, endorsing and approving schedules and budgets, evaluating the athletic program, investigating complaints, interviewing and recommending coaches to athletic directors, developing eligibility guidelines, considering postseason play, approving code of ethics, reviewing scholarship program, and deciding if sports should be added or dropped.

Selected athletic associations

National Association for Girls and Women in Sport (NAGWS). The National Association for Girls and Women in Sport is one of the seven associations of the American Alliance for Health, Physical Education, Recreation, and Dance and is concerned with the governance of sports for girls and women. The specific functions of the National Association for Girls and Women in Sport are:

1. To formulate and publicize guiding principles and standards for the administrator, leader, official, and player
2. To publish and interpret rules governing sports for girls and women
3. To provide the means for training, evaluating, and rating officials
4. To disseminate information on the conduct of girls' and women's sports
5. To stimulate, evaluate, and disseminate research in the field of girls' and women's sports
6. To cooperate with allied groups interested in girls' and women's sports in order to formulate policies and rules that affect the conduct of women's sports

7. To provide opportunities for the development of leadership among girls and women for the conduct of their sports programs*

The National Federation of State High School Athletic Associations. The National Federation of State High School Athletic Associations was established in 1920 with five states participating. With a current membership that includes almost every state, the National Federation is particularly concerned with the control of interstate athletics. According to its constitution:

The object of this Federation shall be to protect and supervise the interstate athletic interests of the high schools belonging to the state associations, to assist in those activities of state associations, which can best be operated on a nationwide scale, to sponsor meetings, publications and activities which will permit each state association to profit by the experience of all other member associations, and to coordinate the work so that waste effort and unnecessary duplication will be avoided.

The National Federation has been responsible for many improvements in athletics on a national basis, such as doing away with national tournaments and working toward a uniformity of standards.

The National Council of Secondary School Athletic Directors. The American Alliance for Health, Physical Education, and Recreation established the National Council of Secondary School Athletic Directors. The increased emphasis in sports and the important position of athletic directors in the nation's secondary schools warranted an association where increased services could strengthen the Council's contribution to the nation's youth. Membership in the National Council is open to members of AAHPERD who have primary responsibility in directing, administering, or coordinating interscholastic athletic programs. The purposes of the Council are

To improve the educational aspects of interscholastic athletics and their articulation in the total educational program

To foster high standards of professional proficiency and ethics

---

*The national office can supply further information: American Alliance for Health, Physical Education, Recreation, and Dance, 1900 Association Drive, Reston, Va. 22091 (Telephone: 703-476-3400).

To improve understanding of athletics throughout the nation

To establish closer working relationships with related professional groups

To promote greater unity, good will, and fellowship among all members

To provide for an exchange of ideas

To assist and cooperate with existing state athletic directors' organizations

To make available to members special resource materials through publications, conferences, and consultant services

Self-assessment tests

These tests are designed to assist students in determining if material and competencies presented in this chapter have been mastered.

1. Prepare an essay of 250 words that describes the relationship of the basic instructional and adapted components of the secondary school physical education program to the intramural, extramural, club, and interscholastic athletic programs.
2. List and evaluate the values that are claimed for sports as well as the harm that can occur.
3. Describe the physical and emotional characteristics of a typical junior high school boy or girl and draw implications from those characteristics that have implications for the conduct of sports in which either will participate.
4. The principal of a high school has asked you to prepare a report for the next faculty meeting, setting guidelines for an intramural and an interscholastic athletic program for the school. Prepare the report and present it to your class.
5. Indicate how a sports program for girls in the secondary school would differ from a sports program for boys.
6. Identify the key provisions of Title IX and also the implications each has for sports programs.
7. What personnel are generally associated in high schools with the intramural, extramural, club, and interscholastic athletic programs?

Points to remember

1. Workable definition of intramurals and extramurals
2. Values associated with participation in sports
3. Harmful results that can occur from participation in sports
4. Characteristics of secondary school boys and girls
5. Guidelines for girls' sports programs

6. Provisions of Title IX
7. Intramural, extramural, club, and interscholastic athletic programs

Problems to think through

1. Why do sports programs have potential to harm as well as benefit participants?
2. Why is it important to develop sports programs in light of the characteristics and needs of the participants?
3. What reservations can be stated regarding interscholastic athletic programs for junior high school students?
4. What are the reasons for the growth of sports for girls?
5. Why was Title IX passed by the federal government?

Case study for analysis

Select a secondary school and make a careful study of its intramural, extramural, club, and interscholastic programs. Make a list of commendable features of these programs and a list of weaknesses that require attention.

Exercises for review

1. Define intramurals and extramurals.
2. Why are intramurals and extramurals recommended for junior high school students?
3. What are some important considerations in developing an effective intramural, club, extramural, and interscholastic athletic program?
4. Make a study of what four physical education leaders consider important policies for sports in the secondary school.
5. Debate the issue—Resolved: Interschool athletics should be banned from all junior high schools.

Selected readings

Banks, O.: How black coaches view entering the job market at major colleges, Journal of Physical Education and Recreation **50:**62, May 1979.

Broyles, J., Hay, J.F., and Hay, R.D.: Administration of athletic programs—a managerial approach, Englewood Cliffs, N.J., 1979, Prentice-Hall, Inc.

Bucher, C.A., and Dupee, R.K., Jr.: Athletics schools and colleges, New York, 1965, The Center for Applied Research in Education, Inc. (The Library of Education).

Bucher, C.A., Thaxton N.: Physical education and sport: change and challenge, St. Louis, 1981, The C.V. Mosby Co.

Bucher, C.A.: Foundations of physical education, ed. 9, St. Louis, 1983, The C.V. Mosby Co.

Colgate, J.A.: Administration of intramural and recreational activities: everyone can participate, New York, 1978, John Wiley & Sons, Inc.

Collison, R.: Master coach certification proposed, The Prep Coach, Feb. 1972 (Publication of Minnesota High School Coaches Association).

Competitive sports for the handicapped, Journal of Health, Physical Education, and Recreation **41:**91-96, Nov./Dec. 1970.

Crowe, W.C., Auxter, D., and Pyfer, J.: Principles and methods of adapted physical education and recreation, ed. 4, St. Louis, 1981, The C.V. Mosby Co.

Deatherage, D., and Reid, C.P.: Administration of women's competitive sports, Dubuque, Iowa, 1977, William C. Brown Co., Publishers.

Division for Girls' and Women's Sports: 1973 guidelines for intercollegiate athletic programs for women, Washington, D.C., 1973, American Association for Health, Physical Education, and Recreation.

Durso, J.: The sports factory: an investigation into college sports, New York, 1975, Quadrangle/The New York Times Book Co., Inc.

Educational Policies Commission: School athletics—problems and policies, Washington, D.C., 1954, National Education Association.

Eitzen, D.S.: Athletics in the status system of male adolescents: a replication of Coleman's *The Adolescent Society,* Adolescence **10:**266-275, Summer 1975.

Eitzen, D.S.: Sport in contemporary society, New York, 1979, St. Martin's Press, Inc.

Encyclopedia of Associations, Detroit, Mich., 1979, Gale Research Co.

Fuoss, D.E., and Troppmann, R.J.: Creative management techniques in interscholastic athletics, New York, 1977, John Wiley & Sons, Inc.

Gerson, R.: Redesigning athletic competition for children, Motor Skills: Theory into Practice **2:**3-14, Fall 1977.

Gilbert, B., and Williamson, N.: Programmed to be losers, Sports Illustrated **38:**60, 1973.

Gould, D., and Martens, R.: Attitudes of volunteer coaches toward significant youth sport issues, Research Quarterly **50:**369-380, Oct. 1979.

Hardy, R.: Checklist for better crowd control, Journal of Physical Education and Recreation **52:**70-71, May 1981.

Hoepner, B.J., editor: Women's athletics—coping with controversy, Reston, Va., 1974, AAHPERD

Hotchkiss, S.: Parents and kids' sports, Human Behavior **7:**35, March 1978.

Howe, H., II: On sports, Educational Record **58:**218-219, Spring 1977.

Hult, J.: Equal programs or carbon copies, Journal of Physical Education and Recreation **47:**24-25, May 1976.

Lopiano, D.A.: A fact-finding model for conducting a Title IX self-evaluation study in athletic programs, Journal of Physical Education and Recreation **47:**26-30, May 1976.

Lumpkin, A.: Let's set the record straight, Journal of Physical Education and Recreation **48:**40, 42, 44, March 1977.

Magil, R., Ash, M., and Smoll, F.: Children in sport: a contemporary anthology, Champaign, Ill., 1978, Human Kinetics Publishers.

Martens, R.: Joy and sadness in children's sports, Champaign, Ill., 1978, Human Kinetics Publishers.

The National Association for Physical Education of College Women and The National College Physical Education Association for Men: Perspectives for sport, Quest Monograph 29, Winter Issue, 1973 (entire issue devoted to sports).

The National Association for Physical Education of College Women and The National College Physical Education Association for Men: Sport in America, Quest Monograph 27, Winter Issue, 1977 (entire issue devoted to sports).

Noble, L., and Sigle, G.: Minimum requirements for interscholastic coaches, Journal of Physical Education and Recreation **51:**32-33, Nov./Dec. 1980.

Orr, R.E.: Sport, myth, and the handicapped athlete, Journal of Physical Education and Recreation **50:**33-34, March 1979.

Parkhouse, B.L., and Lapin, J.: The woman in athletic administration, Santa Monica, Calif., 1980, Goodyear Publishing Co., Inc.

Penman, K.A.: Planning physical education and athletic facilities in schools, New York, 1977, John Wiley & Sons, Inc.

Pflug, J.: Evaluating high school coaches, Journal of Physical Education and Recreation **51:**76-77, April 1980.

Policies on women athletes change, Journal of Health, Physical Education, and Recreation **44:**51, 1973.

Poorman, D.: Should A.D.'s coach? Juco Review **25:**10, 1973.

Rarick, G.L., editor: Physical activity: human growth and development, New York, 1977, Academic Press, Ltd.

Reed, J.D.: A miracle! or is it a mirage? Sports Illustrated, April 20, 1981.

Resick, M.C., and Erickson, C.E.: Intercollegiate and interscholastic athletics for men and women, Reading, Mass., 1975, Addison-Wesley Publishing Co., Inc.

Sabock, R.J.: The coach, Philadelphia, 1979, W.B. Saunders Co.

School athletics face austerity budgets, Sportscope, Sept./Oct. 1973.

Seefeldt, V., coordinator: Youth sports, Journal of Physical Education and Recreation **49:**38-51, March 1978.

Sisley, B.L.: Women in administration—a quest for leadership, Journal of Physical Education and Recreation **52:**77-78, April, 1981.

Shults, F.D.: Toward athletic reform, Journal of Physical Education and Recreation **50:**18-19, 48, Jan. 1979.

Smoll, F.B., and Smith, R.E.: Behavioral guidelines for youth and sport coaches, Journal of Physical Education and Recreation **49:**46-47, March 1978.

Smoll, F.B., and Smith, R.E., editors: Psychological perspectives in youth sports, Washington, D.C., 1978, Hemisphere Publishing Corp.

Stevenson, C.L.: Socialization effects of participation in sport: a critical review of the research, Research Quarterly **46:**287-301, Oct. 1975.

Talamini, J.T., and Page, C.H.: Sport and society—an anthology, Boston, 1973, Little, Brown & Co.

Tutko, T., and Burns, W.: Winning is everything and other American myths, New York, 1976, Macmillan, Inc.

Underwood, J.: The writing is on the wall, Sports Illustrated, May 19, 1980.

Vanderzwaag, H.J., and Sheehan, T.J.: Introduction to sport studies, Dubuque, Iowa, 1978, William C. Brown Co., Publishers.

Weber, M.: Title IX in action, Journal of Physical Education and Recreation **51:**20-21, May 1980.

Wilkerson, M., and Dodder, R.A.: What does sport do for people? Journal of Physical Education and Recreation **50:**50-51, Feb. 1979.

6

Legal liability and physical education

Instructional objectives and competencies to be achieved

After reading this chapter the student should be able to

1. Define each of the following terms: legal liability, tort, negligence, *in loco parentis* (in place of parents), "save harmless" law, assumption of risk, immunity
2. Indicate the legal basis for physical education programs and its implications for requiring all students to participate in physical education
3. Illustrate what constitutes negligent behavior on the part of physical educators and coaches and what constitutes defenses against negligence
4. Identify common areas of negligence in the conduct of physical education and athletic programs, and explain what can be done to eliminate such negligence
5. Appreciate the relationship of Title IX to legal liability in the conduct of physical education and athletic programs
6. Interpret the law regarding P.L. 94-142 in respect to the handicapped
7. Discuss recent court interpretations regarding sports product liability, violence, and physical education activities that are conducted off-campus
8. Discuss safety precautions that physical educators can take in order to prevent accidents and provide for the safety of students

According to Bouvier's *Law Dictionary*, liability is "the responsibility, the state of one who is bound in law and justice to do something which may be enforced by action." Another definition states: "Liability is the condition of affairs that gives rise to an obligation to do a particular thing to be enforced by court action."

Leaders in the fields of physical education and ath-

letics should know (1) how far they can go with various aspects of their programs and (2) what precautions are necessary to avoid legal liability in the event of an accident.

This information is particularly important to physical educators because 67% of the boys and 59% of the girls who are injured in school-related accidents sustain their injuries in physical education and recreation programs. It is alarming to note that 50% of student injuries occur during supervised physical education activities. The facts that millions of boys and girls participate in athletic programs and that every year one out of every 33 students attending school is injured make these statistics of special significance for the field of physical education.

When an accident resulting in personal injury occurs, the question often arises as to whether damages can be recovered. All employees run the risk of suit by injured persons on the basis of alleged negligence that causes bodily injury. Such injuries occur on playgrounds, on athletic fields, in fitness laboratories, in classes, or in any place where physical education and athletic programs take place.

The legal rights of the individuals involved in such cases are worthy of study. Although the law varies from state to state, it is possible to discuss liability in a general way that is relevant to all sections of the country. First, it is important to understand the legal basis for program requirements in physical education, athletics, and allied areas.

The legal basis for physical education, athletics, and allied areas

Surveys concerning mandatory physical education requirements in elementary, junior, and senior high schools indicate certain interesting facts. One survey showed that all but five states have physical education requirements. In 46 states, some degree of physical

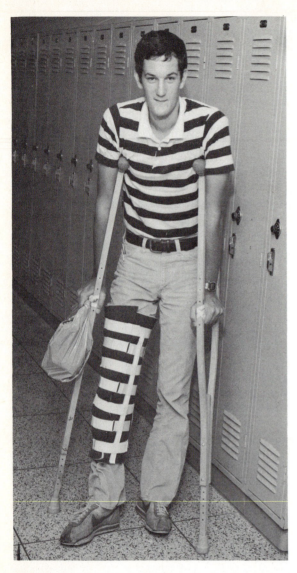

Fig. 6-1. Accidents occur in physical education and athletic programs.

Courtesy Brockport Central Schools, Brockport, N.Y.

education instruction—from 1 to 4 years—is required in grades 9 through 12. Forty-four states have some type of required program in grades 7 and 8, and some degree of physical education is required in all grades (1 through 12) in 14 states.

LEGAL IMPLICATIONS FOR REQUIRING PHYSICAL EDUCATION

Shroyer* made a study of the legal implications of requiring pupils to enroll in physical education classes and found that the courts have handed down decisions from which the following conclusions may be drawn:

1. Students may be required to take physical education. However, there should be some flexibility to provide for those cases where an individual's constitutional rights might be violated if such activities are against his or her principles, for example, dancing.
2. Where reasonable parental demands for deviation from the physical education requirement are requested, every effort should be made to comply with the parent's wishes. However, unreasonable demands should not result in acquiescence.
3. Where rules and regulations may be questioned, the board of education should provide for a review of the rationale behind the rule or regulation and need for the policy.
4. A student may be denied the right to graduate and receive a diploma when a required course such as physical education is not taken.

LEGAL LIABILITY

Some years ago the courts recognized the hazards involved in the play activities that are a part of the educational program. In hearing a case where a boy was injured while he was playing tag, the court recognized the possibility and risk of some injury in physical education programs and would not award damages. However, it pointed out that care must be taken by both the participant and the authorities in charge. It further implied that the benefits derived from participating in physical education activities such as tag offset the occasional injury that might occur. The court's decision was handed down at a time when the legal attitude held that no government agency, which would include the school, could be held liable for the acts of its employees unless it so consented.

Since that time a changing attitude in the courts has been evident. As more accidents occurred, the courts frequently decided in favor of the injured party when

*Shroyer, G.F.: Legal implications of requiring pupils to enroll in physical education, Journal of Health, Physical Education, and Recreation **35**:51, 1964.

negligence could be shown. The immunity derived from the old common-law rule that a government agency cannot be sued without its consent is slowly changing in the eyes of the courts so that now both federal and state governments may be sued.

Those elements of a school curriculum that are compulsory, such as physical education, prompt courts to decide on the basis of what is in the best interests of the public. Instead of being merely a moral responsibility, safety has become a legal responsibility. Those who uphold the doctrine that a government agency should be immune from liability maintain that payments for injury to constituents are misapplications of public funds. On the other hand, some persons feel it is wrong for the cost of injuries to fall on one or a few persons and, instead, should be shared by all. To further their case, these persons cite the constitutional provision that compensation must be given for the taking or damaging of private property. They argue that it is inconsistent that the government cannot take or damage private property without just compensation, yet can injure or destroy the life of a person without liability for compensation. This view is being used more and more by the courts.

The rule of immunity is still legal in many states. Because school districts are instrumentalities of the state, and the state is immune from suit unless it consents, the state's immunity extends to the districts. However, as has already been pointed out, the doctrine of immunity is starting to crumble. In some states governmental immunity has been annulled either by legislation or judicial decision. In other states schools may legally purchase liability insurance protecting school districts that may become involved in lawsuits, although this does not necessarily mean that governmental immunity has been waived. Of course, in the absence of insurance and "save harmless" laws (laws that require that school districts assume the liability of the teacher, whether negligence is proved or not), any judgment rendered against a school district must be met out of personal funds. School districts in such states as Connecticut, Massachusetts, New Jersey, and New York have "save harmless" laws.

There are still states, however, where school districts have governmental immunity, which means that as long as they are engaging in a governmental function they cannot be sued, even though negligence has been determined.

School districts that still enjoy governmental immunity usually are either required or permitted to carry liability insurance that specifically covers the operation of school buses.

There is a strong feeling among educators and many in the legal profession that the doctrine of sovereign immunity should be abandoned. In some states students injured as a result of negligence are assured recompense for damages directly or indirectly, either because governmental immunity has been abrogated or because school districts are legally required to indemnify school employees against financial loss. In those states with liability insurance, students may also recover expenses incurred.

Although school districts have been granted immunity in many states, teachers do not have such immunity. A decision of an Iowa court in 1938 provides some of the thinking in regard to the teacher's responsibility for his or her own actions (*Montanick v. McMillin,* 225 Iowa 442, 452-453, 458, 280 N. W. 608, 1938).

[The employee's liability] is not predicated upon any relationship growing out of his [her] employment, but is based upon the fundamental and underlying law of torts, that he [she] who does injury to the person or property of another is civilly liable in damages for the injuries inflicted. . . . The doctrine of *respondeat superior,* literally, "let the principle answer," is an extension of the fundamental principle of torts, and an added remedy to the injured party, under which a party injured by some act of misfeasance may hold both the servant and the master. The exemption of governmental bodies and their officers from liability under the doctrine of *respondeat superior* is a limitation of exception to the rule of *respondeat superior* and in no way affects the fundamental principle of torts that one who wrongfully inflicts injury upon another is liable to the injured person for damages. . . . An act of misfeasance is a positive wrong, and every employee, whether employed by a private person or a muncipal corporation owes a duty not to injure another by a negligent act of commission. . . .

TORT

A tort is a legal wrong resulting in direct or indirect injury to another individual or to property. A tortious act is a wrongful act, and damages can be collected

Fig. 6-2. Tennis as part of the physical education program at Panama Central School, Panama, N.Y.

through court action. Tort can be committed through an act of *omission* or *commission*. An act of omission results when the accident occurs during failure to perform a legal duty, such as when a teacher fails to obey a fire alarm after he or she has been informed of the procedure to be followed. An act of commission results when the accident occurs while an unlawful act is being performed, such as assault.

The National Education Association points out that

A tort may arise out of the following acts: (a) an act which without lawful justification or excuse is intended by a person to cause harm and does cause the harm complained of: (b) an act in itself contrary to law or an omission of specific legal duty, which causes harm not intended by the person so acting or omitting; (c) an act or omission causing harm which the person so acting or omitting did not intend to cause, but which might and should, with due diligence, have been foreseen and prevented.*

*National Education Research Division for the National Commission on Safety Education: Who is liable for pupil injuries? Washington, D.C., 1950, National Education Association, p. 5.

The teacher, leader, or other supervising individual not only has a legal responsibility as described by law but also a responsibility to prevent injury. This means that in addition to complying with certain legal regulations, the teacher must comply with the principle that children should be taught without injury to them and that prudent care, such as a parent would give, must be exercised. The term *legal duty* does not mean only those duties imposed by law but also the duty that is owed to society to prevent injury to others. A duty imposed by law would be one such as complying with housing and traffic regulations. A duty that teachers owe to society in general consists of teaching children without injury to them. For example, it was stated in one case (*Hoose v. Drumm*, 281 N.Y. 54):

Teachers have watched over the play of their pupils time out of mind. At recess periods, not less than in the classroom, a teacher owes it to his charges to exercise such care of them as a parent of ordinary prudence would observe in comparable circumstances.

It is important to understand the legal meaning of the word *accident* in relation to the topic under discussion. According the Black's *Law Dictionary,*

An accident is an unforeseen event occurring without the will or design of the person whose mere act causes it. In its proper use the term excludes negligence. It is an event which occurs without fault, carelessness, or want of proper circumspection for the person affected, or which could not have been avoided by the use of that kind and degree of care necessary to the exigency and in the circumstance in which he was placed.

The case of *Lee v. Board of Education of City of New York* in 1941, for example, showed that prudent care was not exercised, and the defendant was liable for negligence. A boy, playing football in a street that had not been completely closed off to traffic, was hit by a car during his participation in a physical education program. The board of education and the teacher were found negligent.

NEGLIGENCE

Questions of liability and negligence are a matter of some concern to teachers and leaders in physical education and athletic programs.

The law in America pertaining to negligence is based on common law, previous judicial rulings, or established legal procedure. This type of law differs from statutory law, which has been written into the statutes by lawmaking bodies. Negligence implies that someone has not fulfilled his or her legal duty or has failed to do something that, according to common-sense reasoning, should have been done. Negligence can be avoided with common knowledge of basic legal principles and proper vigilance. One of the first factors that must be determined in event of accident is whether there has been negligence.

Rosenfield* defines negligence as "the failure to act as a reasonably prudent and careful person would under the circumstances involved." The National Education Association's report elaborates further.

Negligence is any conduct which falls below the standard established by law for the protection of others against unreasonable risk of harm. In general, such conduct may be

of two types: (1) an act which a reasonable man would have realized involved an unreasonable risk of injury to others, and (b) failure to do an act which is necessary for the protection or assistance of another and which one is under a duty to do.*

According to Garber, a school employee may be negligent because of the following reasons:

1. He did not take appropriate care.
2. Although he used due care, he acted in circumstances which created risks.
3. His acts created an unreasonable risk of direct and immediate injury to others.
4. He set in motion a force which was unreasonably hazardous to others.
5. He created a situation in which third persons, such as pupils, or inanimate forces, such as shop machinery, may reasonably have been expected to injure others.
6. He allowed pupils to use dangerous devices although they were incompetent to use them.
7. He did not control a third person, such as an abnormal pupil, whom he knew to be likely to inflict intended injury on others because of some incapacity or abnormality.
8. He did not give adequate warning.
9. He did not look out for persons, such as pupils, who were in danger.
10. He acted without sufficient skill.
11. He did not make sufficient preparation to avoid an injury to pupils before beginning an activity where such preparation is reasonably necessary.
12. He failed to inspect and repair mechanical devices to be used by pupils.
13. He prevented someone, such as another teacher, from assisting a pupil who was endangered, although the pupil's peril was not caused by his negligence.†

The National Education Association report includes the following additional comment:

The law prohibits careless action; whatever is done must be done well and with reasonable caution. Failure to employ care not to harm others is a misfeasance. For example, an Oregon school bus driver who parked the bus across a driveway when he knew the pupils were coasting down the hill

---

*Rosenfield, H.N.: Liability for school accident, New York, 1940, Harper & Row, Publishers, Inc.

*National Education Research Division for the National Commission on Safety Education, op. cit., p. 6.
†Garber, L.O.: Law and the school business manager, Danville, Ill., 1957, The Interstate Printers & Publishers, Inc., pp. 205-206. (NOTE: These stipulations obviously apply to women as well.)

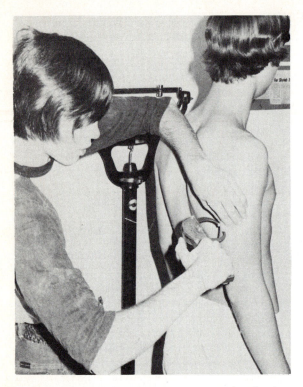

Fig. 6-3. Exercise physiology at Penney High School in East Hartford, Conn. Skinfold test to test for body fat.

was held liable for injuries sustained by a pupil who coasted into the bus. (*Fahlstrom v. Denk,* 1933.)*

Negligence may be claimed when the plaintiff has suffered injury either to self or to property, when the defendant has not performed his or her legal duty and has been negligent, and when the plaintiff has constitutional rights and is not guilty of contributory negligence. The teacher or leader of students in such cases is regarded as *in loco parentis,* that is, acting in the place of the parent in relation to the child.

Because negligence implies failure to act as a reasonably prudent and careful person, necessary precautions should be taken, danger should be anticipated, and common sense should be used. For example, if a teacher permits a group of very young

*National Education Research Division for the National Commission on Safety Education, op. cit., p. 14.

children to go up a high slide alone and without supervision, he or she is not acting as a prudent person would act. In the case previously cited of *Lee v. Board of Education of City of New York,* when the physical education class was held in a street where cars were allowed to pass, negligence was established.

Four factors of negligence must be proved before a lawsuit can be won. First, there must be conformance to a standard of behavior that avoids subjecting a person to reasonable risk or injury. Second, a breach of duty must be shown. Third, the breach of duty must be the cause of injury to the victim. The final factor that must be proved is that injury did occur.

A verdict by the jury in a California district court points up negligence in the sport of football. Press dispatches indicated that the high school athlete who suffered a disabling football injury was brought into court on a stretcher. The court awarded $325,000 (against the school district) in a suit in which the parent charged that the coach "was negligent in having the boy moved to the sidelines *too soon* after he was injured." The newspaper report seemed to imply that the negligence lay not in the *method* of moving the boy from the field but rather in the *time* at which he was moved.

An interesting case where the court ruled negligence occurred in New Jersey. In 1962 a student in the Chatham Junior High School was severely injured in an accident while participating in physical education. The testimony brought out that the physical education teacher was not present when the accident occurred but was treating another child for a rope burn. However, he had continually warned his class not to use the springboard at any time he was out of the room. (The student was trying to perform the exercise where he would dive from a springboard over an obstacle and finish with a forward roll.) The prosecution argued that the warning had not been stressed sufficiently and that the teacher's absence from the gymnasium, leaving student aides in charge, was an act of negligence. The court ruled negligence and awarded the boy $1.2 million dollars for injuries. His parents were awarded $35,140. On an appeal, the award to the boy was reduced to $300,000, but the award to the parents remained the same.

In respect to negligence, considerable weight is given by the law to the *foreseeability of danger.* One authority points out that "if a danger is obvious and a reasonably prudent person could have foreseen it and could have avoided the resulting harm by care and caution, the person who did not foresee or failed to prevent a foreseeable injury is liable for a tort on account of negligence."* If a person fails to take the needed precautions and care, negligence exists. However, it must be established on the basis of facts in the case and not on mere conjecture.

Physical educators must realize that students will behave in certain ways, that certain juvenile acts will cause injuries unless properly supervised, and that hazards must be anticipated, reported, and eliminated. The question that will be raised by most courts of law is: "Should the physical educators have had prudence enough to foresee the possible dangers or occurrence of an act?"

Two court actions point up legal reasoning on negligence as interpreted in one state. In the case of *Lane v. City of Buffalo* in 1931, the board of education was found not liable. In this case a child fell from a piece of apparatus in the schoolyard. It was found that the apparatus was in good condition and that the student was properly supervised. In the case of *Cambareri v. Board of Albany,* the defendant was found liable. The City of Buffalo owned a park that was supervised by the park department. While skating on the lake in the park, a boy playing "crack the whip" hit a 12-year-old boy who was also skating. Supervisory personnel had been instructed not to allow games that were rough or dangerous.

Although there are no absolute, factual standards for determining negligence, certain guides have been established, with which teachers and others engaged in physical education should be familiar. Attorney Cymrot, in discussing negligence at a conference in New York City, suggested the following:

1. The person must be acting within the scope of his or her employment and in the discharge of his or her duties in order to obtain the benefits of the statute.
2. There must be a breach of a recognized duty owed to the participant.

3. There must be a negligent breach of such duty.
4. The accident and resulting injuries must be the natural and foreseeable consequence of the person's negligence arising from a negligent breach of duty.
5. The person must be a participant in an activity under the control of the instructor, or, put in another way, the accident must have occurred under circumstances where the instructor owes a duty of care to the participant.
6. A person's contributory negligence, however modified, will bar his or her recovery for damages.
7. The plaintiff must establish the negligence of the instructor and his or her own freedom from contributory negligence by a fair preponderance of evidence. The burden of proof on both issues is on the plaintiff.
8. Generally speaking, in a school situation, the board of education alone is responsible for accidents caused by the faulty maintenance of plants and equipment.*

Some states have a "save harmless" law. For example, in New Jersey the law reads:

Chapter 311, P. L. 1938. Boards assume liability of teachers. It shall be the duty of each board of education in any school district to save harmless and protect all teachers and members of supervisory and administrative staff from financial loss arising out of any claim, demand, suit or judgment by reason of alleged negligence or other act resulting in accidental bodily injury to any person within or without the school building; provided, such teacher or member of the supervisory or administrative staff at the time of the accident or injury was acting in the discharge of his duties within the scope of his employment and/or under the direction of said board of education; and said board of education may arrange for and maintain appropriate insurance with any company created by or under the laws of this state, or in any insurance company authorized by law to transact business in this state, or such board may elect to act as self-insurers to maintain the aforesaid protection.

Negligence concerning equipment and facilities. Defective or otherwise hazardous equipment or inadequate facilities are often the cause of injuries that lead to court action. If a physical educator has noted that the equipment is defective, he or she should put this observation in writing for future personal protection. A letter should be written to the principal and

---

*National Education Research Division for National Commission on Safety Education, op. cit., p. 14.

*Proceedings of the City Wide Conference with Principal's Representatives and Men and Women Chairmen of Health Education, City of New York Board of Education, Brooklyn, N.Y., 1953, Bureau of Health Education.

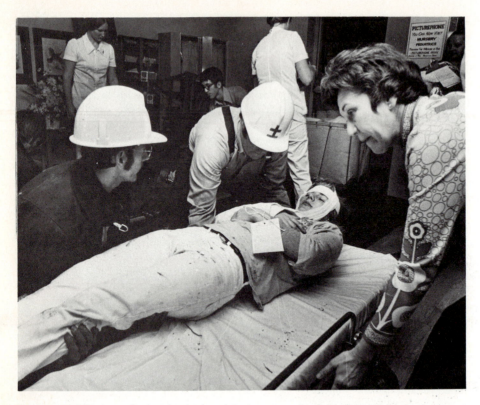

Fig. 6-4. Liability may be involved when injuries occur. Students from College of DuPage, Glen Ellyn, Ill., participating in a local emergency drill in order to be prepared in the event of emergency and injuries.

superintendent of schools or other responsible person stating that danger does exist and noting the areas of such danger. The physical educator should keep a copy for evidence in a possible lawsuit. In these cases the courts tend to agree with the student even if dangerous conditions had been noted. Conditions should not only be recognized but also be corrected.

Negligence concerning instruction. Many cases result from incidents that occur during instruction in an activity. For example, if a student is injured in a fall from a trampoline, a case might ensue where the student and his or her parents may try to show that instruction had been inadequate. These cases often find in favor of the student because of the inherent danger of the activity. Some students and their families have sued teachers because they did not follow a class syllabus that many states require of their teachers. Such a syllabus outlines the course content, and if

injury occurs in an unlisted activity, then a basis for suit is apparent.

Negligence in athletic participation. Many injuries are related to participation in athletics. Since unequal competition is often the cause of accidents, physical educators should consider sex, age, size, and skill of students in grouping players for an activity.

DEFENSES AGAINST NEGLIGENCE

Despite the fact that an individual is negligent, to collect damages the plaintiff must show that the negligence caused or was closely connected with the injury. The legal question in such a case is whether or not the negligence was the ''proximate cause'' (legal cause) of the injury. Furthermore, even though negligence is determined the ''proximate cause,'' there are still certain defenses on which a defendant may base a case.

Proximate cause. The negligence of the defendant may not have been the proximate cause of the plaintiff's injury.

Example: In the case of *Ohmon v. Board of Education of the City of New York,* 88 N.Y.S. 2d 273 (1949), a 13-year-old pupil in a classroom of a public school was struck in the eye by a pencil thrown by another pupil to a third pupil, who stepped aside. The court declared the proximate cause of injury was an unforeseen act of the pupil who threw the pencil and that the absence of the teacher (who was stacking supplies in a closet nearby the classroom) was not the proximate cause of injury. Thus liability for the injury could not be imposed on the board of education.

Act of God. An act of God is a situation that exists because of certain conditions that are beyond the control of human beings. For example, a flash of lightning, a gust of wind, a cloudburst, and other such factors may result in injury. However, an act of God defense applies only in cases where injury would not have occurred had prudent action been taken.

Assumption of risk. This legal defense is especially pertinent to games, sports, and other phases of the physical education and athletic program. It is assumed that an individual takes a certain risk engaging in various games and sports where bodies come in contact and where balls and apparatus are used. Participation in such activity indicates that the person assumes a normal risk.

Example: In the case of *Scala v. City of New York,* 102 N.Y.S. 2d 709, the plaintiff, when playing softball on a public playground, was aware of the risks caused by curbing and concrete benches near the playing fields. It was decided that the plaintiff had voluntarily and fully assumed the dangers and, having done so, had to abide by the consequences.

Contributory negligence. Another legal defense is contributory negligence. A person who does not act as would a normal individual of similar age and nature thereby contributes to the injury. In such cases negligence on the part of the defendant might be ruled out. Individuals are subject to contributory negligence if they expose themselves unnecessarily to dangers. The main consideration that seems to turn the tide in such cases is the age of the individual and the nature of the activity.

The National Education Association's report makes this statement in regard to contributory negligence:

Contributory negligence is defined in law as conduct on the part of the injured person which falls below the standard to which he should conform for his own protection and which is legally contributing cause, cooperating with the negligence of the defendant in bringing about the plaintiff's harm. Reasonable self-protection is to be expected of all sane adults. With some few exceptions, contributory negligence bars recovery against the defendant whose negligent conduct would otherwise make him liable to the plaintiff for the harm sustained by him. Both parties being in fault, neither can recover from the other for resulting harm. When there is mutual wrong and negligence on both sides, the law will not attempt to apportion the wrong between them.

Contributory negligence is usually a matter of defense, and the burden of proof is put upon the defendant to convince the jury of the plaintiff's fault and of its causal connection with the harm sustained. Minors are not held to the same degree of care as is demanded of adults.[*]

Contributory negligence implies a difference in the degree of responsibility held by elementary and high school teachers. The elementary school teacher, because the children are immature, has to assume greater responsibility for the safety of the child, and so the negligence factor is weighed more strictly. The courts might say that a high school student was mature enough to avoid doing whatever caused injury but that in the case of an elementary school child, the teacher should have prevented or protected the child from the injurious act.

Sudden emergency. This legal defense is pertinent in cases where the exigencies of the situation require immediate action on the part of a teacher and, as a result, an accident occurs. For example, an instructor in a swimming pool is suddenly alerted to the fact that a child is drowning in the water. The teacher's immediate objective is to save the child. He or she runs to help the drowning person and in doing so knocks down another student who is watching from the side of the pool. The student who is knocked down hits his head on the tile floor and is injured. This would be a case of sudden emergency and, if legal action is taken, the defense could be based on this premise.

---

[*]National Education Research Division for the National Commission on Safety Education, op. cit., p. 9.

COMMON AREAS OF NEGLIGENCE

Common areas of negligence in physical education and athletic activities, listed by Begley* in a New York University publication, are situations involving poor selection of activities, failure to take protective procedures, hazardous conditions of buildings or grounds, faulty equipment, inadequate supervision, and poor selection of play area. Cases involving each of these common areas of negligence follow.

Poor selection of activities. The activity must be suitable to the child or youth. In *Rook v. New York,* 4 N.Y.S. 2d 116 (1930), the court ruled that tossing a child in a blanket constituted a dangerous activity.

Failure to take protective measures. The element of "foreseeability" enters here, and proper protective measures must be taken to provide a safe place for children and youth to play. In *Roth v. New York,* 262 App. Div. 370, 29 N.Y.S. 2d 442 (1941), inadequate provisions were made to prevent bathers from stepping into deep water. When a bather drowned, the court held that the state was liable.

Hazardous conditions of buildings or grounds. Buildings and grounds must be safe. Construction of facilities and their continual repair must have as one objective the elimination of hazards. In the case of *Novak et al. v. Borough of Ford City,* 141 Atl. 496 (Pa., 1928), unsafe conditions were caused by an electric wire over the play area. In the case of *Honaman v. City of Philadelphia,* 185 Atl. 750 (Pa., 1936), unsafe conditions were caused by failure to erect a backstop.

Faulty equipment. All play and other equipment must be in good condition at all times. In the case of *Van Dyke v. Utica,* 203 App. Div. 26, 196 N.Y. Supp. 277 (1922), concerning a slide that fell over on a child and killed him, the court ruled that the slide was defective.

Inadequate supervision. There must be qualified supervision of all play activities. In the case of *Garber v. Central School District No. 1, Town of Sharon, N.Y.,* 251 App. Div. 214, 295 N.Y. Supp. 850, the court held that a school janitor was not qualified to

*Begley, R.F.: Legal liability in organized recreational playground areas. Safety Education Digest, 1955.

supervise school children playing in a gymnasium during the lunch hour.

Poor selection of play area. The setting for games and sports should be selected with a view to the safety of the participants. In the case *Morse v. New York,* 262 App. Div. 324, 229 N.Y.S. 34 (1941), where sledding and skiing were permitted on the same hill without adequate barriers to prevent participants in the two activities from colliding, the court held that the state was liable for negligence.

LIABILITY OF TEACHERS

The individual is responsible for negligence caused by his or her own acts. With the exception of certain specific immunity, the teacher or leader in programs of physical education and athletics is responsible for what he or she does. The Supreme Court of the United States has reaffirmed this principle, and its important implications should be recognized.

In New York a physical education teacher was held personally liable when he sat in the bleachers and permitted two strong boys, untrained in boxing, to fight through nearly two rounds. The plaintiff was hit in the temple and suffered a cerebral hemorrhage. The court ruled

It is the duty of a teacher to exercise reasonable care to prevent injuries. Pupils should be warned before being permitted to engage in a dangerous and hazardous exercise. Skilled boxers at times are injured, and . . . these young men should have been taught the principles of defense if indeed it was a reasonable thing to permit a slugging match of the kind which the testimony shows this contest was. The testimony indicates that the teacher failed in his duties in this regard and that he was negligent, and the plaintiff is entitled to recover. (*LaValley v. Stanford,* 272 App. Div. 183, 70 N.Y.S. 2d 460).

In New York (*Keesee v. Board of Education of City of New York,* 5 N.Y.S. 2d 300, 1962) a junior high school girl was injured while playing line soccer when she was kicked by another player. The board of educated syllabus listed line soccer as a game for boys and stated that "after sufficient skill has been acquired two or more forwards may be selected from each team." The syllabus called for 10 to 20 players on each team and required a space of 30 to 40 feet. The physical education teacher divided into two teams

Fig. 6-5. Equipment and supplies must be in good repair at all times in order to avoid negligence. Some playground equipment in the elementary school.

Courtesy Playground Corporation of America.

some 40 to 45 girls who had not had any experience in soccer. A witness who was an expert in such matters testified that in order to avoid accidents no more than two people should be on the ball at any time and criticized the board syllabus for permitting the use of more than two forwards. The expert also testified that pupils should have experience in kicking, dribbling, and passing before being permitted to play line soccer. The evidence showed that the teacher permitted six to eight inexperienced girls to be on the ball at one time. The court held that possible injury was at least reasonably foreseeable under such conditions, that the teacher had been negligent, and that the teachers negligence was the cause of the pupil being injured.*

Teachers are expected to conduct their various activities carefully and prudently. If they do not, they are exposing themselves to lawsuits for their own negligence.

The National Education Association's report comments on the role of administrators regarding liability.

The fact that administrators (speaking mainly of principals and superintendents) are rarely made defendants in pupil-injury cases seems unjust to the teachers who are found negligent because of inadequate supervision, and unjust also to the school boards who are required to defend themselves in such suits. When the injury is caused by defective equipment, it is the building principal who should have actual or constructive notice of the defect; when the injury is caused by inadequate playground supervision, the inadequacy of the supervision frequently exists because of arrangements made by the building principal. For example, a teacher in charge of one playground was required to stay in the building to teach a make-up class; another teacher was required to supervise large grounds on which 150 pupils were playing; another teacher neglected the playground to

*School Law Series: The pupil's day in court; review of 1963, Washington, D.C., 1964, Research Division, National Education Association, p. 43.

answer the telephone. All of these inadequacies in playground supervision were morally chargeable to administrators; in none of these instances did the court action direct a charge of responsibility to the administrator. Whether the administrator in such cases would have been held liable, if charged with negligence, is problematical. The issue has not been decided, since the administrator's legal responsibility for pupil injuries has never been discussed by the courts to an extent that would make possible the elucidation of general principles; the administrator's moral responsibilities must be conceded.*

SUPERVISION

Children are entrusted by parents to leaders of physical education and athletic programs, and the parents expect that adequate supervision will be provided in order to minimize the possibility of accidents. Questions of liability in regard to supervision pertain to two points: (1) the extent of the supervision and (2) the quality of the supervision.

Regarding the first point, the adequacy of supervision is questioned. Although the answers vary from situation to situation, it is helpful to ask, "Would additional supervision have eliminated the accident?" and "Is it reasonable to expect that additional supervision should have been provided?"

In regard to the quality of the supervision, it is expected that competent personnel will handle specialized programs in physical education and athletics. If the supervisors of such activities do not possess proper training in such work, the question of negligence can be raised.

WAIVERS AND CONSENT SLIPS

Waivers and consent slips are not synonymous. A waiver is an agreement whereby one party waives a particular right. A consent slip is an authorization, usually signed by the parent, permitting a child to take part in some activity.

A parent cannot waive the rights of a child who is under 21 years of age; the parent is merely waiving his or her right to sue for damages. A parent can sue in two ways—from the standpoint of rights as parent and from the standpoint of the child's rights as an

individual, irrespective of the parent. Thus a parent cannot waive the right of the child to sue as an individual.

Consent slips offer protection in that they show that the child has the parent's permission to engage in an activity.

Title IX and sports for girls—a federal law

Today's relevant physical education program must take into account the passage of a very important law by our national government. On May 27, 1975, the President of the United States signed into law Title IX of the Education Amendments Act of 1972 (effective as of July 21, 1975), which prohibits sex discrimination in educational programs that are federally assisted.

Title IX affects nearly all public elementary, secondary, and postsecondary educational institutions, which includes the nation's 16,000 public school systems and nearly 2,700 postsecondary institutions. As a first step, the regulations provide that educators should perform a searching self-examination of policies and practices in their institutions and take whatever remedial action is needed to bring their institutions into compliance with the federal law.

REASON FOR TITLE IX

The main reason for the enactment of Title IX was such testimony before Congressional and other committees as the following:

• Girls were frequently denied the opportunity to enroll in traditionally male courses and activities.

• Girls and women were frequently denied equal opportunity, such as the case cited where a program for girls was inferior to that provided for boys and another case in which rules in one state prevented the best tennis player (a girl) in a high school from competing on the school's tennis team.

• A national survey conducted by the National Education Association showed that although women constituted a majority of all public school teachers, they accounted for only 3.5% of the junior high school principals and 3% of the senior high school principals.

• A study by the National Center for Educational

*National Education Research Division for the National Commission on Safety Education, op. cit., p. 14.

Gen. No. 1 100M-1-54-3191   **WAIVER FORM**   **Long Beach, California**

Long Beach Public Schools

Date _____

We, _____, are the parents or guardians

of _____, and in consideration of the special benefits
of the extracurricular activity being afforded the student by the Long Beach Board of Education and the school
districts whose school the aforementioned child attends, hereby permit _____

_____

to participate in _____

_____

and we hereby release and discharge the said Long Beach Board of Education, the said school district, and
each and all their agents and employees from any liability whatever to the undersigned resulting from or in
any manner arising out of any injury or damage which may be sustained by the said _____

_____, on account of his participation in

_____

_____ or in the transportation in connection therewith.

  We further agree that in case of any action being brought for, or on behalf of the aforementioned child on
account of any injury received during his participation in the above mentioned events, or in the transportation
connected therewith, that we will be personally responsible to the school district, the Board of Education, and
any of its officials or agents concerned, and will repay to them and hold them harmless against any judgment
recovered in any such action against them or either of them.

  Signed this _____ day of _____, 198 _____

_____   _____
   Signature of Parent or Guardian   Address

_____   _____
   Signature of Parent or Guardian   Address

NOTE: Parents or Guardians, read the reverse side of this form.

Statistics revealed that women college faculty members received average salaries considerably lower than those of their male counterparts.

IMPLICATIONS FOR PHYSICAL EDUCATION AND ATHLETIC PROGRAMS

• *Physical education classes must be set up on a coeducational basis.* This regulation does not mean that activities must be taught coeducationally. Within classes, students may be grouped by sex for such

Fig. 6-6. Girls' volleyball.

Courtesy Barbara Ann Chiles,
Aledo, Ill.

contact sports as wrestling, basketball, and football. Further, within physical education classes, students may be grouped on an ability basis even though such division results in a single-sex grouping. However, sex must *not* be the criterion for grouping. Furthermore, if an evaluation standard has an adverse impact on one sex, such as a standard of accomplishment in a physical fitness test, different evaluation requirements may be used.

• *Schools and colleges must establish separate teams for boys and girls and men and women or provide a coeducational team.* If there is only one swimming team in a particular school, for example, then both boys and girls must be permitted to try out for this team. In other words, if a school fields a team in a noncontact sport for one sex and not for the other, members of both sexes must be allowed to try out for the same team.

The regulation does not enumerate what activities and teams a school should provide. However, under the regulation, equality of opportunity means that schools and colleges must select sports and levels of competition that provide for the interests and abilities of both sexes. This means that where the interests and abilities of members of both sexes are not provided for on one team, the institution is required to provide separate teams for males and females.

• *Schools and colleges must provide equal opportunities for both sexes.* This is true in such matters as facilities, equipment and supplies, practice and games, medical and training services, coaching and academic tutoring opportunities, travel and per diem allowances, and housing and dining facilities.

Equal opportunity means that the sports and activities offered must reflect the interests and abilities of students of both sexes.

Adequate facilities and equipment must be available for both sexes in every sport. Furthermore, one sex cannot dominate the facilities or the new equipment. Adequate time for practice and games must also be provided for both sexes in every sport. Again, one sex cannot dominate.

• *Schools and colleges must spend funds in an equitable manner.* Although equal aggregate expenditures are not required, an educational institution cannot discriminate on the basis of sex in providing proper equipment and supplies.

• *Title IX takes precedence over all state and local laws and conference regulations that might be in conflict with this federal regulation.*

• *If an institution receives federal aid, it must be in compliance with Title IX even though its athletic or physical education program does not directly receive any of this aid. (See Michigan judge's 1981 court ruling later in this chapter.)*

• *There can be no discrimination in respect to personnel standards.* Sex cannot be a consideration for employment, promotion, salary, recruitment, job classification, marital or parental status, or fringe benefits.

• *Scholarships must be awarded on an equitable basis.* The regulations require an institution to award students financial aid on the basis of criteria other than a student's sex.

TITLE IX GUIDELINES

In a fact sheet dated December 4, 1979, the Department of Health, Education and Welfare* sought to clarify the proposed policy, "Title IX and Intercollegiate Athletics," which was issued in 1978† and has implications for secondary schools. This policy interpretation of the Education Amendments of 1972, published in the *Federal Registrar* on December 11, 1979, determines whether a school's athletic program is in compliance with Title IX by assessing three aspects of the athletic program.

1. *Financial assistance*—scholarships and grants-in-aid provided on the basis of athletic ability
—The Title IX regulation requires that:
Colleges and universities provide reasonable opportunities for male and female students to receive scholarships and grants-in-aid in proportion to the number of male and female participating athletes
—The policy explains that:
Schools must distribute all athletic assistance on a substantially proportional basis to the number of participating male and female athletes. (Example: Total scholarship fund = $100,000 in a school with 70 male and 30 female athletes. Male athletes are entitled to $70,000. Female

athletes are entitled to $30,000.) Unequal spending for either the men's or the women's program may be justified by sex-neutral factors, such as a higher number of male athletes recruited from out-of-state.

2. *Athletic benefits and opportunities*—equipment and supplies, travel, compensation of coaches, facilities, housing, publicity, and other aspects of a program
—The Title IX regulation specifies the factors that HEW should assess in determining whether a school is providing equal athletic opportunity. This "equal opportunity" regulation applies to all aspects of athletic programs, such as equipment and supplies, scheduling of games and practices, compensation of coaches, housing and dining services, publicity, travel and per diem costs, opportunities for coaching, locker rooms and other facilities, medical and training services, and other relevant factors.
—The policy explains that schools must provide "equivalent" treatment, services, and benefits in those areas. HEW will assess each of those factors by comparing:
• Availability
• Kind of benefits
• Quality
• Kind of opportunities

3. *Accommodation of student interests and abilities*—the third section of the policy sets out how schools can meet the requirement of the regulation to "effectively accommodate the interests and abilities of both sexes."
—The Title IX regulation requires that schools effectively:
Accommodate the interests and abilities of students of both sexes in the selection of sports and levels of competition
—The policy explains how to accommodate interests and abilities through:
• Selection of sports
  1. When there is a team for only one sex, and the excluded sex is interested in the sport, the university may be required to:
     —Permit the excluded sex to try out for the team if it is not a contact sport; or
     —Sponsor a separate team for the previously excluded sex if there is a reasonable expectation of intercollegiate competition for that team
  2. Teams do not have to be integrated.
  3. The same sports do not have to be offered to men and to women.
• Levels of competition
  Equal competitive opportunity means:
  1. The number of men and women participating in intercollegiate athletics is in proportion to their overall enrollment; or
  2. The school has taken steps to insure that the sex

---

*In 1979, the Department of Health and Human Services and the Department of Education replaced the Department of Health, Education and Welfare.
†HEW Fact Sheet: Title IX and Intercollegiate Athletics Policy, Washington, D.C., December 4, 1979, U.S. Department of Health, Education and Welfare.

underrepresented in athletic programs is offered new opportunities consistent with the interests and abilities of that sex; or

3. The present program accommodates the interests and abilities of the underrepresented sex

and

4. Men and women athletes, in proportion to their participation in athletic programs, compete at the same levels; or

5. The school has a history and practice of upgrading the levels at which teams of the underrepresented sex compete

—Schools are not required to develop or upgrade an intercollegiate team if there is no reasonable expectation that competition will be available for that team.

• Measuring of interests and abilities

The recipient must:

1. Take into account the increasing levels of women's interests and abilities

2. Use methods of determining interests and ability that do not disadvantage the underrepresented sex

3. Use methods of determining ability that take into account team performance records; and

4. Use methods that are responsive to the expressed interests of students capable of intercollegiate competition who belong to the underrepresented sex

These Title IX guidelines require that expenditures on men's and women's athletics be proportional to the number of men and women participating in athletics. This standard of substantially equal per capita expenditures must be met unless the institution can demonstrate that the differences are based on nondiscriminatory factors, such as the costs of a particular sport (for example, the equipment required) or the scope of the competition (national rather than regional or local). This proportional standard applies to athletic scholarships, recruitment, and other readily measurable financial benefits such as equipment, supplies, travel, and publicity.

According to the Secretary of the Department of Health and Human Services, the policy was designed to eliminate, over a reasonable period of time, the discriminatory effects of the historic emphasis on men's sports and to facilitate the continued growth of women's athletics. It requires educational institutions to take specific active steps to provide additional athletic opportunities for women—opportunities that will fully accommodate the rising interests of women in participating in athletics. The staff attorney of the Department of Health and Human Services indicated that the guidelines have three basic parts. First, there must be equal expenditure of money per person involved in athletics; second, there must be comparable standards set where elements are not easily measurable; third, schools must have policies and procedures for upgrading women's athletics, such as showing how they will elevate a women's club team to a varsity team.

The staff attorney also explained that if a school awards 95 full athletic scholarships to men for football, it does not have to give 95 full athletic scholarships to women. The guidelines do stipulate, however, that if a school has 200 male varsity athletes and spends $200,000 on scholarships, which averages $1,000 per scholarship per male athlete, it must spend $1,000 on each athletic scholarship for women. Thus a school that has 50 women in varsity sports must spend $50,000 on women's athletic scholarships. In the same manner, if a school spends $300 for each football helmet, it is not required to spend a similar amount for women's equipment. But it does mean that if tennis racquets cost $40 each, a school with women tennis players must make racquets as available to these women as the helmets are to the football players. Another example given by the attorney is that if a school sends its football team by first-class charter flight to a game it must spend a proportionately similar amount on some component—not necessarily travel—of its women's teams, for example, on living quarters.

COMPLIANCE WITH TITLE IX

Title IX is enforced by the Federal Office of Civil Rights (established under Health, Education, and Welfare—now the Department of Health and Human Services). Administrators of the Office seek voluntary compliance, but if violations are found, federal financial support may be cut off and other legal measures taken, such as referring the violation to the Department of Justice for appropriate court action.

The Office of Civil Rights attempts to approach Title IX in an constructive manner, with the goal of achieving an end to discrimination against women, a policy that is now a legal mandate and must be enforced. The Office utilizes the Department of Education's enforcement machinery by giving priority to systemic forms of discrimination rather than to individual complaints. The total picture of noncompliance is assessed, taking into consideration information from individuals and groups to determine enforcement priorities and compliance reviews. Title IX regulations have been evolving for a long time and should result in increased physical education and athletic opportunities for all students.

TITLE IX AND THE COURTS

There have been numerous cases involving discrimination against women in sports reported in recent years. In 1978 a federal judge in Dayton, Ohio, ruled that girls may not be barred from playing on boys' school athletic teams, even in contact sports such as football and wrestling. In his decision the judge pointed out that there might be many reasons why girls would not want to play on boys' teams, such as "reasons of stature or weight or reasons of temperament, motivation, or interest. This is a matter of choice. But a prohibition without exception based on sex is not." The judge also indicated that his ruling would have national implications—for example, the Ohio High School Athletic Association had barred girls from contact sports.

A ruling by the State Division on Civil Rights of New Jersey (the first state in the nation to have such a ruling) requires Little League baseball teams to permit girls to play. The order also requires that both boys and girls be notified of team tryouts and that both sexes be treated equally. An amendment to the Education Law of New York State provides that no one may be disqualified from school athletic teams because of sex, except by certain regulations of the state commissioner of education.

Another case involved two women coaches who were denied admittance to the North Carolina Coaching Clinic because of their sex. A lawsuit was instituted by the women against the all-male coaching association. The Indiana Supreme Court ruled that it was discriminatory for a high school to sponsor a boys' team and not a girls' team.

Title IX prohibits discrimination by sex. Although it is a federal law, it has still been necessary for many girls and women to go to court to ensure their rights under the law.

A Michigan judge's court ruling in 1981, if allowed to stand, may have serious implications for the implementation of Title IX. Federal District Court Judge Charles Joiner ruled that Title IX can apply only to programs that directly receive federal funds. He ruled that the U.S. Department of Education could not enforce Title IX in the Ann Arbor School District's interscholastic sports program because the program received no federal funding. If such a precedent is established, it will have a far-reaching effect not only on athletics but other areas as well.

The publication *In The Running,* in its Fall 1978 issue, provides advice to girls and women regarding the filing of a Title IX Complaint. Some *pros of filing a complaint* are that it is possible to win; other women may be convinced to take legal action for other complaints; the Title IX compliance plan at the plaintiff's school may become the subject of scrutiny, which can change discriminatory practices at her school to the benefit of many girls and women; and schools that have been cited for complaints are more likely to be closer to compliance with the law. Some *cons of filing a complaint* are that the plaintiff can lose her suit and her position or scholarship. She may become frustrated in dealing with the many organizations involved, and the procedure sometimes takes years to resolve. She also may be labeled a troublemaker.

Organizations that are of help in cases of inequality are the Department of Education; Office of Civil Rights; Equal Employment Opportunity Commission; Office of Federal Contract Compliance; and the U.S. Department of Labor—Wage and Hour Division of the Employment Standards Administration.

COEDUCATIONAL SPORTS AND TITLE IX

Coeducational sports should be provided for students in schools because of the benefits (mainly social and cultural) that can accrue from such participation. However, coeducational sports, in many cases, should be limited to the intramural and recreational levels. As a general rule, highly competitive athletics should not be coeducational. But in instances where one or

Fig. 6-7. Girls' basketball.

Courtesy Barbara Ann Chiles,
Aledo, Ill.

coach said that, although she possessed excellent basketball skills, her weight and overall strength militated against her making the team. The skills of most of the other basketball hopefuls at that level of play were probably also very high. Thus size and strength became critical factors. This would not be the case on the intramural and recreational levels. Females with greater skill than their male counterparts can make up for the differences in strength and size.

When providing coeducational sports for the intramural and/or recreational sports programs, administrators must modify the games to suit both sexes. Several examples of effective coeducational activities are presented in the May 1976 *Journal of Physical Education and Recreation:* basketball, flag football, fencing, water joust, softball, and several other sports. The article describes how intramural basketball was offered on a coeducational basis at Christiansburg High School. Only the following modifications and/or restrictions were required.

1. Teams are comprised of three boys and three girls.
2. The length of the game is two 10-minute halves.
3. Boys are not allowed to shoot from inside the key (free throw circle).
4. Slow break rules are used (that is, when the ball is controlled by the defensive team, everyone must advance. The ball cannot be moved until everyone is down court).
5. Players must alternate passes between boys and girls when the ball is in the forecourt.
6. One set of passes must be completed before a shot can be attempted.
7. Balls are taken out-of-bounds after a foul, unless it was a deliberate or technical foul.

The main consideration in establishing coeducational sports programs is to respond to the interests and ability levels of the participants. Because of their level of skill and other reasons, some males and females will not wish to participate in coeducational sports programs even on an intramural or recreational level. Opportunities should be provided for these individuals to participate on separate teams. When conducting sports on a coeducational basis, physical educators should make appropriate modifications in the rules and conduct of the activities to equalize competition between the sexes. AAHPERD has published a book entitled *Rules for Coeducational Activities and*

two extremely skilled females would not otherwise have the opportunity to participate in a particular sport, they must be allowed to participate with males.

There are several reasons for advocating separate teams for males and females. For instance, if coeducational varsity teams were encouraged, males would comprise most of the teams. Because of the "speed, size, and strength" factors, girls would not be able to make varsity teams in any great numbers. Consequently, there would be mostly male-dominated teams.

The attempt by Ann Myers (a former women's all-American basketball player from UCLA) to make the roster of an NBA basketball team demonstrates the athletic differences between top-level male and female athletes. Myers failed to make the NBA team. The

SAMPLING OF FINDINGS

Q—Do you enjoy P.E.?
A—High ability students—98% yes, 2% no
    Medium ability students—90% yes, 10% no
    Low ability students—87% yes, 13% no
Q—Do you feel that you are good at sports?
A—High ability students—90% yes, 10% no
    Medium ability students—74% yes, 26% no
    Low ability students—65% yes, 35% no
Q—Do you feel that coed gym is worthwhile?
A—Students whose coach is of the same sex as last
    year's—56% yes, 44% no
    Students whose coach is of the opposite sex as
    last year's—74% yes, 26% no
    All male students—53% yes, 47% no
    All female students—80% yes, 20% no

Q—Do you feel comfortable engaging in sports with
    members of the opposite sex?
A—Students whose coach is of the same sex as last
    year's—74% yes, 26% no
    Students whose coach is of the opposite sex as
    last year's—85% yes, 15% no
    All male students—75% yes, 25% no
    All female students—85% yes, 15% no
Q—Compared to last year's class, are the students
    in your class more or less motivated?
A—Students whose coach is of the same sex as last
    year's—52% more, 48% less
    Students whose coach is of the opposite sex as
    last year's—62% more, 38% less
    All male students—52% more, 48% less
    All female students—68% more, 32% less

Sports (1977) that contains many examples of coeducational programs in action and suggestions for modifying coeducational college level team sports for elementary and secondary educational levels.

Mikkelson* conducted a survey of 263 students about coeducational physical education classes. The students included those of "high ability," "medium ability," and "low ability" in terms of class placement (ability level, previous semester's grade, and the sex of their coach). Classes in each group were taught with the following results (See "Sampling of findings" above.)

PROSPECTS FOR THE FUTURE

All institutions, and this includes most schools and colleges, that receive federal financial assistance must comply with Title IX. Furthermore, since it is difficult for the federal government to supervise and make decisions for the 16,000 schools and 2,700 postsecondary educational institutions, a major share of the responsibility rests with individual institutions. Each school district and each college or university or other institution is unique and, as a result, must develop its own plan for compliance. Noncompliance can present many problems and difficulties. The government will no longer tolerate and this nation can no longer justify inequities in the treatment of the sexes.

Each institution and each educational program faces many problems in complying with Title IX. This is true particularly in light of present budget crises. It will be difficult for many institutions to increase items such as the course offerings, budgets, and facilities for an expanded athletic program for girls without curtailing some other parts of the educational program, possibly that of the boys'. It will be difficult to bear the increased costs of adding faculty, facilities, supplies and equipment, and scholarships to provide girls and women with a physical education and athletic program comparable to that of the boys and men.

These problems, however, are being solved in thousands of educational institutions from coast to coast. For example, there are many schools where athletic and physical education activities are being modified so that students may engage in them on a coeducational basis. Basketball is being played, for example,

---

*Mikkelson, M.D.: Coed gym—it's a whole new ballgame, Journal of Physical Education and Recreation **50:**63-64, Oct. 1979.

with three women and two men on a team, with field goals scored by women counting four points and those by men two points, and with men not being permitted to enter the free-throw lane at any time at either end of the court. Volleyball is being played with four men and four women: men are not permitted to spike and must serve underhand. Furthermore, at least one woman must touch the ball before it is volleyed back over the net by her team. Adaptations and modifications can be developed in most activities to make them suitable for coeducational use.

Instructors of physical education classes and coaches of athletic teams assigned to teams of the opposite sex or to coeducational teams have been successful. Budgets have been increased for girls' and women's programs in many cases without harming the overall physical education and athletic program. Schedules have been revised so that both males and females have access to facilities on an equitable basis. Many other changes have also taken place to comply with Title IX.

Compliance may be achieved according to the letter and the spirit of the federal mandate providing there is a willingness to comply and a desire to cooperate with other members of an educational institution. The first and foremost way to achieve desirable results is to work locally through the system. It should be recognized that resistance will sometimes be encountered, since change seldom comes easily. However, the law demands equity for both sexes, and as a result such changes will eventually take place. The Office of Civil Rights is willing to assist school officials in meeting their Title IX responsibilities. Regional offices, where help may be secured, exist in 10 different locations throughout the nation.

Physical education and athletics occupy a very important place in the American culture. The turmoil and reorganization implicit in meeting the federal requirement for equity offer an opportunity to physical educators to contribute to the health and welfare of all human beings rather than to only a few.

The handicapped and the law

There is considerable variation in statistics relating to the number of handicapped school children—from

six to nine million. Gearheart and Weishahn, in their recent book *The Handicapped Child in the Regular Classroom* (1980, The C.V. Mosby Co.), provide the following figures:

Visually impaired (includes blind)—55,000
Hearing impaired (includes deaf)—330,000 to 440,000
Speech handicapped—1,925,000 to 2,750,000
Crippled and other health impaired—275,000
Emotionally disturbed—1,100,000 to 1,650,000
Mentally retarded (both educable and trainable)—
    1,375,000 to 1,650,000
Learning disabilities—1,100,000 to 2,200,000
        Total: 6,160,000 to 9,020,000

The authors also point out that more than half of the handicapped children in the United States do not receive adequate educational services. However, there have been many court decisions and laws passed to ensure equality of educational opportunity for handicapped individuals.

PUBLIC LAW 94-142*

Because of the specific mention of physical education in the final regulations implementing P.L. 94-142 (Education of All Handicapped Children Act of 1975), it is discussed in some detail here.

The final regulations of P.L. 94-142 spell out the federal government's commitment to providing all handicapped children with a free and appropriate education. Specifically, full educational services must be provided for (1) handicapped children not currently receiving a free and appropriate education and (2) severely handicapped youngsters receiving inadequate assistance.

Handicapped children, as defined in P.L. 94-142, are those who require some type of special education and related services. Related services, under the act, are defined as "transportation and developmental, corrective, and other supportive services, including occupational therapy, recreation, and medical and counseling services. . . ." Although gifted children might need special education and related services, they are not covered under the law.

---

*Technical information related to P.L. 94-142 is taken from the Physical Education Newsletter, No. 87, Nov. 1977. By permission.

Fig. 6-8. An individual in a wheelchair stretches to catch a long pass.

Courtesy Julian Stein, American Alliance for Health, Physical Education, Recreation, and Dance (1900 Association Dr., Reston, Va. 22091) and Rehabilitation Education Center, University of Illinois, Champaign-Urbana, Ill.

Special stipulations of P.L. 94-142 require:

1. State and local educational agencies to initiate policies to ensure all handicapped boys and girls the right to a free and appropriate education
2. Planning of individualized educational programs, with conferences among parents, teachers, representatives of local educational agencies, and, where appropriate, children themselves. These conferences must be held at least once a year.
3. Due process for parents and children, to ensure that their rights are not abrogated
4. A per pupil expenditure which is at least equal to the amount spent on nonhandicapped children in the state or local school district
5. The state and local agency shall carry out the mandates of the law according to specific time-tables provided therein

6. The development of a comprehensive system of personnel training, including preservice and inservice training for teachers
7. That handicapped students will be educated in the "least restrictive environment." This means that they will be mainstreamed into the regular class whenever possible.

Aspects of P.L. 94-142 related to physical education

121a.307 Physical Education

(a) *General.* Physical education services, specially designed if necessary, must be made available to every handicapped child receiving a free appropriate public education.

(b) *Regular physical education.* Each handicapped child must be afforded the opportunity to participate in the regular physical education program available to nonhandicapped children unless:

    (1) The child is enrolled full time in a separate facility; or

    (2) The child needs specially designed physical education, as prescribed in the child's individualized education program

(c) *Special physical education.* If specially designed physical education is prescribed in a child's individualized education program, the public agency responsible for the education of that child shall provide the services directly, or make arrangements for it to be provided through other public or private programs.

(d) *Education in separate facilities.* The public agency responsible for the education of a handicapped child who is enrolled in a separate facility shall insure that the child receives appropriate physical education services in compliance with paragraphs (a) and (c) of this section.

The House of Representatives, in a special report on this subject, made the following reference to physical education:

The committee expects the Commissioner of Education to take whatever action is necessary to assure that physical education services are available to all handicapped children, and has specifically included physical education within the definition of special education, to make clear that the Committee expects such services, specially designed where necessary, to be provided as an integral part of the educational program of every handicapped child.

The physical education program for handicapped students must be individualized according to the needs of each person. Students should be included in the regular program whenever possible and special adapted programs established as needed. Students should not be mainstreamed into the regular physical education program when their handicap(s) prevents them from receiving an adequate educational experience. Conversely, they should not be placed in a special class and left there. Handicapped youngsters should be scheduled in and out of regular classes, depending on their ability to cope with the specific activity being taught at a particular time. The final consideration is to provide the handicapped child with the "least restrictive environment" or one that permits the child to achieve his or her maximum potential.

OTHER LEGISLATION

Other legislative acts relating to handicapped persons and affecting physical education programs are Section 504 of the Rehabilitation Act of 1973 (P.L. 33-112) and the Education Amendment Act of 1974 (P.L. 93-380). The provisions of this statute guarantee the rights of handicapped persons in programs for which schools and other sponsoring groups receive federal funds. P.L. 93-380 is designed to ensure that handicapped individuals be placed in the least restrictive alternative environment for educational purposes. Part VIB of the law specifically states that

. . . to the maximum extent appropriate, handicapped children should be educated with children who are not handicapped, and that special classes, separate schooling or other means of removal of handicapped children from the regular educational environment, occurs only when the nature or severity of the handicap is such that education in regular classes with the use of supplementary aids and services cannot be achieved satisfactorily.

MAINSTREAMING

Mainstreaming means that handicapped persons receive their education, including physical education, with persons who are not handicapped, unless the nature of the handicap is such that education in the regular classroom or gymnasium setting cannot be achieved in a satisfactory manner, even with the use of supplementary aids and services. The federal law does not mean that all handicapped children will be a part of the regular class. It does mean that those handicapped students who can profit from taking physical education with regular students should be assigned to regular classes.

Advocates of mainstreaming point out the following advantages:

• Some psychological testing has been questioned, since some tests that have labeled many students as retarded have proved to be unreliable; therefore, many of these students should be in regular classes.

• Fiscal considerations encourage mainstreaming because special education with segregated and special classes increases educational costs.

• Classifying and segregating handicapped students who are retarded result in labeling and cause harm to children.

• The research does not convincingly show that handicapped children advance scholastically faster when segregated than when grouped with children in the regular classroom.

- The American way suggests an integration of all types of children into the classroom situation.
- Many educators are convinced that the nonhandicapped child gains in understanding by exposure to handicapped children.
- Handicapped children benefit socially and emotionally when they are a part of regular classes.

A new concept of mainstreaming. The traditional definition of mainstreaming is to take handicapped students from a special class and make them part of the regular class, along with nonhandicapped students. In recent years, this definition has lost favor among some special educators and other teachers who believe that students are frequently placed in regular classes without any support services or modification of regular class instructional procedures. A new concept of mainstreaming being favored by more educators today is that of providing educational services for handicapped students in the "least restrictive environment." In essence, this means that a handicapped child is placed in a special class or a regular class or is moved between the two environments as dictated by his or her abilities and capabilities. Furthermore, the school assumes the responsibility of providing the necessary adjunct services to ensure that handicapped students perform to their optimum capacity, whether integrated into the regular program or left in a special class.

According to many educators, mainstreaming can be successful if certain basic practices are adhered to before and during the process of mainstreaming. The handicapped person should be placed in the educational environment that produces optimal growth and development, that is, the "least restrictive environment." Stein, of the American Alliance for Health, Physical Education, Recreation, and Dance, states, "The idea behind mainstreaming is that if an individual can safely, successfully, and with personal satisfaction take part in a regular program or in unrestricted activities, no special program is necessary.* However, this should be viewed as the ideal. Some

handicapped students must be educated in special self-contained classrooms while others might benefit from some services in a regular class and some activities in the special class.

The developmental concept—an aid to mainstreaming. The use of the developmental approach to programming for handicapped persons (individual planning of educational programs) will help to promote positive and successful mainstreaming. This developmental concept of education rejects the notion of rigid categories that result in people being stigmatized. Rather it advances the notion that there is a hierarchy of developmental tasks through which each individual must progress. In other words, each person grows and develops in a sequential pattern in all domains—physically, mentally, emotionally, and socially. By observing behavior in each of these developmental areas on an individual basis, instructional programs can be planned. Crowe, Auxter, and Pyfer* have provided a thorough presentation of the application of the developmental concept.

Mainstreaming in a physical education program for the handicapped. Physical education is a subject where a great deal can be done for handicapped students if they are mainstreamed, provided that the physical educators in charge understand handicapped individuals and the type of program that will best meet their needs. Whether or not the program is successful depends on the teacher and his or her ability to individualize the offering to meet the needs of each student in the class. It is essential to select the program of activities carefully, to begin at the student's current level, and to let the capabilities of the individual determine his or her progress.

The physical educator should use several approaches in teaching various types of handicapped students and not expect rapid progress. Handicapped students should feel a sense of achievement and success in their efforts. A thorough medical examination should be a first step, and each student will require assistance from time to time. Modification of the activities will be necessary in many cases. Complete records on each student should be kept, with notations concerning the

---

*Stein, J.U.: Sense and nonsense about mainstreaming. Journal of Physical Education and Recreation **47:**43, Jan. 1976.

*Crowe, W.C., Auxter, D., and Pyfer, J.: Principles and methods of adapted physical education and recreation, ed. 4, St. Louis, 1981, The C.V. Mosby Co.

nature of the handicap, recommendations of the physician, and appropriate and inappropriate activities.

Each handicapped student must be made to feel a part of the physical education program. For example, mentally retarded children should gain self-confidence, and physically handicapped students should have fun meeting the challenges that certain activities and exercises provide. In addition, the activities should be challenging and at the same time rewarding for the development of a positive self-concept. Some handicapped students should be taught leisure-time activities and ways to play. The need for physical fitness should be stressed. Finally, it is important to stress safety, to avoid underestimating a student's abilities, and to remember that many handicapped children have a short attention span, tire easily, and are easily distracted.

SUGGESTED PROCEDURES FOR IMPLEMENTING P.L. 94-142

Cole and Dunn have suggested the following procedures for implementing P.L. 94-142.*

• Develop task forces on a local and regional basis and appoint people to leadership positions who know about the law.

• Appoint someone with responsibility to implement the law and also see that the implementation processes are prescribed in writing.

• Establish a series of workshops to orient administration and staff personnel to the various components of the law and implementation procedures.

• Request information about the law and its implementation from organizations concerned with special education.

• Simulate team placement conferences so that administration and staff may become better informed of their responsibilities, the instructional strategies involved, and other administrative details in providing for handicapped students.

• Prepare a brochure on the program for parents, outlining their rights and the rights of children under the law. Explain procedures that may be used and programs under consideration.

• Organize workshops for administrative and staff

*Adapted from Cole, R.W., and Dunn, R.: A new lease on life for education of the handicapped: Ohio copes with P.L. 94-142, Phi Delta Kappan **59**:3, Sept. 1977.

personnel to familiarize them with different instructional strategies for individualizing instruction and to acquaint them with the relationships between learning-style characteristics and these instructional strategies.

• Visit schools that are already providing excellent programs under P.L. 94-142, find out what practices are successful, and get suggestions for implementing the program.

• Develop a curriculum that meets the needs of various types of handicapped students, including the preparation of such features as learning packages, contract activity packages, multisensory instructional packages, and resource lists for teachers.

• Involve parents and students in the provision of resources and in helping handicapped students.

• Decide carefully which students will be mainstreamed and which ones will not be.

• Encourage all teachers to individualize instruction so that handicapped students will be integrated into their classes as easily as possible.

• Have all teachers, whether teaching regular or special classes, participate on the reevaluation team.

• Simplify instructional materials so that they may be easily understood by the students.

• Participate in regional, state, and national conferences on the implementation of P.L. 94-142 in order to discover new techniques and means of instruction that have proved effective in other schools.

FACILITIES, EQUIPMENT, AND SUPPLIES FOR THE HANDICAPPED

Appropriate and adequate facilities, equipment, and supplies are important to successful programs of physical education for handicapped persons. However, these factors must be emphasized in special or adapted physical education programs because facilities and equipment are usually designed for students in the regular class. Adaptations are also often necessary when handicapped students are mainstreamed into regular programs.

The passage of recent legislation and the results of various legal decisions have prompted school districts to make available the necessary facilities, equipment, and supplies to ensure a quality education for handicapped students. There is some question, however, as to whether handicapped students are in fact being provided with these adequate facilities, equipment, and supplies. They are not, according to Stein, a recognized authority on problems of handicapped persons. He believes that "despite federal legislation, mandates in every state, and regulations in some local areas, facilities of all types continue to be built and renovated without consideration of barriers, accessibility, and availability [to the handicapped person]." Stein states that the major problem and cause of these situations and conditions are "attitudinal barriers."*

The types of facilities and equipment needed for adapted physical education will vary according to the nature of the program (adapted sports, remedial or corrective exercises, or rest and relaxation), the type of student (mentally retarded, physically handicapped, or some other), and the school level at which the program is conducted. For example, the elementary school program in adapted physical education may be taught in the regular gymnasium or, in less desirable circumstances, in the classroom. In secondary schools and colleges, however, a special room for adapted physical education should be provided.

The State of Virginia, in its instructional booklet "Physical Education for Handicapped Students," outlines some of the factors that should be taken into consideration for handicapped students.

Within building
- Doors easy to open
- Ramps with handrails on both sides
- Elevators or chair lifts when necessary
- Floors with non-slip surfaces
- Toilet seats of proper height with rails provided

Outside building
- Loading and parking areas close to entrances
- Convenient parking places
- Ramps suitable for wheelchairs
- Doorways wide enough for wheelchairs
- Emergency exits for wheelchairs

Adaptive physical education equipment (for bowling)
- Providing a wheelchair student with a bowling ball ramp
- Providing a blind student with a bowling rail
- Providing a student with limited strength with lightweight, plastic bowling balls and pins

---

*American Alliance for Health, Physical Education, and Recreation: Making physical education and recreation facilities accessible to all: planning, designing, adapting, Washington, D.C., 1977, The Alliance, p. i.

Child abuse and the law

It is estimated that 652,000 children in the United States are maltreated annually. However, according to the National Center on Child Abuse and Neglect, the numbers are much higher since this figure takes into account only those children "who definitely suffered demonstrable harm." The American Humane Society found 711,142 substantiated cases of abuse and neglect throughout the nation in 1979, a 71% increase from the 1976 total. Child abuse and neglect means "the non-accidental physical or mental injury, sexual abuse, negligent treatment or maltreatment of a child under the age of 18 years by a person who is responsible for the child's welfare under circumstances which indicate the child's health or welfare is harmed or threatened in any way." Among the more frequent types of abuse and neglect are
- *Physical abuse*—beating, punching, shaking, or burning by a person taking care of a child. Such abuse could result from overdiscipline or from some sort of punishment.
- *Sexual abuse*—any interaction or contact between child and adult for sexual stimulation. Sexual abuse also includes incest, rape, or lewdness with a minor.
- *Physical neglect*—chronic inattention to such necessities as food, clothing, shelter, medical care, and supervision
- *Emotional neglect/abuse*—denial of needs essential to the child's emotional well-being, feelings such as being loved, secure, wanted, and valued
- *Improper supervision*—failure to safeguard the child's health and welfare
- *Emotional maltreatment*—the rejection, blaming, or belittling of a child
- *Destitution*—inability of the family to provide physical care for child
- *Alcohol/drug abuse*—impairment of a minor's health as a result of excessive use of drugs and/or alcohol by adults
- *Abandonment*—failure of legal parent or guardian to assume responsibility for a minor
- *Exploitation*—use of child by adult for personal gain, such as forcing child to beg or to overwork
- *Environmental neglect*—conditions in the home that are not in the child's best interests: lack of clean-

liness, overcrowding, safety hazards, and/or other dangers

The schools represent one of the best sources for reporting cases of child abuse and neglect. For example, in Clark County schools in Nevada, it is estimated that more than 70% of the schools' reports of child abuse turned out to be legitimate. According to Dr. Fred Kirschner, Professor of Education at the University of Nevada, Las Vegas, ''Teachers are agents who promote better learning and they are obligated to observe a child's welfare.'' He goes on to state that ''we are talking about better mental health for our children. A child can't be attentive in school if he's worried about his homelife or scared of going home. If a child is afraid to dress in gym class because he's battered, what's this going to do to his behavior? You simply can't play the denial game. We've got to help children in any way we can.''

Child abuse is illegal, and physical educators should be on the lookout for cases involving physical abuse, physical neglect, sexual abuse, or emotional maltreatment. These cases should be reported to the proper authorities.

New interpretations of legal liability by the courts

In recent years the courts have heard cases involving physical education and athletics that have resulted in a new look at liability in such areas as sports products, violence, and physical education classes held off-campus.

SPORTS PRODUCT LIABILITY*

The sale of sporting goods is a multibillion dollar industry today. The desire of many people to engage in physical fitness and sports activities is one reason for this growth in sales. In turn, recent years have seen the subject of sports product liability arise. The term ''product liability,'' according to Arnold, refers to the liability of the manufacturer to the person who uses the manufactured product and who sustains injury or damage as a result of using the product. What is

most important to physical educators, athletic directors, and coaches is that they are being named as co-defendants in approximately one-third of all liability suits involving sports product liability.

Years ago the buyer was responsible for inspecting the product before making the purchase and assumed the risk of injury or damage to property. Today, however, the courts are placing more and more responsibility on the manufacturer to discover weaknesses and defects in products. The manufacturer is required to exercise due care in such matters as design, manufacture, and packaging of the product, guaranteeing it safe for consumer use.

According to Arnold, within the last 25 years an estimated 42 states have used the *strict liability doctrine* for some products. Under this doctrine the plaintiff must establish proof that the product contained a defect that caused injury or damage. In addition to this doctrine, a breach of the manufacturer's warranty can also be just cause for awarding damages. The number of suits involving product liability has increased dramatically in the last few years. One reason is that persons involved in injury suits feel it is possible to get a large award from the courts. As a result of these enormous amounts of money to successful plaintiffs, insurance rates have skyrocketed.

Arnold lists 10 ways that the risks associated with sports product liability may be reduced and that will help in successful product liability litigation. The individual should

1. Become involved in the collection of pertinent facts and information associated with illness and injury, which can result in discouraging unwarranted claims
2. Purchase the best quality equipment available. Equipment should be carefully evaluated and tested and records kept regarding such items as date of purchase. Reconditioning and repair items should also be recorded.
3. Purchase only from reputable dealers, who stand behind their products and provide replacements when necessary
4. Utilize only reputable reconditioning equipment companies that have high standards. For example, the NOCSAE stamp of approval should appear on reconditioned football helmets.

*Arnold, D.E.: Sports product liability, Journal of Physical Education and Recreation **49**:25-28, Nov./Dec. 1978.

5. Follow the manufacturer's instructions in regard to the fitting, adjusting, and repair of equipment, particularly protective equipment, and urge participants to wear protective equipment regularly

6. Be careful not to blame someone or something for the injury without just cause. Furthermore, it is best to confine such remarks to the accident report.

7. Follow good teaching and supervising procedures and avoid drills or techniques that are disapproved by professional associations and respected leaders in the field

8. Prepare an emergency care plan and be ready to implement it when needed

9. Purchase and/or make available to all parties, including athletes, staff members, and schools, insurance coverage for accident and general liability

10. Preserve items of evidence, such as pieces of equipment, associated with any serious injury

VIOLENCE AND LEGAL LIABILITY*

An increasing number of injuries resulting from sports contests are intentional rather than accidental. When such an act occurs, it is referred to as battery and "involves the harmful, unpermitted contact of one person by another." Carpenter and Acosta point out that the courts are making large awards for violence in sports cases. They cite the 1979 case of the professional basketball player who was hit in the face with a lethal punch and was awarded in excess of $3 million in damages.

Carpenter and Acosta also point out that the coach is not necessarily free from liability in such cases of violence. They cite two theoretical situations where the coach may be held liable. The first is where a coach knows that a player is likely to commit a violent act in a sports situation, yet puts the player into the lineup. In this case the coach is not taking the necessary precautions to protect opponents from harm and injury, and in the event injury does occur, the coach may be found negligent. In the second instance,

a coach may instruct a player "to take 'X' out of the game." In this case, the player who follows such instruction is acting as an agent of the coach. As a result, a person who causes battery to be committed (in this case the coach) is just as negligent as the person who commits the act. In both cases, the coach who is a good leader will see that his or her players conduct themselves in accordance with proper standards of conduct.

PHYSICAL EDUCATION CLASSES HELD OFF-CAMPUS AND LEGAL LIABILITY*

Off-campus physical education activities have become popular in many schools. In such cases, instruction in the activity may be provided by the faculty, or the faculty may provide supervision only, with a specialist not associated with the school in charge.

Although instruction by nonfaculty members may take place in off-campus settings, considerable responsibility and control still rest with the administration and staff of the organization that sponsors these activities. Arnold cites the case of a college that hired a person not affiliated with the college to teach a course at an off-campus equestrian center. The plaintiff was injured in a fall from a horse while receiving instruction in horseback riding. The plaintiff's attorney argued that the college was vicariously liable for the negligence of the riding academy. The court ruled in favor of the college, which did not have to pay damages on the grounds that a master-servant relationship did not exist between the plaintiff and the college. To show such a relationship, the plaintiff would have had to prove that, among other things, the college could control the instruction that was taking place. Furthermore, the court ruled that the agency relationship did not result in the college authorizing the fall that led to the injury and that no complaints had been lodged regarding the instruction.

Where off-campus physical education activities are conducted, a primary consideration is whether *due care* is provided. The type of activity offered would indicate the amount of care that should be provided.

---

*Carpenter, L.J., and Acosta, R.V.: Violence in sport—is it part of the game or the intentional tort of battery? Journal of Physical Education and Recreation **51**:18, Sept. 1980.

---

*Arnold, D.E.: Legal aspects of off-campus physical education programs, Journal of Physical Education and Recreation **50**:21-23, April 1979.

For example, according to Arnold, bowling in a town bowling alley in most cases would not require as much care as a skiing class. It is the responsibility of physical educators to exercise caution and prudence in the selection of sites to be used for off-campus activities, to control the quality of the instruction, and to provide adequate supervision. Failure to observe proper care can result in negligence on the part of the school. Physical educators should also look into other aspects of off-campus activities, such as transportation for students to participate in these activities.

Avoiding lawsuits

GENERAL PRECAUTIONS

The physical educator should
1. Be familiar with the health status of each person in the program
2. Consider the individuals' skills when teaching new activities
3. Group participants together on equal competitive levels
4. Be sure that both equipment and facilities are safe
5. Organize and carefully supervise the class. Never leave the class unattended—even in emergencies. If an emergency occurs, get a replacement before leaving the room
6. Administer only first aid—never prescribe or diagnose
7. Use only qualified personnel to aid in classrooms
8. Keep accurate accident records
9. Provide adequate instruction, especially in potentially dangerous activities
10. Make sure that any injured person receives a medical examination

COACHING PRECAUTIONS

The Coaches' Handbook of the American Alliance for Health, Physical Education, Recreation, and Dance lists some of the ways by which a reasonable and prudent coach can avoid a lawsuit. In addition to the general precautions listed above, the coach should
1. Require medical clearance of players who have been seriously injured or ill

2. Render services only in those areas where fully qualified
3. Follow proper procedures in case of injuries
4. See that medical personnel are available at all games and on call for practice sessions
5. See that all activities are conducted in safe areas
6. Be careful not to diagnose or treat players' injuries
7. See that protective equipment is properly fitted and worn by players who need such equipment
8. Use coaching methods and procedures that provide for the safety of players
9. Be sure only qualified personnel are assigned responsibilities
10. Make sure proper instruction is given before players are permitted to engage in contests
11. See that a careful and accurate record is kept of injuries and that procedures are followed
12. Act as a prudent, careful, and discerning coach whose players are his or her first consideration

ADMINISTRATIVE PRECAUTIONS

The following exercise should provide personal guidance in establishing a degree of prudence commensurate with the professional as well as legal responsibilities of the contemporary administrator in physical education and/or athletics (see p. 181).

SAFETY

It is important to take every possible precaution to prevent accidents by providing for the safety of students and other individuals who participate in programs of physical education, athletics, and recreation. If such precautions are taken, the likelihood of a lawsuit will diminish and the question of negligence will be eliminated.

1. Instructor should be properly trained and qualified to perform specialized work.

2. Instructor should be present at all organized activities in the program.

3. Classes should be organized properly according to size, activity, physical condition, and other factors that have a bearing on safety and health of the individual.

4. Health examinations should be given to all pupils.

	Degree of compliance			
	Always	*Frequently*	*Rarely*	*Never*

The prudent administrator:

1. Seeks to prohibit the situation which may lead to litigation through constant foresight and care inherent in the professional role he/she holds ____ ____ ____ ____

2. Assigns instructional and supervisory duties concerning an activity to only those people who are qualified for that particular activity ____ ____ ____ ____

3. Conducts regular inspections of all equipment used and insists on full repair of faulty items prior to use ____ ____ ____ ____

4. Establishes procedures and enforces rules concerning safe use of equipment and proper fitting of all uniforms and protective gear ____ ____ ____ ____

5. Has written plans with adequate review procedures to assure that participants do not progress too rapidly into areas of skill performance beyond their present skill level ____ ____ ____ ____

6. Selects opponents for each participant/team with care to avoid potentially dangerous mismatching ____ ____ ____ ____

7. Establishes and scrupulously enforces rules regarding reporting of illness or injury, to include compilation of written records and names and addresses of witnesses ____ ____ ____ ____

8. Does not treat injuries unless professionally prepared and certified to do so ____ ____ ____ ____

9. Regularly updates first aid and emergency medical care credentials ____ ____ ____ ____

10. Does not permit participation in any activity without medical approval following serious illness or injury ____ ____ ____ ____

11. Readily recognizes the presence of any attractive nuisance, and initiates firm control measures ____ ____ ____ ____

12. Posts safety rules for use of facilities, then orients students and colleagues to danger areas in activities, facilities, and personal conduct ____ ____ ____ ____

13. Does not place the activity area in the control of nonqualified personnel for *any* reason ____ ____ ____ ____

14. Relies on waiver forms not as a negation for responsibility for injury but only as a means of assuring that parents/guardians recognize students' intent to participate ____ ____ ____ ____

15. Does not permit zeal for accomplishment or emotion of the moment to suppress rational behavior ____ ____ ____ ____

16. Provides in letter and spirit nondiscriminatory programs for all students ____ ____ ____ ____

17. Cancels transportation plans if unable to be thoroughly convinced of the personal and prudent reliability of drivers, means of transportation and adequacy of insurance coverage ____ ____ ____ ____

18. Does not conduct a class/or practice/or contest without a plan for medical assistance in the event of injury regardless of the setting ____ ____ ____ ____

19. Holds professional liability insurance of significant dollar dimensions and pertinent applicability to professional pursuits involving physical activity ____ ____ ____ ____

20. Does not permit excessive concern about legal liability to prohibit the development of a challenging and accountable physical education experience for each participant ____ ____ ____ ____

From Parsons, T.W.: What price prudence? Journal of Physical Education and Recreation **50**:45, Jan. 1979.

5. A planned, written program for proper disposition of participants who are injured or become sick should be followed.

6. Regular inspections should be made of such items as equipment, apparatus, ropes, or chains, placing extra pressure on them and taking other precautions to make sure they are safe. They should also be checked for such hazards as deterioration, looseness, fraying, and splinters.

7. Overcrowded athletic and other events should be avoided, building codes and fire regulations should be adhered to, and adequate lighting for all facilities should be provided.

8. Protective equipment such as mats should be used wherever possible. Any hazards such as projections or obstacles in an area where activity is taking place should be eliminated. Floors should not be slippery. Shower rooms should have surfaces conducive to secure footing.

9. Sneakers should be worn on gymnasium floors and adequate space provided for each activity.

10. Activities should be adapted to the age and maturity of the participants, proper and competent supervision should be provided, and spotters should be used in gymnastics and other similar activities.

11. Students and other participants should be instructed in the correct methods of using apparatus and performing in physical activities. Any misuse of equipment should be prohibited.

12. The buildings and other facilities should be inspected regularly for safety hazards, such as loose tiles, broken fences, cracked glass, and uneven pavement. Defects should be reported immediately to responsible persons and necessary precautions taken.

13. A detailed report should be prepared if an accident occurs.

Insurance management

There are three major types of insurance management that schools and other organizations use to protect themselves against loss. The first type is insurance for *property.* The second type is insurance for *liability protection,* a safeguard against financial loss arising from personal injury or property damage for which the school district or organization is liable. The third type, *crime protection,* insures against a financial loss that might be incurred as a result of theft or other illegal act. This section on insurance management is primarily concerned with the second type of insurance, liability protection.

A definite trend can be seen in school districts toward having some form of school accident insurance to protect students against injury. The same is true wherever physical education programs are conducted. This trend has had an impact on casualty and life insurance companies that offer insurance policies. The premium costs of accident policies vary from community to community and depend on the age of the insured and type of plan. Since accidents are the chief cause of death among students between the ages of 5 and 18, it can readily be seen that some protection is needed, and interscholastic athletics has stimulated the development of many state athletic protection plans as well as the issuance of special policies by commercial insurance companies.

Self-assessment tests

These tests are designed to assist students in determining if material and competencies presented in this chapter have been mastered.

1. Without consulting your text, write a one-sentence definition of each of the following terms: legal liability, tort, negligence, *in loco parentis,* "save harmless" law, assumption of risk, immunity.
2. Prepare a legal brief for a case in your state that justifies a rule requiring all students in grades 1 through 12 to attend physical education classes.
3. Arrange a mock trial in your class. The case before the court is that, in the final minutes of a game, the coach of a high school football team used a player who had incurred a brain concussion in the first quarter. The player later died from the injury.
4. Survey a physical education program in a junior or senior high school, and identify any areas of negligence that might exist in the conduct of the program.
5. Discuss the legal aspects of Title IX and P.L. 94-142.
6. Outline recent court interpretations of sports product liability, violence, and physical education activities that are held off-campus.
7. Prepare a list of safety procedures that should be followed by every physical education person in order to provide for the welfare of all students and players.
8. Indicate to your class why insurance is necessary in a physical education program.

Points to remember

1. A workable definition of various legal liability terms
2. The legal basis for physical education in the schools
3. The nature and scope of negligent behavior
4. The defenses that can be used in litigation against negligence
5. Provisions of Title IX
6. Provisions of P.L. 94-142
7. Safety procedures to be followed in a physical education program

Problems to think through

1. Why is it essential for a physical educator to understand legal liability?
2. What are common areas of negligence in the conduct of physical education programs?
3. What is the legal basis for physical education?
4. What constitutes negligent behavior on the part of a physical educator?
5. What are the implications of mainstreaming the handicapped?
6. How have girls benefited from Title IX legislation?
7. What safety precautions should physical educators observe in the conduct of their programs.

Case study for analysis

Select a secondary school, and make a careful study of its physical education and athletic program in light of Title IX regulations. Make one list of commendable aspects of the program and another list that indicates any points of noncompliance. Prepare a report that shows how full compliance with Title IX can be achieved.

Exercises for review

1. Define legal liability.
2. Discuss the implications of physical educators acting *in loco parentis* as teachers in the junior and senior high schools.
3. What can a physical educator do to avoid a lawsuit?
4. What are the implications of sport product liability, violence, and off-campus courses for physical educators?
5. Prepare a list of safety precautions you would take in order not to be guilty of negligent behavior.

Selected references

Appenzeller, H.: Bench and bar, Kendal Sports Trial **28:**12, 1973.
Arnold, D.E.: Sports product liability, Journal of Physical Education and Recreation **49:**25-28, Nov./Dec. 1978.
Arnold, D.E.: Legal aspects of off-campus physical education programs, Journal of Physical Education and Recreation **50:**21-23, April 1979.
Bird, P.J.: Tort liability, Journal of Health, Physical Education, and Recreation **41:**38, 1970.
Bucher, C.A.: Football can be made safer, New York World-Telegram and Sun, Saturday Feature Magazine, Sept. 1, 1956.
Carpenter, L.J., and Acosta, R.V.: Violence in sport—is it part of the game or the intentional tort of battery? Journal of Physical Education and Recreation **51:**18, Sept. 1980.
Chambless, J.R., and Mangin, C.: Legal liability and the physical educator, Journal of Health, Physical Education, and Recreation **44:**42, 1973.
Coping with the "sue syndrome," The Athletic Educator's Report, Aug. 1980.
Deatherage, D., and Reid, C.P.: Administration of women's competitive athletics, Dubuque, Iowa, 1977, William C. Brown Co., Publishers.
Foraker, T., et al.: School insurance, School and Community, Oct. 1967, p. 28.
Fuoss, D.E., and Troppmann, R.J.: Creative management techniques in interscholastic athletics, New York, 1977, John Wiley & Sons, Inc.
Garber, L.O.: Yearbook of school law, Danville, Ill., 1963, The Interstate Printers & Publishers, Inc.
Gauerke, W.E.: School law, New York, 1965, The Center for Applied Research in Education, Inc. (The Library of Education).
Grieve, A.: Legal aspects of spectator injuries, The Athletic Journal **47:**74, 1967.
Grieve, A.: State requirements for physical education, Journal of Health, Physical Education, and Recreation **42:**19, 1971.
Guenther, D.: Problems involving legal liability in schools, Journal of the American Association for Health, Physical Education, and Recreation **20:**511, 1949.
Hall, J.T., et al.: Administration; principles, theory and practice—with applications to physical education, Pacific Palisades, Calif., 1973, Goodyear Publishing Co., Inc.
Hamilton, R.R.: School liability, Chicago, 1952, National Safety Council.
Jensen, G.O.: State requirements in health and physical education, The Society of State of Health, Physical Education, and Recreation, July, 1973.
Johnson, T.P.: The courts and eligibility rules; is a new attitude emerging? Journal of Health, Physical Education, and Recreation **44:**34, 1973.
Parsons, T.W.: What price prudence? Journal of Physical Education and Recreation **50:**45, Jan. 1979.
Rosenswieg, M.: Want to file a title IX complaint? In the Running **50:**2, Fall 1978.

7

Interpreting the physical education program

Instructional objectives and competencies to be achieved

After reading this chapter the student should be able to

1. Recognize and understand the need for interpreting the educational value of physical education
2. Discuss the role of the Physical Education Public Information (PEPI) project in interpreting physical education to the public
3. Apply sound principles and policies of public relations to physical education
4. Identify various groups of people who need to be reached in interpreting the value of physical education and the basic considerations that need to be utilized in planning a public relations program for these groups
5. Utilize various communication media to interpret the value of physical education
6. Evaluate his or her own role in interpreting the worth of physical education

The challenge

Today, as never before, the specialized area of physical education is being challenged in the form of opportunities which, if met, will enable physical educators to render a major contribution to the nation. The public is spending millions of dollars to achieve health and fitness goals, many of which are closely related to this special field. Men and women throughout the country want to control their weight, understand scientific movement concepts, develop physical skills, prevent heart attacks, understand their bodies, and stay healthy. The physical education program can play an active role in helping people to achieve these and other goals.

The public has never been more interested in phys-

ical education, health, fitness, recreation, dance, exercise physiology, and athletic training than it is today. The challenge facing the physical education profession in light of this public interest is how to get greater support for its particular programs. Health care legislation is being proposed that costs billions of dollars a year. Federal and state governments are allocating millions of dollars for physical education for handicapped persons. More than 100 million people in the United States are now actively engaged in physical fitness activities. An estimated 1,300 books on fitness are currently in print. At least 50,000 United States firms spend an estimated $2 billion a year on fitness and recreational programs for their employees. Millions of joggers are a common sight on the highways, streets, and sidewalks of the country. Men and women, young people and the elderly, and the able as well as the disabled want to be involved.

The medical profession has indicated it can treat only 10% of the health problems that affect Americans. Physicians maintain they cannot do anything about the other 90% since the individual is responsible (that is, accountable) for making decisions about such health factors as diet, physical activity, drugs, alcohol, and tobacco. Americans—and particularly the young people attending our schools who have their lives ahead of them—need to be educated in health risk factors so that they can make informed decisions as well as develop useful physical skills that will give them a better chance of living happy, healthy, and productive lives.

Physical education at times has been the victim of the economy, taxpayers' rebellion, and fiscal pressures. Some budget officials and boards of education view physical education as a nonacademic subject and therefore low on the priority list when it comes to allocating money for new staff and equipment. Other educators have noted that, with an austerity budget, physical education is one of those extras they will have to do without.

A few years ago the city of Philadelphia decided to cut all extracurricular activities and reduce the physical education program requirement to the minimum mandated by state law. Fortunately, pressures exerted by responsible individuals and groups and a concerted effort to interpret the physical education program and its worth to students resulted in the programs being partially restored. As one student of the Philadelphia High School for Girls said before an important meeting, "When Board of Education members meet with budget officials, I hope they will be able to convince them that physical and mental conditioning go hand in hand and are equally necessary."

Need for interpreting physical education

There is an urgent need to interpret physical education to students, academic teachers and other educators, and the public in general. Accurate and sig-

nificant facts must be presented to them so that they will understand the purposes and worth of our profession in the educational process as well as in their personal lives.

Physical education is frequently a misunderstood profession. Surveys conducted among lay persons show that physical education is misconceived by some as "calisthenics done to command," "athletics," and "arms and legs and good intentions." Only if physical educators interpret their profession effectively will it be possible to obtain public support and to achieve their goals.

It is vital for teachers, students, parents, and the community-at-large to have a clear understanding of the important place of physical education in general education. This can be accomplished only when there is cooperation within the department, within the school, and within the community. A public that is not informed is not likely to lend its support to furthering physical education.

Teachers, to be effective participants in public relations, must be guided by well-considered, sound

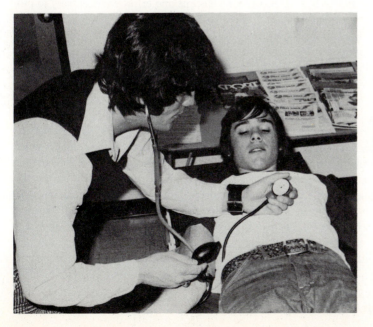

Fig. 7-1. Checking blood pressure. Exercise physiology at Penney High School in East Hartford, Conn.

educational policies. This chapter concerns itself with policies and suggestions that will assist each physical educator to be an effective public relations worker, recognizing that it is important not only to teach but also to interpret the program and its worth to various groups of people.

School-community relations

Community relations is a much-defined term and is interpreted in various ways by experts in this field. Philip Lesly speaks of it as comprising the activities and attitudes used to influence, judge, and control the opinion of any individual, group, or groups of persons in the interest of some other individuals. Professor Harwood L. Childs defines it as a name for those activities and relations with others that are public and that have significance socially. J. Handly Wright and Byron H. Christian refer to it as a program that has the characteristics of careful planning and proper conduct, which in turn result in public understanding and confidence. Edward L. Bernays, who has written widely on the subject of public relations, lists three items in his definition: first, information that is for public consumption, second, an attempt to modify the attitudes and actions of the public through persuasion, and third, an attempt to integrate the attitudes and actions of the public and of the organization or people conducting the public relations program. Benjamin Fine, a former specialist in educational community relations, defines it as the entire body of relationships that make up our impressions of an individual, an organization, or an idea.

These selected definitions of community relations help clarify its importance for any organization, institution, or group of individuals trying to develop an enterprise, profession, or business. Community relations deals with such important factors as consumers' interests, human relationships, public understanding, and good will. In business, it attempts to show the important place that specialized enterprises have in society and how they exist and operate in the public interest. In education, it is concerned with public opinion, with the needs of the school or college, and with acquainting constituents with what is being done in the public interest. It also concerns itself with ac-

quainting the community with the educational problems that must be considered in order to render greater service.

Some of the purposes of school community relations include (1) serving as a public information source concerning school activities, (2) aiding the promotion of confidence in the schools, (3) gathering support for school funding and programs, (4) stressing the value of education of all individuals, (5) improving communication between students, teachers, parents, and community members, (6) evaluating school programs, and (7) correcting misunderstandings and misinformation concerning the aims and objectives of the school.

Community relations considers the opinions of the populace. Public opinion is powerful, and individuals, organizations, and institutions succeed or fail in terms of its influence. Therefore, in order to have good community relations, the interests of human beings and what is good for people in general must be considered.

The practice of community relations is pertinent to all areas of human activity: religion, education, business, politics, military, government, labor, and other affairs. A sound community relations program is not hit-or-miss. It is planned with considerable care, and great amounts of time and effort are necessary to produce results. Furthermore, it is not something in which only the ''top brass,'' management, executives, or administrative officers should be interested. In order for any organization to have a good program, all members must be community relations–conscious.

The extent to which interest has grown in the field of community relations is indicated by the number of individuals specializing in this area. The *Public Relations Directory and Yearbook* lists such personnel. A recent edition of this publication contains the names of nearly 1,000 individuals who are working in this area on an independent basis, approximately 5,000 who are directors of public relations with business firms, approximately 2,000 who are associated with trade and professional groups, and nearly 1,000 who are with social organizations. In a recent Manhattan telephone directory, there are over 500 names listed under the heading of ''Public Relations.'' In contrast, in 1935, there were only 10 names.

The importance of community relations is being increasingly recognized for the part it can play in educational, business, or social advancement: helping these areas obtain vital public support and understanding.

PLANNING THE COMMUNITY RELATIONS PROGRAM

Community relations programs are more effective when they are planned by many interested and informed individuals and groups. Such individuals and groups as school boards, management personnel, teachers, administrators, and citizens' committees can provide valuable assistance to physical educators in certain areas of the community relations program. These people, serving in an advisory capacity to physical education and athletic departments, can help immeasurably in planning a community relations program by following specific steps identified by one expert in community relations.

1. Establish a sound public communications policy.
2. Determine what services will yield the greatest dividends.
3. Obtain facts about what citizens do and do not know and believe about educational values and needs.
4. Decide what facts and ideas will best enable citizens to understand the benefits obtained from good programs and what improvements will increase these benefits.
5. Make full use of effective planning techniques to generate understanding and appreciation.
6. Relate cost to opportunity for participants to achieve.
7. Decide who is going to perform specific communication tasks at particular times.

After the community relations plan is put into operation, it is important to test and evaluate its results and then improve the educational program accordingly.

COMMUNITY RELATIONS MEDIA

There are many media that can be employed in a community relations program. Some have more significance in certain localities than others. Some are

Fig. 7-2. Track-and-field events require adherence to basic movement principles in order to achieve best physical performance.

Walt Whitman High School, South Huntington Schools, N.Y.

more readily accessible than others. Physical educators, athletic directors, and coaches should survey their communities to determine media that will be most effective.

The *program* and the *staff* represent the best advertisement for an effective community relations program. Through the activities and experiences provided and the leadership given, good will may be built for any school, department, or profession. The most effective community relations are accomplished on a person-to-person basis. This might be teacher to student, student to parent, teacher to citizen, or physical educator to participant. In all cases the participant is an important consideration, indeed the most important agent of communication.

PEPI project

The Physical Education Public Information (PEPI) project is one of the major efforts by the profession to interpret physical education to the public. The project has identified some 600 coordinators situated in each of the nation's largest metropolitan areas who organize and interpret physical education in their own geographical area through such means as radio, television, newspapers, and other media.

The PEPI project was initiated on the premise that the tendency to curtail physical education programs can be reversed if people become aware of such basic values of physical education as:

- Physical education is health insurance.
- Physical education contributes to academic achievement.
- Physical education provides experiences and skills that last a lifetime.
- Physical education helps in developing a positive self-image and the ability to compete and cooperate with others.

PEPI has mobilized its efforts to get these messages across to the public, particularly taxpayers, students, teachers, administrators, school boards, parents, and funding agencies.

Coordinators have been carefully selected on the basis of their interest in the profession and in public relations, their reputation for working with people, and their ability to get the job done. All coordinators are required to attend several workshops for orientation in the use of materials, the procedure for obtaining time on television and radio, and other matters pertaining to the effective carrying out of their responsibilities.

Currently, PEPI is stressing a "new" physical education—that physical education has changed and is more relevant to the times. Those who are interested in further information or who wish to help in this project may contact the American Alliance for Health, Physical Education, Recreation, and Dance.

General public relations policies for physical education

1. Each school within an educational system should develop its own public relations program, which should be an integral part of the larger school organization.

2. Before attempting to foster good public relations between the school and the community, good internal public relations should be developed, involving students, teaching personnel, nonteaching personnel, and administrators.

3. The public relations program should recognize that there are many kinds of people to be reached, such as pupils, parents, alumni, physicians, and administrators and that each group requires its own unique procedures and approach for effective results.

4. The public relations program should present an articulate philosophy of physical education that clears away the misconceptions and stresses the objectives and worth of the field through the presentation of scientific evidence.

5. The physical educator should recognize that how he or she relates to other individuals within and without the department has implications for the public relations program. Consequently, such factors as a pleasing personality and appearance and harmonious relations with students and parents are very important.

6. Before using communications media, such as radio or television, advanced planning is essential.

7. Evaluation of the effectiveness of the public relations program and the attitudes of the various sectors of the public should be determined through a carefully planned research program.

Fig. 7-3. Movement education in New Zealand.

Department of Education, Wellington,
New Zealand.

Public relations in practice

Fifteen school systems in New York State were questioned about their public relations programs for physical education. They cited these factors in the conduct of their program.

1. Each physical education department operates an active public relations program.
2. Definite policies are established to guide the public relations program.
3. Responsibility for public relations is shared by all members of the department, with the central authority residing with the director.
4. Many media are used to interpret the program to the numerous groups to be reached.
5. Preparation and planning are essential in the use of all public relations media.
6. The total physical education program, in action, is recognized as the most effective medium of public relations.
7. Effort is made to communicate to the public accurate information concerning physical education.

The directors of physical education programs at 15 school systems surveyed were asked, ''What message are you trying to convey to the public?'' The answers include:

1. The aims and objectives of the total physical education program

2. The value of the total physical education program
3. The importance of the program to the student
4. Recognition and achievement of all students in physical education classes and in intramural and extramural activities—not athletics only
5. The importance of the physical education program for each child
6. The efforts and energies that are directed toward providing a sound program of physical education for each child
7. The contributions of the physical education program to all children, not just athletes
8. The fact that even though interschool athletics receive most of the publicity, these activities are not given priority in the program of physical education
9. The ability of the physical education program to enhance the health and welfare of the student

The New York schools used numerous media to convey their message. The most effective were (1) the physical education program itself, (2) personal contact, (3) newspapers, (4) public speaking, and (5) demonstrations and exhibits.

Groups needing information

Interpretation (or public relations) is basically concerned with communication. One person has defined it as getting the right facts to the right people at the right time and in the right way. Another has said it is "doing good" and receiving credit for it. One important consideration, regardless of definition, is to recognize that there are different kinds of people to be reached, and therefore different procedures and techniques are necessary in reaching these various groups. Six important groups that should be contacted are identified here.

YOUTH

Students in our schools who are exposed to physical education programs should be our best supporters. They should graduate from our schools and depart from our programs feeling that they have had worthwhile, enjoyable, and educational experiences. They should believe that the subject of physical education needs support and should be recommended to other people. Students grow up to be presidents of boards of education, directors of banks, industrial chairmen, and other important citizens in our communities from coast to coast. Their experience in physical education will help to determine how much they will support these programs as adults.

COLLEAGUES

Faculty members in other subject matter areas are an important group to reach. The absence of coaches and other physical education personnel at faculty meetings and various academic gatherings frequently results in a lack of adequate communication and interpretation of the program to teachers of history, science, English, and other subjects. Physical education will not be considered an essential part of the school educational program if the department is not represented at important meetings. Physical educators need the support of their colleagues. They should exploit every opportunity to reach these influential individuals, whether in faculty meetings or in informal discussions in the teachers' room.

ADMINISTRATORS

School administrators make decisions affecting physical education programs, they determine budget allocations, they approve facility allocations, and in many other ways they help or hinder our professional progress. It is important to reach this powerful group

and impress them with the benefits of physical education to the total education of the student.

PARENTS

Mothers and fathers should understand that physical educators contribute to their children's health and welfare. If they believe that their youngsters are receiving a worthwhile educational experience in physical education, they will be strong supporters, but if they believe that it is a waste of time because of poorly planned programs, they may fail to provide needed support.

ALUMNI

The alumni of a school can be a valuable asset to any physical education program, provided they are kept informed.

GENERAL PUBLIC

Of course, the general public, consisting of business and professional people, taxpayers, and other citizens is interested in its schools. Outstanding educational systems are marks of good communities; therefore, it is important to interpret to community members how physical education contributes to a strong educational program.

Basic considerations

Numerous factors, plans, and projects are involved in informing the various groups of people mentioned above.

STUDIES AND RESEARCH

The results of investigations of various aspects of the physical education program, such as improvement in the students' physical fitness or skills, provide excellent publicity material. These studies should help place physical education on defensible ground as to its worth in the educational program.

WRITTEN MATERIAL

Newsletters, reports, memoranda, brochures, and other forms of written material that have been accurately and neatly prepared are excellent media for reaching the various groups.

SOUND DEPARTMENTAL POLICIES

If the department of physical education has given time and study to policies concerning excuses, uniforms, athletic participation, class participation, grades, and other important matters, the wide dissemination of such material will reflect efficiency and a well-functioning program.

CONFERENCES

Student, parent, administrator, or teacher conferences are important avenues for explaining purposes of programs, indicating interests, eliminating problems, and planning projects.

INTEGRATED PROGRAMS

Planning interdepartmental programs is an effective educational and interpretive device. A folk dance festival, for example, that integrates the resources of the physical education, art, music, home economics, history, geography, and other departments is an excellent medium.

INVOLVEMENT

"As you share you care" is a saying that has much merit. Administrators, townspeople, colleagues, students, and others can be involved in many aspects of the physical education program, ranging from athletics to a "careers day" project.

INTERNAL CONSIDERATIONS

Public relations should be considered internally before being developed externally. The support of everyone within the organization, from the top administrator down to the last worker, should be sought. Furthermore, such items as defining the purpose of the program, designating the responsible person or persons, considering the available funds, deciding on the media to be utilized, and procuring the wherewithal to carry on the program are vital considerations.

PUBLIC RELATIONS PLAN

The public relations program should be outlined in writing, and every member of the organization should become familiar with it. The better it is known and understood, the better chance it has of succeeding.

FUNDS

There should be adequate funds to do the job. Furthermore, the person or persons in charge of the public relations program should be given freedom to spend this money in whatever ways they believe will be most helpful and productive for the organization.

PERSONS RESPONSIBLE

Individuals assigned to public relations responsibilities should modestly stay in the background, keep abreast of the factors that affect the program, develop a wide acquaintance, and make contacts that will be helpful.

WIDE COVERAGE

A good interpretative program will utilize all available resources and machinery to disseminate information in order to ensure adequate coverage.

OUTSTANDING PROGRAM

The physical education program itself is the most important public relations medium. Good news travels fast but bad news spreads even faster. If the program is good, people will hear about it and, in turn, will give their support and help.

Interpretive media

Fifteen school systems, surveyed to determine specific media utilized by the departments of physical education in interpreting their programs to the various groups of people they were attempting to reach, listed:

Total physical education program	Personal contact
Newsletter	Demonstrations and exhibits
School publications	Films
Radio	Pictures
Television	Magazines
Newspapers	Window displays
Posters	Brochures
Letters to parents	Sport days
Public speaking	Bulletin boards
Slogans	Professional associations

A discussion of some of these media follows.

SLOGANS

The strength of a slogan, a distinctive phrase used to signify a purpose, lies in its emotional appeal. Slogans should be informational, factual, colorful, appealing, and easily understood and remembered, and they should impel people to act. In addition, slogans should be timely, practical, personal, challenging, simple, truthful, short, imaginative, and concrete. They can be used in radio, television, speeches, songs, posters, letterheads, billboards, displays, rallies, exhibits, advertisements, and handbills.

Our nation's political history has produced slogans: "Walk softly and carry a big stick," "Keep cool with Coolidge," "Make the world safe for democracy," "A chicken in every pot," "54-40 or fight," "Over the top," "Remember the Maine," "Taxation without representation is tyranny."

Slogans have been used effectively in advertising, noticeably affecting our economic development: "It's smart to be thrifty," "We will not be undersold," "What helps business helps you," "All the news that's fit to print," "Progress is our most important product," "The pause that refreshes."

Ways of life are reflected in slogans: "A stitch in time saves nine," "Time and tide wait for no man," "He who hesitates is lost," "Spare the rod and spoil the child."

Slogans have also been used successfully in health, physical education, and recreation: "It pays to play," "Give your child's mind his body's support," "Cross at the green, not in between," "Brush today to check decay," "A sound mind in a sound body," "Health, energy, and power are yours," "Fitness—a basic goal of education," "You can't sit and be fit."

POSTERS

Posters should catch and hold the attention of the viewer. They require an eye-catching design and should have a message that is short, punchy, and well-worded. Color is one of the most important agents that help to convey a poster's messages, if effectively used.

Posters should be simple, interesting, attractive, and convincing and should leave a specific message with the viewer. They should guide an observer's view

from one part of the display to the other. This can be done through color, line, and various layout techniques. Posters should be placed at eye level if possible and should have good balance, with essential features in the most prominent places.

RADIO

A radio program should hold the listener's attention from start to finish. Since many radio stations today broadcast little other than music and news, programs must fit into such a pattern to hold listeners rather than lose them. Very few persons turn on the radio today to listen to a dramatic play or a long discourse on some topic of the day. Thus the program should be short, informative, and entertaining.

Language must be simple and direct; human interest and anecdotal material are always effective. It is better to discuss one idea in depth rather than cover many ideas and only scratch the surface of each. Program developers should know their audience and talk *with* rather than *to* the listener.

Those responsible for managing publicity on radio programs should consult with the broadcasters such as producers and program directors and find the most effective methods for radio broadcasting. They should have a definite message to put across to the public and be thoroughly familiar with the method they choose to relay the information: spot announcements, editorials, news broadcasts, reporting of school activities, panels, interviews, plays, or quiz programs. They should also determine the time of day when the most receptive audience would be listening and publicize the radio program in advance through advertisements, announcements on other broadcasts, school publications, and press releases.

TELEVISION

The program developers should:

• Explore the possibility of obtaining free time. The idea of performing a public service will influence some television station managers. Consult television stations that are reserved for educational purposes.

• Be prepared with written plans that can be put into operation immediately so they can take advantage of opportunities for television time on short notice.

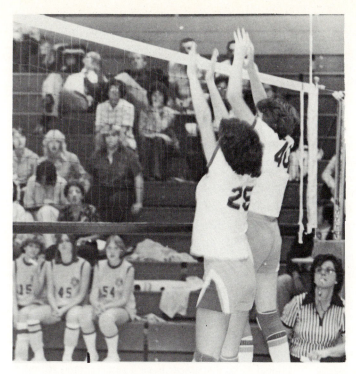

Fig. 7-4. Girls' volleyball.

Courtesy Barbara Ann Chiles,
Aledo, Ill.

Being ready may make the difference between acceptance or rejection for such an assignment.

• Understand that television programming requires rehearsals, preparation of scenery, and other work.

• Include boys and girls as participants in the program. When youngsters are in the act, the attention of mothers, fathers, aunts, uncles, grandparents, and friends is immediately attracted.

MOTION PICTURES

One of the most powerful means of informing and enlightening the public in regard to physical education is the use of motion pictures. Good shots of daily class activity are tangible evidence of the worth of the program to parents and others. They are excellent for groups such as PTO and civic clubs. Motion pictures usually receive better audience attention than does television, where there is opportunity to change to another program.

Before making a film, those in charge should analyze important factors such as the potential audience and the message to be conveyed. They should survey the entire program of physical education in order to select the most significant and typical activities for photographing.

Homemade film depicting daily operation of the school can be useful in interpreting the program to the public. In a do-it-yourself operation, the filmmakers should try to obtain some professional advice—perhaps from a photography club or a camera shop, and they should use good equipment and material. Nothing is more annoying than watching a poorly planned movie that consists of shots that are blurred or unfocused or going through an unpleasant experience with a projector that does not work properly.

Many films on physical education are available through professional organizations, college and university film libraries, commercial organizations, and state departments of education.

EXHIBITIONS AND DEMONSTRATIONS

An exhibition or a demonstration can be a culminating school activity to show what has been accomplished and learned in the physical education program. Exhibitions and demonstrations can focus public attention and stimulate action in support of the program.

Exhibitions can take the form of bulletin board displays, showcases, scrapbooks, drawings, or posters to point up such subjects as physical fitness or some sport or skill. They can also be used to show how expert performers have acquired outstanding skill in a particular sport.

An exhibition, for best results, should be limited to one type of activity or purpose and should be original; it should present facts, stimulate participation, provide new ideas, and create action. Demonstrations, utilizing all the students regardless of skill, also present a picture of what actually goes on in day-to-day classes.

NEWSPAPER AND MAGAZINE ARTICLES

Articles can be published in local papers or periodicals or in national publications. They should be factual, arouse and secure attention, contain human interest material, and be written in the language of the reader. Magazines have many advantages since they have excellent color and layout, are read many times by different persons, reach a wide range of people varying in income and intelligence, and are found in many offices and homes.

The writer should know the subject, the ideas to be put across, and the type of persons to be reached before placing the article in a suitable publication, since newspaper material is often read hurriedly. Therefore, the writer must consider the style of writing. All copy should be in typewritten form—neat, double spaced, and on one side of the paper only.

Ideas may also be suggested to magazines and newspapers to be staff written.

LETTERS

Next to personal contact, correspondence is the best interpretive medium. Letters can be direct, they are economical, and they may be adapted to any situation. Letters should be individually typed, and it is impor-

tant to use correct grammar and spelling. The message contained in the letter should be friendly, cordial, warm, courteous, sincere, enthusiastic, and natural. It should be written as though the writer were speaking to the individual in person.

Letters can be used to announce special programs, to indicate the necessary skills and understanding expected of students, and to interpret desired objectives. Letters should be written in terms of the reader's wishes and needs.

PUBLIC SPEAKING

Public speaking can be a very effective medium of interpreting. Through public addresses to civic and social groups in the community, public gatherings, professional meetings, and any organizations or groups that desire to know more about the work being performed, the physical educator is afforded a good opportunity for interpreting the physical education profession to the public.

A public speech must be effective, or it may result in poor public relations. The speaker should know the subject to be discussed; have a sincere interest in the topic; be enthusiastic, direct, straightforward, and well prepared; and give a brief presentation, using clear and distinct enunciation.

For a well-organized talk, the speaker should prepare an outline of the talk in advance, use correct English, and have an interesting beginning and conclusion as well as a theme or central point.

PROFESSIONAL ASSOCIATIONS

Professional associations on local, state, and national levels can do a great deal to interpret physical education to the public at large. Professional groups hold meetings to upgrade programs; prepare films, publications, and other materials; establish professional standards; sponsor radio, television, and other programs; publish articles in periodicals; and in many ways inform the community, state, and nation about the physical education profession. They deserve constant support.

Professional organizations are valuable in reaching boards of education, the general public, colleagues in the profession, other teachers, pupils, and other groups.

Fig. 7-5. High school students helping the elderly with physical education activity.

Courtesy Westwood Home, Clinton, Mo.

Some methods each physical educator can use to interpret the field of physical education

1. Join professional associations and help them to achieve their goals.

2. Attend faculty meetings after becoming a member of a school staff, and enter into discussions.

3. Become well informed about physical education as a professional field and about education in general.

4. Seek out school administrators, other members of the faculty, and the consumers of physical education's products and services. Help them to better understand the profession of physical education.

5. Understand the scientific foundations underly-

ing physical education: the latest research and new trends and developments. Find out what the latest thinking is and translate it into action at the grassroots level.

6. Develop the best possible program of physical education. See that satisfied children and youth leave the program.

7. Utilize every opportunity to sell someone else on the worth of your field. If the physical educator is sold, it will not be difficult to sell someone else.

8. Exploit every medium of communication to put the message across.

9. Think in positive terms. Think success, and the profession's chances of achieving great things will be better assured!

Self-assessment tests

These tests are designed to assist students in determining if material and competencies presented in this chapter have been mastered:

1. Conduct a survey of 25 lay people on a public street in your town. Ask each person what he or she understands is meant by the term "physical education" and to what extent it has value in an educational program. Summarize the results of your survey and relate your findings to the need for interpreting the educational value of physical education to the public.
2. What do the letters PEPI stand for? What is the purpose of PEPI? How is it organized and what does it accomplish?
3. Given a secondary school program of physical education, prepare a set of guiding principles that you feel will help in educating the public as to the worth of a physical education program.
4. As a faculty member in a secondary school where the physical education program has little public respect, what groups of people would you try to reach and what specific types of information would you try to communicate to these groups to gain more respect for your field?
5. Identify the various communication media that exist in your home community. Construct a plan indicating how you would use four of these media in interpreting physical education to the public.
6. Perform a self-assessment by listing on a piece of paper in *column 1*, what you are actively doing to interpret the worth of physical education to the public and, in *column 2*, what additional things you could do in this regard that you are not now doing.

Points to remember

1. Some of the basic principles underlying a sound program of interpretation and public relations
2. The various groups of people to whom the profession should be interpreted
3. A knowledge and understanding of the following interpretative media: slogans, posters, radio, television, motion pictures, exhibitions, demonstrations, newspapers, magazines, letters, public speaking, and professional associations
4. Some methods to interpret the professional field of physical education

Problems to think through

1. What are some of the common misconceptions about physical education? How did these misconceptions originate, and how can they be corrected?

2. What constitutes an adequate public relations program for a secondary school?

Case study for analysis

Choose some product that has gained national recognition, such as an automobile, cigarette, soap, and so on. Do an in-depth study to discover what techniques were used to promote it and to persuade the public to accept this product.

Exercises for review

1. Define the term "public relations."
2. What are the groups of people with which physical education is most directly concerned?
3. What are five principles to recognize in interpreting your profession to the public?
4. What do we mean by the statement, "As you share you care"?
5. Develop a slogan that can be used to promote physical education.
6. Prepare a poster to stress the importance of physical fitness.
7. Write a series of 10 one-minute spot announcements for a radio station.
8. Write a letter that could be used to inform parents about the physical condition of their son or daughter.
9. What is the difference between an exhibition and a demonstration?
10. Write a 500-word magazine article on the topic, "It pays to play."

Selected references

American Association for Health, Physical Education, and Recreation: PEPI-GRAMS, a series of communications on the Physical Education Public Information Project, 1972, The Association.

Bucher, C.A.: Administration of health and physical education programs, including athletics, ed. 5, St. Louis, 1983, The C.V. Mosby Co.

Bucher, C.A.: Back to school—what kind of education is relevant? (syndicated newspaper column), Washington, D.C., Sept. 1972, President's Council on Physical Fitness and Sports.

Bucher, C.A.: Foundations of physical education, ed. 7, St. Louis, 1983, The C.V. Mosby Co.

Bucher, C.A.: Play and your child's report card (syndicated newspaper column), Washington, D.C., May, 1972, President's Council on Physical Fitness and Sports.

Bucher, C.A., and Thaxton, N.: Physical education and sport: change and challenge, St. Louis, 1981, The C.V. Mosby Co.

Caldwell, S.F.: Toward a humanistic physical education, Journal of Health, Physical Education, and Recreation **43:**31, 1972.

Clay, W.B.: First class and getting better, Journal of Physical Education, Recreation, and Dance **52:**19-21, June 1981.

Geyer, C.: Physical education for the electronic age, Journal of Health, Physical Education, and Recreation **43:**32, 1972.

Marsh, D.B.: Program promotion, Journal of Physical Education, Recreation, and Dance **52:**24-25, June 1981.

McLaughlin, R.D.: "Chip-n-block" for parental involvement, Journal of Physical Education, Recreation, and Dance **52:**22-23, June 1981.

Muller, P., et al.: Intramural-recreational sports: programming and administration, New York, 1979, John Wiley & Sons, Inc.

Smith, N.W.: Community involvement through a curriculum study project, Journal of Physical Education, Recreation and Dance **52:**16-17, June 1981.

Torpey, J.: Interpreting physical education for the public, Physical Educator **24:**131, 1967.

Wagenhals, J.G.: Involving parents in after school activity programs, Journal of Physical Education and Recreation **51:**13, Oct. 1980.

Willet, L.: Physical education—alive, well, and growing, Journal of Physical Education, Recreation, and Dance **52:**18, June 1981.

Ziatz, D.H.: Practical-realistic public relations, Journal of Physical Education and Recreation **46:**69, 1975.

PART THREE

The teacher

8

A philosophy of physical education to guide the teacher*

Instructional objectives and competencies to be achieved

After reading this chapter the student should be able to

1. Understand the reasons for having a sound philosophy of physical education
2. List the principles on which a philosophy is composed
3. Discuss why philosophy is important in articulating a professional's beliefs
4. Identify general and educational philosophies
5. Implement the step-by-step procedure for developing a philosophy
6. Develop a philosophy of physical education for the secondary school

One of the tasks that each student should accomplish before entering the field of teaching is to develop a well-thought-out philosophy of general and physical education. Too often the student develops the skills and accumulates the pertinent knowledge about a field of endeavor but fails to develop a sound philosophy for using these skills and this knowledge in the most effective way. The result is that the student, like a ship without a rudder, lacks direction.

The beginning teacher faces many difficult problems and decisions. A philosophical approach to solving these problems and reaching sound decisions will be helpful. Philosophy provides physical educators with a rational basis for examining society and the

role of general and physical education in that society. It will help in evaluating the actions of human beings in light of ethical and moral values. It will help in determining the truth. It will provide a method for critically viewing the many situations and problems that physical educators face from day to day in the secondary schools of the nation.

Why each teacher should have a sound philosophy of physical education

In today's changing society, there must be a sound philosophy of physical education for the profession to survive. Physical educators must ask themselves such important questions as: What has value in today's society? What is relevant to the needs of today's youth and adults? A philosophy of physical education serves several functions.

A philosophy of physical education is essential to professional education. Persons who claim to be physical educators should have developed carefully thought-out philosophies. In so doing, it will help them to have a common basis for thinking about their profession, to properly articulate the meaning and worth of their field of endeavor to the public at large, to become motivated to achieve greater professional accomplishments, and to better evaluate physical education programs and practices.

A philosophy of physical education guides people's actions. To function as intelligent individuals, people need a philosophy that will guide their actions. They need knowledge about moral judgments before any program can be created. A philosophy will help teachers decide what they want to have happen to students in the gymnasium.

A philosophy of physical education provides the direction for the profession. Today in physical ed-

---

*Some of the material in this chapter has been adapted or reprinted from the following sources: Bucher, C.A.: Foundations of physical education, St. Louis, 1978, The C.V. Mosby Co.; Bucher, C.A., and Thaxton, T.: Physical education and sport: change and challenge, St. Louis, 1981, The C.V. Mosby Co.

Fig. 8-1. Boys' basketball.

Courtesy Barbara Ann
Chiles, Aledo, Ill.

ucation many programs lack order and direction. When assumptions are made by the physical education teacher, for example, that physical education strengthens human relationships because children play together, they should be based on a system of reflective educational thinking that embraces logic and other philosophical tenets. A philosophy of physical education will help to provide this system.

A philosophy of physical education makes society aware that physical education contributes to its values. Physical educators must realize that people are not going to be satisfied with only facts that show that students who participate in physical education improve in such things as endurance. This is important, but it does not go far enough. In today's changing society, people want to know how physical education can contribute to human performance, quality of life, and productivity. A thoughtful philosophy of physical education will assist in interpreting those values important in society so that programs can be established to help meet these needs.

A philosophy of physical education aids in bringing the members of the profession closer together. Many members of the physical education profession are dissatisfied with what they see happening in their field today. A philosophy of physical education will enable them to determine how they can best contribute to society and thus provide them the opportunity to work together in making such a contribution.

A philosophy of physical education explains the relationship between physical education and general education. A philosophy of physical education will help in the development of a rationale showing that its objectives are closely related to those of general education. In the definition of physical education, the importance of education ''of and through the physical'' is stressed.

Physical educators must strive to develop their educational philosophies in a rational, logical, and systematic manner and to represent the best interests of all humans. This means that scientific facts must be assembled and workable theories applied that support the worth of physical education as an important and necessary service to humanity.

A philosophy of physical education articulates the worth of physical education. Philosophy is a process through which people search for truths, reality, and values. Through philosophy, physical educators are able to study the meaning, nature, importance, and source of values in physical education. Philosophy guides the physical educator in determining the aims, objectives, principles, and content of physical education and provides a logical means of determining whether physical education is providing worthwhile services in the education of human beings.

A philosophy of physical education results in the improvement of educational practices. When educational practices are based on intuition or emotional whim and fancy, they are usually not sound. However, when they are based on a thoughtful philosophy, they are much more likely to be defensible. This is especially true if physical educators develop their philosophies in a rational, logical, and systematic manner and if they represent the best interests of human beings.

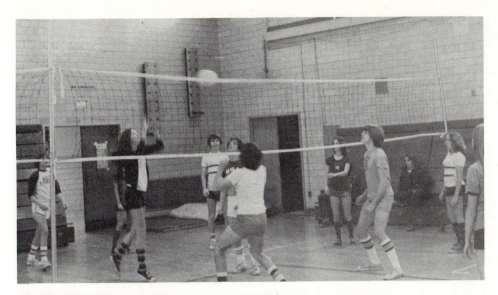

Fig. 8-2. High school volleyball.

Courtesy Bill Henderson,
Toms River, N.J.

What is philosophy?

The essence of any discipline can only be appreciated by a thorough consideration of philosophy in general and the philosophies of the particular field being investigated. Philosophy is a field of inquiry that attempts to help individuals evaluate, in a satisfying and meaningful manner, their relationships to the universe. Philosophy seeks to help people evaluate themselves and their world by giving them a basis from which to deal with the problems of life and death, good and evil, freedom and restraint, and beauty and ugliness.

According to Aristotle, philosophy is the grouping of the knowledge of universals. A dictionary definition reports that it is the love of wisdom and the science that investigates the facts and principles of reality and of human nature and conduct. Copleston* writes: "Philosophy . . . is rooted in the desire to understand the world, in the desire to find an intelligible pattern in events and to answer problems which occur to the

mind in connection with the world." In defining the word *philosophy*, Randolph Webster* says, "Love of wisdom means the desire to search for the real facts and values in life and in the universe, and to evaluate and interpret these with an unbiased and unprejudiced mind." As can be seen from these definitions, philosophy offers an explanation of life and the principles that guide human lives.

Some questions that reflect the concern of philosophers include the following:

What is the role of human beings on this earth?
What is the origin and nature of the universe?
What constitutes good and evil, right and wrong?
What constitutes truth?
Is there a God?
Do human beings have souls, that is, something which exists but cannot be seen?
What is the function of education in society?
What relationship exists between mind and matter?

---

*Copleston, F.: Contemporary philosophy, Westminister, Md., 1966, The Newman Press.

*Webster, R.W.: Philosophy of physical education, Dubuque, Iowa, 1965, William C. Brown Co., Publishers.

To comprehend more clearly the meaning of philosophy, it is important to examine the major branches of philosophy.

METAPHYSICS

Metaphysics is based on the principles of being. This school of philosophy attempts to answer a series of related questions: What is the meaning of existence? What is real? How are human actions governed? How and why did the universe evolve? What is the nature of God? The question, What experiences in the physical education program will better enable students to meet the challenges of the real world? is metaphysical in nature. Philosopher Will Durant says that metaphysics investigates the reality of everything concerned with human beings and the universe.

EPISTEMOLOGY

Epistemology is concerned with methods of obtaining knowledge and the kinds of knowledge that can be gained. It is a comprehensive study that attempts to define the sources, authority, principles, limitations, and validity of knowledge. Physical education is concerned with knowledge regarding the role of physical activity and its impact on the physical, mental, emotional, and social development of individuals. Students are seeking the truth about physical education, and epistemology seeks to answer the question, What is true?

AXIOLOGY

Axiology helps to determine to what use truth is to be put. It asks, How do we determine what has value, and on what criteria is this judgment based? Axiology is concerned with the aims and values of society and is extremely important in physical education because the aims and values set by society become the basis of the curriculum used in schools and colleges. In physical education the following question must be answered: How can the values that society cherishes be embraced in the physical education program? American society, for example, holds dear the value of "equality for all," which is exemplified by having students from all walks of life playing together and developing tolerance for one another. Students who learn to respect one another on the playing fields, it is hoped, will be more likely to carry those feelings off the field.

ETHICS

Ethics is a more individualized and personalized subdivision of axiology. It helps to define moral character and serves as a basis for an individual code of conduct. Ethics attempts to answer the question, What is the highest standard of behavior each person should strive to attain? The strengthening of moral conduct is an important function of physical education. In physical education the following questions must be answered: How can games and sports be utilized to help the individual learn right conduct? Is character education through physical education possible? Since physical education places individuals in situations that reveal their true nature and character, those who play on a team with an excellent coach may soon realize that using four-letter words is not acceptable. The student who plays by the rules and acts like a sportsman or sportswoman at all times is more likely to win the respect of teammates. It is hoped that the relationships formed and the character developed will carry over to out-of-school situations.

LOGIC

Logic seeks to provide human beings with a sound and intelligent method of living. Logic describes the steps that should be taken in thinking and puts ideas into an orderly, structured sequence that leads to accurate thinking. It helps to set up standards by which the accuracy of ideas may be measured. Logic concerns itself with the orderly connection of one fact or idea with another. It asks the question, What method of reasoning will lead to the truth? Physical educators must use logical thought processes in arriving at the truth. When students ask questions, such as "Why should I play football?" the physical education teacher should not answer by saying, "Because it's in the program." The teacher should explain the benefits and risks associated with playing football, since only then will the student really understand its true value.

ESTHETICS

Esthetics is the study and determination of criteria for beauty in nature and the arts, including dance, drama, sculpture, painting, music, and writing. Esthetics, which is a less scientific branch of axiology, is concerned not only with art but also with the artist and the appreciation of what he or she has created. In an attempt to determine the close relationship of art to nature, esthetics asks the question, What is beauty? There is esthetic appreciation involved in watching a gymnast perform on the trampoline, a football player leap high to catch a pass, or a baseball player dive to catch a line drive, just as there is an esthetic appreciation gained from viewing great works of art or listening to a symphony orchestra. The physical movements that one can view in athletics are often a source of great pleasure.

· · ·

The branches known as metaphysics, epistemology, axiology, ethics, logic, and esthetics represent aspects of philosophy. They can be applied in formulating a philosophy for any particular field within the educational endeavor such as health, physical education, recreation, or dance. Philosophy yields a comprehensive understanding of reality, which, when applied to education or any other field of interest, gives direction that would likely be lacking otherwise.

Philosophy and the physical educator's articulation of beliefs

Broudy* lists four levels of discussion applicable to a progressive step-by-step exploration of educational problems. These levels of discussion help to clarify the implications of philosophy for the physical educator.

EMOTIONAL OR UNCRITICAL LEVEL

On the emotional level individuals discuss the advantages or disadvantages of an issue mainly in terms of their own limited experience. The arguments presented are not based on reflective thinking but, instead, on impulse and emotional feeling. A statement by a high school basketball coach that "All boys who play high school basketball perform better in the class-

room than those who do not play" may be an emotional or uncritical statement. The coach may only have had experience with his own team and cannot be certain that all boys who play high school basketball perform better in the classroom than those who do not play. It is generally agreed that the emotional level of thinking is the most unreliable one and that few differences of opinion can be settled by using it.

FACTUAL OR INFORMATIONAL LEVEL

The factual level of discussion involves the gathering of evidence to support the individual's arguments. By mobilizing statistics and other factual evidence, tangible support is often given to a particular argument. However, this level of discussion can be unreliable and misleading, since it depends on the facts used—whether they are valid, applicable, and significant—and other conditions that exist in any particular situation. A statement by a physical education teacher that "in an experiment, students who participated in the physical education program showed greater improvement in strength than those who did not participate" is a factual statement. Although the teacher can introduce all kinds of impressive statistics to prove this point, the listener cannot be sure whether the experiment was properly conducted. Nevertheless, the mobilizing of accurate facts in a discussion can frequently result in the solution of a problem and the satisfactory conclusion of a discussion on a controversial topic.

EXPLANATORY OR THEORETICAL LEVEL

Facts provide solid support, but they are most effective when they are associated with theories that make them dynamic and applicable. A statement by a physical educator that "the jump shot in basketball should be taught as a whole and not broken down into its component parts" is theoretically valid. The teacher's statement can be supported by reference to the Gestalt theory and such thinkers as Kurt Koffka and Wolfgang Kohler, whose theories stress the idea that learning takes place as a whole (rather than in fragments) because of the essential unity that exists in nature. At this level of discussion, the introduction of a reliable scientific explanation provides strong evidence for rational individuals.

*Broudy, H.S.: Building a philosophy of education, New York, 1954, Prentice-Hall, Inc., pp. 20-24.

Fig. 8-3. High school student practicing archery at University School of Nashville, Nashville, Tenn.

PHILOSOPHICAL LEVEL

The highest level of discussion involves asking questions relative to what is really true, valuable, right, or real. The application of such values is universal and eternal; it is the ultimate to which any discussion can go. The physical education teacher's question, ''Do students participating in team sports develop strong human relationships?'' is characteristic of the philosophical level. At this level there is self-criticism of programs, and physical educators try to decide what they want for their students in the gymnasium. This level of discussion is of greatest use when problems fail to yield a clear solution and when facts and science are limited and inconclusive. (Many such problems in general and physical education merit a philosophical discussion.)

General philosophies

Five general philosophies have prevailed through the years and have influenced educational thinking.

IDEALISM

Idealism is a branch of philosophy that deals with such general concepts as: The mind is the focus of a person's being. In the scheme of the universe, people are more important than nature. Values exist independently of individuals and are permanent. Reasoning and intuition help individuals to arrive at the truth.

When these general principles of idealism are applied to educational thinking, they result in such concepts as: Education develops the personality of the individual. Knowledge and the development of the mind are important. Education is a process that originates within the self. The curriculum is centered around ideals. The student is a creative being who is guided by the teacher.

When these general principles of idealism are applied to the area of physical education, they result in such concepts as: Physical education involves more than the "physical." Strength and fitness activities contribute to the development of one's personality. Physical education is centered around ideals. The teacher is a model for students. The teacher is responsible for the effectiveness of the program. Education is for life.

REALISM

Realism is a branch of philosophy that deals with such general concepts as: The physical world is the real world. All physical events that occur in the universe are the result of the laws of nature. The truth may be best determined through the scientific method. The mind and the body have a close and harmonious relationship. Religion and philosophy can coexist.

When these general principles of realism are applied to educational thinking, they result in such concepts as: Education develops one's reasoning power. Education is for life. Education is objective. The educational process proceeds in an orderly fashion. The curriculum is scientifically oriented. There should be standardization of measurement techniques in education.

When these general principles of realism are applied to the area of physical education, they result in such concepts as: Education is for life. Physical fitness results in greater productivity. Programs are based on scientific knowledge. Drills play an important part in the learning process. Interscholastic athletic programs can lead to desirable social behavior. Play and recreation aid in life adjustment.

PRAGMATISM

Pragmatism is a branch of philosophy that deals with such general concepts as: Human experience causes changes in the concept of reality. Success is the only criterion of the value and truth of a theory. Individuals are an integral part of a larger society, and their actions reflect on that society.

When the general principles of pragmatism are applied to educational thinking, they result in such concepts as: The individual learns through experience. Education is for social efficiency. Education is child centered. Problem solving is necessary in a world of change.

When these general principles of pragmatism are applied to the area of physical education, they result in such concepts as: More meaningful experiences are presented when there is a variety of activity. Activities are socializing in nature. The program is determined by the needs and interests of the learner. Learning is accomplished through the problem-solving method. The teacher is a motivator. Standardization is not a part of the program.

NATURALISM

Naturalism is a branch of philosophy that deals with such general concepts as: Any reality that exists exists only within the physical realm of nature. Nature is a source of value. The individual is more important than society.

When these general beliefs of naturalism are applied to educational thinking, they result in such concepts as: Education must satisfy the inborn needs of the individual. Education is geared to the individual growth of each child. Education is not simply mental in nature. Students educate themselves. The teacher has an understanding of the laws of nature. The teacher is a guide in the educational process.

When these general principles of naturalism are applied to the area of physical education, they result in such concepts as: Physical activities are more than just "physical" in nature. Learning is accomplished through self-activity. Play is an important part of the educational process. Highly competitive performance between individuals is discouraged. Physical education is concerned with the whole individual.

EXISTENTIALISM

Existentialism is a branch of philosophy that deals with such general concepts as: Human existence is the only true reality. Individuals must determine their own systems of values. Individuals are more important than society.

When the general principles of existentialism are applied to educational thinking, they result in such concepts as: Individuals discover their "inner selves." Education is an individual process. The curriculum is centered on the individual. The teacher acts as a stimulator. Education is to teach responsibility.

When these general principles of existentialism are applied to the area of physical education, they result in such concepts as: There is freedom of choice. There should be a variety of activity. Play results in the development of creativity. Students should "know themselves." The teacher is a counselor.

Educational philosophies

Several educational philosophies have been developed to deal specifically with the problems and conduct of educational thought and practice. Philosophers of education usually state their philosophical beliefs in the context of broad cultural orientations. These educational philosophies are very briefly identified.

PROGRESSIVISM

Progressivism is a philosophy that is based on many of the concepts of pragmatism. This educational philosophy is also identified by some as instrumentalism and experimentalism. Progressivists view education as inherently a social experience, with students at the center of learning. Cooperative effort is stressed instead of competition, and the democratic process is practiced by progressive educators. Furthermore, progressivists encourage students to actively participate in the decision-making process involving curriculum and related areas of the educational program. Problem-solving methods of instruction are used and the teacher acts as a guide and facilitator. The student is taught to be an independent, self-reliant thinker.

PERENNIALISM

Unlike progressivism, which is based on the changing nature of things, perennialism rests on the concept of an unchanging and constant universe. Some of the practices of this philosophy are based on idealistic concepts. Education is based on principles and concepts that are permanent and unchanging. The curriculum is constant and universal. It includes subjects such as art, philosophy, music, and literature; great books from the past are used to instruct students in this liberal tradition. Teaching methods stress the traditional lecture and demonstration. The perennialist would teach the great lessons of the past by example and precept. Individualization of instruction is not a part of the teaching strategy of perennialist teachers; they teach the same material in the same manner to all students.

ESSENTIALISM

Essentialism is an outgrowth of idealism and realism. It also shares some of the concepts of perennialism. Thus it might be considered eclectic in its orientation. Essentialist educators believe there is a core of knowledge, skills, and values that are essential for all people to learn. They also maintain that learning involves hard work and the application of discipline. The teacher must set firm controls so that students will put forth the effort necessary to succeed in learning essential material. If the student puts forth the necessary effort to succeed, interest will be heightened. However, students must be directed by the teacher to learn even though interest is low: effort is more important than interest. Mental discipline is maintained in the schools through traditional methods such as drill and recitation. Logical organization and presentation of course materials are stressed, and the

Fig. 8-4. Students helping the elderly in physical education activities.

Courtesy Westwood Home, Clinton, Mo.

scientific method is used to arrive at data, with emphasis placed on the physical sciences.

RECONSTRUCTIONISM

Reconstructionism is an outgrowth and extension of pragmatism and progressivism. Its proponents maintain that the major purpose of education is to "reconstruct" society to meet the cultural crisis of our time. To achieve this goal, the school must reinterpret the basic values of western society in light of the scientific knowledge available to human beings. The reconstructionist curriculum contains material and courses that enable teachers to impart the most humane values of the culture, all designed to rebuild the social structure. It is futuristic curriculum, emphasizing preparation for life in a "reconstructed" society. Social self-realization is the predominate goal in the curriculum. The community-school concept where adults as well as children participate is a reconstructionist idea. Teaching strategies stress group discussion, debate, and dialogue. Students are given opportunities to make group decisions about curriculum matters, but the teacher makes forceful arguments for the acceptance of the reconstructionist point of view. In the area of physical education, little time is devoted to competitive sports; emphasis is, rather, on intramural activities.

Establishing a personal philosophy

Developing a philosophy of physical education is a consuming, tedious, and often difficult task. Oftentimes, such a quest is never completed. But each person should be "somewhere on the journey," to use Zeigler's terminology, to the arrival of a personal and professional philosophy.

Although it is difficult to think through and indicate a personal philosophy in a logical and systematic manner, the process should be attempted. The goal is to move through the various stages until the individual arrives at the stage of philosophical maturity—a personal philosophy. This personal philosophy will provide the guidance and foundation on which a professional philosophy rests.

The development of a personal philosophy provides a foundation for guiding and directing the individual, in thought and action, toward a professional philosophy.

A sound philosophy serves several purposes. It forces a person to think logically, critically, and analytically about life, people, education, and physical education; it explains the worth of physical education and sport; it provides a basis for relating physical education to general education; and it provides a means of professional growth and development.

There are several approaches to developing a philosophy. The following brief discussion of a procedure for developing a philosophy of physical education for school programs may be used to develop any type of philosophy.

PROCEDURE FOR DEVELOPING A PHILOSOPHY

This approach for developing a philosophy uses what Morris describes as the "Outside-In" or deduc-

tive method.* The specific steps involved in this procedure are outlined, and then directions and suggestions are provided for the development of each step.

1. Think through logically, analytically, systematically, and comprehensively your personal views on reality (metaphysics), truth or knowledge (epistemology), and value (axiology).
2. Indicate the educational theory to which your convictions will lead.
3. Indicate what you think should be the aims of education.
4. Indicate what you think should be the functions of the school in a democratic society.
5. Indicate the concrete practices and behavior patterns you would use in teaching as a result of the educational theory you espouse.
6. Compare what you have done in the previous steps and the ideas you have established with the general philosophies and the educational philosophies or theories described in this chapter.

1. Each of the steps in this process of developing a well-thought-out philosophy is important and requires careful attention. The first step takes on added significance, however, because it is the foundation on which an entire philosophy rests. Personal views on metaphysics, epistemology, and axiology must be comprehensively and clearly developed. Because each of these divisions of philosophy is related, a logical, consistent development of ideas regarding each one is important to the proper development of later stages of a personal philosophy. Those who develop incompatible ideas by taking eclectic viewpoints will encounter problems later. For example, it would be incompatible to adhere to the views of both realists and pragmatists concerning value. Whereas realists believe that values are permanent and unchanging, pragmatists believe that values change with experience. There are many other opposing ideas among the adherents of varying schools of philosophy. Thus the individual must be careful not to embrace contradictory ideas.

How does someone go about preparing for this first

---

*Morris, V.C.: Philosophy and the American school, New York, 1961, Houghton Mifflin Co.

step in building a philosophy? There are several means of developing ideas regarding reality, truth or knowledge, and values. A starting point might be to read what philosophers have said about these questions and problems. This reading might be related to a college course in philosophy and/or the philosophy of education. An individual should also think about and apply these questions to experiences in personal life. From these sources, a basic foundation should emerge on which to build a comprehensive and clear philosophy.

2. After developing a set of compatible ideas regarding reality, truth, and value from one or two schools of philosophy, the individual may proceed to the second step. This step involves the development of an educational theory that follows fundamental convictions. At this point, the information in this chapter or an educational philosophy textbook may be helpful—a text that explains the basic philosophies from which educational philosophies have been developed or to which they are connected. Thus the individual can formulate an educational theory by examining general philosophical ideas. Someone with ideas that are mainly pragmatic, for instance, would probably be considered a progressivist or even a reconstructionist in terms of educational philosophy. The same careful, analytical, and comprehensive assessment of a position is as necessary at step 2 as it was in the first step. Views regarding the various divisions of educational philosophy must be compatible and consistent.

3. An individual who has been rigorous and comprehensive in carrying out the tasks of the first two steps should find it fairly easy to state his or her aims of education. These aims or purposes of education have differed, according to the philosophical persuasion of various individuals, groups, organizations, and philosophers. The essentialists' purpose of education would be to transmit those enduring aspects of our social heritage and the verified knowledge of the past. On the other hand, progressivists believe that education should help students to discover the qualitative experiences that will lead to the good life.

One might examine several statements of aims or purposes of education (such as the Cardinal Principles

of Education, the statements of aims by the Educational Policies Commission, and professional groups of educators) to determine those consistent with a personal educational philosophy. The importance of basing educational views on a critical assessment of personal philosophical views is reemphasized at this point. Butler, in *Four Philosophies and their Practice in Education and Religion,* underlines such an approach when he writes that ''We must have a value theory if in turn we are to embrace aims or functions for education which will stand up against the ravages of time and the challenge of the uneducated of all levels and ages.''

4. This step should be a natural outgrowth of the previous one. Having developed the aims or purposes of education, the individual should find it easy to state the school's function in helping to achieve these aims. He or she may use personal experience as a student, the knowledge gained from courses in the foundations of education, and any other means to increase knowledge of the various functions of schools in different societies. In the final analysis, what the individual believes is the function of the school should be consistent with personal philosophical ideas. The school, as one of many social institutions, should be viewed as a vehicle for helping to achieve the aims of education. These aims of education should be based on views of reality, truth, and value. The interconnectedness of the ideas is very important, and they must be compatible.

5. Now the individual is ready to indicate the specific behavior patterns and techniques to use in the classroom or gymnasium as a result of personal ideas of educational theory. What kind of curriculum should be developed? What kind of teaching methods should be used? All of these, as well as other questions, should be answered at this point. In working out this step, students or teachers with very little experience will have to rely on what their teachers taught and how they have behaved in the classroom.

It is very important in this step, as in other phases of the development of philosophy, to be consistent in connecting the various stages in a logical and harmonious manner. Careful study of philosophical questions concerned with reality, truth, and value should be compared to educational questions related to the aims of education, the values of the school in this process of education, and the specific strategies to use to accomplish ultimate goals. A specific example of the importance of philosophical consistency is in teaching methodology. The teacher whose ideas are compatible with realism would probably not use problem solving as a method of teaching or social experience as the major curriculum material since these are antithetical to the ideas of most realists, (in terms of general philosophy) and most essentialists (in terms of educational theory). Such methods would be more consistent with the philosophy of pragmatists and the educational theory of progressivists.

6. In the final and summarizing step, the individual should be aware that if views on aspects of philosophy or educational theory or practice are too incompatible, it may be necessary to do some rethinking. There should be a consistent relationship between ideas at each stage and among ideas in the various stages. In speaking of the importance of a logical and consistent movement from philosophy to educational theory to practice, Morris said, ''In the degree to which you can draw a deductive argument from your philosophic position to your educational theoretical position to the kinds of specific behavior patterns you feel a teacher would follow according to such a view, in that degree you will have put down a complete 'work paper' for the next stage.''*

The next step to which Morris refers is the comparison of the kinds of teaching behavior the teacher exhibits and the various stages of philosophy development, an unnecessary stage for students majoring in physical education. At this point, the student should have developed a comprehensive philosophy and can compare actual teaching practices with philosophical position and educational theoretical position when he or she begins teaching.

Although Morris proposes the deductive method for the development of a philosophy of education, it can be used to develop a philosophy of physical education. By thinking through each step, with physical education as the focal point, the physical educator can develop a philosophy that is consistent with the basic goals and objectives of general education. An example of the use of this process in developing a philosophy of physical education follows.

A philosophy of physical education for school programs*

I shall attempt to present a description of my personal philosophy of physical education for programs in schools. My personal philosophy has helped me to clarify my thinking about the main aims or purposes of education, the function of the school in society, the relationship of physical education to general education, and whether my teaching is based on sound philosophical ideas and educational theory. Furthermore, it is hoped that my statement of philosophy will help students who are majoring in physical education and beginning teachers to think about their philosophy of physical education in a logical and comprehensive manner.

In terms of what is real, I believe that true reality is to be found in the experience and nature of human beings, even though it is constantly changing because of the changing social, political, economic, and religious conditions and situations. As individuals begin to understand and account for the impact of cultural forces on human beings, they will develop the type of culture that is best suited for humanity.

I believe that knowledge comes from both sense experience and the insight of reason. Truth can be established by the scientific method, problem solving, and intuitive thinking, or a combination of these. Truth or knowledge, like reality, is transitory; it changes as circumstances and conditions change. Knowledge should continually be revised and updated as new experiences and information dictate. Human beings should seek the truth to enable them to develop as social beings in a democratic society.

Human beings are capable of making value judgments because they have free will. In fact, it is vitally necessary that these value judgments be made. It must be realized, however, that certain actions and behaviors are better for human beings than are others. Through group experience, one can determine those values that may be used as a starting point for making value judgments. Determining what is good or right, for example, should reflect the effect such actions might have on the group as well as the individuals in the group. An action would be considered good if it were to work out in practice.

Before indicating my beliefs about physical education in particular, I think that some statement about the central

---

*Morris, *op. cit.*

*Philosophy of Nolan Thaxton.

Fig. 8-5. High school girls participating in track activities.

Courtesy Barbara Ann Chiles,
Aledo, Ill.

purpose of education is necessary. I believe that the aim or goal of education is to transmit the desirable cultural traits of a people and to equip them with the necessary skills, knowledge, and total fitness to enable them to discover new truths that will make for a satisfying and productive life in a democratic society. The Educational Policies Commission, expressing the same sentiments about the purpose of education, indicated in 1946 how this aim might be achieved. This group wrote that it

> . . . involves the dissemination of knowledge, the liberation of minds, the development of skills, the promotion of free inquiries, the encouragement of the creative or inventive spirit, and the establishment of wholesome attitudes toward order and change. . . . *

To achieve this central purpose of education, all people should be developed to their optimum level of ability—

physically, mentally, emotionally, and socially. I believe that the four groups of objectives (self-realization, human relationships, civic responsibility, and economic efficiency) stated by the Educational Policies Commission in 1938 and reiterated in 1961 are worthy for today's education. The widely used ''taxonomic system'' developed by Bloom* and Krathwohl and coworkers,† which is divided into three domains (cognitive, psychomotor, and affective), provides an excellent framework for communicating instructional objectives.

The school should unite with other agencies in the community (churches, community centers, hospitals, and others) to achieve its central mission. However, the school should be the most vital and vibrant learning and resource center in the community. It should provide services for all persons, including the community—the young and old, the rich and poor, and the healthy and disabled.

Physical education, I believe, can aid in the development of the ''total person.'' Specifically, the purposes of physical education are to develop individuals who: (1) use their bodies efficiently and effectively in movement situations generally and in sports and games specifically, (2) develop the necessary skills for participation in leisure time activities, (3) develop a positive attitude toward self, others, and physical activities, (4) understand, appreciate, and value physical activity as an adjunct to healthful living, and (5) are socially well-adjusted.

I believe that the purposes and specific objectives of physical education can be achieved with a competent professional educator who offers a variety of activities and experiences for people. These activities and experiences should be based on sound principles of growth and development and the resultant needs, interests, and capacities of each individual. Furthermore, I believe that the ''why'' of physical education should be taught in addition to the skills and fitness activities. Teaching the ''why'' of physical education means teaching the cognitive aspects as well as the psychomotor and affective-social aspects. For example, I would teach the students about the worth of physical education in their overall school program and especially about the values of physical activity to their total development. The sequencing of curriculum material would be based on the present level of student achievement, and the principle of progression—

---

*Educational Policies Commission: Policies for education in American democracy, Washington, D.C., 1964, National Education Association and American Association of School Administrators, p. 60.

*Bloom, B.S., editor: Taxonomy of educational objectives, Handbook I: cognitive domain, New York, 1956, David McKay Co., Inc.

†Krathwohl, D.R., and others: Toxonomy of educational objectives, Handbook II: affective domain, New York, 1956, David McKay Co., Inc.

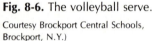

Fig. 8-6. The volleyball serve.
Courtesy Brockport Central Schools,
Brockport, N.Y.)

from simple to more complex—would be stressed. I would teach concepts rather than isolated skills and knowledge.

In addition to the instructional program, I would have an intramural, extramural, and varsity athletic program. I believe also that physical education should be adapted to meet the special educational needs of individuals with handicapping conditions, such as those with impaired vision or hearing, low fitness levels, obesity, and so on. I also believe that coeducational activities should be offered at all levels.

In the elementary school, I would stress the development of basic movement skills. These skills would include lo-

comotor, nonlocomotor, and manipulative skills and would be developed in a movement education environment. The specific structure of the program would conform to Laban's Theory of Movement, which stresses four major components: body awareness (what can the body do?), spatial awareness (where does the body move?), qualities of movement (how does the body move?), and relationships (with whom or what does the body move?)

At successive grade levels, I would apply these skills to specific sport forms such as dance, gymnastics, tennis, field hockey, and so forth. As stated previously, I believe that students should also be aided in the development of objectives in the cognitive and affective/social domains as well as the psychomotor area.

Varsity level sports competition would not be provided for students at the elementary school level. I would stress play days and sport days and intramural sports for those students in the upper elementary grades. The main part of the program in the elementary school would be instruction in movement skills and opportunities for the development of social self-realization. The program of sports at the junior high school level would stress intramural and extramural activities, deemphasizing large crowds, excessive traveling, and expensive awards. When varsity sports are offered at the junior high school level, the program would be adapted to meet the needs, interests, and developmental level of boys and girls. Varsity sports would be provided for youngsters at the senior high school level. The emphasis in this program would be on helping the persons with superior skill levels to display those skills in socially acceptable activities. This would be an educational sports program rather than a commercial venture.

I believe that several teaching styles should be tried to develop students to their optimum level of ability. With some students, a more direct approach might be necessary; with others a more informal approach might prove more successful. I would strive to move toward the discovery method in my teaching. As students become more mature in making decisions, they would be allowed increasingly more freedom in directing their own education. I do not interpret this as meaning that I, as a teacher, would cease teaching once students were able to direct their own learning at a more independent level. On the contrary, I would help the students to reach even greater heights in learning by challenging them with more complex concepts. For example, as soon as individuals mastered the requisite skills, they would be challenged to improvise novel movements and create unique and new movement patterns.

Finally, I believe that the physical education program must be expanded beyond the boundaries of the school if all of its objectives are to be met. For instance, instruction in golf, equestrian arts, swimming, and other specialized activities might best be taught by specialists who are affiliated with schools, if they have the necessary personal qualities and professional competencies.

Self-assessment tests

These tests are designed to assist students in determining if material and competencies presented in this chapter have been mastered.

1. Prepare a report to be given to the class orally in which convincing arguments are presented stressing the fact that each major student in physical education should have a sound philosophy of physical education before graduating from college.
2. Define the terms metaphysics, ethics, esthetics, epistemology, axiology, and logic.
3. Using the statement, ''Highly competitive athletics of the varsity type should not be permitted in the junior high school,'' present arguments on both an emotional and a philosophical level for its adoption.
4. Define five general philosophies and four educational philosophies. What are the implications of each for physical education?
5. List the various steps that might be followed in developing a personal philosophy of physical education.
6. Prepare a written statement of your philosophy of physical education. Present it to the class for their appraisal.

Points to remember

1. A well-thought-out philosophy is essential for each physical educator.
2. An understanding of philosophy is essential in defending the worth of a profession.
3. General and educational philosophies provide a background for many practices that exist in education today.
4. A philosophy can be developed in a logical manner.
5. A philosophy of physical education should be clarified before a teacher accepts a teaching position.

Problems to think through

1. To arrive at the truth, on what principles would each of the following depend: idealist, realist, naturalist, pragmatist, and existentialist?
2. How can a sound philosophy of physical education help the teacher to solve problems and make day-to-day decisions?
3. How would you classify yourself in respect to a general philosophy and an educational philosophy?

Case study for analysis

Analyze the philosophy that has been presented in this chapter. Critically evaluate it in respect to the step-by-step procedure that was used in developing the philosophy, the ideas presented, the practical aspects of this philosophy, and the value of the philosophy in guiding behavior in the conduct of a physical education program at the secondary school level.

Fig. 9-1. The teacher.

jects to obtain almost completely predictable results is used by Gage to illustrate a scientific endeavor. He says, however, that when scientists conduct research, they are themselves practicing an art. He concludes by denying the existence of a science of teaching, since teachers are not able to predict with a high degree of certainty the outcome of learning.

Siedentop characterizes the science of teaching as a process in which teaching is amenable to systematic evaluation and capable of being broken down into a series of tasks that can be mastered.* The science of teaching involves an understanding of human behavior, behavior modification, and instructional design, delivery, and management. Furthermore, the science of teaching involves strict adherence to principles of

learning such as readiness, motivation, practice, feedback, and progression and sequence.

Siedentop states that another characteristic of the science of teaching is the possibility of examining teaching from a theoretical-scientific perspective. He believes that, in order to develop a theory of teaching, teaching should be studied from the theoretical-scientific perspective. Although Siedentop states that we are a long way from having such a theory in physical education, we should be moving in that direction in our attempt to understand the teaching process.

Based on Gage's and Siedentop's characteristics of a science of teaching, there obviously is a lack of a unified science of teaching in physical education. Although Gage speaks only of the inability of teachers to produce the outcomes sought in a science of teaching and Siedentop approaches the teaching of skills

*Siedentop, D.: Developing teaching skills in physical education, Boston, 1976, Houghton Mifflin Co., p. 3.

Fig. 9-2. Teacher at Hampton Institute, Hampton, Va., in physical education class for students.

as if there were a science of teaching, other educators believe it does not exist. For example, Pease indicates that ''until there becomes a scientific body of knowledge about teaching, or as long as teaching remains an art and not a science, then the behavior of teachers will be subject to the behavioral reinforcers operating at any given time.''*

Career options within physical education

There are areas of concentration in physical education at both the undergraduate and graduate levels where specialization can take place. Those areas com-

*Pease, D.A.: Physical education: accountability for the future. In Welsh, R., editor: Physical education: a view toward the future, St. Louis, 1977, The C.V. Mosby Co., p. 153.

monly include athletic training, athletic coaching, and athletic administration; elementary and/or secondary school physical education; physical education for the handicapped; dance; exercise physiology; ergonomics and biomechanics; the behavioral aspects of sports; and motor learning.

ATHLETIC TRAINING

Professional preparation and certification in athletic training comprise relatively new concepts in physical education programs. Athletic trainers usually complete a 4-year college curriculum that emphasizes the biological and physical sciences, psychology, coaching techniques, first aid and safety, nutrition, and other related areas. The National Athletic Trainers Association (NATA) recommends a certification program that provides for a major area of study in physical

Table 9-1. Ten career choices in physical education and sport*

Occupation	*Brief job description*	*Recommended educational preparation*	*Compensation range†*	*Occupational outlook†*
Athletic trainer	Works in schools and colleges or with professional athletic teams in the prevention and care of injuries associated with competitive athletics	College preparation in curriculum approved by the National Athletic Trainers Association and National Certification Examination	Schools: $7,000-30,000 Professional teams: $12,000-30,000	Good
Sports official	Employed by schools, colleges, sport clubs and recreation departments to conduct athletic contests in all sports. Those with outstanding ability may be eligible for assignment to professional contests	Training and qualifying examination in each sport. Must hold membership in official's organization for each sport	Clubs, schools, recreation depts: $10-50 per contest Professional: $50-500 per contest	Good
Professional athlete	Plays baseball, football, basketball, hockey, softball, track & field, tennis, golf, skates or bowls before paying audiences	High school, college for most sports. Intensive coaching and practice	$2,500-1,000,000+	Very few opportunities, heavy competition
Recreation leader	Organizes and directs leisure activities in public agencies, parks and institutions (e.g., YMCA, Scouting, churches, etc.) and corporations. Works with part-time and volunteer workers and supervises their training and activities	2-4 year college degree in recreation and/or related fields	$7,500-25,000	Fair
Physical education teacher	Prepares lesson plans and tests, works with students evaluating skills, sportsmanship, effort and participation Position available with preschool through adult levels	College degrees and appropriate teaching credentials	$8,000-30,000	Fair
Athletic coach	Coaches team or individual sports. May specialize in one sport or one aspect of a sport plan, organize practice sessions and strategy. May teach P.E., health or other subjects; makes business arrangements, gives press interviews Opportunities exist in schools, colleges, community and professional sports	College degree with credits in physical education, education and coaching techniques	$300 (part-time) to $100,000+	Excellent for part-time. Fair for full-time
Sports journalist or photographer	Works with all media in interpreting the sports world to the public through written, oral or visual communication Opportunities exist at local or big city newspapers, T.V., radio stations, magazines, or as sports information director at colleges or universities	College degree with credits in communications Sports experience helpful Photography experience	$6,000-30,000+	Good

*From American Alliance for Health, Physical Education, Recreation, and Dance: Careers in physical education and sport, 1900 Association Dr., Reston, Va.
†Variations in compensation and occupational outlook (availability) depend on geographic area. (Salaries updated by author.)

Table 9-1. Ten career choices in physical education and sport—cont'd

Occupation	Brief job description	Recommended educational preparation	Compensation range†	Occupational outlook†
Sporting goods dealer	Sells sporting goods or manages a department or store. Is in charge of purchasing and marketing, supervises office employees and sales personnel. May represent a manufacturer	College degree or management training programs Sports experience helpful	$9,000-25,000 +	Excellent
Physical therapist	Works with patients who have been physically disabled through birth, illness or accident. Evaluates physiological functions and selects therapeutic procedures for treatment	College degree and state licensing	$8,000-30,000	Good
Physical education and/or athletic administrator	Organizes and supervises competitive and/or instructional programs in clubs, schools, colleges & professional sports. Has responsibility for transportation, budget, facilities, personnel, equipment, scheduling and community relations. PE administrator develops curriculum, athletic director participates in fund raising	College degrees with credits in administration Experience in education and athletics helpful	$10,000-40,000 +	Good

education and health and/or another secondary education field, with the necessary courses required for state licensure. To become an NATA certified athletic trainer, the student must complete the recommended course of study, present proof of 1-year active membership in the NATA, and pass practical and written examinations.

ATHLETIC COACHING AND ADMINISTRATION

Those persons who are particularly interested in coaching various sports and/or the administration of athletic programs will find that some institutions of higher learning offer these as areas of specialization. Usually there is a core of general and physical education requirements and then an in-depth offering of courses concerned with methods and materials for coaching various sports, officiating, first aid and care of injuries, administration of athletic programs, financial management, public relations, and the legal aspects of athletic programs.

ELEMENTARY AND/OR SECONDARY SCHOOL PHYSICAL EDUCATION

The latest surveys show that many institutions offering professional preparation still combine specialization in elementary and secondary school physical education. However, more and more of these schools are offering their students an opportunity to specialize in elementary school physical education. With the current emphasis on movement education, perceptual-motor learning, and interdisciplinary analysis, there is a need to provide experiences that will prepare the physical educator with the expertise to work with children in an effective and meaningful manner.

PHYSICAL EDUCATION FOR THE HANDICAPPED

Teaching handicapped persons is becoming a rewarding area for specialization among physical educators who are interested in working with the mentally and physically handicapped and other types of atypical individuals. Such specialization is becoming increasingly evident since the passage of Public Law 94-142, which provides for the education of the handicapped at public expense.

DANCE

Dance is becoming a popular and rewarding area of specialization for physical educators who wish to render a service by helping young persons to better understand their bodies and to express themselves through rhythmical activity. Although many opportunities present themselves in elementary and secondary schools and also in dance studios and community agencies and recreation programs, the college and university levels (where more often than not dance teachers work in departments, divisions, or schools of physical education) also offer many opportunities. There has been considerable expansion of dance programs in recent years in institutions of higher learning. Liberal arts colleges are offering expanded programs of dance experiences for their students, professional preparation programs are training teachers of physical education with an emphasis in the area of the dance, and other institutions are providing instruction in modern, ballroom, and folk dancing for the general student body.

As the dance program in schools and colleges becomes increasingly popular, there is a demand for teachers of physical education who are specialists in the various phases of dance. Prospective teachers in this area will find more positions available if they prepare themselves to teach the other activities in the physical education program as well since opportunities for teaching dance alone are limited.

In addition to schools and colleges, dance personnel are needed in other places such as the theater, private studios, recreation centers, armed forces, summer camps, and hospital therapy. Roles that dance personnel play include that of teacher, performer, dance therapist, choreographer, notator, and director of a concert group and in television, movie, and theater productions. Teaching dance effectively requires a study of the scientific principles of body movement; an understanding of dance forms, dance composition, and technique; skills of notation; theories relating to costuming, staging, and lighting; and a good grounding in the scientific foundations of physical education and a sound general education.

EXERCISE PHYSIOLOGY

In recent years there has been a great deal of interest in exercise physiology. The fitness explosion has given even further impetus to specialization in this area. Industrial fitness programs are seeking exercise physiologists, and the involvement of increasing numbers of girls and women in athletic programs has provided a challenge to specialists and researchers in this area to determine the physiological characteristics and the potentialities of the female athlete.

ERGONOMICS AND BIOMECHANICS

The desire to know more about the anatomical and physiological bases of human performance is causing more physical educators to seek expertise in these areas. Biomechanics is receiving considerable attention throughout the United States and the rest of the world and has become a viable subdiscipline of physical education.

BEHAVIORAL FOUNDATIONS OF SPORT

Emphasis on the psychology and sociology of sport continues to increase. As a result, some physical educators are specializing in these areas, although the number of institutions that provide appropriate indepth preparation is limited.

MOTOR LEARNING

Since motor learning is directly related to the teaching of physical education skills, it is of vital importance to members of the profession and therefore an important area of specialization in physical education.

Personal qualifications necessary to become a physical educator

The personal qualifications of the physical educator are extremely important. Administrators value such characteristics as professionalism, promptness, and the ability to maintain control, while students hold patience, understanding, and fairness as desirable qualities in a teacher.

There is no formula for a successful teacher to follow. The "coach" who is like a father or mother to his boys or girls may be as highly respected as the one who is a strict disciplinarian and dictator. The physical educator who is highly organized and efficient may be as well liked as the young graduate who can participate with the students.

Is being "highly respected" and "well liked" the key to successful teaching? Perhaps these characteristics are a part of the overall picture. Certainly maintaining discipline and imparting information are equally important qualities for the teaching process. The personality traits exhibited by the teacher and the relationship established with the students are the vital links between the subject and its recipients. All four aspects of the teacher's character—physical, social, emotional, and intellectual—should be worthy of emulation by the developing adolescent.

PHYSICAL QUALIFICATIONS

The physical educator frequently has many more students in classes than do other teachers. Close relationships with students develop through the intramural and interscholastic programs. Because of the

Fig. 9-3. Physical education teachers should have good relationships with their students.

Courtesy Bill Henderson of Toms River, N.J.

number and type of these relationships between student and teacher, it is important that the appearance of the physical educator be worthy of adolescent respect and admiration. Uniforms should be spotless and all clothing should be neat, clean, appropriate, and in good taste. Health, good hygiene, and cleanliness are so closely associated with physical education that the instructor must represent these ideals to the students.

The physical skills and abilities of the physical educator should be exemplary. To conduct satisfactory demonstrations and teaching lessons, teachers should be able to perform well in as many areas as possible. This does not mean that they must "star" in all events, but their background of physical skills should be above average.

SOCIAL QUALIFICATIONS

Because of the many social objectives of physical education, it is important that the teacher be a model of mature social development, meet people easily, mix well, and treat all individuals with respect and consideration. It is these qualities that the teacher reveals in the classroom and that the students should be able to recognize.

As a leader the physical educator should strive to control but not dominate the group and to plan with but not for students. Thus leadership qualities are promoted, and students in turn may learn to lead well.

EMOTIONAL QUALIFICATIONS

It is important that every teacher be a stable and mature individual, well adjusted to life in his or her chosen occupation. This is particularly true of the physical educator. The nature and tenor of the work require an emotional control and a responsiveness that are not easily defined.

To establish effective teaching rapport, the teacher must have patience and understanding mixed with firmness and composure. To meet all the individual problems that arise daily with students—their maladies, their excuses, their upsets—the teacher must offer a sympathetic, understanding ear, indicating a sincere interest in students' personal difficulties. In handling everyday occurrences in the classroom, the teacher should display firmness and quiet confidence so that students realize that the situation is well under control.

The many frustrations that beset the physical educator striving for winning teams and competitive excellence must be met with calm self-assurance. Administrative and community pressures should not become so strong that other teaching responsibilities are neglected or that self-concern replaces consideration for the students.

INTELLECTUAL AND OTHER PROFESSIONAL QUALIFICATIONS

Intellectually, the physical educator needs many qualities that are equally important for a teacher and a model for young people.

As a teacher the physical educator should be efficiently organized and able to maintain order in handling the myriad administrative details. An ability to express ideas clearly and distinctly orally and on paper is also important, for students learn from what is imparted to them, and therefore materials must be intelligently presented. A professional manner and outlook enhance the profession itself in the eyes of the students, and this, too, becomes an important aspect of the teacher's personality. The image that a physical educator is a person of all brawn and no brains is slowly being overcome, and new teachers entering the field should further enhance this newer picture of the teacher as an intelligent educator.

As a model for young people, the teacher should have many interests in and out of the field. This is important because it affords more opportunities for sharing various student interests. As a broader interpretation of physical education in its relationship to life is presented to the students, the physical educator is respected for more than just coaching abilities or professional skills. In this role of a counselor influencing students in their approach to life, the physical educator should have an outlook worthy of respect and imitation.

Ideally, the physical educator should have a wholesome personality, sharing a deep knowledge and interest in the subject with students who are respected as people and led with sympathetic understanding. The personality that the teacher presents to the students may be as important as the material to be learned. Ideally, the physical educator should also meet other qualifications and standards in addition to those of a personal nature.

According to the Eighth Annual Gallup Poll of the Public's Attitude Toward The Public Schools,* the following personal qualities are most important.

1. *Communication*—the ability to relate to, understand, and to communicate with students, parents and the public in general
2. *Discipline*—the ability to maintain discipline in a fair but firm manner
3. *Motivation*—the ability to motivate a student to work up to his or her capacity—the ability to inspire boys and girls to do their best
4. *Character*—since the child emulates the teacher, moral character is essential
5. *Love*—the teacher should love children, be sympathetic to their needs, and have a concern for them
6. *Dedication*—the teacher should be enthusiastic about teaching, like to teach, and find a challenge in doing so
7. *Personality*—the teacher should have a friendly, warm personality
8. *Appearance*—the teacher should have a clean and attractive personal appearance

Becoming certified to teach physical education

Among the many problems encountered by any prospective teacher are those concerning the initial step of becoming properly certified. Often the confusion and red tape involved in finding appropriate information and determining personal status are so disheartening that the new teacher is bewildered before starting. The prospective physical educator is not different from other teachers in this respect, and knowing in advance about state requirements and qualifications can save a great deal of worry and frustration. Certification problems are complicated further by the continuous study and change of specifications.

Some of the newer approaches to teacher certification include a competency-based approach, a freer movement of qualified teachers across state lines, a simplification of the types of certificates issued, an

*Gallup, G.H.: Eighth Annual Gallup Poll of the Public's Attitudes Toward the Public Schools, *Phi Delta Kappa* **58**:187, 1976.

approved-program approach where the preparing college or university has its teacher-preparing program endorsed and then accepts the responsibility for training and certifying the teachers who pursue and graduate from that program, and certification based on a teacher's demonstrated abilities rather than on the completion of courses in a collegiate program.

CERTIFICATION REQUIREMENTS

All states have established minimum requirements that must be met by prospective teachers before they become legally certified to teach. These certification requirements correspond to similar requirements in other professions, such as the licensing of doctors and dentists after state or national examinations.

The certification of teachers serves several purposes: protecting schoolchildren by ensuring a high quality of teaching, employing only superior and qualified personnel, and unifying teaching standards. The students therefore benefit from these requirements. For teachers, however, the task of meeting the varying state requirements complicates professional preparation and certification procedures.

There are nine general areas in which most states have governing regulations for teacher certification. While many states may agree on certain factors, they may disagree on others. The prospective teacher should therefore inquire directly of the state education department (division of teacher certification) for exact requirements. To summarize these nine general areas and the current requirements in the 50 states, the following information is presented.

Citizenship. More than one half of the states have citizenship requirements or a declaration of intention clause. The teacher must be a citizen of the United States to qualify.

Oath of allegiance or loyalty. Approximately one half of the states do not require a loyalty oath for teacher certification. The others require a signed statement.

Age. The age requirement varies among states. The lowest minimum age is 17 years. In general 18 or 19 years of age is acceptable in states specifying a particular age although some states have no stipulation in this matter.

Professional preparation. It is in this area that the greatest differences in state requirements may be found. Many states are moving toward a competency-based approach. Several states have particular courses that must be taken by candidates for certification. For example, in one state teachers must have studied American government and/or history; in another, state and federal government; and in still another, school health education. Some of these special state requirements must be complete before the first year of teaching, while others may be fulfilled within a certain period of time.

Recommendation. Most of the states require a teaching candidate to have a recommendation from college or from the last place of employment.

Fee. A fee for certification, ranging from $1 to $25, is required in a majority of the states.

Health certificate. A certificate of general good health is necessary in many states. Some states require a chest x-ray report instead of or along with this certificate.

Employment. Candidates from *other* states may need to have secured employment to become certified within some states.

Course of study. Besides the general areas of state requirements, there are basic and minimum regulations regarding the course of study that must be followed to qualify for specific certification in physical education. Again, the states differ in their requirements of hours of study and competencies necessary within the field of physical education.

Because of these curriculum differences and the variation among states in regard to the nine basic factors outlined, a certificate to teach in one state is not necessarily valid in another state. However, reciprocity among states in the same region of the country is a growing reality, particularly for graduates of an accredited teacher preparation program.

A further problem in certification presents itself where localities within a state have specific regulations governing selection of teachers. These are often more rigid than the standards established within the state itself. Detroit and New York City, for example, have their own sets of qualifications that must be met by their teachers, and many southern cities and states require high scores on the National Teacher Examinations. Local regulations usually involve such factors as teacher preparation and experience. An applicant may also be required to pass written and oral examinations for local licensing. Information regarding local teaching requirements may be secured by writing to the board of education in the city in question.

Prospective teachers should try to determine state and local regulations far in advance, if possible. In so doing they may guide their course of study in college to meet the requirements. They should then send in their records far enough ahead of time to become certified before accepting a position.

TYPES OF CERTIFICATES

The type and value of certificates issued by the states vary nearly as much as do their regulations. In some states, for example, there are merely two categories of certification, permanent and probationary, while another state may have 22 variations of certificates. The certificate to teach physical education is generally limited to this special field of work, but its validity may be for one year (probationary) or for life. Some states grant temporary, provisional, or emergency certificates to teachers who do not fully meet all requirements, with the understanding that within a certain period of time the candidate will become fully qualified.

The value of the certificate again depends on state regulations. It enables the teacher to teach in any public school system within that state, except those where local standards require further qualifications. It may qualify the teacher to teach in neighboring states, depending on reciprocity agreements. It may also permit him or her to teach in private schools within the state or at least in private schools seeking state accreditation.

Neither the prospective nor the experienced teacher seeking employment in a different state should let these differences in state requirements and qualifications become a hindrance. An inquiry to the state or local department of education should bring the necessary information in time to facilitate certification.

Making application for a teaching position

Recent surveys and statistics indicate that teaching jobs will be difficult to obtain in the future. However, positions will still be open to those who are highly qualified and prepare themselves well for their responsibilities. Furthermore, there are many bright job opportunities in such places as the inner city and poor rural districts, in teaching the handicapped, in early childhood education, in educational research, in industry, and in health spas.

The next series of problems faced by the prospective teacher revolves around finding a job—writing a proper letter of application, having an interview, and attending to the details important in obtaining any teaching position. The superintendent who is forced to choose between two or more candidates for a physical education opening may allow the decision to rest on appearance, on spelling, or on the smallest of details. The applicant should therefore take great care in all phases of the process of finding and obtaining a position.

LETTER OF APPLICATION

The prospective teacher usually hears of job openings through friends, the college bureau of appointments, an employment agency, or direct application by letter to a specific locale. The letter of application serves as an introduction to the prospective employer and should be carefully composed to contain appropriate information.

The letter should be neat, typewritten, and grammatically correct. Pertinent details should be included in such a manner that the personality of the individual is conveyed to the reader. The employer wants to know about the applicant's educational background, experiences related to the field of education, and interests. Personal information such as age and health should also be included, together with names and addresses of references. If possible, the applicant should also state his or her availability for an interview.

In response to this letter of application the candidate should receive a letter reporting either that there are no vacancies or that the position is open and an interview is desired. A printed application form is often included with this reply, and it should also be filled out neatly and carefully.

INTERVIEW

Interviews of teacher-applicants generally take place either at the school itself, providing candidates an opportunity to see the school in action, or at the college of the graduating candidate. In the latter case a field representative of the school system usually interviews several candidates from the college, and a request from the superintendent for a school visitation interview follows.

In either type of interview the prospective teacher should expect to ask and to answer questions of all types, for it is the purpose of the interview to allow the new teacher to learn about the school system, as well as to give the employer an opportunity to screen the applicant.

While the employer is questioning the applicant, he or she will be observing the teacher's bearing, outlook, speech, personal mannerisms, and general effectiveness as a person. Needless to say, the applicant should be prompt, well groomed, and neatly dressed for this occasion. The prospective teacher should be ready to answer in a concise and intelligent manner questions about any phase of teaching physical education: What is the most important attribute of a good teacher? What is the philosophy behind the inclusion of physical education in the school curriculum? What are some specific objectives of the program? How are the needs of the children determined?

The range of possible questions is very broad, and the candidate can make little actual preparation for them other than to know and sincerely believe in the field of physical education.

The answers given by the applicant at the interview are not the only determining factor. The employer may judge to some extent on the basis of intelligent questioning by the candidate about the type of education being offered in the school and the community's interest in school affairs. Inquiries about scheduling, class groupings, extramural duties, community activities, and school organizations indicate to the superintendent or person doing the interviewing that the prospective teacher knows what is involved in a teaching position. At the same time the applicant is, of course, determining whether this particular school administration is genuinely interested in physical education and if this type of position is the most desirable and suitable in comparison to other available jobs.

The physical educator should consider the various types of teaching jobs. Is a large or small school system preferable? In a small school the teacher often has classes from grades one through 12, while in the larger, multiple-building systems, a position may be limited to elementary, middle school, junior high, or senior high teaching. Is teaching in a large, departmentalized situation with several other persons a better position in which to start than one in which the teacher is the only physical educator? These are questions that the teacher must settle in his or her own mind, in terms of personal preferences, after several school visitations and interviews have revealed the differences.

Unfortunately, the prospective teacher does not always receive the position of first choice. A poor impression during the interview or a poor letter of application may make the difference. Other factors also enter into a failure of final appointment. Lateness of application or heavy competition for a position may be a determining factor. The teacher seldom knows the real cause of failure.

Appointments are not generally made at the interviews themselves, for the board of education must give final approval, and the applicant should have additional time to think about such an important decision. Later the applicant may receive a letter from the superintendent or other school official stating that the position has been filled or offering an appointment and perhaps some type of contractual agreement.

CONTRACTUAL AGREEMENTS

Contractual agreements between employer and teacher vary in style, form, and content, but essentially they signify a promise of payment for services rendered. In some areas a single word or handshake is the only type of agreement used, while in other areas a formalized contract carefully specifying duties and assignments is required. Each board of education has its own particular method. However, the prospective teacher should inquire about certain aspects of the agreement in order to know exactly what responsibilities and fringe benefits are contained in it.

Term of employment. The initial contract is usually a provisional one, covering one year of teaching. In many schools there is a three- or five-year provisional period for new teachers, and at the end of that time a more permanent type of contract may be issued. Some boards of education provide *tenure* for teachers, which means that following the provisional period

Fig. 9-4. High school girls participating in track activities.

Courtesy Barbara Ann Chiles, Aledo, Ill.

teachers may be assured of a permanent position in their schools, if so desired.

Persons going into teaching should be aware that teacher tenure is under nationwide attack. A Gallup poll indicates that the public in general—61%—does not approve of the idea of tenure. For those who are parents and have children in school, 64% disapprove of tenure. Among professional educators 53% approve of tenure, 42% disapprove, and 5% have no opinion.

Responsibilities. In some instances contracts contain detailed outlines of teaching responsibilities, including, for example, the number of hours of intramural activities or the number of coaching assignments required of the teacher. These duties must be performed by the teacher if he or she enters into such an agreement, unless unusual circumstances permit exemption.

Release from a contract. Unusual circumstances, such as forced leave of absence or call to military

service, may release the teacher from the contract. This is possible in most cases by application to the board of education. The prospective teacher should realize, however, that except in these unusual situations it is not wise to break an agreement with the board of education. As professionals in the field of education, teachers are expected to be reliable and dependable people, with high ethical standards, and therefore able to live up to agreements.

Salary. Written agreements between teachers and employers usually indicate exact salary arrangements. In most schools a salary scale has been established with definite regulations governing the placement of teachers on that scale. Years of service or merit usually determine increments in salary, although differentiated staffing is changing this practice in some places. Where years of service are used as a basis for raises in pay, teachers usually receive regular increments in salary. In schools where a merit plan is in effect, the better teachers usually receive higher pay on the basis of certain standards of teaching that have been established for evaluation of services. A third type of salary schedule has emerged from schools using the team-teaching program. In this case the person or persons shouldering major responsibility for a course of study receive higher salaries.

Benefits. Some school systems also establish additional teacher benefits that make them more desirable and attractive places in which to work. Sick leave policies and personal days are examples of administrative consideration for teacher welfare. Provisions for sabbatical leave, health insurance, and retirement are also benefits that vary among schools and states. The new teacher should try to find out as much as possible about these fringe benefits for teachers in the particular school system offering employment.

When the prospective teacher accepts an appointment and signs a contractual agreement, if one is necessary, the benefits and terms are settled and the problems of job application cease. The teacher has now assumed new responsibilities and obligations that must be met. These responsibilities encompass the physical education department itself, the school faculty, the community, and the profession—all equally important to a successful career.

The first year

As the day of birth is one of the most critical for the newborn baby, so is the first year of teaching one of the most critical for the newly trained teacher. The neophyte instructor has spent four or more years in college learning a great amount of theory from professors, talking about what to do when discipline problems arise with students, and discussing how to function with inadequate facilities. Now the new teacher in the classroom or gymnasium faces a live and restless group of students. These boys and girls know that an inexperienced teacher is handling the class, and many seek opportunities to disprove all the theory that has been learned in four years of training.

The big test has come. Will the beginning teacher be successful in meeting the challenge? Will the class be organized for effective instruction? Will the teaching techniques that have been mastered be equal to

the existing situation? The answer to these and similar questions depends on many factors, including whether or not the beginning teacher has been alerted to some of the problems that may arise and some of the procedures that may be followed in handling them. This chapter is aimed at helping the new teacher meet difficulties encountered the first year on the job. Although those problems are infinite, many are common and recommendations by experienced teachers will assist the beginning teacher in successfully completing the first critical year.

There is a high turnover rate among first-year teachers. Some teachers change jobs to improve their status; others leave the profession because of dissatisfaction and discouragement and because they have found the job of adjusting to the hard realities of teaching too difficult for them to master.

PROBLEMS OF BEGINNING TEACHERS

Several research studies have been conducted to determine the reasons for job satisfaction or dissatisfaction among teachers. They include such factors as relationships between teacher and administrator, teacher and community, teacher and faculty, teacher and student, and teacher and parent; physical conditions; and salary and security concerns. An example of one such study cites three areas of difficulties encountered by teachers: difficulties related to personal characteristics, difficulties related to instructional activities, and difficulties related to community environment and relationships. Most of the difficulties pertain to pupil control, teaching assignment, adaptation to pupil needs, records and reports, deficiencies in equipment, teacher-principal relationships, and personality.

According to a study conducted by the National Education Association, the five major problems of teachers were identified as (1) insufficient time for rest and preparation in the school day, (2) large class size, (3) insufficient clerical help, (4) inadequate salary, and (5) inadequate fringe benefits. Less stress was placed on such problems as lack of public support for schools, ineffective faculty meetings, and poor administration.

A representative number of directors of physical education in school systems across the nation was

AN ACTUAL DAY IN THE LIFE OF ONE PHYSICAL EDUCATOR

PRE-FIRST PERIOD ACTIVITIES

8:20   Sign in
8:20   Confer with other teachers
8:35   Set up and check of equipment to be used that day

FIRST AND SECOND PERIODS—8:50-10:20 (double period for ninth graders)

Locker room supervision
Attendance check by student leaders
Fifteen-minute exercise period in preparation for physical fitness test
Presentation of the skills and techniques involved in the sprint start
Individual practice—instructor and the student leaders checking student progress
One-hundred-yard sprint—students demonstrating the skill that they have just learned
Shower and change clothes—locker room supervision

THIRD AND FOURTH PERIODS—10:22-11:48 (double period for tenth graders)

Locker room supervision
Attendance check by student leaders
Fifteen-minute exercise period in preparation for physical fitness test
Review of the basic skills and techniques involved in the sprint start with student demonstration
Presentation of the basic skills and techniques involved in the long jump: the run, the gather, the take-off
   (float style in the air, hang style in the air, and the hitch-kick style in the air), and the landing
Student leader demonstration
Question-answer period on basic skills and techniques
Student individual practice with suggestions offered by instructor to improve individual performance
Shower and change clothes—locker room supervision

FIFTH AND SIXTH PERIODS—11:50-1:10

Preparation of new skills for future presentation, review of new library materials, films, and so on, setting
   up skill scales for evaluation purposes, and preparation of written test questions on the activity being
   covered
Lunch

SEVENTH PERIOD—1:11-1:53 (single period for twelfth graders)

Locker room supervision
Attendance check by student leaders
Fifteen-minute exercise period in preparation for physical fitness test
Review of previous class instruction (beginning skill, the relay race, or intermediate skill, long jump)—
   student demonstration and explanation
Presentation of the basic skills and techniques involved in the shot put—8- and 12-pound shot puts available
Individual student practice with suggestions offered by instructor to improve student performance
Question-answer period on the basic skills and techniques of this activity
Shower and change clothes—locker room supervision

EIGHTH PERIOD—1:55-2:40

Preparation period—continuation of activities begun in the fifth and sixth periods surveyed to determine the most difficult problems faced by beginning teachers. These administrators, whose views, because of firsthand observation, should be of value to teachers embarking on professional careers, indicate that the problems relate to organization, teaching, teacher-student relationships, teacher-teacher relationships, and ability to adjust to problems associated with the position.

A few of the more common professional problems experienced by the beginning physical educator, with recommendations for meeting them, are discipline, difficulty in working effectively with colleagues, lack of respect for physical education, inequitable use of facilities, problems relating to sex roles, and extra school assignments.

Discipline. Lack of discipline is one of the most common problems cited by beginning physical educators in the secondary school. Poor neighborhoods, parental neglect and indifference, overcrowded classes, student transiency, poor economic conditions, and pampered children have been cited as contributing factors. Teachers have mentioned that some students are guilty of inattention, unpreparedness, smoking, drug use, cutting classes, refusing to follow instructions, talking, and many other infractions.

If a teacher is to be a success, classes must be conducted in an orderly manner, and the teacher must have the respect of the pupils. Part of the difficulty in regard to discipline problems may be caused by the youthful appearance of the teacher and the desire on the part of the students to test the new teacher.

Some beginning teachers are more sensitive than others to the reasons why discipline problems arise. For example, one teacher stated that poor planning on his part was quickly recognized by the pupils, causing many discipline problems. Another teacher noted that in some schools the beginning teacher must work three times as hard as an experienced instructor to establish proper student-teacher relations. A third teacher related that the previous teacher was not respected, which made it more difficult for her to work effectively. A fourth teacher made an excellent point when she said that she did not understand the boys and girls with whom she was working. She pointed out that she lacked knowledge of their stages of growth and development and therefore of what to expect at each age

level. She recognized that this problem could be alleviated only by a thorough study and understanding of the physical, mental, social, and emotional characteristics of children and youth.

Experienced teachers have recommended many techniques that should be helpful to the physical educator in working with groups of students.

1. Be firm when first meeting a group. It is easy to relax after a good relationship has been established, but it is difficult to gain control over a group that has not known discipline.

2. Maintain poise with a noisy group. Call for silence and then wait for the order to be obeyed. If necessary, call to one or two individuals to be quiet. This will often have the desired effect on the class.

3. Use a whistle only when necessary. Blow it sparingly, but require attention whenever it is used.

4. Wait for silence before talking. A murmur can multiply quickly if it is not stopped.

5. Know the pupils well in order to determine the best approach to each individual.

6. Maintain self-control. No situation should be allowed to deteriorate into a personal duel with the students.

7. Give all pupils a feeling of belonging. Show the boys and girls that they are all part of the group and will receive your interest and attention.

8. Be liberal in praise. Every child wants to be praised by the teacher, and accomplishment should be recognized.

9. Be friendly and relaxed. The atmosphere that the teacher establishes in class will be quickly copied by the pupils.

10. Be sympathetic. Show an awareness of the difficulty of the stunt or skill and encourage the student to continue.

11. Know the subject matter; have a sense of humor; have the courage of your convictions; work for challenging, exciting programs; and be consistent, fair, and democratic.

12. Know the pupils' interests, abilities, parental and family backgrounds, and achievements.

13. Make physical education activities interesting, meaningful, and vital.

14. Find out what the pupils' problems are and try to help them solve their difficulties.

Working effectively with colleagues. A problem frequently cited by beginning teachers is the problem of working effectively with other members of the department of physical education and with other faculty members. One beginning teacher commented that it was particularly difficult to gain the cooperation of older teachers because they were inflexible. Another teacher said that some colleagues do not cooperate because a new teacher is too ambitious and too much of an "eager beaver." Another teacher believed that physical education teachers are frowned on as not being very scholarly. Finally, another teacher commented that being young and inexperienced makes it difficult to adjust—that the teacher is looked on more as a student than as a faculty member.

Probably the best advice is the comment of one beginning teacher on this problem. She said: "Whether or not you get along with colleagues depends on you."

Human relations can be effective when a person is considerate, tries to help others, it not overly critical, listens to advice, becomes a member of the team, and tries in every way to contribute effectively to the achievement of the goals of the school.

It is important for the new teacher to understand that the experienced instructors have amassed practical knowledge in addition to their formal training, which places them well ahead of teachers just out of college. There are many techniques that can be learned from colleagues. The beginning teacher should watch closely and select the methods that can be of value.

The new teacher should try to follow accepted procedures and systems, fitting into the existing pattern as much as possible. Being willing to work, anxious to learn, and able to get along increases the possibility of obtaining quick acceptance by colleagues.

Another aspect of this problem is the distribution of the work load. There is the question of whether, at first, the new teacher should carry a heavier or a lighter load than the older teachers and do more or less committee work.

The new teacher should willingly accept assignments of teaching and nonteaching duties but should feel free to ask questions when there is some phase of the program or duties that is not clear. New teachers often run into difficulty because they are afraid to ask questions. They think this would indicate ignorance, and instead of seeking the answers, they blunder ahead, making mistakes and intensifying problems.

Each teacher is primarily responsible for his or her own preparation for the job. There is also the responsibility of the administrator, however, to help prepare the new teacher for the experiences to be encountered. Some steps that administrators can take that, in the opinion of their Association,* would benefit a beginning teacher are

1. To provide all the necessary pertinent information
2. To establish workshops for teachers
3. To assign an adviser for each new teacher
4. To hold seminars for new teachers
5. To have new teachers observe excellent teaching
6. To demonstrate teaching techniques to improve skills

Lack of respect for physical education. Sometimes physical educators are referred to as "jocks," "muscular women" or "muscle men," or they are given other uncomplimentary names, separating them from other teachers who are considered educators. It is important to break down this stereotyped thinking. Only when administrators, colleagues, and the public in general understand the true purpose and philosophy of physical education will this attitude change.

Physical educators should be educators first—well-educated people who are interested in the total development of students, not just their physical development. Although the work may concern itself more with the physical than the work of other teachers, it should not deter them from an appreciation of the importance of giving high priority to the mental development of youngsters, recognizing that the physical is only a means to an end. The end must be the education of the total child.

The dress of physical educators as well as their manners will help to support or disprove the stereotype. The working uniform should be restricted to the gymnasium. Teachers would not, of course, be expected to change clothes every time they leave the gymnasium for a few minutes, but they should be properly attired for every school function, whether it

---

*American Association of School Administrators.

is an assembly, a faculty meeting, or a conference, as well as for merely leaving school. Furthermore, in all actions physical educators should try to show that they are well-mannered, cultured, educated human beings who rank on the same level with other educators.

Another major task for teachers is to interpret the program of physical education wherever they go. There is much misunderstanding in regard to the goals and values of the profession. All phases of the program—classes, adapted programs, intramural and extramural activities, and interscholastic athletics—should be accurately explained in terms of its specific worth in the educational program.

Physical educators must be professional in every respect. This means joining local, state, and national organizations, recruiting outstanding personnel for the profession, continually seeking opportunities for self-improvement, being effective teachers, continually keeping abreast of the latest developments and thinking in the field, and being good public relations ambassadors. If physical educators would fulfill their responsibilities in these areas, physical education would soon be respected throughout the country.

Inequitable use of facilities. The use of the available facilities, according to many beginning teachers, seems to be a common problem throughout the country. Several beginning teachers point out that too often women are asked to give up facilities in favor of the varsity interscholastic program. It may be that a separate gymnasium or field is not available for a girls' intramural sport or that, because of the varsity schedule the area is free only during the late afternoon hours. The equipment shared may also be divided inequitably. Finally, the budgetary allotments may be apportioned in such a way that the men obtain the lion's share and the women a bare minimum.

The underlying cause of such inequity may be little administrative enthusiasm for what has traditionally been considered girls' activities. Such a problem may take considerable time to correct, and the new teacher must work slowly and patiently to build up a more favorable administrative attitude. An effort should be made to develop student and community interest in activities in which girls will participate. When interest is aroused, it may be possible to convince the admin-

istrator of the importance and value of providing a strong coeducational program as well as activities in which girls are interested. Since Title IX (see Chapter 6) prohibits discrimination against girls and women, a strong program in this area is a better possibility than it used to be. As a result girls and women are having much more say in the administration of the program, which in itself will hurry the solution of many of these problems. The best possible program for all girls and boys is what is needed.

Problems relating to sex roles. Male physical educators experience many different types of problems when they begin to teach. They may be required to take on additional responsibilities in the community, working with recreation, church, and various youth groups. Or they may not be assigned teaching and coaching duties in accordance with their wishes. Those who are married may have personal responsibilities that require additional funds when starting salary schedules do not adequately provide for family considerations.

There are many problems faced by the beginning male teacher, but the most common seems to be associated with an overemphasis on interscholastic athletics. (Under Title IX this may also become true for some female physical educators.) The pressures involved in sports, when they are influenced by local newspapers, radio, television, community, and alumni, place undue importance on this phase of the physical education program. The physical educator wants to be an effective teacher in regular classes and intramural activities but finds that community pressures often force him to spend a disproportionate amount of time on the interscholastic athletic program.

Under such conditions the teacher should steer a steady course, realizing that he is associated with educational, rather than professional, athletics. The coach who puts a winning team above all else, tries to pressure teachers to keep players eligible, teaches how to win at any cost, is rude to officials, is not completely honest, and closes his eyes to improper conduct will be a credit neither to his school nor to the profession of physical education. There are many valuable contributions that sports can make to the student, such as teamwork, skill, sportsmanship, respect for ability, and greater understanding of the value and place of sports in our society. These worthy goals must receive the main emphasis as the total physical education program for all students is kept in proper focus.

Women physical educators also have many problems with which to contend during their first year on the job. Some of these, including inequitable use of facilities, have been mentioned. Other problems may involve her professional as well as personal life.

Male physical education teachers sometimes receive extra pay for extra coaching duties, but the time spent by female teachers with intramural and interscholastic programs sometimes remains unrecognized. The Title IX clause prohibiting salary discrimination may help change this trend. When an unequal pay scale exists, the female physical education instructor—together with other teachers in the school who devote extra work to the band, orchestra, dramatics group, school newspaper, or other activity— should strive to impress the administration with the need for added salary benefits.

The beginning female teacher may find an obvious lack of interest in physical education among secondary school girls. The students may be more interested in dates and social obligations than in physical education.

Personal problems may also confront beginning teachers. If they are married, there is the problem of time to devote to the home. Physical education requires long hours, and home life may be neglected. Good planning and organization in the home as well as at school may relieve this situation. Unmarried teachers may allow their social lives to interfere with work at school. Those who enjoy their work, however, find that self-preoccupation disappears as soon as the morning bell sounds and that the problems of the students replace their own.

Not all these problems will be faced by all new (male and female) teachers, but some of them will be present. The teacher who keeps in mind his or her responsibilities to students, school, and profession, who gets along with others, and who does quality work should encounter little difficulty.

Extra school assignments. One of the most pressing problems facing beginning teachers of physical education is assignment of extra duties during the school day. It is not uncommon for the physical educator to supervise a lunchroom period, to keep an eye on the entrance or exit where the students congregate, to handle traffic at school functions, to manage school dances, to monitor study halls, or to supervise the parking lot. Too often the number and type of such assignments place an unfair burden on the teacher, sometimes to such a degree that they interfere with the primary responsibility of a physical educator. It is important, of course, to perform all duties to the best of one's ability. It is also reasonable to point out to the administrator in charge those instances when such assignments affect teaching, infringe upon hours that could be put to better professional use, or take an unfair amount of a teacher's free time.

It is readily evident that problems of beginning teachers are numerous and varied. It would be of great value to the new teacher to study each of these problems in as much detail as possible and to determine their meaning in relation to adjusting satisfactorily to the job.

Many of the problems of teachers are ''across the board'' types of difficulties affecting all teachers regardless of subject matter. However, the teacher of physical education encounters some problems caused by the nature of this special field of endeavor. Some of the more common problems of beginning physical education teachers that have been identified through research are associated with:

Discipline
Facilities
Adjustment to the school
Class organization
Student hostility toward the program
Methods of teaching
Legal liability
Numbers of students in class
Insufficient space
Equipment
Behavior problems
Introduction of new ideas and techniques
The intellectually inferior label associated with
    physical education
Program planning
Status

Role of physical education in general education
Personal relationships
Interscholastic athletics
Budget
Scheduling
Grouping in classes
Time allotment
Insurance

Many problems of the beginning physical education teacher appear to recur over and over again. Thus it is important to consider how selecting the right position and having a better understanding of the new teacher's school, community, and job can reduce or alleviate the problems.

Eliminating some problems before assuming the position

The teacher should carefully evaluate the position before accepting such a responsibility. Unfortunately, some teachers accept positions in schools and communities in which they do not fit or belong and, consequently, problems are bound to arise. If an individual is going to be unhappy and ineffective on the job, it may be better not to accept such a position in the first place. The many complex factors related to job adjustment are usually associated with the nature of the person, the nature of the environment, and the interaction of the two. It is therefore important that the candidate carefully weigh a position in terms of his or her abilities and personal characteristics for handling it effectively. Thus many of the problems can be foreseen, and the qualities and preparation needed to manage them successfully can be evaluated realistically.

ADVANCE CONSIDERATIONS

Two advance considerations important to the beginning teacher before assuming the job are knowledge of the conditions of employment and pertinent factors about the school and community.

Knowledge of employment conditions. It is imperative for the new teacher to understand the numerous details, duties, and responsibilities that he or she is about to assume, including a knowledge of classes to be handled, sports to be coached, clubs to

be sponsored, homeroom assignments, study halls, length of the school day, after-school obligations, compensation to be received, salary schedules in force, sick leave, tenure, sabbaticals, health insurance, and other relevant facts. Only as the teacher has a clear understanding of the responsibilities will he or she be able to prepare sufficiently, mentally and physically, for the position. Information can be obtained from other teachers, members of the administration, and school literature that contains pertinent school policies.

Lack of advance knowledge of unfavorable working conditions has caused many teachers to be unhappy in their positions. The following are some of the conditions most often mentioned.

1. Classes are too large.
2. The work week is too long.
3. The daily schedule is too long.
4. Clerical duties are excessive.
5. Community demands for out-of-school activities are too heavy.

In some studies it has been shown that the teacher is required on the average to spend approximately an hour each day in nonteaching schooltime duties. Many school systems are attempting to minimize such unfavorable conditions and will undoubtedly eliminate some of them. The beginning teacher should not become discouraged but should understand these problems and be prepared to meet them.

The importance of ample preparation and knowledge of conditions of employment cannot be overemphasized. Teachers who know and understand the circumstances of their jobs are less likely to be discouraged when they do not find the optimum or theoretical standards they have been studying in college.

Pertinent factors about school and community. A beginning teacher should have a thorough knowledge of the new school and community. He or she should know the school and community—history, traditions, curricular offerings, economic status, philosophy of education, industrial development, size, political structure, problems, and projected growth. These factors will have implications for the type of students to be taught, the parents with whom the teacher will work, the community of which the teacher is to be a part, and the social, political, and educational climate within which the teacher must work.

Responsibilities after assuming position

RESPONSIBILITIES TO THE DEPARTMENT

Whether the school system is large or small, the physical educator has many responsibilities to the department, each of which is essential in administering a successful teaching program. These responsibilities demand the teacher's time and thoughtful consideration, but because they relate directly to the students, the results of the teacher's efforts are apparent.

In a large school. As one member of a team of physical educators, the individual instructor has definite responsibilities in relation to teaching regular classes, conducting the after-school program, and working with other members of the department. In all three areas these duties require constant cooperation and mutual understanding for a smoothly functioning program.

Teaching classes. Each teacher is officially in charge of the instructional program in assigned classes. This responsibility entails far more than just teaching or conducting classes, however. Some of the other duties entailed in class management are

1. Program planning and evaluation
2. Grading and pupil evaluation
3. Testing
4. Motivating (through such media as charts and diagrams)
5. Checking health problems
6. Counseling on student problems
7. Conferring with students and parents
8. Caring for shared equipment and facilities
9. Maintaining departmental standards in locker room, showers, and gymnasium
10. Keeping records

These duties are performed in cooperation with other members of the department, and the same or similar approved methods are used by all. For example, one teacher would not keep one form of record on a student while another teacher in the same department followed a different system.

Conducting the after-school program. In addition to regular teaching responsibilities, the members of the department share in carrying out the many extra duties that are a natural component of the physical education program. Conducting an after-school program of intramural and extramural activities, as well as interscholastic athletics, involves many details, such as

1. Coaching assignments
2. Scheduling games
3. Handling publicity
4. Scheduling facilities
5. Caring for uniforms and equipment
6. Arranging transportation
7. Handling finances
8. Checking custodial maintenance
9. Ordering awards
10. Keeping records

In a large school a single instructor would not be able to manage all these details alone. With the entire staff working together, however, a well-organized after-school program serving all the students may be effectively conducted.

Working with the staff. Conducting the after-school program is only one of the ways in which the members of the department cooperate. The director of the department usually considers the staff a policy-making body that proposes and carries out progressive ideas. It plans together the direction the program will take and shares with the administrator of the department the many details of budgeting, scheduling, making inventory, and so forth. In some schools the team teaching approach to physical education has been implemented. In this case the staff cooperates and coordinates all its efforts in order to capitalize on the special abilities of each of its teachers.

Cooperation promotes harmonious relationships among members of the department, and when disagreements or problems arise, they should be handled within the department itself. Ethical standards of conduct indicate that mutual support of colleagues be presented to outsiders and that individual problems of a member be taken to the department chairperson first, rather than to the principal or superintendent.

The new teacher should realize at the outset the nature of the role he or she must play as a member of a large school staff. Schools may differ in the actual delegation of responsibilities, but the teacher's obligation to share and cooperate remains the same.

Fig. 9-5. Physical education class playing soccer in Lexington Public Schools, Lexington, Mass.

In a small school. In a small secondary school it is customary to find one man and one woman on the physical education faculty. While such a situation simplifies the problems of group planning and departmental organization, the same administrative responsibilities outlined for a large school remain, and they must be carried out by these two individuals. Because the number of students served by the program is small, it may be possible for one teacher to handle the many details involved in the teaching program.

A new teacher will find that the job of teaching in a small-school situation requires a great deal of coordination between the boys' and girls' activities. The physical education program is more effective if the instructional procedures and requirements of the two teachers are similar and methods of pupil evaluation agree. Their policies on intramural and interscholastic activities should also be consistent, with schedules for the use of facilities for these programs mutually and equitably arranged, as provided for in Title IX.

When problems or difficulties develop concerning the sharing of facilities, for example, the two teachers should try to work out the solutions together. If the answers cannot be found, the teachers should both seek advice from the next higher authority. If there is no officially designated chairperson of the department, the school principal would be the person to ask for guidance.

Working together effectively is of primary importance to a smoothly functioning program of physical education in a small-school situation. When the two teachers mutually assist and support each other in all phases of their work, this worthy objective is achieved.

RESPONSIBILITIES TO SCHOOL FACULTY

Beyond being a member of a physical education department, a teacher is also a member of a school faculty. This position carries with it many responsibilities related to administering a program of education for children. All teachers must share in this endeavor, which includes three general areas of obligation: upholding school policies, sharing mutual faculty responsibilities, and respecting the educational curriculum.

Upholding school policies. Administration of a secondary school program involves the establishment of well-defined policies concerning all phases of school life: the curriculum, school regulations, homework, activities, and sponsored functions. In most school situations teachers play an important part in regard to these policies.

In a democratically administered school system, the teachers share in the establishment of school policies. Decisions are formulated on the basis of group discussion and majority opinion. The physical educator should share with the other teachers in formulating policies at teachers' meetings.

Once they are determined, school policies must be upheld by all members of the staff. This includes the physical education teacher, who should not expect special privileges for members of varsity teams in respect to academic standards, or request athletic considerations contrary to school regulations.

Sharing mutual responsibilities. In large and small school systems alike, the faculty shares many administrative duties. These are essential to a sound educational program, although they have no relationship to the school curriculum, and are a necessary component of school administration. For example, there are many instances in which a teacher is called on to act as a supervisor or sponsor of student activities. Teachers may be required to take bus duty or cafeteria supervision or to be responsible for noon-hour activities. Homerooms, study halls, club activities, and student council are all additional responsibilities, and the physical educator should expect to serve with the other teachers in any of these areas.

In many schools, faculty committees are established to study current educational problems, such as education for the gifted or elementary foreign language teaching. Committees to handle administrative details, such as class scheduling, grouping, or safety, may also be set up. Membership in these committees is usually voluntary, but all teachers are expected to serve in some capacity. While the conduct of the after-school program may make it difficult for the physical educator to attend committee meetings, every effort should be made to share in this phase of school organization.

Respecting the curriculum. Just as physical educators should support the methods and procedures of their colleagues within the department, so should they respect those of the other teachers in all areas of education. The teacher should exhibit a genuine and sincere interest in all phases of the curriculum and respect the work and accomplishments of the other teachers.

In return, the physical educator should expect from other teachers similar respect and appreciation of the work being accomplished by the department. This regard should be deserved, however. Teachers in other subject areas do not necessarily evaluate the physical education program in the same manner that physical educators would. Instead of rating program content with which they are unfamiliar, other teachers tend to value the teacher's seriousness of approach to teaching, the manner in which the instructor fulfills educational responsibilities, the concern shown for student welfare, and general attitudes toward the profession. The physical educator who meets all these responsibilities as a member of the teaching staff actually promotes appreciation for physical education as a profession.

There is one further obligation of physical educators that is directly connected with their particular field and deserves special mention at this time. Good working relations with members of the school custodial staff are of vital importance to the program and are clearly as important as relations with other teachers. The service of the custodians in gymnasium maintenance and in care of equipment adds significantly to the quality of physical education and should not be forgotten.

RESPONSIBILITIES TO THE PROFESSION

Membership in a profession such as physical education carries with it certain responsibilities that the new teacher should expect and accept. These responsibilities are concerned mainly with professional advancement for the teacher and the growth of the profession itself.

Professional organizations. Professional associations are the media through which members mutually assist each other in achieving benefits for the group and promoting advancement.

As educators, physical education teachers should join the educational organizations active in their district or local area. This includes the faculty association, the local education association, and the county or district group—whichever organization has been formed. It is also considered the mark of a professional to join the state education association and the National Education Association. Membership in these associations is usually made available to the teacher through the school office at the beginning of each school year.

Physical educators should also join their own special local and state organizations and the American Alliance for Health, Physical Education, Recreation, and Dance. It is through these channels that the teacher is able to keep up with the latest advancements within the profession. There are also specialized organizations on the local level for coaches, women, or teachers of a particular activity. It is in these local, small groups that the greatest benefits are derived, for the members have the opportunity to know each other well and to share mutually in the problems and issues at stake.

Membership in these associations and alliances is made possible through literature sent to the school in each locale, in most cases. If not, teachers in neighboring districts are ready to provide the necessary information to newcomers.

Professional advancement. Membership in various associations is not the only professional responsibility of the physical educator. To reap the greatest benefits and to aid in advancing the profession itself, each member must make valuable contributions to these associations, which are usually organized into committees that function in a particular area, such as planning, research, fitness, and publications. Working on these committees can be a very satisfying and rewarding experience and one that should not be missed.

Even greater contributions to the profession as a whole can be made through research on problems in the field. Sharing results or findings on a particular method of teaching or testing is a real service to other members that should be willingly performed.

Personal advancement. Continued study for personal growth and development is another major responsibility of every member of a profession. In addition to individual study, the physical education teacher has two developmental paths open: inservice education and graduate study.

Inservice education takes many forms within the school system and neighboring districts. It is found in individual and staff conferences and in workshops, clinics, and study institutes. Planning sessions, orientation programs, and interschool visitations are all phases of inservice education. Any opportunity in which teachers join together with associates to consider school problems may be considered to be inservice education. Real values stemming from these sessions are seen when teachers change and grow together for the improvement of the school program and the profession.

Graduate study is the other method of personal and professional advancement. Some of the purposes of graduate study include the development of a higher degree of competence and the development of the ability to evaluate, interpret, and draw conclusions from the scholarly work of others.

There are several types of graduate degrees available to the physical education teacher.

1. Master's degree. A master's degree in physical education usually requires one year of study beyond a bachelor's degree. In some universities a thesis is part of the required program for a degree, while in other schools several related extra credits or a comprehensive examination is required in its place.

2. Doctor of philosophy, doctor of education, or doctor of physical education. The doctoral degrees usually require three or four more years of study. In the curriculum for a doctorate, a formal dissertation or documented paper is a requisite.

Some institutions offer a professional or specialist's certificate for 30 hours of graduate work above the completion of the master's program.

The prospective teacher of physical education should realize that a professional attitude is another important responsibility that must be developed through associations and study programs with other

Fig. 9-6. Girls' hockey.

Courtesy Cosom Corp., Minneapolis, Minn.

professionals. In this way the teacher serves himself or herself and the profession as a whole.

RESPONSIBILITIES TO THE COMMUNITY

Another important responsibility of the physical educator is the relationship established with the community. This is a two-way association, for the support a physical education teacher gains for the program depends largely on the program itself and the way the citizens interpret it. The responsibilities of the physical education department in promoting this community relationship are three: presenting a sound program, joining community-sponsored activities, and supporting community standards.

Presenting a sound program. The physical educator is employed by a community's board of education to teach physical education in the finest manner possible. The program of physical education can be a comprehensive source of good public relations between a school and its community because of the many contacts that are a natural by-product of this program. It is in this field that an entire student body may be drawn together by interscholastic competitive activities, and parents, too, share in these enjoyable events. Through the intramural programs, the demonstrations, and the testing program, the parents become very much aware of and interested in the total program of physical education. The entire school administration benefits from a sound physical education program because of community interest; therefore, it is essential that the program be thoughtfully planned, presented, and evaluated.

Joining community activities. The physical educator has definite obligations to become a part of the community by joining selected community organizations, including the parent-teacher organization. Furthermore, because of the close association between recreational activities and physical education, the teachers often are called on to conduct evening programs and assist in sponsoring special events. While sharing in these activities, the teacher has an opportunity to know the people of the community and what it is that they want from their schools. This is an advantage to the school, for it must serve its own particular community. At the same time the physical educator helps the school administration by serving as an interpreter of its philosophy to the community and helping the people understand what the schools are trying to do.

Serving the community in which they teach is a responsibility that must be met by all teachers. Good school-community relations are of primary importance to a school that is meeting the needs of its students. Physical educators must do their share by contributing in as many ways as possible, and the results will bring greater support to the program.

Supporting community standards. Through the many contacts established with community citizens, the physical educator should support and honor the standards expected of teachers in that particular community, where they are in accordance with high professional standards. It is important to remember, for example, that relating school gossip or information of a personal nature about a particular student does not earn respect for a teacher in the schools and that by wiser action the respect and status of teachers may be upheld in the community.

Code of ethics

The teacher is far more than a teacher of physical education. His or her responsibilities extend to all relationships established with people, and all actions are governed in almost every area by a code of professional ethics. Many important principles in this code of ethics have been pointed out in relation to particular situations. The code of the National Education Association has been endorsed by the American Alliance for Health, Physical Education, Recreation, and Dance. This code represents the combined thinking of experienced leaders in the field and therefore should be respected. Furthermore, it provides a framework of guidelines for all professional physical educators, thereby guaranteeing the professional freedom it is designed to preserve.

The code consists of four principles. *Principle 1* outlines the commitment to the *student* and indicates the cooperative, helpful, and professional relationship that exists between the student and teacher. *Principle 2* outlines the commitment to the *public* and spells out the important role of educators in the development of educational programs and policies and their interpretation to the public. *Principle 3* outlines the commitment to the *profession* and indicates the need to raise educational standards, improve the service to people, and develop a worthwhile and respected profession. *Principle 4* outlines the commitment to *professional employment practices* and explains the importance of acting in accordance with high ideals of professional service that embody personal integrity, dignity, and mutual respect.

The code is designed to show the magnitude of the education profession and to judge teachers in accordance with the provisions of this code.

Teacher accountability

Most educational systems are giving increased attention to teacher accountability. The high cost of education and the rise in taxes to support it are causing the public, which pays the bill, to demand accountability in terms of what a teacher produces. The aim of such a movement is to develop objective standards as a means of improving school effectiveness. Among other things, it is designed to show which teaching and school methods have proved most effective in achieving specific educational goals. It protects successful teachers against unfair criticism by providing proof of their effectiveness; for those teachers who are not effective, it will indicate the additional training and help they need to become effective teachers.

It may help the prospective teacher to know the educational goals that the public thinks are important for them to attain. According to the Fourth Annual Gallup Poll of Public Attitudes Toward Education, the public wants education

- To help children get better jobs
- To help children develop better human relations
- To help children be financially successful
- To help children be satisfied with themselves
- To help children be mentally stimulated

This Gallup poll also indicates that approximately three out of every four persons surveyed stated that they would be very happy to have their offspring take up teaching as a career. In other words, teaching is a very popular vocation today among all classes of people.

New teachers in today's modern secondary schools face tasks and responsibilities far different from those of several years ago. Whereas a teacher used to work alone, today's teacher may work with a team of several teachers and with many different groups. Whereas, at one time, a teacher had only one set of textbooks at his or her disposal, today there are films, television, cassettes, transparencies, computers, and programmed materials to assist in teaching. Once the teacher had to rely on subjective judgments to recognize pupils' attitudes, aptitudes, and interests, but today's extensive testing programs offer comprehensive guidance information. Yet these technological advances have not made the teacher's tasks in education any easier, for they have brought with them additional responsibilities. The teacher must learn how to operate specialized equipment. He or she must keep up with new materials and know when and how to utilize them appropriately.

Teachers presently graduating from professional institutions are being trained to meet these innovations in modern education. First of all, courses of study within their fields of interest are greatly specialized. For example, a prospective teacher may specialize in such areas as health, the dance, elementary school teaching, athletic training, or coaching. Moreover, some institutions offer teacher-internship programs in which a student lives and teaches in a community while gaining firsthand teaching experience. Increased knowledge of child development and the learning process has made another substantial contribution to the training of today's teachers.

Yet even these improvements in teacher training have not made the teacher's task any easier, for administrators of modern secondary schools are expecting more from their staff members. Administrators expect the teacher to keep abreast of the advances in knowledge, application of the latest teaching methods, and utilization of modern equipment. Furthermore, administrators want increased professionalism through inservice workshops and advanced study as well as increased commitments to their teaching field through faculty associations and organizations.

Although the task of teaching has not become any easier, progress in education has brought benefits not only to students but also to the teachers themselves. Today's teachers now enjoy greatly improved standards and practices. Many schools offer valuable fringe benefits in terms of retirement plans, medical and life insurance coverage, and tenure. Teacher organizations such as the National Education Association are developing increased power to demand improved health standards for children and improved working conditions for teachers, such as lighter class loads, fewer nonteaching duties, and smaller classes.

Preventing teacher burnout

More stable school faculties, shrinking employment opportunities, austere budgets, the back-to-basics movement, public criticism, lack of community support, heavier teaching loads, accountability, discipline problems, and inadequate salaries are a few of the conditions that are resulting in teacher burnout. This term has been defined as "a physical, emotional, and attitudinal exhaustion." Some teachers are unhappy with their work and the many educational problems they are having to face. As a result, in many cases the students are being shortchanged and the teachers are complacent, dissatisfied, restless, and suffering emotionally and sometimes physically.

What can be done to cope with "teacher burnout"? What procedures will result in self-renewal for teachers? Most importantly how can "teacher burnout" be prevented?

Many suggestions have been made for eliminating

and avoiding this malady. Susan E. Langlois* of the College of Our Lady of the Elms in Chicopee, Massachusetts, has found that fitness is one answer. She has initiated faculty fitness classes at her college that have paid dividends in eliminating and avoiding faculty burnout.

Darrell Crase† suggests the following activities as antidotes to faculty burnout and complacency:

- Reassess teaching technologies
- Reevaluate curricular offerings
- Participate in visitations and exchange programs
- Participate in structured learning experiences
- Become involved in professional organizations
- Reassess reading habits
- Contribute to professional publications
- Develop quest for new knowledge
- Get involved in local service functions
- Explore additional development opportunities

Janice Wendt,‡ in her article on ''Resistance to Change,'' implies that change may help in avoiding ''teacher burnout.'' Dean A. Austin§ lists several methods that can bring about teacher renewal: using holidays and vacations for personal and professional revitalization, changing the way material is taught, transferring to another school, playing a new role within the educational structure, finding a job outside education, and participating in inservice education.

Self-assessment tests

These tests are designed to assist students in determining if material and competencies presented in this chapter have been mastered.

1. Distinguish between the art and science of teaching. Why is teaching not a science?
2. List six career options within the field of physical education and the nature and scope of each.
3. Conduct a self-evaluation of your qualifications for teaching by writing down what you consider to be your present status in each of the following areas: physical, social, emotional, intellectual, and professional. Opposite your qualifications in each of these four groupings, list desirable competencies for a teacher. Compare your qualifications to this list.
4. Without consulting your text, prepare an extensive list of major problems faced by beginning teachers.
5. Take the list prepared in number 4 and, opposite each problem, indicate if it could have been eliminated before the teacher assumed the position. Describe how the problems could have been eliminated. Under what conditions should the teacher not have accepted the position?
6. Imagine that you are a member of the physical education faculty in a junior or senior high school. Indicate what responsibilities you would assume to ensure that you would be a respected member of the faculty.
7. Prepare a plan indicating how you would cope with five of the problems that face beginning teachers.

Points to remember

1. There is a need to make the teaching of physical education a science.
2. Students training for a career in physical education should evaluate their interests and abilities to determine what career option is best for them.
3. Specific qualifications are needed to be a success in the field of physical education.
4. By investigating before accepting a position, the beginning teacher may avoid many potential problems.
5. The probability exists that discipline will be a major professional problem.
6. The beginning teacher should know how to conduct a program when facilities are limited.
7. A physical educator is governed by a code of ethics that suggests standards of behavior to protect members of the profession.

Problems to think through

1. When is a teacher not a teacher?
2. What personal qualities are most important for a teacher of physical education—qualities that may not be as essential in teaching other areas?
3. With whom would a new physical education teacher discuss a disagreement relating to procedures in grading students (a) in a small school? (b) in a large school? With whom would he or she not discuss it?
4. In August a new teacher receives another job offer at a higher salary in a preferred locale. What course of action, if any, should be taken?

*Langlois, S.: Faculty fitness; a program to combat teacher burnout, Update, March 1981.

†Crase, D.: Developmental activities: a hedge against complacency, Journal of Physical Education and Recreation **51**:53-54, Nov./Dec. 1980.

‡Wendt, J.: Resistance to change, Journal of Physical Education and Recreation **51**:56, Nov./Dec. 1980.

§Austin, D.A.: Renewal, Journal of Physical Education and Recreation **51**:57-59, Nov./Dec. 1980.

5. What community clubs or agencies have a direct interest in the school physical education program? How would the teacher who lives outside the school's community indicate an interest in the activities of such groups?

6. An after-school intramural game conflicts with a special faculty committee meeting. The physical education teacher, as a member of this committee, must choose where his or her time will be spent. What factors enter into this decision?

7. Why is the problem of acceptance of great importance to any beginning teacher?

8. How can one best prepare for the first day of teaching?

9. What do you anticipate as your greatest problem on entering the teaching profession? Why?

Case study for analysis

Unfavorable working conditions are causing many teachers to leave the profession. Some of these conditions relate to the size of classes, the length of the daily schedule, workload, and clerical duties and afterschool obligations. Determine the degree to which adverse conditions prevail in a school system of your choice. Analyze factors that contribute to these conditions. How may the beginning teacher help to combat this problem?

Exercises for review

1. What specific information should be included in an application to a superintendent of schools? Write a sample letter.

2. Investigate the requirements for teaching in another state and determine in what ways these requirements are being met, if they are, and in what ways professional preparation may be lacking.

3. What questions may a candidate for a physical education position in a large school system expect to be asked during an interview with the administrator?

4. What school policies should this candidate inquire about during this interview?

5. A school system is planning to build a second junior high school and the administrator asks the physical education department to share in the formulation of plans for the physical education facilities. What steps would a new teacher take in order to offer real assistance in this project?

6. A new physical education teacher discovers that the community fathers run a highly competitive Little League program. If this teacher disagrees with the type of management the program is receiving, what procedures might be followed to combat this community enterprise?

7. List some outside interest and hobbies that would add to the professional growth of a physical educator.

8. In what areas of teaching physical education would further scientific research be particularly valuable?

9. In what ways does a professional code of ethics protect the teacher of physical education?

10. What responsibilities to the profession of physical education would be most difficult for a teacher to meet?

Selected references

Austin, D.A.: Renewal, Journal of Physical Education and Recreation **51:**57-59, Nov./Dec. 1980.

Berg, K.: Maintaining enthusiasm in teaching, Journal of Physical Education and Recreation **46:**22, 1975.

Bronson, D.B.: Thinking and teaching, The Educational Forum **39:**347, 1975.

Bucher, C.A.: Physical education for life, New York, 1969, McGraw-Hill Book Co.

Bucher, C.A.: Administration of heath and physical education programs, including athletics, ed. 8, St. Louis, 1983, The C.V. Mosby Co.

Bucher, C.A.: Foundations of physical education, ed. 9, St. Louis, 1983, The C.V. Mosby Co.

Bucher, C.A., and Thaxton, N.: Physical education and sport: change and challenge, St. Louis, 1981, The C.V. Mosby Co.

Cheffers, J.R.F.: Pedagogy, Journal of Physical Education and Recreation **51:**50-52, Nov./Dec. 1980.

Crase, D.: Development activities; a hedge against complacency, Journal of Physical Education and Recreation **51:**53-54, Nov./Dec. 1980.

Dillon, S.V., and Franks, D.D.: Open learning environment: self-identity and coping ability, The Educational Forum **39:**155, 1975.

Dougherty, N.J., and Bonanno, D.: Contemporary approaches to the teaching of physical education, Minneapolis, 1979, Burgess Publishing Co.

Dowell, L.J.: Strategies for teaching physical education, Englewood Cliffs, N.J., 1975, Prentice-Hall, Inc.

Field, D.: Accountability for the physical educator, Journal of Health, Physical Education and Recreation **44:**37, 1973.

Fisher, M.: Assessing the competence of prospective physical education teachers, The Physical Educator **29:**93, 1972.

Forker, B., and Fraleigh, W.W.: Graduate study and professional accreditation: applications to physical education, Journal of Physical Education and Recreation **51:**45, March 1980.

Frith, G.H., and Roswal, G.M.: Teacher aides—a discussion of roles, Journal of Physical Education and Recreation **52:**37, 70, June 1981.

Gallup, G.H.: Fourth Annual Gallup Poll of Public Attitudes Toward Education, Phi Delta Kappan, Sept. 1972, p. 33.

Graham, G.: Acquiring teaching skills in physical education, Journal of Physical Education and Recreation **52:**19-20, April 1981.

Healey, J.H., and Healey, W.A.: Physical education teaching problems for analysis and solution, Springfield, Ill., 1975, Charles C Thomas, Publisher.

Langlois, S.: Faculty fitness; a program to combat teacher burnout, Update, March 1981.

Menzies, I.: The touchy teacher's benefit issue, The Boston Evening Globe **207:**18, 1975.

O'Hanlon, J.: Leadership for tomorrow's physical education program, Journal of Physical Education and Recreation **49:**37-39, Nov./Dec. 1978.

Richardson, H.: Academic preparation of athletic coaches in higher education, Journal of Physical Education and Recreation **52:**44-45, March 1981.

Sabock, R.J.: The coach, Philadelphia, 1979, W.B. Saunders Co.

Siedentop, D.: Developing teaching skills in physical education, Boston, 1976, Houghton Mifflin Co.

Singer, R.N.: Teaching physical education—a systems approach, Boston, 1980, Houghton Mifflin Co.

Toffler, A.: Future shock, New York, 1970, Bantam Books.

University of the State of New York, The State Education Department: Competence based certification, Newsletter of the Division of Teacher Education and Certification, No. 1, June 1972, Albany, N.Y.

Vittetoe, J.O.: Why first year teachers fail, Phi Delta Kappan **58:**429-430, 1977.

Wendt, J.: Resistance to change in physical education, Journal of Physical Education and Recreation **51:**56, Nov./Dec. 1980.

10

The physical educator and teaching style

Instructional objectives and competencies to be achieved

After reading this chapter the student should be able to

1. Demonstrate those aspects of teacher-student relations necessary to effective teaching
2. Define the term "teaching style" and describe the various styles
3. Evaluate the worth of teacher-centered and student-centered styles
4. Relate various general philosophies to teaching style
5. Demonstrate that he or she has developed a viable teaching style

Research studies have shown that the behavior and personality of one person closely interacting with another can have an effect on behavior and personality. This is true of many human relationships, whether in a family or business setting or some other relationship. It is especially true of the relationship between teacher and student since the teacher's personality and behavior can affect the pupil's classroom behavior. It follows, therefore, that the differences in teachers' personalities have a different impact on their students.

Although in some occupations personality is secondary to professional goals (carpentry, for example), teaching success in great measure depends on the teacher's style. Indeed, the teacher's personality and the way he or she behaves in the classroom, gymnasium, or playfield may be one of the most important factors in determining what the student accomplishes in the physical education experience. The excellent teacher is not only one who has command of the skills, subject matter, and other requirements for specialized fields; he or she also successfully transmits these skills and this subject matter to the students.

Alexander M. Mood* points out that some authorities believe that about 10% of the teachers may be classified as excellent, 10% as hopeless, and the other 80% as having varying degrees of competence and effectiveness. Mood states that a characteristic of most excellent teachers is that they are sympathetic to students and deeply concerned about their welfare and interests. He further reports that research verifies principles teachers should understand if they wish to teach effectively and professionally.

- *The teacher should listen to what the students have to say and put this information to use.* The teacher should pay attention to each question or comment no matter how trivial it may be. Each student should be given a feeling that he or she is participating in the learning process and has something worthy to contribute.
- *Each student should be encouraged to develop a sense of personal worth.* Teachers should go out of their way to instill in each student the feeling that he or she has some knowledge, skill, or attitude that is important and therefore deserves to be complimented.
- *Each student should be imbued with a feeling of confidence, particularly in respect to ability to learn.* The teacher must be very careful not to erode the student's self-confidence. Thus the teacher must understand that some students will learn faster than others and that students are also different in other ways that affect the learning process.
- *The teacher should not appear to be superior morally or intellectually.* This attitude builds up antagonism between student and teacher; then students tend to become overprotective of their egos.

*Mood, A.M.: How teachers make a difference, Washington, D.C., 1971, U.S. Office of Education, Department of Health, Education, and Welfare.

- *Conflicts of interest with students should be minimized*. If students are convinced that the teacher feels goodwill toward them, conflicts of interest should be reduced to a minimum. Although some conflicts will naturally exist—for example, attendance may be considered unnecessary by pupils but important by the teacher, and disruptive behavior cannot be tolerated—the teacher should aim at enlarging, rather than decreasing, a community of interests with students.

- *Lecturing should be kept to a minimum*. Students learn more readily if they can grapple with questions and problems. Although this process is slower than having the teacher present information, it is generally agreed that learning is more effective when the students do some thinking and arrive at answers themselves.

- *The gymnasium, swimming pool, playground, or classroom should be characterized by a relaxed atmosphere*. Greater student participation and learning will take place in an open, relaxed atmosphere than in one that is rigid and formal.

- *Students should be kept active*. Physical movement is needed by all students throughout the school day to enhance learning.

- *Genuine concern should be shown by the teacher for each student in the class*. Each student should be given the feeling that the teacher cares about him or her as a person.

- *Individual students should not be permitted to fall behind*. Everything possible should be done to make sure each student makes progress in learning. The whole class should be aware of this attitude so that when a student starts to falter, not only the teacher but the whole class plays a part in seeing that the student moves ahead.

- *Apathy and boredom should be combated*. They are deterrents to learning. Students should be kept interested and learning made an exciting experience.

- *Teaching should be diversified*. A variety of methods, such as films, slides, curriculum packages, programmed devices, and records, should be used. The teacher must keep abreast of new teaching ideas.

- *Student participation should be encouraged to make learning attractive*. Students should be consulted about teaching and how to make it more interesting. Many of their experiments and ideas should be utilized.

- *The teacher should do the best possible type of teaching*. Each teacher must do the very best job each day. Effective teaching is an important responsibility, and pupils should not be cheated.

- *Colleague interaction will help*. An exchange of ideas, discussion of problems, and joint ventures with other teachers are excellent ways to improve teaching.

- *Grading systems should be questioned*. Grades create problems between teacher and student. If possible, they should not be used, or at least the importance of grades should be minimized.

- *The teacher should be a model*. Setting a good example of what is right, honest, and scholarly is important to the learning process.

Teaching style and methods and materials

Courses in methods and materials in professional preparation curricula are typically concerned with instructing the future physical educator how to teach a particular skill, how to correct student errors in skill performance, and how to direct the practice of a skill. Such courses are said to be skill-centered. The methods unique to team, individual, and dual sports are taught as independent units, for example, soccer. Methods and materials courses are also concerned with patterns of class organization for the teaching of a skill. The future physical educator learns how to teach the left-handed student, how to line the students up for instruction so that they do not face into the sun, and how to efficiently organize a class for various drills and lead-up games.

Rarely do methods and materials courses consider the individuality and creativity of the teacher, and even more rarely do they take into account the individuality of the students to whom the methods will be applied. These courses do, however, serve an essential purpose as part of the professional preparation curriculum. They introduce the future physical educator to effec-

Fig. 10-1. In the student-centered style the attention is focused on the student. Student in physical education class at Hampton Institute, Hampton, Va.

tive methodology in teaching and class management, and they help him or her prepare for the student teaching experience. What methods and materials courses frequently do not do is to provide the future teacher with experiences in developing a system and style of teaching that is unique to the individual.

DEFINITION OF THE TERM "TEACHING STYLE"

Teaching style and teaching methodology are two separate yet complementary phenomena. Teaching methodology is based on a standard philosophy of physical education and on the objectives of the phys-

ical education program. A physical educator's style of teaching is an expression of his or her individuality and is related to personal philosophy and objectives. A physical educator should adapt methodology to teaching style rather than the reverse.

We may thus define teaching style as an observable phenomenon that is an expression of the physical educator's individuality in relation to teaching philosophy and program objectives. Teaching style is also reflected in methodology of teaching and in class organization and management.

Originally, the term "style" was applied to a pen

Fig. 10-2. High school students engaging in a new activity developed by Cosom Corp., Minneapolis, Minn.

or stylus. Later, it referred to handwriting and eventually to the quality and nature of a literary work. In the psychological sense, as it is used in this chapter, it refers to personality and to individual behavior. Specifically, it refers to the behavior of the teacher in the classroom, gymnasium, swimming pool, playground, or other setting where learning takes place. It encompasses the basic characteristics of teachers as reflected in their personalities and has implications for their relations with students and their outlook on learning and teaching.

Some persons have confused teaching style with teaching method. Teaching method refers to the techniques and procedures used by the teacher, such as textbooks and audiovisual aids, to present certain subject matter or skills. Although these methods are outside the range of personality structure, their selection

is of course influenced by a teacher's personality and behavior.

Personality and teaching styles

Several types of teaching styles have been identified by researchers in the field. Hamachek* discusses four prominent personality styles that are reflected in teacher behavior, which he points out were categorized clinically by Shapiro.† These styles are the compulsive style, the suspicious style, the hysterical style, and the impulsive style.

COMPULSIVE STYLE

Hamachek refers to these teachers as "living machines." They are rigid in their schedules and ways of behaving and thinking. A compulsive teacher might be called "dogmatic," "opinionated," or "bullheaded." He or she frequently does not listen to what a student is saying but instead spends time thinking about what to say in response. This type of teacher is obsessed by detail, whether it be erasing the blackboards every night before going home, insisting that students perform a particular skill in exactly the way demonstrated, or giving back in an examination the same information initially passed on to them. He or she directs and tells students rather than interacts with them. This type of teacher is not sensitive to the individual differences among students and has limited interests. The classroom is devoid of a social tone; education is serious business, and interpersonal dynamics are not considered part of the learning process. It is very difficult for this teacher to have fun with students. He or she tends to prescribe for students in light of personal feelings and needs instead of in terms of the students' feelings and needs.

SUSPICIOUS STYLE

The suspicious style is, according to Hamacheck, characterized by some paranoidlike features. These teachers often feel the students are plotting against them. They also have a guilty and tense feeling about many things that happen and imagine colleagues or

*Hamachek, D.E.: Personality styles and teacher behavior, The Educational Forum **36:**313, 1972.
†Shapiro, D.: Neurotic styles, New York, 1965, Basic Books, Inc.

other persons are trying to find out about their personal life and are very wary. Because of these suspicions, it is difficult to enjoy teaching students. Such teachers see very little fun in teaching and rarely laugh. Since they cannot accept or place trust in themselves, they find it difficult to do the same with others. Therefore, they are reluctant to have faith in other people, whether students or colleagues. Such teachers are also very conscious of those who possess power or position and may have an antagonistic relationship with these authority figures. They are particularly wary of administrators who evaluate them. They feel that the principal or superintendent may evaluate their teaching, for example, in terms of their character or personal habits rather than in terms of their teaching performance.

HYSTERICAL STYLE

The teacher characterized by the hysterical style is particularly different from others in respect to awareness of the more colorful events that occur. In fact, the colorful events may be so highlighted by this person that the substance of teaching may be overlooked. In other words, the reactions of such a teacher may be more in terms of impressions than facts. Such teachers are easily influenced by other persons' feelings, prejudices, fads, and objects or circumstances that excite them. Their attention is captured not so much by accurate details as by the headlines and sensational happenings that occur. They are the teachers who accentuate rumors about students and colleagues using drugs, engaging in sex, getting traffic tickets, or squandering money at the races. They are apt to think of students in terms of these emotional characterizations and judgments, and in turn these characterizations may affect the manner in which they treat their students. It should be recognized that although the hysterical style may cause many teaching problems, it may also result in teaching behavior that is enthusiastic, colorful, and lively.

IMPULSIVE STYLE

The teacher with this style is characterized by quick action that is unplanned and not carefully thought through. In such cases, judgment may be poor and reckless and result in poor decisions. In turn, these decisions may provide many disappointments. Such persons are unpredictable since behavior is often the result of whim or impulse. They usually are motivated by the immediate concerns of their own lives rather than permanent goals or values. As contrasted with the compulsive teacher, who critically evaluates a problem, the impulsive teacher acts on the spur of the moment, with initial impressions frequently becoming the basis for action.

REFLECTIVE STYLE

Murphy and Brown* discuss a teaching style that is referred to as the "reflective" style. This is a style aimed at getting the students to think, analyze, reflect, and conceptualize. It encourages questioning and hypothesizing. The questioning and discussing take place in a climate of freedom and tolerance, with the teacher serving as a guide rather than a dispenser of truth. There is a very warm, respectful relationship between this kind of uninhibited instructor and student that results in a high degree of student motivation since the student experiences a feeling of freedom to discuss the subject in terms of his or her own attitude, experience, and opinion. The subject becomes interesting and exciting to students in such a democratic atmosphere.

Basic teaching styles

There are two basic kinds of teaching style: teacher-centered and student-centered with, of course, some overlapping with the five styles already discussed.

TEACHER-CENTERED STYLE

The teacher-centered physical educator is often described as autocratic. He or she states the philosophy of physical education in terms of personal attitudes to the profession and a personal conception of the goals of the profession. Program objectives are planned in terms of what the teacher wishes to accomplish. Evaluation is made in terms of what was achieved. For example, the teacher-centered physical educator might

---

*Murphy, P.D., and Brown, M.M.: Conceptual systems and teaching styles, American Educational Research Journal **7:**529, 1970.

list some of the daily objectives of a unit in basketball in the following manner:

1. To teach the dribble
2. To teach the hook shot
3. To teach foul shooting

The autocratic physical educator will evaluate the basketball unit as a successful learning experience if he or she has indeed taught the dribble, the hook shot, and foul shooting *and* has taught the class to perform these skills to a common standard. The satisfaction for the autocratic physical educator, then, is based not on student success but on teacher accomplishments in terms of teacher-centered objectives. The program evaluation is not derived from observing student success but rather from an analysis of the teaching and its effectiveness in terms of student learning.

The teacher-centered physical educator is somewhat of a perfectionist and expects that all students will be able to perform a certain skill in the same way. This teacher does not realize that all students do not have the ability to meet a single standard of performance. Thus teaching is frequently geared to those students who can measure up to the physical educator's criteria for success. This teacher tends to experience a sense of failure when a student falls short of the expected goal. The teacher-centered physical educator strives to guide students toward the response or action he or she views as the correct one in any given situation. In a rules quiz, for example, all the students may correctly answer that there are nine players on a baseball team. They may not know why there are nine players or what the players' duties are, but they have given the correct response, and that accomplishes the goal.

The teacher-centered physical educator is generally a rather rigid individual, and this rigidity is transferred to the teaching situation. Classes tend to be dull rather than exciting, and students are more often externally motivated by fear of failure than by an inner-directed desire to succeed. This teacher is often the delight of supervisors and administrators because he or she demands excellent discipline and maintains tight control over classes. It is difficult to assess, however, whether the students in such classes derive any enjoyment from their physical education experience.

In a teacher-dominated physical education class, the instructor is most likely to strictly follow tried and tested methodology. This teacher, feeling that only proved methods and techniques will work, finds innovation threatening and resists it. He or she sometimes refers to educational changes as fads that will not be fully accepted because their lasting value has not been demonstrated. A capsule analysis of this kind of teacher is one year of teaching experience repeated ''x'' number of times.

The teacher-centered physical educator is less interested in the individual student than in the student group. The class is viewed as simply a group of bodies that need to be physically educated. For this reason, the teacher-centered physical educator is less apt to know students by name than to know them by their physical abilities. This teacher frequently can describe accurately the tumbling, softball, or other skills of the fourth student in the second squad but may not know the student's name. Students often feel that they are less important to the teacher than the condition of the gymnasium floor, the cleanliness of the locker room, or the height of the grass on the playing field.

The teacher-centered physical educator is chiefly concerned with the cognitive areas of teaching and less often with the affective areas. Therefore, this teacher chooses the body of knowledge to be imparted to students and is interested only in their grasp of it, depending on observable motor skills and scores on written and skills tests to tell whether the knowledge is being absorbed. He or she is not particularly interested in whether students appreciate, enjoy, or want to participate in certain physical education activities. The right of choosing activities is reserved for the teacher, and the activity is taught for the sake of the activity.

The teacher-centered educator feels the need to conform to the philosophy of the school administration, which is frequently a traditionalistic philosophy. Thus the physical educator believes that students too must conform in terms of traditional teaching methods. In the gymnasium or on the playing field, it is the physical educator who demonstrates new skills, and the students are expected to mimic the instructor's technique. Student evaluations are thus subjectively determined in terms of ability to conform—not only in regard to performing techniques but in the areas of behavior and attitude as well. The results of written tests are sometimes discounted if they diverge either way from the physical educator's subjective evaluation of the student.

This style of teaching physical education often helps to stereotype the field as one that stands apart from the rest of the school program. The teacher-centered physical educator is primarily concerned with his or her own field and tends not to keep abreast of changes. This person does not consider innovations in general education any more seriously than he or she considers that changes in physical education are important to teaching and professional growth.

Intramural and interscholastic sports programs and physical education clubs are also influenced by the teacher-centered physical educator in much the same way as the class program is influenced. Often the intramural and club activities offered are not decided on the basis of student need and interest but rather on the basis of what the physical educator thinks the students ought to have.

Under the teacher-centered approach, students may be barred from joining clubs and intramural teams if they also have an interest in other school clubs and activities. In some instances, a student whose band rehearsal makes him or her a few minutes late for a club meeting or game may be locked out of the gymnasium or locker room. The teacher-centered physical educator tends to theorize that the student cannot be seriously interested in the afterschool program in physical education without making the effort to arrive at the activity on time. This labels the student as a nonconformist in the eyes of the teacher and effectively drives the student away from afterschool physical education activities. In some secondary schools, this lack of a cooperative relationship on the part of the physical educator with other school activities results in a marked failure of the intramural and club programs in physical education. Students will seek out and participate in those school activities that answer their needs and interests and that welcome them as individuals who have something to contribute.

With a teacher-centered physical education program, intramural teams are frequently highly and rigidly coached. Contests are instructional extensions of the class period rather than games played purely for enjoyment. The physical educator will supervise very closely and at times will remove a student from a game if the student is not "giving his or her all." A contest may also be stopped to correct errors of several players. Frequently, the physical educator will have formed the teams and appointed a captain for each without any student participation and will exercise the right to shift players from one team to another.

In varsity sports the teacher-centered physical educator will dominate the game completely. The physical educator in the coaching role will decide all lineups and lineup changes and direct all game strategy from the bench. In a sport such as football, for example, the coach will send the plays in to the quarterback rather than letting the quarterback direct the offense. A game in which this kind of team goes on to victory is another example of guiding students to the response desired by the teacher. The victory serves as proof for the physical educator of the worth of the teacher-centered style of teaching, but such a victory makes a questionable contribution to the physical, mental, emotional, and social growth of the players involved.

STUDENT-CENTERED STYLE

The student-centered physical educator is sometimes thought of as a democratic teacher. The student-centered physical educator's philosophy is stated in terms of the relationship of physical education to the total educational field and its goals. Goals of physical education are conceived as parallel to those of general education. The student-centered physical educator's program objectives are established in terms of student needs and interests, and evaluation is based on how well the program has succeeded in meeting those needs and interests. Some of the daily objectives of a unit in tennis might be listed in the following manner:

1. To be able to execute the forehand
2. To be able to serve
3. To be able to play a game of doubles

The student-centered physical educator will be pleased with this unit if, among the other basic tennis skills, students can return the forehand shot into the playing court, serve well enough to keep the ball in play, and cooperate with a partner in playing a game of doubles. This physical educator is not satisfied with teaching minimal skills. Rather, students learn skills as well as they can so that they will find success and pleasure in physical activity. Such a teacher does not attempt to develop champion players in a sport such as tennis but instead is concerned with the ability of students to play a recreational game of tennis, even if it is played on a beginning level. The student-centered physical educator does not expect or demand that all students attain a common level of skill; rather, each student attempts to reach his or her own potential. The satisfaction for this teacher is based on student success in terms of student-centered objectives. The program evaluation is derived from an observation of student success and from an objective analysis of teaching in terms of meeting student needs and interests. This physical educator uses evaluation as a guide to adaptations and modifications that might help to meet those needs even more effectively.

The student-centered physical educator is especially cognizant of differences in student ability and avoids setting common criteria for skill performances. Instead, the teacher prefers to devise charts or other devices that show the beginning, intermediate, and advanced levels of performance for each skill or combination of skills. Each student can use these criteria to judge personal progress and performance and to attempt to move from the beginning to the more advanced levels according to individual potential. Thus each student progresses at his or her own most comfortable rate and can find success that is meaningful. Because there are no artificial or induced standards toward which each student must strive, there is less chance for failure. The student-centered physical educator attempts to gear teaching to each individual in the class rather than to any one similarly skilled group of individuals. Teaching takes place on a more personal basis, and there is a decided emphasis on remedial help for those who need it as well as on coaching tips for those who are more advanced. The student-centered physical educator strives to help students reach their own goals in regard to motor skill ability.

The student-centered physical educator is usually very flexible, altering or adapting a lesson if it is not accomplishing its purpose. Other on-the-spot changes will be made if the class seems unusually tired or if a dreary day leads to student lethargy. The teacher will devise unique games or activities that will help to rekindle student interest and enthusiasm or will place a unique lesson in the program merely to provide a break in routine. Classes are exciting to watch, and students are enthusiastic about the class because they find it stimulating and challenging. These students have an inner motivation to succeed because they are encouraged to behave and succeed as individuals, which helps them to discipline their own behavior. At times, this physical educator is criticized by supervisors and administrators because the noise from the gymnasium or playing field is interpreted as a lack of teacher control rather than as the sounds of boys and girls responding enthusiastically to their physical education experience. Yet discipline is an undertone, not a fear-inducing characteristic of the class period.

The student-centered physical educator welcomes innovations because the latest techniques and methodology can contribute to student well-being, to the profession, and to the teacher's own professional growth. This teacher will, for example, adopt the principles of movement education, giving them an objective and sufficiently lengthy trial before either accepting or rejecting them as a permanent part of the program because they are either valuable or questionable. This type of person judges innovations in terms of student relevance rather than on how they satisfy the teacher. Although appreciative of traditional methodology, this teacher does not view it as unchanging or unchangeable. Each new school year represents an opportunity to test new techniques and methodologies, to introduce new activities, to guide new individuals through the physical education experience, to meet new challenges, and to gain new personal experiences.

The student-centered physical educator is interested in each student and realizes that physical education makes a unique contribution to the individual made by no other phase of the school program. This physical educator knows students by name and can accurately describe the physical education needs, interests, and abilities of each one. The teacher is interested in students as human beings and willingly gives time for individual guidance and counseling. Students prize this person because they know their teacher views them as the most important part of the physical education program.

This physical educator attempts to teach students to think for themselves, to be creative, to express themselves, and to ask questions. He or she is concerned with the cognitive objectives of physical education but is also especially aware of the affective objectives. This teacher is vitally interested in having students understand the values and varieties of physical activity. He or she wants them to enjoy and appreciate such activity, to seek out new activities, and to participate in them on their own. This teacher employes a conceptual approach to physical education so that students will be able to base their knowledge of physical activity on scientific understanding. When new activities are introduced or new units initiated, the students know the value of that activity and the need for it, aside from the fact that the activity is listed on a syllabus.

The student-centered physical educator believes in a balance of activities presented in a logical progression but also very strongly feels that students should be able to select the activities that appeal to them. Rather than dictating the activity for each unit, the physical educator will present students with a list of several activities that will fulfill the needs indicated by the students' test scores in motor ability and physical fitness. If there is more than one teacher, the class may be divided into two interest groups. If there is only one teacher, the class may decide to select one activity, or the classes may be so arranged that two activities can be covered. Some student-centered physical educators will extend the number of class periods allocated to a unit to assure meeting the needs and interests of the students.

The student-centered physical educator is also interested in conforming to administrative dicta but does not view them as a hindrance to the program or to the adoption of the latest thinking in physical education. Before adopting any new method or technique that might be viewed as radically different, this teacher will present a plan to superiors for approval, showing how the innovation will make the physical education experience more meaningful for students. This physical educator further realizes that there are many alternatives in teaching and is willing to test those that seem pertinent and logical. The teacher also knows that his or her performance of a skill is not necessarily the best way for students to perform it. Variations in body build, flexibility, strength, endurance, and experience are taken into account and students are asked to demonstrate a variety of techniques for their fellow classmates. This helps students to understand that there is more than one acceptable technique in performing a skill.

Student evaluations, for the student-centered physical educator, are based on many objective measures. He or she does not believe that one single grade should be given to a student, especially when the grade is expected to include skill, attitude, and behavioral outcomes. This physical educator prefers to evaluate students in a written, comprehensive statement that is more meaningful than a letter or number grade. Some secondary schools have permitted their physical education staffs to devise a separate evaluation form based on just such a statement and including places for noting test scores and other factors. Such evaluation forms give a total picture of student progress.

The student-centered physical educator is interested in other areas of the curriculum as well as in physical education. He or she reads professional journals and attempts to understand the changes being made in general education. He or she views education and physical education as dynamic and is aware of their many interrelationships and interdependencies. Through reading and meetings with other professionals, he or she strives to grow as a teacher in conjunction with the growth of general and physical education as professional fields of endeavor.

Intramural and interscholastic sports, as well as physical education clubs, are student-centered when the physical educator is student-centered. The intramural and club activities offered are directly related to student needs and interests. There are frequently different programs for students in different grades. For example, in the fall season ninth-grade students may be offered soccer and speedball, while senior students may be offered field hockey and lacrosse.

The student-centered physical educator wants students to be interested in all phases of the school program. He or she will work cooperatively with the art, drama, or music teacher to plan a schedule of after-school events that will not conflict with each other or may set aside a special day for students whose diversity of interest makes cooperative scheduling difficult.

Intramural teams are organized by the students under the supervision of the physical educator, and captains are elected by the vote of team members. The games are played for their recreational value, regardless of the skill levels of the various players. While the intramural program is considered to be an extension of the class program, it is regarded not as a formal teaching-learning situation but as an opportunity for each student to practice skills and to enjoy using them in a chosen activity. Team lineups, substitutions, and the conduct of the intramural games will be student-directed. The teacher will supervise but never control or dominate the games.

Varsity sports will also be student-directed. Although the physical educator will be directly responsible, as coach, for the overall administration of the team, the players themselves will take the most important role. Lineups, lineup changes, and game strategy will evolve from a dialogue between the players and the physical educator. Additionally, the quarterback in football or the catcher in baseball will have the responsibility for calling the game plays, with the physical educator suggesting plays only when the situation demands it. In victory, the glory belongs wholly to the players, and in defeat they will have learned invaluable lessons that will lead to future victories. The student-centered approach makes a definite contribution to the physical, mental, emotional, and social growth and development of the students and athletes in such a program because student initiative is the keynote.

TEACHER-CENTERED STYLE VERSUS STUDENT-CENTERED STYLE

The teacher-centered physical educator and the student-centered physical educator are equally knowledgeable about their subject matter. It is only their *approach* to teaching that really differs. Although the subject matter is the prime focus of the former, the latter focuses on the student in the teaching-learning situation.

Neither style of teaching is perfect, nor is either free of disadvantages. Both styles have their merits, and both have been used successfully by many teachers of different subjects. Each style has been described from a puristic, theoretical point of view so that differences would be more easily recognized and understood, but it must be remembered that teachers tend to borrow elements of both styles and incorporate them into their own unique teaching systems.

In practice, physical educators may shift from style to style, depending on the particular lesson. In teaching team and dual sports, the physical educator may use an approach that is closer to the teacher-centered style and may do this for a variety of reasons. For example, he or she may have a class, or several classes, that have not developed the maturity required for a student-centered approach or may want to teach a skill and have only a limited amount of time. This same physical educator may find that these same classes benefit most from the student-centered approach when its use is limited to such creative, expressive activities as dance, tumbling, gymnastics, swimming, and other individual sports. It is also possible to use the teacher-centered style during one part of a class period and the student-centered style during another part of the same class period.

A physical educator may use the teacher-centered style in the class program and in a varsity coaching situation but prefer the student-centered style for the intramural and club program, or the reverse may be true. Any number of combinations of teaching style may be observed in the individual physical educator, depending on the activity, the needs of the students, and the physical educator's assessment of the most appropriate style for the situation.

The two teaching styles are not exclusive, and they do overlap. A physical educator may, in fact, state objectives and goals in student-centered terms, yet instruct through the teacher-centered style. However, the predominating style in use at the time will be readily identifiable to the observer.

Mosston's teaching styles*

Mosston has developed seven styles of teaching that provide a continuum from the teacher-centered to stu-

*Mosston, M.: Teaching physical education, Columbus, Ohio, 1966, Charles E. Merrill Publishing Co.; Mosston, M.: Teaching: from command to discovery, Columbus, Ohio, 1981, Charles E. Merrill Publishing Co.

dent-centered styles. Each style is related to the decision-making process, whether by teacher or student, concerning motor responses, social interaction, emotional growth, and intellectual involvement. Furthermore, Mosston indicates that teaching decisions revolve around three areas: the preimpact or planning phase, the impact or execution phase, and postimpact or evaluation phase.

THE COMMAND STYLE

The command style is very similar to the teacher-centered style: essentially all of the decisions are made by the teacher. The student complies with the teacher's wishes and commands. In the execution of a skill, for example, the teacher demonstrates and the student mimics the teacher. The command style may have its greatest advantage when a limited amount of time is available. However, it has such disadvantages as placing a damper on self-motivation and creativity and is designed basically for the average student, without accounting for the poorly coordinated or the gifted student.

THE TASK STYLE

During the impact and execution phase of the lesson, the task style of teaching allows more student involvement, some limited decision-making, and less teacher dominance than the command style. The task style provides, where feasible, the use of task sheets that free students to move at their own rate. This style also provides for more individualization of instruction and feedback and better utilization of equipment. Two disadvantages of this style are that a student can, under some conditions, avoid involvement in the lesson and that, in order to be most effective, it requires greater preparation.

THE RECIPROCAL STYLE

The reciprocal style of teaching provides for one student to serve as the performer and another student to serve as the evaluator who assesses the performance in light of criteria developed by the teacher. Evaluation is limited to the correction of performance errors. This style provides for immediate feedback, greater student involvement, enhancement of students' self-image, and potential for greater skill improvement. At the same time, there are potential dangers in that the student evaluator may be overcritical of the performance and thus present a danger to the emotional state of the performer. There may also be negative feed-back and the possibility that incorrect performance may be reinforced.

THE SMALL-GROUP STYLE

The small-group style is an extension of the reciprocal style. The main difference is that it involves more students. In the reciprocal style only two students are involved whereas in the small-group style, three or more students may be involved. Therefore, the advantages and disadvantages that existed under the reciprocal style are also applicable to the small-group style. The small-group arrangment provides each student with a separate functional task to perform in the lesson, whether as a performer, evaluator, scorer, spotter, or other capacity.

THE INDIVIDUAL-PROGRAM STYLE

The individual-program style extends student involvement to the point where there is greater opportunity for decision-making, particularly in the area of evaluation. In other words, the student is given more responsibility for self-assessment. Such self-assessment can take qualitative or quantitative form. This style of teaching requires that students be previously exposed to participating in the decision-making process and thus ready to cope with self-assessment. It also requires that the teacher develop and prepare specific cues to help students evaluate themselves objectively and effectively. The individual-program style at times uses programmed instruction, where goals are broken down and a sequence of tasks outlined by the teacher for the students to accomplish. An important advantage of adopting such a style is that the teacher gains time and freedom for individual attention to those students who need extra help.

THE GUIDED-DISCOVERY STYLE

The guided-discovery style is designed to develop the intellectual capacity of the student. This method involves questioning and the use of inquiry to lead students to discover the ultimate goal, solution, or answer. The questions must be carefully phrased so that, in a sequence, the answer to one question is based on the information gained from the solution to the previous question. Furthermore, it is important to permit students to respond and then reinforce their responses. The advantage of this style is the intellectual involvement that takes place. Of importance to the student is arriving at the correct answer or solution. Of equal value is the process itself. Although time-consuming and difficult to use with large groups of students, it is very worthwhile.

THE PROBLEM-SOLVING STYLE

The problem-solving style enables students to use their creative talents. Students are presented with a problem situation and then given the criteria for solving it. As a result, students can propose a variety of solutions. As long as the solution meets the teacher-presented criteria, they must be considered correct. Although this style is not designed to teach specific skills, it provides the student with worthwhile opportunities for conceptualization and acclimatization.

Philosophy and teaching style

There are five major philosophies that influence educational thought and teaching style. These philosophies are idealism, realism, pragmatism, naturalism, and existentialism. The ability to understand the key concepts of these philosophies and to relate these concepts to education help physical educators to articulate a professional philosophy and guide them in developing a teaching style that reflects their personal philosophy.

IDEALISM AND TEACHING STYLE

Idealism is a heritage from the ancient Greek philosophers. The idealist places universal ideas at the center of the universe and says that these ideas represent absolute and universal reality. Further, the idealist believes very strongly in human powers of reasoning and intuition.

In regard to education, the idealist feels that the quest for knowledge is inner-directed and that the creativity and thought processes of the student are personal. The role of the teacher is to supply a learning atmosphere and mold the mind of the learner.

The idealist regards physical education as more than a purely physical experience. The physical education program is expected to provide opportunities for mental, social, and emotional growth as well. The idealist would strongly support a physical education program that encouraged student initiative and creativity and furthered intellectual attainment. Having the student understand the *why* of the activity would be approved. The teacher would be looked on as a cultural model worthy of emulation by the student. The emphasis would be centered on seeing how nearly the pupil could achieve the ideal.

REALISM AND TEACHING STYLE

Realism as a philosophy took hold during the late nineteenth and early twentieth centuries, although its roots are as old as those of idealism. The realist places the laws of nature at the center of the universe and supports the scientific method as the best way of seeking and gaining knowledge.

Mathematics and science are, to the realist, the core of the educative process. The educative process as a whole is thought of as a system of learning how to acquire knowledge, acquiring knowledge, and putting knowledge to use. The teacher's role is to be objective in methodology, testing, and student evaluation. The development of standardized tests, for instance, was influenced by the philosophy of realism.

The realist values physical education because experiencing it helps the student learn to adjust to the world, which is of prime importance to the realist. The realist prefers a scientifically formulated program that follows a logical sequence. However, any activities offered in the program would have to be justified as valuable on the basis of scholarly research. This person would require that student evaluations be derived from the results of objective tests. The realist would approve of a physical education program that had a teacher strong in scientific procedures.

PRAGMATISM AND TEACHING STYLE

Pragmatism, in its modern concept, is considered to be an American philosophy. The word "pragmatism" was first used in the 1800s, the approximate time this philosophy began to evolve from its earlier form, which was known as experimentalism. Pragmatism is the philosophy associated with John Dewey.

The pragmatist is a flexible person who believes in change, in the integration of human beings with their world, and in the scientific method. The pragmatist places experience at the center of the universe because an individual cannot know or prove anything that has not personally been experienced.

Dewey said that experience is the key to learning and that the problem-solving method gives the student the experience he or she needs in order to learn. The pragmatist stresses individual differences among students and demands a student-centered school. The role of the teacher is to inspire, guide, and lead the student through a variety of problem-solving activities.

The pragmatist demands a physical education program that meets the needs of the individual student. A wide variety of activities, with emphasis on creativity, is of prime importance. Rigidity and formality, which are inherent in drills and exercises, would not receive the approval of the pragmatist. The pragmatist believes in providing activities that arise from the interests and experiences of the student and in adapting the activity to the student. He or she also prefers that students sample innovative activities, that they be involved in deciding curriculum content, and that they participate as equals in program planning.

NATURALISM AND TEACHING STYLE

Naturalism is the oldest philosophy known to the western world. It shares many of the concepts of realism and pragmatism because it has had a strong influence on the development of these philosophies.

The naturalist places at the center of the universe only those things that exist in actuality. In other words, only material or physical things have significance. The naturalist values society as a whole but is more concerned with each human being as an individual.

Naturalist thought has influenced the development of the educational philosophies of realism and pragmatism. The naturalist desires a student-centered school in which the educational process is geared to the growth, needs, and interests of each individual student. The problem-solving method is important to the naturalist, who feels that the role of the teacher is to guide the student through the process of investigation by the use of example and scientific demonstration.

The naturalist believes in a wide variety of physical activity and in vigorous exercise. All activities in the program must be geared to the student as an individual rather than as part of a larger group. The program should follow the natural pattern of the student's growth and development.

EXISTENTIALISM AND TEACHING STYLE

Existentialism emerged as a philosophy in the late nineteenth century but did not receive significant recognition until after World War II. Thus it is a thoroughly modern philosophy.

The concept of the individuality of human beings forms the core of existentialism. The existentialist believes that each person guides his or her own destiny, determines his or her own system of values, and occupies a place that is superior to that of the society at large.

The existentialist says that education is an adventure in the discovery of self and that the schools must be totally student-centered so that the individual student will not be hindered in attempts at discovery. The existentialist advocates that the student be given full freedom to learn what he or she is interested in learning at the time he or she is interested in learning it. The student selects not only the subject matter but also the method by which learning will take place. Norms, standardized tests, and group tests would be entirely eliminated in favor of an individual evaluative process. The role of the teacher is to monitor the learning environment and to supply the needed tools and opportunity for learning, as well as to serve as a stimulus for the student.

In regard to physical education, the existentialist would prefer a balanced and varied program that offers something for everyone. Additionally, the existentialist would prefer that each student have freedom in the choice of activities and that he or she be responsible for self-discipline, guiding learning, and evaluating progress. The teaching approach most preferred by the existentialist is that of the physical educator who is completely student-centered.

Development of a teaching style

A teaching style develops gradually and is unique to each physical educator because of myriad individual variations and shadings. There are various influences, however, that affect the development of an individual's teaching style. Two of the most important influences are the undergraduate professional preparation program and the student-teaching experience. A third influence is the philosophy of the school system in which the beginning teacher matures.

INFLUENCE OF THE UNDERGRADUATE PROFESSIONAL PREPARATION PROGRAM

It is in the undergraduate years that the future physical educator first explores the nonactivity aspects of physical education. Courses in the history and philosophy of education, psychology and other of the behavioral sciences, and physical education; in principles and practice of physical education; and in organization and administration of physical education form a foundation of understanding and comprehension of the breadth and depth of the field. Through such courses the future physical educator begins to form a personal philosophy of physical education. He or she is often required, as an adjunct to these courses or in methods and materials courses, to formulate a series of objectives for physical education, to plan course outlines and curriculum content, and to write lesson plans.

The philosophy and teaching style of the undergraduate instructors have a profound influence on the development of the student's teaching style. In general, the faculty of a department will decide how the students in that department are to write their objectives and construct the lesson plans that will carry out these objectives. The decision may dictate student-centered terminology or teacher-centered terminology or some kind of compromise terminology. However, the point is too infrequently made that there is more than one way of writing objectives and that there is more than one style of teaching that will satisfactorily carry out objectives. Experience gained in methods courses influences and reinforces teaching style. It is this method of phrasing objectives and this style of teaching that is brought to the student-teaching experience.

INFLUENCE OF THE STUDENT-TEACHING EXPERIENCE

The student-teaching experience is often described as the culminating event of the future physical educator's undergraduate preparation. This experience is at times a traumatic one for the student teacher, but it is invaluable because it provides an opporunity for further development of teaching style or drastic modification in it.

Not all the master teachers associated with a particular undergraduate school will state their objectives or design their lesson plans in exactly the same way. There may be many variations, and the student teacher who has begun to develop a student-centered style may find that his or her master teacher advocates a rigidly teacher-centered style. These stylistic differences can be a source of friction between the student teacher and the master teacher. It is typically the student teacher who adapts teaching style to gain the approval of the master teacher and to ensure a favorable evaluation at the end of the student-teaching experience.

The master teacher has an obligation to the student teacher but an even stronger obligation to the students being taught. Secondary school students are adaptable, and a change in teaching style at the beginning of a new unit should not have a detrimental effect on the students. A change in the middle of a unit, however, could be less than beneficial. It is of no value to the student teacher to follow the example of the master teacher without question. Conferences between the two individuals can open doors to understanding, however, and may result in an enjoyable and worthwhile experience for the master teacher and the student teacher.

INFLUENCE OF THE PHILOSOPHY OF THE SCHOOL SYSTEM

The beginning teacher may or may not have a well-defined teaching style, depending on the strength of his or her undergraduate experience and willingness to express himself or herself as an individual in the teaching situation. The initial weeks of full-fledged teaching give the beginning teacher an opportunity to evaluate further undergraduate and student-teaching experiences.

In a one-teacher department, the beginning teacher will be free to test both teaching styles and to make adaptations, modifications, and compromises. Where there are several teachers in a department, the probationary teacher may be required to adhere to a preferred departmental style. In either case the philosophy of the school system as a whole will give the beginning teacher clues as to how much innovation to attempt.

The beginning teacher may find that he or she is free to innovate and to teach by any style or that it is better to shift teaching style frequently until comfortable and until students react favorably. An experienced teacher, too, will modify and change teaching style from time to time as student needs and interests change.

Ideal teaching style

There is no ideal teaching style. Each physical educator may find that the suitability of a particular style depends on the circumstances and the teaching situation.

Teaching style must be the physical educator's unique expression of his or her role in relation to the role of students. The value system of the students balanced against the value system of the physical educator will help to influence the choice of a teaching style.

Teaching style should be viewed as dynamic rather than static. As student needs change and as the profession of physical education grows, the teaching style should be adapted to keep abreast of this growth and change. Fear of attempting the new and untried impedes the professional growth of the physical educator, but a willingness to be flexible enhances the teacher as a member of a professional field of endeavor.

The kind of teacher a person becomes will depend on the kind of person he or she is. These two factors cannot be separated because they are so closely interwoven and related. The student-teaching experience, as well as the actual teaching experience that comes later on, should reflect this important concept. The methods and materials used are important. However, it should never be forgotten that the process of teaching is never more important than the person who is doing the teaching. It is necessary for the prospective teacher to know about personality theories, but it is even more important to understand his or her own personality.

Self-assessment tests

These tests are designed to assist students in determining if materials and competencies presented in this chapter have been mastered.

1. Identify and list examples to prove the validity of each of the principles identified by Alexander M. Mood as being important in developing a teacher-student relationship conducive to optimum learning.
2. Demonstrate to the class the behavior of a teacher who reflects each of the styles discussed in this chapter.
3. Compare the advantages and disadvantages of a teaching-centered and a student-centered style. Which do you recommend and why?
4. Describe the relationship of general philosophies to teaching style. Provide illustrations to show how each of the several philosophies are reflected in a teacher's style.
5. Assume the role of the teacher of one of your classes to demonstrate what you consider to be a viable teaching style. Have the class evaluate your performance.

Points to remember

1. The teacher should be able to exercise his or her individuality and creativity.
2. The student should be able to exercise his or her individuality and creativity.
3. A physical educator's style of teaching is an expression of himself or herself as an individual.
4. Teaching style is an observable phenomenon.
5. The teacher-centered physical educator is often autocratic.
6. The student-centered physical educator tends to be democratic.
7. The physical educator's philosophy of education influences teaching style.
8. There is no ideal teaching style.

Problems to think through

1. How can methods and materials courses be changed so that they take more cognizance of individual teaching styles?
2. How closely aligned are teaching style and teaching methodology?
3. How can the area of affective learning take place more effectively under the teacher-centered style?
4. How can we objectively evaluate teaching style in terms of student need?
5. How can we justify the teacher- or coach-dominated activity or sport in terms of contributions to student creativity and initiative?

6. How can a physical educator determine whether his or her teaching style is unique?

Case study for analysis

A student teacher finds that his teaching style and that of his master teacher are directly opposite. The student teacher feels that he is obligated to follow the example set by the master teacher, but he wishes to test his own theories, methods, and style of teaching. He hesitates to assert himself because he fears that he may be given a poor evaluation as a result. What steps should he take to resolve his dilemma?

Exercises for review

1. What are the characteristics of the teacher-centered style?
2. What are the characteristics of the student-centered style?
3. Under what circumstances should a physical educator change his or her teaching style?
4. How do the individual philosophies of education influence teaching style?
5. What factors help to determine the development of a teaching style?
6. Show why it is true that teaching style is dynamic rather than static.

Selected readings

Bruner, J.S.: Toward a theory of instruction, Cambridge, Mass., 1966, Harvard University Press.

Bucher, C.A., and Thaxton, N.: Physical education and sport: change and challenge, St. Louis, 1981, The C.V. Mosby Co.

Conant, J.B.: The education of American teachers, New York, 1963, McGraw-Hill Book Co.

Dougherty, N.J., and Bonanno, D.: Contemporary approaches to the teaching of physical education, Minneapolis, 1979, Burgess Publishing Co.

Gage, N.L.: Can science contribute to the art of teaching? Phi Delta Kappan 49:339, 1968.

Hamachek, D.E.: The self in growth, teaching and learning: selected readings, Englewood Cliffs, N.J., 1965, Prentice-Hall, Inc.

Hamachek, D.E.: Personality styles and teacher behavior, The Educational Forum 36:313, 1972.

Healey, J.H., and Healey, W.A.: Physical education teaching problems for analysis and solution, Springfield, Ill., 1975, Charles C Thomas, Publisher.

Hyman, R.T.: Teaching: triadic and dynamic, The Educational Forum 32:65, 1967.

Joyce, B., et al.: Conceptual development and information processing: a study of teachers, Journal of Educational Research 59:219, 1966.

Kagan, J.: Understanding children; behavior, motives and thought, New York, 1971, Harcourt Brace Jovanovich, Inc.

Katz, J.M.: Seniors view their student teaching, Kappa Delta Pi Record 4:75, 1968.

Lemen, M.: Implications of the problem-solving method for physical educators, Journal of Health, Physical Education, and Recreation 37:28, 1966.

Mood, A.M.: How teachers make a difference, Washington, D.C., 1971, U.S. Department of Health, Education and Welfare.

Mosston, M.: Teaching physical education, Columbus, Ohio, 1966, Charles E. Merrill Publishing Co.

Mosston, M.: Teaching: from command to discovery, Belmont, Calif., 1972, Wadsworth Publishing Co., Inc.

Murphy, P.O., and Brown, M.M.: Conceptual systems and teaching styles, American Educational Research Journal 7:529, 1970.

Shapiro, D.: Neurotic styles, New York, 1965, Basic Books, Inc.

Siedentop, D.: Behavior analysis and teacher training, Quest 18:26, 1972.

Singer, R.N. and Dick, W.: Teaching physical education—a systems approach, Boston, 1980, Houghton Mifflin Co.

Solomon, D.: Teaching styles and learning, Chicago, 1963, The Center for the Study of Liberal Education.

Washburne, D., and Heil, L.M.: What characteristics of teachers affect children's growth? Scholastic Review 68:420, 1960.

Webb, D.: Teacher sensitivity-affective impact on student, Journal of Teacher Education 22:4, 1971.

PART FOUR

Teaching physical education

11

The teaching process

Instructional objectives and competencies to be achieved

After reading this chapter the student should be able to

1. Describe learning theories that provide the underlying foundation of teaching methodology
2. Identify internal and external conditions found in any instructional setting that may influence the effectiveness of learning activities
3. Explain the law of readiness and the law of transfer as applied to the teaching of a physical education skill
4. Compare a variety of teaching methods in terms of student and teacher roles in each
5. Evaluate a variety of teaching methods in terms of their advantages and disadvantages in an instructional setting
6. Interpret the nature of the activity, the group, and its goals in relation to selection of appropriate teaching methodology

In the previous chapter an extensive analysis of the teacher-centered and student-centered styles of teaching was offered. These teaching styles are sometimes called the direct versus indirect or the structured versus unstructured approaches to teaching.

The present chapter will be devoted to descriptions of teaching methods, with a detailed analysis of advantages and disadvantages of each. The conditions that influence the teaching process—conditions within the learning environment as well as within the learner—will also be discussed. It is important for the teacher of physical education to recognize the variety of conditions that affect instruction in order to select appropriate teaching methods from the many types presented here. Selection of teaching methodology should also be based on a sound knowledge and understanding of *how* students learn. Inasmuch as the-

ories of learning mark the initial point from which a teacher should start this selection process, these theories will be presented first.

Theories of learning

Psychologists have attempted to explain the phenomenon of learning and to answer such questions as how it best takes place and to identify the laws under which it operates. The basic theories of learning, for purposes of discussion, may be divided into two broad categories. The first category may be called the connectionist theories. These theories hold that learning consists of a bond or connection between a stimulus and a response or responses. The second category may be labeled cognitive theories. Those psychologists that support these theories believe that a human being's various perceptions, beliefs, or attitudes (cognitions or mental images) concerning his or her environment determine behavior. The manner in which these "cognitions" are modified by experience indicates the learning that takes place. The basic principles underlying the cognitive theories were developed by the Gestalt psychologists.

THE CONNECTIONISTS

Thorndike's laws. E.L. Thorndike, a psychologist whose theories of learning have had a great impact on educators and education, believed in a stimulus-response theory, or S-R bond theory. Thorndike's laws of readiness, exercise, and effect describe the conditions under which learning best takes place. Because psychology is a relatively new science and because there are many contradictory views as to various psychological principles, laws of learning should not be regarded as the final word. However, they are working principles and, as such, deserve the attention of all physical educators who desire to seek the most efficient and effective ways of teaching.

Law of readiness. The law of readiness means that an individual will learn much more effectively and rapidly if he or she is "ready" and has matured and if there is a felt need. Learning will be satisfying if materials are presented when an individual meets these criteria. This law also works in reverse. It will be annoying and dissatisfying to the individual to do something he or she is not ready to do. The closer an individual is to reaching the point of readiness, the more satisfying the act.

In physical education activities, the teacher should determine whether the child is ready in terms of various sensory and kinesthetic mechanisms and, in some cases, in strength. The teacher should ask such questions as: Does the student have the capacity, at this time, for certain skills? Does he or she have the proper background of experience? Is the material that is being presented timely—that is, should it be postponed until some future time, or is now the time to present it? Most physical educators agree, for example, that athletic competition on an interscholastic basis should not be part of the program for elementary school children. The child is not mentally, emotionally, and physically ready for such an experience. There is also considerable agreement that fine-muscle activity should not play too pronounced a part in the program for young children. Instead, their program should consist mainly of activities that involve the large muscles.

The law of readiness also has implications for the learning of skills. An adult has difficulty hitting a baseball, riding a bicycle, throwing a football, and performing other physical activities if he or she has not developed some skill in these activities during youth. During youth, on the other hand, individuals can perform reasonably well in these skills without too much difficulty. They are at the proper maturational level for the learning of such skills, and their neuromuscular equipment has developed to a point where skills are learned more economically and effectively. They do not mind passing through an awkward trial-and-error period. Physical educators should bear this in mind and set as their goal the development in youth of many interesting and varied skills. In this way students will have the foundational equipment when they reach adulthood to engage in a variety of physical activities that will provide many enjoyable hours of wholesome recreation.

Law of exercise. The law of exercise, in respect to the development of skills in physical education, means that practice makes for better coordination, more rhythmical movement, less expenditure of energy, more skill, and better performance. As a result of practice, the pathway between stimulus and response becomes more pronounced and permanent.

In many ways this law of learning is similar to the law of use and disuse. As a result of continual practice, strength is gained, but as a result of disuse, weakness ensues.

Learning in physical education is acquired by doing. To master the skill of bowling, swimming, or handball, a person must practice. However, it should be restated that practice does not necessarily ensure perfection of the skill, and mere repetition does not mean greater skill. Practice must be meaningful, with proper attention to all phases of the learning process. The learner, through repetition and a clear concept of what is to be done, steadily makes progress toward a specific goal, since it is during the *process* of repetition that learning takes place.

Law of effect. The law of effect maintains that an individual will be more likely to repeat experiences that are satisfying than those experiences that are annoying. If experiences are annoying, the learner will shift to other, satisfying responses.

This law of learning, as applied to physical education, means that every attempt should be made to provide situations in which individuals experience success and have a satisfying and enjoyable experience. Leadership is an important factor. Under certain types of leadership, undesirable experiences may be satisfying. A coach who approved of hitting an opponent might make such an act enjoyable, while other coaches would not tolerate it. Their condemnation would make the act an annoying experience. Therefore quality of leadership is the key to good teaching.

Guthrie's contiguity theory. Edwin R. Guthrie* developed the contiguity theory of learning, which emphasizes the stimulus-response association. Contiguity means that a response evoked by a stimulus will be repeated whenever that same stimulus recurs. The strengthening of the connection between the stim-

---

*Guthrie, E.R.: The psychology of learning, rev. ed., New York, 1952, Harper & Row, Publishers, Inc.

Fig. 11-1. Teaching physical education.

ulus and the response takes place in a single trial. Guthrie believed that, since associations can occur with one trial and last forever, the process of learning requires neither reward nor motivation. However, although Guthrie holds that full connection is established in one trial, it usually appears to take place gradually. This means that all stimuli cues are not always presented in the same manner, and for this reason many stimulus-response associations must be made. In every learning situation, for example, various combinations of stimuli are presented; thus the correct responses need to be established for each situation. Guthrie believes that repetition and practice are essential for learning in order for the individual to become aware of the stimuli that will evoke the correct response.

In physical education we can apply Guthrie's theory to the learning of a skill such as the high jump. If a youngster desires to be proficient in this skill, he or she must make sure that bodily movements are always the same with each approach to the bar. The individual must be aware of all the surrounding stimuli, such as the runway and position of the bar. The proficient high jumper will have established a successful movement pattern and will not deviate from it. Even the slightest change in a stimulus can evoke an incorrect response. The youngster accustomed to practicing in complete silence becomes distracted by the noise of the spectators and finds it difficult to clear the bar. According to Guthrie's theory, this youngster should practice under competition conditions, for to achieve optimal performance, the competitor must be aware of all the stimuli that are present at the time of competition.

Hull's reinforcement theory. Clark L. Hull* sees learning as a direct influence of reinforcement. He has established his theory on the influence of need and its reduction as the prime elements in learning. Hull emphasizes that learning occurs when the individual adapts to the environment and that such adaptation is necessary for survival. When needs arise, the individual's survival is threatened, which motivates acting in a certain manner to reduce the need. Thus the responses the individual makes that lead to the reduction of the need are reinforced, resulting in habits or learning. To elaborate, a stimulus causes a response that results in a need. The need evokes a response on the part of the individual, which reduces the need. The response that resulted in the reduction of the need is then reinforced, which develops habits or learning. Hull employed drive and primary reinforcement in his early work. Later he used ideas such as drive stimulus reduction and secondary reinforcement.

Hull's theory emphasizes that habits or learning result from reactions set into motion by needs. In physical education the teacher plays an important part in satisfying the needs of the student. Teachers who explain the psychological and sociological bases for participating in an activity may stimulate students to a greater degree than those who present the activity without any rationale. To elicit correct responses from students, the teacher presents material that is meaningful, and therefore lesson plans consist of material important to the learner.

Since the child learns by doing, drive reduction is a ''doing'' phenomenon. In physical education the child arrives at the solution to many problems through individual effort. For example, the student practices the ''kip'' on the low bar and after many attempts becomes aware of not achieving success because of the position of the arms or other weakness. On discovering the correct position, the student repeats it over and over to reinforce it. The result is the correct movement on the low bar, and the habit is learned. Further repetition of the activity with the correct response leads to a feeling of satisfaction on the part of the student, for the need is no longer a problem.

One of the major implications of Hull's theory to physical education is his finding that practice periods that are extremely long or lacking in reinforcement inhibit learning. An example is the pole vaulter who practices hour after hour. After a long period of practice without any reinforcement, he finds it difficult to clear his usual height. However, Hull states that the inhibitions decrease after rest periods, and the next day the vaulter can again clear his accustomed height. Thus practice periods play an important role in determining the performance of an individual.

Skinner's operant conditioning theory. The main feature of B.F. Skinner's* operant conditioning theory is the fact that the stimulus that reinforces the responses does not precede it but follows it. That is, the individual organism first makes the desired response and then is rewarded. Thus reinforcement is contingent on response. Skinner's main emphasis is that the individual repeats at a future time the behavior that has been previously reinforced. Behaviors that are not reinforced are not usually repeated. When the individual is rewarded, he elicits that behavior again. Extinction occurs when the behavior is no longer reinforced.

Skinner makes the point that since teachers cannot always wait for desirable behavior, they must sometimes shape the behavior of the individual. In teaching any physical skill, it is recognized that reinforcement is extremely valuable. For example, the teacher who desires that a student learn how to make the jump shot encourages that student to learn the proper form. When the student is shooting at the peak of the jump, in the correct manner, the teacher indicates approval to the student. The student becomes aware of the proper form and continues to use it, knowing that the skill is performed according to the teacher's standard.

Skinner has placed great emphasis on the use of audiovisual aids and teaching machines because of

---

*Hull, C.L.: Principles of behavior, New York, 1943, Appleton-Century-Crofts.

*Skinner, B.F.: The behavior of organisms, New York, 1938, Appleton-Century-Crofts.

their reinforcement value. Since the teacher cannot reinforce the behavior of all children in a class, such machines may be useful, although some psychologists believe that they may interfere with the organization of materials into structural wholes. Through the use of such new innovations as the videotape replay, students see themselves in action and discover their deficiencies. Such devices prove beneficial in reinforcing learning in large classes where the teacher cannot cope with all the individual problems that arise.

THE COGNITIVE THEORISTS

Gestalt theorists. The Gestalt psychologists, such as Max Wertheimer, Kurt Koffka, Wolfgang Kohler, and Kurt Lewin, are greatly concerned with form and shapes. Gestalt theory is more concerned with perception than learning. One of the most important Gestalt principles having implications for physical education is the whole method theory. This theory is based on the premise that a person reacts totally to any situation—that is, the whole individual attempts to achieve a goal. Furthermore, the greater the individual's insight or understanding concerning the goal to be attained, such as paddling a canoe or guiding a bowling ball to a strike, the greater the degree of skill in that activity. An individual reacts differently each time he or she performs a physical act. Therefore it is not just a question of practice, as it would be if performed the same way each time. Instead, the more insight a student has of the complete act, the greater his or her skill. The individual performs the whole act and does it until gaining an insight into the situation or until getting the ''feel'' or the ''hang'' of it. Since insight is so important, dependent conditions such as a person's capacity and previous experience—as well as environmental factors—are very important considerations.

Psychoanalytic theory of learning. Psychoanalysis is based on genetic as well as dynamic theory. Learning, related to the psychosocial stages of development, must account for the effects of unconscious forces that, in certain cases, lead to repression, fixation, and regression. Sigmund Freud, who developed the theory of psychoanalysis, stressed the importance of cognitive control in the development of a rational ego.

INFORMATION-PROCESSING THEORIES

More recently, educational psychologists have been investigating the relationship of central nervous system processes to learning itself. Two groups of information-processing theorists have been looking at neurophysiological and neurochemical functioning in the brain, giving particular attention to the feedback mechanisms involved from that center.

Of particular interest to physical educators is the work of a third group of investigators, the cyberneticists, whose theory on feedback mechanisms relates specifically to motor learning. According to cybernetic theory, a motor response is the result of a three-phase process: (1) sensory input, (2) information processing through the central nervous system wherein selective attention to appropriate stimuli is evoked and then followed by (3) motor responses. Included in this process is kinesthetic feedback from the proprioceptors (sensitive nerve endings in muscle fibers), which, together with a knowledge of results from previous experiences, combine to produce improved motor performances.

There is a critical need in our profession for further research in this area of motor learning and the conditions and factors that influence it. Because acquisition of motor skills is a primary objective throughout physical education activities, it is essential that teachers continue to further their understanding of motor learning concepts. Although many gaps in knowledge still exist, the following material and answers to critical questions may be helpful for development of motor skills in the gymnasium.

Motor learning

The term ''motor learning'' is generally used in reference to the improvement of a motor performance or the development of a skill. For example, when, through practice, a golfer improves putting skill, an archer improves aim, or a pitcher improves delivery, motor learning has taken place.

Movement is a fundamental aspect of human behavior, and skills may be categorized in several different ways. Two frequently used categories of skills are types of action and function.

Motor skills, as they relate to types of action, may

be divided into fine versus gross motor skills or into sensory versus perceptual motor skills.

Fine motor skills are those requiring manual dexterity, such as typing, whereas *gross motor skills* involve large muscle activity, as in running.

Sensory motor skills are those that develop as a result of sensory cues (feeling, tasting, hearing, seeing, and smelling). Serving a volleyball would involve a sensory cue, for example. *Perceptual motor skills* are developed whenever the perceptual process is involved (judgments concerning speed, depth, and background information). In archery, both types of skill are involved because cues of feeling and seeing are used, as well as judgments concerning distance and point of aim.

Motor skills may also be categorized according to their function in human existence. Although some motor skills are essential for normal existence (walking, self-care), others may be classified in terms of their self-improvement or educational values (reading, writing), and others are recreational in nature. Physical education skills would generally be classified in this last division.

How does a student learn a motor skill? Is motor skill ability inherited or acquired? Is it transferable from one type of activity to another? Researchers are beginning to find answers to some of these questions.

PROCESS OF MOTOR LEARNING

Motor learning involves the establishment of pathways within the complex neuromuscular system of the human body. The very simplest human movement, such as clapping the hands, involves a pathway that may be divided into three distinct parts: the sensory, the connecting, and the motor neurons. These neurons form a pathway to bring about muscular innervation, making the hands come together. Neuromuscular skills are merely different sets of pathways that have been established through practice. The following questions immediately come to mind concerning the development of skill.

• *Are all skills acquired, or are some movements inherited?* Some movements may be categorized as inherited. For example, under normal circumstances, individuals walk, and they perform "swimming" movements in the water. Refinements of these motions

can be acquired. Examples include hopping, skipping, and stroking in the water. Other inherited movements include those reflexes that are automatic and involuntary, such as the knee jerk, eye wink, and breathing.

• *Once learned, are motor skills always remembered?* Retention of motor skills is dependent on many factors. Those skills that are easily acquired, are natural, are used frequently, or are "overlearned" usually remain with an individual for a long period of time. For example, riding a bicycle, swimming, skating, and throwing are rarely forgotten. The degree of perfection in performance may vary, but usually a well-refined skill may be reacquired in a relatively short period of time.

• *How much should a skill be practiced?* The amount of practice necessary to learn a skill depends on the individual's quickness in acquiring the skill and the degree of perfection desired (See Chapter 12 on mastery learning). It has been found helpful to practice a motor skill in a series of a few attempts followed by rest and then to return to a series again. By distributing practice and rest intervals, neural pathways may be developed and stabilized.

• *What about injuries?* In injuries where muscle tissue has been damaged, usually rest will allow a return to normal functioning. In instances where nerve endings are damaged, new neural pathways may need to be established, and relearning may take a little longer.

PRINCIPLES AND CONDITIONS THAT ASSIST IN THE LEARNING OF MOTOR SKILLS*

• *Perception is important in motor learning.* Perception refers to the process of receiving and distinguishing among the available stimuli in any situation. It is essential in motor skill learning for an individual to perceive speed, distance, and shapes of objects. Deficiencies in any of these areas make the learning of motor skills more difficult. Various communication devices and techniques assist the learner in acquiring motor skills. Motion pictures, live demonstrations, knowledge of mechanical principles, and a realization

---

*Adapted in part from material in Bucher, C.A.: Foundations of physical education, ed. 8, St. Louis, 1979, The C.V. Mosby Co.

Fig. 11-2. Teacher from Hampton Institute, Hampton, Va., conducting physical education class for secondary school students.

and clear understanding of what is expected of the learner in performing a skill will be of particular value to beginners.

• *Effective motor learning is based on prerequisite factors.* Such factors as strength, dynamic energy, ability to change direction, flexibility, agility, peripheral vision, visual acuity, concentration, an understanding of the mechanics of the activity, and an absence of inhibitory factors are essential to motor learning.

• *Skills should not be taught unless students have reached a level of development commensurate with the degree of difficulty of the skill.* Maturation is growth that takes place without any special training, stimulus, or practice—it just happens. It is closely associated with the physiological development of all individuals. Therefore the material must be adapted to individual maturational levels.

• *Each individual is different.* Teachers must be aware of the fact that individuals are different from one another and that these differences must be recognized if learning is to occur.

• *The learning curve is a consideration in motor*

learning. Learning curves are not always constant, and they are different for each individual. The learning curve depends on the person, the material being learned, and the conditions surrounding the learning. Learning may start out with an initial spurt and then be followed by a period in which progress is not so rapid, or there may be no progress at all.

• *Learning takes place most effectively when the student has a motive for wanting to learn.* Motivation is an inducement to action. Usually the greater the motivation, the more rapid the learning. Motives should be intrinsic rather than extrinsic. That is, the worth of the activity itself should be the motivating factor rather than rewards, awards, and grades.

• *Learning takes place much more effectively when the student intends to learn.* If a boy or girl decides to learn a certain skill and sees a need for it, he or she is much more open to learning.

• *The student should know the goals toward which he or she is working.* Learning progresses much faster when goals are clear. The student should have a clear picture of what constitutes a successful performance. For example, if high jumping is being taught, the proper form and technique should be clearly demonstrated and discussed.

• *The student should receive feedback about progress.* There are basically two kinds of feedback available to the student during the performance of a motor skill. Internal feedback is related to the concept of *kinesthesis,* whereas external feedback is related to the concept known as *knowledge of results.* Kinesthesis is associated with the feeling of the movement and has been recognized as conscious muscle sense. External feedback or knowledge of results is also extremely valuable to the student during and after the completion of a motor skill. Knowledge that one is progressing toward a set goal is encouraging and promotes a better learning situation.

• *Progress will be much more rapid when the learner gains satisfaction from the learning situation.* Satisfaction is associated with success. As the learner is successful in mastering a particular physical skill, the desire to learn increases.

• *The length and distribution of practice periods are important considerations for effective learning. Massed practice* refers to long and continuous practice periods, whereas *distributed practice* refers to practice periods interrupted by rest intervals. There is some agreement that practice periods are most profitable when they are short and spaced over a period of time. The number of repetitions, such as shots at the basket or serves in tennis, should be considered as the unit of practice rather than the total number of minutes spent in the practice session.

According to some psychologists, when subject matter is very interesting and meaningful to the learner, practice periods may be made longer. Therefore it seems that the length and spacing of periods should be adjusted to the class and material being learned.

• *As a general rule, learning is more effective when skills are taught as whole skills and not in parts.* In physical education it seems that the whole method should be followed when the material to be taught is a functional and integrated whole. This means that in swimming, which is a functional whole, the total act of swimming is taught. Individuals learn to swim by using their arms and legs. However, research indicates that complex skills should be broken down into their

basic parts. In a sport such as football, which consists of such elements as blocking, broken-field running, tackling, passing, and punting, each skill represents a part of the whole. But since each represents a functional and integrated whole by itself, each one should be taught separately.

• *Overlearning has value in the acquisition of motor skills.* The initial practice in the learning of a motor skill is important in determining how long the skill remains in the possession of the learner. The learner does not retain a partially learned skill as long as one that is overlearned—that is, practiced until it establishes a pattern in the nervous system. If a skill is mastered and there is continual practice of the accomplishment, considerable time elapses before such a skill is lost to the learner.

• *Speed rather than accuracy should be emphasized in the initial stages of motor skill learning.* Physical educators are often required to make a judgment as to whether speed or accuracy should be emphasized in the initial stages of skill learning. Although some psychologists maintain that speed may lead in some cases to blindness in thinking, other researchers advocate speed. Desirable though it is to emphasize both speed and accuracy, this is not always possible. In physical education, many skills are carried on primarily by momentum, and according to some research, speed should be emphasized in the initial stages of such learning. At this stage an emphasis on accuracy interferes with the development of momentum needed to carry on the movement. In teaching golf and tennis skills that require momentum for successful performance, it is important to emphasize speed in the early stages of learning.

• *Transfer of training can facilitate the learning of motor skills.* Transfer of training is based on the premise that a skill learned in one situation can be used in another situation. For example, the student who knows how to play tennis takes readily to badminton because both skills require similar strokes and the use of a racquet. Most psychologists agree that positive transfer is more likely to occur when two tasks have similar part-whole relations.

Physical educators must be aware of the concept known as *negative transfer.* Negative transfer occurs when one task interferes with the learning of a second task. For example, a young man being introduced to the game of golf for the first time experiences difficulty in swinging the club because of his previous experience in a skill such as baseball. He may be told, "You're swinging the golf club like a baseball bat."

• *Mental practice can enhance the learning of motor skills.* Mental practice is the symbolic rehearsal of a skill with the absence of gross muscular movements. The physical educator should be concerned with the role of mental practice in skill learning. Research seems to indicate that although physical practice is superior to mental practice, mental practice is better than no practice at all. A combination of physical and mental practice is best.

• *A knowledge of mechanical principles increases the student's total understanding of the activity in which he or she is participating.* A knowledge of principles that involve levers, laws of motion, gravity, and other factors is closely related to skills performance. Physical educators should be able to give their students a knowledgeable rationale for the skills they are performing.

• *Implementation of the principle of reinforcement will enhance learning.* One of the most fundamental laws of learning is reinforcement, which means that the behavior most likely to emerge in any situation is one that is reinforced or found successful in a previous, similar situation. Therefore the best-planned learning situation will provide for an accumulation of successes. The reinforcement (reward) should follow the desired behavior almost immediately and should be associated with the behavior in order to be most effective.

• *Errors should be eliminated early in the learning period.* When instructing in such skills as field hockey and softball, the physical education teacher should attempt to eliminate incorrect performance as early as possible so that errors do not become a fixed part of the participant's performance. Inefficient methods, once learned, are difficult to correct.

• *Optimum conditions in the learning situation result in more efficient learning.* To create a challenging teaching situation, distracting elements should be eliminated from the setting, the proper mental set established in the mind of the student, the appropriate equipment and facilities available, and the learner pro-

vided with the proper background to understand and appreciate the material to be presented.

• *A learning situation is greatly improved if the students diagnose their own movements and arrive at definite conclusions about their errors.* Self-criticism is much more conducive to good learning than teacher criticism. Students correct mistakes they discover on their own more readily than those discovered by someone else. Thus a sign of good teaching is the ability to create situations that lead to self-criticism.

IMPLICATIONS OF RESEARCH FOR TEACHING MOTOR SKILLS

The application of scientific research findings to program planning and the teaching of physical education activities is important. There is a gap between what is known and what is applied to teaching motor skills. Bell* has listed the results of some research and applied it to the teaching of selected physical education activities. A sampling of Bell's work is presented here in adapted form to show its implications for the teaching of motor skills.

• *Archery:* Four days per week of massed practice was shown to be better than two days of distributed practice.
• *Badminton:* During the early stages of learning 30 minutes a day of distributed practice was found to be better than 60 minutes of massed practice per day twice a week.
• *Baseball:* Knowledge of results helped to improve speed and accuracy in the baseball throw.
• *Basketball:* Learning the foul shot improved as a result of mental practice in basketball.
• *Bowling:* Demonstration via the motion picture was of help if the learners had already had some practice.
• *Football:* Mental practice in the football pass by reading an instruction sheet improved performance.
• *Golf:* The whole method of practice (total swing) was superior to the part method.
• *Gymnastics:* Videotape replay resulted in better performance.

*Bell, V.L.: Sensorimotor learning, Pacific Palisades, Calif., 1970, Goodyear Publishing Co., Inc.

Fig. 11-3. Physical education class in lacrosse at Wheaton High School in Wheaton, Md.

- *Softball:* Instruction in mechanical principles enhanced performance.
- *Swimming:* The whole method of teaching was found to be superior to the part method.
- *Tennis:* The best results were achieved where emphasis on speed and accuracy was equal.
- *Tumbling:* No difference was found in the performance of two groups, one of which utilized motion pictures while the other did not.
- *Volleyball:* A knowledge of mechanical principles assisted in the performance of volleyball skills.

Conditions for learning

Knowledge of how students learn and how they acquire motor skills provides the background for all methods of teaching. But an understanding of those conditions favorable to the learning process is also needed to ensure success with selected methodology. Conditions that influence learning experiences are internal and external to the instructional setting. Internally the student contributes hereditary influences and an individualistic learning style, whereas the home and school community provide influences of an external nature.

HEREDITY

Nature versus nurture as a contributing factor in personality development has long fascinated educators and psychologists. They are especially interested in the extent to which the genetic makeup of an individual affects the outcome of his or her developmental nature. Present-day scientific knowledge has reached the point where genetic makeup may someday be altered to produce individuals who have desirable predetermined characteristics. In their studies of the makeup of intelligence, psychologists are finding that it may be possible to control portions of the intellect through the administration of such agents as ribonucleic acid. The significance of these discoveries holds many implications for education and physical education. Teachers should remain up-to-date on discoveries and advances in these vital areas and know how these changes will affect the classrooms of the future and the physical abilities of the students in them.

HOME ENVIRONMENT

Community and governmental agencies have long been striving to improve the environmental factors that serve as strong educational forces. Better homes, better jobs, better wages, and improved working conditions have been denied large segments of the population. In the typical middle-class home, books and conversation are a part of everyday life. In the homes of the disadvantaged, books are a rarity, and the home can be of little aid in preparing the child for school and an education. A few significant advances have been made. Project Head Start, for example, is considered helpful in preparing preschoolers for their first formal educational experience by offering childhood opportunities lacking in the home. Improved living conditions for the lower socioeconomic groups may someday make these home environments helpful to the educational process. Teachers must realize that not all students come from homes in which education is a potent force and that not all students are prepared for the challenge of school.

SCHOOL ENVIRONMENT

Computerized education is bringing about many changes in school methods. Through computers, a student, rather than spending hours of research with a variety of books and reference materials, is now able to obtain references from sources across the country or retrieve information in a short period of time. The teacher is often a guide through the machine-controlled process, giving the praise, encouragement, and personal help that the machine cannot give. In spite of the move toward computers, the teacher will continue as the center of the educational process, for it is the teacher who must decide what the machine can do for each student, and it is the teacher who must evaluate what the machine is doing for the student. It is also the teacher who provides the human factor on which good teaching and learning will always depend.

The school must ask itself what vital conditions and characteristics of a learning situation most influence a student during the developmental years. By knowing these determinants, the school can adjust and adapt to future educational developments in every curricular area and will be better able to meet its responsibilities to its students.

If the teaching process is to be enhanced, several environmental factors need careful consideration. Each factor stems from basic individual needs and may be categorized according to four major areas of concern.

1. Physical needs
   a. Heat. Temperatures should be maintained within a comfortable range so that students do not become drowsy from too much heat or overstimulated from too much cold.
   b. Light. Proper lighting in all classroom areas protects and aids students' vision.
   c. Ventilation. Proper circulation of fresh air is important to the health and comfort of everyone in the classroom.
   d. Equipment. Equipment should be in safe condition, adequate to the number of students in the class, and of the proper size and weight for the particular age level.
   e. Facilities. Adequate and safe facilities are a necessity for proper conduct of classes.
2. Emotional needs. A positive approach should be maintained in the handling of students and their problems. The National Association for Mental Health lists several factors essential to good mental health that have significance in the school situation.
   a. Acceptance. Students should feel accepted as persons of worth by teachers and peers.
   b. Security. Students should know what is expected of them as persons and students.
   c. Protection. Students should not be made to feel that peers or teachers have marked them as failures or potential failures.
   d. Control. Students should understand and abide by proper standards of good conduct and courteous behavior.
   e. Independence. Students should feel free to express themselves as individuals as long as they do not impinge on the rights of others.
   f. Guidance. The student's efforts and successes need to be constructively criticized, praised, and recognized.
3. Social needs. Democratic group processes recognize both the larger group and the individual within the group.
   a. Cooperation. Through cooperative efforts with peers the students should feel they are making individual contributions to the larger group.
   b. Competition. Through controlled competition with peers the student should feel gratification

in success, experience the adventure of competing, gain pride in accomplishment, and know the satisfaction that comes from wholehearted effort.

   c. Grouping. Through grouping techniques students should be placed where they will feel most comfortable and where they will be encouraged to work to their capacity.

   d. Rapport. Good teacher-student relationships help the students to feel that they are respected as individuals.

4. Intellectual needs. Not all students' intellectual needs can be met in the same way, and not all students function best in a single kind of learning situation. Some students learn best in a democratic environment where they are encouraged to be creative through a problem-solving approach. These students have the maturity to be able to conceptualize knowledge and come to their own conclusions through personal discovery. Other students function best in a rather rigidly teacher-dominated situation because they are not as yet ready to help guide their own learning. A single classroom may contain either type of student, or students who alternate between the two systems, depending on the material to be learned. Only through a comprehensive knowledge of each student can the teacher determine how each individual learns best and adapt the teaching methods as the need dictates.

CREATION OF A FAVORABLE ENVIRONMENT

The preceding discussion outlines the basic factors necessary for the creation of an environment in which learning may take place. Yet each of these components must be combined for an effective teaching-learning atmosphere. If, for example, each factor is present save one, the atmosphere will not be as conducive to the educational process as it might be. An overheated gymnasium, a poorly ventilated locker room, or a teacher who concentrates only on the students with high motor skill ability will each have a negative effect on the teaching-learning atmosphere. The physical needs, such as heating, lighting, and ventilation, are often only minor problems that can be corrected at once if difficulties arise. However, the social, emo-

tional, and intellectual needs of the students need much more care and attention. The complexity of these needs and their interdependencies demand far greater consideration from the teacher and far more time and effort. Meeting these needs usually is possible only through the establishment of effective teacher-pupil relationships. Unless the teacher is willing to become sincerely involved with students, effective learning cannot take place, no matter how ideal the physical environment may be. This genuine involvement with the student sets the teacher apart from the teaching machine and gains for him or her professional respect. Good teacher-student relationships provide one of the most vital keys to successful teaching and learning. This particular relationship is probably most noticeable in the physical education classroom or on the athletic field, where the physical educator is not only a teacher of skills but a counselor of students as well.

LEARNING STYLES

Learning does not take place simply because the proper atmosphere exists or because the physical tools for learning, such as books, pencils, or athletic equipment, are available. In order for learning to take place, there must first of all be an individual who is motivated to learn, incentives that will increase the motivation, challenges that make reaching the learning goal an adventure, and continued effort on the part of the individual to overcome obstacles and arrive at the goal.

Although all individuals are capable of learning, not all individuals learn at the same rate or in the same manner. Not all learners can be reached by a common methodology or teaching style. Many different kinds of learning styles have been identified, and learners tend to use each of these styles in varying degrees, depending on the material or concepts to be learned. Some learners are completely verbally oriented, for example, while others succeed best when the problem-solving technique is used. Memorization, concept formation, and trial-and-error learning are other examples of learning styles.

The incentives offered for learning are vital to the educational process because they enhance motivation. Grades for achievement, placement in a higher ability group, and teacher praise and recognition are forms of incentives commonly used in education.

The challenges presented to the learner also help to increase the individual's motivation to solve a learning problem. If a learning task is too easy and the goal is reached without much effort on the part of the learner, very little real learning can take place. As the individual meets a variety of challenges and draws closer to a goal, he or she learns—that is, each individual's success in surmounting difficulties is a true learning experience. However, no challenge should be made so difficult that eventual goal attainment is impossible.

To learn and retain what has been learned, the individual must put forth a continued effort in order to arrive at a goal. A learner may experience failure in the first attempts at learning, but continued efforts will bring a successful response in a given situation. As the learner continues to put forth effort, he or she will continue to make more and more successful responses that lead to goal attainment.

Methods of teaching

FACTORS AFFECTING METHOD SELECTION

The proper selection of an appropriate teaching method involves consideration of several factors. Although class size, equipment, and facilities merit some thought, these factors are more often considered in connection with organization of the class. Methods of teaching are determined by the nature of the activity itself, the particular purposes or goals to be achieved, and the age level and ability of the group.

Nature of the activity. The wide variety of activities included in a well-rounded physical education program necessitates utilization of different teaching methods, depending on the nature or type of activity. Teaching an individual stunt such as a handspring requires a personal approach to improve an individual's performance, whereas teaching offensive team tactics requires total group knowledge. Therefore the selection of a method must take into account the nature of the activity.

Nature of the group goals. The nature of the group goals is an extremely important element to be considered in teaching methods. What do the students

themselves expect to learn and achieve in a particular unit of work? In basketball, for example, they all want to play the game and to improve their skills through playing. The creative teacher needs to develop exciting drills for skills practice, thus improving abilities of the individuals and upgrading game play while maintaining class enthusiasm.

Frequently the teacher needs to determine student objectives and goals for classwork. Providing an opportunity to hear students express their interests and desires will often bring out special individual hopes. Some may want to lose weight, and some may want to improve game skill. Meeting these individual goals, revealed through democratic group processes, makes physical education a more meaningful experience for all.

Nature of the group. It is important to keep in mind the characteristics and interests of the students in the class. The differences between boys and girls, their physical abilities, their interests, and their attitudes all need consideration if teaching methods are to be appropriate. For example, on the junior high level, a variety of methods should be utilized to appeal to the students' widespread interests. Whereas a lengthy lecture would serve only to bore these younger students, it might be appreciated as a time-saver by older adolescents. The ability level of the students also needs clarification when methods are selected. Advanced students move rapidly through introductory and review sessions in a unit and should move on quickly into the advanced skills presentations.

WAYS OF PRESENTING MATERIAL

The theories of learning discussed previously provide the basis for all instructional methods. Methods discussed next will reflect such theories as laws of readiness, laws of transfer, and motor learning principles. There is no single best method of teaching physical education. Instead, the teacher will need to bring to each individual teaching situation a knowledge of growth and development, hereditary and environment, and theories of learning and combine it with the best methods available under the given circumstances. Judgment and experience bring quality instruction to the teaching process. Fig. 11-4 represents a "cycle of learning" established when a se-

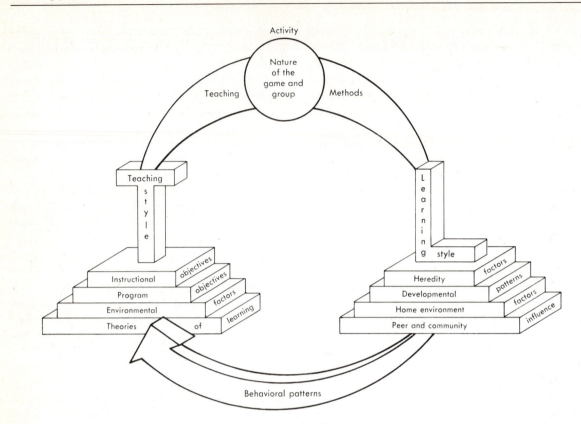

Fig. 11-4. Cycle of learning.

lected method of teaching forms the bridge between teacher and learner. Evaluation of behaviors provides feedback to complete the cycle.

The following descriptions of teaching methods include several factors that may be helpful to students and teachers in planning daily classes of physical education. The role of the teacher and the role of the student are pinpointed, and teaching style is identified as teacher-centered or student-centered. Important advantages and disadvantages are also listed with each method, followed by a question that is worthy of consideration.

First, however, two essential principles of teaching should be stressed as an introduction to methodology. The teacher of physical education should remember that instruction should progress from the known to the unknown with every class meeting. Whichever method of teaching is finally selected for presentation of

material, the introductory activities should include a review of previous learnings to ensure progress.

A second principle involves the whole-part-whole organization of teaching materials. It has been found that learning may be more effective if students know or at least have an acquaintance with the total activity being studied. For example, an introduction of the entire game on the opening day of a new unit on individual or team sports provides an intellectual framework or background of concepts from which the student may be led toward learning the component parts. In the same way, viewing a folk or square dance in its entirety gives students a mental image of how the various steps and patterns combine to create the whole dance. Thereafter, working on the steps or parts of the dance makes more sense to the student and creates a feeling of orderliness in the practice sessions. This whole-part-whole concept in teaching and the idea of going from what is known toward the unknown are basic principles underlying the teaching process. Once the appropriate material has been selected, providing for sequential, progressive progamming by these principles, a method of teaching can be selected from those described below.

Lecture

• *Purpose*. To present information, usually cognitive in nature, such as facts (rules, history, etiquette) or concepts (physical laws, physiological effects of exercise). It is also used to discuss the application, analysis, synthesis or evaluation of ideas and concepts.

• *Role of the teacher*. Speaker

• *Role of the student*. Listener

• *Style*. Teacher-centered

• *Description*. A lecture is a verbal presentation of a body of knowledge. The material should be well organized and the mode of delivery clear and interesting. The speaker should be easily seen by all students, and the students should be comfortably seated within range of the speaker's voice or audio system.

• *Advantages*

1. A great deal of information may be presented to a very large audience in a single presentation, making very efficient use of time available.

2. The cognitive content of lecture later provides materials for evaluation purposes.

• *Disadvantages*

1. No interaction is allowed between students and teacher during lecture.

2. Students may not all be able to receive the information or assimilate the materials to the same degree.

• *Question for consideration*. Could the same amount of information be presented to the students as effectively through some other method of teaching? If so, which one(s)?

Verbal explanation

• *Purpose*. To explain the nature of a single concept or to analyze a single skill that has immediate relevancy to the activity of the class period

• *Role of the teacher*. Explainer

• *Role of the student*. Listener

• *Style*. Teacher-oriented

• *Description*. Verbal explanation provides information on a single problem or topic. It is similar to a lecture but briefer, and it addresses a particular point related to the day's activity. As with a lecture, the teacher should speak clearly and concisely from a position in view of all students. Students may be gathered informally around the teacher.

• *Advantages*

1. May be used in the middle of a game or drill to make additions or corrections during skill learning, to promote more acceptable social behaviors, or to provide additional essential cognitive information

2. May be initiated by the teacher or stem from questions or problems developing during the course of activity

• *Disadvantages*

1. All students may not need the verbal explanation, yet may have their activity interrupted.

2. Time may be lost from activity.

• *Question for consideration*. Could the students acquire the same knowledge, information, or ideas or find solutions to their problems through some other method that does not cut down on activity?

Demonstration

• *Purpose*. To present information through the visual channel by presenting psychomotor examples of activity. Auditory stimuli may also be involved.

• *Role of the teacher*. Demonstrator, planner, or commentator

• *Role of the student*. Receiver or listener

• *Style*. Teacher-centered

• *Description*. A demonstration is one of several types of audiovisual methods of presentation frequently used in physical education. The psychomotor skills and activities are performed by a single individual, by a group, or by a team while the remaining class members view the presentation. A verbal analysis may accompany the demonstration or be given immediately afterward, as in the case of diving or gymnastics, where quiet is necessary for the performer.

When presenting a demonstration certain important factors should be kept in mind.

1. The demonstration should be well planned so that all important points are firmly fixed in the teacher's mind.

2. The demonstration should be organized so that all students are able to see and hear well. If student

but also by developing positive self-concepts in a facilitative learning environment. The two major forms of feedback used in the classroom are verbal and non-verbal communication. Within each classification are categories that are important to practice methodology.

Non-verbal communications. Students sense a teacher's pleasure or displeasure through a variety of non-verbal or unspoken, signals. *Gestures,* such as clapped hands or a pointed finger, carry meanings of their own, as do *facial expressions,* a smile, a frown, a look of surprise. When a teacher *touches* a student with a friendly hug or a pat on the back, feelings of approval are transmitted, while shoves and pushes connote anger. Unspoken messages are also sent through *body language,* as seen in relaxed or tensed *postures* or projected in *vocal intonations,* such as harsh or gentle tones. Space utilization tells a story as well. Does the teacher dare to stand close to students or must he or she hide behind a desk or lectern?

Oftentimes nonverbal feedback paints a more accurate, more believable picture of the teacher's true feelings than the spoken word. The relationship established between student and teacher may well be the result of interpretations of these hidden messages rather than the verbal feedback. Mainstreamed students are particularly sensitive to nonverbal communications. According to Rankin and Weisenstein, handicapped students' perceptions of teachers are based 7% on verbal, 38% on vocal, and 55% on facial communications.

Verbal communication. Several types of feedback occur within this classification. *Simple feedback* may be found in short phrases such as "Keep it up" or "That's the way!" Ordinarily, such communications, unless accompanied by a student's name, have little meaning or value. Frequently students are confused as to the intended recipient or the specific action referred to. *Descriptive feedback* provides accurate, value-free information to the learner. Comments such as "The ball rebounded off the left post" or "The frisbee went over the net," tell the student the results of his or her action without qualitative analysis. Because knowledge of results has been found valuable for motor learning, this type of response can be effective. A third type, *corrective* or *evaluative/prescriptive* feedback, provides students not only with judgments

of their actions but also indicates specific ways to improve or develop effective motor skill. Suggestions, such as "Your back is too arched, John. You need to straighten your body, making it as long as possible," help correct faulty performance. Whether corrections are given by partners or teachers, it is important that they be accurate and well timed to be most effective. Comments offered while students are still underwater or out of breath may lose some of their value.

For best results all feedback should be appropriate, accurate, immediate, and personalized. In addition, where possible, it should carry with it *positive reinforcement* only of desired behaviors and *negative reinforcers* of actions considered undesirable. Research indicates that a positive learning environment produces greater results in the form of achievement. Therefore, teachers should strive to provide positive communications, whether verbal or nonverbal, to as many students as possible within a given lesson.

• *Advantages*

1. Practice-drill combined with reinforcement-feedback may be a challenging and interesting method of improving skill.

2. The controlled drill situation provides equal practice opportunities for all students.

• *Disadvantages*

1. Practice should be monitored to ensure correct performance of skills. It is sometimes difficult to monitor performances of many students in one class period.

2. Younger or less mature students may lose interest quickly when drilling over and over in the same pattern. Variations may be necessary.

• *Question for consideration.* On what factors does an instructor base a decision when balancing time allocations for game play and drill practice in a single class session?

Task (individualized approach)

• *Purpose.* To provide the student with an independent learning opportunity for acquisition of skill, for discovery of concepts, or for solving problems

• *Role of the teacher.* Task designer

• *Role of the student.* Task performer

• *Style.* Student-centered

• *Description.* The task method of teaching allows the individual student to work singly or in small groups toward the accomplishment of specific tasks designed for achievement of particular learning objectives. The tasks themselves are generally of two types: (1) performance tasks or (2) information plus performance tasks. They may be simple in nature, with structured tasks described on reading cards or posters, or they may be more elaborate packets or a series of study units in task form. Such study units would be information-plus-performance tasks, sometimes described as an individualized instructional packet, including activities for skill development plus outside reading requirements, audiovisual aids, and self-evaluation instruments. This packet method of teaching, according to recent research, has proven to be very effective.

Task teaching may be organized at learning centers and designed specifically for independent study by one or more students. Necessary materials should be available at the center, along with instructions for proceeding through the learning activities. Specific objectives to be achieved should be carefully outlined in sequential form, with evaluation measures incorporated therein (see behavioral objectives). The student at the learning center is responsible for his or her own rate of achievement and is free to progress to different learning centers or other activities after completing the prescribed tasks.

• *Advantages*

1. Tasks provide an independent, self-directed learning situation.

2. Students are free to progress at their own rate and according to their own ability levels.

• *Disadvantages*

1. The teacher needs to design tasks and learning packets appropriate for the widespread variation in ability levels and interests of adolescents.

2. Other measures of evaluation beside the self-evaluation tests may be necessary to check on progress of students.

• *Question for consideration*. To what extent should individualized learning experiences be balanced with team and large group activities in the total physical education curriculum?

Reciprocal teaching (partner-small group)

• *Purpose*. To provide independent learning experiences in all three domains of learning

• *Role of the teacher*. Facilitator

• *Role of the student*. Performer-helper

• *Style*. Student-centered

• *Description*. In the reciprocal method of teaching, the student has a greater responsibility for achievement of many learning objectives than is found in some of the previous methods. The word reciprocal, as it is used here, indicates that at least two partners work together to accomplish established goals. While one partner is performing or practicing the desired activity, the second partner watches and assists the learner by evaluating performance and offering suggestions. The teacher, as facilitator, encourages the second partner by assisting in the correction phase of the experience. In the case where a third person is involved in the group, this third member may help with equipment or scoring procedures and later change places (roles) with all the other partners.

It may be seen from this description that objectives within all three domains of learning are involved in this method of teaching. The partner who analyzes and evaluates is forced to use high level cognition. At the same time, sharing and working closely with a partner bring affective objectives into play. The psychomotor domain is utilized in the actual performance of tasks or activities.

• *Advantages*

1. Self-directed learning experiences are provided for all three learning domains.

2. The teacher is freed to guide the learning of all the small groups.

• *Disadvantages*

1. At first some students may feel strange in the role of evaluator and be hesitant about correcting a partner's performance.

2. It may be difficult for the teacher to hear all partners when they are acting in the role of evaluator.

• *Question for consideration*. In what ways might the problem-solving and guided discovery methods be combined with reciprocal types of teaching?

Guided discovery

• *Purpose*. To allow students opportunities to discover for themselves appropriate solutions to a given series of sequential problems

• *Role of the teacher*. Designer-sequencer

• *Role of the student*. Explorer-discoverer

- *Style*. Student-centered
- *Description*. The guided discovery method of teaching requires a student to seek solutions to sequentially designed problems that will lead to discovery of an appropriate result. In this method the teacher never provides an answer. Instead, the instructor designs a series of tasks on a given subject, such as facts, concepts, relationships, or movements, and through experimentation the student progresses step-by-step, finally arriving at a desirable result. This method of teaching has been receiving widespread acceptance since the time that movement education programs were introduced into the United States during the 1960s.
- *Advantages*
1. The student is allowed to discover the answers to given problems, thus achieving more permanent learning.
2. The teacher is freed to assist all students in the class.
- *Disadvantages*
1. Proper design of sequential problems is essential if students are to be guided to discover correct solutions. This is a difficult and time-consuming task for the teacher.
2. The process of discovery itself is time-consuming.
3. Some students may have difficulty in being motivated by this teaching method.
- *Question for consideration*. What about those students whose learning style is one that requires motivation by teacher-centered methods?

Problem solving
- *Purpose*. To provide students with independent opportunities to find for themselves one or more solutions to problems provided them in various learning experiences
  - *Role of the teacher*. Designer
  - *Role of the student*. Inventor
  - *Style*. Student-centered
- *Description*. The problem-solving method of teaching promotes student inquiry and exploration to find new solutions to problems that have no predetermined answers. It is the responsibility of the teacher to design tasks that will require these cognitive processes and force the student to discover from several possible solutions that which is most appropriate.

Many types of problems can be designed in physical education activities: for example, skill problems, concepts, limitations of movement, and variations of movement. Through the process of experimentation, the student (either singly or in a small group) arrives at possible solutions, all of which may be correct, providing they meet the limitations of the given problem. This method, like guided discovery, has been highly successful in movement education activities.
- *Advantages*
1. There are many opportunities for success in problem solving, thus contributing to a positive learning experience.
2. Students are responsible for directing their own learning experiences.
3. The teacher is freed to assist all students in the class.
- *Disadvantages*
1. Designing appropriate tasks without preconceived solutions is difficult and time consuming.
2. The process of problem solving is a time-consuming one for students.
- *Question for consideration*. How may the problem-solving method of teaching be adapted to suit those students who are less imaginative and creative than others?

Contract
- *Purpose*. To provide a self-directed learning experience in an area of personal interest to the student wherein the element of success is generally assured
  - *Role of the teacher*. Evaluator
  - *Role of the student*. Contractor
  - *Style*. Student-centered
- *Description*. A contract is a form of individualized study in which the student embarks on a self-directed learning experience. After previous agreement with the instructor, the student identifies specific objectives to be achieved in the contract. These objectives may be in one, two, or all three learning domains. Included in the contract are specific tasks associated with accomplishment of each objective, and a time format indicating dates for completion. The standards for evaluation are usually identified with each task so that a final grade is automatically derived.

Contracts may be one of three types, depending on

the role played by the student: (1) the student is required to fulfill all tasks, (2) the student is allowed to select from the total number of tasks a specific number of assignments to meet contract requirements, and (3) the student is allowed to design the total contract, including all tasks, assignments, and evaluation techniques. Content of the tasks may be derived from the cognitive, affective, and psychomotor domains.

• *Advantages*

1. The contract method allows the individual student to be responsible for his or her own learning experiences.

2. Measures of evaluation are previously detailed. Students generally know in advance exactly what is expected and what grades they will receive for their accomplishments. Therefore success is generally assured if qualitative and quantitative criteria are met.

3. Interaction between the teacher and student is usually an important ingredient, particularly in the planning stages of contracts.

4. The student is meeting personal needs and interest through individualization of contracts.

• *Disadvantage*. Implementation of this method is difficult.

• *Question for consideration*. Are there enough resources and materials available to meet the variety of needs and interests of students in the class?

Independent study

• *Purpose*. To provide an elective, self-directed learning opportunity (usually in upper secondary levels)

• *Role of the student*. Initiator-performer

• *Style*. Student-centered

• *Description*. Independent study offers alternative program opportunities to students who are eligible according to prerequisites of the curriculum. These alternatives frequently are offered in the eleventh and twelfth years of school after required academic and performance standards have been met.

There are many types of independent study programs offered within elective phases of physical education. Contracts, as discussed in the previous section, represent one type of independent offering. Another type of elective being experimented with in some states is called an out-of-school program, in which

students are allowed to attend activities sponsored by local Ys, JCCs, private classes, or similar programs. Courses taken as part of this alternative educational program are generally limited to one or two a year and only to cases where certain established criteria are met. Activities might include figure skating, judo, horseback riding, or special swimming classes. Participation in such a course of study might be used to meet *some* of the total physical education requirements in a secondary school curriculum but only with prior administrative approval and for very limited periods of time. Establishment of appropriate criteria is essential before the implementation of such a program to ensure quality instruction. The checklist below outlines some important factors that must be considered for proper administration of out-of-class programs.

Important, too, are decisions regarding the percentage of time that may be fulfilled by out-of-class programs. Some schools have found 10% or at most 20% to be reasonable allocations. In the same way, procedures for evaluation and grading must be predetermined before contracts with out-of-school personnel can be established. The problem of insurance coverage for accidents occurring on off-school property is particularly serious and must be carefully investigated before the introduction of these programs.

• *Advantages*

1. The student is allowed to pursue an area of study of particular interest to him or her.

2. The student is responsible for his or her own learning experience.

3. Program offerings of the secondary curriculum may be greatly expanded.

• *Disadvantages*

1. The responsibility for the instructional program is shifted to outside personnel. The teacher's responsibility becomes one of supervision and evaluation.

2. Record keeping needs to be carefully administered to cover both in-school and out-of-school requirements.

• *Question for consideration*. Should a school sanction programs taught by persons other than those on the regular teaching staff?

Question-answer

• *Purpose*. To stimulate cognitive processes in the students as well as to provide information on physical education activities

CHECKLIST FOR QUALITY AND CONTROL FOR ALTERNATIVE OUT-OF-SCHOOL PHYSICAL EDUCATION PROGRAMS*

	Completed(✔)
1. Proposed program meets standards and qualifications set by Commissioner's regulations in respect to alternatives allowed.	☐
2. Description of program contains	
a. Nature of program	☐
b. Who is eligible	☐
c. Credit plan	☐
d. Cost facts for pupils	☐
e. Liability aspects	☐
f. Transportation responsibilities	☐
g. Time demands	☐
h. Procedure for student to make arrangements with community agents	☐
i. Clarification of evaluation procedures	☐
j. Need for goal setting by pupil	☐
k. Nature of supervision of program	☐
l. Expectations for attendance	☐
m. Nature of final report at end of experience	☐
n. Range of activities and experiences accepted	☐
3. Pupils receive description of program before planning experience.	☐
4. Parents receive description of program before planning experience.	☐
5. Community participants receive description of program and final agreement between school and pupil.	☐
6. Form designed for agreement or contract between pupil and school contains time, credit, objectives and goals, starting and ending dates, evaluative procedures, signatures of pupil, community, instructor, authorized school personnel, and due date for final report	☐
7. Authorized physical education personnel confer with community personnel and clarify institutional expectations, pupil attendance, supervision, evaluation procedures.	☐
8. Authorized physical education personnel check qualifications of community instructors.	☐
9. Authorized physical education personnel make recommended visit to most frequently used instructional sites and make periodical phone calls.	☐
10. Form designed for pupil evaluation of out-of-school experience and situation	☐
11. Form designed for record keeping of out-of-school experience	☐
12. Time allotted for physical education personnel for supervision and evaluation of program	☐
13. Clerical services provided for record keeping	☐
14. Plans for periodical evaluation of program and procedure and subsequent revision if necessary	☐
15. Approval of administration of school and school board of program	☐
16. Periodic report on progress of program to the faculty administration and school board	☐
17. Occasional publicity releases describing program given to local media	☐

*Developed by Evelyn L. Schurr, State University of New York College at Brockport, Nov. 1975. Reprinted with permission.

Fig. 11-6. The dance—a popular physical education activity.

Courtesy Barbara Ann Chiles, Aledo, Ill.

• *Role of the teacher.* Questioner
• *Role of the student.* Respondent
• *Style.* Teacher-centered
• *Description.* Questioning may be a very effective method of teaching, particularly when the instructor is knowledgeable in the techniques of conducting a worthwhile question-and-answer session. This method may be utilized at the beginning of a class period as a means of imparting information or at the close of activities as an analyzing and synthesizing technique. There are several factors the teacher needs to keep in mind.

1. Questions should be clearly stated.

2. Questions should be stated so that all students can hear, and they should *all* feel that their responses are welcome.

3. Questions should be addressed to all students

and a specific respondent named after the question has been asked.

4. Questions should be asked only once, and sufficient time should be allowed for answering.

5. Questions should be interesting, pertinent, and challenging and should incorporate different levels of cognitive responses. For example, questions asking for simple *facts* would be categorized at the first level of cognitive development, requiring only a recall of knowledge. Higher levels of questions would require an *analysis* of skill, perhaps, or a discussion of differences in performance. Top level questions would demand the highest cognitive processes, such as synthesis and evaluation. To answer such a question, the student must use imagination and creativity. Then new ideas will result (see Bloom's taxonomy).

6. Question-and-answer periods should be carried on in a dignified atmosphere, with only relevant answers tolerated. Off-subject responses should be discouraged as often as necessary, and all appropriate answers should be treated with respect.

• *Advantages*

1. High-level thought processes are encouraged in well-designed question-answer sessions.

2. High-level affective responses may also be fostered as students learn to value and respect one another's responses.

• *Disadvantages*

1. Questions must be carefully planned and outlined, which may be a time-consuming task for teachers.

2. Questioning may take an extended period of time, thus limiting activity sessions.

• *Question for consideration.* Which method provides a more effective learning experience: a brief verbal explanation followed by a long practice or a long question period followed by a brief practice session?

Evaluation

• *Purpose.* To provide self-evaluation opportunities for students through various in-class and out-of-class experiences.

• *Role of the teacher.* Administrator, evaluator
• *Role of the student.* Respondent
• *Style.* Teacher-centered
• *Description.* Evaluation may be classified as a

method of teaching, inasmuch as the instructor, through careful selection of appropriate testing instruments, may afford students the opportunity to evaluate their own personal progress. In so doing, students come to know themselves and to view realistically their achievement of personal and course goals. Selected instruments may measure accomplishment of objectives in all three learning domains.

In the cognitive domain, evaluation instruments may be developed in the form of standardized or teacher-made tests or written reports on reading assignments. In the affective domain, the student may be brought to deeper self-awareness through values clarification techniques and sociometry. Psychomotor testing in the form of skills and fitness testing provides a clear indication of progress to the student in the third learning domain.

• *Advantages*

1. Tests may serve diagnostic, prescriptive, and final evaluation purposes.

2. The teacher is able to become better informed with student development in all three learning domains.

3. The student better understands his or her own development.

• *Disadvantages*

1. Testing takes time away from instructional periods.

2. In an individualized program the teacher will need to construct a variety of evaluation instruments, all of which will require correction and recording of results. With large classes this may be difficult.

• *Question for consideration*. What percentage of class time should be devoted to evaluation procedures during the course of a school year?

Media-assisted instruction

• *Purpose*. To supplement the learning process through interesting methods of presenting materials. This method relies on auditory and visual channels for sensory input.

• *Role of the teacher*. Arranger

• *Role of the student*. Listener/viewer

• *Style*. Teacher-centered

• *Description*. The use of teaching aids and materials supplements the learning process. Students who are not stimulated by other teaching methods may be motivated by films, charts, or other resource materials, and highly skilled students may broaden the scope of their knowledge by studying enrichment materials. Well-chosen teaching aids are of special value in teaching the culturally disadvantaged or other students whose formal experience with physical education has been limited. Acquaintance with the wealth of outside resources and information from which all members of a class may benefit is an invaluable aid in teaching, and the physical educator should make good use of such information.

In recent years considerable progress has been made in regard to teaching aids. The equipment and tools have been vastly improved and the resources and services greatly extended so that all schools may take advantage of these instructional materials.

• *Advantages*

1. They enable the student to better understand concepts and the performance of skills, events, and other experiences. The cliché, ''One picture is worth a thousand words,'' has merit. The use of a film, pictures, or other materials gives a clearer idea of the subject being taught, whether it concerns how a heart functions or how to perfect a golf swing.

2. They help to provide variety to teaching. There is increased motivation and attention span, and the subject matter of a course is much more exciting when audiovisual aids are used in addition to other teaching techniques.

3. They increase student motivation. To see a game played, a skill performed, or an experiment conducted before their eyes in clear understandable form helps motivate students to engage in a game, perform a skill more effectively, or want to know more about the relationship of exercise to health. This is particularly true in video replay, for example, where students can actually see how they perform a skill and then compare this performance to the ideal.

4. They provide for an extension of what can normally be taught in a classroom, gymnasium, swimming pool, or playground. Audiovisual aids enable the student to experience other countries and sports events in other parts of the United States. All of these are important to both physical education and the general instructional program.

5. They provide a historical reference for the field

of physical education. Outstanding events in sports and physical education that have occurred in past years can be brought to life before the student's eyes. In this way the student obtains a better understanding of how physical education plays an important role in American society and in other cultures of the world.

• *Disadvantages*

1. Necessary equipment is expensive and bothersome to assemble or repair.

2. Films may become outdated.

3. There is little interaction between student and teacher.

4. The teacher may become overly dependent on these aids.

• *Questions for consideration.* Is a performance by an expert on film of greater value than a live demonstration by peers or teacher?

Teaching aids and materials

When selecting audiovisual aids or other resources and materials, the teacher of physical education should consider certain principles that make utilization of these aids effective and valuable. The similarity between these principles and those suggested in other methods of teaching should be noted, for the aim in each case is to create a worthwhile learning situation.

• *Materials should be carefully selected and screened.* The teacher should preview the materials to make sure they are appropriate for the unit and age level of the students and that they present information in an interesting and stimulating manner.

• *Proper preparation of materials should be made.* The teacher should check all necessary equipment for the presentation of materials to make sure that it is in operating condition. Record players and movie projectors, in particular, need to be carefully inspected before they are used.

• *The presentation of materials should be planned and integrated into the lesson.* Students should be properly introduced to the materials so that they know what to expect and so that they understand their relationship to the unit of study.

• *Materials should be presented to the students in a proper learning situation.* Students should be located so that all may hear, see, and learn from the material. They should realize that they will be held responsible for the information being presented.

• *Materials should be varied.* Different types of materials should be chosen for presentation to stimulate the varying interests of the students. A teacher using films or slide films exclusively does not take full advantage of supplementary materials.

• *Use of supplementary materials should be limited.* The teacher should place a reasonable limit on the use of extra teaching materials to maintain a balance between supplementary and regular instructional materials.

• *Care should be taken to avoid excessive expenses.* A reasonable part of the instructional budget should be set aside for supplementary materials—in accordance with the emphasis placed on this phase of the teaching program.

• *Records and evaluations of materials should be maintained.* All supplementary materials should be carefully evaluated and records kept on file for future reference. This should save the unnecessary expense of reordering or duplicating materials and in maintaining outdated materials. By following these principles the teacher is able to supplement learning with materials that are valuable and interesting to the students.

A recent study by one of Bucher's students concerns current practices and trends in the use of audiovisual media for the teaching of motor skills in professional physical education programs. This study has implications for secondary school physical education programs in that it reveals the number of responding schools that offer or require a course in audiovisual media and techniques in their professional preparing programs.

The researcher developed and mailed a questionnaire that was returned by 63 physical education directors in a variety of colleges and universities. Of these respondents, five required a course in audiovisual media and techniques, and 35 offered such a course on an elective basis. A total of 54 of the individuals answering the questionnaire indicated that they felt audiovisual media serve as a valuable supplement to instruction in the learning of motor skills.

The study also found that the use of videotaping as

an instructional tool is increasing. The audiovisual media used with the most frequency by the respondents in this study were, in order of frequency, 16-mm and 8-mm films, loop films, cartridge films, chalkboards, wall charts, slide films, filmstrips, and instructional television.

On the pages that follow, six categories of materials and resources are discussed in terms of their purposes, problems, and specific sources. Suggestions are listed under *reading materials, audiovisual aids, special aids, professional personnel, community activities,* and *clinics.* Although these are recent and fairly inclusive listings, new types of materials are always being placed on the market. Teachers should be on the lookout for the very latest items available as listed in journals, catalogs, and advertisements.

READING MATERIALS

• *Purposes.* To provide up-to-date information and enrichment materials on all aspects of the program

• *Problems.* To keep track of materials and assignments. A checkout system should be developed so that the teacher knows where materials may be located. In addition, some method of annotating particularly beneficial articles or resources should be devised, thus simplifying assignments.

• *Types*

1. Textbook

Bucher, C.A.: *Physical Education for Life,* New York, 1969, McGraw-Hill Book Co.

This text for high school boys and girls provides information about physique, posture, physical skills, physical fitness, safety and first aid, and the body in motion. The book also includes basic instruction about 20 different sports and activities. Additional information is provided on the purchase and care of equipment. The textbook is informative and motivating and is an excellent means of giving high school students a rich physical education experience.

2. Magazines (research, historical, educational, informational, or supplementary)

All-American Athlete, Dept. J, 801 Palisade Ave., Union City, N.J. 07087

Athletic Journal, Athletic Journal Publishing Co., 1719 Howard St., Evanston, Ill. 60202

The Coach, Lowe and Campbell Athletic Goods, 1511 Baltimore Ave., Kansas City, Mo. 64108

Coach and Athlete, 1421 Mayon St., N.E., Atlanta, Ga. 31324

Dance Magazine, 268 West 47th St., New York, N.Y. 10036

Journal of Health, Physical Education, Recreation, and Dance, 1900 Association Ave., Reston, Va. 22091

Research Quarterly, 1900 Association Ave., Reston, Va. 22091

Scholastic Coach, Scholastic Magazine, Inc., 50 West 44th St., New York, N.Y. 10036

U.S. Gymnast Magazine, P.O. Box 53, Iowa City, Iowa 52240

3. Booklets, pamphlets, and catalogs (educational and supplemental information about health, safety, and related areas)

American Alliance for Health, Physical Education, Recreation, and Dance, 1900 Association Ave., Reston, Va. 22091

American School and University, Product Catalog File, American School Publishing Co., 470 Fourth Ave., New York, N.Y. 10016

The Athletic Institute, 200 Castlewood Drive, North Palm Beach, Fla. 33408

American Medical Association, 535 N. Dearborn St., Chicago, Ill. 60610

Metropolitan Life Insurance Co., 1 Madison Ave., New York, N.Y. 10010

National Dairy Council, 111 N. Canal St., Chicago, Ill. 60606

Science Research Associates, 259 E. Erie, Chicago, Ill. 60611

AUDIOVISUAL AIDS

• *Purposes.* To give information to a large group at one time in such areas as skill break-downs, game play, techniques and rules of sports, and enrichment materials and to provide musical or other rhythmical accompaniment

• *Problems.* To keep an accurate and up-to-date file on current materials, with evaluative suggestions. Individual file cards are helpful for this purpose. Large school systems and new schools generally maintain departments for audiovisual instruction, with personnel specifically hired for the maintenance, distribution, selection, and follow-up of all equipment and materials in this area.

• *Types*

1. Motion pictures. Motion pictures for use in physical education classes are available in every area. They may be purchased in color or black and white or rented for nominal fees. Catalogs issued by film companies contain listings of films available for rental or purchase and generally include brief descriptions of the films themselves to help the teacher in making selections.

Guides are also available for filmstrips and for tapes, scripts, and transcriptions.

2. Slide films. Slide films—both sound and silent—have been developed for rental and purchase.

A source of full-color slide films is The Athletic Institute, 200 Castlewood Drive, North Palm Beach, Fla. 33408. To rent their slide films, contact must be made with Ideal Pictures, Inc. at one of their regional offices:

102 West 25th St., Baltimore, Md. 21218

58 E. South Water St., Chicago, Ill. 60601

1840 Alcatraz Ave., Berkeley, Calif. 94703

Slide films are available in sports, including beginning archery, beginning badminton, beginning baseball, beginning bowling, campcraft, beginning fencing, beginning golf, beginning table tennis, gymnastics, beginning soccer, beginning softball, swimming, beginning tennis, track and field, beginning volleyball, and beginning wrestling, plus individual recreational sports such as fishing, ice skating, skiing, and judo. Excellent booklets accompany each of these slide films.

3. Learning loops. Several 8-mm learning loops may be purchased from the Athletic Institute. An 8-mm loop film projector is also available directly from the Institute. These loops are excellent for specific instruction in skills performance. They are available in each individual event in track and field for men, track and field for women, gymnastics, and tennis.

4. Loop movies. Loop movies consist of several 16-mm loops spliced together, end to end, for continuous projection. They are available for purchase

from Champions on Film, 3666 South State St., Ann Arbor, Mich. 48104. These films cover such subjects as basketball, wrestling, swimming, baseball, golf, tennis, trampoline, and track.

5. Television. Although educational television (ETV) has widespread appeal at various age levels in all phases of the curriculum, its use as a teaching technique in physical education is still rather limited.

Physical educators agree that the full potential of television has not been reached and recognize that recent developments in physical education, such as movement efficiency and sensory-perceptual experiences, contain concepts adaptable to television production.

6. Videotape. Videotapes are being used more frequently in many educational endeavors and are recognized as an invaluable teaching aid in physical education activities. Because of its adaptability, this special type of recording device may be used in the following ways:

a. To videotape sports performances for later study of still frames for closer analysis of action

b. To supervise several outdoor play areas from one location through a closed-circuit television monitoring device

c. To provide objective evaluation of an individual performance, such as diving or trampolining, through instant replay

d. To build up a school library of tapes for specific instructional purposes at later dates

These are only a few of the instructional possibilities of this versatile teaching tool. Its popularity will continue to increase because of its flexibility, the ease with which it may be operated, and its effectiveness. Current problems caused by tapes that fit improperly in some machines are being solved.

7. Phonographs and audiotape recorders. For extensive use in physical education classes, phonographs and audiotape recorders must be durable, portable, and provided with discrete volume controls. Transportation and storage of this valuable equipment may be a problem if safe closet space is not available relatively near the gymnasium.

8. Records (available in all speeds, some in un-

breakable nylon materials, for teaching all rhythmic activities)

9. Drum (dance drum, bongo drum, and similar percussive devices). Drums are used extensively to provide rhythmical measures for creative activities. They should be kept in a dry place, for extreme dampness causes loss of tone. In such instances, placing the drum on a radiator for a few minutes restores tautness.

SPECIAL AIDS

• *Purposes*. To provide graphic, illustrative material to students in an interesting and educational manner

• *Problems*. To find time to utilize displays effectively, to change displays for added interest, and to keep up-to-date with current events. Student assistants should be utilized to prepare and maintain the displays.

• *Types*

1. Charts, diagrams, and photographic materials (for materials in several different sports)

   National Association for Girls' and Women's Sports, American Alliance for Health, Physical Education, Recreation, and Dance, 1900 Association Dr., Reston, Va. 22091

   Nissen Corp., 930 27th Ave., S.W., Cedar Rapids, Iowa 52416

2. Bulletin boards and chalkboards (cork or beaver board, stationary or movable). These are excellent teaching devices for educational and motivational purposes. They should be colorful, interesting, neat, clear, uncluttered, and changed often. School administrators generally provide these materials.

3. Erasable boards (blank-surfaced boards suitable for specific sports, such as soccer, football, or basketball, or all-purpose types of boards, suitable for all sports). These boards are excellent teaching devices for team sports. Although the initial expense ($12.95 to $20.00) seems rather expensive, the lasting value of this item makes it a worthwhile investment.

PROFESSIONAL PERSONNEL

• *Purposes*. To provide an interesting incentive to students by having a visiting professional demonstrate, teach, or discuss a sports or related experience

• *Problems*. To plan and organize for thorough effectiveness and safety. Preplanning with the guest is essential, and preparation with students allows them to gain more fully from the experience.

• *Types*. The directors and personnel of professional organizations such as the National Golf Foundation, United States Lawn Tennis Association, and Amateur Athletic Association

COMMUNITY ACTIVITIES

• *Purposes*. To promote good public relations with the community and to provide additional activities for student participation

• *Problems*. To find time to plan and organize carefully the various details of the activities with community leaders

• *Types*. Recreational activities (tennis meets), PTO-sponsored special events and programs, benefit athletic demonstrations

CLINICS

• *Purposes*. To provide additional and valuable learning experiences to students attending these clinics as participants or observers. Taking an honor team, a leaders' club, or an entire class to a special program of this type offers information and an opportunity for appreciation that the students will never forget because of the specialized nature of the experience.

• *Problems*. Planning, organizing transportation, obtaining parental permission, and providing supervision of the students. In many schools definite procedures for taking students on field trips are outlined, and they should be carefully followed.

• *Types*. Special games and programs put on by visiting professional clubs (basketball or football teams), special clinics sponsored by local or state teaching organizations, traveling college groups and community organizations

Self-assessment tests

These tests are designed to assist students in determining if material and competencies presented in this chapter have been mastered.

1. Draw a diagram of the components of the information-processing theory of learning. Compare this with a diagram of the stimulus-response theory.

2. Given two columns headed "internal conditions" and

"external conditions," list those factors and subfactors that affect the learning environment.

3. Select a psychomotor skill (underhand pitching) and explain how the principle of transfer affects learning this skill.

4. Describe a minimum of five different teacher roles, relating them to teaching methodology, including a description of the responsibilities of the teacher and student in each example.

5. Cite one advantage and one disadvantage to the following teaching methods:
   a. Contract   e. Reciprocal
   b. Lecture   f. Evaluation
   c. Demonstration   g. Task
   d. Audiovisual   h. Problem solving

6. You are assigned a group of beginning swimmers who have expressed a desire to learn water polo. Would you incorporate this activity when planning their learning experiences? In what ways?

Points to remember

1. Selection of teaching methods depends on many factors internal and external to the teaching environment and the learner.

2. Two important principles of teaching involve progressing from known to unknown material and introducing material first in its entirety and then part by part.

3. There are many effective methods of presenting information to learners, each having its own unique set of advantages and disadvantages.

4. Acquisition of motor skills is dependent on a variety of factors requiring consideration for instruction.

5. Individualized methods of instruction allocate responsibility for learning to the student and allow the teacher freedom to facilitate the teaching process.

6. An understanding of learning theories should lay the foundations for planning effective instructional activities.

Problems to think through

1. Why is there no single best method for the teaching of physical education?

2. Which teaching methods would probably be more effective with students who have poorly developed motor coordination?

3. Which methods would probably be more effective with highly skilled boys and girls?

4. To what extent should students be allowed choices in the selection of activities?

5. To what extent should students be allowed to elect independent study in physical education?

Case study for analysis

You have accepted a teaching position in a small high school where there is only one other physical education teacher for all four high school grade levels. This teacher has been on the faculty for many years and may best be described as the "commander" or "drill sergeant" type of teacher. How would you effectively go about incorporating newer teaching methodology in this situation without causing friction between the two of you?

Exercises for review

1. What is teaching?

2. What environmental factors enhance the teaching process?

3. What are the values of individualized learning experiences?

4. Why should a teacher be familiar with a variety of teaching methods?

Selected readings

American Association for Health, Physical Education and Recreation: Guidelines for secondary school physical education, Washington, D.C., 1970, AAHPER.

American Association for Health, Physical Education, and Recreation: Physical education for high school students, ed. 3, Washington, D.C., 1982, AAHPERD.

American Association for Health, Physical Education, and Recreation: The new physical education, Journal of Health, Physical Education and Recreation, 42:24-39, Sept. 1971.

American Association for Health, Physical Education and Recreation: Personalized learning in physical education, Washington, D.C., 1976, AAHPER.

Heitmann, H.M., and Kneer, M.E.: Physical education instructional techniques: an individualized humanistic approach, Englewood Cliffs, N.J. 1976, Prentice-Hall, Inc.

Kalakian, L., and Goldman, M.: Introduction to physical education; a humanistic perception, Boston, 1976, Allyn & Bacon, Inc.

Locke, L.F., and Jensen, M.: Pre-packaged sports skills instruction: a review of selected research, Journal of Health, Physical Education and Recreation 42:7, 57-59, Sept. 1971.

Mosston, M.: Teaching physical education, Columbus, Ohio, 1981, Charles E. Merrill Publishing Co.

Rankin, K.D. and Weisenstein, G.R.: Communicating nonverbally with mainstreaming, Quest 31(2):294-301, 1979.

Siedentop, D.: Developing teaching skills in physical education, Boston, 1976, Houghton Mifflin Co.

Shulman, L.S., and Keisler, E.R., editors: Learning by discovery: a critical appraisal, Chicago, 1966, Rand McNally & Co.

Willgoose, C.E.: The curriculum in physical education, ed. 3, Englewood Cliffs, N.J., 1979, Prentice-Hall, Inc.

12

Teaching for mastery

Instructional objectives and competencies to be achieved

After reading this chapter the student should be able to

1. Differentiate between the Carroll and Bloom models for mastery learning
2. Identify and explain the six components of mastery learning strategy
3. Delineate six or more advantages and disadvantages of mastery learning
4. Discuss research findings related to mastery learning
5. Outline implementation procedures for mastery learning for administrators and teachers in physical education
6. Define and discuss active learning time as it relates to achievement

During the last two decades a "new" learning theory has emerged in public education. Called "mastery learning theory," this strategy for teaching incorporates many of the earlier, accepted components of learning theory but organizes them into what has become recognized as an effective instructional system.

Definition and development

Mastery learning has been variously identified as a "theory," a "method," a "technique," "an instructional system," "a model," and "a process." Most frequently it is labeled an instructional strategy, one which originated from the Model of School Learning by John Carroll in the early 1960s. Carroll asserted that when given appropriate amounts of *time,* all students could learn up to *mastery* levels. In his conceptual model, *aptitude* for learning is essentially equated with *rate* or *time* needed for learning to take place, thus acknowledging differences between slow and fast learners. He further stated that the amount of time necessary for learning could be reduced if the quality of instruction were adapted to meet individual student needs. According to Carroll's theory, degree or amount of learning is a function (f) of the time spent to learn in relation to time needed to learn, symbolized in the formula

$$\text{Degree of learning} = f\ \frac{\text{Time spent to learn}}{\text{Time needed to learn}}$$

By substituting sample figures in the above model, it can readily be understood that if a student is allowed only 7 of the 10 minutes that he or she needs to learn material, he or she will achieve only a 70% level of mastery.

Benjamin Bloom of the University of Chicago expanded Carroll's conceptual model by suggesting that if appropriate conditions before and during learning are provided, high levels of mastery will result—in addition to other affective outcomes. Bloom was taking into account the role of affective characteristics (motivation, interest, esteem) and cognitive characteristics (readiness and aptitude) in the learning process, along with quality in the instructional environment. He added to Carroll's strategy a system of *procedures* for enhancing the quality of instruction by increasing student involvement and eventually reducing individual differences. The critical factor to be underscored in mastery learning theory is *active learning time* (ALT). When educators accept the philosophy that, given appropriate conditions and sufficient amounts of time, all students can achieve high levels of mastery, educators are recognizing that active student *involvement* in learning is the key to achievement.

Components of mastery learning

Bloom's adaptation of Carroll's model requires systematic implementation of important procedures in

Fig. 12-1. Learning a difficult dance movement.

Courtesy Barbara Ann Chiles, Aledo, Ill.

order to provide for high levels of mastery learning. He organizes six essential components into an instructional system that acknowledges individual differences, promotes quality instruction, and provides the variations in time necessary to learn. Taken singly, each component has long been recognized as an essential factor in the educational process. It is the structuring of these essentials into an organized process that is the essence of this new approach to learning.

Step one: the writing of specific objectives. The logical first step in curricular design is the establishment of instructional objectives. In mastery learning it is essential that teachers identify, as part of each unit objective, minimum passing levels that define for the student what constitutes mastery. According to research investigations of the mastery learning approach, between 80% and 95% of students can achieve 80% of material. Therefore criteria can be established at high levels in this initial step.

Step two: preassessment. Following the establishment of unit objectives, the teacher preassesses students to determine entry levels. This may be done

through reviewing past performances, administering tests, observing, or using other forms of teacher judgment or evaluation. The significance of this step relates to Bloom's insistence that prior learning of appropriate skills and knowledge—"readiness"—must be established for subsequent mastery to higher levels of attainment (see also Thorndike's Law of Readiness).

Step three: Initial instruction. Instruction within the mastery learning system may take many forms. At this point (early in the unit), all students are proceeding simultaneously toward mastery of established objectives. The teacher may use any one of a variety of teaching methods or perhaps a combination of methods, as appropriate.

Step four: diagnostic assessment. This is an extremely important step in mastery learning. Assessment at this midpoint in the unit tells the teacher how well the instructional system is working and how well the students are progressing toward mastery. This assessment, also known as formative evaluation, should evaluate the degree of mastery of established criteria for the unit. It should *not* be graded. Students should know that scores on this evaluation will not be included in any final marking for the unit. Bloom insisted on this procedure, pointing out the need for students to feel comfortable in a nonthreatening test situation in order to determine accurate levels of mastery which, in turn, provide the basis for grouping in the next phase of the process.

Step five: prescription. Based on test results in step four, students are grouped into one of the following areas.

a. *Enrichment.* For those students who have already achieved mastery levels, enrichment materials and activities related to the skills and knowledges of the unit under study are provided.

b. *Remediation.* Students requiring more time are now allowed a second chance to achieve mastery levels. During this phase it is essential that the teacher accurately analyze student deficiencies, locating areas of weakness and offering appropriate corrective feedback. Here again Bloom insisted that the *needs* of students and their individualized learning styles must be recognized. For this phase of the process, teachers prepare a variety of *alternative* instructional activities

Fig. 12-2. Learning to climb trees requires strength.

Courtesy Jerry Taylor.

and materials that acknowledge student differences. Students work independently in small groups, alone or with partners, to master those facets of the unit that were originally difficult for them. This second chance gives them additional time, according to their needs.

c. *Relocation*. For those few students whose diagnostic assessment shows excessive difficulties, there may be a need for teachers to modify objectives or to select alternative (related) unit objectives for which the student shows evidence of prerequisite skills and interest. Again, individualized instructional modules are essential.

Step six: postassessment. In this last phase of mastery learning the teacher administers final tests or summative evaluations to all students at the conclusion of the unit. At this point in the process, it is hoped that 80% to 95% of the students will have achieved mastery levels and therefore will be ready to move on to the next unit of study. The length of any given unit may be five to six weeks, or it may be broken down

into smaller instructional subunits. As new units or work are introduced, the overall process is repeated.

It should be evident from this brief summary of the six-step system that it is essentially an individualized method of instruction, allowing students a second (or more) chance to achieve mastery.

Research on mastery learning

During the decade of the 1970s, mastery learning strategies were implemented in the teaching of sciences, mathematics, and languages, particularly at the elementary school level. In general, it was found that mastery learning enables at least 80% of the students to reach a level of attainment that fewer than 20% of the students attain under nonmastery. Measures of the time-cost factor showed only 10% to 20% additional time was necessary to implement mastery learning procedures, a figure that steadily decreased as corrective feedback methods improved. In Johnson City,

N.Y., where mastery learning has been in use for 10 years, there has been remarkable improvement shown in test scores on the Pupil Evaluation Program. In large cities, such as Chicago and Denver, where large-scale projects have been instituted, test scores have also been raised, along with increased attendance and improved student and teacher morale.

Torshen (1977) reported on the results of some 40 studies of mastery learning, concluding that there were "marked effects" on students' cognitive and affective development as well as their learning rates. Specific cognitive consequences, when all six components of mastery learning were utilized, included higher levels of performance on objective-referenced posttests, increased instructional time spent in active learning, and greater retention among high mastery students. In terms of affective consequences, the teachers indicated that they felt they did a better job of teaching, had a better knowledge of the subject, and, most importantly had higher expectations of students. This last point is particularly significant in light of research on teacher expectations of students, which shows that students, in general, fulfill those expectations, whether low or high. The teacher who perceives that a particular student will do poorly will, in most cases, view his or her performance as below standard. Under mastery learning, where teachers expect high levels of achievement, these expectations tend to be met.

Research reveals that students under a mastery learning approach show more favorable attitudes toward instruction, devote more time to their studies, and withdraw from school less frequently. A positive self-concept as well as a positive school cycle is established, and both continue to affect achievement. Little evidence has been collected on the parents' perceptions of mastery learning although one questionnaire showed that 70% to 80% of the parents responded positively to their child's elementary schooling.

Advantages of mastery learning

To date, advantages of mastery learning, from the students' point of view, include
1. Improved levels of mastery
2. Improved retention
3. Increased levels of involvement

4. Self-paced learning
5. Immediate feedback
6. Heightened teacher expectations
7. Improved attitudes toward school
8. Improved self-concepts
9. Improved learning habits
10. Improved grades

While the contribution of each of these advantages to learning is important, their synthesis into a positive cycle of learning should be emphasized. Because of its particular significance to learning and because of recent research in this area, further discussion of increased levels of involvement follows later in the chapter.

From the teacher's point of view, mastery learning incorporates a large number of those teaching skills essential for student achievement. According to Torshen, the following nine teaching variables are recognized in a mastery learning approach:
1. Clarity of teacher's presentation
2. Variety of teacher-initiated activity
3. Enthusiasm of teacher
4. Teacher emphasis on learning and achievement
5. Avoidance of extreme criticism
6. Positive responses to students
7. Student opportunity to learn criterion material
8. Use of structuring comments by teachers
9. Use of multiple levels of questions in cognitive discourse

For administrators faced with parental concerns about accountability, the structured mastery learning approach provides many positive solutions. The coordination of curricula into logical, sequential units, combined with cooperation of teachers for the development of instructional materials, leads to much stronger, more unified educational outcomes. To be effective, however, administrators must provide support to faculty in terms of planning and development time as well as providing testing instruments and assessment opportunities.

Disadvantages of mastery learning

Opponents of the mastery learning approach have identified several disadvantages to its use.
1. Extra time and effort are needed to prepare materials for instruction.

A   B   C   D

Fig. 12-3. The tennis serve.

From Armbruster, D.A., Musker, F.F., and Mood, D.: Sports and recreational activities for men and women, ed. 7, St. Louis, 1979, The C.V. Mosby Co.

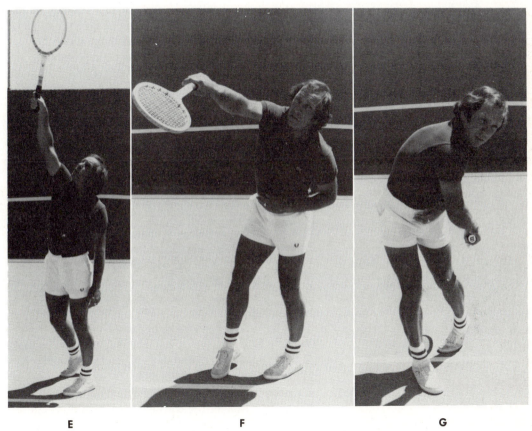

E   F   G

Fig. 12-4. High school girls participating in physical education activity at University School of Nashville, Nashville, Tenn.

2. The cost of assessment instruments and materials may be unreasonable.
3. Mastery levels are difficult to determine.
4. Students may not be exposed to all activities.
5. Appropriate assessment tools may not be available.
6. Some students may not respond well to this strategy.
7. All subject areas may not be suitable for this treatment.
8. While a larger portion of the class may achieve mastery, those in the top 20% may be unjustifiably restrained while waiting for classmates to catch up.
9. Students who fail to meet mastery levels become isolates.
10. There are too few ready-made materials available for this approach.

Critics on both sides of the question agree that mastery learning is no panacea for all educational problems. Obviously, more research is needed, they say, but, with the positive results recorded so far, this method certainly warrants further investigation.

Implications for physical education

At the present time very little research has been conducted on mastery learning in physical education. The work of Annarino in curriculum development and of Siedentop in Active Learning Time research shows evidence of introducing components of its structure into programs. Bloom has indicated that psychomotor tasks should be easy to define according to mastery learning strategy but adds that evidence of this application is not readily found in the literature.

Full implementation of mastery learning strategy into physical education would require coordinated efforts on the part of administrators and faculty within a school district. After recognizing its value in the instructional process, administrators would have to provide teachers with planning time, materials, assessment instruments, and means for program evaluation. Teachers would then have to work together to produce organized sequential units of instruction, using a variety of alternative instructional materials and activities found within the physical education curriculum. Answers to hard questions would need to be found: Should all students experience all movement forms? What criteria should the physically educated secondary student meet? What specific skills, attitudes, and knowledge should a graduate of high school acquire?

By organizing instructional units according to identified outcomes, and including the six components of mastery learning strategy, students should achieve an appropriate level of skills and knowledge suitable for a lifetime of satisfying activity.

Role of the teacher. Once procedures for mastery learning units have been designed, the role of the teacher is to promote and foster active learning on the part of each student. Matching activities and tasks to the motivations and needs of the individual takes careful organization and grouping. Accurate diagnostic assessment and corrective feedback are key elements to successful achievement of objectives. Therefore the observational and analytical skills of the teacher are critical. If each lesson is to be truly individualized, the teacher must interact with every student to the greatest extent possible.

Role of the student. In mastery learning, the school is responsible for providing a quality instructional en-

Fig. 12-5. Racquetball is becoming a popular sport.

Courtesy State University College of Arts
and Science, Potsdam, N.Y.

vironment through appropriate instructional materials and media, while the student is responsible for individual achievement of designated objectives. Work is independently accomplished, self-paced, and, most importantly, available learning time is effectively used—that is, the student is actively involved in learning.

ACTIVE LEARNING TIME (ALT)

Bloom's adaptation of Carroll's model stresses the importance of student involvement in the learning process for mastery levels to be attained. True involvement is recognizable in either overt (observable) or covert (unobservable) learning behaviors and may be measured in three ways:

1. Length of time needed for completion of task (for example, 30 minutes)
2. Time spent on the task in relation to time available (for example, 20 out of 30 minutes)
3. Number of trials on given task (for example, 7 out of 10 attempts)

Siedentop's research in ALT indicates that students spend only 15% of available class time actively involved in learning. The problem for the teacher, then, is to increase to the greatest extent possible the ALT of individuals as well as the class group.

Logical instructional procedures maximize effective use of time: teachers should be adequately prepared for class; give clear, concise instructions; and arrange groups appropriately to facilitate student-teacher interactions. Also vital are fluid transitions between activities that are selected for maximum participation.

It should be pointed out that results of this increased student involvement play a significant role in Bloom's theory. He holds that improvements in the conditions of learning bring changes in those cognitive and affective entry behaviors mentioned earlier in his model—that is, motivation, esteem, and aptitude for learning. These changes, in turn, decrease learning times necessary for mastery, thus improving the learning rate and further promoting a positive learning cycle. Eventually, according to Bloom, individual differences among students gradually diminish, and the well-known bell-shaped curve, commonly used in grading, would no longer be appropriate in evaluating

learned behavior. All or nearly all students would achieve mastery. Implications for grading and evaluation systems in schools are indeed significant.

Self-assessment tests

These tests are designed to assist students in determining if material and competencies presented in this chapter have been mastered.

1. Compare the advantages and disadvantages of mastery learning from the point of view of the student. Develop a position statement based on your comparison.
2. Develop a unit of study following mastery learning procedures.
3. Determine three organizational patterns for instruction that are consistent with mastery learning theory.
4. Observe an activity class. Determine active learning time of one participant.
5. List those conditions for learning that might enhance cognitive and affective behaviors.

Points to remember

1. According to mastery learning theory, learning is a function of opportunity to learn in relation to time needed to learn.
2. For mastery learning to be effective, all six components should be implemented.
3. Aptitude for learning is no longer thought to be predicated on intelligence but is instead determined by learning rate.
4. Individualized instructional materials provide the basis for mastery learning.
5. School administrators play an extremely responsible role in fostering mastery learning within the school.

Problems to think through

1. Is mastery learning strategy appropriate for extremely large classes? Athletic teams?
2. Will coeducational groups be able to work effectively together to achieve unit objectives?
3. In what ways can mastery learning strategy change aptitude for learning?
4. When a student fails in a mastery learning program, what subsequent procedure(s) should the teacher follow?

Case study for analysis

Physical education teachers in a large public school district were skeptical about the implementation of mastery learning strategies in physical education. The administration suggested pilot testing of mastery procedures over one semester to a selected group of classes. What procedures would you and your colleagues follow to implement the administration's ideas? What criteria would you establish for evaluation?

Exercises for review

1. Why does Carroll equate aptitude for learning with rate or time for learning?
2. Why does Bloom insist that formative evaluation should not be graded?
3. Diagram a "positive cycle of learning."
4. Compare the role of the teacher in a mastery learning classroom with that of one of your own past teachers.
5. What kind of student might have difficulty with a mastery learning approach to activity?

Selected readings

Annarino, A.A.: Instructional strategies and activities for elementary and middle schools, The Physical Educator **36**(3):134-138, 1979.

Annarino, A.A.: Accountability—an instructional model for secondary physical education, Journal of Health, Physical Education, Recreation, and Dance **52**(3):55-56, 1981.

Annarino, A.A., Cowell, C.C., and Hazelton, H.W.: Curriculum theory and design in physical education, ed. 2, St. Louis, 1980, The C.V. Mosby Co.

Aufderheide, S.K., Knowles, C.J., and McKenzie, T.: Individualized teaching strategies and learning time: implications for mainstreaming, The Physical Educator **38**(1):20-25, 1981.

Block, J.H., editor: Mastery learning—theory and practice, New York, 1971, Holt, Rinehart & Winston.

Bloom, B.S.: Human characteristics and school learning, New York, 1976, McGraw-Hill Book Co.

Bloom, B.S.: Changes in evaluation methods. In Glaser, R., editor: Research and development and school change, Hillsdale, N.J., 1978, Lawrence Erlbaum Associates, Publishers.

Dolan, L.: The status of mastery learning research and practice, The Administrators Notebook (Midwest Administrators Center: The University of Chicago) **34**(3):1-4, 1978.

Frederick, W.C., and Walberg, H.J.: Learning as a function of time, Journal of Educational Research **73**(4):183-194, 1980.

Gettinger, M., and White, M.A.: Which is the stronger correlate of school learning? Time to learn or measured intelligence? Journal of Educational Psychology **71**(4):405-412, 1979.

Knowles, C.: Concerns of teachers about implementing individualized instruction in the physical education setting, Research Quarterly for Exercise and Sport **52**(1):48-57, 1981.

Levin, T., and Long, R.: Effective instruction, Alexandria, Va., 1981, Association for Supervision and Curriculum Development.

Martinek, T.J.: Pygmalion in the gym: a model for the communication of teacher expectations in physical education, Research Quarterly for Exercise and Sport **52**(1):58-67, 1981.

Siedentop, D.: Physical education curriculum, an analysis of the past, Journal of Health, Physical Education, Recreation, and Dance **51**(7):40-41, 50, 1980.

Torshen, K.P.: The mastery approach to competency: based education, New York, Ltd. 1977, Academic Press.

13

Learning outcomes—end results of the teaching process

Instructional objectives and competencies to be achieved

After reading this chapter the student should be able to

1. Define the terms *learning, instructional objective,* and *behavioral objective*
2. List the taxonomies of instructional objectives in the three domains of learning
3. Apply the taxonomies of instructional objectives to physical education
4. Describe three values of instructional objectives
5. Demonstrate an ability to write behavioral objectives, including all four basic components
6. Discuss four specific values to the learner of behavioral objectives

Learning is generally defined as an observable change in behavior as an outcome of the teaching process. In the previous chapter learning theories were presented, and several methods of teaching were described. In this chapter the results of this teaching process, or the *outcomes* of learning, will be analyzed. The recent trend to hold teachers accountable for what takes place within the classroom makes it imperative that actual learning be identified. How does a teacher know that learning has occurred in the gymnasium or on the playing field? How does a teacher know for certain that a student has achieved specified educational goals?

It is the purpose of this chapter to help the teacher evaluate the teaching process by identifying learning outcomes. These learning outcomes are in the form of observable, measurable behaviors that the teacher has brought about through the establishment of two types of objectives: instructional and behavioral. The first section of this chapter deals with *instructional* objectives—those goals or aims that the *teacher de-*

fines for the program of activities or unit under study. The second part of this chapter concerns the writing of specific *behavioral* objectives—those outcomes of the learning process that the *student* should *achieve* during a particular class session.

Development of instructional objectives

To meet the current demands for accountability, several significant changes in teaching methodology have taken place. For example, the introduction of programmed learning materials, flexible schedules, and individualized instructional programs represents an attempt on the part of educators to improve educational methodology. These improved teaching approaches provide answers to the demands for measurement of teacher effectiveness by offering evidence that educational changes have indeed taken place.

Of the many innovations that have been introduced, perhaps one of the most significant is the classification of educational objectives into three domains of learning. These educational or instructional objectives may be defined as those goals of the instructional process that the teacher has identified as essential to learning.

EDUCATIONAL OBJECTIVES IN THE LEARNING DOMAINS

The first publication of educational objectives by Bloom and his associates in 1956 was the result of intense work by many educators to bring modern psychological thinking into the educational sphere. Although objectives have long been a part of the educational process, the classification of educational objectives into a taxonomy, or hierarchical form, using developmental theories as a basis for structuring objectives, was a totally new approach.

The first taxonomy deals with learning in the cognitive or thinking domain of learning. From the research of developmental psychologists (Piaget and others), theories about stages of development emerged, indicating when or at what point in the developmental process a child would begin to assimilate facts and then proceed to higher levels of cognitive activity. Development of specific cognitive skills could then be fostered at appropriate stages of intellectual development.

Educators like Bloom and Krathwohl further recognized that an individual does not learn facts or develop cognitive abilities without the influence of other factors. Realizing that how a person feels—both about self and surroundings—has a definite relationship to learning, they next developed a taxonomy of educational objectives in the affective or feeling domain. Here again the developmental nature of the individual was taken into account in classifying objectives in hierarchical form.

The third learning domain, the psychomotor do-main, has recently been classified by educators in the fields of physical education and home economics, as well as by developmental psychologists. One of the first to publish a psychomotor taxonomy was Elizabeth Simpson, a home economist from Illinois, in 1966-1967. This was followed by publications from several physical educators, such as Cratty, Jewett, and Fleischman, who presented their ideas on the structures of psychomotor functioning. Because of the complex nature of development in this third domain, the process of identification of a single taxonomy of educational objectives has been slow. However, the taxonomy published by Anita Harrow in 1972 seems to be receiving acceptance among physical educators at the present time. Therefore her classification of instructional objectives will be utilized in this discussion of learning in the psychomotor domain.

A fourth domain of learning, the emotional domain, has been suggested by some educators but has not as yet received widespread application. Inasmuch as

Fig. 13-1. Volleyball class being conducted for students at Hampton Institute, Hampton, Va.

many of the objectives within this fourth domain are subsumed within the sociological aspects of the affective domain, the discussions that follow will be limited to the taxonomies of instructional objectives within just three domains: the cognitive, the affective, and the psychomotor.

Physical educators historically have been dedicated to the teaching of the *whole* person. Therefore it might seem that a discussion of objectives within three learning domains would be in no way innovative to teachers in the field. Yet, to meet the widespread demands for accountability, physical educators, like all teachers, have to prove that learning has indeed taken place in their gymnasiums and classrooms. Therefore the development of a taxonomy of instructional objectives, leading towards *measurable* behaviors, helped to answer these demands. With the utilization of the following series of instructional objectives in the three learning domains, the teacher of physical education is able to take the first step toward promoting changes in behavior. The second step, measurement of the specific outcomes of the learning process through behavioral objectives, will then be presented.

Cognitive learning domain

Developers of the taxonomy of educational objectives* within this learning domain recognized that cognition increases in complexity at each developmental stage of the individual. Initial stages of development allow learning of basic facts, while the mature individual is later able to understand and apply total concepts. Six basic levels or stages of cognitive learning are identified so that teachers can incorporate educational objectives on a hierarchical basis. The taxonomy of objectives in the cognitive domain is organized under the following six headings: (1) knowledge, (2) comprehension, (3) application, (4) analysis, (5) synthesis, and (6) evaluation.

APPLICATION TO PHYSICAL EDUCATION

To apply this taxonomy of cognition to the instructional physical education program, teachers must first

keep in mind its hierarchical nature and develop objectives appropriate to the intellectual development of their students. For example, the cognitive development of first graders would allow simple objectives at the first level, that is, knowledge objectives. In other words, 6-year-olds are capable of learning *facts* about games, about their bodies, or about equipment. Therefore the teacher would write instructional objectives suitable to this level of intellectual development. In secondary schools, where students' intellectual skills and abilities are more fully developed, the teacher should expect achievement of higher levels of cognition—application of strategy to game play, for example, or creation of new movements or games at the synthesis level. Thereafter, instructional objectives demanding higher intellectual skills would be written.

To further clarify the utilization of this cognitive taxonomy in physical education, it may be helpful to identify possible instructional objectives in a sample unit on tennis. The teacher must first think through the body of knowledge in the game of tennis, identifying specific information to be included in the unit—that is, intellectual skills essential to the game. The teacher must ask, ''What should the students *know* at the beginning tennis level?'' The answer might include a knowledge of the rules of the game, knowledge of scoring, the history of the game, and knowledge of tennis etiquette. These four areas of knowledge would fall in level 1 of the cognitive taxonomy, requiring merely a recall of facts on the part of the student.

The next question the physical educator must ask is, ''What do the students need to comprehend?'' Here, at level 2 of the taxonomy, the teacher might identify basic concepts in tennis that the student should understand, such as concepts of spin, concepts regarding levers, and concepts of force applied to a moving object.

At the third level the student would have to apply this knowledge and understanding to playing the game. For example, the student might have to keep score during a game, explain rules to a partner, or move to anticipate spin of the ball appropriately.

The three remaining higher levels of intellectual skills may also be used to formulate instructional ob-

---

*From Bloom, B.S., editor: Taxonomy of educational objectives. Handbook I. Cognitive domain, New York, 1956, David McKay Co., Inc.

jectives in a beginning tennis unit. At the analysis level the teacher might seek to develop the students' abilities to examine certain aspects of their own or their opponent's playing strategies, finding weaknesses or strengths in game play. Then, when providing opportunities for students to utilize this information by synthesizing and evaluating what they have learned, the teacher can expect the highest intellectual levels to operate.

This is a very brief, and by no means complete, application of the cognitive taxonomy of educational objectives to a unit on beginning tennis. From this brief presentation, however, it should be understood that the levels of intellectual development form a foundation for writing specific instructional objectives for any unit of study or activity.

TEACHING COGNITIVE CONCEPTS

The importance of introducing physical education concepts from AAHPERD's *Basic Stuff Series I* should be reiterated here. Achievement of objectives in this domain, incorporating current knowledge related to exercise physiology, kinesiology, and motor skills and their development in activity situations should provide a basis for lifetime participation in sports and game-like activities. Satisfactory understanding of this knowledge depends at least in part on logical and *appropriate* sequencing of objectives throughout a progressive physical education curriculum. Requiring students to explain cardiorespiratory function in each of 4 successive high school years, or expecting low achievers to comprehend Newton's laws of motion, promotes only minimal learning. Careful and thoughtful development of a viable cognitive curriculum that matches student needs and interests is necessary.

Concepts from *Basic Stuff Series I* that may be acquired through cognitive objectives are

- Aggression is defined as intent to injure.
- Muscle soreness occurs from connective tissue damage.
- The center of gravity is located in the pelvis on a line with the hip points.
- Proper alignment of body segments is necessary to optimum balance and efficient movement.
- Temperature affects performance.
- Heat exhausts body fluids.

Affective learning domain

The affective learning domain encompasses the development of attitudes and appreciation for a particular subject or activity. The writing of educational objectives in this domain by Krathwohl, Bloom, and Masia in 1964 followed previous work in the cognitive domain. With acceptance of affect into the educational scene came recognition of the role of a student's feelings and interests in relation to achievement and a heightened awareness among educators of the importance of this learning domain.

Formulation of the taxonomy of instructional objectives* in the affective domain combined recent work of developmental psychologists like Abraham Maslow, who developed a hierarchy of needs, with the work of sociologists studying the changing patterns of society. It will be noticed that within this taxonomy the developing individual is aware first of his or her own self and his or her own responses to surroundings, gradually developing a value structure in an ever-increasing social sphere. The taxonomy of objectives in the affective domain is organized under the following headings: (1) receiving, (2) responding, (3) valuing, (4) organization of values, and (5) characterization by value.

APPLICATION TO PHYSICAL EDUCATION

The affective domain of learning formulates a significant part of physical education objectives. Traditionally teachers in this field have claimed that physical education activities contribute greatly to character development through the social skills of cooperation, leadership, and sportsmanship. However, there was little evidence to support these claims. Now, with the application of instructional objectives through an affective taxonomy and measurement of learning outcomes, proof is available that students develop attitudes and values in physical activity.

To understand the application of the affective taxonomy to a particular instructional activity, the following hierarchy of objectives in an introductory unit

---

*From Krathwohl, D.R., Bloom, B.S., and Masia, B.B.: Taxonomy of educational objectives. Handbook II. The affective domain, New York, 1964, David McKay Co.

Fig. 13-2. Relay race being conducted for students at Hampton Institute, Hampton, Va.

on team handball is presented. The teacher's general objective is to develop positive feelings and attitudes on the part of the students toward this new activity.

The first instructional procedure might be to establish a setting where the student would be exposed to a game of handball, perhaps in the form of a film or demonstration game. This class activity would meet the teacher's instructional objectives at the first level on the taxonomy in that the students would be *receiving* information on team handball. The next set of instructional objectives would necessitate a response from the students regarding the game of team handball, such as following directions or becoming involved in certain aspects of the game. As each student's interest in the game increases, the third level of objectives, valuing, would be achieved. The student might voluntarily practice the skills of the game or participate in a demonstration of the game, thus indicating his or her own valuing of the activity. At the fourth level of the taxonomy, the student might show increasing valuing of the game by indicating a

preference for the game over and above other elective activities. In so doing, the student points out inner feelings for the game by placing it in an *organizational structure* of those activities he or she most highly prizes. Finally, when this same student becomes dedicated to the furtherance of this activity by proclaiming a devotion to the game over a long period of time, incorporating it into a total life-style, he or she has reached the highest level in the taxonomy, *characterization by value*. The teacher must recognize that these higher levels in the affective domain may not be reached within a single unit of activity and that evidence of their achievement might be presented at some future time. The teacher also must realize that all students will not highly prize all activities but will develop these attitudes and appreciations for only certain programs in the curriculum. Therefore the teacher might set these top-level instructional objectives for a few of the students, with the hope that all students would achieve them in at least one or two activities during a secondary school career.

TEACHING AFFECTIVE CONCEPTS

Here again it is important that current materials from AAHPERD's *Basic Stuff Series I* be incorporated into unit instructional objectives. For example, the developing awareness of the self in activity settings, fostering appreciation for the beauty of movement in the self and others, and promoting a valuing of survival skills become affective characteristics of a lifetime.

Concepts from *Basic Stuff Series I* that may be acquired through affective objectives are

- Knowing what feels good increases understanding of movement experiences.
- Affiliation is a very important human need.
- Reciprocity of liking helps affiliation.
- Cooperation toward a common goal helps affiliation.
- Movement experiences rely on cooperation as well as competition.
- Competition depends on cooperation.

Psychomotor learning domain

The taxonomy of objectives in this third domain of learning, the psychomotor or "doing" domain, provides the foundation of programs of physical activities. Again, the taxonomy presented here is developmental in nature, relying on theories of physical development for its hierarchical structure.

APPLICATION TO PHYSICAL EDUCATION

Although physical educators have traditionally used objectives in their instructional programs, the application of this hierarchy of objectives can provide an appropriate individualization of programming. By allowing students opportunities to develop motor tasks organized from simple to complex, a distinct progression in psychomotor abilities can be achieved.

The following taxonomy has been suggested by Harrow.* Its relevance to physical activity and to development of physical skills is easily recognized, and its application to physical education is obvious. The taxonomy of educational objectives in the psycho-

*From Harrow, A.: A taxonomy of the psychomotor domain, New York, 1972, David McKay Co., Inc.

motor domain is organized under the following headings: (1) involuntary reflex movements, (2) voluntary purposeful movements such as locomotor movements, (3) perceptual abilities where sensory stimuli are communicated to the brain for interpretation, (4) physical abilities, which are the foundation of skilled physical movements, (5) skilled movements characterized by proficiency in performing a physical skill, and (6) nondiscursive communication as in dance.

TEACHING PSYCHOMOTOR SKILL CONCEPTS

According to research, learning to move effectively, efficiently, and expressively may be best achieved if there is concomitant understanding of and about movement. Using Harrow's taxonomy as a guide for developing movements—first simple adaptive, then compound adaptive, and finally complex adaptive skills (found at the 5.0 level and above)—in concert with performance concepts should cement learnings of secondary school students.

Sample concepts from *Basic Stuff Series I* that may be learned through psychomotor objectives are

- Training must be progressive.
- Anaerobic performance can be influenced by training.
- Static stretching improves flexibility.
- Force is needed to produce or change motion.
- The body can rotate in three planes.
- Speed of movement of body parts affects amount of force developed.

Values of instructional objectives

For the teacher of physical education or of any subject matter area, these taxonomies of educational objectives provide concrete guidelines to develop *levels* of behavior or improvement in the learner. Moreover, the organization and systematic ordering of behaviors found within each taxonomy also provide a framework for other important teaching functions. For example, the taxonomic framework of a unit of study may serve as a basis of comparison of that program with a similar program, allowing for judgment and evaluation of curricular offerings. Taxonomic instructional materials also provide necessary information for test development, which may be similarly organized to measure levels of development in the three learning domains and at the same time pinpoint needs of individual students.

Classifications of instructional objectives have already been successfully used for the development of physical education programs and for the organization of activity units within those programs. In Ohio, a guide for the teaching of secondary school girls' physical education was developed, based on key concepts that the teachers thought should be included from physiology, sociology, and psychology.

Development of instructional objectives in taxonomic form for the many activities incorporated in a program of physical education is a very demanding task. Yet the outcomes, as evidenced by concrete measurement of learning by students, are of extreme importance to the students and to the parents. Evidence that learning has indeed taken place because instructional objectives have been met thus answers their demands for accountability.

But how does the teacher determine that instructional objectives have been met? The second step, that of writing specific objectives for students based on outlined instructional objectives, is essential for completion of the teaching process. The students in the classroom must show evidence of learning by *doing* something specific and measurable. Therefore, after developing instructional objectives for a unit of study, the teacher must next formulate specific behavioral objectives for students to accomplish in each daily lesson.

Behavioral objectives

WRITING BEHAVIORAL OBJECTIVES

A behavioral objective, sometimes referred to as a performance objective, may be defined as an intended learning outcome achieved through the performance (an observable, measurable behavior) of a specified task. When a student accomplishes the established task, this behavior represents an outcome of the educational process; in other words, the student shows that learning has taken place.

In the tennis unit described previously, the instructional objective in the cognitive domain was written from the viewpoint of the teacher, who hoped that the students would know the rules of tennis. However,

for the teacher to determine that this learning has taken place, the students have to demonstrate this knowledge by doing something, such as taking a written test, answering questions orally in class, or performing some similar measurable behavior. These test results or performances in the cognitive domain would then indicate not only what each student had learned but also would indicate to the teacher how well instructional objectives had been met. Proof of higher levels of cognitive skills should also be evaluated while students actually play their tennis matches and while they are analyzing each other's play. Student activities or performances should be based on written behavioral objectives, established to ensure that learning has taken place.

Translation of intructional objectives (the teacher's goals) into behavioral objectives (the students' goals) requires careful and thoughtful planning, for these behavioral objectives become the formula for planning a daily lesson. The fact that behavioral objectives then become the organizers of the instructional process must not be overlooked, for herein lies the implementation of the several methods of teaching described previously. If a student's behavioral objective in the psychomotor domain involves learning to stroke a tennis ball, then within the daily lesson plan some activities must be organized that will develop that stroking. If an affective objective for the day is to develop sharing of equipment with a partner, then the activities during class must require sharing opportunities. Student achievement of established behavioral objectives, therefore, is synonymous with the learning process. They *are* the outcomes of learning.

COMPONENTS OF BEHAVIORAL OBJECTIVES

The writing of a behavioral objective based on instructional objectives requires careful delineation of four specific components or elements. It must first be stated *who* will be performing the behavior—the student, the tenth-grade girl or boy, or whoever it might be. In the second place, *what* the student will be doing must be identified, and third the *conditions* under which the activity will be performed must be described. The fourth element is perhaps the most significant from the instructional standpoint. Here the quality of performance is measured by including a description of *how well* the performance has to be demonstrated.

Following are three behavioral objectives taken from a beginning tennis unit and drawing from each learning domain. All four elements are incorporated in each objective.

- *Cognitive.* After studying instructional materials, the student will correctly explain (according to a partner's judgment) the concept, "sweet part of the racket."
- *Affective.* The ninth-grade boy or girl will choose to practice the forehand stroke against the tennis backboard throughout the class period.
- *Psychomotor.* The beginning tennis student will execute a controlled stroke against the tennis backboard by not losing the ball for 5 minutes.

Each of the above objectives contains the four necessary components. To clarify the factors, these objectives have been rewritten with each element defined (Table 13-1).

When writing a behavioral objective, the teacher must be careful to include

1. A behavior that can be *performed*. The student must *do* something. Knowing how to do it is not enough, because it is hard to be sure what a student knows.

2. A behavior that is *measurable*. The student must do something that is observable. If the student *develops* a stroke, that is difficult to measure, so a different word should be selected.

Selection of verbs is an important factor. General verbs, such as know, learn, appreciate, and comprehend, are appropriate for instructional objectives. However, more specific verbs that involve *action* must be included in behavioral objectives. In the cognitive domain, such verbs as explains, describes, lists, identifies, diagrams, analyzes, and evaluates are acceptable. In the affective domain a student might follow, respond, answer, obey, practice, select, volunteer, share, or prefer an activity. Psychomotor verbs are more easily included, in that they already involve actions, as in run, walk, swing, hit, catch, pass, and jump.

3. A behavior that is *described,* with limiting specifications. How did the student explain? Verbally? In writing? Where did the student *run?* On the track? Out of the stadium?

4. A behavior that can *meet* certain established *criteria* or standards for evaluation purposes. Judgment of the quality of performance is required here, as in a score of 80% or better to pass a written test or successfully hitting a target in three out of five attempts.

The evaluation element is a critical component of a behavioral objective. If the major underlying purpose for establishing these behavioral objectives is to identify results of the teaching process—the learning outcomes—then measurement of performance must be obtained.

Table 13-1. Components of behavioral objectives

	Objective		
Component	*Cognitive*	*Affective*	*Psychomotor*
Who will do it?	Student	Ninth-grade boy or girl	Beginning tennis student
What will be done?	Will explain verbally the concept of "sweet part of racket"	Will choose to practice the forehand	Will execute a controlled forehand stroke
Under what *conditions?*	After studying the instructional materials	Against the tennis backboard	Against the tennis backboard
How well will it be done? By what *criteria?* To *what extent?*	Correctly, according to judgment of a partner	Throughout the class period	By not losing the ball for 5 minutes

RELATIONSHIP TO TEACHING METHODS

Taking a closer look at the three behavioral objectives from a beginning tennis unit, it is easy to recognize teaching methodology incorporated within each one. In the cognitive domain, the student has been given instructional materials and is working with a partner. Therefore this behavioral objective might be found with a reciprocal teaching arrangement, with small groups working at the centers. By having students work on stroking at the tennis backboard, the teacher has allowed students opportunities to practice—an affective response that shows valuing of the activity—throughout the entire class period. The teacher's intent in expecting students to stroke without losing the ball is that the students work for control, again at a learning station established for the individualization of instruction.

In most cases more than three objectives would be incorporated into a single lesson plan for physical education. Often these objectives would overlap by contributing to learning in more than one domain. (In the lesson above, the objective of practice might also be classified in the psychomotor domain, or working with a partner might be categorized as an affective objective.) Moreover, there may be a need for several objectives, stated at different achievement levels for an individualized learning experience described previously.

Of the utmost importance, however, is the *need* for writing objectives in all three learning domains, for learning takes place in all three of these domains constantly within any classroom. If the outcomes of the teaching process are to be educational in nature, then the *planning* of each learning experience is essential to the achievement of appropriate educational goals.

VALUES OF BEHAVIORAL OBJECTIVES

The utilization of behavioral objectives offers the teacher of physical education concrete evidence of learning outcomes. At the same time, many other values are also afforded the student participant.

1. Guidelines for sequential learning and performance, from simple to complex, are generally developed in this behavioral format, thus allowing the student to select the appropriate task level, promoting individualized, self-directed learning.

2. Knowledge of the results of effort are almost immediate as the evaluation or measurement process is included in each objective.

3. A model of appropriate behaviors is often provided in the form of written or audiovisual materials. The "condition" element expressed within each behavioral objective ensures this.

4. Meeting of a behavioral objective requires *action.* Therefore the student is learning by doing something specific, with actions specified in the instructional verbs.

Critics of behavioral objectives point out that this standardization of performances is very mechanical and nonhumanistic and leaves little room for individualization and student interaction. Proponents of behavioral objectives answer these criticisms by emphasizing that one of their key values is individualization. When relevant behavioral objectives are established in terms of individual needs and interests and students are provided options regarding what learning to pursue, these behavioral objectives become their guides and resources for further learning. With thought and careful planning, the teacher can write behavioral objectives for all students at whatever stage of development they may be and may plan execution of these objectives through appropriate individualized teaching methodology. Certainly not *all* learning that takes place within the classroom is measurable or even anticipated. But the utilization of instructional and behavioral objectives provides guidelines for teachers and students that in turn give evidence of results of that teaching process—the learning outcomes.

Self-assessment tests

These tests are designed to assist students in determining if material and competencies presented in this chapter have been mastered.

1. Without consulting your text, state in your own words a definition of the terms *learning, instructional objective,* and *behavioral objective.* Give a sample of each.
2. Prepare a chart showing the levels of instructional objectives in taxonomic form for each of the three domains of learning. Cite an action verb appropriate for each level.
3. Select a physical education activity, such as basketball, and prepare a unit of instruction incorporating the tax-

onomy of instructional objectives in each learning domain.

4. An experienced teacher on your school faculty claims that traditional objectives are as effective as the newer behavioral objectives. Prepare a justification for behavioral objectives to convince this teacher of their value.

5. Write two behavioral objectives for measurement of learning outcomes in each of the three domains of learning. Select verbs from different levels in the hierarchy so that the developmental aspect of behaviors will be incorporated into your objectives.

6. You have just finished explaining testing procedures to a class of seventh-grade boys and girls who then begin to question you about the need for so many tests. Cite four reasons you might use to convince these learners of the value of assessment to them.

Points to remember

1. Through the writing of instructional objectives, a teacher is better able to promote measurable changes in behavior.

2. Through the achievement of goals outlined in behavioral objectives the student is better able to assess his or her own learning.

3. Utilization of a taxonomy of instructional objectives will ensure sequential and progressive learning activities.

4. Achievement of behavioral objectives lays the foundation for planning subsequent individualized learning experiences.

5. Achievement of behavioral objectives in one domain often may be dependent on simultaneous achievement of objectives within the other learning domains.

Problems to think through

1. How are the needs and interests of each learner in the classroom met by behavioral objectives?

2. How much daily class time should be allocated to assessment procedures?

3. To what extent may students be relied on to carry out self-assessment procedures? At what level may these procedures be introduced?

4. How do behavioral objectives become the "organizers" for teaching methodology within a daily lesson plan?

Case study for analysis

Parents in the high school community were concerned that students were not learning anything in physical education class. Explain how unit and lesson objectives might be utilized to answer these criticisms.

Exercises for review

1. Why does a teaching method become a bridge between teacher and learner?

2. How can a cognitive or affective concept from the *Basic Stuff Series I* be changed into a behavioral objective within a daily lesson?

3. Why is a learning outcome also called a behavioral objective?

Selected readings

American Alliance for Health, Physical Education, Recreation, and Dance: Basic Stuff Series I, Reston, Va., 1981, AAHPERD.

American Association for Health, Physical Education and Recreation: Organizational patterns for instruction in physical education, Washington, D.C., 1971, AAHPER.

American Association for Health, Physical Education and Recreation: Curriculum improvement in secondary school physical education, Washington, D.C., 1973, AAHPER.

Bloom, B., editor: Taxonomy of educational objectives. Handbook I. Cognitive domain, New York, 1956, David McKay Co., Inc.

CSC Media Book: The cognitive domain, Washington, D.C., 1972, Gryphon House.

CSC Media Book: The psychomotor domain, Washington, D.C., 1972, Gryphon House.

Davis, R.: Writing behavioral objectives, Journal of Health, Physical Education and Recreation **44:**47-49, April 1973.

Gronlund, N.E.: Stating behavioral objectives for classroom instruction, New York, 1970, Macmillan Publishing Co., Inc.

Gruben, J.J., and Kirkendall, D.R.: Effectiveness of motor, intellectual and personality domains in predicting group status in disadvantaged high school pupils, Research Quarterly **44:**423-433, Dec. 1973.

Harrow, A.J.: A taxonomy of the psychomotor domain, New York, 1972, David McKay Co., Inc.

Hartman, B., and Clement, A.: Adventures in key concepts, The Ohio Guide for Girls Secondary Physical Education, Journal of Health, Physical Education and Recreation **44:**20-22, March 1973.

Krathwohl, D.R., Bloom, B.S., and Masia, B.B.: Taxonomy of educational objectives. Handbook II. Affective domain, New York, 1964, David McKay Co., Inc.

Kryspin, W.J., and Feldhusen, J.F.: Writing behavioral objectives, Minneapolis, 1974, Burgess Publishing Co.

Simpson, E.: The classification of educational objectives, psychomotor domain, Illinois Teacher **10:**110-144, Winter 1966-1967.

Singer, R.N., and Dick, W.: Teaching physical education: a systems approach, Boston, 1980, Houghton-Mifflin Co.

Snider, R.C.: Should teachers say no to MBO? Today's Education **65:**44-46, March/April 1976.

Tanner, D.: Using behavioral objectives in the classroom, New York, 1972, Macmillan Publishing Co., Inc.

14

Class management—organization for instruction

Instructional objectives and competencies to be achieved

After reading this chapter the student should be able to

1. Encourage development of self-management techniques in the classroom through activities designed for that purpose
2. Explain several important purposes for good class management
3. Identify important details that should be prepared before the beginning of the school year
4. List the characteristics of a well-managed classroom
5. Identify several methods of grouping students
6. Describe verbal and nonverbal communications, both positive and negative, that promote discipline and control in the classroom
7. Explain four aspects of an individual's "learning state" that indicate readiness to be motivated
8. Differentiate between intrinsic and extrinsic motivations

The well-managed physical education classroom may best be described as one that allows desired educational goals to be achieved. From the point of view of the teacher, this means making effective and efficient use of each minute of class time. For the student it means developing good self-management skills and assuming responsibility for his or her own learning. The teacher's role in class management has therefore changed, according to current educational practices. Instead of maintaining tight control over student performances throughout a single class period, the teacher has now become an effective planner and organizer of each daily session, and the responsibility for learning has shifted to the student. Management of the class

is the result of individual self-management by each student, whose active involvement and productivity promote accomplishment of educational goals.

Although effective class management is a primary concern of all educators, it is perhaps an even greater concern of the physical educator because of the special equipment, facilities, and programs that must be coordinated for a large school population. Moreover, the partial loss of class time to dressing and showering procedures necessitates particularly efficient management of class time.

Class management includes attention to all the necessary procedures and routines that are a part of the daily instructional program. Roll call, excuses, and showers all require certain procedures to make the most effective use of the available time. Class management should not be confused with teaching method. The preparation of the setting and the organization of the class is the major concern. Thus the main purposes of good class management are:

1. To make the most effective and efficient use of class time
2. To ensure the safety of the group through class routines and procedures
3. To provide a controlled classroom atmosphere in which instruction may take place
4. To promote self-discipline and self-motivation on the part of each individual in the class
5. To develop within the students a sense of responsibility toward themselves and toward each other
6. To enhance rapport between teacher and student that will promote learning
7. To create a group spirit in which each individual feels good within himself or herself and comfortable with the group
8. To recognize and provide for the needs and

interests of each individual within the group

9. To make the most effective use of the teacher's time and energy

10. To provide the most effective organization and arrangement of the class in order that instruction may be given and learning take place

Effective class management is brought about through careful and thoughtful planning by the teacher with the students. This mutual and cooperative planning should be the backbone of class organization so that students willingly maintain the standards they have established. Boys and girls understand and respect the mutual benefits derived and in a sense they manage themselves. When this happens it is class management at its best.

The teacher's role in developing this ideal type of class management is one of guidance and leadership during the planning periods and orientation of students at the beginning of the school year. Advance preparation, class orientation, and class procedures are the main areas with which the teacher must be concerned. These three topics will receive detailed attention in the first part of this chapter.

Advance preparation

Early preparation includes attention to the many details to which the physical education teacher should attend before school opens in the fall. The opening program, the equipment, the lockers, the records, and the schedule all need to be prepared. This readiness is a basic step to good class management, for it prepares the teacher in advance, and he or she is then able to devote full attention to the requirements of the students when they arrive.

PROGRAM PLANNING

An outline of the program for the year should be formulated in view of departmental objectives. Plans for the opening unit and the first week of school should be drawn up in detail so that the teacher knows exactly what needs to be accomplished in the first meeting of all classes. In schools where team teaching is practiced, the entire team should be involved in the planning. Of course, the program should remain flexible so as to provide for student involvement in the final plans.

EQUIPMENT AND FACILITIES

All equipment and facilities should be checked against the inventory that was made the year before. The teacher should make sure that all necessary repairs have been completed and that everything is ready and safe for use, including playing fields, gymnasiums, swimming pools, and other facilities. The special equipment needed for the first teaching unit, whether it concerns hockey, soccer, or football, should be taken from storage and placed in an appropriate place where it is easily accessible. The teacher will thus be prepared to use it as soon as the class is organized.

LOCKER ROOM

Necessary preparations should be made in the locker room. A check to ensure that the lockers are clean and in working order will save the confusion and frustration of assigning a locker to a student only to find that it does not work.

If there are bulletin boards in the locker rooms, they should be attractively prepared with appropriate pictures and materials. When the students come into the locker room and see these careful preparations, it will help to establish an atmosphere that is conducive to effective learning in physical education.

CLASS LISTS AND RECORDS

The physical education teacher will find class lists very helpful. Preparing record files and grade books ahead of time saves confusion later on. It is usually quite difficult to find time to take care of these clerical duties once school has begun. There are always other urgent matters that require immediate attention, which means that sometimes paper work remains undone. The mental attitude of the teacher is greatly improved, too, when these details have been cared for beforehand, because he or she is not burdened with thoughts of additional work that needs to be accomplished.

SCHEDULES

Another detail that should be given attention before school opens is the teaching schedule. Any changes or errors that occur regarding teaching stations and assigned instructors should be provided for in advance of the initial class meeting. The scheduling of facilities should be cooperatively worked out by the men's and women's departments so that the instructional classes as well as the after-school program can be organized without delay. This includes games scheduled with other schools.

Class orientation

Proper orientation of each physical education class is important because it affects the outcome of the classwork thoughout the year. It is during the first week of school that the students are introduced to physical education and are made aware of their personal responsibilities. This period of orientation also includes student registration, locker assignments, and group planning sessions and discussions.

REGISTRATION OF STUDENTS

Usually at the first class session some form of class registration is necessary. The required information and the form of registration vary, depending on the uses for which the registration is held. Customarily it is valuable to have on file the following items about each student:

Name

Address

Home telephone number

Age and birthday

Locker number and combination

Health status

Record of fee payments

Family physician

Activities (electives, intramural activities, honor teams)

Test scores and achievement records from previous grades

Awards, varsity letters

Only a part of this information is recorded during the registration period. Other factors regarding such matters as electives and awards would be reported later on. By maintaining a personal record of each student from year to year, an overall picture of his or her accomplishments is readily available.

The form on which information is recorded should be a printed card where appropriate details can be filled in. The cards may be used to call the roll until squad cards are made out (if this is the procedure),

and then they may be filed in the physical education office.

LOCKER ASSIGNMENT

Another item of business that can be taken care of during the orientation period, when students do not yet have uniforms and sneakers available, is the assignment of lockers. This routine procedure becomes difficult when combinations to built-in locks must be explained, but even in such instances no more than one class period should be necessary to accomplish this task.

Locker rooms are generally organized according to a regular pattern, with rows of lockers and benches arranged alternately. The room itself should be well lighted and ventilated and kept as clean as possible. There are different types of lockers used in school locker rooms: baskets, full-length lockers, half-size lockers, and combinations of baskets or small lockers. In each of these types, locks may be built in, with the teacher having a master list of combinations and a master key, or individual locks may be provided by the students. If students provide the locks, the teacher must keep an accurate record of students' locker combinations, for occasions arise when it is essential that the teacher have access to all lockers.

A major point to be kept in mind when assigning lockers is the spacing of class members. Aisles and sections must not be overcrowded, in order to guard against accidents and to facilitate dressing as rapidly as possible.

Lockers may be selected by the individuals in the class or specifically assigned by the teacher, but whichever method is used, it probably should be consistently followed by the teacher with all class groups. The choice of method depends on class size, locker room conditions, and departmental procedures that may have been established.

GROUP PLANNING

The teacher may wish to devote part of one of the orientation periods to a discussion of the physical education program so that the students will understand the objectives and purposes of the program and have an opportunity to ask questions. The teacher should prepare in advance a general outline of points to be

Fig. 14-1. Strength building exercises.

Courtesy Brockport Central Schools,
Brockport, N.Y.

used in the discussion to ensure that all phases of the program are covered.

The extent of the discussion depends largely on the course of action the teacher intends to follow. During the orientation a discussion with the students about the year's program may bring out suggested elective units or special requests in regard to the intramural and interscholastic programs. On the other hand, the teacher may use the time to introduce the program the class will be following, as determined by departmental requirements. The nature of the discussion will therefore depend on the degree of flexibility in program arrangement, as determined by the philosophy of the department concerning student planning.

During the discussion, time should be taken to orient students about school regulations governing such concerns as medical excuses, dress codes, shower procedures, attendance regulations, grading, and pro-

cedures for fire drills. Formal regulations are generally outlined on a handout that facilitates discussion and clarification of these matters. In some cases, where older students or special groups demonstrate sufficient self-discipline, these codes of conduct may be developed by the students themselves. In general, self-regulatory systems promote more effective class management and should be implemented wherever possible.

During the discussion period, time should be taken to determine, through class suggestion and selection, the rules and regulations that will be a necessary part of class organization. The students themselves should establish a code of conduct for the locker room, the showers, roll call, and other class situations in order to give them an opportunity to realize the need for such codes and, it is hoped, to accept their own regulations more willingly. The teacher must carefully moderate the discussion to ensure a constructive approach to the problems under consideration and to give all individuals an opportunity to express opinions.

The orientation period may also be an appropriate time for the election or appointment of class leaders or captains. Valuable pointers on the qualifications of leaders may be brought out at this time.

Class procedures

Proper management of a class is brought about by giving considerable attention to many small details covering teacher and student behavior. The suggestions that follow govern various phases of a single class period except for actual instruction. It is this class organization that is the key to promoting a valuable instructional period. Important factors in class procedure include locker room regulations, roll call, shower procedures, costume regulations, excuses, and preclass preparations.

BEFORE CLASS

When students come to a class in physical education the teacher should be completely prepared for them. The teacher should be properly dressed for class and stationed where students may easily locate him or her for advice or questioning. Plans for class organization should be fixed in the teacher's mind, and all equipment should be in readiness. The students should come to class in an orderly fashion, just as they proceed to all school classes. This businesslike atmosphere should continue throughout the dressing time.

LOCKER ROOM REGULATIONS

Locker room regulations, determined and enforced by the class, should cover:

Benches. Benches between lockers should remain clear of books and clothing to prevent these items from being crushed, pushed around, or lost. Benches are to be used for sitting while students change clothes.

Books. A special place should be set aside where students may place their books—usually on top of the lockers, provided the lockers are not too high. Such a location helps to prevent damage or loss.

Clothing. All clothing should be hung up neatly in long lockers and shoes placed on the floor of the locker to protect clothing and prevent it from becoming dirty or damaged. Even where half-size lockers are used, this regulation should be enforced as far as possible. Lockers should be closed and locked during class to ensure the protection of all belongings.

Valuables. Valuable jewelry and wallets should, of course, be placed in lockers during the physical education class. Some teachers require all jewelry to be locked up in this manner, thus preventing damage or loss.

Lights. Locker room lights should be turned out when all students leave for the gymnasium. A member of the class may be given this particular responsibility, or the job may be shared by many students during the course of the school year.

Routine. The routine followed by students in the locker room should provide for changing clothes in the quickest and easiest manner. Students should attend to the business at hand without any undue nonsense or loud and raucous behavior.

Time. The time allotted for changing clothes before class should be established by the students in the orientation week discussions. Customarily, 5 minutes is sufficient time for all students to change and proceed to their places.

Safety. For overall safety it is generally accepted standard procedure that only unbreakable containers of liquids such as shampoos and lotions be stored in lockers. Glass bottles and jars constitute unnecessary hazards, which can easily be avoided through group cooperation.

Costume. The costume or gymnasium uniform may vary in style and color. Requirements, preferably established by the group, may also vary, from rigid to loose restrictions. In general, boys wear shorts, a T-shirt, and athletic supporter, while girls may be outfitted in a uniform of shorts and top. Both wear sneakers and socks. Safety is the major concern—one that should be emphasized with students. Clothing for active participation should be comfortable and loose fitting, allowing full range of motion. Jewelry, nylons, gum, hats, toothpicks, or other accessories may be inhibitory or hazardous to activity. In addition, all belongings should be identified with names.

ROLL CALL

The teacher responsible for the group should keep an accurate record of attendance for each class session. Symbols are usually used to denote excuses, absences, tardiness, and other reasons for nonattendance. Roll call can be a complicated and time-consuming process and therefore needs careful consideration.

Methods. Teachers of physical education have devised various means of calling roll to save time and promote efficiency. Some of the better methods are worthy of attention.

1. *Number check.* The students are assigned a certain number painted on the floor and must be standing on it when roll is taken. The numbers are painted in sequence along the sidelines of the gymnasium floor or bleachers, and the teacher merely notes vacant numbers.

2. *Number call.* The students are given a certain number that they must call out at the appropriate time. Numbers not mentioned are then noted by the teacher as absences.

3. *Roll call.* The teacher calls out the names of all students and listens for their responses.

4. *Squad call.* Names of the students are checked according to organized squads, with leaders assisting the teacher by checking attendance.

5. *Sign in.* With older students a self check-in sys-

tem may be established. As they enter the gymnasium, students simply check their names off on a chart placed by the gymnasium door.

6. *Attendance card.* Students pull an attendance card and hand it to the teacher on entering class.

Each of these methods has its own merits. However, the first suggestions are rather impersonal, and a more friendly atmosphere can be promoted through the use of the latter methods. Furthermore, the use of student leadership—while requiring more of the teacher's time for instruction and training—has the advantage of fostering leadership qualities.

Systems. There is no established rule about when class roll should be taken or what symbols should be used. It is customary for attendance to be taken at the beginning of a class period so that a report of students absent from class but not listed on the daily absence list may be sent to the office. This is an important function of every teacher. Offenders should be discovered as soon as they are found absent from any part of the school day. Besides fulfilling the responsibility for taking roll at the beginning of the class, the teacher will find proceeding from roll call formations to the next activity a convenient way of organizing the group for instruction.

Taking roll during a brief rest in the middle of the period may be an effective technique in small classes if there is no prolonged interruption to activity and class continuity. In addition, an occasional check at the conclusion of class helps to identify students who may have left class before dismissal time.

In regard to the use of symbols, most teachers develop their own systems. The main criteria that should be kept in mind are speed, clarity, uniformity, and exactness. If leaders are used, they must be able to understand the procedure, and in the case of a teacher's absence the substitute should be able to interpret the system. Symbols most often required cover the following items:

Absence	Uniform cut
Tardiness	Suit
Excuse	Sneakers
Office	Not clean
Illness	
Observing	

Safety. Roll call is a very convenient time for checking on safety regulations. This important factor needs special emphasis in physical education, and it is at this point in the daily lesson that equipment rules and safety regulations can be reviewed. Each class member should know and accept personal responsibility for the safety of others.

EXCUSES FROM CLASS

The problems concerning temporary and permanent excuses from class are always prevalent in physical education. Methods of handling these problems depend on the size of the department, the department's philosophy, the facilities available, and the teacher.

Basic philosophy. A physical education program should include some kind of modified or adapted activities program for individuals who are injured, disabled, or recently recovered from illness. Limited activities under these circumstances should be prescribed by a physician and supervised by the teacher. Because most physical education teachers understand the need for an adapted program, it is possible for them to carry out such instructions. When this type of program is in operation, there is no need for temporary or permanent excuses.

Methods of handling excuses. Temporary or permanent excuses from physical education class may be accepted by the teacher but should have the authorization of nurse or physician. This procedure channels health problems through health services that are aware of health deficiencies. Some teachers send excused students directly to a study hall if there is neither in-class alternate program nor adapted program. However, this is a questionable practice. Theoretically, students should participate in as much of the regular class activity as possible or in a program specially adapted to their needs. Whenever a particular activity is more difficult than the student should undertake, he or she should have an assignment related to physical education. Students should be engaged in a purposeful activity. If it is possible to assign a remedial type of exercise, with permission of the physician, this should be done. Whatever course of action is taken, the teacher needs time and patience to motivate excused students to spend class time wisely and to help them achieve educational objectives.

SHOWERS

The amount of time allotted for dressing at the close of the physical education class depends on the shower requirement. Because of the health-teaching opportunity provided by a showering program, students should be encouraged to meet this regulation. However, certain rules and procedures for enforcement should be established. A well-run showering program requires restrictions for efficiency, safety, and consistency. Towels, too, may become a problem unless properly handled.

Twelve to 15 minutes is the usual amount of time allotted for efficient showering. However, this guideline is relative to the number of students in the class and the number of shower stalls available. Another consideration is that girls generally require a longer period of time to shower than boys.

Because of the danger of slipping on a wet locker room floor, students should dry completely in the drying area, usually adjacent to the showers. Lacking such an area, the teacher should designate a particular portion of the locker room, near the shower exit, ''for drying only.'' In terms of safety, it is also essential that soap, deodorants, and other personal items be kept in unbreakable plastic containers.

The problem of towels can best be solved when the school provides them. Each student is then given a clean, dry towel that is returned at the end of the period. When students bring their own towels from home, they frequently allow them to mildew in the lockers. Squad captains should assist the teacher in the collecting and counting of towels, especially when towels are rented and the teacher is responsible for the exact number supplied by the rental company. If showers are required of all students, the teacher may find it of value to send students into the showers by squads. In schools where no individual shower stalls and dressing areas are provided, girls who are menstruating should be permitted to sponge off at the sinks while partially dressed. In addition, a doctor's excuse from showering should be honored. All other students well enough to be in school and to participate in physical activity should be encouraged to take a shower.

GRADING

Grading in physical education, as in any academic subject, is a very difficult matter. It should be kept in mind that the purpose of grading is to report progress to the individual and to his or her parents. Each party should understand exactly what the grade represents if it is to have any real meaning and subsequent effect. It must be pointed out that a grade in physical education represents many different factors—not skill alone. For an extensive discussion of this topic, see Chapter 19.

CUMULATIVE RECORDS

Record keeping in physical education, as in every field of endeavor, is a time-consuming process. However, time devoted to this aspect of the program is well spent if the material collected is pertinent, useful, and up-to-date.

The registration card referred to in connection with class orientation is the basic item to be included in the individual record file. Each year a new registration card is added to the file with current information. Other data that should be on file—either on the same card if there is room, or separately—should include such information as medical excuses, grades, skill accomplishment, attendance, awards, and honors.

Records, efficiently kept from year to year, provide an accurate picture of an individual's growth and development and a meaningful basis for determining particular needs.

PROBLEMS AND INTERRUPTIONS

Flexibility in the management of classes should be a byword for all teachers but particularly for physical educators. Many unforeseen occurrences create interruptions in the established school routine, and the teacher who can remain flexible and adapt suddenly yet wisely is a real master. There are several types of interruptions that merit attention: assemblies, class outings, fire drills, and injuries. (Weather may sometimes cause an interruption if the teacher has not considered this factor when planning.)

Assemblies. In schools where a combination auditorium-gymnasium is used, assemblies become a major source of interruptions. Book week, the science fair, and special examinations are all held in the auditorium, in addition to the regular assembly programs. Even when assemblies do not interfere with the scheduled physical education classes, the chairs may have to be put up or taken down. In this event

Fig. 14-2. Archery class at Paul J. Gelinas Junior High School in Setauket, N.Y.

Courtesy Gwen R. Waters.

the physical education teacher must have alternate plans to follow: written work, textbook assignments, the use of audiovisual materials, or discussion. Fortunately, in good weather classes can be held outdoors.

Class outings or trips. When class groups are taken on special field trips or outings, the physical education teacher is often left with half a group. In this instance the regular classwork should be adapted to the smaller group.

Fire drills and shelter drills. Safety drills are essential in all schools, and regular, prescribed procedures should be followed when such drills occur during physical education class. Instructions are usually issued by the administration as to where the groups should exit. The teacher is responsible for his or her particular group and must see that orders are carried out. These drills can be a source of confusion, particularly when students are showering. The teacher should try to point out this difficulty to the principal so that the situation may be avoided.

Injuries. Injuries occur even with safety precautions. The teacher must be calm in following regular accident procedures. All instructions—to send for the nurse, carry out an activity, or dismiss the class—should be given with unruffled authority to prevent students from becoming unduly alarmed or excited. At no time should the teacher, while tending injuries, leave the class unsupervised. Each accident, no matter how minor, should be appropriately reported to the school health office.

Characteristics of good class management

Careful observation of a single physical education class should reveal to a large extent the degree of management the teacher has established. Thoughtful analysis of the conduct of the *students* and their application to the day's work should point out certain characteristics of good class management. The following questions provide a guideline for such an analysis.

1. How much time is used in locker room procedures before class? After class?

2. How much time is required to check attendance?

3. How much time is required for students to become organized into working groups?

4. Are transitions from one activity to the next accomplished smoothly and quickly?

5. Are the students properly prepared for participation?

6. Are the students motivated to improve, and are they engaged in purposeful activity?

7. Do the students display eagerness? Enthusiasm? Cheerfulness? Attentiveness? Respect?

8. Are *all* students thoughtfully engaged in some form of activity related to the unit or classwork for that day?

9. Do the students display an understanding of the purpose(s) of the day's lesson?

10. Are the students aware of their responsibilities for the safety and welfare of the group?

Observation of teacher behavior should also serve as an indicator of the extent to which the teacher has promoted the development of self-management skill in the students. The following questions on *teacher* behavior relate to these class management skills.

1. To what extent does the teacher feel the need to impose controls on student behavior?

2. To what extent does the teacher feel the need to control the conduct of all activities?

3. How much time does the teacher spend introducing activities? In presenting information? In organizing groups? In repeating instructions or directions?

4. How much time does the teacher spend controlling disturbances rather than assisting students with activities?

The degree to which a teacher is able to reduce time spent in managerial activities and management of behavior represents the extent to which self-management skills have been developed in students—skills essential to effective teaching.

It has been suggested by some physical educators that self-management skills, which are themselves learned behaviors, should be specifically taught to secondary students early in the school year. For example, management *games* may be used, in which members of a group or team must appropriately react to signals for quiet in order to earn points, praise, or a reward of some kind. Participation in *elective activities* is another reward offered for appropriate team conduct due to self-management by its members.

The important point that perhaps should be underscored here is that good class management allows for an effective teaching environment in which *students assume responsibility for learning*.

Development of self-management skills is one of several factors that contribute to a learning environment. The teacher must also give careful consideration to techniques of *grouping, discipline,* and *motivation* in the conduct of the class. These additional three components of the classroom setting, because of their contributions to the instructional scene, need particular attention here.

Grouping

The problems of grouping within an educational setting are not new. Researchers have been arguing the values of heterogeneous and homogeneous grouping for many years and are still seeking conclusive answers to these problems. In a recent 2-year study of 150 Philadelphia schools involving some 1,896 student researchers, Summers and Wolfe found that low achievers performed better in classes that included high achievers. Moreover, they concluded that classes of 34 or more were detrimental to all types of students, whereas small classes were particularly helpful to those students classified as disadvantaged.

Traditionally, students have been grouped by grade level, and physical educators, like other classroom teachers, have designed programs progressively on a grade level basis. More recently, however, emphasis has been placed on individualized, humanistic instruction, as was practical in the one-room school house. In physical education there are many techniques for grouping available to the instructor. Selection of an appropriate scheme would depend on several factors, such as class objectives and the number of students and equipment. Recently AAHPERD identified many organizational patterns for instruction, citing several purposes of grouping, including health, competition, safety, effective learning, and interaction for students. Although grade level distribution of students continues to be a customary pattern in school, the teacher may be able to reallocate students according to some of these other categories. Or class groupings may be based on some of the following criteria: social structures, anthropometric data (height, weight, and age), ability preferences, interest groups, achievement levels, physical capacity scores, or some other learning characteristics. In general, administrative procedures determine the type of grouping, although in some school systems, teachers may request special groupings. However, even if the teacher is unable to request certain types of class groupings, he or she may still organize smaller subgroups within each class unit, according to the above purposes or criteria.

The major goal of any grouping procedure is to establish an instructional setting wherein increased learning opportunities may take place. It is the responsibility of the physical education teacher to choose the method of grouping that is most appropriate to his or her teaching situation. In the discussion that follows the various *types of groups* and *factors* affecting procedures for grouping will be analyzed in greater depth in order to help the teacher make enlightened decisions on this important matter.

TYPES OF GROUPS

Methods of grouping may be classified according to the type of *control* that determines the selection of the group. Control may be in the hands of the teacher or the student, or it may be left to chance. Each type of grouping has its own particular advantages and problems, and each should be considered carefully by the teacher when he or she is grouping a class for instruction.

Teacher-controlled methods of grouping. In teacher-controlled grouping the teacher determines the groups. Teams or squads are selected according to

scores on fitness tests, according to a particular skill or ability such as basket-shooting or speed, or on the basis of some other single underlying factor such as height or weight. The teacher then places students, by homogeneous or heterogeneous grouping, into squads.

Homogeneous groups
Samples
1. Low, average, or highly skilled gymnasts
2. Slow, average, or fast runners
3. Tall, medium, or short students

Advantages
1. The teacher knows individual needs in the area under study.
2. The teacher can select teaching methods appropriate to the levels and abilities of a particular group.
3. Individual students feel at home in their group when the abilities of all are similar.
4. Opportunities for leadership are provided students in the low and medium groups that otherwise may not be available.
5. The teacher may control cliques of students through their distribution on teams.
6. Students formulate realistic assessments of their own abilities and may be motivated to improve.

Problems
1. It is an unrealistic classroom setup: groups are not generally composed of people of like ability.
2. There may be a lack of motivation and incentive among some students in the lower groups.
3. There may not be adequate leadership in low ability groups.
4. Teachers may have a difficult time finding opportunities to retest and change groups of students showing improvement.
5. Record keeping and evaluation of students may become complicated if groups change frequently within a unit.

Heterogeneous groups
Samples
1. Highly skilled students evenly distributed
2. Tallest players evenly distributed
3. Leaders evenly distributed

Advantages
1. The teacher controls the distribution of students of high, average, and low skills to make even teams.

2. The teacher may control cliquishness in the same manner.

3. Leadership in all groups may be assured.

4. Students of high ability are motivated to assist others on their own team, and those of low ability are motivated to improve.

5. Opportunities are provided for students to learn how to work together effectively with others.

Problems

1. Students dissatisfied with the group may be resentful and blame the teacher.

2. It is a very time-consuming method of grouping for the teacher because it requires a great deal of thought and preparation; well-balanced teams may not be the result.

3. A team or squad that does not perform well together immediately loses its spirit instead of trying harder.

4. It is difficult to teach groups composed of different levels of skills.

NOTE: Schools presently engaged in the team-teaching approach have found teacher-controlled methods of grouping most helpful in dividing large classes into smaller study groups.

Student-controlled methods of grouping. In the student-controlled method of grouping, students select the teams. Captains previously elected by the class or appointed in some other manner select the members of their own teams. Rather than selecting teams in front of the group (a practice physical education teachers use too often and one that destroys the self-concept of those last chosen), captains may choose their teams out of class from the teacher's roll book. Another method is to have captains choose four teams; then the teacher assigns each team to a captain. In a third method, captains select only a few team members, and remaining students choose the team they wish to join, provided that resulting teams are even.

Advantages

1. Captains are generally well-respected individuals and good leaders, for they have been elected by the group or otherwise selected for their abilities.

2. Initial selections by the captains generally provide an even distribution of highly skilled players to effect balanced teams.

3. Team spirit is promoted because players are generally pleased about being chosen or having an opportunity to select their own team.

Problems

1. Students waiting to be chosen by captains often feel left out and uncomfortable while hoping to be selected.

2. This is a time-consuming method if the entire class waits for teams to be selected.

3. The teams that result from this method are not necessarily balanced.

4. Cliques are not necessarily broken up by this method.

5. Some animosity may develop between students and captains.

NOTE: This method may be used most effectively to select teams for tournament games that end a special unit of study, such as basketball or volleyball, especially if captains select entire teams without the class in attendance.

Methods controlled by chance. In this type of grouping, chance is the determining factor. Teams or squads are formed on the basis of homeroom groups or from numbers drawn from a hat. The system of lining students up and having them number off by "threes" or "fours" is frequently used. The line itself then offers a new factor of control, in that students may be lined up by alphabet, by height, or just haphazardly. The resulting teams are all heterogeneous in nature.

Advantages

1. Groups are realistic and competitive.

2. Skilled players assist others in their group.

3. Intraclass games and tournaments are usually interesting.

4. Students learn to play and get along well with all other students in their class.

5. Groups may be created and changed quickly and easily.

6. Many leadership opportunities are allowed if teams are changed often and if individuals are not allowed to serve as leaders a second time.

7. The teacher maintains standards of fairness and quality because chance is the controlling factor.

Problems

1. It is difficult to meet the needs and interests of the individuals in these groups.

2. Teaching methods may not be appropriate for all students.

3. Teams may come out unbalanced, thereby hampering class tournaments and games.

NOTE: A teacher must vary methods for selecting groups, for students are quick to catch on to repetitive methods. For example, if a teacher always divides groups by having students number off by fours, the students will soon begin to station themselves at intervals of fours as they line up.

These various methods of grouping have their advantages and problems. Before selecting the type of grouping most suitable to his or her teaching situation, the teacher needs to give careful consideration as to what is best for the students.

OTHER FACTORS INVOLVED IN GROUPING

• *How many squads or teams should be established?* The teacher should keep in mind the ultimate goal of providing the greatest number of practical opportunities by creating as many as available equipment permits. The activity itself, the number of students, the number of teachers, and the facilities and teaching stations available are all determinants in answering this initial question. The samples given in Table 14-1 indicate the different numbers of teams that may result because of the difference in the arrangement rather than the activity.

• *With which type of working groups may the objectives for physical development best be met in this unit?* Some units of study may require special group-

ings for drills—for example, forwards and guards in basketball, defensive and offensive players in football, and heavyweight and lightweight students in wrestling. Therefore the teacher must determine whether heterogeneous or homogeneous groupings would be more suitable for the activity.

• *With which type of working groups may the objectives for social development in this unit best be met?* Teams providing opportunities for leadership and for establishing harmonious relationships may result from selections made by either teachers or students. Perhaps there are special cliques that need to be separated for a more smoothly functioning class, and the teacher may therefore prefer to control the groupings for a particular unit.

• *With which type of working groups may the objectives for intellectual development best be met?* Homogeneous groups may understand certain types of instruction more quickly when it is geared to each group's particular level. For example, rules and historical development of games may be learned more quickly by groups of lower abilities when audiovisual aids (such as charts and magnetic boards) are utilized. However, lectures would probably be suitable in giving this information to other groups.

• *With which type of grouping may the objectives for emotional development in this unit best be met?* With a class of highly stimulated junior high school girls, for example, who are just being introduced to the game of speedball, squads may best be selected by the teacher in order to maintain calm and control. Then, at the end of the unit, the students may select teams for a tournament to climax the unit.

The teacher must weigh the answers to these questions before deciding which method to follow in grouping the class. The problem of heterogeneous versus homogeneous grouping in education has been and still is being argued from many different viewpoints. However, each teacher must determine the most suitable method in terms of existing circumstances.

Table 14-1. Factors involved in grouping

Activity	Number of students	Number of teachers	Teaching stations and equipment	Squads/ members
Volley-ball	48	1	2 courts 8 balls	4/12
	120	2	2 courts 8 balls	8/15
Basket-ball	60	1	6 goals 10 balls	6/10
	120	2	6 goals 10 balls	10/12

Discipline

According to the 1980 Gallup Poll of the Public's Attitudes Toward the Public Schools, lack of discipline was cited most often as the biggest problem in school communities, well ahead of drug use and poor curriculum standards. Martinek, in his studies of aggressive behavior in children, points out that during the last decade, aggression and disobedience have greatly increased in schools—to the extent that teachers now must focus on handling discipline problems rather than offering purposeful instruction.

What is discipline? Is it something the teacher does to a student, or is it a characteristic of a student or group? The word has a variety of meanings. For the purposes of this discussion, discipline is a term used to describe controlled behavior, a quality demonstrated by students in classroom situations. One aim of physical education teachers is to develop controlled behaviors in students so that instructional time will be effectively used for the benefit of all participants.

Any discussion of discipline or control in a classroom generally involves two aspects of this problem—encouragement of behavior that is consistent with educational goals and discouragement of disorderly conduct that interferes with the instructional process. Student behavior that would be classified as appropriate to an educational setting includes concentrating on a task, listening and responding to signals and directions, and engaging in productive activity. Inasmuch as behavior is learned, it is the goal and responsibility of the teacher to promote student learning of these self-management skills using techniques similar to those for motivating other educational behavior. For example, verbal and nonverbal communications (praise or a pat on the back) and grades are frequently used. All of these techniques will be discussed further in the motivation section of this chapter. However, it is important for the teacher to realize that self-management skills are acquired in much the same way as other learning. It should also be realized that the maintenance of a warm, humanistic climate where self-control and self-discipline predominate is an ideal setting for the accomplishment of educational goals.

Alternately, the discouragement of disruptive behaviors is the other side of the problem of discipline in the classroom. Again, verbal and nonverbal communication techniques may be used, as well as punishment and grades. Whereas techniques utilized to promote appropriate behavior are generally classified as positive in nature, those required to discourage disturbances are usually negative. Because of the negative quality to these interactions between student and teacher, contemporary educators suggest the following guidelines for their use.

1. Negative interactions or "chides" should be used sparingly, for they accomplish very little. It is generally more effective to ignore disruptive behaviors and offer positive communication when appropriate.

2. If negative comments seem necessary, they should be directed carefully at the offender, timed immediately following the misdemeanor, and be severe enough to be effective.

Teachers need to develop real skills for handling discipline problems so that, rather than reacting ineffectively out of anger and perhaps mistakenly calling down the wrong individual or the wrong behavior, the teacher will respond properly to the appropriate person or persons. It should be kept in mind that negative interactions of any kind—verbal disdain, sarcasm, lowering of grades, corporal punishment, removal of rewards, removal from the classroom, or additional assignments—are generally ineffective and contribute only further to hostility.

STEPS TO FOLLOW

When discipline problems recur in the classroom, the teacher needs to take appropriate steps in order to prevent further difficulties from arising. He or she should

1. *Determine causes.* Disruptive behavior generally stems from the anxieties and frustrations experienced by students as they try to adjust to their school environment. Immediate causes may be categorized under the following headings:

   a. The student: illness, fatigue, hunger, confusion, lack understanding of what is expected, feelings of inadequacy or insecurity

   b. The teacher: inappropriate or uninteresting lesson, lack of good preparation, organization, and ability to explain clearly

   c. The environment: not well ventilated or well lighted, too noisy, too hot, too crowded, insufficient equipment

   d. Miscellaneous: problems at home, difficulties

with other school subjects, worries over grades, money, friends

2. *Take appropriate action*. Once causes are identified, steps should be taken, where possible, to assist the student in making appropriate adjustments or changes. Within the class itself, the teacher may need to establish policies cooperatively with students to serve as guidelines for the handling of discipline problems. Possible procedures might include:

   a. First infringement—loss of points or privileges
   b. Second infringement—special assignment (not physical exercise, however)
   c. Third infringement—notify parents or administration
   d. Fourth infringement—isolation, inhouse suspension

These suggestions of course can be altered to fit a given situation. In many schools there are district-wide policies that must be implemented by all teachers in every subject matter area. Whatever the action taken, it is important that students know exactly what they did wrong and what is expected of them before returning to class. Punishments should be meted out fairly, consistently, and in such a way that students realize it is their actions, not themselves, that are undesirable.

3. *Prevention*. In order to avoid recurrences of disruptive behaviors the teacher should try to establish a climate of learning that

   a. Avoids long periods of frustration
   b. Provides opportunities for success
   c. Provides opportunities for interaction and feedback from peers
   d. Establishes a reward system for appropriate behaviors (additional responsibilities, status, choices)
   e. Promotes increased decision making on the part of the student
   f. Provides frequent positive reinforcement

According to Gallahue (1978),

Rewarding desired behavior when it occurs is much more effective in increasing the desired behavior than is punishing the undesired behavior and hoping that the punished person will automatically change for the better.*

---

*Gallahue, D.L.: Punishment and control, part 2: alternatives to punishment, The Physical Educator **35**(3):114, Oct. 1978.

Problems unique to physical education

Physical educators face several problems stemming from the unique nature of the program that often contribute to frustrations of students. In most other subjects, the learning environment is an ordinary classroom. In physical education, problems arise from lack of space in locker rooms or shower facilities, lack of equipment, or overcrowded classes. Such conditions require special control and management due to their inherent potential for disruptions. In addition, problems arise when students try to avoid participation in activity by sitting on the sidelines, skipping class, or feigning illness. Here again are potential problems requiring special handling.

One problem of discipline that needs further discussion here concerns the administration of corporal punishment. Most educational theorists agree that corporal punishment is not a useful way to maintain discipline because of its negative effect on the classroom atmosphere as well as on the student involved. Although some school boards have established definite rules forbidding its use, others have established policies permitting paddling or similar punishment under certain restrictive conditions. It is the responsibility of the teacher to find out school policy in regard to this important issue and to govern his or her disciplinary responses accordingly.

Ultimately teachers should seek to develop self-management skills in students, thereby creating a controlled setting. It is generally advisable to establish only a few rules for conduct—with *seven* regulations being a suggested limit—and to be consistent in enforcing them. Manner of enforcement should be as humanistic and individualized as possible, using personal conferences whenever possible, as well as other management techniques. Just as the best defense is often described as a strong offense, so might effective discipline begin with *prevention* of problems. The development of self-management skills is therefore a key to a disciplined classroom.

Motivation

It has often been stated that the key to good discipline in the classroom is good motivation, or that discipline problems generally stem from problems in motivation. What is motivation? It has been defined as a desire within an individual to act and continue to be involved in learning. It has also been identified as ''that which gives both direction and intensity to human behavior.''*

Recent studies into the complex nature of motivation find it strongly related to achievement needs as they are developed through childhood. In homes where great emphasis is placed on achievement, mastery, and self-direction, motivation to learn is high. Differences between the sexes in achievement needs indicate that females want love more than mastery.

The *Basic Stuff Series I* booklet on achievement identifies important concepts underlying motivation, pointing out the relationship between needs and fears of success and failure and their effect on performance in physical activity. The role of anxiety as it affects performance is also discussed, along with stress reduction factors that help promote achievement. Understanding these concepts may lead students toward improved performance. Knowing about their own thresholds or optimum motivation levels is another important factor in learning, particularly when tasks are difficult and lower levels of stimulation are preferable. Teachers can help students recognize these internal needs and, further, can provide external motivators for those who need it. Because styles of learning vary—some are visual, some aural, others physical—the teacher should attempt a broad range of motivational techniques.

INTRINSIC MOTIVATORS

Intrinsic motivators are factors found within the individual that prompt practice, review, and improvement in any phase of learning. A sincere desire to learn without thought of reward, because of a genuine need to use the material or skill, is probably one of the greatest forces promoting learning. When students strive to improve performance for their own sake—when they believe it is important to know how to swim or to play golf, for example—then they will be more likely to master the subject and retain skills.

Intrinsic motivation brings about the more desirable type of learning, learning that will not be disturbed by the emotional tensions of competition or external

*Frymier, J.R.: Motivating students to learn, NEA Journal **57**:37, 1968.

stress. This type of motivation produces learning that in and of itself is its own greatest reward. The student recognizes improvement and is satisfied with the results of the effort. The transfer of knowledge is more likely to take place when learning is self-motivated. The student who drives himself or herself to a better performance in one skill area, such as ball handling, will probably do better in other ball games as a result. Transfer and retention of knowledge and skill are vital aspects of any educational endeavor, and the teacher should strive to promote them.

How does the teacher foster intrinsic motivation to promote learning? Educators generally believe that students who share in the planning of their programs of study are more likely to have a greater interest in it. The goals and objectives that students set for themselves are usually those they will sincerely strive to attain. Teachers who establish goals and objectives that take into account the needs and interests of their students and who allow students to share in specific program planning can expect more effective learning.

Halliwell points out that when people feel their actions are self-determined and gain a sense of personal competence, the higher their level of intrinsic motivation will become. Moreover, in cases where external rewards are offered to intrinsically motivated learners there may be a subsequent loss of attention or interest in the activity. To maintain and increase intrinsic motivation, the teacher needs to provide a large number of successful sports experiences.

EXTRINSIC MOTIVATORS

While some students are perhaps more highly motivated from within, teachers realize that extrinsic motivational factors are not without value. Grades, awards, trophies, and point systems fall into the category of extrinsic motivators—factors that originate outside the individual. There are some students who will work hard just to earn the coveted ''A'' or the trophy. Yet learning does take place.

Pressure from the peer group may also be classified as an extrinsic motivator. The desire of adolescents to be a part of the team or a star on the athletic field promotes a great deal of learning in physical education.

A third extrinsic motivator is especially important for a teacher to understand and use. Genuine praise

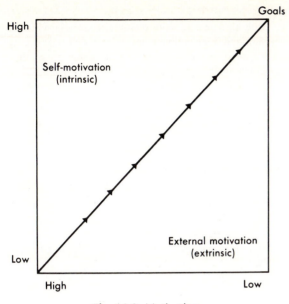

Fig. 14-3. Motivation.

may do more to promote individual learning than all the ribbons and medals the school can provide. When students know they are performing correctly, several things happen: they continue to perform in the same manner, thereby creating a pattern of automatized movement in performing a skill; they feel pleased with themselves; and they develop a positive self-image that further promotes the learning process. Educators generally agree that punishment (fear or threat) in some way actually shatters the entire learning situation and disturbs the total teaching-learning process. This seems to hold true for every age level in all subject matter areas. Particularly, though, it is applicable to physical education, in which a confident self-image and a skilled performance (achieved through practice that has been guided by constructive criticism and praise) combine to help produce better physically educated individuals.

In connection with this discussion of intrinsic and extrinsic motivational factors, it is interesting to speculate about the aptness of Fig. 14-3. Assuming that individuals are motivated both from within and without in an inverse relationship, the ideal student would be one whose intrinsic motivation is so high that over-

all goals of education are nearly achieved. Students fall somewhere in the middle of this line as they approach the general purpose of education. It is for teachers in their role as planners, organizers, and motivators to move students upward on this ladder, or scale, toward effective behavior.

Keeping in mind that feelings of competence and self-determination promote increased intrinsic motivation, the teacher should strive to encourage students to establish their *own* realistic, attainable goals, and then hold students accountable for them. Asking for student input is the key.

A knowledge and understanding of the motives, interests, and needs of students will assist the teacher in motivating them toward learning appropriate behaviors in the classroom. Because students' motives, needs, and interests vary, the teacher must attempt to reach each individual class member through a variety of motivational techniques.

PLANNING MOTIVATIONAL TECHNIQUES

Success in using *intrinsic* or *extrinsic* motivational techniques is dependent on selection of a technique appropriate to the "learning state" of the individual students. This learning state may be identified by answering the following four questions.

1. Are they *capable* of learning the behavior?
2. Are they *motivated* to learn the behavior?
3. Do they have the *incentive?*
4. Can they expect *success?*

These four aspects describe the learning state or readiness of the individual student to be motivated. The final element, that of success, is of particular importance because of its relationship to the self-concept that the student is developing. To ensure successful experiences that will further contribute to the developing self-concept, it may be helpful for the teacher to assess the needs, interests, and attitudes of students toward physical education.

STUDENT ASSESSMENT TECHNIQUES

Student assessment is a broad area in educational process—too broad to be completely covered within a single chapter of a specialized text. However, physical educators should be knowledgeable about the many assessment techniques available that will enable them to understand the attitudes, interests, and needs of students. Teacher-devised instruments, such as rating systems, reports, records, and simple question-and-answer tests, have been found to be very effective in this area. The information thus acquired can be most useful in program planning and motivating students toward desirable educational goals. (See Chapter 19.)

A final note

Good class management is the result of many interrelated factors. The overall goal of self-management by students may best be accomplished by development of these skills and by careful attention to grouping, discipline, and motivational techniques. If a student is motivated by reachable, interesting goals and by positive interactions from the teacher, the classroom will become self-managed and the teacher will then be free to make effective and efficient use of all instructional time.

Self-assessment tests

These tests are designed to assist students in determining if material and competencies presented in this chapter have been mastered.

1. Develop a procedure for utilization at the beginning of class that will promote quiet and orderly behavior while students are dressing for class.
2. Prepare a 2-minute lecture for students explaining why self-control and self-management are essential to the learning environment.
3. Design a bulletin board for the opening day of school on which is displayed important information about the program and procedures for class.
4. Write a brief paragraph describing the behaviors of the student and the teacher in a well-managed classroom.
5. Draw up two plans for grouping 30 students in basketball, giving reasons for procedures used.
6. You have a new student in class who is hard of hearing. List five ways in which you would communicate praise for improvement in skill performance.
7. A disruptive student continually interferes with the conduct of your class. Cite three possible actions you might take to correct the situation.
8. Given a choice, several students in your class would prefer to sit on the bleachers rather than participate in any active game or contest. Explain what your first step would be in trying to change their attitudes.

Points to remember

1. Good class management means effective and efficient utilization of class time.
2. Self-management skills are learned behaviors and may be developed in the classroom.
3. Grouping patterns may have helpful or detrimental effects on the conduct of activity.
4. Discipline is an individual problem.
5. Motivational techniques should be geared to the needs and interests of the students.

Problems to think through

1. Why should self-management techniques be encouraged in the classroom?
2. Why should negative verbal communication be avoided in controlling disruptive behavior?
3. Why should students be responsible for their own learning?
4. Of what value is the element of "success"?

Case study for analysis

In a large high school there are two men and two women physical education instructors assigned to each class of 120 students. To fulfill Title IX regulations for providing equal programs to boys and girls, the administration has scheduled coeducational classes in all subject matter areas, including physical education. Design a grouping arrangement that would satisfy coeducational activity requirements for a fall semester in which three lifetime sports (archery, bowling, and tennis) are offered along with field hockey and soccer.

Exercises for review

1. Identify all appropriate information that should be recorded on a registration card for each student enrolling in physical education at the beginning of a school year.
2. Develop a recording system that would efficiently record absences and excuses from class and any other information that you feel might be pertinent for evaluation and other purposes.
3. Determine a set of standards for desirable behavior to be followed in the locker rooms before and after class, and draw up a list of possible actions that could be carried out in instances of undesirable behavior.
4. Devise one or more motivational schemes other than grading that would promote minimal levels of participation by less skilled and disinterested students scheduled in a daily, required program of physical education.
5. In the case where chance groupings result in squads of vastly unequal abilities, what action should the instructor take?

Selected readings

Carron, A.V.: Motivating the athlete, Motor Skills: Theory Into Practice 1(1):23-34, 1977.

Czikszentmihalyi, M.: Beyond boredom and anxiety, San Francisco, 1975, Jossey-Bass, Inc. Publishers.

Daughtrey, G., and Lewis, C.: Effective teaching strategies in secondary school, ed. 3, Philadelphia, 1979, W.B. Saunders Co.

Deci, E.L.: Intrinsic motivation: theory and application. In Landers, D.M., and Christina, R.W., editors: Psychology of motor behavior and sport, Champaign, 1978, Human Kinetics Publishers.

Gallahue, D.L.: Punishment and control: part 2: alternatives to punishment, The Physical Educator 35(3):114, Oct. 1978.

Gallup Poll of the Public's Attitudes Toward Schools, The New York Teacher Magazine, Oct. 5, 1980.

Halliwell, W.: Intrinsic motivation in sport. In Straub, W., editor: Sport psychology: an analysis of athlete behavior, Syracuse, 1978, Movement Publications.

Levin, T., and Long, R.: Effective instruction, Alexandria, Va., 1981, Association for Supervision and Curriculum Development.

Martinek, T.J.: Aggressive behavior in children: new concerns for the physical educator, Motor Skills: Theory Into Practice 3(2):94-101, Spring 1979.

McKenna, B.H., and Olson, M.N.: Class size revisited, Today's Education 64:29-31, March/April, 1975.

Pratt, T.M.: A positive approach to descriptive behavior, Today's Education 64:60-62, March/April, 1975.

Seidentop, D.: Developing teaching skills in physical education, Boston, 1976, Houghton Mifflin Co.

Shepardson, R.D.: Don't just say great! Today's Education 64:32-33, Nov./Dec., 1975.

Summers, A.A., and Wolfe, B.L.: Schools do make a difference: The Federal Reserve Bank of Philadelphia study, Today's Education 64:24-27, Nov./Dec., 1975.

Van DerBur, M.: Motivating students, Today's Education 63:68-70, Sept./Oct., 1974.

PART FIVE

Methods and materials for teaching physical education

15

Methods and materials for team sports

Instructional objectives and competencies to be achieved

After reading this chapter the student should be able to

1. Identify the values of team sports in a secondary school program of physical education
2. Apply methods of teaching to team sports normally found in a physical education program
3. Write instructional objectives in the three domains of learning for each of the team sports normally included in a program of physical education
4. Select methods of teaching appropriate for the accomplishment of instructional objectives in each of the three domains of learning
5. Incorporate considerations for the nature of the game and the nature of the group into selection of teaching methodology
6. Derive behavioral objectives from instructional objectives in each of the three domains of learning

It is the purpose of this chapter to discuss the implementation of teaching methods in activities classified as team sports. A team sport is one that generally involves the combined efforts of three or more players competing in a game situation against an equal number of opponents.

Team sports normally found in secondary school physical education include baseball, basketball, field hockey, football (touch football and flag football), ice hockey, lacrosse, recreational games such as dodgeball, soccer, softball, speedball, team handball, volleyball, and water polo. Often favorite activities of adolescent students, they are taught extensively through the upper levels of a progressive program. To meet standards now required by Title IX regulations, boys and girls are participating together in many of these team games. Therefore, selected teaching methods must take into consideration the extreme variations in needs, abilities, and the extreme variations classes.

The values of football, softball, soccer, and the many other team sports are numerous. The physical skill and fitness benefits, the opportunities for intellectual growth and development, and the multitude of social interactions combine to make team sports an excellent educational experience. Because of these inherent values and their widespread appeal, physical educators should strive to present team sports to students in a manner that will provide meaningful experiences throughout the secondary curriculum. To help teachers accomplish this end, a brief discussion of each of the teaching methods presented in an earlier chapter, with a description of their applications to the teaching of team games, follows.

Team sports

METHODS FOR TEACHING TEAM SPORTS

Lecture may be used effectively to introduce a new game or unit to a large number of students in one class period. The content may include a history of the game, the nature of the game or activity, and objectives for the unit.

Verbal explanation may be used at the beginning of a class period to present new material briefly to either a large or small number of students. Content of verbal explanation may include skill development hints, strategy concepts, team formations, promotion of social interactions, and cooperation.

Verbal explanation may also be used effectively in the middle of a class period to redirect group interactions or to stress or highlight important concepts to be learned. At the close of a period verbal explanations may be used to review specific daily objectives and to announce plans for future lessons.

Fig. 15-1. Basketball game as part of physical education program at Regina High School in Cincinnati, Ohio.

Demonstration may be used to introduce the activity as a whole, as in a demonstration of a total game, or to introduce specific skills and concepts involved in the game. Offensive and defensive strategies may also be explained by means of a demonstration of teamwork and position play. Demonstrations may be given for large or small groups of players, and although they may be presented at any point during a class period, they are usually more effective at the beginning of a session, thus avoiding interruptions of activity.

Practice-drill and reinforcement-feedback are often used following demonstration of a specific skill being developed in a team game. Small groups may be organized for the practice of a single skill, or several skills may be practiced simultaneously, with groups rotated to various drill stations. Feedback from practice sessions may be provided by group leaders, part-

ners, or teachers, as well as by knowledge of results from the performance itself (see soccer skill module).

Tasks may also be used to develop skills needed in team games. Individuals, singly or in small groups, may independently seek to improve their skills by striving to accomplish specific tasks (behavioral objectives) established from the game or activity. Because this method consists of independent modules, students may develop skills in their weak areas. Further, because of the design of task experiences, students may have *more* developmental *opportunities* than in practice-drill situations. However, because of the larger number of students who usually elect or are assigned to team activities, the task method may be more difficult to organize than practice-drill.

Reciprocal teaching requires the use of partners or small groups for skills development, as in the task method. Again, because of large numbers involved in team activities, this method may be difficult to organize for all class members. However, it may be incorporated into game play by giving players the responsibility of analyzing a partner's playing skills and then alternating into an active role while the partner becomes the passive observer. Small groups may work effectively together to develop game strategies—offensive plays or defensive maneuvers during team scrimmages organized in class.

Guided discovery may be used to allow individuals or small groups to accomplish specific skill development objectives or, more creatively, to discover teamwork patterns that use each member's skills most effectively.

Problem solving may be used to allow individuals or small groups opportunities to devise new strategies or game play regulations that may provide new challenges for competition as well as for changing the game. For example, changing field dimensions, the number of objects used in a game, or the limitations on players may vary a game structure in a way that demands greater skill or teamwork. This method may also be used to develop totally new game situations based on given sets of equipment, facilities, and conditions.

Contract teaching may be adapted for individuals within a team setting. For example, cognitive objectives may be met through establishment of contracts

Fig. 16-3. Table tennis in the Brockport Central Schools, Brockport, N.Y.

METHODS

Cognitive

• The student will acquire knowledge of the game through televised programming, audiovisual loop films, and textbooks, rule books, and articles appearing in magazines and newspapers.

• The student will obtain information from class discussions and verbal explanations.

• While working in small groups students will discuss and develop effective strategies for singles and doubles play.

Affective

• During class the student will exhibit knowledge of tennis etiquette by showing given suggestions and teaching other students.

• Following pretest the student will group himself or herself with players of similar skill level and will set up a tournament for these players to enjoy during and after class.

Psychomotor

• The student will develop basic physical skills for tennis through audiovisual aids, individualized learning programs for skill development, pretesting and posttesting evaluations, and practice-drill combined with reinforcement feedback. The student may also select his or her own best methods for performing tennis skills through the problem-solving and guided discovery approach.

• Before class the student will warm up with a series of exercises that promote development of physical abilities necessary to the game of tennis. These exercises should be individually prescribed, according to the personal development of the student.

Special considerations	Problems	Solutions
Nature of game		
Movement pace	Slow for beginners; rapid for skilled	Work in homogeneous groups at progressive tasks.
Equipment	Insufficient quantity	Students may supply own; alternate with other activities.
Safety	No problem	
Nature of group		
Size of group	Too large	Drills in large groups; alternate officiating and playing of a short game.
Skill level	Varied	Stronger players occasionally can assist weaker ones.
Coeducational	Boys too strong	Separate for practices; occasionally allow options for mixed practices and tournament play.

INDIVIDUAL SPORTS, ACTIVITIES, AND RHYTHMS

One definition of an individual sport or activity stems from the type of competition or competitive element that exists. For the purpose of this text, an individual sport or activity is one that is *not* played against an opponent. Instead the participant is competing against himself or herself, trying to perform to the best of his or her capability. This may be accom-

plished by improving on earlier personal records or scores as in swimming times, by beating bowling, golf, and archery scores, or by presentation of perfected routines as in dance or synchronized swimming. Personal efforts may be combined with those of other team members for scoring purposes, as at a gymnastics or swimming meet, or may be combined with a partner or group, as in such activities as figure skating and folk dancing. Nevertheless, the individual engages in the activity or sport alone, facing a challenge inherent in the activity itself rather than a challenge provided by external opponents.

Included in this category are aquatics, archery, bicycling, bowling, conditioning, environmental education (hiking, camping, orienteering, pioneering), figure skating, golf, gymnastics, rhythms (folk dance, square dance, ethnic dance, and aerobic, modern, jazz, and social dancing), track and field (including cross country), skiing, and weight training.

METHODS OF TEACHING INDIVIDUAL SPORTS AND ACTIVITIES

Teaching methods for these individualized activities are similar to those used in the teaching of dual sports. Lectures, demonstrations, audiovisual materials, and evaluation instruments may all be used with large classes, but essentially, the nature of these games necessitates using more of the student-centered methods of presenting materials. Cognitive concepts, affective values, and psychomotor skills may be more readily learned through individualized approaches and through teacher-student interaction within small groups.

One distinctive feature of individual sports lies in the realm of feedback mechanisms, for in these activities there is an immediate relay of knowledge of results to the performer. For example, scores from archery, golf, and bowling are known after each motor act, providing the student with instant feedback on accuracy. Feedback may also be transmitted readily to a performer through videotape, as with gymnastic stunts, diving, or figure-skating routines. This teaching method, although applicable to team games, is particularly useful for filming single performances. Analysis of form by the individual, peers, older students, and the teacher will assist the learner in meeting educational objectives.

Like dual sports, individual activities have tremendous carry-over value and are becoming increasingly popular in school programs. In instances where schools may not be able to provide all of the necessary facilities and equipment to organize individual sports, as in bowling and golf, arrangements may be made to utilize nearby community facilities. Independent study programs of this type greatly increase the curricular offerings in secondary schools and thus provide students with enough skills and satisfying experiences to motivate them to continue participation in these activities in later life. When these affective goals are achieved, whether by in-school or out-of-school programs, physical education has made a lasting contribution to the growth and development of adolescents.

Special mention should be made of the increased interest in environmental education, or adventure programming, in schools throughout the country. Taking their cues from the Outward Bound programs in Great Britain, where individuals developed inner security through survival training, today's high schools are now providing similar challenging experiences in the wilderness and the out-of-doors. These programs include survival techniques on land, mountains, desert, and water, orienteering, ecological studies, and recreational skills in the out-of-doors. Students acquire greater insights into their own personalities as they develop self-control and self-discipline, in addition to a sense of cooperation through group process. The problem-solving method of teaching is incorporated into these programs, with small groups being forced to seek answers to group survival situations.

SUGGESTED INSTRUCTIONAL OBJECTIVES FOR INDIVIDUAL SPORTS AND ACTIVITIES

On the pages that follow are activities listed in the introduction to this section. Because of duplication in teaching methodology and activities in objectives, specific methods will not be discussed for each topic except in the area of rhythms. It should be clear at this point that cognitive objectives are generally achieved through reading assignments, films, lectures, verbal explanations, and question-answer, whereas psychomotor objectives are generally met through individualized tasks, through audiovisual

materials, problem solving, guided discovery, reciprocal teaching, and, of course, practice-drill with reinforcement feedback and evaluation. In each case, subject matter needs careful preparation, according to the types and availability of materials. Inasmuch as these are individual areas of study, independent methods and contract methods can easily be utilized. For the accomplishment of affective objectives, grouping arrangements and out-of-class opportunities should be organized. For all teaching, the instructor should strive to use a variety of teaching methods in order to appeal to the wide range of learning styles found in every classroom.

Although specific methodology for the activities has been omitted, special considerations have been outlined as in the previous chapter, with selected problems and solutions highlighted. Factors drawn from the nature of the sport or activity and the nature of the group again provide categories for the problems themselves.

Aquatics (instructional, competitive, synchronized)

INSTRUCTIONAL OBJECTIVES

Cognitive

• The student will acquire knowledge of safety regulations in a swimming area, cardiorespiratory functioning, component parts of basic strokes and adaptations for competition and rhythmic presentation, and American Red Cross standards for performance.

• The student will understand and apply basic concepts of force, propulsion, buoyancy, and resistance as related to moving through water.

Affective

• The student will observe all safety regulations and be alert to the safety of others.

• The student will recognize the value of developing swimming abilities for greater life-long enjoyment of swimming and other related recreational activities (boating, canoeing, sailing, water-skiing).

Psychomotor

• The student will develop skills in basic swimming strokes, basic entry and exit skills in water, basic reach and rescue techniques, and artificial-resuscitation procedures.

• The student will develop specific swimming abilities for aquatics, including strength, endurance, flexibility, and breath control.

Special considerations	Problems	Solutions
Nature of activities		
Safety (the first consideration)	Hazardous	Teach proper reach and resuscitation techniques; assign many lifeguards; enforce safety rules.
Equipment	Pool maintenance	Get outside help.
Movement pace	Exhaustion (with fright in beginners)	Allow rest periods; use buddy system.
Nature of group		
Size of group	Too large	Use buddies; take turns in water
Skill level	Extremely varied	Group according to abilities, as in American Red Cross; arrange low pupil-teacher ratio.
Coeducational	Not necessarily a problem	Use grouping procedures to overcome any difficulties.

Archery

INSTRUCTIONAL OBJECTIVES

Cognitive

• The student will acquire knowledge of selection of equipment, care and storage of equipment, rules of tournaments, etiquette and terminology, history of the sport, and names of Olympic leaders and other record holders in the field.

• The student will understand concepts of flight (as related to point of aim-distance) and will apply to his or her own shooting stance.

Affective

• The student will become aware of personal body structure and postures in determining his or her own most appropriate shooting stance.

• The student will appreciate the value of archery as a life-time recreational activity.

Psychomotor

• The student will develop appropriate stance for

archery, together with proper shooting technique at increasing distances.

• The student will try to increase strength in arms and shoulders as well as eye-hand coordination.

Special considerations	Problems	Solutions
Nature of sport		
Safety (first consideration)	Injury from equipment	Teach *group* shooting and recovery in wave formations.
Equipment	Varied for size, skill	Purchase some bows and arrows of each size; share.
Movement pace	Slow	Combine with more active sports or preliminary running.
Nature of group		
Size of group	Too large; left-handedness	Work in pairs, trios; put at far end of shooting line.
Skill level	Varied	Group homogeneously; shoot at increasing distances.
Coeducational	No problem	

Bicycling

INSTRUCTIONAL OBJECTIVES

Cognitive

• The student will acquire knowledge of the structure and function of bicycle parts, traffic rules and safety regulations for cycling, and repair of equipment.

• The student will understand and apply concepts of cardiovascular development as related to cycling activity.

Affective

• The student will choose to cycle to and from school, weather permitting.

• The student will be aware of personal safety and of safety of others during all cycling experiences.

Psychomotor

• The student will develop cycling skills.

• The student will improve physical abilities, especially endurance and leg strength, through cycling experiences.

Special considerations	Problems	Solutions
Nature of activity		
Safety	Traffic hazards	Teach rules of the road.
Equipment	Many types and styles	Teach functioning of all types; let students supply own.
Movement pace	Tiring	Allow rest stops.
Nature of group		
Size of group	Too large	Plan alternative learning stations for non-cyclers.
Skill level	No problem	
Coeducational	No problem	

Bowling

INSTRUCTIONAL OBJECTIVES

Cognitive

• The student will acquire a knowledge of the history and development of the sport, the rules and scoring of the game, etiquette and terminology, care and selection of equipment, and the conduct of tournaments.

• The student will understand concepts of force as applied to straight-line and hooking techniques in bowling.

Affective

• The student will assist other students in the development of skill, keeping score, and setting of pins.

• The student will appreciate the recreational value of this activity for later leisure time.

Psychomotor

• The student will develop physical skills necessary for bowling, including four-step approach, smooth back-swing, and release.

• The student will develop eye-hand coordination plus strength to improve his or her bowling technique.

Special considerations	Problems	Solutions
Nature of sport		
Safety	No problem	Teach caution, control; bowlers release simultaneously.

Special considerations	Problems	Solutions
Equipment	Plastic type, unlike real equipment	Use local facilities whenever possible.
Movement pace	Slow	Use more active activities to meet other physical objectives.
Nature of group		
Size of group	Too large	Work in groups; alternate roles of scorer, setter, bowler.
Skill level	Varied	Pretest; use skilled to assist except in tournament play.
Coeducational	No problem	

Conditioning/weight training

INSTRUCTIONAL OBJECTIVES

Cognitive

• The student will acquire knowledge of the physiological structure and function of the human body and its systems (particularly muscular development), diet and exercise and their relationships to one another, and exercise equipment.

• The student will understand and apply principles of weight control, conditioning exercises, and weight training.

Affective

• The student will become aware of personal deficiencies and design a program for improvement.

• The student will incorporate personal conditioning or weight training program into his or her daily routine.

Psychomotor

• The student will perform daily conditioning-weight training exercises at increasing degrees of difficulty.

• The student will develop physical abilities through weight training and conditioning programs, especially muscular strength, endurance, and control, according to his or her own needs.

Special considerations	Problems	Solutions
Nature of activity		
Safety	Muscle strains	Teach proper care; exercise in increments.

Special considerations	Problems	Solutions
Equipment	Expensive (universals, etc.)	Convince administration of its long-lasting values; have fund-raising projects involving all students.
Movement pace	Steady	Allow self-pacing.
Nature of group		
Size of group	Too large	Restrict numbers; rotate groups, number of meetings, provide independent work.
Skill level	Varied	Individualize.
Coeducational	No problem	Individualize.

Environmental education (camping, orienteering, hiking)

INSTRUCTIONAL OBJECTIVES

Cognitive

• The student will acquire knowledge associated with local environment, particularly regarding ecology and pollutants.

• The student will understand and apply techniques for safety, survival, and conservation, particularly those related to local environments.

Affective

• The student will experience (singly and in small groups) challenging situations that involve an understanding of factors within given environments and a realization of his or her own capacities.

• The student will contribute to the safety of others in small group situations while cooperating with them for the solutions to problems and challenges presented by environments.

Psychomotor

• The student will perform camping, orienteering, and hiking tasks (dependent upon available environments).

• The student will develop physical skills necessary for accomplishing tasks in the given environments, including strength, endurance, and speed.

Special considerations	Problems	Solutions
Nature of activities		
Safety	Hazardous	Teach safety and first aid pertinent to given environments.

Special considerations	Problems	Solutions
Equipment	Complex (bridges, ropes, etc.)	Dependent on environment; adapt.
Movement pace	Challenging; tasks too strenuous	Adapt to abilities and capacities of individuals.
Nature of group		
Size of group	Too large	Restrict; work in small groups at many given problems.
Skill level	Varied	Vary degree of challenge in tasks.
Coeducational	No problem	Students assist each other.

Gymnastics

INSTRUCTIONAL OBJECTIVES

Cognitive

• The student will acquire knowledge of the care, structure, and function of various types of apparatus and of the scoring systems of various types of apparatus in competition.

• The student will understand and apply concepts of balance, force, and flow in combining moves on various apparatus and mats.

Affective

• The student will become aware of weaknesses in personal techniques and strive to correct them in practice sessions.

• The student will appreciate the esthetic qualities of gymnastics.

Psychomotor

• The student will develop specific physical skills for apparatus and mats: *unevens,* mount (back-pull-over), back hip circle, dismount; *balance beam,* chasse, stag leap, scales, support mount, hitchkick, dismounts; *vaulting,* bent-hip squat, straddle; *parallel bars,* mounts, traveling, swings, dismounts; *trampoline,* bounces, knee-drop, seat drop, hand-and-knee drop, front drop, back drop, twists; *floor exercise,* basic tumbling (rolls, cartwheels, headstands); movements, walk, run, leap, hop, jump, slide, chasse, turns, falls.

• The student will develop necessary physical abil-ities for gymnastics, including strength, balance, agility, flexibility, endurance, and power.

Special considerations	Problems	Solutions
Nature of activities		
Safety	Injury	Teach spotting.
Equipment	Varied; expensive	Acquire singly; teach proper care.
Movement pace	Steady	Individualize.
Nature of group		
Size of group	Too large	Work in small groups; use films at centers.
Skill level	Varied	Individualize tasks.
Coeducational	No problem	Boys assist.

Figure skating (beginning)

INSTRUCTIONAL OBJECTIVES

Cognitive

• The student will acquire knowledge of proper selection, lacing and tightening of boots, structure and function of edges, school figures, terminology, types of competition, and leading personalities.

• The student will understand and apply the concepts of balance (on inner and outer edges) related to body positioning for control.

Affective

• The student will develop confidence in his or her ability to skate with control through practicing to music.

• The student will appreciate the aesthetic qualities inherent in rhythmic skating patterns.

Psychomotor

• The student will develop physical skills necessary to figure skating, including stops and starts, falls, stroking (forward and backward), turning (crossovers, clockwise, and counterclockwise), and combinations.

• The student will develop physical abilities necessary to figure skating, including strength, endurance, balance, speed, power, flexibility, and agility.

Special considerations	Problems	Solutions
Nature of sport		
Safety	Injury (falling on ice)	Teach proper way to fall; teach stops and starts.

Special considerations	Problems	Solutions
	Momentum	
Equipment	Figure and ice hockey skates	Let students provide own; teach about differences.
Movement pace	Rapid, after learning basics	Allow rests.
Nature of group		
Size of group	Not usually a problem (depends on size of arena)	Work in homogeneous groups at tasks; share areas.
Skill level	Varied	Group by pretesting in homogeneous groups.
Coeducational	Not a problem	

Special considerations	Problems	Solutions
Equipment	Expensive; varied	Ask students to bring some in; use practice golf balls.
Movement pace	Slow	Provide running or other more active activities during part of class.
Nature of group		
Size of group	Too large	Alternate active and passive groups.
Skill level	Varied	Use skilled players to assist nonskilled; provide competition by skill level.
Coeducational	No problem	

Golf

INSTRUCTIONAL OBJECTIVES

Cognitive

• The student will acquire a knowledge of the history and development of golf, golf terminology, etiquette, tournament regulations, care and selection of equipment, and current champions of leading tournaments.

• The student will understand and apply to his or her playing the correct stance in addressing the ball and the correct club selection in relation to lie of the ball and remaining distance.

Affective

• The student will become aware of personal strengths and weaknesses in golf stroking and will practice on his or her own for improvement.

• The student will develop an appreciation for the recreational values of golf as a lifetime activity.

Psychomotor

• The student will develop proper technique and skills for golf, including stance, grip, swing, chipping, and putting.

• The student will try to improve flexibility and strength as well as eye-hand coordination.

Special considerations	Problems	Solutions
Nature of sport		
Safety	Injury from others practice swinging	Watch overcrowding; organize students to face in same directions.

Skiing

INSTRUCTIONAL OBJECTIVES

Cognitive

• The student will acquire knowledge of equipment and its care and selection, clothing and other gear, types of ski tows, and types of environmental conditions.

• The student will understand types of skiing conditions and will apply appropriate safety measures and techniques.

Affective

• The student will appreciate the many values inherent in skiing activities.

• The student will voluntarily ski outside of class, conditions permitting.

Psychomotor

• The student will develop basic skiing skills, including walking, straight running, gliding, snowplowing, wedge turns, and basic christie.

• The student will develop necessary physical abilities necessary for skiing, including endurance, leg strength, and balance.

Special considerations	Problems	Solutions
Nature of activity		
Movement pace	Rapid	Allow rests.
Equipment, area	Varied conditions	Plan alternate learning activities.
Safety	Falls	Teach caution with equipment and conditions

Special considerations	Problems	Solutions
Nature of group		
Size of group	Too large	Alternate active-passive groups.
Skill level	Varied	Pretest; group by skill.
Coeducational	No problem	

Special considerations	Problems	Solutions
Skill level	Varied	Individualize.
Coeducational	No problem	Establish separate standards.

Track and field

INSTRUCTIONAL OBJECTIVES

Cognitive

• The student will acquire knowledge of at least four events (including both field and running events), plus knowledge of effects of performance on cardiovascular efficiency.

• The student will comprehend and apply concepts of force to throwing and jumping events.

Affective

• The student will become aware of personal capacities in selecting types of events (both track and field) that he or she is best able to perform.

• The student will practice for improvement in times and distances in the running and fielding events.

Psychomotor

• The student will develop physical skills related to running, hurdling, passing a baton, throwing, and jumping.

• The student will develop physical abilities essential to the activities, including strength, endurance, speed, agility, flexibility, balance, and eye-hand coordination and power.

Special considerations	Problems	Solutions
Nature of activities		
Movement pace	Fast and slow	Alternate stations.
Equipment	Varied	Teach care, handling.
Safety	Injuries from others or from strains	Organize practice sessions carefully; space activities generously; condition carefully; progress by degrees.
Nature of group		
Size of group	Too large	Group at several activities; alternate passive-active roles.

Rhythms (including folk, square, social, dances-without-partners, creative)

The objectives of developing rhythmic skills in secondary students may be met through a wide variety of activities. In an earlier chapter on movement education, rhythms were utilized as stimuli to create and develop movement. Within the total physical education curriculum students should be exposed not only to creative, expressive rhythms but also to folk, square, social, ethnic, aerobic, jazz, and other forms of dance. Because of the wide variation of interests and abilities found in high school students, elective and selective options should be offered to serve student needs.

Methods for teaching rhythms are equally varied, ranging from command-style for audience-centered or structured activities, such as folk or square dancing, to problem-solving methodology for student-centered, creative forms of dance. For example, when teaching a specific folk dance such as the *troika,* the teacher introduces each step successively to the entire group, first without and later with appropriate accompaniment, and finally runs through the entire dance as described. All students perform in unison, responding, as directed, to verbal commands and rhythm.

In contrast, at the other end of the teaching spectrum, problem-solving methodology may be incorporated into dance lessons by providing various stimuli that invite rhythmic movement responses. Stimuli such as rhythmic sounds or props such as pictures, stories, scarves, balloons, or thematic problems may be used effectively to spark creative activity.

The innovative teacher may also find ways of combining both structured and unstructured activities. For example, by teaching specific steps and then allowing students to create their own final dance patterns, creative and affective objectives may be achieved along with psychomotor outcomes.

Selection of appropriate methodology is determined

Table 16-2. Suggested behavioral objectives for individual sports and activities*

Cognitive	Affective	Psychomotor
Aquatics		
Student will explain concept of buoyancy to the satisfaction of teacher.	Student will join a synchronized swimming group that meets after school.	Student will bob 20 times in a row without supporting self on side of pool for 20 to 25 seconds.
In a written paragraph, student will analyze correct form for performing flutter kick.	Student will practice on own until time on 100-yard freestyle improves by 2 seconds.	Student will perform jackknife dive in good form, according to rating of three judges.
Archery		
After studying diagram of bow and arrow, student will correctly name all parts of bow and arrow.	After receiving instructions student will respond by assuming correct body position in preparation for shooting with each arrow.	Student will hit target with 3 out of 6 arrows from 25 feet away.
After studying materials on relationship of point of aim to increased distances, student will apply this concept by adjusting point of aim at three distances and hitting target with 60% accuracy.	After reading information provided, student will select bow and arrows appropriate to personal size, weight, strength, and abilities.	Student will shoot 5 out of 6 balloons on target face from distance of 30 yards.
Gymnastics (beam)		
After reading materials on scales, student will describe 4 scales to partner while performing on beam.	Student will voluntarily demonstrate 1-minute routine on beam for class.	Student will walk length of beam without falling.
Student will evaluate performance of classmates according to official standards and will be in agreement with an expert panel 85% of time.	The student will organize and join a gymnastic club meeting twice a week during lunch hour.	Student will perform a 1-minute routine judged satisfactory by panel of classmates.
Skating		
Following review of material, student will describe to class four methods of stopping forward motion on ice.	Student will feel difference between inside and outside edges and assist partner in discovering same.	Student will skate backward, without falling, from one end of rink to another.
Cycling		
Student will correctly reassemble gears according to diagram and get bicycle in proper working order.	Student will cycle to school and home whenever weather permits.	Student will control bicycle by staying in line while bicycling through traffic during class trip.
Folk dance		
Given test of five musical themes, student will recognize and correctly distinguish between 3/4 and 4/4 tempo by doing appropriate foot patterns.	Student will stay in step with partner while performing polka once around the gymnasium.	Student will correctly perform three out of five basic folk dance steps according to previous instruction.
Student will interpret 5-minute musical selection by combining axial and locomotor movements that, in judgment of teacher, match rhythm of selection.	Student will, in combination with three other classmates, create an original ending to given dance routine.	Student will be able to control a balance on one-half toe for 15 seconds.

*Sample objectives for some of the individualized sports and activities are included, showing various teaching methods applied to a daily classroom session.

Fig. 16-4. Dance is an important part of the physical education program at the Bel Air Middle School in Bel Air, Md. Videotape equipment is being used here to analyze student performance.

by objectives of the lesson. If students are learning the *troika* for the purpose of performing it or to learn about Russian folk dance form, the teacher may choose the command style of teaching. If, on the other hand, the purpose of the lesson is to learn to perform three uneven locomotor patterns, a problem-solving approach may be utilized.

Cognitive, affective, and psychomotor objectives are easily included in instructional units on rhythm.

Cognitive

• To define rhythm, beat, tempo, measure, and phrase

• To appropriately match even and uneven loco-motor or axial movements to given rhythms

• To design movement patterns appropriate to given stimuli

Affective

• To experience feelings of completeness and satisfaction when performing individually designed movement patterns

• To become aware of the matching of sequenced movements with a partner for 32 measures

• To cooperate with a small group in the development of an uneven locomotor pattern in a 32-measure selection

Psychomotor

• To perform three to five folk (square or other) dances

• To perform a 3-minute routine created by the individual (alone or with others)

Special considerations	Problems	Solutions
Nature of activities		
Movement pace	Tiring	Allow rest periods.
Equipment	Records; apparatus limited	Allow students to provide; develop partner routines.
Safety	No problem	Keep apparatus under control.
Nature of group		
Size of group	No problem	Work in alternating groups.
Skill level	Varied	Group by interest, ability
Coeducational	No problem	

MATERIALS FOR TEACHING INDIVIDUAL AND DUAL SPORTS
Special reading materials

National Association for Girls' and Women's Sports (NAGWS), P.O. Box 870, Lanham, Md. 20801

  Guides

    Aquatic guide

    Archery-golf guide

    Bowling-fencing guide

    Gymnastics guide

    Tennis-badminton-squash guide

    Track and field guide

  Selected articles

    Archery

    Gymnastics

    Riding

    Track and field

Wm. C. Brown Co., Publishers, 2460 Kerper Blvd., Dubuque, Iowa 52001

  Advanced badminton

  Advanced tennis

  Archery

  Badminton

  Bowling

  Circuit training

  Conditioning and basic movements

  Dance: from magic to art

  Fencing

  Figure skating

  Folk dancing for students and teachers

  Gymnastics for men

  Gymnastics for women

Handball
Judo
Karate
Modern dance
Raquetball
Skiing
Skin and scuba diving
Swimming
Tumbling and apparatus stunts
Weight training

Mayfield Publishing Co., 285 Hamilton Ave., Palo Alto, Calif. 94301

Ballet basics
Beginning diving
Bowling
Fitness and figure control
Golf
Introduction to women's gymnastics
Practical personal defense
Tennis, anyone?
The dancer prepares (modern)
This is ballroom dance

National Federation of State and High School Athletic Associations, 7 South Dearborn St., Chicago, Ill. 60603

Track and field rules
Wrestling official's manual

The Athletic Institute, 200 Castlewood Dr., North Palm Beach, Fla. 33408

Sports technique books (paperback and hard cover)
Archery
Badminton
Bowling
Golf
Gymnastics—floor exercise
Gymnastics—horizontal bars
Gymnastics—parallel bars
Gymnastics—rings
Gymnastics—side horse and long horse vaulting
Women's gymnastic—balance beam
Women's gymnastic—floor exercise-vaulting
Women's gymnastic—uneven parallel bars
Skiing
Tennis
Track and field
Women's track and field

Other sources of reading materials

Amateur Athletic Union, 233 Broadway, New York, N.Y. 10007
Allyn & Bacon, Inc., 470 Atlantic Ave., Boston, Mass. 02210
Goodyear Publishing Co. (now Scott, Foresman & Co., 1900 E. Lake Ave., Glenview, Ill. 60025)
Prentice-Hall, Inc., Englewood Cliffs, N.J. 07636
United States Figure Skating Association, 178 Tremont St., Boston, Mass. 02158 (figure-skating kit by Mary Maroney)

Slide films (sound and silent—for purchase or rental)

The Athletic Institute, 200 Castlewood Drive, North Palm Beach, Fla. 33408

Archery (4 units)
Badminton (6 units)
Bowling (4 units)
Camp craft (4 units)
Competitive swimming (3 units)
Cycling (8 units)
Diving (3 units)
Fencing (4 units)
Gold (6 units)
Gymnastics (girls and women, 4 units)
Ice skating (4 units)
Judo (6 units)
Life-saving (3 units)
Skiing (6 units)
Skin and scubadiving (6 units)
Swimming (4 units)
Table tennis (2 units)
Tennis (6 units)
Track and field (9 units)
Track and field (girls, 2 units)
Trampolining (3 units)
Tumbling (3 units)
Tumbling—advanced (3 units)
Wrestling (5 units)
Student manual with each sport
Instructor's guide

Special aids

American Alliance for Health, Physical Education, Recreation and Dance, P.O. Box 870, Lanham, Md. 20801 (fitness emblems, awards)
American Red Cross, local chapters (charts, skill sheets, and other free instructional materials)
Castello's, 30 East 10th St., New York, N.Y. 10003 (fencing, judo, and karate equipment)
Educational Activities, Inc., Box 392, Freeport, N.Y. 11520 (records, instructional kits)
Harvard Table Tennis Co., 265 Third St., Cambridge, Mass. 02142 (table tennis tournament charts and booklet)
Hoctor Products for Education, Waldwick, N.J. 07463 (records)
Kimbo Educational, P.O. Box 246, Long Beach, N.J. 07723 (records)
National Association for Girls' and Women's Sports, AAHPERD, P.O. Box 870, Lanham, Md. 20801 (swimming and diving charts)
Nissen Corporation, 930 27th Ave., S.W., Cedar Rapids, Iowa 52406 (gymnastic technique charts)
Youngjohn Enterprises, Inc., P.O. Box 4522, Cleveland, Ohio 44124 (instructional swimming charts)

Self-assessment tests

These tests are designed to assist students in determining if material and competencies presented in this chapter have been mastered.

1. List instructional objectives from each domain of learning for a selected individual or dual sport, and list methods that might be utilized for their achievement.
2. Plan a demonstration for the introduction of an individual sport to a large class of ninth-grade boys and girls.
3. Design a bulletin board that would include motivational materials for students participating in an individual sport or activity.
4. Make a list of reading materials appropriate for assignments to meet cognitive objectives in individual or dual sports.

Case study for analysis

You are a new teacher in a "traditional" physical education program that includes only team sports plus limited gymnastics and rhythms. Identify objectives and activities that you would select to expand the program, giving the rationale you would use to convince the administration and the local community of the need for them.

Exercises for review

1. Identify basic types of instructional objectives that should be achieved in the cognitive learning domain, the affective domain and the psychomotor domain.
2. Write a behavioral objective that tests learning of an individual sport in the cognitive domain, the affective domain, and the psychomotor domain.
3. Select a specific manipulative skill, and write a series of tasks designed to improve an individual's skill level.
4. Write a short answer test on rules and regulations of a selected individual or dual sport that consists of at least 10 questions.
5. Develop an answer that would explain your denial of seventh graders' requests to participate in teams of their own selection in a tournament ending a unit on a dual sport.

Points to remember

1. Individual and dual sports should be an integral part of a well-rounded program of physical education.
2. Instructional objectives from all three learning domains may be achieved through individual and dual sports.

3. Through adaptations of teaching methodology, the special problems inherent in individual and dual sports may be eliminated.
4. Many materials are now available to help in the individualization of instruction in these activities.

Problems to think through

1. How may large classes be organized to afford adequate instruction and skills development in individual and dual activities?
2. How may environmental activities be incorporated into the physical education curriculum?
3. Should beginning levels of swimming be required for graduation from high school?
4. Should class organization be homogeneous or heterogeneous for skill practices? For games?
5. In how many individual and dual sports should a high school student become proficient?

Selected readings

American Alliance for Health, Physical Education and Recreation: Ideas for secondary school physical education, Washington, D.C., 1976, AAHPER.

American Alliance for Health, Physical Education and Recreation: Personalized learning in physical education, Washington, D.C., 1976, AAHPER.

American Association for Health, Physical Education and Recreation: Physical education and recreation: phyical education for high school students, Washington, D.C., 1970, AAHPER.

American Association for Health, Physical Education and Recreation: Organizational patterns for instruction in physical education, Washington, D.C., 1971, AAHPER.

Harris, J.A., Pittman, A.M., and Waller, M.S.: Dance a while, ed. 5., Minneapolis, 1978, Burgess Publishing Co.

Heitmann, H.M., and Kneer, M.E.: Physical education instructional techniques: an individualized humanistic approach, Englewood Cliffs, N.J., 1976, Prentice-Hall, Inc.

Knapp, C. and Leonhard, P.H.: Teaching physical education in secondary schools, New York, 1968, McGraw-Hill Book Co.

Vannier, M., and Fait, H.F.: Teaching physical education in secondary schools, ed. 4, Philadelphia, 1975, W.B. Saunders Co.

Walker, J.: Cowell and Schwehn's modern methods in secondary school physical education, Boston, 1973, Allyn & Bacon, Inc.

Methods and materials for mainstreaming and teaching the handicapped student*

Instructional objectives and competencies to be achieved

After reading this chapter the student should be able to

1. Define the terms "adapted," "handicapped," and "mainstreaming"
2. Explain the advantages and disadvantages of mainstreaming and the principles that should apply when this concept is practiced
3. Identify the various kinds of handicapped students, their characteristics and needs, and the type of physical education activities and programs that are most adaptable to each
4. Demonstrate how each type of handicapped student should be provided for in a mainstreamed physical education class
5. Define and outline a program for the physically gifted and creative student

In a recent annual report to Congress, a member of the President's Cabinet indicated that change is prevalent throughout the field of education and that increased educational opportunities should be provided the gifted and the handicapped.

During recent years a considerable amount of legislation has been enacted by Congress to meet the educational needs of the handicapped student. This legislation has encouraged such practices as stronger cooperative ties between school and community guidance services, interdisciplinary cooperation in educational programs, and pilot studies designed to improve the lot of the approximately 7 million preschool and school-age handicapped children in the nation.

*See also Chapter 6 on legal liability.

Much of this legislation has implications for the adapted program in physical education.

The public attitude, as reflected in governmental action designed to provide equal education for all persons, has been changing. Today there is a strong public conviction that the handicapped student not only has a moral but a legal right to a sound education. This changing public opinion also affects the definition of the handicapped child. For example, in New York State the handicapped child is defined as one who can benefit from special services and programs for mental, physical, or emotional reasons. The American Alliance for Health, Physical Education, Recreation, and Dance interprets adapted physical education in terms of a physical activity program that is diversified and suited to students with varying disabilities, limitations, and capacities.

Mainstreaming

Mainstreaming is a term applied to programs concerned with handicapped persons, such as those who are health impaired, mentally retarded, blind and visually deficient, deaf or hard of hearing, brain damaged, emotionally disturbed, or learning disabled because of such conditions. In substance mainstreaming means developing programs to include handicapped students in regular educational programs and activities—that is, taking handicapped students from special or segregated status and integrating them with so-called normal children in regular school programs. It also implies that although handicapped students will be scheduled in regular classes whenever and to whatever extent possible, a special education program will be provided to include those selected educational experiences for which they are capable.

The legal aspects of mainstreaming have been established in various court cases, ruling that handicapped children have the same right to public education as other children and that special provisions must be made for them. As a result of such court decisions, laws and guidelines have been passed and established in most states mandating such services and providing appropriate education for this segment of the population. For example, according to Kansas law, "The board of education of every school district shall provide special education services for all exceptional children in the school district . . . not later than July 1, 1979." The State of Wisconsin school code requires that "preference is to be given whenever appropriate to education of the [special] child in classes along with children who do not have exceptional educational needs. . . ." In Maine the law states that "if after the compliance date (July 1, 1975) all eligible children have not been provided with the necessary education by the appropriate administrative unit, the state commissioner of education may withhold all in such portion of the state aid as, in his judgment, is warranted."

Federal legislation provides for mainstreaming in such statutes as Public Law 93-380, Education Amendments of 1974, which was signed into law by President Ford on August 21, 1974, Part VI, B of the law, Education of the Handicapped, states that "to the maximum extent appropriate handicapped children should be educated with children who are not handicapped and that special classes, separate schooling or other means of removal of handicapped children from the regular educational environment occurs only when the nature or severity of the handicap is such that education in regular class with the use of supplementary aids and services cannot be achieved satisfactorily."

In November, 1975, the Education of all Handicapped Children Act became Public Law 94-142, appropriating $100 million for the handicapped, increasing to $3.1 billion by 1982. (In some instances budget cutbacks have terminated the availability of these funds.) In regard to physical education, a survey by AAHPER showed that 27 states in 1973 provided physical activities to children with various handicapping conditions, but only 12 states required special preparation of physical educators working with hand-

icapped children. The number of states providing for mainstreaming in physical education has increased since 1973 as has the emphasis on adequate teacher training.

SOME HISTORICAL FACTS CONCERNING EDUCATION FOR THE HANDICAPPED AND MAINSTREAMING

It is estimated by the United States Office of Education that there are 7.8 million handicapped children in this nation between the ages of 3 and 21. Of this number, it is estimated that 1 million are not receiving any education and only about one-half of them are enrolled in satisfactory educational programs. The nation has been slow to recognize the importance of

In 1817 Thomas Gallaudet opened a special school for deaf children in Hartford, Connecticut. At that time it was generally thought that such students could be best served in institutions where they were segregated from the rest of society. By the early twentieth century, however, boards of education began to accept some responsibility for the education of the handicapped. As a result, by 1911 more than 100 cities had established special schools within public school districts for the handicapped, and colleges began to prepare teachers to instruct them. World War II provided an impetus to this trend when large numbers of disabled soldiers returned to civilian life.

Mainstreaming, although practiced to a very limited degree in the 1920s, developed into a major emphasis in the 1950s when Lloyd Dunn and others questioned the practice of special classes for the handicapped. With the prominence of the civils rights movement, parents of handicapped children and special education personnel went to court to ensure fairer treatment for this group of students. In 1971 a United States district court reached a momentous decision in the case involving the Pennsylvania Association for Retarded Children versus the Commonwealth, ordering the state to provide education at public expense for all retarded children. As a result of this court decision, almost all of the states now have laws mandating special education.

ADVANTAGES OF MAINSTREAMING

Reasons for the trend toward mainstreaming, in addition to those already mentioned, include the fact

that studies on the effectiveness of special class versus regular class placement have failed to come up with any conclusive results. In addition, many educators believe that, among its many advantages, mainstreaming helps handicapped students improve their interpersonal relationships while nonhandicapped children also benefit from their association with handicapped children. Other advantages of mainstreaming are that it helps handicapped students to better meet life situations, gives them a better feeling of belonging, makes them feel more self-sufficient, eliminates labeling, which has a detrimental effect on all students, enhances the learning situation, provides a more diversified program for all children, and enriches the lives of all children.

DISADVANTAGES OF MAINSTREAMING

Some of the disadvantages of mainstreaming, as pointed out by educators, include the arguments that it will restrict the educational growth of the average child, that it places more pressure on teachers, and that the handicapped student requires more time and attention by teachers than does the so-called normal child. The rationale for this last argument is that the scholastic pace and projects must be tailored to meet the needs of the handicapped. In addition, scheduling is a major problem. Many teachers do not feel adequately prepared to teach handicapped children in their classes, and class size becomes a problem.

PRINCIPLES THAT SHOULD APPLY TO MAINSTREAMING

Certain principles should guide mainstreaming.

• All students should be provided satisfactory learning experiences whether they are handicapped or "normal" students.

• Class size should allow for adequate educational opportunities and effective instruction for all students.

• Facilities should be adapted to meet the needs of all students, including the handicapped (for example, building ramps, if necessary).

• Mainstreaming should be used only for those students who can benefit from such a practice. Severely handicappped students, for instance, may profit more from special classes. Handicapped students generally should be placed in the least restrictive environment possible.

• Periodic evaluation should take place to objectively determine the effectiveness of mainstreaming in terms of students' progress.

Fig. 17-1. Equipment and facilities can be altered to accommodate handicapped persons.

Provided through Unit on Programs for the Handicapped, American Alliance for Health, Physical Education, Recreation, and Dance, 1900 Association Dr., Reston, Va.

• Adequate supportive services should be provided for handicapped students—for example, a speech therapist or a specially trained physical educator, if necessary.

• The administration should support the program and make it possible for those teachers involved in such a program to have the necessary instructional supplies, space, time, and other resources necessary to adequately do the required job.

• Adequate preservice and inservice teacher preparation should be provided for all teachers who are or who will be involved in working with handicapped students.

• In order that full public support can be assured, an adequate public information program should be carried on by the school to ensure that parents, the community, and the public in general are aware of the program, its needs, and what it is doing for children.

PHYSICAL EDUCATION PROGRAM FOR HANDICAPPED WITH MAINSTREAMING

Physical educators must be aware of the various mainstreaming concepts that have been discussed thus far. Physical education is a subject that can help handicapped students who are mainstreamed, if the physical educators in charge understand them and the type of program that will best meet their needs. Whether the program is successful will depend on the teacher's ability to individualize the offering to meet the needs of each student in the class. The program of activities must be carefully selected, it must account for the student's current starting point, and it must allow for progress within the capabilities of the individual.

The physical educator should utilize several approaches in teaching various types of handicapped students, offering personal assistance when it is needed and modifying activities, as necessary. Rapid progress in skills development should not be expected, yet handicapped students should feel they have achieved and are successful in their efforts. Complete records on each student should be kept with notations concerning the nature of the handicap, recommendations of the physician, and activities that are appropriate or inappropriate. Individual education programs require planning by a team of knowledgeable educators.

Each handicapped student must be made to feel a part of the physical education program and understand the need for physical fitness. Mentally retarded children should gain self-confidence, and physically handicapped students should have fun meeting the challenges that certain activities and exercises provide. At the same time, activities should be challenging and rewarding for the development of a positive self-concept. Some types of handicapped students should be taught leisure-time activities and ways to play. Finally, some points that physical educators should remember are that safety must be stressed at all times and that it is important not to underestimate a student's abilities, while recognizing that many handicapped children have a short attention span, tire easily, and are easily distracted.

The adapted physical education program

The emphasis on adapted physical education has resulted in many innovations in school systems in the United States and provisions for students with all types of handicapping conditions. A select few are listed here, particularly for the blind and visually handicapped, to indicate the nature and scope of such changes throughout the nation. It should be recognized, however, that adapted physical education programs are needed and exist for all kinds of handicapped students, including the mentally retarded, emotionally disturbed, culturally disadvantaged, and physically handicapped.

A junior high school in Los Angeles, California. Blind children are provided a physical education program that enables them to participate in such activities as track and field, tug-of-war, weight lifting, combatives, rope skipping, basketball, and wrestling.

A school in Long Beach, California. Blind children are enrolled and participate in the same activities as those offered normal children. The normal classmates assist the blind children in such activities as the 50-yard dash and softball.

A school in Walnut Creek, California. At this school when the blind student is at bat in softball, a batting tee is used. Other activities in which the student engages are whoopla ball, folk dancing, tether ball, and flag football.

Public schools in Fargo, North Dakota. Visually handicapped students in the schools of this community meet with the regular physical education classes and engage in such activities as tumbling, self-testing activities, balance beam exercises, ice skating, relays, physical fitness tests, rope jumping, and conditioning exercises.

Physical education in the State of Michigan. The program is designed to help students become aware of personal potential. They do not participate in those activities for which they are not physically fit. This goal applies to handicapped and normal children.

A school in Wheeling, Illinois. In the physical education program at this school, blind students play softball with sighted classmates. Such modifications are made as roping off the diamond to guide the blind student running bases, sighted classmates giving signals to blind students to bat and to throw to a particular base, using a 23-inch soft playground ball, and rolling rather than throwing the ball to the batter.

Other activities, events, and associations that have been organized and developed for the handicapped person on national and international levels include International Special Olympics for the Mentally Retarded, National Wheelchair Basketball Association, International Paralympics, Pan American Wheelchair Games, and National Mail-A-Graphic Bowling Tournament.

These innovative programs have many implications for physical education at the secondary school level. Educators now teach in an era in which adapted physical education has come into its own and in which federal subsidy is extensive. Of course, the key to success of the adapted program, as is the case in all physical education programs, is the teacher, who, in this program, must be particularly well prepared, dedicated, and sensitive to the needs of handicapped students.

Individualized educational programs

According to federal guidelines regulating P.L. 94-142, every handicapped student must be regularly scheduled for physical education activities. It is the responsibility of the instructor, after consultation with the student's physician, parents, and classroom teach-

er, to develop an Individualized Education Program (IEP) appropriate for meeting performance goals during the school year. Parental conferences are scheduled periodically throughout the year to assess student progress.

Seven steps should be followed in drawing up an IEP.

1. *Statement of student's present level of performance.* Formal and/or informal assessment techniques are used to evaluate physical and motor development and serve as a basis for planning the individual's program.

2. *Annual goals.* These are broad statements that provide direction for the school year. For example, the handicapped nonswimmer might have, as an annual goal, learning to swim across a pool, or the noncyclist might try to learn to cycle on a two-wheeler.

3. *Instructional objectives.* There is need for developing a series of short-term performance objectives that provide specific direction to instructional units. Learning to perform specific motor skills, such as kicking and throwing for required distances, are examples of individualized instructional objectives.

4. *Media and supportive aids.* Each handicapped student may have need of special materials, mechanical equipment, and supportive personnel to assist in reaching goals. These must be designated at the beginning of the school year so that appropriate plans may be made. For example, special personnel such as speech therapists or physical therapists may have to be included in planning.

5. *Regular education.* Plans for mainstreaming the handicapped student in regular classroom activities, according to his or her special needs and interests, should be developed. Whereas the youngster may safely engage in certain units or activities such as rhythms, other instructional units may not meet individual limitations. Thus alternative activities must be designed.

6. *Evaluation procedures.* Steps for assessing progress toward established goals should be outlined. These may be informal or standardized instruments, arranged at appropriate intervals throughout the year.

7. *Dates of service.* Specific dates for starting and ending special physical education services must be

identified. A time line should be established for meeting both long-term and short-term objectives.

Physical education is the *only* curricular area specifically mandated for mainstreamed students. Because of this legislation, physical educators have a unique opportunity to provide much-needed service to a special population. Active involvement in developing appropriate IEPs is an essential prerequisite to this process and a responsibility that the physical education teacher must accomplish.

The challenge of the handicapped student

A beginning physical educator soon discovers that the students in any single physical education class do not form a homogeneous group. While all the boys or all the girls in one physical education class may be in the same secondary grade and while all of them may fall within a certain narrow age range, they will not possess the same physical and mental abilities.

INDIVIDUALIZED EDUCATIONAL PROGRAM*

I. Student name __John Doe, Jr.__ Date of birth __1-24-67__ Age __16__ School division __Stony Point__
Parent/Guardian __Mrs. John Doe__ Date of eligibility __6-15-83__ Date of IEP implementation __9-6-83__
Address _____1736 Bay Street_____ Categorical identification __E.M.R.__

II. Present level of performance (summary data)

Academic:	*Piat*		*AAHPERD Physical Fitness Test Items* (Refer to charts/age group)	
Key math	Reading recognition	2.3	Pull-up/flexed arm hang	5
3.8	Reading	3.6	Sit-ups (flexed legs)	41
Dolch sight	Spelling	2.0	Shuttle run	10.1
Word inventory	Reading comprehension	4.8	50-year dash	6.7
263 Words mastered	Mathematics	4.2	600-yard run-walk	1:55
	General knowledge	5.9	Standing broad jump	6'9"

Behavior:
John is very shy and lacks physical fitness. There is little eye contact with others. He is well mannered. John gets discouraged easily when working in language areas. He performs well in math. His social skills are limited. John is interested in woodworking. Carpentry may provide a setting for advancement and training after he has obtained the necessary prevocational orientation.

III. Long-term goals
  1. All items of the AAHPERD Physical Fitness Test will increase to the 50th percentile (above satisfactory) by the end of the school year.
  2. a. To increase sight word vocabulary and survival words
     b. To increase skills in reading through spelling skills and decoding skills
     c. To increase math processes skills to include banking and savings
     d. To demonstrate planning of careers, duties of specific jobs, and survival forms of applications
     e. To provide instruction in local, state, and national governments
     f. To increase self-confidence and social adaptability

---

*From Division of Special Education, Health, and Physical Education Service, Department of Education, Richmond, Va., 1977, Virginia Department of Education.

INDIVIDUALIZED EDUCATIONAL PROGRAM—cont'd

IV. Education and/or related services

	Date to begin	Anticipated completion date	Environment	Location	Personnel
E.M.R.	9-6-83	through high school	4 periods— self-contained	Virginia High School	Mrs. Green
Physical education	9-6-83	through grade 10	1 period— regular	Virginia High School	Mr. Dean
Vocational orientation	9-6-83	through high school	1 period— regular	Virginia High School	Vocational rehabilitation W.I.N. Program

V. Short-term objectives

Objectives	Methods	Special materials and equipment	Dates		
			Begun	Comple- tion	Continuation and/or modification
Physical education	Establish warm-up stations to be used for following activities:				
1. Student's performance levels should show improvement in efforts to obtain the 50th percentile	1. To perform sit-ups three times per week	Tape, stop watch, horizontal bar	9/6	5/4	Mastered/ maintain
	2. To perform pull-ups three times per week		9/6	5/4	Cont. (inc. no. per week)
	3. To perform shuttle-run two times per week		9/6	5/4	Cont. (inc. no. per week)
	4. To run three 50-year wind sprints per week		9/6	5/4	Cont./ Modif. no.
	5. To jump vertically 1 minute three times per week		9/6	5/4	Exercise
	6. To run one 600-year run-walk per week		9/6	5/4	Mastered/ Cont.
Academic					
1. To master Dolch sight vocabulary and survival words		Flash cards, word finds, crossword puzzles	9/15	6/3	Cont./In- crease
2. To spell and define 10 words per week	Cover and write method		9/15	6/3	Modif.
			9/15	6/3	Cont.

Continued.

INDIVIDUALIZED EDUCATIONAL PROGRAM—cont'd

VI. Participants

Date	Signature of persons present	Relationship to student
9-1-83	*Mrs. Ann Long*	Guidance counselor
9-1-83	*Mrs. Louis Green*	E.M.R. teacher
9-1-83	*Mr. George Dean*	Physical education teacher
9-1-83	*Mrs. John Doe*	Parent
9-1-83	*Ms. Matilda Snodgrass*	Psychologist
9-1-83	*Mr. Oscar Rinklefender*	Director of special education

I GIVE PERMISSION FOR MY CHILD _____John Doe, Jr._____ to be enrolled in the special program described in the individualized education program plan. I understand that I have the right to review his/her record and to request a change in his/her individualized education program at any time. I understand that I have the right to refuse this permission and to have my child continue in his/her present placement pending further action.

I did participate in the development of the individualized education program. YES __X__ NO _____

I did not participate in the development of the individualized education program, but I do approve of the plan. YES _____ NO _____

9/1/83	*Mrs. John Doe*
Date	Signature of parent or guardian

I DO NOT GIVE PERMISSION FOR MY CHILD _____ to be enrolled in the special education program described in the individualized education program. I understand that I have the right to review his/her records and to request another placement. I understand that the action described above will not take place without my permission or until due process procedures have been exhausted. I understand that if my decision is appealed, I will be notified of my due process rights in this procedure.

_____	_____
Date	Signature of parent or guardian

Not all of them will have developed to the same levels of emotional and social maturity. Most of these students will fall into the classification "average" or "normal" for their age and grade. Other students will deviate considerably from their peers in a specific physical, mental, emotional, or social area or in a combination of these areas. This latter group may be said to be handicapped.

Handicapped students in physical education present a challenge to the teacher, for they may fall into any of several different categories. The culturally disadvantaged child is atypical, as are the physically gifted student, the creative student, and the awkward student with low motor ability. Atypical groupings also include emotionally disturbed as well as mentally retarded students. Each of these groups needs a strong and well-planned physical education experience. In schools where facilities and teaching personnel are available, adapted programs are developed especially to meet the needs of the handicapped student. With mainstreaming the physical educator must be prepared to make both program and instructional adaptations to meet special physical education requirements.

It is a rare secondary school that does not have at least a few handicapped students on its class rolls. It is a definite possibility that some day each physical educator may have to teach at least some students who fall outside the norm. Thus each physical educator should know how to best provide for the following types of handicapped students.

The culturally disadvantaged student

Culturally disadvantaged students have always made up a segment of the school population, but it is only recently that they have become a real concern to various communities and to the schools serving these communities. It is a common error for the public to associate only the black child with cultural deprivation. Professional educators, especially, must realize that cultural deprivation crosses all color lines and ignores none of them.

The blight of poverty is especially apparent in the large urban centers. Ten years ago 1 in 3 city children was classified as culturally disadvantaged, according to the Ford Foundation. At the present time an estimated 50% of the children living in cities are culturally disadvantaged as are many of the inhabitants of Appalachia, suburban communities, and isolated small towns and rural villages all across the United States.

CHARACTERISTICS OF THE CULTURALLY DISADVANTAGED STUDENT

The culturally disadvantaged student feels isolated from the mainstream of life. Home and neighborhood environment are negative influences that destroy confidence, rob the student of a chance for success, and defeat aspirations. The goals of middle-class culture, as represented by the school, seem unreachable to someone who lives in poverty.

A culturally disadvantaged student may not achieve success in school because the cultural standards of the school and the home environment are usually inconsistent. Even schools in inner city areas are staffed by teachers who represent the middle-class segment of society.

In a classroom situation the culturally disadvantaged student is unable to compete successfully scholastically, emotionally, or socially. Because reading and conversation have not been encouraged at home, the student is severely restricted in ability to communicate and finds it extremely difficult to use logic, form concepts, or think in abstract terms. The culturally disadvantaged student is, for these reasons, often behind proper grade level in achievement. This boy or girl frequently makes low scores on intelligence and standardized tests because these tests are not designed to accurately measure atypical individuals. As the culturally disadvantaged student continues to fail, he or she loses any motivation to achieve, which results in declining levels of ambition and aspiration.

Continual failure in the classroom negatively affects the school behavior of the culturally disadvantaged student. Short attention span, emotional instability, excitability, and restlessness often contribute to disruptive behavior patterns.

EDUCATIONAL NEEDS OF THE CULTURALLY DISADVANTAGED STUDENT

Many culturally disadvantaged students come from itinerant families. The children of migratory workers, in particular, attend several different schools throughout the course of a single school year. Other culturally disadvantaged families are mobile because they constantly search for higher-paying jobs or better living conditions. This mobility further increases the educational deprivation of the culturally disadvantaged student.

Conventional middle-class curricula with conventional middle-class objectives and goals are not adequate for the culturally disadvantaged. The teacher cannot employ traditional middle-class methodology and impose middle-class standards of discipline. These approaches succeed only in driving the culturally disadvantaged student into an even narrower existence.

Many authorities have criticized the unrealistic educational atmosphere to which the culturally disadvantaged student is systematically exposed. On the elementary school level especially, it is pointed out, reading books and textbooks illustrate and espouse a way of life that is totally alien to the culturally disadvantaged. It is further noted that if the student does indeed continue education in a secondary school, the curriculum choices offered are really only weak attempts to resolve long-standing educational inequities. On the secondary school level the culturally disadvantaged student is sometimes arbitrarily channeled into a terminal vocational program, without regard to hidden potential for seeking a higher education and a professional career.

Educators are constantly seeking to adjust or innovate curricula that will better serve the culturally disadvantaged. As yet, definite answers about realistically meeting the needs of culturally disadvantaged students have not been found. However, educators have been able to identify three broad curricular designs in secondary education for the disadvantaged. These three educational patterns, which are not mutually exclusive, may be termed remedial education, curriculum adjustment, and methodological modification.

Remedial education is a genuine need of the dis-

advantaged, but an entire secondary school curriculum cannot be based on such a program. However, many communities are engaged in out-of-school remedial education through a program such as Upward Bound.

Curriculum adjustment involves a slowing down of the educational pace. Curriculum content is identical for all segments of the school population, but classes made up of disadvantaged students spend proportionately greater amounts of time in each subject area. A regularly paced class will cover a unit of work in mathematics, for example, in many fewer class periods than will a slower-paced class of disadvantaged students. In these latter classes, discipline is very rigid—a concession to the teacher but not necessarily the most conducive atmosphere for the students. This slower method of teaching makes a questionable contribution to the disadvantaged student. It does not guarantee that educational or vocational needs are being met. However, it does allow the student to move into regularly paced classes when ability permits and to move more slowly in those courses where there is a need to increase confidence and knowledge.

Methodological modifications are nothing more than the extreme adaptation of existing standard courses or specially designed standard courses. This educational technique is sometimes known as "tracking." When this method of educating disadvantaged students is adopted, the curriculum is made up almost entirely of vocationally oriented subject matter designed to prepare the student for the job market. Very few courses with a purely academic orientation are included in the programs, which may close the door on higher education. For example, courses in mathematics will be geared toward learning to make change, while courses in English will concentrate on writing a business letter or going for an interview. In the former there will be no attempt to teach the concepts of secondary school mathematics, such as algebra and geometry, and in the latter there will be no attempt to teach literature or theme writing. In some secondary schools, placement of a student in a program of this sort is undertaken in spite of the student's personal aspirations or untapped academic ability that might be revealed through exposure to a more academic curriculum.

These three systems may have more disadvantages

than advantages, but they will continue to be used until better methods are found to meet the needs of these youth in secondary schools. Culturally disadvantaged students do need vocational training, but they should also be free to select courses that meet their individual needs and interests. The culturally disadvantaged student will not succeed educationally if all courses are dictated or if he or she is confined by a tracking system or is otherwise educationally isolated. The secondary schools must be as dedicated to educating culturally disadvantaged students as they are to educating the more advantaged segments of the school population.

THE PHYSICAL EDUCATOR AND THE
CULTURALLY DISADVANTAGED STUDENT

In the physical education classroom the culturally disadvantaged student can be given an opportunity to meet success. Physical activity has a strong appeal for these youngsters, whether they are students in a school in their neighborhood or community or part of the student body in a school in an advantaged area.

The physical educator is the most important single factor in a secondary school physical education program for the disadvantaged. This teacher must have a sincere interest in the students and must be willing to assume the responsibility for physically educating them. He or she should have an adequate background and special training in general and physical education courses concerned with teaching the disadvantaged. These courses will help in gaining a fuller understanding of culturally disadvantaged students and the educational problems they face. The physical educator must have the ability to develop rapport with them in order to better respect, understand, and help them. He or she must also be able to provide an enriched program that will help motivate these students to make the best use of their physical, intellectual, and creative abilities.

THE PHYSICAL EDUCATION PROGRAM
AND THE CULTURALLY DISADVANTAGED
STUDENT

The school physical education program frequently is the only supervised physical activity program for the culturally disadvantaged student. These students usually do not have a neighborhood recreational facility available and must conduct their sports and games on unsupervised streets or in dangerously littered lots. Thus the school experience must be designed to afford them the physical education and recreational activities denied them elsewhere.

• *The physical education program must be carefully tailored to meet the needs and interests of the students.* Culturally disadvantaged students enjoy vigorous activity as well as creative and self-testing activities. They must be given a wide choice so they can select not only those experiences they find pleasurable but also those in which they can find success. As fundamental challenges are met successfully, new challenges must be presented in a logical progression.

• *The physical education program must be designed to increase the physical fitness and motor skills abilities of the students.* The program should include activities that will help the students increase their physical fitness levels. Lack of structured programs outside the school denies culturally disadvantaged students the opportunity to participate in a regular program of physical activity, which often prevents them from maintaining even minimum fitness levels. In addition, motor skills and abilities are often inadequate simply because some students may never have had the benefit of a good physical education program in school.

• *There must be provision for suitable competition.* Culturally disadvantaged students need and enjoy competition. Although competitive sports and games must be a part of the class program, time must also be allotted the individual to compete with himself or herself in order to raise a physical fitness test score or to improve in a skills performance. Intramural programs are an invaluable extension of the class program, and the culturally disadvantaged student should be encouraged to participate and to seek membership on interscholastic teams as well.

• *The program must provide for carry-over interests.* The culturally disadvantaged students need to develop a background in the lifetime sports: swimming, dancing, and tennis, as well as other recreational activities such as bowling.

• *Equipment must be carefully purchased to suit the program.* There should be records, a phono-

graph, and a variety of rhythm instruments. Culturally disadvantaged students enjoy rhythmical activities and often find that they are successful in such areas as dance, gymnastics, and tumbling, where they can demonstrate their creativity and express their individuality. Many warmup activities, as well as many games, can be done to a musical accompaniment.

• *The program must allow for each student to be treated as an individual.* Culturally disadvantaged students are especially conscious of their difference, and the program should allow ample opportunity for self-expression and creativity. Teacher recognition and praise for the most minor accomplishment are of utmost importance to the continued success of these students.

• *The program should help to instill good health habits and attitudes.* Where possible, showers should be available to the students. Each student should be provided with an individual locker, and cleanliness and proper maintenance of uniforms should be required.

• *The size of classes should be so arranged that discipline is easy to maintain.* Secondary school physical education classes are frequently overcrowded, and discipline is a major problem. If possible, culturally disadvantaged students should not be in a large class because little teaching takes place and the individual student becomes lost in the mass. These students need and want to follow firm, consistent, and appropriate disciplinary standards. As much as any student, they must know what is expected of them and should be made to conform to established standards. However, any disciplinary standards imposed must be relevant since artificial rules will result in a total lack of discipline.

• *The physical education program should attempt to instill values that will extend into the classroom situation.* Through the activities of physical education, culturally disadvantaged students can obtain a release of tension in an acceptable way. They can also learn, from the give and take of sports, how to get along with others, and they will become more aware of the needs, abilities, and talents of their classmates. If these experiences are provided in the physical education class, at least some of the lessons may be transferred to the academic classroom.

• *The program should be correlated with the general education program of the school.* Through physical education activities, a great deal of general educational knowledge and many skills and abilities can be reinforced. Through folk dances, for example, it is possible to acquaint the student with the dress and customs of various cultures. This knowledge will make a class in history more interesting to the student and will help develop pride in his or her own culture. Through a sport such as baseball, mathematics can be brought to life. The students will be able to see the relationship between mathematics and its uses for such practical purposes as determining baseball batting averages, computing team won-lost percentages, and understanding angles so that this knowledge can be applied to laying out a baseball diamond.

The physically handicapped student

The physically handicapped student may have a temporary disability, such as a broken arm, or may be in a postoperative stage of recovery. Other physically handicapped students suffer from more permanent disabilities, such as blindness, deafness, or irremediable orthopedic conditions. The range of physical handicaps extends from minor to major in severity and directly affects the kinds and amounts of participation in physical activity.

Whatever the disability, a physical education program should be provided. Some handicapped students will be able to participate in a regular program of physical education with certain minor modifications. A separate, adapted program should be provided for those students who cannot participate in the basic instructional program of the school. The physically handicapped student cannot be allowed to sit on the sidelines and become only a spectator. He or she needs to have the opportunity to develop and maintain adequate skills abilities and fitness levels.

There are about 3 million children and youth between the ages of 4 and 19 years in the United States who are physically handicapped in varying degrees. About 500,000 of these handicapped individuals are of secondary school age. These figures are based on estimates made by the Bureau of the Census through its ongoing United States National Health Survey. Many authorities believe, however, that accurate sta-

tistics are not as yet available and that the number of physically handicapped youth may be somewhat higher than these estimates. Further, these surveys sometimes classify mental retardation under the broad category of physical handicaps.

Many of the more severely handicapped secondary school children attend special schools where their unique needs can be met by highly trained staff members. The remainder are enrolled in the public secondary schools. It is this latter group with which the physical educator must be especially concerned.

CHARACTERISTICS OF THE PHYSICALLY HANDICAPPED STUDENT

The presence of a physical handicap does not mean that the student also has a mental handicap, although this is sometimes true. Physical handicaps may stem from congenital or hereditary causes or may develop later in life through environmental factors, such as malnutrition, or from disease or accident. Sometimes negative psychological and social traits develop because of the limitations imposed on the individual by a severe physical handicap.

A physically handicapped student is occasionally ignored or rebuffed by classmates who do not understand the nature of the disability or who ostracize the student because a disability prevents full participation in the activities of the school. These attitudes toward handicapped persons force them to withdraw to avoid being hurt, which results in their becoming further isolated from the remainder of the student body. Some experts have noted that the limitations of the handicap often seem more severe to the observer than they in fact are to the handicapped individual. When this misconception occurs, the handicapped student must prove his or her abilities to gain acceptance and a chance to participate and compete on an equal basis with nonhandicapped classmates.

The blind or deaf student or the student with a severe speech impairment has different problems from those of the orthopedically handicapped student. The student who is partially sighted, blind, deaf, or impaired in speech cannot communicate with great facility. The orthopedically handicapped student is limited in the physical education class but not necessarily in the academic classroom. The student with vision, hearing, or speech problems may be limited in the physical education classroom and the academic classroom.

EDUCATIONAL NEEDS OF THE PHYSICALLY HANDICAPPED STUDENT

Physically handicapped students in general have the same academic needs, interests, and abilities as do their nonhandicapped peers. While special arrangements must be made for students who have speech, hearing, or visual disabilities, these students are capable of competing successfully in the classroom.

Physically handicapped students need preparation for vocations, technical schools, or colleges. They can contribute to the school through participation in social and service activities. They are far less limited in the general education program and activities of the school than in the physical education program.

THE PHYSICAL EDUCATOR AND THE PHYSICALLY HANDICAPPED STUDENT

There is a lack of physical educators who are specifically trained to teach the physically handicapped. School systems find that the cost of providing special classes taught by specially trained physical educators is prohibitive. Where there are no special classes, the physical educator must provide, within the regular instructional program, those activities that will meet the needs of the handicapped student. Further, placing the physically handicapped student in a regular physical education class will help in providing a feeling of belonging. This advantage is not always possible where separate, adapted classes are provided.

To be able to furnish an adequate program for physically handicapped students, the physical educator needs special training. Advanced courses in anatomy, physiology, physiology of activity, and kinesiology are essential, along with special work in psychology and adapted physical education. The professional preparation curriculum should also include courses in movement education and body mechanics.

The physical educator must have an understanding of the physical disability of each handicapped student and must be aware of any psychological, social, or behavioral problems that may accompany the disability. The physical educator must know the capacities of each handicapped student so that he or she can provide an individualized program.

THE PHYSICAL EDUCATION PROGRAM AND THE PHYSICALLY HANDICAPPED STUDENT

No two physically handicapped students will have the same limitations in regard to the activities of the physical education program. Under no circumstances can the physical educator diagnose the disability and prescribe a physical activity program. This must be accomplished by the student's physician. The physician's recommendations for students whose conditions have been diagnosed should be followed. If, in the course of the year, the physical educator observes that a student seems to have some kind of physical handicap that is not noted on the record cards of the school, he or she must refer the student to the family physician or the proper agency through the normal administrative process of the school. After the disability has been medically diagnosed and activity recommendations made, it becomes the responsibility of the physical educator to provide the proper program.

Some handicapped students will be able to participate in almost all the activities that nonhandicapped students enjoy. Blind students, for example, have successfully engaged in team sports where they can receive aural cues from their sighted teammates. Some athletic equipment manufacturers have placed bells inside game balls, and the blind student is then able to rely on this sound as well as on the supplementary aural cues. Ropes or covered wires used as hand guides also enable the blind student to participate in track-and-field events. Still other activities, such as swimming, dance, calisthenics, and tumbling, require little adaptation or none at all, except in regard to heightened safety precautions.

In general, deaf students will not be restricted in any way from participating in a full physical education program. Some deaf students experience difficulty in activities requiring precise balance, such as balance-beam walking, and may require some remedial work in this area. The physical educator should be prepared to offer any extra help that is needed.

Other physically handicapped students will have a variety of limitations and a variety of skills and abilities. Appropriate program adaptations and modifications must be made in order to meet this range of individual needs. The following general guidelines are helpful in physically educating the physically handicapped on the secondary school level.

- *Cooperate with the physician in planning each student's program.* The physician is the individual most knowledgeable about the history and limitations of a student's handicap. He or she is therefore in the best position to recommend a physical activity program for the student.

- *Test the motor skills ability and physical fitness levels of each student.* The student's abilities and levels of fitness should be tested in areas where medical permission for participation has been granted. This will not only ensure a proper program for the individual but will help in placing the student in the proper class or section of a class.

- *Keep the program under constant evaluation.* Careful records should be kept showing the student's test scores, activity recommendations, activities engaged in, and progress through the program. In this way, the physical educator will know whether the program is reaching its objectives, the student will be able to discuss progress with the physical educator, and the school health team and the student's physician can be kept up to date on the student's progress and needs.

- *Keep the adapted and regular programs as similar as possible.* Where the two programs are totally divergent, the physically handicapped student is isolated from classmates. When the programs are as similar as possible, the handicapped student can be made to feel a part of the larger group and will gain self-confidence and self-respect. Similarity in the programs will also effectively serve to motivate the physically handicapped student.

- *Provide challenges for the student.* Physically handicapped students need the challenge of a progressive program. They welcome the opportunity to test their abilities and should experience the fun of a challenge and the success of meeting it.

- *Provide time for extra help.* Handicapped students should be given an opportunity to seek extra help and extra practice after school hours. During this time they can benefit from more individualized instruction than is possible during the class period.

- *Select activities on an individual basis.* Although several handicapped students in a single class may be able to participate together in certain activities, they may not have a common interest in them. The fitness level and ability, recreational needs, sex, age, and

interests of each student will help to determine the activities the student will engage in pleasurably.

• *Adapt the activity to the student rather than the student to the activity.* The student's disability determines the activities in which he or she can participate. Therefore any modifications or adaptations that are made must be made in the activity.

• *Provide safe facilities and safe equipment.* Although safe facilities and safe equipment are essential in any physical education program, extra safeguards must be taken in a physical education class that includes physically handicapped students.

• *Provide suitable extraclass activities.* Experts feel that physically handicapped students are placed in an unduly hazardous situation when they engage in highly competitive activities. Intramural and club programs should be provided, but they must be of such a nature that physically handicapped students can enjoy them in a safe, controlled atmosphere that precludes the danger of injury.

The mentally retarded student

There are special schools in many states that serve mentally retarded students either on a residential or a day-care basis. Public secondary schools also offer specially designed curricula and employ teachers who have the comprehensive background and training needed to teach in programs for the retarded. In some public schools, special physical education classes are offered for these students, while in still other schools, mentally retarded students participate in the regularly scheduled physical education classes.

Mental retardation can be a result of hereditary abnormalities, a birth injury, or an accident or illness that leads to impairment of brain function. There are degrees of mental retardation ranging from the severely mentally retarded, who require custodial care, to the educable mentally retarded, who function with only a moderate degree of impairment.

Each year in the United States an estimated 126,000 babies are born who have some degree of mental retardation. At present, there are approximately 7 million mentally retarded children and adults in the United States.

Many agencies are conducting research in the field of mental retardation in an attempt to discover the causes of mental retardation, the nature of mental retardation, and the methods through which it may be prevented. Some agencies are operating innovative training schools for mentally retarded students. The Joseph P. Kennedy, Jr. Foundation spearheads much of the research concerned with mental retardation and also leads in providing camping and recreational programs for the mentally retarded. In addition, the Kennedy Foundation has sponsored training programs for teachers of the mentally retarded. The United States government too has supported an experimental physical education program for the mentally retarded at the Austin State School in Austin, Texas. This program is cooperatively conducted by a staff of special education teachers, specially trained physical educators, vocational rehabilitation technicians, and architectural engineers. A special program and special equipment have been designed especially for use with the mentally retarded. Climbing devices, obstacle courses, and unique running areas, as well as a swimming pool, are part of the special facilities. The objectives of this program include social and personal adjustment, as well as the development of physical fitness, sports skills, and general motor ability.

CHARACTERISTICS OF THE MENTALLY RETARDED STUDENT

Mentally retarded students show a wide range of intellectual and physical ability. The experts seem to agree that a mentally retarded child is usually closer to the norm of chronological age in physical development than in mental development. Some mentally retarded students are capable of participating in a regular physical education class, while others have been able to develop only minimum motor ability. In general the majority of mentally retarded students are 2 to 4 years behind their normal peers in motor development alone.

Despite a slower development of motor ability, mentally retarded students seem to reach physical maturity faster than do normal boys and girls of the same chronological age. Mentally retarded children tend to be overweight and to lack physical strength and endurance. Their posture is generally poor, and they lack adequate levels of physical fitness and motor coordination. Some of these physical problems develop because mentally retarded children have had little of

the play and physical activity experiences of normal children. The problems of some mentally retarded youngsters are further multiplied by attendant physical handicaps and personality disturbances.

A mentally retarded student does not have the ability to think abstractly or to remember isolated facts well. A short attention span, a tendency to overreact emotionally, and a low threshold of irritability also contribute to the classroom problems of the mentally retarded student. While not all mentally retarded students have the same personal characteristics, some of them also tend to be very restless, destructive, and impulsive.

EDUCATIONAL NEEDS OF THE MENTALLY RETARDED STUDENT

Mentally retarded students require a sound foundation in educational skills. Many of them will seek and be able to hold jobs at the conclusion of their secondary education, and vocational training courses must be provided for them. Girls in particular need and enjoy courses in home economics, while both boys and girls benefit from instruction in money management and the techniques of using the telephone and writing acceptable letters.

While special classes are usually conducted in many subject areas of the school curriculum, it has been found that the mentally retarded student can join with peers in some subjects. Vocational and shop courses, art, music, home economics, and physical education are a few of the subjects in which mentally retarded students can find success outside of the special class. The mentally retarded student can also enjoy intramural activities and school clubs and can contribute to special events, school committees, and service organizations.

THE PHYSICAL EDUCATOR AND THE MENTALLY RETARDED STUDENT

The mentally retarded student requires a physical educator with special training, special skills, and a special brand of patience. Such a student lacks confidence and pride and therefore needs a physical educator who will help to change his or her negative self-image. The physical educator must be able to provide a program designed to give each student a chance for success. The goals of the program cannot be so high that they are unreachable.

The physical educator must be ready to praise and reinforce each minor success. He or she should be capable of demonstrating each skill and giving simple and concise directions and be willing to participate in the physical education activities with the students. Discipline must be enforced and standards adhered to, but the disciplinary approach must be a kind and gentle one.

The physical educator must be especially mindful of the individual characteristics of each mentally retarded student. Students who need remedial work should be afforded this opportunity, while students who can succeed in a regular physical education program should be placed in such a class or section. Above all, the physical educator must remember not to advance with a class of mentally retarded students in the same manner as he or she would proceed with a class of students with average intelligence and physical ability.

THE PHYSICAL EDUCATION PROGRAM AND THE MENTALLY RETARDED STUDENT

Most mentally retarded students need to be taught how to play. They are frequently unfamiliar with even the simplest of childhood games and lack facility in the natural movements of childhood, such as skipping, hopping, and leaping. They are often seriously deficient in physical fitness and need work in postural improvement. Further, mentally retarded students find it difficult to understand and remember game strategy, such as the importance of staying in the right position, and they cannot relate well to the rules of sports and games.

Many mentally retarded students require a specially tailored physical education experience. For those who can participate in a regular physical education class, care must be taken that these students are not placed in a situation where they will meet failure. In a special physical education class, the mentally retarded student can be exposed to a variety of physical education experiences. Physical fitness and posture improvement, along with self-testing activities and games organized and designed according to the ability and interests of the group, will make up a vital part of the

AAHPERD
KENNEDY FOUNDATION

SPECIAL FITNESS TEST for the mentally retarded

A manual explaining the purpose of this test, administrative procedures, and how to record and use the results is available from:

AAHPERD
1900 ASSOCIATION DRIVE
RESTON, VA. 22091

It presents graphs showing changes in the performance of retarded children with age, national norms for educable retarded boys and girls 8 to 18 years of age, and suggestions for improving their physical fitness.

It is highly recommended that anyone using this test obtain a copy of the manual.

Special Fitness Record Forms (score cards) are also available

1. FLEXED ARM HAND

—horizontal or doorway gym (about 3½" dia.) bar adjusted to approximately the student's height.

—overhand grasp, pull chin above bar and hold as long as possible

—may use stool or tester may lift to position

—score is time *in seconds* from when he hangs unaided until his chin touches or falls below bar.

2. SIT-UP

—student lies on back, fingers interlaced behind head, legs extended. Partner holds ankles down

—sit up, touch elbow to knee and return keeping fingers behind head.

—"curl up;" no pushing off with elbows, back flat on mat each time.

—score is *number of complete sit ups in one minute*

3. SHUTTLE RUN

—2 lines, 30 feet apart, 2 blocks of wood (2" x 2" x 4") behind far line.

—on "GO!" student runs down, picks up one block, runs back and *places* it behind starting line, runs down and picks up second block, runs back and *carries* it across starting line

—score is time in *seconds to the nearest tenth* from "GO!" until he crosses finish line.

4. STANDING BROAD JUMP

—toes behind take-off line with feet several inches apart

—bend knees and swing arms backward

—jump by extending legs and swinging arms forward

—score is distance *in feet and inches* from take-off line to back of heel *nearest* take-off line

5. 50-YARD DASH

—Starter raises hand, says "READY?—GO!" and sweeps hand down to signal timer who stands at finish line

—any starting position may be used

—score is time *in seconds to the nearest tenth*

6. SOFTBALL THROW FOR DISTANCE

—12" softball thrown from between two parallel lines, six feet apart (see figure)

—must be thrown overhand

—score is distance *in feet* from *point* of *throwing* to *point* of landing

START AND FINISH

25'

50'

START AND FINISH

RESTRAINING LINE

50 YDS

7. 300-YARD RUN-WALK

—if indoors, six times around 50' x 25' course

—if outdoors, three times up and back a 50-yard shuttle course

—walking permitted but object is to cover distance in shortest possible time.

—score is the elapsed time *in minutes and seconds*

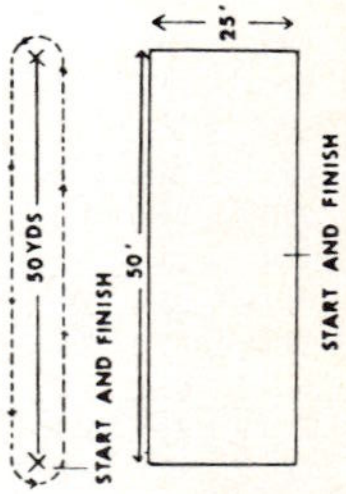

Special Note

Some retarded children must be restricted in their physical activity for medical reasons. It is strongly recommended that each child be examined by a medical doctor before beginning any physical testing or training program.

Fig. 17-2. Kennedy Foundation Special Fitness Test for mentally retarded.

STANDARDS FOR AAHPER SILVER AWARD

(Qualified by achieving the standard on any five test items)

GIRLS

Age	Flexed Arm Hang (sec.)	Sit-Ups (no.)	Shuttle Run (sec.)	Standing Broad Jump (ft.—ins.)	50-yd. Dash (sec.)	Softball Throw (ft.)	300-yard Run-Walk (min.—sec.)
8	5	13	15.0	3' 1"	11.3	27	1:34
9	6	15	14.2	3' 4"	10.5	34	1:33
10	8	18	13.3	3' 10"	9.3	41	1:23
11	7	18	12.9	4' 0"	9.1	46	1:23
12	5	19	12.2	4' 3"	8.8	56	1:18
13	5	18	12.3	4' 3"	8.9	57	1:16
14	6	20	12.1	4' 6"	8.7	63	1:15
15	5	20	12.0	4' 6"	8.6	65	1:20
16	5	21	12.1	4' 8"	9.0	67	1:18
17	4	20	12.5	4' 9"	9.0	62	1:22
18	7	20	12.2	4' 9"	9.0	61	1:20

BOYS

Age	Flexed Arm Hang (sec.)	Sit-Ups (no.)	Shuttle Run (sec.)	Standing Broad Jump (ft.—ins.)	50-yd. Dash (sec.)	Softball Throw (ft.)	300-yard Run-Walk (min.—sec.)
8	7	16	14.0	3' 4"	10.5	43	1:33
9	8	17	13.1	3' 10"	9.9	58	1:24
10	8	20	12.6	3' 11"	9.2	66	1:20
11	11	22	11.9	4' 6"	8.9	80	1:15
12	12	24	11.6	4' 10"	8.3	95	1:12
13	10	25	11.3	5' 0"	8.2	104	1:10
14	13	26	11.0	5' 3"	8.0	112	1:07
15	12	31	11.2	5' 9"	7.5	137	1:01
16	17	29	11.1	6' 1"	7.3	154	0:59
17	17	30	10.6	6' 2"	6.9	159	0:56
18	25	31	10.6	6' 6"	7.1	159	0:57

STANDARDS FOR AAHPER GOLD AWARD

(Qualified by achieving the standard on any five test items)

GIRLS

Age	Flexed Arm Hang (sec.)	Sit-Ups (no.)	Shuttle Run (sec.)	Standing Broad Jump (ft.—ins.)	50-yd. Dash (sec.)	Softball Throw (ft.)	300-yard Run-Walk (min.—sec.)
8	10	18	13.8	3' 8"	10.1	33	1:28
9	11	21	12.9	3' 9"	9.1	46	1:24
10	13	25	12.1	4' 5"	8.8	52	1:16
11	12	24	11.9	4' 8"	8.4	65	1:15
12	10	24	11.5	4' 11"	8.1	71	1:09
13	11	22	11.6	4' 10"	8.3	72	1:10
14	12	25	11.3	5' 1"	8.2	86	1:08
15	11	25	11.0	5' 1"	8.0	84	1:12
16	11	24	11.2	5' 3"	8.1	82	1:11
17	10	24	11.7	5' 3"	8.2	81	1:13
18	10	24	11.5	5' 3"	8.5	84	1:11

BOYS

Age	Flexed Arm Hang (sec.)	Sit-Ups (no.)	Shuttle Run (sec.)	Standing Broad Jump (ft.—ins.)	50-yd. Dash (sec.)	Softball Throw (ft.)	300-yard Run-Walk (min.—sec.)
8	11	20	12.6	3' 9"	9.4	57	1:23
9	13	23	12.1	4' 5"	8.9	73	1:17
10	16	26	11.8	4' 8"	8.5	81	1:13
11	19	27	11.1	5' 1"	8.2	99	1:08
12	19	30	11.0	5' 4"	7.9	114	1:05
13	19	30	10.8	5' 6"	7.7	125	1:04
14	22	30	10.4	5' 11"	7.4	142	1:00
15	26	34	10.7	6' 4"	7.1	159	0:58
16	29	34	10.2	6' 9"	6.9	181	0:55
17	29	35	9.8	7' 2"	6.3	176	0:51
18	39	36	9.9	7' 1"	6.5	187	0:52

STANDARDS FOR KENNEDY FOUNDATION CHAMP AWARD

(Qualified by achieving the standard on all seven test items)

GIRLS

Age	Flexed Arm Hang (sec.)	Sit-Ups (no.)	Shuttle Run (sec.)	Standing Broad Jump (ft.—ins.)	50-yd. Dash (sec.)	Softball Throw (ft.)	300-yard Run-Walk (min.—sec.)
8	14	22	13.0	3' 10"	9.6	36	1:26
9	16	25	12.4	4' 1"	8.8	58	1:19
10	16	29	11.9	4' 8"	8.5	59	1:12
11	17	27	11.5	5' 0"	8.2	75	1:13
12	14	28	11.1	5' 4"	7.8	82	1:06
13	14	25	11.2	5' 1"	7.9	81	1:07
14	16	27	11.0	5' 6"	7.8	95	1:04
15	15	27	10.6	5' 6"	7.8	94	1:06
16	14	26	11.0	5' 7"	7.9	97	1:05
17	13	27	11.1	5' 6"	7.9	98	1:10
18	13	28	11.2	5' 8"	8.1	93	1:09

BOYS

Age	Flexed Arm Hang (sec.)	Sit-Ups (no.)	Shuttle Run (sec.)	Standing Broad Jump (ft.—ins.)	50-yd. Dash (sec.)	Softball Throw (ft.)	300-yard Run-Walk (min.—sec.)
8	15	22	12.4	4' 1"	9.1	61	1:22
9	19	27	11.9	4' 9"	8.6	85	1:14
10	21	29	11.4	4' 11"	8.2	89	1:08
11	24	29	10.9	5' 4"	8.0	108	1:05
12	25	32	10.7	5' 6"	7.5	123	1:03
13	25	33	10.5	5' 10"	7.5	140	1:00
14	32	34	10.1	6' 4"	7.1	151	0:56
15	36	36	10.3	6' 9"	6.9	181	0:56
16	37	38	9.9	7' 0"	6.5	188	0:52
17	34	38	9.6	7' 5"	6.1	187	0:49
18	49	38	9.7	7' 4"	6.3	204	0:49

For boys and girls who achieve the CHAMP standards on all seven test items and engage in at least 30 hours of sports and recreational activity.

Fig. 17-2, cont'd. Kennedy Foundation Special Fitness Test for mentally retarded.

special program. In such a class, activities can be easily modified and new experiences introduced before interest wanes. Research has indicated that specially tailored physical education classes can help mentally retarded students to progress very rapidly in their physical skill development.

Physical education can make a very positive contribution to the mentally retarded. Not only must the program be a suitable one, but the physical educator must also be adequately prepared and emotionally and intellectually dedicated to teaching these students.

• *The program should provide opportunities for increasing physical fitness*. Mentally retarded students do not usually initiate play experiences or seek out physical activity. Lack of a regular program of physical exercise, as well as lack of understanding of the need for such a program, means that the mentally retarded student may be lacking in physical fitness. A sound program that includes physical fitness activities can help these students become more physically fit.

• *Provide a background of basic motor activities*. Movement education is especially suited to mentally retarded students. These students have often not engaged in the natural play activities of childhood and need to develop their gross motor skill abilities in order to find success in some of the more sophisticated motor skills.

• *Provide a wide variety of self-testing activities*. Mentally retarded students enjoy even the smallest success in physical activity. Given an opportunity to compete against himself or herself, such a student will gain confidence and pride in accomplishment.

• *Provide a carefully structured, progressive program*. Mentally retarded students have the same physical activity needs as do normal students. Thus a progressive program will help to interest and motivate them in a variety of physical activities.

• *Provide opportunities for competition in games of low organization*. Mentally retarded students enjoy the give-and-take of competition, but any competition must be geared specifically to their needs and abilities. The experience of competing will aid in the development of desirable social traits.

• *Introduce new activities at the beginning of a class period*. Mentally retarded children tire easily and

have a short attention span. New activities will be learned more easily and will be enjoyed more before fatigue sets in and while interest is still high.

• *Provide for a choice of activities*. This will help the mentally retarded student to feel important. Further, if a choice of activities is offered, motivation, morale, and discipline will remain higher.

• *Provide for lifetime recreational skills*. These skills are essential for any student, but mentally retarded students especially need to learn the value of recreation. Through specially designed intramural and club programs, additional recreational experiences can be introduced.

• *Stress positive health and safety habits*. Provide each student with a locker and require that proper care be taken of the physical education uniform. Where possible, provide time in the program for showers. Stress should be placed on the relationship between health and physical activity. Safety must be constantly stressed in all activities and must be related to other phases of the school program.

• *Keep accurate, up-to-date records*. Records will help in guiding students and in assessing their abilities and limitations. The students' parents are also interested in their children's progress, and keeping them informed of gains will help to establish good public relations. Accurate and complete records will be invaluable to the students' guidance counselor, school health team, and personal physician. Complete records will also help the physical educator in making an objective evaluation of the program.

The disruptive student

The disruptive student may suffer from deep-seated emotional disturbances or may simply be in need of guidance and counseling to help resolve less serious problems that lead to disruptive behavior. Some students who dislike school will be disruptive in classes even though there is no serious emotional problem involved. In any case, such a student presents special problems for the physical educator, who must be concerned not only with teaching but also with the safety of the students in the class.

A single disruptive student can have a disastrous effect on the conduct of a class as well as on the

behavior of the rest of the students in that class. Effective teaching cannot take place when discipline deteriorates (see Chapter 14 on class management).

CHARACTERISTICS OF THE DISRUPTIVE STUDENT

Emotionally unstable students have difficulty in maintaining good relationships with their classmates and teachers. Some of their abnormal behavior patterns stem from a need and craving for attention. Sometimes the disruptive student exhibits gross patterns of aggressiveness and destructiveness. Other emotionally unstable students may be so withdrawn from the group that they refuse to participate in the activities of the class, even to the extent of refusing to report for class. In the case of physical education, the disruptive student may refuse to dress for the activity. These measures elicit both student and teacher reaction, focusing the desired attention on the nonconforming student.

Emotionally unstable students are often restless and unable to pay attention. In a physical education class they may poke and prod other students, refuse to line up with the rest of the class, or insist on bouncing a game ball while a lesson is in progress. These are also ploys to gain attention, and the student behaves similarly in the academic classroom for the same reason.

Some disruptive students may have physical or mental handicaps that contribute to their behavior. Others may be concerned about what they consider to be poor personal appearance, such as extremes of height or weight or physical maturity not in keeping with their chronological age. Still other disruptive students may simply be in the process of growing up and finding it difficult to handle their adolescence.

EDUCATIONAL NEEDS OF THE DISRUPTIVE STUDENT

The disruptive student is in need of guidance and counseling. Therefore the school should not impose discipline on the disruptive student before the causes for his or her behavior have been ascertained. The school has many services available to help such a student. School psychologists can administer tests, and social welfare agencies can assist by working with both student and family. Case studies of the student and conferences with all involved teachers can be invaluable in determining the student's needs. The school health team will also have pertinent information to contribute, as will guidance counselors. Conferences with the student also help to open the doors to understanding.

The school cannot take the responsibility for arbitrarily expelling or suspending the disruptive student without first carefully and comprehensively examining the causes for such behavior. Expulsion or suspension often serve to heighten the student's negative feelings and make it more difficult to draw him or her back into the life of the school.

THE PHYSICAL EDUCATOR AND THE DISRUPTIVE STUDENT

The physical educator faced with many disruptive students in a single class must first examine his or her relationship to that class. Rapport with the entire class, relationships with individual students, disciplinary standards, and program will all affect student behavior to some degree.

If negative student behavior stems from some aspect of a student's personality, then the physical educator must take positive steps to resolve the problem so that teaching can take place. The teacher must deal with each behavioral problem on an individual basis and seek help from the school personnel best equipped to give aid. A conference with the student's guidance counselor may reveal methods that have proved effective with the student in the past. Further, the observations made by the physical educator will be of value to the guidance counselor's continuing study of the student.

The physical educator will find that not all disruptive students present continual and serious behavior problems, since students as well as teachers have their good and bad days. The physical educator should have a private conference with the student whose behavior suddenly becomes negative and try to understand why the student has reacted in such a way. Such a conference will lead to mutual understanding and often help to allay future problems with that student.

Much of the physical educator's task is student guidance. In individual cases of disruptive behavior, the physical educator should exhaust personal resources in order to alleviate the problem before enlisting aid from other sources. Any case of disruptive

behavior demands immediate action to prevent minor problems from becoming major ones.

THE PHYSICAL EDUCATION PROGRAM AND THE DISRUPTIVE STUDENT

A majority of secondary school pupils enjoy physical activity and physical education. They look forward to the physical education class as one part of the school day in which they can express themselves and gain a release of tension in an atmosphere that encourages it. For this reason, physical education can be of special help to the student who is disruptive in the classroom but is often one of the best participants in the physical education class. Most of these students profit from the activities of physical education, and their behavior in such a class may help their other teachers gain many insights into student behavior.

• *Know each student by name and as an individual.* Individual knowledge of each student is of utmost importance in physical education and in understanding individual behavior patterns. Recognizing a student's needs and problems early in the school year will help prevent future behavior problems.

• *Be certain that students understand the behavior required of them.* While physical education classes are conducted in a less formal manner than are classroom subjects, this does not mean that lower standards of behavior are acceptable. Students should know what the standards are on the first day of class and should be expected to adhere to these standards in all future classes.

• *Discipline must be firm and consistent.* When rules are rigid one day and relaxed the next, students will not know how to react. Discipline must be enforced in a firm and consistent manner for all students during all classes.

• *Discuss behavioral problems with the individual student.* Respect for the individual student is a necessity. No student likes to be criticized or embarrassed in front of peers. When a student is singled out from a group and used as a disciplinary example, the atmosphere in the class will deteriorate. Respect for the student helps maintain respect for the teacher. If disciplinary matters are handled on a one-to-one basis, rapport is enhanced.

• *Expect good behavior from all students.* If the disruptive student knows that the physical educator expects bizarre behavior, the student will react in just this way. Good behavior should be expected until the student acts otherwise.

• *Try to ensure that the disruptive student will be successful in the physical education class.* Constant failure only abets disruptive behavior. If a student is known to be hostile and disruptive, an attempt should be made to avoid situations where he or she feels inadequate. If, for example, a disruptive student does not run well, he or she may still make a superior goalie in soccer, a position that would not require running.

• *Give praise as often as possible.* If the disruptive student has a special skills talent, ask him or her to demonstrate for the class. This will provide the recognition and attention needed. Give praise for a skill that is well performed and notice the minor accomplishments of the student.

• *Allow the student to help with equipment.* Make the position of equipment leader a reward rather than a punishment. See that each deserving student, including the disruptive ones, receive this honor when they merit it.

• *Welcome the disruptive student to intramural and club activities.* No student is going to participate in extraclass activities unless so motivated. Set behavioral standards for these activities and open them to all students in the school who meet the standards. Acceptance into a club or participation on an intramural team may help the disruptive student gain self-respect and peer recognition and approval.

• *Keep the student's guidance counselor informed of his or her progress.* The guidance counselor should know of any progress made by the pupil. Too often these individuals are informed only of failures or increasing behavior problems. Progress in one area of the school curriculum may have a positive effect on progress in other areas of the curriculum.

The poorly coordinated student

Well-coordinated students are the bright lights of the physical education class. Often held up as examples by the physical educator, they find success easily and receive much individual attention because they respond well to instruction and coaching. There is another segment of the school population, however, that needs individual instruction even more—the awk-

ward, uncoordinated students who are frequently left to learn skills as best they can.

The student with low motor ability is often ignored by the physical educator and frequently unpopular with classmates because he or she is considered a detriment in team sports. This student is undesirable as a partner in dual sports and therefore is often paired with equally uncoordinated and awkward partners. The student with low motor ability needs special attention so that physical skills performances can be improved and success gained in the activity.

Although physical educators make special arrangements for the physically handicapped, the mentally retarded, and the athlete, very little is done for the poorly coordinated student.

CHARACTERISTICS OF THE POORLY COORDINATED STUDENT

The poorly coordinated student exhibits a measurable lack of physical ability. Less often considered is the psychological effect of this deficiency. The poorly coordinated student who is not given special help in the secondary school often becomes the adult who abhors any physical activity and is reticent about participating in adult recreational activities.

Poorly coordinated students are usually placed in regular physical education classes when they have no mental or physical handicaps. The only concession made to their problem is through ability grouping in schools where facilities and personnel are adequate. Even then, ability grouping sometimes is used only to separate the "duds" from the "stars," thus increasing the poorly coordinated student's feelings of inadequacy. Such a student may be held up to ridicule by other students as well as by physical education teachers, who tend to use him or her as an example of how not to perform a physical skill.

The student with poor coordination will resist learning new activities because the challenge offers little chance for success. The demands of a new skill or activity may create such tension within the student that he or she becomes physically ill. In other instances this tension may result in negative behavior.

Poor coordination may be the result of several factors. The student may not be physically fit, may have poor reflexes, or may not have the ability to use mental imagery. For some reason, such as a lengthy childhood illness, the poorly coordinated student may not have been normally physically active. Others enter the secondary school from an elementary school that lacked a trained physical educator, facilities for physical education, or an adequate physical education program. A single factor or a combination of any of them will help to retard motor skill development.

EDUCATIONAL NEEDS OF THE POORLY COORDINATED STUDENT

The physical education program frequently motivates students with specific problems to perform better in the academic classroom by offering an opportunity for success in physical activity. This process may work in reverse with the poorly coordinated student. A student's dread of physical education class will have a detrimental effect on ability to perform well in the classroom. Both behavior and academic achievement may be adversely affected.

When classroom performance declines, it is the classroom teacher who will become aware of the problem first. As with any other student problem, the first step in resolving that problem is a conference with the student and then with the student's guidance counselor. It may be only through such conferences that the cause of the problem is revealed and the physical educator made aware of his or her contribution to the problem, and thus help remedy it. Many problems of this nature cast doubt on the value of the physical education program, its philosophy, and objectives. If measures are not taken to adequately resolve the problems, poor relations will develop between the physical educator, the student body, the remainder of the school faculty, the administration, and the community.

THE PHYSICAL EDUCATOR AND THE POORLY COORDINATED STUDENT

The physical educator must understand child growth and development and formulate a physical education program that is based on sound principles of growth and development. A knowledge of adolescent growth and development and of adolescent psychology are prerequisites to teaching on the secondary school level. Additionally, the physical educator must be able to use personal knowledge to select activities

and devise progressions that are appropriate to the age and grade level of the students in the program.

In working with poorly coordinated students, the physical educator must exercise the utmost patience. He or she must know why the student is poorly coordinated and be able to devise an individual program that will help the student to move and perform more effectively. The physical educator must be sure that the student understands the need for special help and should try to motivate him or her to succeed. When a skill is performed with even a modicum of improvement, the effort must be praised and the achievement reinforced.

With a large class and only one instructor, there can be relatively little time spent with each individual. The buddy system, in which a poorly coordinated student is paired with a well-coordinated partner, often enables both students to progress faster. Immediate successes will not be forthcoming for the poorly coordinated student, and the physical educator must be careful not to push the student beyond desirable limits. An overly difficult challenge, coupled with the fatigue that results from trying too hard, may result in retarding, rather than accelerating, improvement. Any goal set for the poorly coordinated student must be an attainable goal.

The physical educator has a very definite responsibility to the poorly coordinated student. Negative attitudes concerning physical activity can too easily be carried over into adult life. If such attitudes can be reversed by the physical educator early in the student's secondary school career, the student may be motivated to develop abilities in several of the lifetime sports.

THE PHYSICAL EDUCATION PROGRAM
AND THE POORLY COORDINATED STUDENT

The objectives of the program for poorly coordinated students will not differ from the objectives of any physical education program, but the emphases will lie in different areas, and many activities will be modified or adapted as the need arises.

Before a program is devised, students' individual abilities and needs should be identified. Physical fitness and motor ability testing must be ongoing phases of the program. Through the physical education program, students must realize that their special needs are being met because they are as important as the well-skilled students in the eyes of the physical educator.

• *Carefully weigh the advantages and disadvantages of ability grouping.* Separating students into ability groups may cause poorly coordinated students to feel that they are being pushed out of the way. If ability grouping is used, all must receive adequate instruction and a meaningful program and have equal access to good equipment and facilities.

• *Select the proper activities.* If a student has poor eye-hand or eye-foot coordination, it will be difficult to succeed in such activities as tennis or soccer. Activities must be chosen that suit the abilities of the students and at the same time help them to develop the needed coordination.

• *Offer a varied, interesting, and progressive program.* Work on improving fitness and self-testing activities should form only a part of the program. Games of appropriate level, rhythmics and dance, and such activities as swimming and archery will help to stimulate and maintain interest.

• *Offer a club program for all students.* Physical fitness clubs, swimming clubs, and other clubs open to all students will benefit poorly coordinated students. If ability grouping is used in class, a common club program will help to remove the stigma of separateness.

• *Include competition in the program.* With carefully arranged teams and schedules in an intramural program, poorly coordinated students can be given a chance to compete on their own level. Preparation for intramural competition should be a part of the class program.

• *Include some activities of a coeducational nature.* Dancing in particular lends itself to coeducational instruction. When classes can be combined and coeducational instruction offered, poorly coordinated students have an opportunity to develop social skills.

• *Group students on a flexible pattern.* Different groupings for different activities will stimulate interest and provide students with a variety of partners.

• *Provide for upward progression.* Reassess the students periodically to see how they are progressing. When an adequate level of success has been attained

in a particular activity, move the student into a faster-moving and more highly skilled group.

• *Involve the students in program planning.* Offer a selection of activities that will appeal to poorly coordinated students and guide their selections in relation to their abilities.

• *Provide for lifetime sports skills.* Swimming and dance are ideal for future recreational use. Poorly coordinated students need a background of lifetime sports skills to help them to offset the tensions that will arise in their lives and to receive the fullest enjoyment from life. Rather than attempting to develop championship-level skill, these students need to develop enough skill to appreciate and engage voluntarily in physical activity.

The physically gifted or creative student

By what criteria do we judge the gifted or creative student in physical education? Is it the boy who captains the basketball team, the girl who scores the most goals for the field hockey team, the boy who wins a state gymnastics title, or the girl who aspires to a career as a professional dancer? Is it the student who decides to be a professional physical educator? The gifted or creative student in physical education has a combination of many qualities, the depth of each quality varying with the individual. Gifted and creative students in physical education are handicapped when they do not receive a specially tailored physical education experience.

In this section we are not concerned with the secondary school student who is gifted intellectually. These students may also be gifted physically, but some intellectually gifted students have only low or average motor ability. We are concerned here with the student who is exceptional because of his or her motor skill abilities and who perhaps is also gifted intellectually.

CHARACTERISTICS OF THE PHYSICALLY GIFTED OR CREATIVE STUDENT

The physically gifted student is not the student who is a star athlete in one sport or activity. The physically gifted student has superior motor skills and abilities in many activities and maintains a high level of phys-

ical fitness. He or she may be a star athlete but in general is simply a good all-around performer.

The physically gifted student learns quickly and requires a minimum of individual instruction. This student is usually enthusiastic about physical activity and practices skills of his or her own volition. Any individual instruction required is in the form of coaching rather than remedial correction. The physically gifted student has a strong sense of kinesthetic awareness and understands the principles of human movement. The student may not be able to articulate these latter two qualities, but observation by the physical educator will reveal that the student has discovered how to exploit the body as a tool for movement.

The physically creative student also has a well-developed sense of kinesthetic awareness. This student is the girl who dances with ease and grace or who is highly skilled in free exercise. It is the boy who is the lithe tumbler or gymnast. These students develop their own sophisticated routines in dance, tumbling, gymnastics, apparatus, and synchronized swimming. They may or may not be extraordinarily adept in other physical education activities but are as highly teachable as are the physically gifted.

EDUCATIONAL NEEDS OF THE PHYSICALLY GIFTED OR CREATIVE STUDENT

The physically gifted student or the physically creative student may or may not exhibit similar extraordinary abilities in the academic classroom. A student who is doing very poorly academically may be a superior student in physical education or may be superior in all phases of the secondary school program.

For the academically gifted student, most secondary schools offer honors courses, opportunities to conduct independent research, or courses that lead to college credits. Where a student shows exceptional talent in physical education but none in the classroom, appropriate measures must be taken to discover, and perhaps remedy, the cause of this disparity. Exceptional students in physical education should be identified to the guidance personnel by the physical educator in a conference, since grade reports will reveal a superior mark only and reveal little of the student as an individual. Guidance personnel should be informed of these exceptional students as early in the school year as a reliable and valid judgment can be made.

A   B

Fig. 17-3. The physical educator must meet the needs of physically gifted and creative students. **A,** Student at Walt Whitman High School, South Huntington Schools, New York. **B,** Student at Mount Pleasant Senior High School in Wilmington, Del.

THE PHYSICAL EDUCATOR AND THE PHYSICALLY GIFTED OR CREATIVE STUDENT

The beginning physical educator, especially, may find it difficult to teach a student who seems to possess many more physical abilities than the teacher. However, there is no student in a secondary school who knows all there is to know about an activity. Students' knowledge is limited by what they have been taught or have learned on their own. Many experiences will still be new to them.

The physically gifted student or the physically creative student may not have attempted participation in a wide range of activities; he or she may have experienced only those activities offered in the school physical education program. Both the physically gifted and the physically creative student, as well as the average student, will be stimulated and challenged by the introduction of new activities. The creative student in dance may be introduced to a new kind of music, or the boy who is skilled on apparatus may enjoy adding new moves to his routines. The athlete may be a good performer but, because of a tendency to rely on superior skills rather than on a complete knowledge of the rules and strategies of sports and games, may need to become a better team player.

The physical educator has a contribution to make to each student in the physical education program. The challenges presented by students of exceptional ability will help to keep the physical educator alert, stimulated, and enthusiastic about teaching.

THE PHYSICAL EDUCATION PROGRAM AND THE PHYSICALLY GIFTED OR CREATIVE STUDENT

A well-planned physical education program will be adaptable to the needs of all the students it serves. Before the program can be definitely developed, however, the specific needs, limitations, and abilities of the students in the program must be defined. The activities offered must be adapted to the needs of the students, since the students cannot be adapted to the program. Objectives are not achieved in the latter manner.

The exceptional student needs a structured program of physical activity, since this is a vital part of his or her mental, social, emotional, and physical development. Some schools have made it a policy to excuse athletes from the activity program when their varsity sport is in season. This is a disservice to the student, especially when the varsity sport and the unit being

taught in class are different. A student benefits from physical activity in a regular program. The physical educator can keep the interest of the exceptional student high by adopting some tested methods.

• *Develop a leaders' program.* This type of activity has proved valuable in many secondary schools. Leaders can assist the physical educator in innumerable ways and develop a sense of responsibility for the program because they are directly involved. Members of leaders' clubs have served as gymnastics and tumbling spotters in classes other than their own and can assist as officials in the class program and during intramural contests. Members of leaders' clubs still participate in the activities of their own class but at the same time receive the benefit of extra exposure to activities.

• *Utilize audiovisual materials.* Movies, filmstrips, loop films, and slides interest and benefit all students, but by watching these materials the exceptional student can compare performance with those of experts, gain new insights into skills, and discover new techniques of performing skills.

• *Provide special challenges.* Textbooks in physical education are not in wide use in secondary school physical education programs. While all students could benefit from the use of a textbook, special outside readings, assignments, and research problems would provide an additional challenge for the exceptional student. Bucher's physical education textbook for high school boys and girls, *Physical Education for Life*, should be especially helpful (see Selected Readings at end of this chapter).

• *Encourage the exceptional student to assist in class.* Many of the highly skilled or creative students will be able to assist students who have low motor skill abilities. By working on a one-to-one basis, the amount of individualized instruction will be increased. The student with low motor ability will receive the special assistance needed, and the gifted student will be helped to realize that not all students possess high levels of ability.

• *Assign the student to coaching responsibilities.* The exceptional student can assist in the intramural program by acting as a coach on a day when the team is not playing. Coaching a team will help the student to become more cognizant of the importance of team play, sportsmanship, and the need for rules. Such coaching, however, should be done under the close supervision of the physical educator.

• *Provide challenges within the program.* A skilled gymnast would not benefit from a beginning unit in tumbling. If the class is on this unit, the exceptional student might be assigned to work on advanced skills or on an advanced routine. A girl who shows great creativity in dance could be assigned to design a new dance or to devise some new steps.

Self-assessment tests

These tests are designed to assist students in determining if material and competencies presented in this chapter have been mastered.

1. Write a definition in your own words of the terms "adapted," "handicapped," and "mainstreaming."
2. Your classmates maintain that handicapped students should be segregated from so-called normal students. Present a report to your class outlining the advantages and disadvantages of mainstreaming. Furthermore, assume it is required by law in your state and therefore must be implemented. Provide in your report the guidelines you feel are necessary in implementing this concept in physical education classes.
3. Prepare a chart. For each of the following classifications of handicapped students, list their characteristics, needs, the physical education activities that meet their needs, and the methods and materials that will assure a viable physical education program for each.
   Culturally disadvantaged
   Mentally retarded
   Physically handicapped
   Disruptive
   Poorly coordinated
4. Given a physical education class where mentally retarded and physically handicapped students are enrolled, outline a program of physical education and the methods and materials you would use.
5. Justify why physically gifted and creative students should also be provided for in the physical education program.

Points to remember

1. Every physical educator will at some time have handicapped students in class.
2. There are many different categories of handicapped students.

3. Physical education has a strong appeal for the culturally disadvantaged.
4. Physically handicapped students may exhibit a wide range of disabilities.
5. Some mentally retarded students can participate in regular physical education classes.
6. A disruptive student may affect the safety of a physical education class.
7. A poorly coordinated student may become a behavior problem if he or she does not receive special assistance.
8. The physically gifted or physically creative student can benefit from participation in regular physical education classes.
9. Mainstreaming influences the nonhandicapped as well as handicapped students.

Problems to think through

1. Should the objectives of physical education be the same for all secondary school students?
2. What is the advantage of having specially trained physical educators for special students?
3. What are the advantages and disadvantages of having special physical education classes for handicapped students?
4. What special concerns should physical education have for the student with average physical ability?
5. How can physical educators best plan a program for the resistive student?
6. What implications does ability grouping have for the handicapped student? for mainstreaming?

Case study for analysis

You are a beginning physical educator in a medium-size secondary school and the only member of your department. On the first day of activity in the fall, one of your students refuses to put on the physical education uniform. The remainder of your class is dressed for activity and ready to report to the playing area. What steps will you take to resolve this problem?

Exercises for review

1. What special responsibilities does the physical educator have for the handicapped student?
2. How can the physical educator best adapt the program to the needs of the mentally retarded student?
3. What special physical education needs does the creative student have?
4. To what other resources can the physical educator turn for assistance in understanding and working with the handicapped student?
5. Through what means outside of the class program can physical education contribute to the handicapped student?
6. What special challenges does the physically gifted student present?

Selected readings

Adams, R., et al.: Games, sports and exercises for the physically handicapped, Philadelphia, 1975, Lea & Febiger.

American Alliance for Health, Physical Education, and Recreation: A guide for programs in recreation and physical education for the mentally retarded, Washington, D.C., 1968, AAHPER.

American Alliance for Health, Physical Education, and Recreation: Guidelines for professional preparation programs for personnel involved in physical education and recreation for the handicapped, Washington, D.C., 1973, AAHPER.

American Alliance for Health, Physical Education, and Recreation: Practical pointers: individualized education programs, Washington, D.C., Dec. 1977, AAHPER.

Arnheim, D., and Sinclair, W.: The clumsy child: a program of motor therapy, ed. 2, St. Louis, 1979, The C.V. Mosby Co.

Barach, R.: Achieving perceptual motor efficiency, Seattle, 1968, Special Child Publications.

Bucher, C.: Physical education for life, New York, 1969, McGraw-Hill Book Co.

Buell, C.: Physical education and recreation for the visually handicapped, Washington, D.C., 1973, American Alliance for Health, Physical Education, and Recreation.

Cratty, B.: Motor activity and the education of retardates, Philadelphia, 1969, Lea & Febiger.

Cratty, B.: Active learning, Englewood Cliffs, N.J., 1971, Prentice-Hall, Inc.

Cratty, B.: Remedial motor activity for children, Philadelphia, 1975, Lea & Febiger.

Crowe, W.C., Auxter, D., and Pyfer, J.: Principles and methods of adapted physical education, ed. 4, St. Louis, 1981, The C.V. Mosby Co.

Fait, H.: Special physical education, Philadelphia, 1972, W.B. Saunders Co.

National Advisory Council on Education Professions Development: Mainstreaming: helping teachers meet the challenge, Washington, D.C., 1976, The Council.

Vodola, T.: Individualized physical education program for the handicapped child, Englewood Cliffs, N.J., 1973, Prentice-Hall, Inc.

Wheeler, R., and Hoally, A.: Physical education for the handicapped, Philadelphia, 1969, Lea & Febiger.

Winnick, J.P.: Early movement experiences and development: Habilitation and remediation, Philadelphia, 1979, W.B. Saunders Co.

18

Methods and materials for developing physical fitness

Instructional objectives and competencies to be achieved

After reading this chapter the student should be able to

1. Define the term "physical fitness" and discuss its relationship to total fitness
2. Demonstrate effective methods and techniques for teaching adolescents in the area of physical fitness
3. Discuss with students the value of being physically fit
4. Identify the ways in which the various in-class and out-of-class parts of the physical education program can contribute to the physical fitness of secondary school students

How fit are young people today? Recent information indicates that although there was a real improvement in the general physical fitness of American youth from 1958 to 1965, there has been very little gain since that time. These results are based on a six-part youth fitness test taken by 12 million girls and boys between the ages of 10 and 17. A national sampling of 7,800 of these boys and girls revealed that more girls than boys showed improvement, especially in endurance tests, but that girls' performances on all but one test were not as good as that of boys. The President's Council on Physical Fitness and Sports reports that there are 9 million students in school physical education programs. Four out of every five of these students are able to pass standard physical fitness tests, while only two out of three could pass in 1961.

There is still much progress to be made in improving the physical fitness of young people. Many students do not take part in school physical education programs or in other fitness programs, and many such students are unable to pass certain parts of physical fitness achievement tests.

The terms "physical fitness" and "fitness" have been defined and interpreted in many different ways during the past few years. Some persons believe that these terms refer only to body building and motor performance. Others, including most physical educators, prefer to think in terms of *total fitness* of the individual—physical, social, emotional, and intellectual—and recognize this as a more valuable educational goal.

Physical educators have a very real responsibility to their students and the community in the area of physical fitness and its role in total individual fitness. Increased public awareness and curiosity about what is being done in the schools have forced teachers in this field to come up with concrete programs and answers. However, the public does not yet realize that physical fitness is but a part of the total fitness picture, and thus teachers have a dual educational role: explaining to both students and parents the overall story of total fitness and one of its components, physical fitness.

The current high level of interest in fitness is the result of a massive campaign sponsored by the President's Council on Youth Fitness, established first during President Eisenhower's administration and later changed by President Kennedy in 1961 to the President's Council on Physical Fitness. It is now known as the President's Council on Physical Fitness and Sports. Under the leadership of such men as Shane McCarthy, Bud Wilkinson, Stan Musial, James A. Lovell, Jr., and George Allen, the Council has attempted to raise the standards and level of physical fitness of people across the entire country. Their nationwide campaign reached out in many different ed-

ucational areas, striving to accomplish several objectives:

1. To improve programs of physical education, with increased emphasis on physical fitness
2. To increase state leadership and supervision of physical fitness and sports programs
3. To increase the number of school personnel doing physical education work
4. To conduct regional clinics in physical fitness
5. To establish demonstration centers in schools where high-level fitness programs were already organized
6. To develop adult fitness programs
7. To improve standards in Armed Forces testing and training programs
8. To publish pamphlets, booklets, and other resource materials
9. To inform the public and develop its interest in physical education through advertising in public media

Statistics indicate the remarkable effectiveness of the Council's work. Not only have physical education programs been improving, but the number of teaching specialists has increased, state supervision and leadership has been extended, and the physical fitness levels of students has substantially improved. Many states now have a governor's physical fitness council or commission. Fitness programs for cycling, swimming, jogging, and running specified distances have been developed across the country, with badges and awards issued to those who qualify.

Yet physical educators and Council members realize that only a beginning has been made. Other statistics reveal that much more has to be done in the many states that do not yet have full-time people employed in the department of education to supervise the program and in nearly 40% of schools where no daily physical education classes are held for all students.

In March of 1968, President Johnson, to extend the scope of the Council and promote sports and fitness in America, changed the Council's name to President's Council on Physical Fitness and Sports. In addition to the important work of the President's Council on Physical Fitness and Sports, the American Alliance for Health, Physical Education, Recreation, and Dance recently developed a new testing program entitled *Lifetime Health-Related Physical Fitness*. This new test, published in 1980, was the result of a careful review by a specially appointed task force of the AAHPERD Youth Fitness Test. Its members made up of representatives of the Physical Fitness, Research, and Measurement and Evaluation Councils of AAHPERD, had been charged with the responsibility of investigating the validity of the current test in measuring physical fitness according to its contemporary definition. Because the committee recognized a distinction between physical *fitness*, as it relates to health, and physical *performance*, as demonstrated in athletic ability, it determined the former to be a more appropriate definition of fitness for broad educational purposes.

In order to evaluate the relationship between health and physical activity, test items had to be identified to show a range of fitness levels and capacities that could be affected by physical activity. Three areas of physiological functioning were isolated: (1) cardiorespiratory function, (2) body composition (leanness/fatness), and (3) abdominal and low back–hamstring musculoskeletal function. By looking at these essential fitness components, the Committee members believed that physical fitness rather than motor performance abilities could be assessed. The general health status of the individual student, rather than athletic prowess, would be the focus of attention. The resulting battery of tests consists of four items: distance runs, sum of skinfold fat, modified sit-ups, and the sit and reach (see Chapter 19 on evaluation).

Teaching for physical fitness

The task of teaching for physical fitness to adolescent students is particularly difficult because of

- *Lack of interest.* Adolescent girls are sometimes more interested in matters other than physical pursuits, and boys often want to become star athletes without extensive effort.
- *Lack of understanding.* Adolescents do not fully understand the term "physical fitness" as it relates to their growth and development and their all-round health and total performance.

Fig. 18-1. Modified push-up for women—an item in some physical fitness tests.

From Hockey, R.V.: Physical fitness, ed. 4, St. Louis, 1981, The C.V. Mosby Co.

Fig. 18-2. Students using Universal Gym.

Courtesy Bill Henderson, Toms River, N.J.

• *Lack of uniformity.* Physical fitness is an individual attainment and cannot be achieved by a total group through a single process.

Furthermore, the very nature of physical fitness requires maintenance. It is not a fact, like the multiplication tables, that once learned may be set aside. Physical fitness is a condition that must be maintained. Healthful attitudes toward fitness must be developed in students, along with an appreciation for its significance. In addition, fitness itself varies in relation to the individual's personal requirements. The scholar needs physical skills different from those of the football player and therefore requires a different level of fitness. However, the basic components of fitness—such as good posture, desirable health habits, and social, emotional, and mental well-being—are necessary for all. It is the responsibility of the physical education teacher to promote the development of these qualities to their fullest degree. Students must be made aware of their need for physical fitness and led toward achievement of this goal through both the instructional

and the noninstructional phases of the total physical education program.

Teaching concepts

Physical fitness objectives provide an excellent vehicle for the teaching of concepts from the disciplines of physical education, as identified in AAHPERD's *Basic Stuff Series* I (see Chapter 3). This foundational knowledge, when organized and sequenced throughout a progressive school curriculum, should develop in students a sound understanding and vital attitude toward fitness. Specifically, concepts dealing with health (feeling good) and appearance (looking good) as presented in five of AAHPERD's six booklets, plus those in the motor learning booklet, should provide ample material for the development and promotion of fitness. Concepts may be incorporated across content areas or taught as a separate unit. Samples of objectives for teaching these concepts may be found later in this chapter.

Teaching methods and techniques*

There are many methods and techniques useful for teaching adolescents in the area of physical fitness. The instructional program itself should contain definite steps for appraisal, guidance, and testing throughout the school year, and related discussions, assignments, and studies should be included for special emphasis.

APPRAISAL

The appraisal of physical fitness in secondary school is an important teaching technique that serves many purposes. It provides the teacher with a picture of the fitness level of each student and the over-all school population. These data may then be helpful in determining individual student needs and the needs of the total program. Statistics on speed, accuracy, and other components of fitness should be used throughout the year to aid in program planning and to promote fitness.

The process of appraisal should be beneficial to the student, providing an understanding of the true nature of fitness. Endurance, efficiency, and coordination should be recognized as objectives that will enable the secondary school student to satisfactorily complete required everyday school tasks. Students also need to recognize that physical fitness is not the same for each individual, and this attitude may be promoted through the appraisal process. Furthermore, assessment helps to motivate students toward self-improvement. Instead of mistaking physical fitness for mere muscular strength, they see that exercise is necessary for proper growth, development, and resistance to disease.

Many materials, which will be discussed in greater detail later in the chapter, have been developed for appraisal of physical fitness. However, it should be noted here that some of the physical fitness tests include norms, or scoring scales, for evaluation of physical performance. These are helpful in student assessment because they offer a more precise technique for comparing scores of students of the same age, height, and/or weight. Students, too, prefer to compare their own test results in terms of the achievements of hundreds of their peers rather than only their classmates.

Norms do not provide the total picture in the assessment of physical fitness, however. A physical education teacher should be cautious in applying norms since these scores vary according to the criteria used for their development (factors such as age and height). One study indicates that both physique (height and weight) *and* developmental level (accelerated, normal, or retarded growth pattern) are important determinants in physical performance levels. Norms that do not reflect the overweight factor, for example, may be scaled too high for accomplishment by such persons.*

A study of 7,600 boys and girls, 10 to 18 years of age, analyzed the relationship of age, height, and weight to performances in the California Physical Fitness Test. Results brought about recommendations that *age* be used as a basis for test norms, for steady progress was shown by students each year in nearly all test items.†

Obviously, more research is needed in this area of testing physical fitness and establishing norms for guidance. The physical educator should recognize the limitations while taking advantage of the values.

GUIDANCE

The teaching program should provide an opportunity for individual guidance of students in the area of physical fitness. This may be done in connection with the appraisal program, with individual conferences scheduled for each student to discuss personal problems and weaknesses. When a teacher is able to offer this personal attention to each student and can suggest exercises and methods of improvement, the boy or girl consciously puts forth effort to improve.

Group guidance in the general aspects of physical fitness should also be included in the instructional program through a unit of study. For girls, stress should be placed on proper posture and good body mechanics in daily activities—for example, in stand-

---

*See also Chapter 19 on evaluation.

*Wear, C.L., and Miller, K.: Relationships between physique and developmental level to physical performance, Research Quarterly **33**:4, 1962.

†Espenschade, A.S.: Restudy of relationships between physical performance of school children and age, height and weight, Research Quarterly **34**:2, 1963.

Fig. 18-3. Running is an excellent developer of physical fitness.

Courtesy Barbara Ann Chiles, Aledo, Ill.

ing, sitting, walking, lifting, carrying books, and studying. By appealing to the girls' desire to be attractive and to develop balance, grace, and poise in movement, the teacher may motivate these students toward improved fitness. Physical fitness for boys should stress increasing their achievement levels in strength, endurance, flexibility, accuracy, balance, and other physical traits. In this way they, too, are motivated toward improving physical fitness. A successfully taught unit should have carry-over value, not only into daily life but also into college and later years, by developing a wholesome attitude toward fitness and its importance in effective living.

Guidance in physical fitness should not only be included as a unit of study for students but should also be emphasized in each class in the *daily* instructional program. The value of daily calisthenics and warm-up exercises should be stressed in terms of their role in developing physical fitness. A study comparing the physical fitness of Japanese children to boys and girls in Iowa showed that Tokyo children scored higher in nearly all motor performance tests. Furthermore, it was shown that Japanese students had longer and more frequent physical education classes in which to de-

velop these skills. Students in the United States must recognize the importance of daily workouts for developing and maintaining a high level of performance in physical fitness activities. Guidance of this kind is of utmost importance to students while in school, for in later years, as they organize themselves for adulthood, exercise will form an integral part of daily living.

TESTING

Testing should be a regular part of the total physical education program, and testing for physical fitness should be included as one phase of evaluation. The materials for testing different components of physical fitness are extensive. One of the best tests for boys and girls is the Lifetime Health-Related Physical Fitness Test developed by the American Alliance for Health, Physical Education, Recreation, and Dance. The motivational and educational value of this test should be recognized.

DISCUSSION

Students in secondary school should have an opportunity to discuss various aspects of physical fitness

as part of their instructional program. Related problems such as dieting, relaxation, and menstruation are topics that interest girls. Narcotics and alcohol studies provide excellent learning possibilities for both boys and girls. Special studies in these and similar subjects related to physical fitness in everyday life should be a regular part of the instructional program.

ASSIGNMENTS

Homework assignments on fitness that are coordinated with the regular instructional program should be given. These assignments may be in the form of improving performance of particular physical fitness exercises such as push-ups or sit-ups, or they may be in the form of readings related to this particular subject. Studying about young girls and boys who have accomplished unusual feats in athletics is both interesting and inspiring to adolescents. In schools using teaching teams, where students have an opportunity to do independent research, the topic of physical fitness may well be a fitting assignment. Bucher's physical education textbook for high school students, *Physical Education for Life,* devotes considerable space to the subject of physical fitness and how it can be developed and maintained (see Selected Readings at the end of the chapter).

OTHER TECHNIQUES

Some supplementary techniques are particularly helpful in emphasizing physical fitness in the instructional program. The use of audiovisual aids, for instance, is an excellent way to stimulate student interest. Bulletin boards, performance charts, records, and similar devices serve as reminders when they are displayed prominently. In addition, allowing students to conduct drills and take turns in leading the class permits personal experience in promoting physical fitness. Of most importance is making physical fitness enjoyable, for when students see that activities are fun, they will profit more fully from the instructional program.

Materials for developing physical fitness

At the present time the quantity of materials for teaching physical fitness continues to increase as a result of nationwide interest, fostered by the President's Council on Physical Fitness and Sports and increased emphasis on health status, drugs, and medical care. Physical educators, finding greater interest in and reception for their programs among parents and lay people consider this an ideal time to expand and extend fitness objectives in curricula.

There is a wealth of material presently available to teachers for use in physical education classes. The President's Council on Physical Fitness and Sports, Washington, D.C. 20201, and the American Alliance for Health, Physical Education, Recreation, and Dance, 1900 Association Dr., Reston, Va. 22091, are excellent sources for such materials.

There are numerous other materials available in the area of physical fitness. Many state departments of education have developed their own testing instruments (California, Oregon, Washington, Iowa, Virginia, New York), as have some cities (Tucson, Denver, Omaha, Louisville, Kansas City). Teachers should also investigate their own state departments of education, for not only have testing programs been initiated from their offices but also publications on courses of study, programs, and clinic suggestions.

The physical fitness checklist included here is another helpful educational tool for teachers interested in this type of material for their students.

Chapter 16 contains other films and records, listed according to manufacturers, that may be useful in the area of physical fitness.

ISOMETRICS

Widespread attention has been focused on isometrics, an exercise system developing one particular facet of physical fitness—strength. Physical education teachers should understand the principle behind isometrics and recognize its values and limitations in order to place it in its proper perspective within the physical education program.

Definition. Isometrics consists of a series of exercises designed to develop strength in particular muscle groups. The individual contracts a muscle group against an immovable force, or resistance, and "holds tight" before relaxing after a count of 6 to 10. The tension produced in the muscles increases their strength through this isometric contraction. Isometric

A PHYSICAL FITNESS CHECKLIST

Medical aspects

	Yes	No
1. Thorough dental and health examination each year	☐	☐
a. Fit heart and circulatory system, digestive system, nervous system	☐	☐
b. Proper body development, according to age and sex (height and weight)	☐	☐
2. Correction of remediable health defects—vision, hearing, overweight	☐	☐

Physical activity

	Yes	No
1. At least $1^{1}/_{2}$ to 2 hours a day spent in vigorous physical activity, preferably outdoors	☐	☐
2. Adequate muscular strength and endurance*	☐	☐
3. After running 50 yards, heart and breathing return to normal rates within 10 minutes.	☐	☐
4. Average skill in running, jumping, climbing, and throwing	☐	☐
5. Control of body in activities involving balance, agility, speed, rhythm, accuracy	☐	☐
6. Skill in recreational activities—arts and crafts, bowling, dancing	☐	☐

Posture

	Yes	No
1. When student is standing upright, string dropped from tip of ear passes through shoulder and hip joints and middle of ankle.	☐	☐
2. When student is sitting in a chair, trunk and head are erect, weight balanced over pelvis, or trunk slightly bent forward.	☐	☐
3. When student is walking, slumping is avoided, body is in proper balance, and excessively wasteful motions of arms and legs are eliminated.	☐	☐

Health habits

	Yes	No
1. Rest: at least 8 hours of sleep each night	☐	☐
2. Diet: four servings daily from each of the four basic food groups	☐	☐
a. Meat, poultry, fish, and eggs		
b. Dairy products		
c. Vegetables and fruits		
d. Bread and cereals		
3. Cleanliness		
a. Daily bath	☐	☐
b. Teeth brushed after every meal	☐	☐
c. Clean hair, nails, and clothing	☐	☐
4. Abstain from use of tobacco and alcohol	☐	☐

*The school health or physical education teacher can help to determine proper standards.

contractions should not be confused with isotonic, or dynamic, contractions, in which the muscle groups work against a resistant force that is overcome, as in weight lifting.

Values. An important value of isometric exercise is conditioning. Through daily application of isometrics, muscles learn to work efficiently and effectively in performance of activity. It is believed that increased muscular strength improves speed, power, and flexibility, all of which are important components of body conditioning and fitness. For this reason, isometrics has gained in popularity not only in school programs but also in amateur and professional athletics as well.* It is important, however, to evaluate carefully the equipment and literature that are on the market on isometrics.

Isometric exercises are also valuable in corrective, or remedial, programs of physical education. Whenever a student has identifiable weakness in specific muscle groups, such as arm and shoulder muscles, isometric routines are particularly helpful.

Limitations. Certain limitations exist in the isometric program of exercise when it is applied to a school program of physical education. As has been previously stated, the value of isometrics lies in meeting *individual* needs for strengthening and conditioning. In large physical education classes it would be very difficult to individualize this program sufficiently for instructional purposes.

Furthermore, while students may become motivated at first with this approach to exercising, enthusiasm may soon fade if no tangible results are seen. Dynamometers, machines that measure strength, are not standard equipment in most schools, and students may not recognize the progress they are making without them. Further, emphasis should not be placed merely on isometrics. Isometrics, like weight lifting, has specific values that should be utilized whenever possible, within the limits of proper programming for physical fitness.

---

*Some manufacturers have developed special exercise kits, charts, and handbooks of isometrics. Bucher's book, *Physical Education for Life*, lists many excellent isometric and isotonic exercises for high school boys and girls (see Selected Readings at the end of the chapter).

ISOTONICS

Like isometrics, isotonics is a series of exercises designed to develop strength in particular muscle groups. However, in isotonic exercises muscle groups are repeatedly contracted against movable weights in a series of repetitions. The recent popularity of Nautilus and Universal machines attests to community-wide interest in this form of workout. The addition of weight training and conditioning programs to high school physical education curricula also reflects its widespread appeal. Its limitations and values parallel those regarding isometric exercise. Students should be cautioned to avoid muscle strain or injury by following appropriate progressive exercise routines individually designed for them.

CLASS PROGRAMS

Physical fitness objectives, including those foundational concepts discussed earlier in the chapter, may be achieved incidentally within daily lessons, within a total unit of instruction or integrated with related subjects. Sample objectives from these three approaches are included below.

Daily lesson. Fitness concepts may be encompassed in warm-up activities. For example, knowing that flexibility is necessary for all movement, that static stretching improves flexibility, or warm-up can help maximize anaerobic performance helps a student accept the need for effectively warming up. When translated into specific objectives of a daily lesson, the following outcomes might be expected.

- The ninth-grade students will perform designated static stretching exercises (according to an individualized worksheet) for the first 10 minutes of class.
- Without direction from the teacher, the eleventh-grade students will complete an individually prescribed series of exercises moving all joints through full range of motion.

Physical fitness unit. In a sample 5-week unit of instruction, with classes meeting three times per week, tenth-grade students might work to improve personal fitness in a variety of activities and laboratory experiences. By concentrating on increasing aerobic performance—through circuit training, jogging, cycling, swimming, cross-country skiing, or other endurance activity—fitness levels could be improved. Concom-

RECORD FORM FOR IDENTIFICATION OF PHYSICALLY UNDERDEVELOPED PUPILS

Teacher _____   School year _____

Period or section _____   Date of 1st test _____

School _____

Girls

Name of pupil	Modified pull-ups ages 10-17; 8			Sit-ups ages 10-17; 10			Squat thrust ages 10-17; 3			Remarks*
	1st test		Retest	1st test		Retest	1st test		Retest	
	Pass	Fail	Date passed	Pass	Fail	Date passed	Pass	Fail	Date passed	

*Enter here any conditions, e.g., obesity, posture, etc., that may affect physical performance.

Fig. 18-4. Record form for identification of physically underdeveloped pupils; used at Guymon Junior High School, Guymon, Okla.

itant learning of appropriate concepts from exercise physiology in laboratory experiences could promote development of important understanding and attitudes. Sample objectives for this fitness unit might include the following.

- The student will identify correct personal target heart rate at the conclusion of the first laboratory session.
- The student will increase by ___% intensity and duration of performance each activity period. Student should consult with physical education teacher.
- The student will correctly differentiate, on a written examination at the conclusion of the unit, between aerobic and anaerobic activity.

Integrated lesson. During a swimming unit, eighth-grade students might investigate different types of breathing in sprint and endurance strokes. By experiencing aerobic and anaerobic activities, fitness objectives could be met and related concepts understood.

- The student will sprint 25 yards in an overhand crawl with only one breath, decreasing time each day.
- The student will record personal physiological effects—increased heart rate and breathing following endurance swimming—on a fitness chart.

OUT-OF-CLASS PROGRAM

The noninstructional program, which includes all activities held outside the regularly scheduled physical education class, is equally important to the promotion of physical fitness. The intramural and extramural activities, clubs, demonstrations, contests, and other activities all serve to focus student attention on physical pursuits.

Intramural activities. The intramural program should be available to as many students as possible. By providing an interesting and exciting program of intraclass games in a wide variety of sports and in an atmosphere in which all students believe their participation is welcome, the teacher is able to increase the overall interest in physical fitness and skills.

Extramural activities. A program of interscholastic competition serves to heighten the interest of boys and girls, and their efforts to make the honor squads or varsity teams also induce improvement in physical fitness.

Clubs. There are several clubs that may be sponsored by the physical education department to provide benefits for physical fitness. Cheerleaders, baton twirlers, drill team, gymnastics, tumbling, cycling, and physical fitness clubs all promote physical fitness. The avid interest that many students have in these types of activities should be developed. Leaders' clubs and modern dance groups also play a role in the physical education program, and membership should be open to all interested students.

Demonstrations. Public demonstrations and performances by club participants, such as those of the modern dance group, not only improve the physical fitness of participants but also serve to increase the interest in and appreciation of these activities.

Contests and campaigns. Sometimes a special contest or campaign to promote good posture or a similar component of physical fitness is an excellent technique for arousing and enhancing interest in physical fitness. Student planning, as well as participation in such events, should be fostered to gain the most value from them.

Organizations. Organizations such as an athletic association, Hi-Y, or scouting and explorer troops may serve to promote fitness both among its members and on a schoolwide basis.

Outings. Field trips, clinics, and outdoor camping expeditions are very popular with students, and they provide fitness experiences not otherwise available. The physical education teacher should try to sponsor such events whenever feasible.

Awards. For students who have shown a great deal of improvement or have performed exceptionally well in specific areas of physical fitness, a ribbon or small award may be presented. The American Alliance for Health, Physical Education, Recreation, and Dance has special awards and certificates that may be given in connection with the administration of their physical fitness test. The President's Council on Physical Fitness and Sports also has presidential sports awards.

Cosponsored activities. Considerable interest can be stimulated with coeducational activities sponsored by both the boys' and the girls' departments or with special events sponsored cooperatively with community organizations. The local Dads' Club or Chamber of Commerce is usually interested in physical fitness

Fig. 18-5. Students playing flag football to develop physical fitness in the Lexington Public Schools, Lexington, Mass.

activities and often willing to conduct field days, contests, and sports days. The physical education teachers should work with the leaders of these organizations to ensure proper management and supervision for the benefit of the students.

Self-assessment tests

These tests are designed to assist students in determining if material and competencies presented in this chapter have been mastered.

1. Give a description to your class of the characteristics you consider to be a part of a physically fit person.
2. Assume your methods class is a group of eleventh-grade students. Demonstrate what you consider to be some effective methods and techniques for stimulating their interest in being physically fit.
3. Arrange a meeting with a group of high school students during which you discuss the values of physical fitness.
4. Prepare a chart that includes a heading for each of the following: (a) the basic instructional class program, (b) adapted program, (c) intramural and extramural program, and (d) interscholastic program. List under each heading the various ways in which that component of the overall program can contribute to the development of physical fitness in secondary school students.

Points to remember

1. The physical fitness goal of physical education requires special emphasis because of increased national concern in this area.
2. The instructional program of physical education should be geared to physical fitness through methods of teaching that include appraisal and guidance.
3. The additional teaching techniques of testing and assignments should stress physical fitness in the instructional program.
4. The noninstructional program should emphasize fitness through its many components.
5. Students in secondary school should be guided in physical fitness to become aware of its importance to everyday living.
6. Students must realize the individuality of physical fitness and should understand their own personal requirements in this area.

Problems to think through

1. How can the results of the appraisal of physical fitness be most effectively used for the benefit of the students?
2. In a community that sponsors few recreational programs, how may the physical education department of the secondary school promote community-wide interest in physical fitness activities?
3. The administration of a secondary school is disturbed about students smoking on school property, contrary to regulations. Students and some members of the community are in favor of a student smoking lounge. In what ways may the physical education department help in solving this problem?
4. In a small secondary school there is only one woman and one man teaching physical education. Activities after school are therefore limited to the supervision and facilities available to these two instructors. How may an adequate intramural program be set up that would promote physical fitness for the greatest number of students?
5. What methods may be used to improve physical fitness in students scoring low on appraisal?
6. In what ways may individual personal guidance be offered to students needing special attention in physical fitness work?

Case study for analysis

The physical education department in a large secondary school plans to promote a year-long campaign for physical fitness, not only for students in the school but also for the community at large. The administration has approved the idea and offered some financial assistance to back its cam-

paign. What steps should the staff take in carrying out the campaign within the instructional program? In the noninstructional program? In the community? What special activities and events may be sponsored? In what ways may students become involved in the program?

Exercises for review

1. What are the advantages and disadvantages in running a physical fitness appraisal program more than once during a year?
2. What particular objectives should be established for a unit on physical fitness with eighth-grade boys and girls?
3. What aspects of physical fitness should be stressed in team sports? Individual sports? Formal activities? Rhythms? Aquatics?
4. What exercises are particularly valuable for developing strength? Endurance? Flexibility? Balance? Other components of physical fitness?
5. What types of charts and diagrams would serve effectively to motivate students in physical fitness?
6. What current outside reading materials may be valuable homework for high school students?
7. In what ways may a leaders' club assist the physical education teacher in testing and promoting physical fitness?
8. What types of awards would be appropriate for performances in physical fitness?
9. What topics for discussions in physical fitness would be of particular interest to high school girls? Boys? Both?
10. What are the advantages and disadvantages to choosing a ''most physically fit'' boy and girl?

Selected readings

Allsen, P.E., et al.: Fitness for life, Dubuque, Iowa, 1976, Wm. C. Brown Co., Publishers.

American Alliance for Health, Physical Education, Recreation, and Dance: Lifetime health-related physical fitness test, 1980, The Alliance.

American Alliance for Health, Physical Education, Recreation, and Dance: Basic stuff series I, Reston, Va., 1981, The Alliance.

Bucher, C.A.: Physical education for life, New York, 1969, McGraw-Hill Book Co.

Bucher, C.A.: Exercise, it's plain good business, Reader's Digest, March 1976, pp. 127-130.

Bucher, C.A., et al.: The foundations of health, Englewood Cliffs, N.J., 1976, Prentice-Hall Inc.

Bucher, C.A.: Foundations of physical education, ed. 9, St. Louis, 1983, The C. V. Mosby Co.

Cooper, K.H.: How to feel fit at any age, Reader's Digest, March 1968, pp. 79-87.

Jones, K.L., et al.: Total fitness, New York, 1972, Harper & Row, Publishers, Inc.

President's Council on Physical Fitness and Sports: Basic understanding of physical fitness, Physical Fitness Research Digest, Washington, D.C., 1971, The Council.

President's Council on Physical Fitness and Sports: Physical activity and coronary heart disease, Physical Fitness Research Digest, Washington, D.C., 1972, The Council.

President's Council on Physical Fitness and Sports: Circulatory-respiratory endurance, Physical Fitness Research Digest, Washington, D.C., 1973, The Council.

President's Council on Physical Fitness and Sports: Introduction to physical fitness, Washington, D.C., The Council.

President's Council on Physical Fitness and Sports: Youth physical fitness, Washington, D.C., The Council.

Evaluation

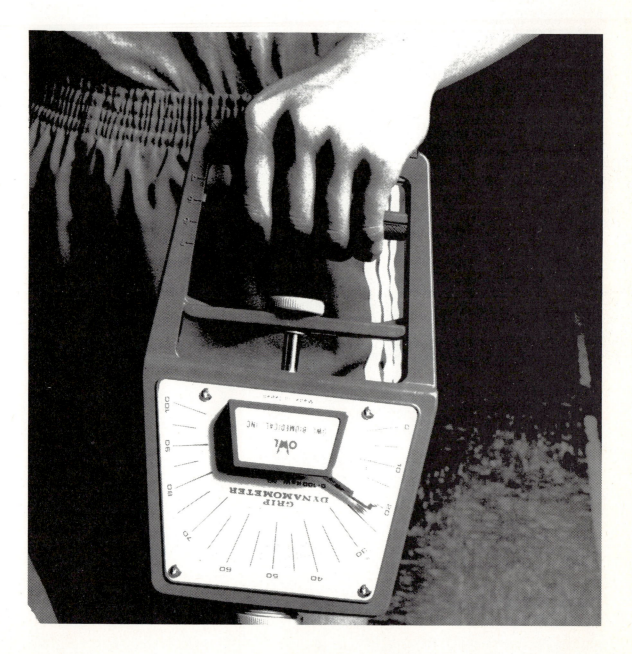

19

Pupil evaluation and grading

Instructional objectives and competencies to be achieved

After reading this chapter the student should be able to

1. Discuss various innovative methods that are being utilized to evaluate students in today's physical education programs
2. Indicate what constitutes a minimum program for evaluating the degree to which students are accomplishing professional physical education objectives
3. List selected methods and materials for evaluating pupil achievement
4. Evaluate physical education tests utilized in the secondary school and select those that best meet established criteria
5. Apply sound principles of evaluation to grading pupils in the secondary school

John is in the twelfth grade at Ft. Pierce, Florida, and is scheduled to take golf as part of his physical education requirement. Before taking the course he has signed a contract with his teacher that spells out in detail the work he must complete to earn a grade of his choice. For example, John knows he can earn 10 points as part of the contract if he learns to swing a club properly, demonstrates proper technique to the instructor, and writes a short report that analyzes the sequence of movements to be followed in using the club effectively. Another part of the golf contract, valued at 20 points, requires John to read a book on golf and write a summary and critique of it. There are other contract options that permit John to earn additional points. To receive a grade of A, John must earn a minimum of 125 points. If he wants a B, he needs 100 points; a C, 90 points; and a D, 80 points. No completed contract receives a failing grade. If the quality is not acceptable, the contract time is extended.

Contract learning is a technique that some teachers are utilizing in various subjects in order to individualize learning and accommodate students who have varying interests and motivations. These teachers have described the "contract-for-grade" system as a way in which they can interact with students and where both have the opportunity to indicate their expectations for the course.

What students accomplish in the contract system depends entirely on their own efforts and how they apply themselves. In physical education at Ft. Pierce, Florida, the sports contracts are designed for students to use on an individual basis, working at their own pace. The goal is not necessarily to create superskilled players but, instead, to have each boy and girl learn the fundamentals, rules, and etiquette of the sport and be able to participate in the activity with some degree of understanding and enjoyment.

To fulfill contract requirements, students frequently use as resources the school library, programmed texts, other supplemental materials, teacher-student discussions, visual aids, the community, and consultants who are familiar with the subject. The teacher is on call to advise students during and after school hours. The sources of information for the students are as great as their imagination and ingenuity. Attendance is not always required. In some schools the students check in to class daily but thereafter are free to go where their resources are located.

Student reaction to contract learning has been favorable. For example, at Madison Consolidated High School in Indiana, about 80% of the students said they enjoyed contract better than traditional learning and wanted to use it again. Three out of every four students felt they learned more under the contract system than under methods that had been in use in past years. Nearly nine out of every ten students liked the independent method of work, the opportunity to earn the grade they wanted, and the statement of exactly what

Fig. 19-1. Measuring physical fitness at Wheaton High School, Wheaton, Md.

must be done to be awarded a specific grade. Some representative student comments include: "You get the grade you want." "It gives the student a chance." "The system helped me more than the teacher." "I knew exactly what was required in order to get a certain grade." "It permitted me an opportunity to work at my own pace." "It places the responsibility on the student, and this is as it should be."

Student contracting for grades is one innovative procedure used to make pupil evaluation more meaningful for the student through personalizing and motivating student learning.

Innovations in evaluation

A physical growth report card has been used by the Abraham Lincoln High School in Philadelphia. The report card consists of 10 different growth items broken down into physical components and personal characteristics. The physical components include muscle strength, muscle endurance, flexibility, cardiovascular endurance, and neuromuscular coordination. The personal characteristics include height, weight, age, posture, muscle tone, health habits, and work habits. Although all of these components are not graded for each marking period, each receives attention in the course of the school year. By the end of the year a physical profile shows the strong and weak points of the pupil. A student receives a grade of A (exceptional), B (above average), C (good), D (poor), or E (very poor) for each component.

At Jessie M. Clark Junior High School in Lexington, Kentucky, each member of the physical education class participates in the evaluation of other students and also rates himself or herself. In addition, the teacher rates each student. Thus far there is considerable agreement among all three ratings. A conclusion reached by those who utilize this method is that the student feels more a part of the learning process and as a result is more concerned and plays a more active role in class.

At Framingham North High School in Framingham,

```
    YOU EARN YOUR MARK IN PHYSICAL EDUCATION
       (You earn 6 points a day for full participation)

Participation and Health   -   -   -   -   -   -   240  points
Skills (ability)   -   -   -   -   -   -   -   -   60  points
Knowledge of the Rules   -   -   -   -   -   -   20  points
         Maximum Total   -   -   -   -   -   -  320  points
────────────────────────────────────────────────────────────
A  -   -   320 - 306     Bonus Points—
B  -   -   305 - 286     Class Intramural Champ    -    10
C  -   -   285 - 261     Leader in Decathlon    -    -     5
D  -   -   260 - 241     Satisfactory Captain    -    -    10
F  -   -   240 - Below   Oiler Leader    -    -    -    -   15
Make-Up — 6 points a week on scheduled day.
```

Fig. 19-2. How a student earns grade in physical education at Richmond Union High School, Richmond, Calif.

Massachusetts, the members of the physical education class formulate goals they wish to achieve. Then they plan the steps by which they will achieve these goals, and, finally, they are rated on the degree to which the goals are achieved.

At Herrick Public School in Herrick, Long Island, New York, students also think through and write out the goals they wish to achieve. They are told they should take a look at themselves, decide what they wish to achieve in physical education, plan goals for themselves in light of their wishes, plan how to achieve these goals, and, finally, evaluate what they have accomplished. Student and teacher grades are averaged together in order to arrive at the final grade.

It would appear that evaluation and grades will continue to be used in our schools. At the same time, methods must be devised that will judge more accurately the work accomplished by students and, in addition, help the student to better understand himself or herself and the degree to which progress is being made toward desirable educational and personal goals.

J. Lloyd Trump, in his latest book dealing with the secondary school curriculum, asks educators to try to find better ways to assess student progress toward desirable educational and personal goals. If educators hope to develop interpretative skills and habits of intellectual inquiry, then these skills require evaluation, along with knowledge in specific subjects. While it is important to determine what students know, it is also necessary, Trump says, to find out what they do. Are students reading outside of class? What are they reading? Do they engage in worthwhile small group discussions on topics other than the latest rock hit? How are their independent study habits? Are they learning responsibility for their own educational accomplishments? Do they see a high school diploma as the end of their education or merely as a stepping-stone toward lifelong learning?

Physical educators should ask similar questions about what students are really learning in physical education. Are they learning to dislike physical activity because doing laps is a punishment for tardiness or because they had to wait in line so long they never had enough chance to practice? Insight into student attitudes and values is critical to effective curriculum development and instruction for the decade ahead.

Evaluation in physical education

Physical education teachers have the responsibility for evaluating the degree to which they are accomplishing professional objectives. This process of evaluation should cover two general areas: pupil achievement, which includes the progress report or grade, and program administration. In Chapter 20 details of the evaluation of program administration and teaching

are discussed, whereas in this chapter the main topic is pupil evaluation and grading.

Evaluation of pupil achievement should determine to what extent program objectives are being met. Evaluation should reveal levels of student development toward each of the four major goals: physical fitness, physical skills, knowledge and appreciation, and social development. The results of this evaluation process should serve many purposes. Besides providing a basis for grading pupil progress, evaluation techniques should also provide essential information for the motivation, guidance, and grouping of students and for program planning and curriculum building.

Current emphasis on meeting individual needs has increased the importance of evaluation, particularly for the purpose of identifying exceptional children. In order for orthopedically handicapped, gifted, and retarded children to receive equal opportunities in ed-

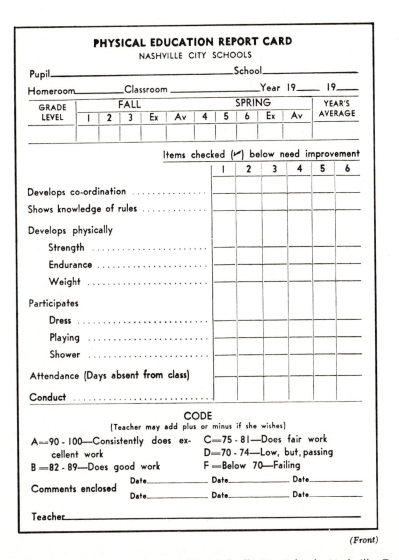

Fig. 19-3. Physical education report card in Nashville City Schools, Nashville, Tenn.

ucation, special adapted programs, both in physical education and in general education, are being developed.

There are many useful techniques of evaluation to measure pupil achievement. Selection of a particular instrument depends on several factors, including time, facilities, and type and purposes of information sought. The development of a program of evaluation for a particular school requires a great deal of thought and study on the part of the staff. Physical education teachers must devise at least minimum evaluation procedures suitable to the philosophy and objectives of their own schools and physical education programs. A minimum program of measurement and evaluation in physical education should include at least a medical examination and some objective means of determining a student's progress toward each goal established for the physical education program. A more comprehen-

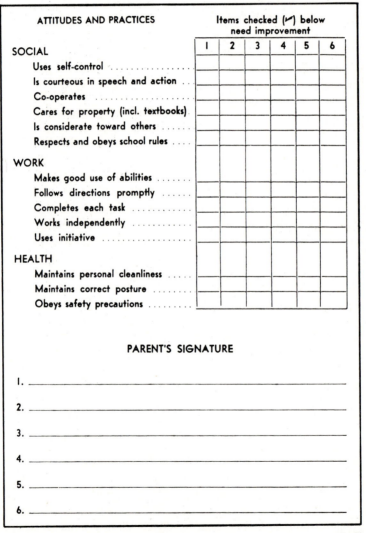

ATTITUDES AND PRACTICES	Items checked (✔) below need improvement					
	1	2	3	4	5	6
SOCIAL						
Uses self-control						
Is courteous in speech and action						
Co-operates						
Cares for property (incl. textbooks)						
Is considerate toward others						
Respects and obeys school rules						
WORK						
Makes good use of abilities						
Follows directions promptly						
Completes each task						
Works independently						
Uses initiative						
HEALTH						
Maintains personal cleanliness						
Maintains correct posture						
Obeys safety precautions						

PARENT'S SIGNATURE

1. _____

2. _____

3. _____

4. _____

5. _____

6. _____

(Back)

Fig. 19-3, cont'd. For legend see opposite page.

sive program of measurement and evaluation would include several other testing techniques, such as sports skill tests, attitude and interest inventories, checklists, and questionnaires.

Methods and materials for evaluating pupil achievement

An evaluation program of pupil achievement should be designed to determine level of achievement in relation to the four principal objectives of the physical education program: physical fitness, physical skills, knowledge and appreciation, and social development. The following testing techniques, resources, and materials, plus methods of devising tests, are included for the physical education goal for which they are most suitable and applicable.

ORGANIC DEVELOPMENT AND PHYSICAL FITNESS

Medical examination. Ideally, each student should have a medical examination at least once a year, and parents should be encouraged to schedule them. School districts generally require physical examination at regular intervals—for example, in grades 2, 6, and 10. Athletes participating in each sports season must of course have current records on file with the athletic director.

Physical fitness tests. Physical fitness tests should be given early in the school year and again in the spring to determine pupil progress toward fitness goals. It is important that comparisons of the two sets of scores be made on an *individual* basis so that each student recognizes his or her own areas of weaknesses. Standardized norms may be useful to the teacher to provide a basis for classification of students in certain activities.

The new AAHPERD Lifetime Health-Related Physical Fitness test has been received favorably by teachers since its publication in 1980. The test, comprised of only four items, uses very little equipment, making it simple to adminster to large groups in a short period of time. It consists of

1. *Distance runs*. Either a 1-mile run or a 9-minute run for distance may be given to young students to measure maximum functional capacity and endurance

of the cardiorespiratory system. Students 13 years of age and older may choose a 1½-mile run for time or the 12-minute run for distance, if administratively feasible.

2. *Sum of skinfold fat*. This test evaluates the levels of fatness of boys and girls by totaling amounts of subcutaneous adipose (fat) tissue in specific regions of the body. Skinfold calipers, available for a reasonable cost, are used to make these evaluations.

3. *Modified sit-ups*. The number of sit-ups completed in 60 seconds is counted by a partner who braces the student's feet, while knees are flexed and arms crossed on the chest. Abdominal muscular strength and endurance are measured.

4. *Sit and reach*. Flexibility (extensibility) of the low back and posterior thighs are measured by this test, in which the student, with feet braced against a box and legs straight, reaches his or her fingertips as far as possible on a ruler placed on the top of the box. (A simply constructed box for this test item is described in the test manual.) Tables of norms for students between the ages of 5 and 17 are available for each test item in the test manual. Also included are special exercises and activities for the development and maintenance of physical fitness. Suggestions for cumulative fitness records and individual profile charts are pictured.

Many state education departments have developed test batteries that have been successfully used in school programs—for example, the Texas Physical Fitness–Motor Ability Test and the New York State Test of Physical Fitness. Another test that may be easily administered to large groups is the Kasch Three-Minute Step Test, where a measure of increased pulse rate is taken. Another is Cooper's well-known 12-minute run test for cardiovascular fitness, which classifies fitness from very poor to excellent, depending on the distance covered. Other instruments are available to test particular components of fitness, such as the Illinois Agility Run Test.

PHYSICAL SKILLS

Because a major portion of the physical education class is devoted to the teaching of skills, many skills tests in each of the various sports have been developed. They cover a wide range of age levels and grades

in some sports, while in other activities there may be no suitable test available. General tests of physical capacity and motor efficiency have also been developed for evaluation of student performance and capacity.

Suggested general skills tests. Leaders in the field have devoted considerable time and research to testing *motor educability, motor capacity, physical capacity, motor ability,* and *motor efficiency.* These terms may appear at first to be synonymous with physical fitness. The beginning teacher should understand, however, that the work done in each of these areas is not to be confused with physical fitness testing. Some of the skills tests measure inherent aptitudes of pupils, while others measure achievement in basic motor skills. The beginning teacher wishing to use some of these tests should become familiar with the purposes of such tests as the Rogers Strength Test and McCloy's General Motor Ability and Capacity Tests.

Suggested sports skills tests. Leaders in the field of physical education have developed testing instruments for skills in such sports as archery, badminton, baseball, basketball, bowling, football, golf, gymnastics, handball, field hockey and ice hockey, riding, rhythms, figure skating, soccer, softball, speedball, squash, stunts and tumbling, swimming, tennis, and volleyball. Descriptions of these tests, including age level, equipment needed, and administrative directions, are given in most physical education tests and measurement books (see references at end of chapter).

Other suggestions for testing may be found in the individual sports rule books, current literature, periodicals, and booklets on sports. In looking over these tests, the teacher finds that certain basic skills necessary to the games themselves have been selected, and the testing procedures that have been devised for these skills are closely related to the game situation. Suggested methods for rating or scoring individual performances on a specified number of trials, as well as norms for grade level performances, are usually included. These tests, however, are limited. In many instances too much time is required for their administration, their reliability or validity is questionable, or the norms listed may be for the college years. It is necessary, therefore, to study these prepared tests

carefully to determine their suitability or adaptability to a particular teaching situation.

Perhaps the most significant development in the area of skills evaluation occurred under the sponsorship of the American Alliance for Health, Physical Education, Recreation, and Dance. Its Research Council devised tests and norms for effective evaluation of boys and girls, grades 5 through 12, in physical education programs across the United States. Complete with instructional manuals, they include skills tests for

Archery	Lacrosse
Badminton	Soccer
Baseball	Softball
Basketball	Swimming
Field hockey	Tennis
Football	Track and field
Golf	Volleyball
Gymnastics	

The sports skills test manuals are very helpful not only for testing purposes but for instructional pointers as well. Sample class composite record forms, data forms, and profile forms are available from the Alliance.

Teacher-made tests. When acceptable testing devices are not available, teachers may want to create sports skills tests that are appropriate and accurate for their teaching situations. This is a long and involved process, but the following suggestions may be helpful in developing sports skills tests for personal use.

1. The sport should be analyzed to determine skills for measurement.

2. Special procedures should be devised for the administration of a test of a skill or skills.

3. A preliminary test should be administered to a group and a check made to review if those of acknowledged superior ability score higher than others in their performances.

4. If the above check suggests validity, complete rating of the group should be made and the validity coefficient computed.

5. The test results should again be checked, this time against the rules of the particular game, with higher scorers playing against lower scorers.

6. One group should be retested to compute the reliability coefficient.

7. To make results most useful, the raw scores from the test should be converted to some type of comparable scoring system.

A teacher following these procedures can be better assured that the results of the test are valid and reliable.

Other testing techniques. Sports skills tests are only one method of evaluating physical skills. In some types of activities there are no objective tests available for use, and more subjective measures must be made. There are also some skills that in themselves are difficult to measure objectively. Other techniques, such as teacher ratings and progress charts, must be used.

Teacher ratings are generally necessary in evaluation of the form used in completing a skill. For example, diving, ski jumping, and figure skating must be judged partially or totally on the basis of form. Form in batting, shooting baskets, playing tennis or badminton, hockey dribbling, and swimming is also important to achievement level and must be judged by teacher rating. The teacher should therefore determine a scale for judgment—1 to 5 or 1 to 10—and establish specific standards for rating individual performance. More acceptable results are obtained if there is more than one judge and averages of ratings are computed.

Teacher ratings are also necessary in the evaluation of creative movement or performance. Establishing certain criteria, or evaluative standards, provides a basis for rating on a predetermined point scale by the teacher or judges. Criteria such as use of space, use of body, use of focus, use of types of movement, and degree to which the given problem is solved should be developed by the teacher and explained to the students.

Student progress in a particular skill is another factor that is sometimes difficult to measure. In some sports, such as bowling and archery, the scores themselves may be used to indicate improvement. The teacher can keep a record of scores on charts to measure individual progress. Charts are also useful in measuring progress because keeping track of the number of baskets shot and missed or the number of goals attempted indicates performance skill and progress.

However, the performance of each individual must be assessed separately when charts are used to determine improvement for grading purposes. Some students may intentionally score low early in the season in order to exhibit great progress when tested at the end of the unit. In addition, several students may have identical progress scores, such as 3 more baskets on the second testing round. The teacher must then consider which student making a score of 3 evidenced greater improvement: the low scorer who managed to make 3 more baskets or the expert who scored high originally, yet still increased his score by 3. Only by evaluating each student's total performance can a teacher make proper use of charts in grading.

KNOWLEDGE AND APPRECIATION

In the area of knowledge and appreciation, tests differ from those of physical fitness and skills in that an intellectual process, rather than a motor performance, is involved. Standardized written tests are available in some of the sports and may be found in rule books and source books of the various sports. Unfortunately, many standardized tests are limited to the college level. Teachers may therefore have to devise their own tests, using either the oral, essay, or objective form. In so doing, the teacher can make sure that the test covers assigned materials and that it is suitable for the age level being tested.

Principles of test construction. There are certain principles of test construction that should be followed when developing a knowledge test.

1. The items selected should cover the entire subject matter, with emphasis placed on the most important facets of the game.

2. The length of the test should be related to the time available for testing.

3. The test should be appropriately worded and geared for the age level to be tested.

4. Directions should be simple and clear.

Techniques of testing. There are different techniques that may be utilized in test construction. True-and-false items, matching questions, sentence completion, multiple-choice, and diagrams, as well as short essays, may be combined to make an interesting and comprehensive examination of knowledge.

The following are a few suggestions regarding the wording of objective tests.

1. Questions or test items should be worded to avoid ambiguity and triviality.

2. Statements should be simple and direct and not tricky, involved, or based solely on opinion.

3. Words such as *never, always, none,* or *all* should be omitted in sentences requiring true or false answers.

Content tests are generally developed in objective form, but evaluation of appreciation requires other techniques. Considerable attention has been paid during the last decade to the collection of information in this affective domain. Helping students to know themselves better through values clarifications techniques has become an accepted evaluative procedure that not only helps the students but also gives important information to teachers regarding the *feelings* of students about program content and other instructional concerns.

Self-appraisal techniques, checklists, anecdotal records, opinion polls, questionnaires, and surveys have all been successfully used to test affect. Responses on teacher-made tests may take the form of a simple preference list (sample: I would rather play tennis than swim), a Likert Scale (1 to 7), or semantic differential (good–bad) to determine feelings of students and thus aid the teacher in program planning and development. The Attitude toward Physical Activity Inventory developed by Kenyon at the University of Waterloo in Canada, the Physical Estimation and Attraction Scale developed by Sonstroem, and the Sport Competition Anxiety Test developed by Martens are three standardized instruments now available to teachers that, according to Safrit, were founded on reasonably sound measurement theory and could prove useful to the instructor.

Because the development of positive attitudes toward and appreciation of physical education is an important programmatic objective, measurement of progress toward its achievement should be an integral part of the evaluation process. With the addition of *Basic Stuff Series I* into programs, assessment of core knowledge, attitudes, and skills becomes essential.

Administration of tests. When a written test is administered, directions should be read aloud as well as written on the test paper. A few questions as to the timing or scoring of the test may be answered, but they should be limited. Following the signal ''go,'' no further questions or talking should be allowed. Nothing is more disconcerting to the teacher or the students than unnecessary discussion. If directions are clear and the test well constructed, a satisfactory examination should result.

SOCIAL DEVELOPMENT

Social development is a goal of the physical education program that also requires evaluation, but, unfortunately, it is one aspect that is often neglected by teachers. The social development of the adolescent is a complex process. However, various techniques of testing have been devised to measure some of its aspects: social adjustment, attitudes and interests, social efficiency, and social status.

Testing social adjustment. Measurements of social adjustment may be made through the administration of standardized inventories (such as the Bell Adjustment Inventory) that have been developed specifically for this purpose. Such inventories should be used cautiously, however, and the results regarded only as clues to or indications of adjustment problems. The guidance department of a large school system is probably better equipped to administer and interpret these tests, but the physical education teacher should be familiar with them. A list of some of the other tests for social adjustment includes Science Research Associates Inventory, Minnesota Multiphasic Personality Inventory, Washburne's Social Adjustment Inventory, and the Bernreuter Personality Inventory. These tests are usually concerned with common adolescent problems or worries about the home, health, friends, and so on. Such tests or inventories are for general educational use, not for physical education personnel alone; therefore, the school psychologist or guidance counselor should be consulted in regard to this phase of testing.

Testing attitudes and interests. The guidance department should also be able to assist the physical educator in testing the attitudes or interests of adolescents. Attitudes may be measured in different ways—for example, through (1) teacher evaluation (observation of students, with an anecdotal record kept by the teacher), (2) opinion polls, and (3) rating scales. The physical education teacher should ask for the assistance of other teachers, particularly the guidance personnel, in this type of testing. Teachers work together because of a mutual interest in student problems, and sharing test results promotes greater understanding among all concerned. This type of faculty cooperation would apply also to interest inventories

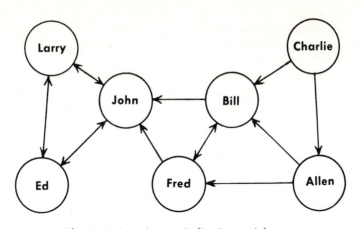

Fig. 19-4. A sociogram indicating social status.

such as the Strong Vocational Interest Blank or the Kuder Preference Record. The development of social interests, attitudes, and adjustment, while a goal of physical education, is also a general educational goal, and testing such development is the concern of the entire teaching staff.

Testing social efficiency. In regard to testing social efficiency, rating scales have been developed by leaders in the field of physical education specifically for use within the program. In these tests, ratings of the frequency of various types of behavior are measured by observer judgment. By referring to the original sources indicated, the teacher may learn the techniques of administering these tests for social efficiency.

Testing social status. Sociometrics is the measurement of social relationships as determined by use of a sociogram. The sociogram is useful in physical education as a method of teaching and of testing the social status of individuals in a class, team, or squad. The results of the sociogram pinpoint the natural leaders in the groups and the outsiders trying to become members. When the device is used more than once with the same group, a comparison of the results indicates social growth or change. A sociogram may be taken, for example, by asking all members of a team to list two people whom they would most like to have as their friends, with their choices limited to a given group or team.

Results may be pictured with arrows pointing to the names listed, as shown in Fig. 19-4. It may be interpreted from the sociogram shown here that John is the strongest leader, with Bill following closely behind. John, Larry, and Ed seem to form a rather small social clique, while Bill, who would like to join them, returns friendship with Fred only. It may be said also that Allen may be trying to break up this friendship and that Charlie, who was chosen by no one, would be happy with either Bill or Allen for a friend.

An indication of social development in such a group would be the movement of Charlie and Allen into an acceptable position in the group and the enlargement of the clique so that friendships are more spread out. A second sociogram would then show partial proof of social development and accomplishment through teamwork in whatever the group activity may have been. This is a simple technique of testing social development. It is useful as a tool in teaching because it indicates social interactions and points out potentially dangerous cliques, as well as those individuals who need assimilation into the group. The teacher, knowing this, can gear teaching to avoid social upsets and to improve social relationships.

PROBLEMS IN EVALUATING STUDENT ACHIEVEMENT

The testing of student achievement and the analysis of results necessary for their future application are essential to the teaching program. For the new teacher,

five main problems stem from this responsibility: (1) allotting time for testing, (2) selecting tests, (3) administering tests, (4) keeping records, and (5) using the results.

Allotting time. The time necessary for adequate evaluation of students' achievements must be set aside as a regular part of the teaching program. In situations where classes meet every day, one class period every other week may be devoted to testing. When classes meet only two or three times a week, the teacher should plan for evaluation procedures at least at the beginning and end of each unit of study in order to obtain accurate records of growth and progress.

Selecting tests. In selecting tests the new teacher should survey the available instruments to determine whether they are pertinent to his or her school situation. Proper selection of tests helps to overcome the problems of large classes, short periods, and individual rating needs. Because good organization and wise use of leaders also help to eliminate loss of valuable time, the beginning teacher should plan testing periods very carefully in order to make the most of them. Testing itself is a teaching method, with its promotion of good performances and its motivational purposes; thus time taken for evaluation is not wasted.

In selecting a test the teacher should be concerned with five elements: validity, objectivity, reliability, norms, and administrative feasibility. If the test is satisfactory in all these respects, the teacher may be assured that the results will be accurate.

Validity. The test should measure what it is supposed to measure. If the teacher is measuring balance, for example, the test should measure balance and not some other physical characteristic, such as speed or endurance.

Objectivity. The scoring of the test should be exact and well defined and as free as possible from personal opinion or subjective judgment. If two or more judges evaluate the performances of a class group, their answers or scores should be similar. This is an important factor in testing, and it affects the students to a great extent. They recognize the value of exact scoring methods for particular performances and generally prefer them to scaled value judgments.

Reliability. The testing device should consistently produce the same results. If a test were repeated under very similar conditions with the same group, the results should be equivalent—with the better performers again scoring high and the weaker performers low. Extraneous factors such as practice, distance, or time should not influence the results.

Norms. The test should have an accepted scale of performance scores normal for particular age levels and groups. Norms are useful for comparison of the achievements of one group with those of a similar group. Norms are valuable, however, only if they are based on a large population, which ensures a wide range of performance levels.

Administrative feasibility. It should be possible to administer a test to a class group without too much expense, loss of time, or other complication. It is logical to expect that testing student achievement consumes a reasonable amount of time, expense, and consideration. Evaluation should not, however, result in an excessive loss of teaching time, which would be detrimental to the program. This factor often determines the feasibility of administering a particular type of test. Taking into account class size, available equipment, and length of class periods may eliminate an otherwise sound testing device.

Selection of a testing instrument according to these five factors is necessary if accurate and worthwhile results are to be obtained. The teacher of physical education should take great care in surveying available tests before making a final choice.

Administering tests. The feasibility of administering a particular testing instrument is not the only consideration. Other factors, unrelated to the test itself, may become problems during test administration and therefore should be anticipated by the teacher.

• *What provisions can be made in regard to changing climatic conditions?* For example, in a test for accuracy in archery or punting in football, wind direction and velocity may be disturbing factors. Can retests be administered?

• *What provisions can be made for make-up testing of pupils who may be absent on the day the test is given?* Will time be set aside after school or during the regular class program to accommodate these pupils? Will the identical test be given, or will a substitute be used to prevent student preparation on the basis of rumors or gossip?

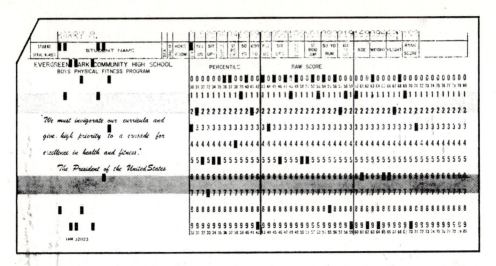

Fig. 19-5. IBM card used in Evergreen Park Community High School, Evergreen Park, Ill.

• *What provisions can be made to correct errors made by student assistants in timing, for example, or in scoring test results?* Will retesting solve this problem, or will the advantage of previous practice produce a higher score by the testee?

• *What provisions can be made for the maintenance of such factors as testing targets and line makers during the test administration?* Chalk lines frequently become blurred or erased during test administration. Can masking tape be used, or is it possible to assign a student leader the task of keeping lines or circles visible?

• *What provisions can be made for students who err throughout the entire test, either through a misunderstanding of the directions or through a lack of sufficient time?* Should such students automatically fail because of their unacceptable performances, or should they be allowed the opportunity to take the test again in the makeup period?

These are questions that the teacher must answer when administering tests, whether they be written or performance tests of student achievement.

Keeping records. The clerical duties attached to the testing program pose other difficulties. Records should be kept up-to-date and new test results constantly analyzed in terms of student progress and program planning for most effective use. The teacher

must take time to do this if the true values of evaluation are to be realized.

To ease this difficulty somewhat, schools have been making use of community volunteers or teacher aids to free regular teachers from these clerical duties that consume so much time. The physical education teacher should investigate this possibility. The form of the record itself may also help to make the task less burdensome. Some schools have been finding the use of IBM cards a real help in solving the problem of recording test results (see Fig. 19-5). The Evergreen Park Community High School uses this system to record physical fitness test results and to send reports home as well.

It may also be helpful for the teacher to maintain a record file of evaluative tests used, adding comments concerning possible success or problems involved in their administration. This procedure would prevent repetition of unsuitable tests.

Using test results. The results of all types of tests of student achievement should be put to use if the process of evaluation is to have any direct value for the students. There are several ways in which this may be done, and the choice depends on the purpose of the particular test.

Tests administered at the beginning of a unit—whether skills, knowledge, or fitness tests—serve as

prognostic devices to determine the needs of the group in relation to a specific activity. The teacher should interpret test results immediately and use them in planning the unit of study. Special groups may have to be formed on the basis of skills, or a special area of the activity may need emphasis because of a general weakness of the group. The motivational aspect of prognostic tests is also a valuable teaching tool.

Tests administered in the middle of a unit serve a diagnostic purpose, since results can indicate to the teacher those areas where teaching has not been sufficiently clear to make learning complete. The teacher then knows that the remaining class sessions should include review and clarification of ideas to cement learning.

Tests at the close of a unit of study indicate pupil progress and achievement. When they are compared with preliminary tests, a vital measure of improvement and effort is obtained.

Evaluation of student achievement should do more than produce figures of present status. It should promote improvement of this status. This can be accomplished only through appropriate use of accurate test results.

Scores on all tests administered within a given unit, course of study, or semester should be averaged and combined with other determinants to constitute a student's grade for a specific report period. The problems of using test results and developing a grading system are extremely important ones, and the physical education teacher must consider them very carefully and thoughtfully.

Special considerations

Before discussing application of measurement to grading procedures, there are four additional problems that the physical educator should consider with respect to pupil evaluation.

Formative evaluation. The importance of formative evaluation as standardized instructional procedure should again be emphasized. Daily or frequent nongraded assessments guide the student toward achievement of goals and assist the instructor by pointing out weaknesses in teaching methodology. With formative or diagnostic assessment, as explained in mastery

learning, changes through corrective feedback can be implemented before the end of the unit.

Self-assessment. Teachers should be reminded that the person most concerned with student progress is the pupil. Therefore the student should be allowed to participate, where possible, in evaluating his or her own achievement. Allowing students to set goals and measure their own results removes some of the anxiety and stress from the evaluation process. In addition progress can be measured in terms of the individual's own previous scores rather than in comparison with others', providing motivation to achieve. It is hoped that with this personalized teaching style, the student will be trying to do his or her best, and test results will be an accurate measure of learning.

Norm-referenced tests. According to mastery learning theory, criterion-referenced tests produce higher levels of achievement than norm-referenced tests. Other theorists point out that the use of standardized norms create additional testing difficulties. For example, with the advent of Title IX, should boys and girls be judged on the same or different norms? Specific gender differences have been identified in body structure, in cardiorespiratory function, and in certain physical skills. The practice of establishing different norms for boys and girls only prolongs or reinforces cultural distinctions. Yet having identical norms for boys and girls forces girls to achieve beyond their capabilities.

Assessment of pupil progress. Accurate assessment of pupil progress is not easily accomplished in the public school setting. Clark and Starr, in their text on secondary school teaching methods, suggest that teachers plan carefully for the evaluation of each unit *before* the start of instruction to ensure that measures of progress toward each objective are in proportion to its importance within that unit. This procedure allows the teachers to translate test scores of pupil achievement into an appropriate estimation of progress for grading purposes.

The abused child. One further problem that should not be overlooked is the abused child. Recent figures show that as many as 1 million abused or neglected children will die within a school year. Teachers, by law, are responsible for reporting any suspected cases of abuse or neglect, even without actual proof of mal-

treatment. The nature of physical education classes (the need to change clothing, for example, or the need to move) may bring to the physical education teacher's attention cases that classroom instructors might easily overlook. Testing procedures and comparisons of individuals' test results may help to pinpoint endangered children. Teachers must be alert to physical signs (injuries, unexplained bruises, withdrawal from activity, difficulty in walking, sudden fears, addiction to drugs, or avoidance behaviors) and report suspected cases immediately to the administration (for more information on child abuse see Chapter 6).

Methods and materials for grading

Grading in physical education is a complex process, for a single grade represents many different facets of pupils achievement, all of them important. In simplest terms, a grade is a teacher's (or teachers') estimation of pupil status. It may take several different forms, it may be arrived at by many different techniques, and it may serve many purposes.

PURPOSES OF GRADING

In general, a grade serves two primary purposes: it informs the student of present status, and it notifies the parents. Grades may also serve several subsidiary functions: (1) a motivational device for some students, (2) a guide to program planning and regrouping of students because grades identify areas of strength and weakness in the curriculum and in the youngsters, and (3) a basis for counseling students, for abrupt changes in a student's grades would probably be indicative of problems. Unfortunately, grades are sometimes used as a threatening device to push or force students into activity, which is not a desirable purpose of grading.

PRINCIPLES OF GRADING

To be of real value, a grade in physical education should be developed according to certain well-defined principles.

• It should be representative of an individual pupil's achievement in relation to the established objectives of physical education. Comparison of achievement with other students should be avoided.

• It should be developed on the basis of all four objectives of physical education. Emphasis should be placed on physical skills and physical development to the same degree that these factors are stressed in the program of instruction.

• It should be understood by the student. He or she should know its components, the derivation of the grade, and how the various items in the test are weighted.

• It should be understandable to parents in terms of the objectives of the program.

• It should be expressed in the same manner as grades in other subject matter areas throughout the school. This not only facilitates record keeping and transfer of credits but also places physical education on the same level as other subjects.

• It should be determined on the basis of several different evaluative techniques. Both subjective and objective measurements should be used.

• It should be fair—a just estimation of the student's achievement, and proper consideration should be given to other factors, such as improvement, effort, sportsmanship, and citizenship.

METHODS OF GRADING

There are several methods utilized in grading, not only in the field of physical education but throughout the general educational system in the United States. Some examples include

1. *Letter grades:* A, B, C, D, and E or F
   H, S, and U
   P and F
2. *Numerical grades:* 1, 2, 3, and so forth
3. *Explanatory paragraphs*
4. *Checklists:* often used to check weaknesses in such areas as effort, improvement, or citizenship

Recent studies of grading methods in motor skills learning indicate that percentile and *A,B,C,D,F* grades are significantly superior to a pass/fail or no-grade system.

PROBLEMS IN GRADING

The main problem is trying to arrive at a single grade that truly represents the pupil's achievement in the various objectives of physical education. To what degree should performance and ability be weighted in relation to achievement in knowledge and social development? Some teachers believe that the former should have twice the value of the latter because phys-

ical skills and development are the primary raison d'être of a program of physical education. Others believe that all four objectives should be considered equally. Another problem in grading centers around improvement. To what degree should improvement in skills affect the final grade? Should the student who has low motor ability but who shows real improvement in a sports unit be rated in the same manner as the highly skilled individual who merely loafs along throughout the unit?

Researchers Hale and Hale have been working on a statistical solution to this problem through conversion of test-retest scores to a progression score. In individualized instruction, as in mastery learning, where students establish personal goals relative to preestablished criteria, a grade for improvement can be mutually agreed on by teacher and student.

A third question arises out of the procedures necessary for participation in physical education classes. Should grading credit be given for having a clean gym suit, for being dressed for participation in every class, for showering, and for attendance? In addition, there is the problem of effort in physical education class. How does a teacher determine maximum effort, and is such effort accorded an automatic A? These are some of the questions the physical educator must answer before developing a grading system suitable for use in his or her school situation. Dr. Lynn McCraw of the University of Texas proposes a plan for grading that offers some solutions to these problems (Table 19-1).

Ideally, the report card should be clear, concise, accurate, and explicit. It should show achievement in physical skills, general ability, social development, and all the objectives that were stressed throughout the program. Perhaps more than one grade is necessary to clarify the many facets of the program for the parents.

In a dual marking system one letter grade can be assigned for achievement in relation to the class and a second grade (perhaps on a numerical scale) given for individual achievement ability. A section should be provided for comments and for setting up conferences with parents when necessary. It should be kept in mind that the report card is one of only a few methods of communicating with parents. When their children are having problems, parents generally want to know, but they need some direction, and they need to know in time. Report cards can provide this information.

It is always revealing to discuss the problem of grading with the students themselves to determine what elements they feel a physical education grade should encompass and to allow them to estimate a grade for themselves. In a survey of high school girls, it is interesting to note that those whom the teacher rated A − or A rated themselves only B or B +, while students whom the teacher ranked C + or lower often rated themselves above the teacher's estimate. This typifies the attitudes of many students toward themselves: those who do little often think they deserve

Table 19-1. Proposed plan for grading*

Components	Weightings	Instruments
Attitude in terms of Attendance Punctuality Suiting out Participation	5% to 25%	Attendance and other records Teacher observation
Skills in terms of Form in execution of skill Standard of performance Application in game situation	20% to 35%	Objective tests Teacher observation Student evaluation
Physical fitness with emphasis on Muscular strength and endurance Cardiovascular-respiratory endurance Agility Flexibility	20% to 35%	Objective tests Teacher observation
Knowledge and appreciation of Skills Strategy Rules History and terms	5% to 25%	Written tests Teacher observation
Behavior in terms of Social conduct Health and safety practices	5% to 25%	Teacher observation Student evaluation

*From McCraw, L.W.: Principles and practices for assigning grades in physical education, Journal of Health, Physical Education, and Recreation **35**:2, 1964.

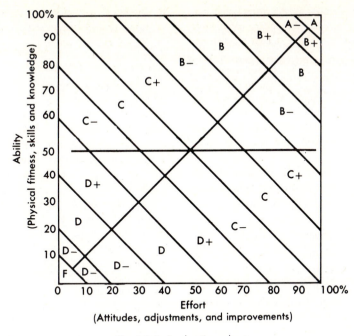

Fig. 19-6. Evaluation chart.

more, while those who put forth real effort rarely feel that they are deserving.

In a survey of eighth graders who were asked about the components of a physical education grade, the element cited with greatest frequency was effort. One astute remark made by an eighth-grade girl included the following observations.

I think that physical education should be graded, but not on a scale, just by the level that one person can reach alone. It is up to the physical education teacher to get to know students and learn just how far their abilities go and then grade each person on the basis of how much he or she is improving. This could probably best be done by having a place on the report card where the physical education teacher can make a statement about the child's improvement.

Table 19-1 depicts one method by which various factors might be weighted in determining an individual's grade. Ability factors such as physical fitness, game skills, and knowledge scores are included in percentages along vertical lines, while attitudes, adjustment, and improvement are diagrammed along the horizontal percentage line. If a student ranks in the fiftieth percentile in ability and in the eightieth per-

centile for attitudes and effort, the final grade would be C+. On the other hand, a student with excellent physical skills and high ability who loafs during class period, putting forth little or no effort, would fall into the C range.

GRADING IN TEAM TEACHING

Grading in schools using teaching teams for instruction has been a difficult problem to solve. It has been found that members of teaching teams must formulate criteria for grades together in order to provide consistency throughout the school. The master teacher in charge of a particular unit, such as volleyball, is responsible for all grades during that grading period and compiles the grades from the helping teachers. In this way a student accumulates several grades in many areas during one grading period. Teachers who have taught under this system seem to believe that it works out satisfactorily for everyone concerned.

Self-assessment tests

These tests are designed to assist students in determining if material and competencies presented in this chapter have been mastered.

1. Close your text and identify at least three innovative methods being utilized in today's secondary school physical education program to evaluate student progress and achievement.
2. Identify each major objective of physical education. For each objective indicate the method or test you would use to determine a student's achievement in regard to this objective.
3. Utilizing one or more of the selective methods discussed in this chapter, evaluate the physical fitness status of one of your classmates.
4. Select five tests utilized in physical education and rate each according to each of the following criteria: validity, objectivity, reliability, norms, and administrative feasibility.
5. Prepare a report card you would recommend to indicate a student's status in each of the major objectives for a physical education class.

Points to remember

1. There are many important factors to be considered when selecting tests for evaluation, such as validity and reliability.
2. There are many types of tests useful in evaluating pupil achievement in the four goals of physical education: physical fitness, physical skills, knowledge and appreciation, and social development.
3. Teacher-made tests of knowledge and skills must be constructed according to certain principles.
4. A system of grading should be developed on the basis of certain well-defined principles.
5. A grade should be a true measure of pupil status and should be expressed in a form similar to that used in other academic areas in the school.

Problems to think through

1. Should skills tests be administered both at the beginning of a sports unit and at the end? What factors should be considered in planning them?
2. Should a written knowledge test be given at the close of every sports unit?
3. When should physical fitness testing be done—at the beginning, middle, and/or end of the year?
4. Should tests of social development be given within a single sports unit? What type? At what other times of the year may they be given?
5. Under what circumstances may teacher-made tests be more valuable than standardized tests?
6. Of what value are tests of social interests and attitudes?
7. To what uses may the results of physical fitness tests be put?

8. Discuss this statement: A student of low motor ability would probably never be graded higher than a C in physical education class.

Case study for analysis

A high school physical education program consists of classes that meet twice a week. The department wishes to gather factual evidence that would convince the administration of the need for expanding the program and the value of a daily class in physical education. What evaluation techniques would be useful to promote this argument?

Exercises for review

1. Define validity of a test, and explain.
2. Define reliability of a test, and explain.
3. Devise a sample knowledge test of volleyball rules for seventh-grade girls or boys.
4. Administer one physical fitness test item to a group and compare the scores with national norms.
5. Prepare a set of directions to be given orally before administering a written knowledge test to a class.
6. Select a specific skill essential to the game of basketball, and devise a simple test for measuring its performance.
7. Look up a standardized skill test in one of the source books and evaluate its suitability for use in a nearby high school.
8. Make a sociometric study of a group or team presently established and evaluate the individual status of participants.

Selected readings

American Alliance for Health, Physical Education, Recreation, and Dance: Lifetime health-related physical fitness test manual, Reston, Va., 1980, The Alliance.

Aten, R.: Formative and summative evaluation in the instructional process, Journal of Health, Physical Education, Recreation, and Dance **51**(7) Sept. 1980.

Bennett, I.C.: Effects of grading systems on learning a fine motor skill, Research Quarterly **50:**715-722, Dec. 1979.

Clark, L.H., and Starr, I.S.: Secondary school teaching methods, ed. 3, New York, 1976, Macmillan Publishing Co., Inc.

Hale, P.W., and Hale, R.M.: Comparison of student improvement by exponential modification of test-retest scores, Research Quarterly **43:**113-120, March 1972.

Hoover, K.: The professional teacher's handbook, ed. 2, Boston, 1972, Allyn & Bacon, Inc.

McDonald, E.D., and Yeates, M.E.: Measuring improvement in physical education, Journal of Health, Physical Education, and Recreation **50**(2):79-89, Feb. 1979.

Paul, J.: For your information, American Educator **4**(2):34, 36, 38, Summer 1980.

Safrit, M.J.: Evaluation in physical education, ed. 2, Englewood Cliffs, N.J., 1981, Prentice-Hall, Inc.

20

Teacher and program evaluation

Instructional objectives and competencies to be achieved

After reading this chapter the student should be able to

1. Identify the reasons why teachers should be evaluated
2. Explain the items on which teachers should be evaluated
3. List and discuss the various methods utilized for evaluating teachers
4. Utilize effective techniques and methods for evaluating the physical education program

Educators today are taking a very close look not only at programs but also at teachers themselves. Recent advances in education have necessitated the development of more accurate methods of rating teachers and their abilities. In this chapter these two important factors, teacher evaluation and program evaluation, are discussed.

Teacher evaluation

Today's educational programs require a system of teacher evaluation that is in tune with the times. Appraisal should be carried out as a mutually desirable procedure for both the student and the teacher. Emphasis should be placed on such items as the teacher's ability to choose effective materials, an understanding of the personalities of the students with whom he or she is working, and knowledge of the subject matter of the teaching field. Appraisals should be conducted by persons who are competent in this area. In a day of specialization it has been suggested that specialists should be the ones to evaluate teachers.

REASONS FOR TEACHER EVALUATION

Castetter* has outlined several reasons why evaluation of personnel is important and necessary. These reasons, presented here in adapted form, are

1. To determine whether a teacher should be retained. Administrators evaluate teachers to determine whether they are making a desirable contribution to the school system where they are employed and whether they should become a permanent part of the faculty.

2. To determine the potential of a teacher. Evaluation can help in indicating the nature and scope of a teacher's potential to the school system.

3. To assign the teacher to responsibilities where he or she can best perform. Through periodic evaluation it will be known where the teacher's abilites can best be utilized in the school system.

4. To improve the performance of the teacher. Evaluation can help the teacher understand his or her weaknesses and strengths and how these weaknesses can be eliminated and strengths best utilized.

5. To uncover abilities. Evaluation offers an avenue for determining teacher abilities that otherwise may go undetected.

6. To serve as a guide for salary raises. Where salary raises are determined on the basis of merit and productivity, evaluation provides important information for these raises.

7. To identify important factors concerning program and students. Evaluation not only determines the teacher's effectiveness but also the desirability and effectiveness of the program and the reaction of students to the program.

8. To test the procedure by which the school recruits teachers. Teacher evaluation can assist in de-

---

*Castetter, W.B.: The personnel function in public administration, New York, 1971, Macmillan Publishing Co., Inc.

termining whether the recruitment procedure for new teachers is effective.

9. To provide motivation for teachers. A sound evaluation procedure can motivate teachers to do better work.

10. To improve the understanding between teachers and administration. Through an effective evaluation system, teachers will be better able to understand the role and responsibilities of the administration, and in turn the administration will better understand the role of the teacher.

11. To provide some basis for the transfer, promotion, or dismissal of teachers. Many objective facts must be mobilized if teachers are to be promoted, dismissed, or transferred in a just manner. Evaluation offers a means of obtaining some of these facts.

12. To motivate self-development. A very important reason for evaluation is to encourage the teacher to develop and become a better teacher.

TEACHER EVALUATION TODAY

Methods and techniques measuring teacher effectiveness and ability have been greatly expanded, and information concerning a teacher's personal history and growth has acquired greater importance, as evidenced by the bulging record folders filed in principals' offices.

Increased stress on the teacher and teaching has resulted from many factors. Educators today have recognized more and more the importance of the teacher-pupil relationship and therefore have been more concerned with the personality patterns of individual teachers. Then, too, with increasing emphasis on teacher accountability, the effectiveness of teaching has assumed greater importance. Other factors, such as merit pay schedules and team teaching programs, have forced principals and supervisors to rate teachers in accordance with their productivity. Increased community pressures and criticisms of educational policies and procedures have brought about the need for greater professionalism among educators and, in turn, has encouraged more effective appraisal of teachers and teaching.

The emphasis today is on teacher competencies in knowledge, skill, and attitudes, and teacher education programs are becoming competency based. In other words, the teacher is evaluated on the basis of developed abilities rather than the traditional criterion of courses taken. Similarly, there is an emphasis on teachers changing the behavior of their students in an observable manner. In other words, teachers are evaluated in more and more school systems on whether their students develop specific competencies in the subject matter and classes they teach. (For a more complete discussion on competency-based learning, see Chapter 13.)

Evaluation of teachers and their effectiveness involves several steps. As in other phases of evaluation, school systems vary in the extent and degree to which they fulfill this requirement. In general, however, a teacher's personal record file includes information regarding

1. Personal status
   a. Health and physical status
   b. Intellectual abilities
   c. Social and emotional stability
2. Professional status
   a. History
   b. Experiences
   c. Teaching effectiveness
   d. Relationship with pupils
   e. Relationship with colleagues
   f. Relationship with the profession
   g. Relationship with the community

The process of evaluation—that is, the actual collection of information—should encompass opinions from several sources. The teacher should be responsible for some self-evaluation; other sources are the administrator and colleagues.

PERSONAL STATUS

Health. A teacher should be in good health and physical condition. Some schools require periodic health examinations and chest x-ray films. The rigors of teaching demand a healthy, vigorous person, particularly in the field of physical education. However, physical perfection is not necessarily a requisite of any teaching position. Countless handicapped persons are effective teachers. (Over a decade ago the New York City schools had a regulation stating that the vision of all swimming teachers had to be 20/20 and that no person wearing corrective lenses could be hired

for this activity. However, this restriction has been lifted.)

Intellectual abilities. A teacher should be well educated, well read, and able to apply knowledge to everyday pursuits. Many schools require evidence of this ability, expecting prospective teachers to take the National Teachers Examination or the Teacher Education Examination Program. Other statistics are also used, such as college entrance examination scores and transcripts of college records.

Social and emotional stability. A teacher should be a well-adjusted person, finding contentment in his or her surroundings while making contributions to it. Administrators have several instruments and methods available to them for comprehensive appraisal of teachers' personalities. The Minnesota Teacher Attitude Inventory, the Minnesota Multiphasic Personality Inventory, and the Rorschach Test are some of the well-known tests that have been used. Other methods are observations, interviews, anecdotal records, and student opinion.

PROFESSIONAL STATUS

Preparation. A teacher should have a broad knowledge of educational psychology and history and be particularly well schooled in his or her subject matter. Administrators are especially interested in the teacher's professional preparation and expect teacher-training institutions to make recommendations on the basis of fair and honest appraisal techniques. Grades in the major field and in student-teaching work may be of special importance. Licensing of teachers may soon become a reality in some states.

Experience. A teacher should seek outside experiences that are both broadening and educational to expand the background brought to a teaching position. Administrators generally take a close look at all summer experiences, such as counseling and recreation work, as well as travels, in assessing a teacher's experiences. Past experiences in the teaching field are naturally important aspects that would also be studied.

Teacher effectiveness. A teacher should be able to apply knowledge and teaching techniques to the classroom situation and be able to communicate effectively with the students.

METHODS OF APPRAISAL

Administrators have several methods of appraisal available for use in teacher evaluation.

New methods. A survey regarding administrator and teacher evaluation procedures in school systems enrolling 25,000 or more pupils and conducted by the Educational Research Service, sponsored jointly by the National Education Association and the American Association of School Administrators, indicates the following new approaches that are being utilized in the evaluation of teachers.

Multiple evaluators. Instead of a teacher being evaluated by one or two persons, in some school systems the evaluation is becoming multifaceted. Teachers are evaluated by a committee, students, subordinates, parents, and/or outside groups. The aim is for consensus evaluations among committee members, for example, or between the teacher and the evaluators.

Performance objectives. Objectives of desirable accomplishments are set by the teacher, administration, or both. Then the teacher is evaluated on the degree to which the objectives are achieved. For example, short- and/or long-range goals are set and stated in terms of measurable objectives. An example of a performance objective might be: "I will provide a special program for my students who are subpar physically." The teacher is then evaluated in terms of whether or not or to what degree this objective is achieved.

Multiple bases for evaluation. Some school systems support a combined evaluation based on performance objectives and a procedure that lists predetermined characteristics of an effective teacher. In other words the teacher is evaluated not only on the achievement of certain objectives but also on the acquisition of the qualities of a model teacher.

In-basket data. In this procedure a file is kept on various incidents and details of teacher performance that occur during the evaluation period. Such a file might contain notations on such matters as class observations, reports from students, complaints from parents, graduate courses taken, and conferences held. Then, on the basis of all these items, the evaluation of the teacher takes place.

Fig. 20-1. Conditioning exercises to music, Campostella Junior High School, Norfolk City Schools, Norfolk, Va.

ADDITIONAL EVALUATION TECHNIQUES

Self-appraisal. Self-appraisal has been identified by some writers as the key to good teaching. The Teacher Self-Appraisal Observation System is one recently developed technique that utilizes a 30-minute video training tape and a self-appraisal manual to provide feedback to the teacher, showing the extent to which classroom procedures actually match the intended plan. The teacher objectively analyzes his or her own performance in the classroom. Adaptations of this instrument for a gymnasium or activity class are yet to be developed. However, it should be pointed out that McNeil and Popham found that teachers are not likely to change behavior on the basis of self-ratings.

Observation techniques. Since the 1960s there has been a marked increase in systematic classroom observation techniques. Earlier tests focused on the process, or normal classroom events, to evaluate teacher effectiveness, while more recent instruments test the outcomes or results reflected in modification of learner behavior. Flander's Interaction Analysis System,

Cheffer's Adaptation of the Flander's Model, and the Ohio State University Behavior Rating Scale are examples of observational systems that colleagues or supervisors might use to tally observable teacher behaviors.

Frequency counts of positive feedback, silence, and questioning are examples of some observable behaviors. Similarly, rating systems showing frequency and quality of specific behavior (for example, seldom/consistently smiles) are also useful.

Student ratings. Use of student ratings of teacher effectiveness has greatly increased in education in recent years, with results partially affecting merit, promotion, and tenure decisions. Many problems surround validity and reliability of these instruments, due to the complex influences of extraneous variables on students. Do students feel they will be earning high grades? Does the teacher like them? Is it a big class? A required class? Has the student recently shown improvement or failed in activity? Correlations between these characteristics are inconsistent.

A Teacher Performance Criteria Questionnaire has

been developed in which students identify whether or not specific teaching behaviors did or did not occur in a given lesson. These behaviors are related to 11 qualities or characteristics identified by Rosenshine and Furst as variables that show a strong relationship to student achievement. Teacher clarity, variability, enthusiasm, task/oriented or business-like behavior, and student opportunity to learn are the first five of 11 important teaching qualities identified in this study.

ADMINISTRATIVE TECHNIQUES

Anecdotal record. An administrator may keep a file on problems that come to his or her attention as a result of a particular teacher's classroom activities. Complaints from students or teachers would fall into this category. (For example: Where was the teacher when those boys started that fight in the locker room? Or why are students always late to classes following gym class?)

Standardized instruments. An administrator may use one of several standardized evaluation charts to appraise teacher effectiveness.

Relationship with pupils. Administrators may take into consideration teacher-pupil relations. Requests for a particular teacher to serve as a chaperone or as a sponsor for a club activity might be indicative of that teacher's concern for students. Complaints from students and parents may also be given due consideration by administrators.

Relationship with colleagues. An administrator may record a teacher's contributions at teachers' meetings, at workshops, or on voluntary committees. Holding an elective office in a faculty association, credit union, or committee would certainly be an indicator of status among one's associates, which administrators would note.

Relationship with profession. Administrators may become acquainted with a teacher's professionalism through his or her activities in local, state, and national organizations (committee work and office-holding). Within the school an administrator may look for innovations and changes in teaching techniques and programming. He or she may also check a teacher's contributions to the current literature in education.

Relationship with the community. Administrators recognize that good public relations are a vital force between a school and its community and that each teacher should foster them. The teacher should show evidence of loyalty to the school and its administrative policies and practices—such as at PTO functions and board meetings—and should be a loyal contributor to the community, working for its betterment through cooperation with residents and promotion of its interests, supporting activities such as the Memorial Day Parade and the summer recreation program.

The appraisal practices set forth here are not intended to be an absolute formula. They are merely suggestions of possible practices that individual school systems may employ. Three other points should be emphasized in this regard.

1. Administrators generally evaluate all teachers in a similar manner. Physical education teachers should not expect special consideration because they have winning teams or bring in valuable gate receipts.

2. Consideration would naturally be given to length of experience in a particular school. The beginning teacher would not be expected to evidence the same degree of effectiveness or competency as the teacher with 5 or 10 years of experience in that school.

3. Standards of evaluation are themselves indicative of the school's expectations. For example, submitting weekly lesson plans or not smoking on the job are regulations with which a prospective teacher may not wish to comply. A teacher who does not agree with these standards would probably be more effective in another school system.

As research into teacher effectiveness continues to explore answers to the question, ''What is a good teacher?'' it may be helpful to remember that ''the effective teacher will not only see, but have vision, he will not only hear, but listen, he will not only touch, but feel.''*

Program evaluation

Evaluation of physical education programs involves not only an internal examination of objectives, content, and other administrative functions but also an external look that compares curriculum with other

*Miller, D.K.: The effective teacher. The Physical Educator 35(3):148, Oct. 1978.

Fig. 20-2. Basketball at Paul J. Gelinas Junior High School, Setauket, N.Y.

groups or standardized norms. While one type is criterion-referenced evaluation, involving judgment of factors unique to a particular setting, the second type of evaluation allows a broader look at accepted determinants of excellence.

The process of evaluation should involve the school staff and be carried out on a regular basis. Bain suggests a 3-year cycle to encompass all facets of the evaluation process and stresses the need for revision to take place based on rating outcomes.

The following sample questions formulated for teacher rating of program administration may be answered poor, fair, good, or excellent, or they may be scored on a scale of 1 to 10. Areas of the program are listed and questions raised concerning various factors.

CLASS PROGRAM

1. Does the teaching program devote equitable time to team sports, individual sports, rhythms and dance, and gymnastic activities?

2. Are the available equipment and facilities adequate to allow maximum student participation?

3. Are reasonable budgetary allotments made for the class teaching program?

4. Are accurate evaluation procedures carried out and worthwhile records kept?

5. Are minimal participation requirements met by all students?

6. Are students meeting proper physical education requirements in regard to dressing and showering?

7. Are proper safety measures taken in all activities?

8. Are opportunities for developing student leadership provided in the class program?

ADAPTED PROGRAM

1. Do adequate screening procedures disclose all possible participants in this program?

2. Are adequate facilities, equipment, time, and space made available to the program?

3. Are proper supervision and instruction afforded each individual participant?

4. Is medical approval obtained for each individual's regimen of activity?

5. Do participants engage in some of the regular

class work, as well as remedial classes, when advisable?

6. Are careful records and progress notes kept on each student?

7. Is the financial allotment to the program reasonable?

8. Does student achievement indicate the value of the program?

INTRAMURAL AND EXTRAMURAL PROGRAMS

1. Are intramural and extramural sports offered to all students in as many activities as possible?

2. Has participation in these programs increased during the past year?

3. Is maximum coaching supervision available to players?

4. Is adequate financial assistance given to this phase of the program?

5. Are accurate records maintained concerning the participants, their honors, award, and electives?

6. Does the reward or point system emphasize the joys of participation rather than stress the value of the reward?

7. Is equipment well cared for and properly stored to gain the most use from it?

8. Are competitive experiences wholesome and worthwhile for all participants?

INTERSCHOLASTIC PROGRAM

1. Is financial support for this program provided by the physical education budget?

2. Is there equitable financial support for all sports in the interscholastic program?

3. Are interscholastic sports available to all students, boys and girls alike?

4. Are adequate health standards being met in respect to number of practices and games, fitness of participants, and type of competition?

5. Is competition provided by schools of a similar size?

6. Is the program justifiable as an important educational tool?

7. Are academic standards for participants maintained?

8. Are good public relations with the community furthered through this program?

AQUATICS

1. Are maximum instruction and participation opportunities made available to all students?

2. Is superior care taken in cleaning and maintaining the pool area—with proper checks on water chlorination, temperature, and filter system?

3. Is adequate supervision by qualified personnel available at all times?

4. Are health standards of cleanliness and rules requiring freedom from infection enforced at all times?

5. Are proper safety regulations enforced at all times?

6. Does student achievement indicate the value of the program?

7. Are competitive swimming and diving events properly officiated and controlled?

8. Is swimming on the intermediate level a requirement for graduation?

ADMINISTRATION

1. Is the teaching staff well qualified and capable of carrying out the program?

2. Is the program run efficiently, with little loss of teaching time or space, and is maximum use made of facilities?

3. Are professional standards maintained as to class size and teacher assignment?

4. Is the departmental organization on a democratic basis, with all members sharing in the decisions?

5. Do members of the staff have a professional outlook, attend professional meetings, and keep up with the latest developments in the field?

6. In what areas have scientific tests and research contributed to the profession?

These are just a few sample questions that may be used for internal program evaluation. A complete instrument requires development based on the particular school program, facilities, school population, and the basic philosophy and objectives of the program, for *those* objectives determine criteria for achievement.

Several instruments are available to teachers to provide further information on standardized assessment tools. In some states—for example, Ohio—evaluative checklists have been developed for statewide use. On a national level, AAHPERD has published an *As-*

sessment Guide for Secondary School Physical Education Programs. This instrument reviews the administrative, instructional, intramural, and athletic programs by eliciting yes/no responses to a series of statements. Its stated purposes are self-study, identification of problem program areas, and eventual improvement of secondary school programs. It assesses knowledge of human movement as a discipline through psychomotor, cognitive, and affective objectives.

Whatever method of program evaluation is selected, it should be realistic, functional, and continuous in order to fulfill its major purpose of benefiting the students.

Self-assessment tests

These tests are designed to assist students in determining if material and competencies presented in this chapter have been mastered.

1. As a prospective teacher, list the ways by which a meaningful evaluation of your performance will assist you in becoming a better teacher.
2. Prepare a list of items on which a teacher should be evaluated. List each of these items in order of priority, giving your reason as to its importance.
3. Utilizing a class situation demonstrate the various methods by which a teacher may be evaluated.
4. Prepare what you consider to be an effective checklist for evaluating each component of a physical education program.

Points to remember

1. Teacher evaluation is a growing responsibility of administrators.
2. Evaluation is a continuing process.
3. Steps involved in teacher evaluation encompass every aspect of a teacher's personal and professional status.
4. Program evaluation may be accomplished within a school system or by a visiting team of specialists.
5. All evaluation procedures must take into account special factors related to the particular community involved.

Problems to think through

1. To what extent should self-rating procedures be included in a teacher's personal record file?
2. What is the primary purpose of program evaluation?
3. Should the teaching staff be informed of the methods of teacher evaluation in use within their school system?

4. For what reasons would test scores be evidence of effective teaching? For what reasons should they not?
5. Should a teacher be well liked by students in order to be an effective teacher?

Case study for analysis

A large new suburban high school is preparing for a visitation from the state accreditation committee. The physical education department is expected to collect concrete evidence of student achievement in all phases of the program. What materials would provide concise information for this purpose?

Exercises for review

1. Take a survey of at least 10 people by asking them to list in order of importance the five most important qualities of a good teacher. Make a composite listing of these qualities.
2. Compare the evaluation instruments presented in this chapter and note the differences among them.
3. Evaluate as completely as possible a high school in your college community.
4. Interview a teacher, and on the basis of that discussion, write a description of the teacher's personal and professional status. What key questions may be used?

Selected readings

American Alliance for Health, Physical Education, and Recreation: Assessment guide for secondary school physical education programs, Washington, D.C., 1977, The Alliance.

Bain, L.L.: Program evaluation, Journal of Health, Physical Education, Recreation, and Dance **51**(2):67-69, Feb. 1980.

Cheffers, J.T.F., and Keilty, G.C.: Developing valid instrumentation for measuring teacher effectiveness, International Journal of Physical Education **17**:15-23, Summer 1980.

Educational Innovators Press: A manual for utilizing the teacher self-appraisal instrument, Tucson, 1973, Educational Innovators Press.

McNeil, J.D., and Popham, W.J.: The assessment of teacher competence. In Travers, R.M.W., editor: Second handbook of research on teaching, Chicago, 1973, Rand McNally & Co.

Miller, D.K.: The effective teacher, The Physical Educator **35**(3) Oct. 1978.

Popham, W.J.: Criterion-referenced measurement, Englewood Cliffs, N.J., 1978, Prentice-Hall, Inc.

Rosenshine, B., and Furst, N.: Research on teacher performance criteria. In Smith, B.O., editor: Research in teacher education: a symposium, Englewood Cliffs, N.J., 1971, Prentice-Hall, Inc.

Safrit, M.J.: Evaluation in physical education, ed. 2, Englewood Cliffs, N.J., 1981, Prentice-Hall, Inc.

Thomas, N.: Thoughts on teacher evaluation, Physical Educator **37**(8):176-178, Dec. 1980.

Index